Dear NFT User,

Welcome back to our sophomore season of dis
dope doesn't typically come without a connection or a price. From Capitol Hill to Columbia Heights, Washingtonians are scrambling to keep up with the frenzied political battles, a booming real estate market, and a raving entertainment scene that's luring in young people from all corners of the country. But fear not—we are here to offer you aid!

This book is not meant for people who sport fanny packs and visors, order overpriced sandwiches, and ask people how to get to "Foggy Bottoms." However, if you're a newbie to the area and are eager to jump in with both feet; if you're a capitol city veteran who wants to elevate to the rank of insider; even if you're a (we cringe to use the word) *tourist* who wouldn't mind breaking away from mom, dad and sis to step into the shoes of the movers, shakers, hipsters and rockers that make this city the most powerful—and one of the most dynamic—in the world, then this book is for you.

What you have in your hand is small. Tuck it in your bag. Toss it in your glove compartment. Ditch the folding map from the Union Station kiosk and take advantage of our detailed page-by-page neighborhood maps to get yourself around. For this edition, we've nearly doubled our restaurant listings, planted our feet deeper into the periphery of the city, and added hundreds of new nightspots, museums, and trendy shopping locales. We've also added new pages for the **National Archives, Catholic University**, and **Local Government**.

We live in a new Washington! Baseball is back, H Street NE is slowly becoming the U Street of the new millennium, Logan Circle is starting to make Dupont seem stiff, and an '08 election buzz has already begun. It's an exciting time to live in the nation's capital, and we hope this book allows you to play a leading part in its most electrifying scene.

Here's hoping you catch the Potomac fever,

Jane, Rob, Diana, John, Dave, and Jim

Table of Contents

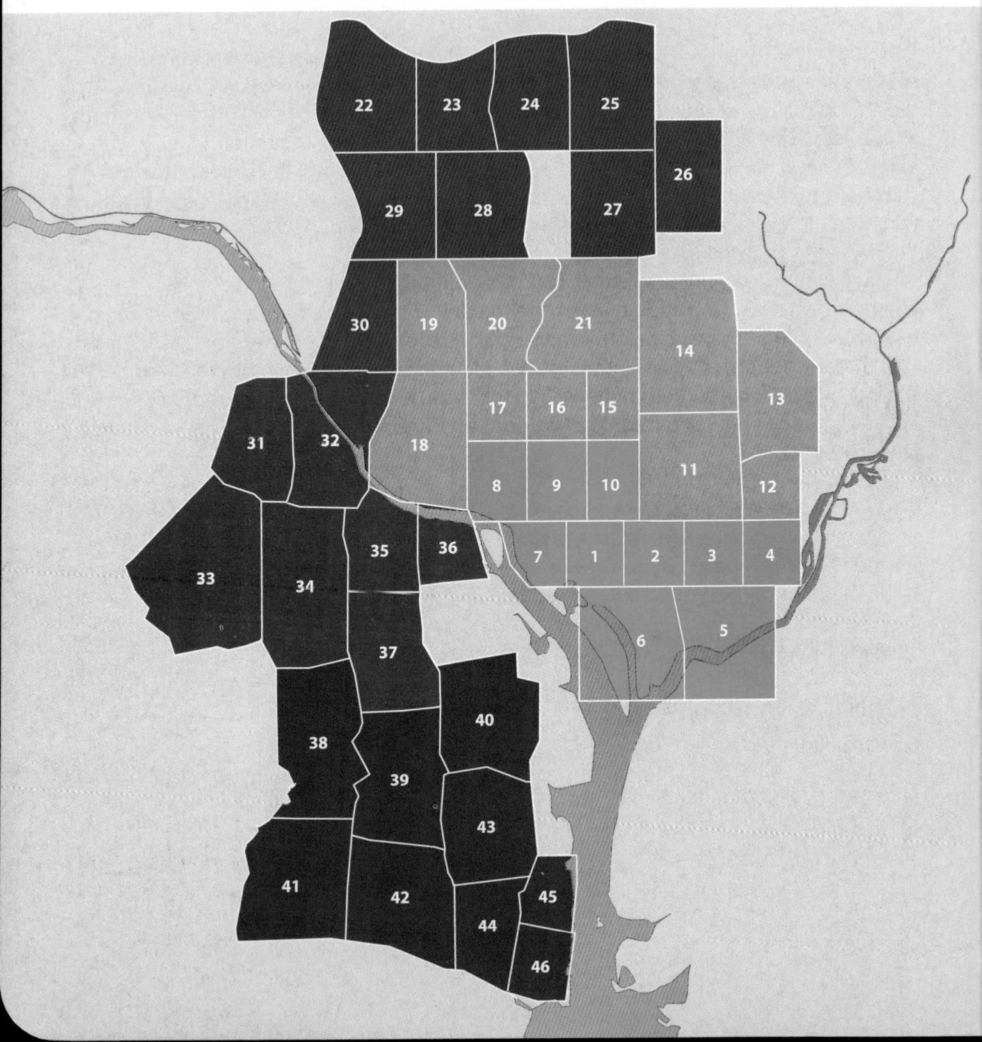

Map 1 • National Mall

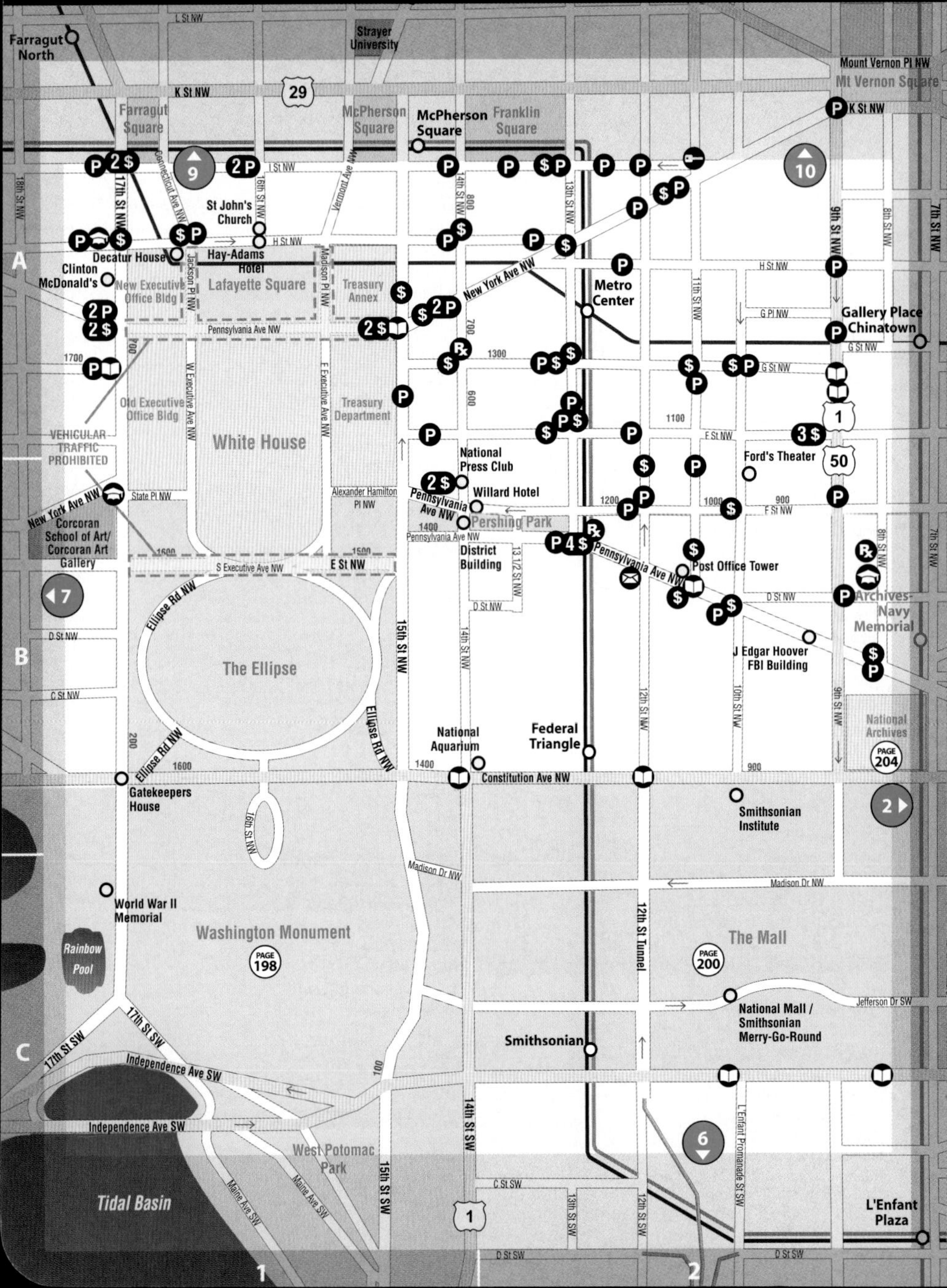

Farragut North
Strayer University
L St NW
Mount Vernon Pl NW
Mt Vernon Square
K St NW
29
Farragut Square
McPherson Square
McPherson Square
Franklin Square
9
10
I St NW
Connecticut Ave NW
Vermont Ave NW
16th St NW
14th St NW
13th St NW
800
St John's Church
17th St NW
18th St NW
H St NW
Decatur House
Hay-Adams Hotel
Jackson Pl NW
Madison Pl NW
New York Ave NW
9th St NW
8th St NW
7th St NW
A
Clinton McDonald's
New Executive Office Bldg
Lafayette Square
Treasury Annex
Metro Center
11th St NW
H St NW
G Pl NW
Gallery Place Chinatown
Pennsylvania Ave NW
700
1300
G St NW
1700
Old Executive Office Bldg
W Executive Ave NW
E Executive Ave NW
Treasury Department
600
1100
1
F St NW
3 $
VEHICULAR TRAFFIC PROHIBITED
White House
National Press Club
Ford's Theater
50
State Pl NW
Alexander Hamilton Pl NW
Willard Hotel
New York Ave NW
Corcoran School of Art/ Corcoran Art Gallery
Pennsylvania Ave NW
1400
1200
1000
900
E St NW
Pershing Park
Pennsylvania Ave NW
1600
1500
S Executive Ave NW
E St NW
District Building
13 1/2 St NW
Pennsylvania Ave NW
Post Office Tower
7
D St NW
Archives-Navy Memorial
D St NW
D St NW
Ellipse Rd NW
B
The Ellipse
15th St NW
J Edgar Hoover FBI Building
C St NW
12th St NW
10th St NW
National Archives
PAGE 204
Ellipse Rd NW
National Aquarium
Federal Triangle
200
Ellipse Rd NW
1600
1400
900
Constitution Ave NW
Gatekeepers House
2
Smithsonian Institute
16th St NW
Madison Dr NW
Madison Dr NW
World War II Memorial
12th St Tunnel
Washington Monument
PAGE 198
The Mall
PAGE 200
Rainbow Pool
National Mall / Smithsonian Merry-Go-Round
Jefferson Dr SW
17th St SW
17th St SW
C
Smithsonian
Independence Ave SW
100
Independence Ave SW
14th St SW
6
L'Enfant Promanade St SW
West Potomac Park
15th St SW
C St SW
Tidal Basin
Maine Ave SW
Maine Ave SW
1
13th St SW
12th St SW
L'Enfant Plaza
D St SW
D St SW
1
2

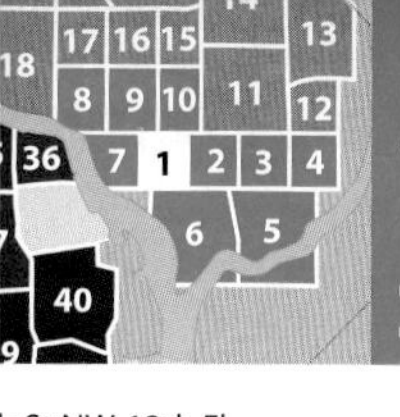

Here are many of the reasons this city is a top tourist destination. The White House, the Washington Monument, the Smithsonian—they're all must visits. But they do get old. Tip: Photocopy this map and give it to visiting relatives, then promise to meet them for a drink later along U Street.

Banks

- **Bank of America** • 1001 Pennsylvania Ave NW
- **Bank of America** • 1501 Pennsylvania Ave NW
- **Bank of America** • 700 13th St NW
- **Bank of America** • 888 17th St NW
- **BB&T** • 601 13th St NW
- **BB&T** • 815 Connecticut Ave NW
- **Chevy Chase** • 1299 Pennsylvania Ave NW
- **Chevy Chase** • 1717 Pennsylvania Ave NW
- **Chevy Chase (ATM)** • 1100 Pennsylvania Ave NW
- **Chevy Chase (ATM)** • 1300 Pennsylvania Ave NW
- **Chevy Chase (ATM)** • 815 14th St NW
- **Citibank** • 1400 G St NW
- **Citibank** • 435 11th St NW
- **Independence Federal Savings** • 1006 E St NW
- **Industrial Bank** • 1317 F St NW
- **M&T Bank** • 555 12th St NW
- **PNC** • 1503 Pennsylvania Ave NW
- **PNC** • 800 17th St NW
- **PNC (ATM)** • 1101 New York Ave NW
- **PNC (ATM)** • 1300 New York Ave NW
- **PNC (ATM)** • 1455 Pennsylvania Ave NW
- **PNC (ATM)** • 900 F St NW
- **Sun Trust** • 1100 G St NW
- **Sun Trust** • 1445 New York Ave NW
- **Sun Trust** • 900 17th St NW
- **United Bank** • 1001 G St NW
- **United Bank** • 1275 Pennsylvania Ave NW
- **Wachovia** • 1300 I St NW
- **Wachovia** • 1301 Pennsylvania Ave NW
- **Wachovia** • 1310 G St NW
- **Wachovia** • 1700 Pennsylvania Ave NW
- **Wachovia** • 740 15th St NW
- **Wachovia** • 801 Pennsylvania Ave NW
- **Wachovia (ATM)** • 529 14th St NW

Car Rental

- **Hertz** • 901 11th St NW • 202-628-6174

Landmarks

- **Clinton McDonald's** • 750 17th St NW
- **Decatur House** • 748 Jackson Pl NW
- **District Building** • 14th St NW & E St NW
- **Ford's Theater** • 511 10th St NW
- **Gatekeepers House** • 17th St NW & Constitution Ave NW
- **Hay-Adams Hotel** • 16th St NW & H St NW
- **J Edgar Hoover FBI Building** • 935 Pennsylvania Ave NW
- **National Aquarium** • Commerce Building, 14th St NW & Constitution Ave
- **National Mall/Smithsonian Merry-Go-Round** • 1000 Jefferson Dr SW
- **National Press Club** • 529 14th St NW, 13th Fl
- **Post Office Tower** • 1100 Pennsylvania Ave NW
- **Smithsonian Institute** • 1000 Jefferson Dr SW
- **St John's Church** • 16th St NW & H St NW
- **Willard Hotel** • 1401 Pennsylvania Ave NW
- **World War II Memorial** • 17th St SW b/w Constitution Ave & Independence Ave

Libraries

- **Dibner Library** • 12th St & Constitution Ave NW
- **Federal Aviation Administration Libraries** • 800 Independence Ave SW # 930
- **Martin Luther King Jr Memorial Library** • 901 G St NW
- **National Clearinghouse Library** • 624 9th St NW # 600
- **National Endowment for the Humanities Library** • 1100 Pennsylvania Ave NW # 217
- **Office of Thrift Supervision Library** • 1700 G St NW
- **Treasury Library** • 1500 Pennsylvania Ave NW #5030
- **US Department of Commerce Library** • 1401 Constitution Ave NW
- **US Department of Energy Library** • 1000 Independence Ave SW

Parking

Pharmacies

- **CVS** • 1275 Pennsylvania Ave NW
- **CVS** • 435 8th St NW
- **CVS** • 717 14th St NW

Post Offices

- **Benjamin Franklin** • 1200 Pennsylvania Ave NW

Schools

- **Corcoran College of Art & Design (Downtown Campus)** • 500 17th St NW
- **Corcoran School of Art & Design (H St Campus)** • 1705 H St NW
- **Marriott Hospitality Public Charter** • 410 8th St NW

Map 1 • National Mall

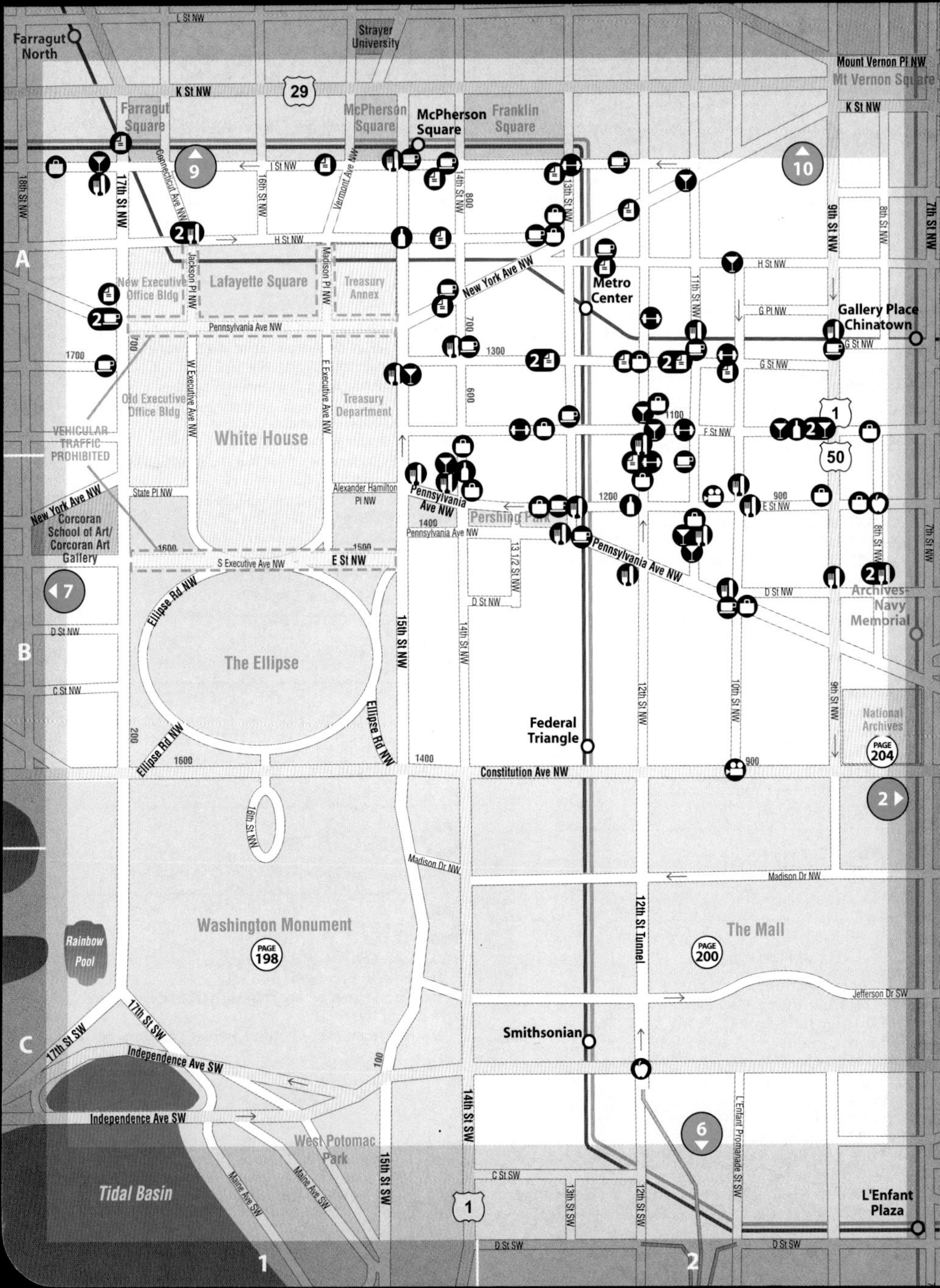

This neighborhood caters mainly to tourists and office workers. Lunch spots (such as the ubiquitous Cosí) and happy hours abound. At night, look harder to avoid tourist and expense account traps and you'll find treasures like soaring architecture and belly dancers at Zaytinya. Not hungry? Catch an indie flick at the Landmark E Street Cinema to build up an appetite.

Coffee

- **Caribou Coffee** • 1701 Pennsylvania Ave NW
- **Caribou Coffee** • 601 13th St NW
- **Coffee Espress** • 1250 H St NW
- **Cosí** • 1001 Pennsylvania Ave NW
- **Cosí** • 1333 H St NW
- **Cosí** • 1700 Pennsylvania Ave NW
- **Cosí** • 700 11th St NW
- **Dean & Deluca Expresso** • 1299 Pennsylvania Ave NW
- **JX Coffee** • 1400 I St NW
- **ME Swing** • 1702 G St NW
- **Starbucks** • 1301 Pennsylvania Ave NW
- **Starbucks** • 1401 New York Ave NW
- **Starbucks** • 555 11th St NW
- **Starbucks** • 700 14th St NW
- **Starbucks** • 701 9th St NW
- **Starbucks** • 901 15th St NW
- **Wally's World Coffee** • 1225 I St NW

Copy Shops

- **Ace Press (9am-6pm)** • 910 17th St NW
- **Advanced Printing (8:30am-5:30pm)** • 1201 New York Ave NW
- **Alpha Graphics Printshop (8:30am-6:30pm)** • 1325 G St NW
- **Docimaging.com (7:30am-8pm)** • 1001 G St NW
- **Ikon Office Solutions** • 1120 G St NW
- **Judicial Copy (9am-5pm)** • 1620 I St NW
- **Metro Press (8:30am-6:30pm)** • 1444 I St NW
- **Minuteman Press (8:30am-5:30pm)** • 1308 G St NW
- **Penn Press II (8:30am-7pm)** • 750 17th St NW
- **Reliable Copy (24 hours)** • 555 12th St NW
- **Reprodoc (8am-8pm)** • 1300 I St NW
- **Sir Speedy Printing (8:30am-5:30pm)** • 1212 G St NW
- **Sir Speedy Printing (8:30am-5:30pm)** • 1429 H St NW
- **Staples (7am-7pm)** • 1250 H St NW
- **Superior Group (24 hours)** • 1401 New York Ave NW

Farmer's Markets

- **Freshfarm Market** • 8th St NW & E St NW
- **US Dept of Agriculture Farmers Market** • 12th St SW & Independence Ave SW

Gyms

- **Club Fitness at Washington Center** • 1001 G St NW
- **Downtown Boxing Club** • 1101 F St NW
- **Fitness Center at Franklin Square** • 1300 I St NW
- **Fitness Co** • 555 12th St NW
- **Washington Sports Clubs** • 1345 F St NW
- **Washington Sports Clubs** • 730 12th St NW

Liquor Stores

- **Central Liquor Store** • 917 F St NW
- **Press Liquors** • 527 14th St NW
- **Washington Wine & Liquor** • 1200 E St NW
- **Woodward Liquors** • 15th St NW & H St NW

Movie Theaters

- **Johnson IMAX Theater** • Constitution Ave NW & 10th St NW
- **Landmark E St Cinema** • 555 11th St NW

Nightlife

- **Capitol City Brewing Company** • 1100 New York Ave NW
- **Eyebar** • 1716 I St NW
- **Gordon Biersch Brewery** • 900 F St NW
- **Grand Slam Sports Bar** • 1000 H St NW
- **Harry's Saloon** • 436 11th St NW
- **Home** • 911 F St NW
- **Old Ebbitt Grill** • 675 15th St NW
- **Pink Elephant Cocktail Lounge** • 436 11th St NW
- **Platinum** • 915 F St NW
- **Polly Esther's** • 605 12th St NW
- **Poste Brasserie Bar** • 555 8th St NW
- **Round Robin Bar** • 1401 Pennsylvania Ave NW
- **Tequila Beach** • 1115 F St NW

Restaurants

- **Bistro D'Oc** • 518 10th St NW
- **Café Asia** • 1720 I St NW
- **Café Atlantico** • 405 8th St NW
- **Caucus Room** • 401 9th St NW
- **Ceiba** • 701 14th St NW
- **Chef Geoff's** • 1301 Pennsylvania Ave NW
- **Equinox** • 818 Connecticut Ave NW
- **ESPN Zone** • 555 12th St NW
- **Gerard's Place** • 915 15th St NW
- **Hard Rock Café** • 999 E St NW
- **Harry's Restaurant and Saloon** • 436 11th St NW
- **John Harvard's Brew House** • E St NW & 13th St NW
- **Les Halles** • 1201 Pennsylvania Ave NW
- **Occidental** • 1475 Pennsylvania Ave NW
- **Old Ebbitt Grill** • 675 15th St NW
- **Ortanique** • 730 11th St NW
- **Teaism** • 400 8th St NW
- **Teaism** • 800 Connecticut NW
- **TenPenh** • 1001 Pennsylvania Ave NW
- **Willard Room** • 1401 Pennsylvania Ave NW
- **Zaytinya** • 701 9th St NW

Shopping

- **Barnes & Noble** • 555 12th St NW
- **Blink** • 1776 I St NW
- **Borders Books & Music** • 600 14th St NW
- **Café Mozart** • 1331 H St NW
- **Celadon Spa** • 1180 F St NW
- **Chapters Literary Bookstore** • 445 11th St NW
- **Coup de Foudre Lingerie** • 1001 Pennsylvania Ave NW
- **Fahrney's** • 1317 F St NW
- **Filene's Basement** • 529 14th St NW
- **H&M** • 1065 F St NW
- **Hecht's** • 1201 G St NW
- **International Spy Museum Gift Shop** • 800 F St NW
- **Penn Camera** • 840 E St NW
- **Political Americana** • 1331 Pennsylvania Ave NW
- **Utrecht Art & Drafting Supplies** • 1250 I St NW

Map 2 • Chinatown / Union Station

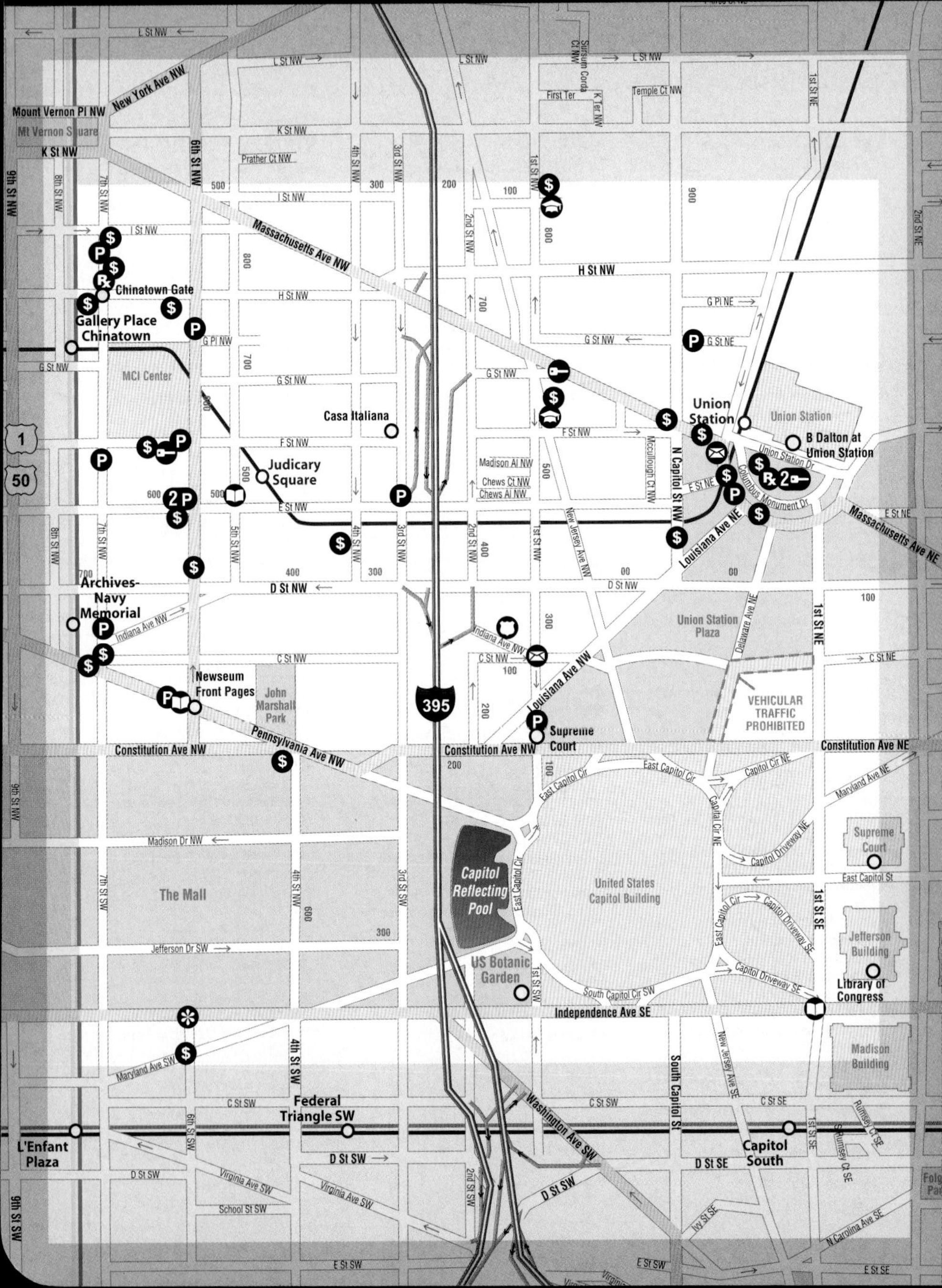

N

Mount Vernon Pl NW
Mt Vernon Square
New York Ave NW
L St NW
K St NW
Prather Ct NW
I St NW
H St NW
G Pl NW
G St NW
F St NW
E St NW
D St NW
C St NW
Massachusetts Ave NW
Sursum Corda Ct NW
First Ter
K Ter NW
Temple Ct NW
9th St NW
8th St NW
7th St NW
6th St NW
5th St NW
4th St NW
3rd St NW
2nd St NW
1st St NW
N Capitol St NW
New Jersey Ave NW
Mccullough Ct NW
Madison Al NW
Chews Ct NW
Chews Al NW
Indiana Ave NW
Louisiana Ave NW
Louisiana Ave NE
Pennsylvania Ave NW
Constitution Ave NW
Constitution Ave NE
G Pl NE
G St NE
E St NE
C St NE
1st St NE
2nd St NE
Delaware Ave NE
Massachusetts Ave NE
Union Station Dr
Columbus Monument Dr
Chinatown Gate
Gallery Place Chinatown
MCI Center
Judiciary Square
Casa Italiana
Archives-Navy Memorial
Newseum Front Pages
John Marshall Park
Union Station
B Dalton at Union Station
Union Station Plaza
VEHICULAR TRAFFIC PROHIBITED
Supreme Court
1
50
395
Madison Dr NW
Jefferson Dr SW
The Mall
East Capitol Cir
Capitol Cir NE
Capital Cir NE
Maryland Ave NE
Capitol Driveway NE
Capitol Reflecting Pool
United States Capitol Building
US Botanic Garden
Capitol Driveway SE
East Capitol St
Jefferson Building
Library of Congress
Madison Building
South Capitol Cir SW
Independence Ave SE
1st St SW
1st St SE
Maryland Ave SW
Washington Ave SW
South Capitol St
New Jersey Ave SE
C St SW
C St SE
Federal Triangle SW
L'Enfant Plaza
Capitol South
D St SW
D St SE
Rumsey Ct SE
Virginia Ave SW
School St SW
Ivy St SE
N Carolina Ave SE
E St SW
E St SE
7th St SW
6th St SW
4th St SW
3rd St SW
2nd St SW
9th St SW

Essentials

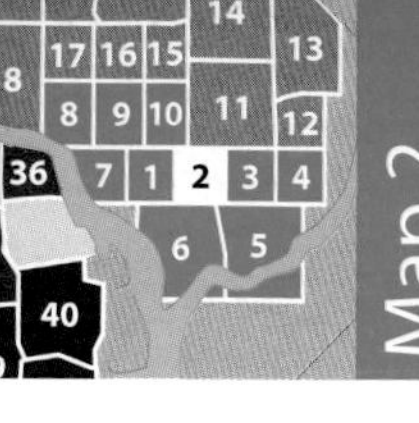

Well, more like China*block*, but the real draw of DC's fastest growing neighborhood is 7th Street, which decided to swap its drug dealers for art dealers and now anchors the development of the most luxurious new apartment complexes in the city. Flanking the palatial MCI Center, the yuppie-christened promenade even plays holiday music in December, uniting suburban revelers with a few pre-boom homeless, who are oddly appreciated for maintaining the neighborhood's urban authenticity.

Banks

- **Adams National** • 50 Massachusetts Ave NE
- **Adams National** • 802 7th St NW
- **BB&T** • 614 H St NW
- **BB&T (ATM)** • 707 7th St NW
- **Chevy Chase** • 650 F St NW
- **Chevy Chase** • 701 Pennsylvania Ave NW
- **Industrial Bank (ATM)** • 441 4th St NW
- **PNC** • 301 7th St NW
- **PNC** • 833 7th St NW
- **PNC (ATM)** • 4th St NW & Constitution Ave NW
- **PNC (ATM)** • 600 New Jersey Ave NW
- **PNC (ATM)** • 601 E St NW
- **PNC (ATM)** • 820 1st St NE
- **Sun Trust** • 2 Massachusetts Ave NW
- **Sun Trust (ATM)** • 30 Massachusetts Ave NE
- **Wachovia** • 444 N Capitol St NW
- **Wachovia** • 600 Maryland Ave SW
- **Wachovia (ATM)** • 417 Sixth St NW
- **Wachovia (ATM)** • 50 Massachusetts Ave NE

Car Rental

- **Alamo** • 50 Massachusetts Ave NE • 202-842-7454
- **Budget** • 50 Massachusetts Ave NW • 202-289-5373
- **National** • 50 Massachusetts Ave NE • 202-842-7454
- **Thrifty** • 601 F St NW • 202-371-0485

Community Gardens

Landmarks

- **B Dalton** • 50 Massachusetts Ave NE
- **Casa Italiana** • 595 1/2 3rd St
- **Chinatown Gate** • H St NW & 7th St NW
- **Library of Congress** • 101 Independence Ave SE
- **Newseum Front Pages** • 6th St NW & Pennsylvania Ave NW
- **Supreme Court of the United States** • 1st St NE
- **US Botanic Garden** • 1st St SW b/w Maryland Ave SW and C St SW

Libraries

- **Federal Trade Commission Library** • 600 Pennsylvania Ave NW # 630
- **National Research Council Library** • 500 5th St NW, Room 304
- **US Library of Congress** • 101 Independence Ave SE
- **US Senate Library** • Russell Senate Office Bldg, B15

Parking

Pharmacies

- **CVS** • 801 7th St NW
- **Tschiffely Pharmacy** • 50 Massachusetts Ave NE

Police

- **MPDC Headquarters** • 300 Indiana Ave NW

Post Offices

- **National Capitol Station** • 2 Massachusetts Ave NE

Schools

- **Georgetown University Law Center** • 600 New Jersey Ave NW
- **Gonzaga College High** • 19 I St NW
- **House of Representatives Page** • 101 Independence Ave SE

Map 2 • Chinatown / Union Station

N

L St NW
New York Ave NW
Mount Vernon Pl NW
Mt Vernon Square
K St NW
K St NW
I St NW
I St NW
Massachusetts Ave NW
H St NW
H St NW
G St NW
G St NW
G St NW
G Pl NW
G Pl NE
G St NE
F St NW
F St NW
E St NW
E St NE
D St NW
D St NW
C St NW
C St NW
C St NE
Indiana Ave NW
Pennsylvania Ave NW
Constitution Ave NW
Constitution Ave NE
Madison Dr NW
Jefferson Dr SW
Independence Ave SE
Maryland Ave SW
Maryland Ave NE
C St SW
C St SE
D St SW
D St SE
Virginia Ave SW
School St SW
E St SW
E St SE
Washington Ave SW
Sursum Corda Ct NW
First Ter
K Ter NW
Temple Ct NW
Prather Ct NW
Madison Al NW
Chews Ct NW
Chews Al NW
Mccullough Ct NW
N Capitol St NW
New Jersey Ave NW
New Jersey Ave SE
Louisiana Ave NE
Louisiana Ave NW
Delaware Ave NE
Columbus Monument Dr
Union Station Dr
Massachusetts Ave NE
East Capitol Cir
Capitol Cir NE
Capitol Driveway NE
Capitol Driveway SE
East Capitol St
South Capitol Cir SW
South Capitol St
Ivy St SE
N Carolina Ave SE
Rumsey Ct SE
9th St NW
8th St NW
7th St NW
6th St NW
5th St NW
4th St NW
3rd St NW
2nd St NW
1st St NW
1st St NE
2nd St NE
9th St SW
7th St SW
6th St SW
4th St SW
3rd St SW
2nd St SW
1st St SW
1st St SE
Gallery Place Chinatown
MCI Center
PAGE 234
Judiciary Square
Archives-Navy Memorial
Union Station
PAGE 264
Union Station Plaza
VEHICULAR TRAFFIC PROHIBITED
John Marshall Park
395
The Mall
PAGE 200
Capitol Reflecting Pool
United States Capitol Building
PAGE 200
Supreme Court
Jefferson Building
Madison Building
PAGE 205
US Botanic Garden
PAGE 194
Federal Triangle SW
L'Enfant Plaza
Capitol South
A
B
C
1
2
10
11
1
3
6
5
1
50

Sundries / Entertainment

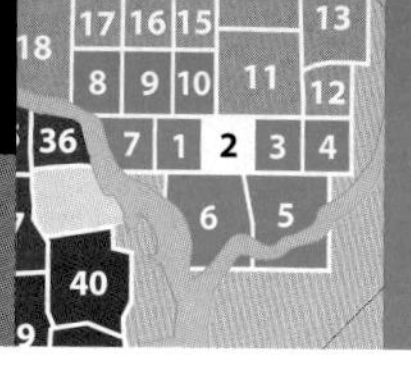

It was exciting when five-star pioneers like Capital Q and Fadó Irish Pub first came onto the scene, but now the fear is that Chinatown soon will become Chain-atown. An outbreak of Fuddrucker's-style restaurants is currently sweeping the neighborhood and threatens to leave behind a scar of Friendship Heights proportions. Thank God for the H Street Chinese restaurants, which still offer amazingly delicious grub at pre MCI-era prices.

Coffee

- **Bucks County Coffee** • 50 Massachusetts Ave NE
- **Café Renee** • 50 Massachusetts Ave NE
- **Cosí** • 601 Pennsylvania Ave NW
- **Starbucks** • 325 7th St NW
- **Starbucks** • 40 Massachusetts Ave NE
- **Starbucks** • 443-C 7th St NW
- **Starbucks** • 800 7th St NW

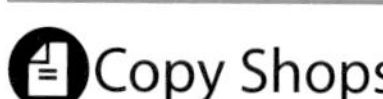

Copy Shops

- **Document Technology Centre (24 hours)** • 50 F St NW
- **Kinko's (7am-11pm)** • 325 7th St NW
- **Lex Reprographics (24 hours)** • 900 7th St NW
- **Minuteman Press (8am-6pm)** • 555 New Jersey Ave NW

Gyms

- **Washington Sports Clubs** • 783 7th St NW

Liquor Stores

- **Corner Store** • 800 N Capitol St NW
- **Kogod Liquors** • 441 New Jersey Ave NW
- **Union Wine & Liquors Store** • 50 Massachusetts Ave NE

Movie Theaters

- **AMC Union Station 9** • 50 Massachusetts Ave NE
- **Lockheed Martin IMAX Theater** • 601 Independence Ave SW
- **Mary Pickford Theater** • Library of Congress, James Madison Memorial Bldg, Independence Ave SE b/w 1st St SE & 2nd St SE
- **Regal Gallery Place Stadium** • 707 7th St NW

Nightlife

- **Bullfeather's** • 410 1st St SE
- **Capitol City Brewing Company** • 2 Massachusetts Ave NE
- **Coyote Ugly** • 717 6th St NW
- **The Dubliner** • 520 N Capitol St (entrance on F St)
- **Fadó Irish Pub** • 808 7th St NW
- **Flying Scotsman** • 233 2nd St NW
- **IndeBleu** • 707 G St NW
- **Juste Lounge** • 1015 1/2 7th St NW
- **Kelly's Irish Times** • 14 F St NW
- **My Brother's Place** • 237 2nd St NW
- **RFD Washington** • 810 7th St NW

Restaurants

- **701** • 701 Pennsylvania Ave NW
- **America** • Union Station, 50 Massachusetts Ave NE
- **Andale** • 401 7th St NW
- **B Smith's** • Union Station, 50 Massachusetts Ave NE
- **Bistro Bis** • 15 E St NW
- **Burma** • 740 6th St NW
- **Capital Q** • 707 H St NW
- **Capitol City Brewing Company** • 2 Massachusetts Ave NE
- **Center Café at Union Station** • Union Station, 50 Massachusetts Ave NE
- **Chinatown Express** • 746 6th St NW
- **District Chophouse** • 509 7th St NW
- **The Dubliner Restaurant** • 520 N Capitol St NW
- **Fadó Irish Pub** • 808 7th St NW
- **Flying Scotsman** • 233 2nd St NW
- **Fuddrucker's** • 734 7th St NW
- **Full Kee** • 509 H St NW
- **Jaleo** • 480 7th St NW
- **Kelly's Irish Times** • 14 F St NW
- **Le Paradou** • 678 Indiana Ave NW
- **Lei Garden** • 629 H St NW
- **Matchbox** • 713 H St NW
- **My Brother's Place** • 237 2nd St NW
- **Rosa Mexicano** • 575 7th St NW
- **Tony Cheng's Mongolian Restaurant** • 619 H St NW, downstairs
- **Tony Cheng's Seafood Restaurant** • 619 H St NW, upstairs

Shopping

- **Alamo Flags** • Union Station
- **Apartment Zero** • 406 7th St NW
- **Comfort One Shoes** • 50 Massachusetts Ave NE
- **Godiva Chocolatier** • 50 Massachusetts Ave NE
- **Marvelous Market** • 730 7th St NW
- **National Air and Space Museum Shop** • 6th St SW & Independence Ave SW
- **Olsson's Books** • 418 7th St NW
- **Urban Outfitters Downtown** • 737 7th St NW

Map 3 • The Hill

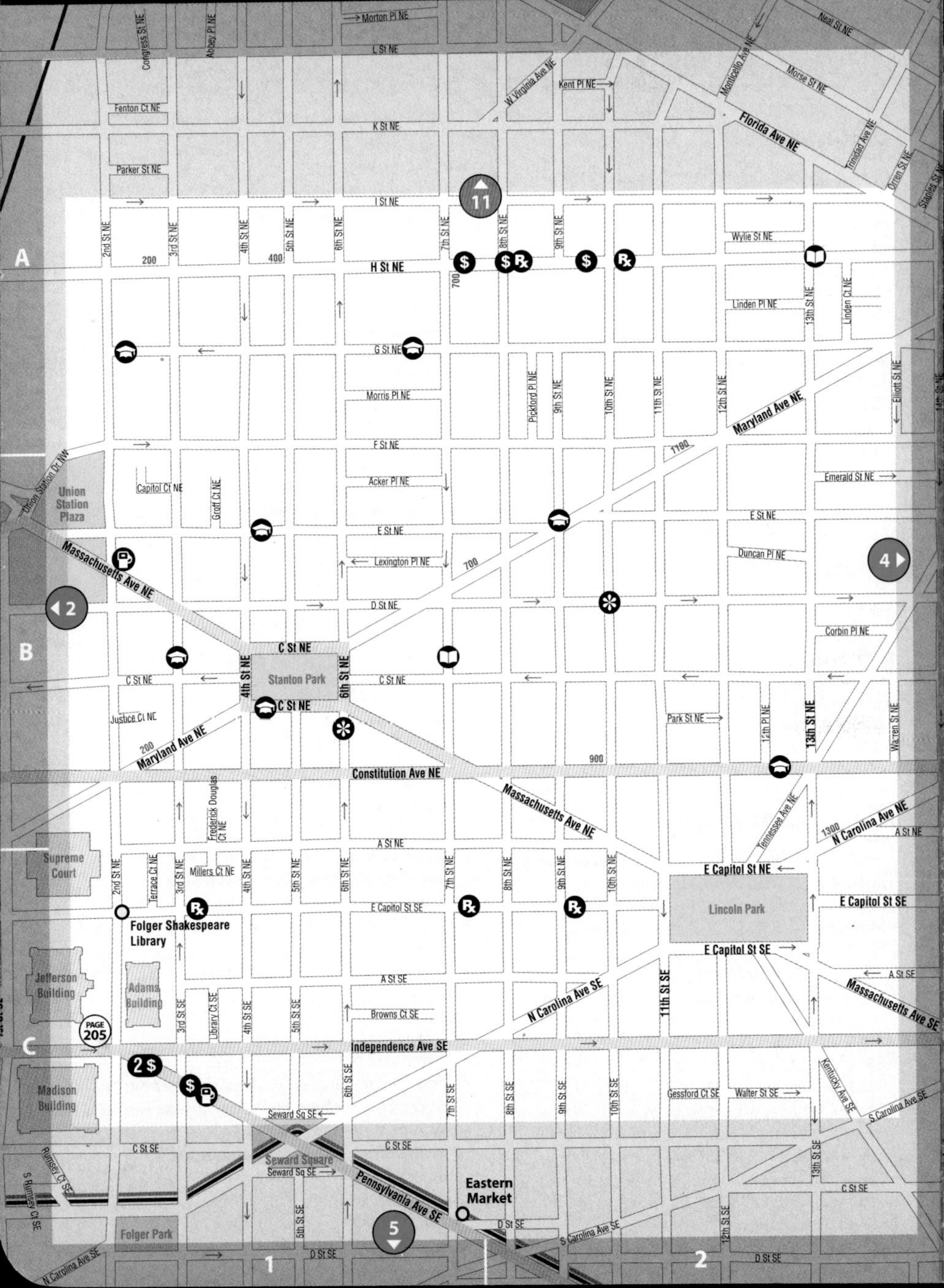

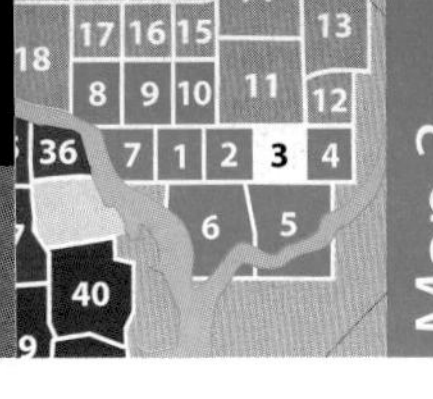

Talk to 10 people on The Hill and you're guaranteed to encounter 10 different accents. These transplant Washingtonians come from all 50 states — amazing because they're all so *similar*. Men: blue shirt and gray suit. Ladies: a very stiff gait and an even stiffer hairstyle. Interns: a backpack worn *over* the blazer. Staffers: seemingly wealthy when getting drunk five nights a week, but suddenly poor when it's time to tip the waiter.

Banks

- **Bank of America** • 201 Pennsylvania Ave SE
- **Bank of America** • 722 H St NE
- **Bank of America (ATM)** • 961 H St NE
- **PNC** • 800 H St NE
- **Sun Trust** • 300 Pennsylvania Ave SE
- **Wachovia** • 215 Pennsylvania Ave SE

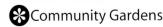

Community Gardens

Gas Stations

- **Exxon** • 200 Massachusetts Ave NE
- **Exxon** • 339 Pennsylvania Ave SE

Landmarks

- **Folger Shakespeare Library** • 201 E Capitol St SE

Libraries

- **Northeast Library** • 330 7th St NE
- **RL Christian Community Library** • 1300 H St NE

Pharmacies

- **Grubb's CARE Pharmacy & Medical Supply** • 326 E Capitol St NE
- **Morton's CARE Pharmacy** • 724 E Capitol St NE
- **Rite Aid** • 801 H St NE
- **Robinson's Apothecary** • 922 E Capitol St NE
- **Super CARE Pharmacy** • 1019 H St NE

Schools

- **Brent Elementary** • 330 3rd St NE
- **Cornerstone Community** • 907 Maryland Ave NE
- **Ludlow-Taylor Elementary** • 659 G St NE
- **Maury Elementary** • 1250 Constitution Ave NE
- **Peabody Elementary** • 425 C St NE
- **Stuart-Hobson Middle** • 410 E St NE
- **Thompson Elementary at Logan** • 215 G St NE

Map 3 • The Hill

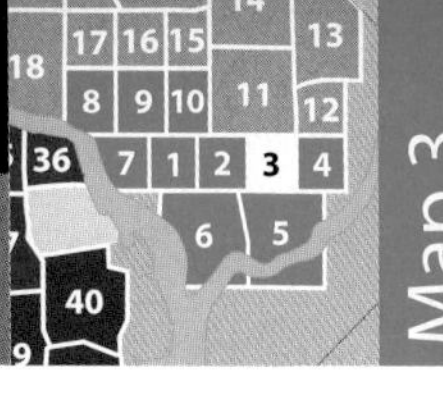

Wealthy young families have infiltrated the now-sleepy streets, pushing 20-something renters down to Eastern Market (hence the better bars). But if you have a sudden urge to warp back to your post-grad days, Capitol Lounge is possibly the diviest dive in America (and we mean it in a good way!). If there's a little more blue in your blood, head to Top of the Hill with a cigar in your pocket, or order one of 40 wines-by-the-glass at Pennsylvania Ave's newest edition, Sonoma.

Coffee

- **Cosí** • 301 Pennsylvania Ave SE
- **Neb's Café** • 201 Massachusetts Ave NE
- **Starbucks** • 237 Pennsylvania Ave SE

Farmer's Markets

- **H Street Freshfarm Market** • 600 H St NE

Hardware Stores

- **Park's Hardware** • 920 H St NE

Liquor Stores

- **Capitol Hill Liquor & Deli** • 323 Pennsylvania Ave SE
- **Gandel's Liquors** • 211 Pennsylvania Ave SE
- **H Street Liquor Store** • 303 H St NE
- **Hayden's Liquor Store** • 700 North Carolina Ave SE
- **Jumbo Liquors** • 1122 H St NE
- **Kelly's Liquor Store** • 415 H St NE
- **Northeast Beverage** • 1344 H St NE
- **Schneider's of Capitol Hill** • 300 Massachusetts Ave NE

Nightlife

- **Capitol Lounge** • 229 Pennsylvania Ave SE
- **Hawk and Dove** • 329 Pennsylvania Ave SE
- **Lounge 201** • 201 Massachusetts Ave NE
- **Politiki** • 319 Pennsylvania Ave SE
- **Top of the Hill** • 319 Pennsylvania Ave SE
- **Tune Inn** • 331 1/2 Pennsylvania Ave SE

Restaurants

- **Café Berlin** • 322 Massachusetts Ave NE
- **Hawk and Dove** • 329 Pennsylvania Ave SE
- **Kenny's Smokehouse** • 732 Maryland Ave NE
- **La Brasserie** • 239 Massachusetts Ave NE
- **La Loma Mexican Restaurant** • 316 Massachusetts Ave NE
- **Pete's Diner** • 212 2nd St SE
- **Ristorante Tosca** • 1112 F St NW
- **Sonoma** • 223 Pennsylvania Ave SE
- **Two Quail** • 320 Massachusetts Ave NE
- **White Tiger** • 301 Massachusetts Ave NE

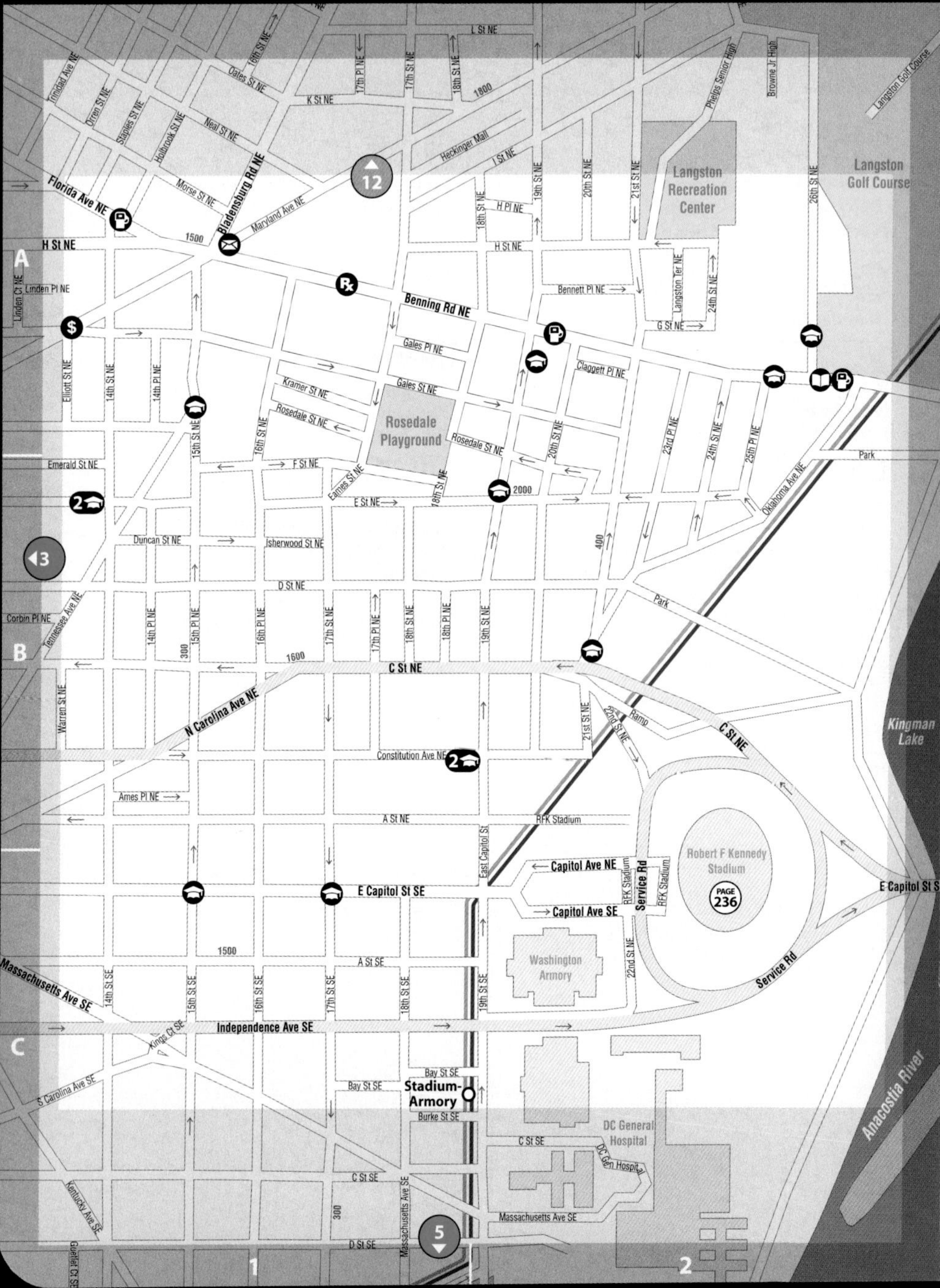

Map 4 • RFK

N
Langston Recreation Center
Langston Golf Course
Rosedale Playground
Robert F Kennedy Stadium
PAGE 236
Washington Armory
DC General Hospital
Stadium-Armory
Kingman Lake
Anacostia River
Benning Rd NE
Bladensburg Rd NE
Florida Ave NE
Maryland Ave NE
H St NE
C St NE
N Carolina Ave NE
E Capitol St SE
Capitol Ave NE
Capitol Ave SE
Independence Ave SE
Massachusetts Ave SE
Service Rd
RFK Stadium
Oklahoma Ave NE
Tennessee Ave NE
Constitution Ave NE
A St NE
A St SE
C St SE
D St SE
Bay St SE
Burke St SE
Kentucky Ave SE
S Carolina Ave SE
Kings Ct SE
Heckinger Mall
Phelps Senior High
Browne Jr High
Langston Golf Course
Park
Ramp
A
B
C
1
2
12
3
5

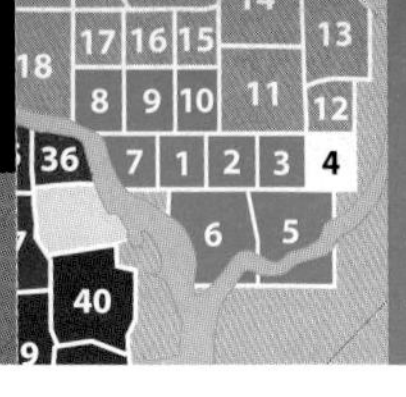

The baby boom to the west has unleashed rampant gentrification that is marching toward the stadium. Crime and newcomer backlash are holding off the pampering amenities that are expected to follow the soaring home prices. Until the pet shops and coffeehouses move in, just be happy that you can walk to Nats games.

Banks

- **Bank of America** • 1330 Maryland Ave NE

Gas Stations

- **Amoco** • 1396 Florida Ave NE
- **Amoco** • 1950 Benning Rd NE
- **Exxon** • 2651 Benning Rd NE

Libraries

- **Langston Community Library** • 2600 Benning Rd NE

Pharmacies

- **Sterling CARE Pharmacy** • 1647 Benning Rd NE

Post Offices

- **Northeast Station** • 1563 Maryland Ave NE

Schools

- **The Academy for Ideal Education Upper** • 702 15th St NE
- **Eastern High** • 1700 E Capitol St NE
- **Eliot Junior High** • 1830 Constitution Ave NE
- **Friendship Edison Blow Pierce Campus** • 725 19th St NE
- **Gibbs Elementary** • 500 19th St NE
- **Holy Comforter-St Cyprian** • 1503 E Capitol St SE
- **Miner Elementary** • 601 15th St NE
- **Options Middle** • 1375 E St NE
- **Phelps Career High** • 704 26th St NE
- **Sasha Bruce Middle** • 1375 E St NE
- **Spingarn Center** • 2500 Benning Rd NE
- **St Benedict of the Moor** • 320 21st St NE
- **Two Rivers Elementary** • 1830 Constitution Ave NE

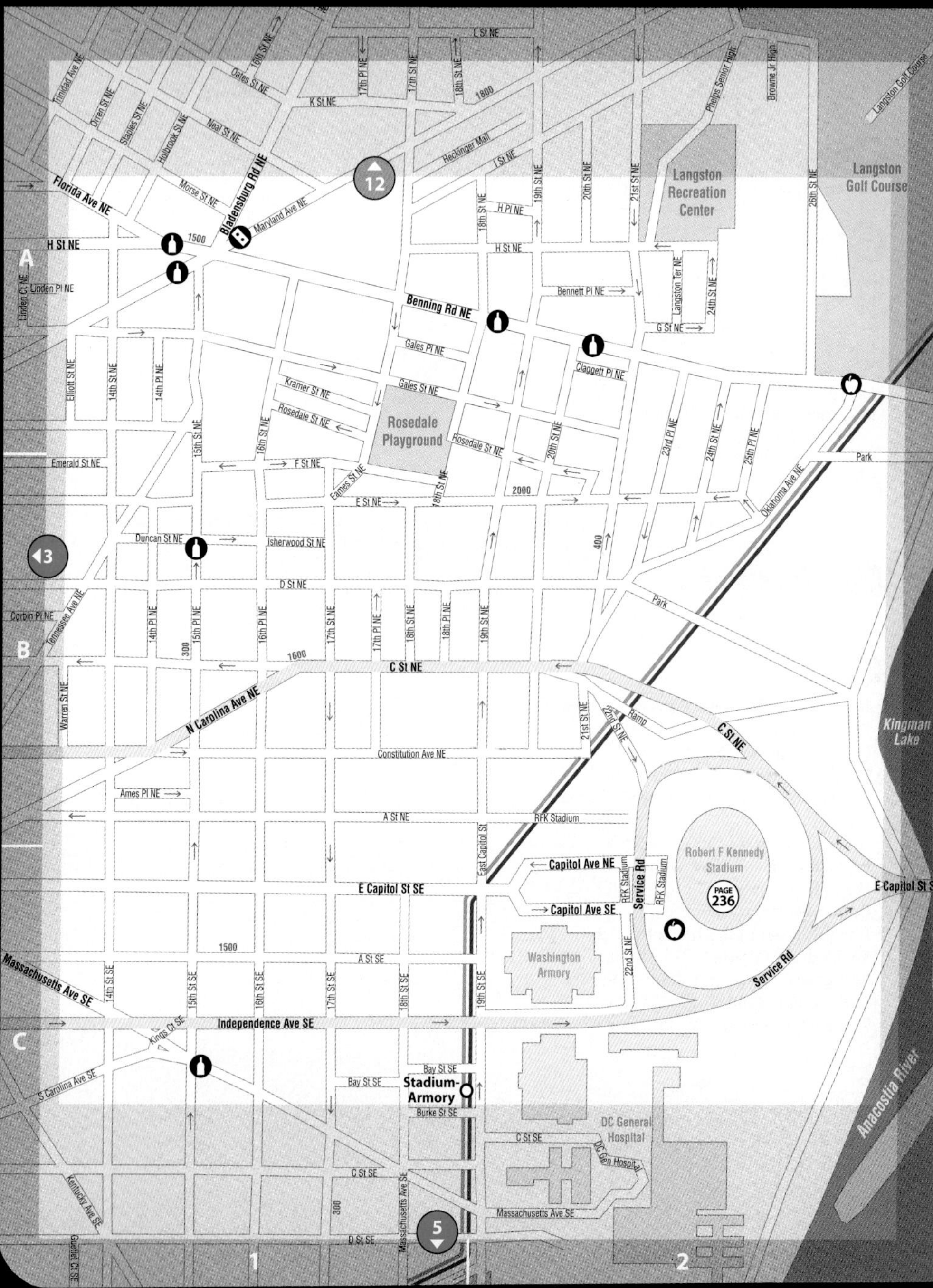

N

L St NE
K St NE
Oates St NE
16th St NE
Trinidad Ave NE
Orren St NE
Staples St NE
Holbrook St NE
Neal St NE
17th Pl NE
17th St NE
18th St NE
1800
Heckinger Mall
I St NE
Phelps Senior High
Browne Jr High
Langston Golf Course
Langston Golf Course
Langston Recreation Center
12
Florida Ave NE
Morse St NE
Bladensburg Rd NE
Maryland Ave NE
1500
H St NE
A
Linden Ct NE
Linden Pl NE
19th St NE
20th St NE
21st St NE
26th St NE
18th St NE
H Pl NE
H St NE
Bennett Pl NE
Langston Ter NE
24th St NE
G St NE
Benning Rd NE
Gales Pl NE
Gales St NE
Claggett Pl NE
Kramer St NE
Rosedale St NE
Rosedale Playground
Rosedale St NE
Elliott St NE
14th St NE
14th Pl NE
15th St NE
16th St NE
20th St NE
23rd Pl NE
24th St NE
25th Pl NE
Park
Emerald St NE
F St NE
Eames St NE
18th St NE
2000
Oklahoma Ave NE
E St NE
Duncan St NE
Isherwood St NE
400
3
D St NE
Park
Corbin Pl NE
Tennessee Ave NE
14th Pl NE
15th Pl NE
16th Pl NE
17th St NE
17th Pl NE
18th St NE
18th Pl NE
19th St NE
300
B
1600
C St NE
Warren St NE
N Carolina Ave NE
21st St NE
22nd St NE
Ramp
C St NE
Kingman Lake
Constitution Ave NE
Ames Pl NE
A St NE
RFK Stadium
East Capitol St
Capitol Ave NE
RFK Stadium
Service Rd
RFK Stadium
Robert F Kennedy Stadium
PAGE 236
E Capitol St SE
E Capitol St S
Capitol Ave SE
1500
Washington Armory
22nd St NE
A St SE
Massachusetts Ave SE
14th St SE
15th St SE
16th St SE
17th St SE
18th St SE
19th St SE
Service Rd
Independence Ave SE
C
Kings Ct SE
S Carolina Ave SE
Bay St SE
Bay St SE
Stadium-Armory
Burke St SE
Anacostia River
DC General Hospital
C St SE
DC Gen Hospital
C St SE
Kentucky Ave SE
300
Massachusetts Ave SE
Massachusetts Ave SE
5
D St SE
Gurtler Ct SE
1
2

Sundries / Entertainment

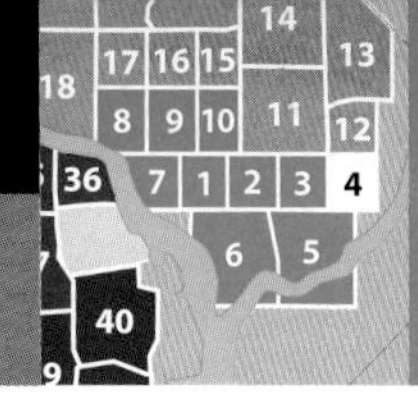

A few entrepreneurs like those behind the Phish Tea Café are making a go of it, catering to a flagging theater crowd along H Street. Otherwise, this is not the area for a moonlit stroll. Better to visit one of the many liquor stores in the daylight hours and plan to gather indoors in the evening.

Farmer's Markets

- **DC Open Air Farmers Market** • RFK Stadium parking lot 6, Independence Ave & 22nd St SE
- **Open Air Farmers Markets** • Oklahoma Ave NE & Benning Rd NE

Liquor Stores

- **Friends Liquors** • 1406 H St NE
- **New York Liquor Store** • 1447 Maryland Ave NE
- **S&J Liquor Store** • 1500 Massachusetts Ave SE
- **Silverman's Liquor** • 2033 Benning Rd NE
- **Sylvia's Liquor Store** • 1818 Benning Rd NE
- **Viggy's Liquors** • 409 15th St NE

Video Rental

- **Blockbuster Video** • 1555 Maryland Ave NE

Map 5 • Southeast / Anacostia

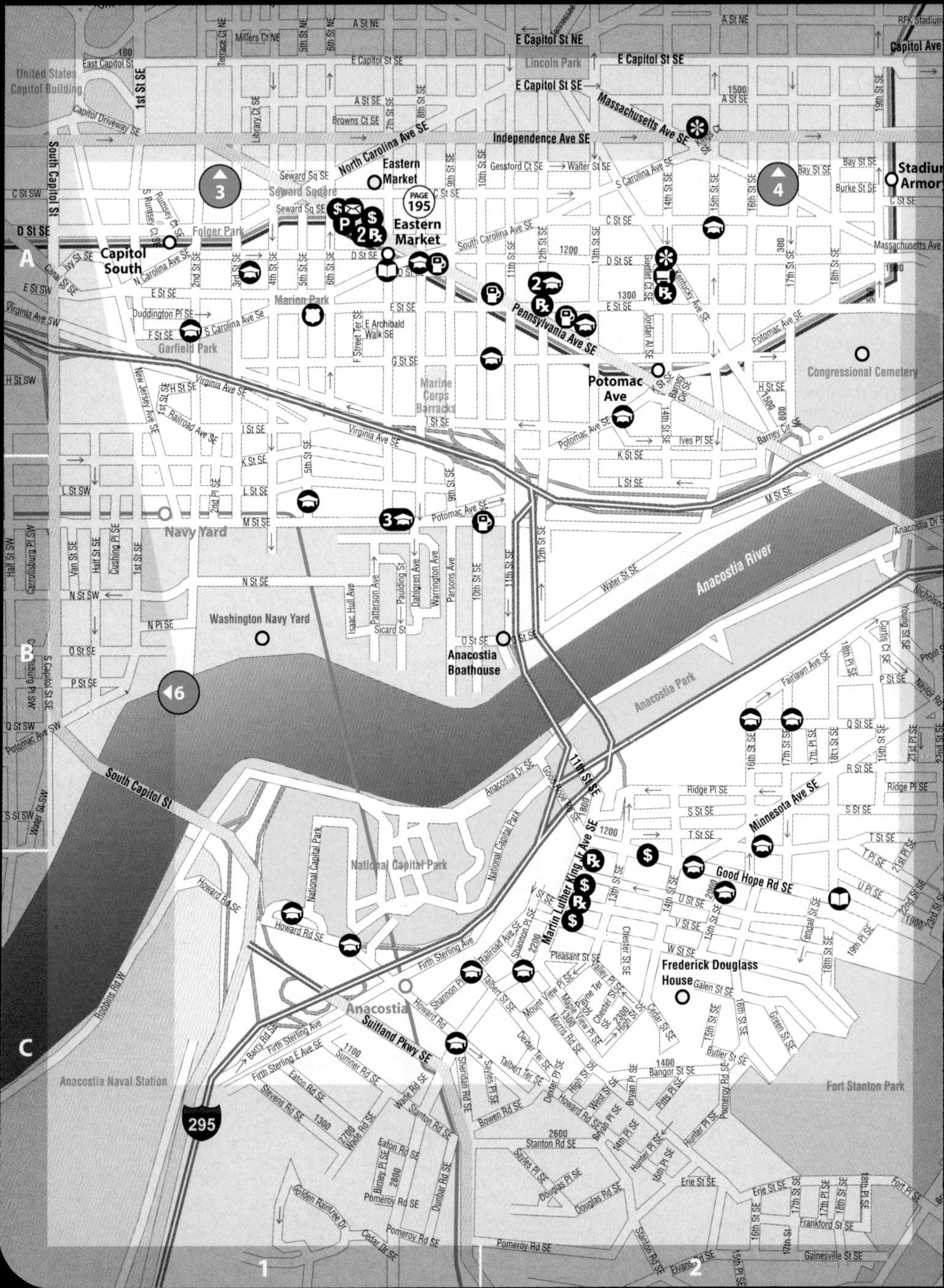

Essentials

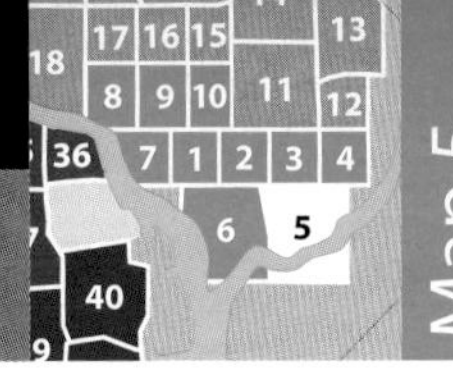

Eighth Street is the center of a funky revitalization, drawing risk-taking residents and retailers. Wandering too far off the main drag can lead you to some dismal stretches because, unlike other, whip-fast, developer-fueled neighborhood turnarounds in the city, the process here seems to be a bit more organic.

Banks

- **Bank of America** • 2100 Martin Luther King Jr Ave SE
- **Citibank** • 600 Pennsylvania Ave SE
- **PNC** • 2000 Martin Luther King Jr Ave SE
- **PNC** • 650 Pennsylvania Ave SE
- **Sun Trust** • 1340 Good Hope Rd SE

Community Gardens

Gas Stations

- **Amoco** • 823 Pennsylvania Ave SE
- **Exxon** • 1022 M St SE
- **Exxon** • 1201 Pennsylvania Ave SE
- **Sunoco** • 1248 Pennsylvania Ave SE
- **Texaco** • 1022 Pennsylvania Ave SE

Landmarks

- **Anacostia Boathouse** • 1105 O St NE
- **Congressional Cemetery** • 1801 E St SE
- **Eastern Market** • 225 7th St SE
- **Frederick Douglass House** • 1411 W St SE
- **Washington Navy Yard** • 8th St SE & M St SE

Libraries

- **Anacostia Library** • 1800 Good Hope Rd SE
- **Southeast Library** • 403 7th St SE

Parking

Pharmacies

- **Capitol Hill CARE Pharmacy** • 650 Pennsylvania Ave SE
- **CVS** • 500 12th St SE
- **CVS** • 661 Pennsylvania Ave SE
- **Neighborhood CARE Pharmacy** • 1932 Martin Luther King Jr Ave SE
- **Safeway** • 415 14th St SE
- **State CARE Pharmacy** • 2041 Martin Luther King Jr Ave SE

Police

- **MPDC 1st District Substation** • 500 E St SE

Post Offices

- **Southeast Station** • 600 Pennsylvania Ave SE

Schools

- **Ambassador Baptist Church Christian Academy** • 1412 Minnesota Ave SE
- **Anacostia Bible Church Christian** • 1610 T St SE
- **Anacostia High** • 1601 16th St SE
- **Birney Elementary** • 2501 Martin Luther King Jr Ave SE
- **Capitol Hill Day** • 210 S Carolina Ave SE
- **Clara Muhammad** • 2313 Martin Luther King Jr Ave
- **Eagle Academy** • 770 M St SE
- **Friendship Edison Chamberlain Campus** • 1345 Potomac Ave SE
- **Hine Junior High** • 335 8th St SE
- **Holy Temple Christian Academy** • 439 12th St SE
- **Howard Road Academy** • 701 Howard Rd SE
- **Ketcham Elementary** • 1919 15th St SE
- **Kipp DC/Key Academy** • 770 M St SE
- **Kramer Middle** • 1700 Q St SE
- **Payne Elementary** • 305 15th St SE
- **Rose Elementary** • 821 Howard Rd SE
- **Savoy Elementary** • 2400 Shannon Pl SE
- **St Peter's Interparish** • 422 3rd St SE
- **Tyler Elementary** • 1001 G St SE
- **Van Ness Elementary** • 1150 5th St SE
- **Washington Math Science Technology High** • 770 M St SE
- **Watkins Elementary** • 420 12th St SE

Supermarkets

- **Safeway** • 415 14th St SE

Map 5 • **Southeast / Anacostia**

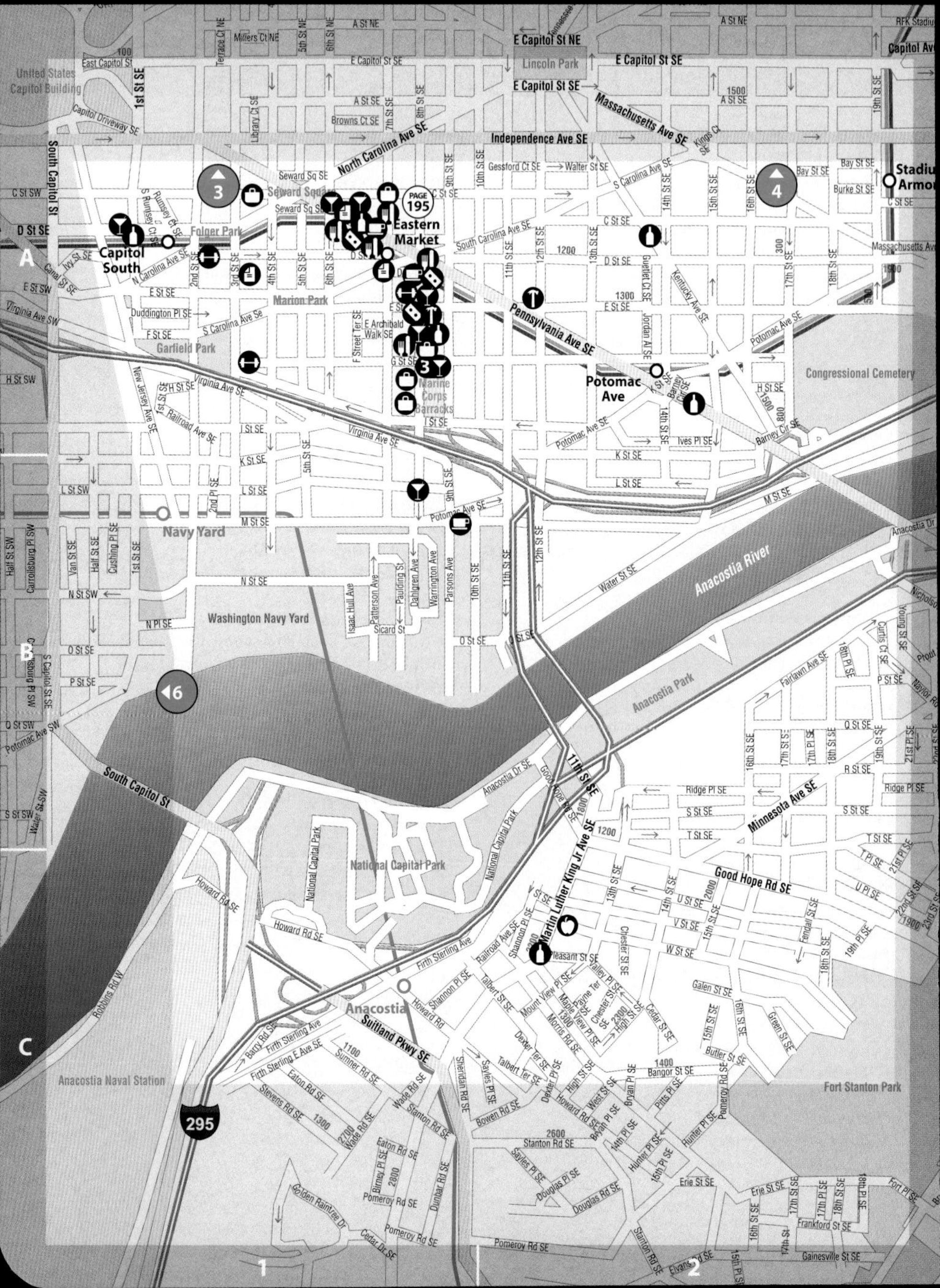

PAGE 195

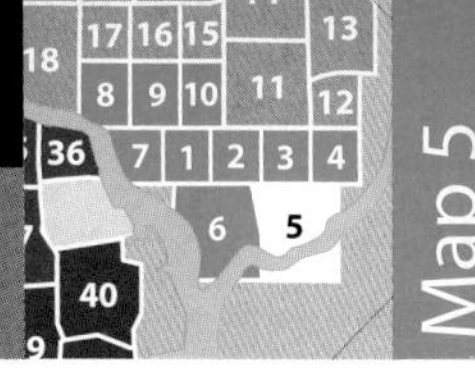

Better and better amenities are pushing out storefront Chinese take-outs along Eighth Street. Banana Café and the more upscale Starfish are owned by the same neighborhood devotee who is doing his bit to remake the area into a citywide draw. Cross Pennsylvania Ave and you'll find yourself in an already polished 'hood where Montmarte calls for special occasions and Bread & Chocolate for a sidewalk brunch.

Coffee

- **Murky Coffee** • 660 Pennsylvania Ave SE
- **Starbucks** • 401 8th St SE
- **William III Gourmet Coffee** • 901 M St SE

Copy Shops

- **Kinko's (6am-11pm)** • 715 D St SE
- **UPS Store (9am-7pm)** • 611 Pennsylvania Ave SE

Farmer's Markets

- **Anacostia Farmers Market** • 1225 W St SE
- **Eastern Market Outdoor Farmers Market** • 225 7th St SE

Gyms

- **Curves** • 407 8th St SE
- **Results the Gym** • 315 G St SE
- **Washington Sports Clubs** • 214 D St SE

Hardware Stores

- **District Lock & Hardware** • 505 8th St SE
- **Frager's Hardware** • 1115 Pennsylvania Ave SE

Liquor Stores

- **Albert's Liquor Store** • 328 Kentucky Ave SE
- **Big K Liquors** • 2252 Martin Luther King Jr Ave SE
- **Chat's Liquors** • 503 8th St SE
- **Congressional Liquors** • 404 1st St SE
- **JJ Mutts Wine & Spirits** • 643 Pennsylvania Ave SE
- **World Liquors** • 1453 Pennsylvania Ave SE

Nightlife

- **Bachelor's Mill** • 1106 8th St SE
- **Ellington's on Eighth** • 424A 8th St SE
- **Finn MacCool's** • 713 8th St SE
- **Marty's** • 527 8th St SE
- **Mr Henry's Capitol Hill** • 601 Pennsylvania Ave SE
- **Remington's** • 639 Pennsylvania Ave SE
- **Tapatinis** • 711 8th St SE
- **Tortilla Coast** • 400 1st St SE
- **Tunnicliff's Tavern** • 222 7th St SE
- **The Ugly Mug** • 723 8th St SE

Restaurants

- **Banana Café & Piano Bar** • 500 8th St SE
- **Bread & Chocolate** • 666 Pennsylvania Ave SE
- **Meyhane** • 633 Pennsylvania Ave SE
- **Montmartre** • 327 7th St SE
- **Starfish** • 539 8th St SE
- **Tortilla Coast** • 400 1st St SE

Shopping

- **Backstage** • 545 8th St SE
- **Capitol Hill Bikes** • 709 8th St SE
- **Capitol Hill Books** • 657 C St SE
- **Eastern Market** • 225 7th St SE
- **Plaid** • 715 8th St SE
- **Woven History & Silk Road** • 315 7th St SE

Video Rental

- **Blockbuster Video** • 400 8th St SE
- **Capitol Video Sales** • 514 8th St SE
- **Penn Video** • 645 Pennsylvania Ave SE

Smithsonian
L'Enfant Plaza
Federal Center SW
Capitol South
Southeastern University
Arena Stage
Waterfront SEU
Navy Yard
Thomas Law House
USS Sequoia
Tiber Island
Gangplank Marina
Odyssey Cruiseline
Spirit of Washington
Fort McNair
Washington Monument
The Mall
United States Capitol Bldg
West Potomac Park
Tidal Basin
Jefferson Memorial
East Potomac Park
East Potomac Park Golf Course
Washington Channel
Potomac River
Anacostia Naval Station
Randall Playground
Garfield Park
Reflecting Pool

PAGE 198
PAGE 200
PAGE 194
PAGE 205
PAGE 198

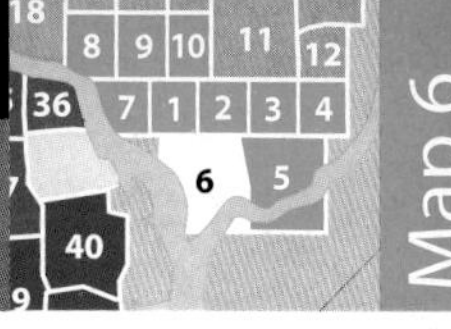

We don't know what's more mishandled in Washington: the White House budget surplus or Waterfront real estate. Bordered by two major waterways, this neighborhood could be the next Georgetown Harbor if it ever got its act together. A new ballpark, a revitalized South Capitol Street and facelifts to Arena Stage and the Waterfront Mall are in the works, so our advice is to sit tight and be sure to buy a copy of *NFT 2008*.

Banks

- **Bank of America** • 401 M St SW
- **M&T Bank** • 500 C St SW
- **M&T Bank (ATM)** • 550 C St SW
- **PNC** • 935 L'Enfant Plz SW
- **Sun Trust** • 965 L'Enfant Plz SW

Car Rental

- **Enterprise** • 970 D St SW • 202-554-8100
- **Rent-A-Wreck** • 1252 Half St SE • 202-408-9828

Car Washes

- **Splash the Car Wash** • 10 I St SE

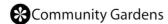

Community Gardens

Gas Stations

- **Amoco** • 1244 S Capitol St SE
- **Exxon** • 1001 S Capitol St SW
- **Exxon** • 950 S Capitol St SE
- **Sunoco** • 50 M St SE

Landmarks

- **Arena Stage** • 1101 6th St SW
- **Ft Lesley J McNair** • 4th St SW & P St SW
- **Gangplank Marina** • 6th St & Water St SW
- **Odyssey Cruiseline** • 6th St & Water St SW
- **Spirit of Washington** • 6th St & Water St SW
- **Thomas Law House** • 1252 6th St SW
- **Tiber Island** • 4th St SW b/w N St SW & M St SW
- **USS Sequoia** • 6th St SW & Maine Ave SW

Libraries

- **Comptroller of Currency Library** • 250 E St SW
- **DOT Law Library, Coast Guard Branch** • 2100 2nd St SW # B726
- **International Trade Commission Library** • 500 E St SW
- **NASA Headquarters Library** • 300 E St SW # 1J20
- **Southwest Library** • 900 Wesley Pl SW
- **US Housing & Urban Development Library** • 451 7th St SW # 8141

Parking

Pharmacies

- **CVS** • 401 M St SW
- **CVS** • 433 L'Enfant Plz SW

Police

- **MPDC 1st District Station** • 415 4th St SW

Post Offices

- **Fort McNair Station** • 300 A St SW
- **L'Enfant Plaza Station** • 437 L'Enfant Plz SW
- **Southwest Station** • 45 L St SW

Schools

- **Amidon Elementary** • 401 I St SW
- **Bowen Elementary** • 101 M St SW
- **Jefferson Junior High** • 801 7th St SW
- **National Defense University** • Ft Lesley J McNair
- **Southeastern University** • 501 I St SW

Supermarkets

- **Safeway** • 401 M St SW

Map 6 • Waterfront

Sundries / Entertainment

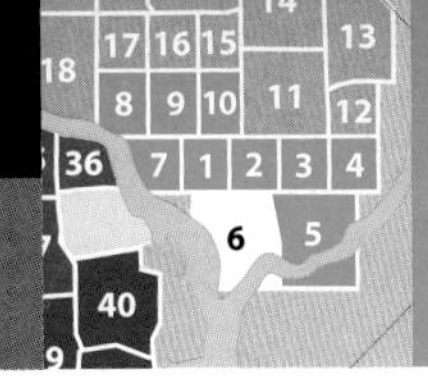

The coolest place to go in Waterfront is not a bar or a restaurant; it's a fish market. You can often smell the crabs from blocks away, and the crowd is always eclectic. As the neighborhood gets younger, Cantina Marina is slowly becoming a solid bar option, 'specially in the summer. But with the exception of salsa night Wednesdays at Zanzibar, the other bars/clubs on Water Street leave much to be desired.

Coffee

- **Olympic Espresso** • 955 L'Enfant Plz SW
- **Starbucks** • 550 C St SW

Farmer's Markets

- **US Dept of Transportation Farmers Market** • 400 7th St SW

Gyms

- **Gold's Gym** • 409 3rd St SW
- **Metro Fitness** • 480 L'Enfant Plz SW
- **Waterside Fitness & Swim Club** • 901 6th St SW

Liquor Stores

- **Bernstein's Reliable Liquor Store** • 39 M St SW
- **Cap Liquors** • 1301 S Capitol St SW
- **Half Street Liquor** • 1260 Half St SE
- **Harry's Liquor Wine & Cheese** • 401 M St SW
- **L'Enfant Wine & Beverage** • 459 L'Enfant Plz SW
- **Shulman's Southwest Liquor** • 1550 1st St SW
- **Tina's Wine Liquor & Deli** • 550 C St SW

Nightlife

- **Cantina Marina** • 600 Water St SW
- **Edge** • 52 L St SE
- **H20** • 800 Water St SW
- **Nation** • 1015 Half St SE
- **Secrets** • 1345 Half St SE
- **Zanzibar on the Waterfront** • 700 Water St SW
- **Ziegfields** • 1345 Half St SE

Restaurants

- **Cantina Marina** • 600 Water St SW
- **H2O at Hogate's** • 800 Water St SW
- **Jenny's Asian Fusion** • 1000 Water St SW
- **Phillip's Flagship** • 900 Water St SW
- **Pier 7** • 650 Water St SW

Shopping

- **Maine Avenue Fish Market** • Maine Ave SW & Potomac River

Map 7 • Foggy Bottom

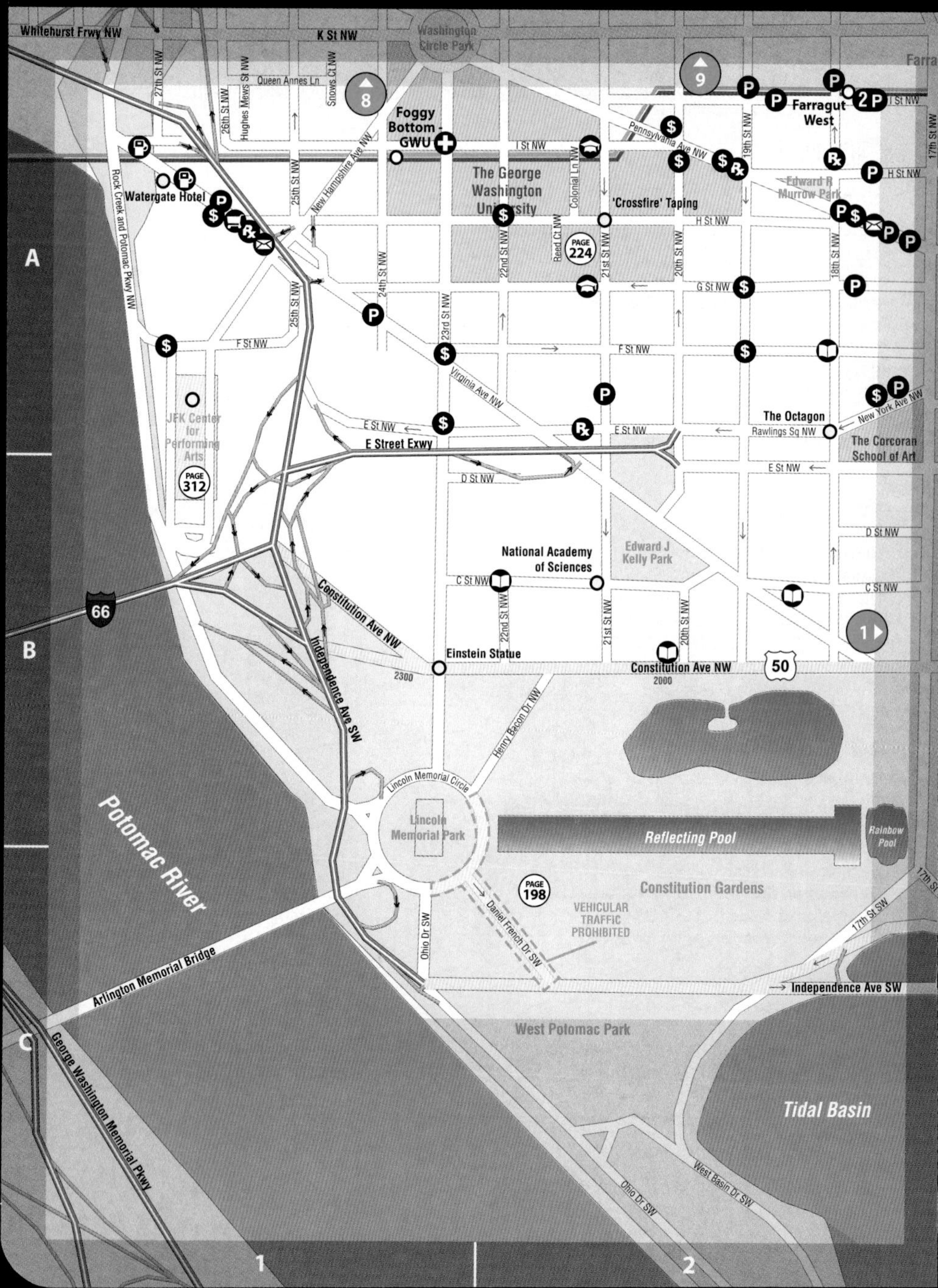

This neighborhood is populated by a mix of George Washington University students, government employees and "old money" Washingtonians who would rather be closer to the Watergate than Georgetown. There are some charming side streets with gorgeous houses in the area, but most of it is dominated by faceless, pseudo-high-rise apartments built in the 1970s. Fun to walk through, but try to end up in Georgetown or Dupont.

Banks

- **Bank of America** • 2001 Pennsylvania Ave NW
- **Bank of America (ATM)** • 1900 F St NW
- **Bank of America (ATM)** • 801 22nd St NW
- **Chevy Chase (ATM)** • 2000 Pennsylvania Ave NW
- **Citibank** • 1775 Pennsylvania Ave NW
- **PNC** • 1919 Pennsylvania Ave NW
- **PNC** • 2600 Virginia Ave NW
- **PNC (ATM)** • 2700 F St NW
- **PNC (ATM)** • 606 23rd St NW
- **PNC (ATM)** • 700 19th St NW
- **Sun Trust** • 1750 New York Ave NW
- **United Bank** • 1875 I St NW
- **Wachovia** • 502 23rd St NW

Gas Stations

- **Chevron** • 2643 Virginia Ave NW
- **Exxon** • 2708 Virginia Ave NW

Hospitals

- **The George Washington University Hospital** • 900 23rd St NW

Landmarks

- **"Crossfire" Taping** • 805 21st St NW
- **Einstein Statue** • Constitution Ave NW & 23rd St NW
- **Kennedy Center for the Performing Arts** • 2700 F St NW
- **National Academy of Sciences** • 2100 C St NW
- **The Octagon** • 1799 New York Ave NW
- **Watergate Hotel** • 2650 Virginia Ave NW

Libraries

- **Ralph J Bunche Library** • Department of State, 2201 C St NW, Room 3239
- **Federal Reserve Board Research & Law Libraries** • 20th St & Constitution Ave NW
- **General Services Administration Library** • 1800 F St NW #1033
- **US Department of the Interior Library** • 1849 C St NW

Parking

Pharmacies

- **CVS** • 1901 Pennsylvania Ave NW
- **CVS** • 2125 E St NW
- **CVS** • 2530 Virginia Ave NW
- **Foer's CARE Pharmacy** • 818 18th St NW

Post Offices

- **McPherson Station** • 1750 Pennsylvania Ave NW
- **Watergate Station** • 2512 Virginia Ave NW

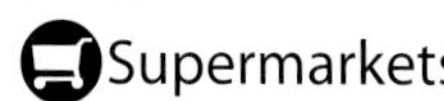

Schools

- **The George Washington University** • 2121 I St NW
- **School Without Walls** • 2130 G St NW

Supermarkets

- **Safeway** • 2550 Virginia Ave NW

Map 7 • Foggy Bottom

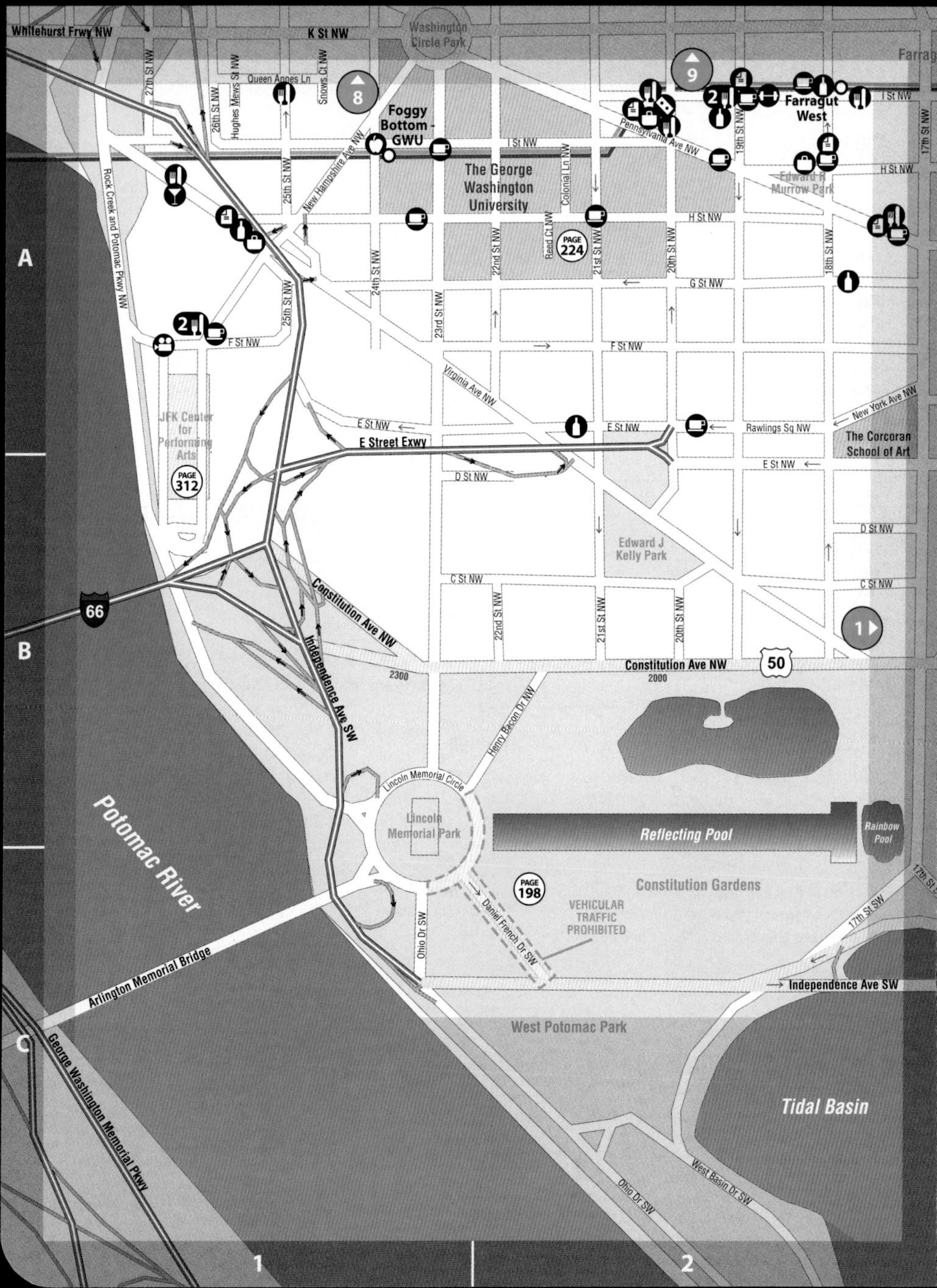

N

Whitehurst Frwy NW
K St NW
Washington Circle Park
Queen Annes Ln
Snows Ct NW
Hughes Mews St NW
26th St NW
27th St NW
25th St NW
24th St NW
23rd St NW
22nd St NW
21st St NW
20th St NW
19th St NW
18th St NW
17th St NW
New Hampshire Ave NW
Foggy Bottom - GWU
I St NW
The George Washington University
Colonial Ln NW
Reed Ct NW
PAGE 224
Pennsylvania Ave NW
Farragut West
Farrag
Edward R Murrow Park
H St NW
G St NW
F St NW
Rock Creek and Potomac Pkwy NW
Virginia Ave NW
E St NW
E Street Exwy
D St NW
Rawlings Sq NW
New York Ave NW
The Corcoran School of Art
JFK Center for Performing Arts
PAGE 312
Edward J Kelly Park
C St NW
Constitution Ave NW
2300
Constitution Ave NW
2000
50
66
Independence Ave SW
Henry Bacon Dr NW
Lincoln Memorial Circle
Lincoln Memorial Park
Reflecting Pool
Rainbow Pool
PAGE 198
Constitution Gardens
VEHICULAR TRAFFIC PROHIBITED
Daniel French Dr SW
Ohio Dr SW
17th St SW
Independence Ave SW
Potomac River
Arlington Memorial Bridge
West Potomac Park
George Washington Memorial Pkwy
Tidal Basin
West Basin Dr SW
Ohio Dr SW

A
B
C
1
2

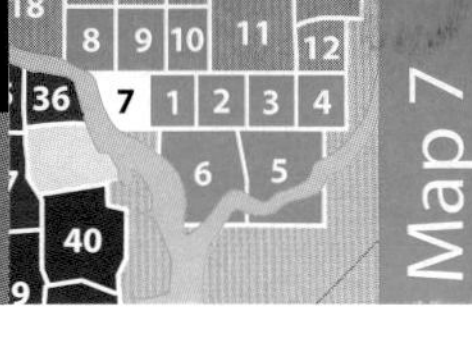

The mix of upscale and college dive is obvious. Aquarelle and Kinkead's are reserved for the power players and their hangers-on. If you forgot your jacket, duck into a gyro joint and then head for the nearest neon window to mingle with the co-ed crowd.

Coffee

- **Cup'a Cup'a** • 600 New Hampshire Ave NW
- **Karma** • 1900 I St NW
- **Starbucks** • 1730 Pennsylvania Ave NW
- **Starbucks** • 1825 I St NW
- **Starbucks** • 1919 Pennsylvania Ave NW
- **Starbucks** • 1957 E St NW
- **Starbucks** • 2130 H St NW
- **Starbucks** • 800 21st St NW
- **Starbucks** • 801 18th St NW
- **Starbucks** • 900 23rd St NW

Copy Shops

- **B&B Duplicators (9am-5:30pm)** • 818 18th St NW
- **Discovery Copy (7am-10pm)** • 2001 Pennsylvania Ave NW
- **Fast Copying & Printing (8:30am-6pm)** • 1745 Pennsylvania Ave NW
- **U Nik Press (9am-6pm)** • 900 19th St NW
- **Watergate Photo & Copy (9am-7pm)** • 2560 Virginia Ave NW

Farmer's Markets

- **Foggy Bottom Freshfarm** • I St NW & 24th St NW

Gyms

- **Fitness Co** • 1875 I St NW

Liquor Stores

- **McReynold's Liquors** • 1776 G St NW
- **Pan Mar Wine & Liquors** • 1926 I St NW
- **Riverside Liquors** • 2123 E St NW
- **S&R Liquors** • 1800 I St NW
- **Watergate Wine & Beverage** • 2544 Virginia Ave NW

Movie Theaters

- **AFI Theater-Kennedy Center for the Performing Arts** • 2700 F St NW

Nightlife

- **Potomac Lounge** • 2650 Virginia Ave NW

Restaurants

- **600 Restaurant at the Watergate** • 600 New Hampshire Ave NW
- **Aquarelle** • 2650 Virginia Ave NW
- **Bread Line** • 1751 Pennsylvania Ave NW
- **Dish** • 924 25th St NW
- **Karma** • 1919 I St NW
- **Kaz Sushi Bistro** • 1915 I St NW
- **Kinkead's** • 2000 Pennsylvania Ave NW
- **Primi Piatti** • 2013 I St NW
- **Roof Terrace Restaurant and Bar** • 2700 F St NW
- **Taberna Del Alabardero** • 1776 I St NW

Shopping

- **Motophoto** • 1819 H St NW
- **Saks Jandel** • 2522 Virginia Ave NW
- **Tower Records** • 2000 Pennsylvania Ave NW

Map 8 • Georgetown

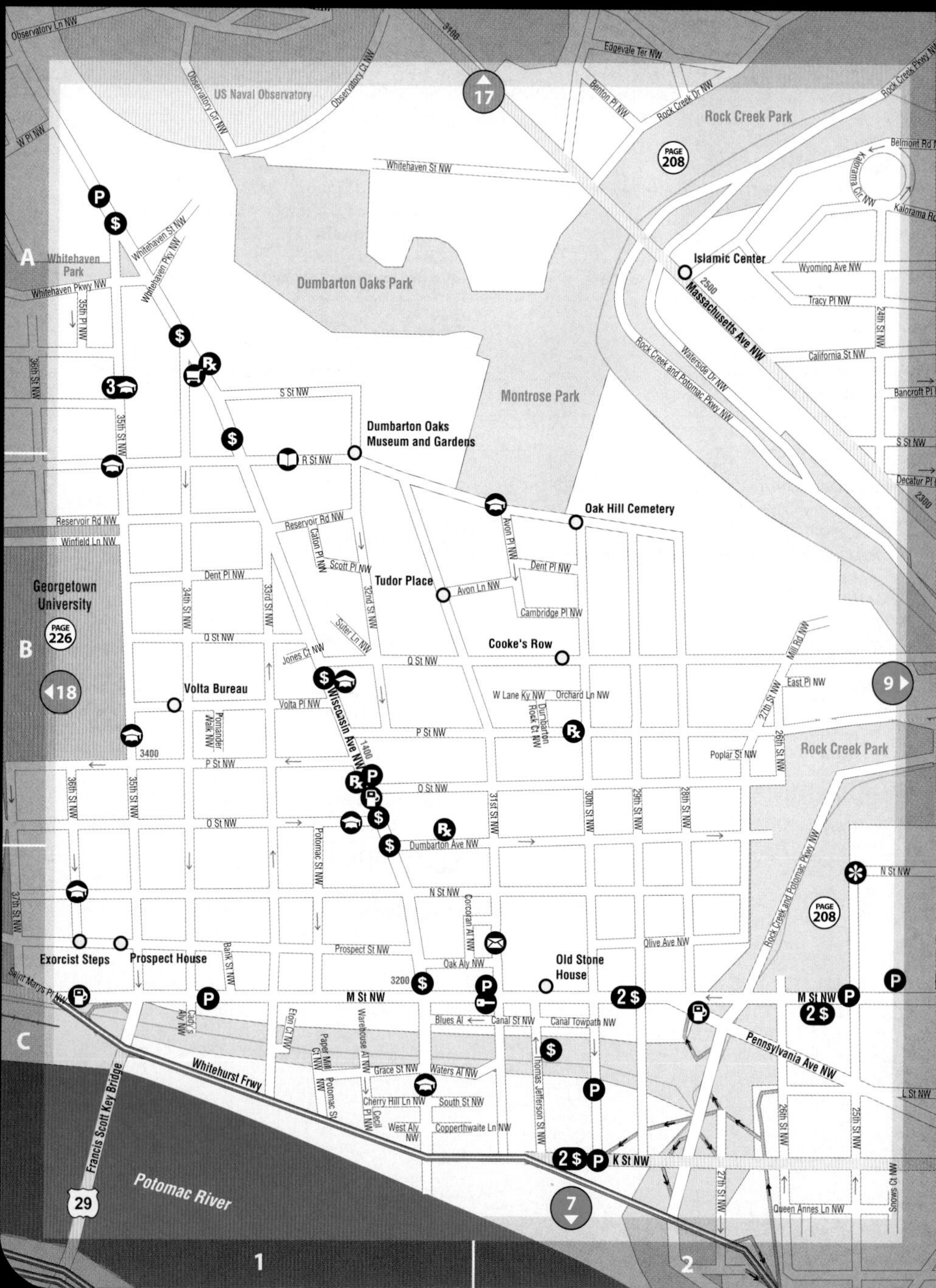

US Naval Observatory

Rock Creek Park

Whitehaven Park

Dumbarton Oaks Park

Islamic Center

Montrose Park

Dumbarton Oaks Museum and Gardens

Oak Hill Cemetery

Georgetown University

Tudor Place

Cooke's Row

Volta Bureau

Exorcist Steps

Prospect House

Old Stone House

Potomac River

Francis Scott Key Bridge

Whitehurst Frwy

Massachusetts Ave NW

Wisconsin Ave NW

Pennsylvania Ave NW

Rock Creek and Potomac Pkwy NW

M St NW

K St NW

PAGE 208

PAGE 226

17

18

9

7

A

B

C

1

2

Essentials

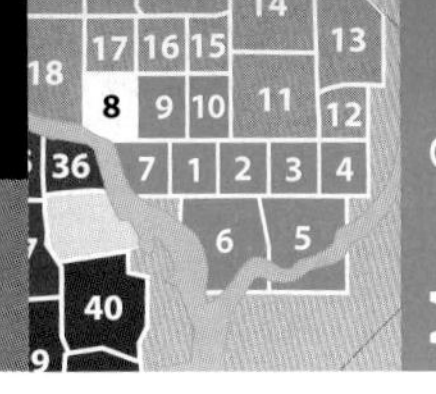

Precious townhouses and stately manses; cobblestone streets and garden tours—yes, darling, this is a beautiful neighborhood. Society matrons have good reason to cluck, though the main drags of K and Wisconsin are another matter altogether. Jammed by car and foot traffic day and night, no one worries that the upper-crust class on the side streets is rubbing off.

Banks

- **Adams National** • 1729 Wisconsin Ave NW
- **Bank of America** • 1339 Wisconsin Ave NW
- **BB&T** • 1365 Wisconsin Ave NW
- **Chevy Chase** • 1545 Wisconsin Ave NW
- **Citibank** • 1901 Wisconsin Ave NW
- **PNC** • 1201 Wisconsin Ave NW
- **PNC** • 2550 M St NW
- **PNC** • 3050 K St NW
- **PNC (ATM)** • 2101 Wisconsin Ave NW
- **PNC (ATM)** • 2550 M St NW
- **PNC (ATM)** • 3050 K St NW
- **Provident Bank** • 1055 Thomas Jefferson St NW
- **Sun Trust** • 2929 M St NW
- **Wachovia** • 2901 M St NW

Car Rental

- **Enterprise** • 3307 M St NW • 202-338-0015

Community Gardens

Gas Stations

- **Amoco** • 2715 Pennsylvania Ave NW
- **Exxon** • 1601 Wisconsin Ave NW
- **Exxon** • 3607 M St NW

Landmarks

- **Cooke's Row** • 3009 - 3029 Q St NW
- **Dumbarton Oaks Museum and Gardens** • 1703 32nd St NW
- **Exorcist Steps** • 3600 Prospect St NW
- **Islamic Center** • 2551 Massachussetts Ave NW
- **Oak Hill Cemetery** • 3000 R St NW
- **Old Stone House** • 3051 M St NW
- **Prospect House** • 3508 Prospect St NW
- **Tudor Place** • 1644 31st St NW
- **Volta Bureau** • 3417 Volta Pl NW

Libraries

- **Georgetown Library** • 3260 R St NW

Parking

Pharmacies

- **CVS** • 1403 Wisconsin Ave NW
- **Dumbarton Pharmacy** • 3146 Dumbarton St NW
- **Morgan CARE Pharmacy** • 3001 P St NW
- **Safeway** • 1855 Wisconsin Ave NW

Post Offices

- **Georgetown Station** • 1215 31st St NW

Schools

- **Corcoran School of Art & Design (Georgetown Campus)** • 1801 35th St NW
- **Devereux Children's Center of Washington, DC** • 3050 R St NW
- **Ellington School of the Arts** • 3500 R St NW
- **Fillmore Arts Center Elementary** • 1819 35th St NW
- **Georgetown Montessori** • 1041 Wisconsin Ave NW
- **Georgetown Visitation Preparatory** • 1524 35th St NW
- **Hardy Middle** • 1819 35th St NW
- **Holy Trinity** • 1325 36th St NW
- **Hyde Elementary** • 3219 O St NW
- **Montessori School of Washington** • 1556 Wisconsin Ave NW

Supermarkets

- **Safeway** • 1855 Wisconsin Ave NW

Map 8 • Georgetown

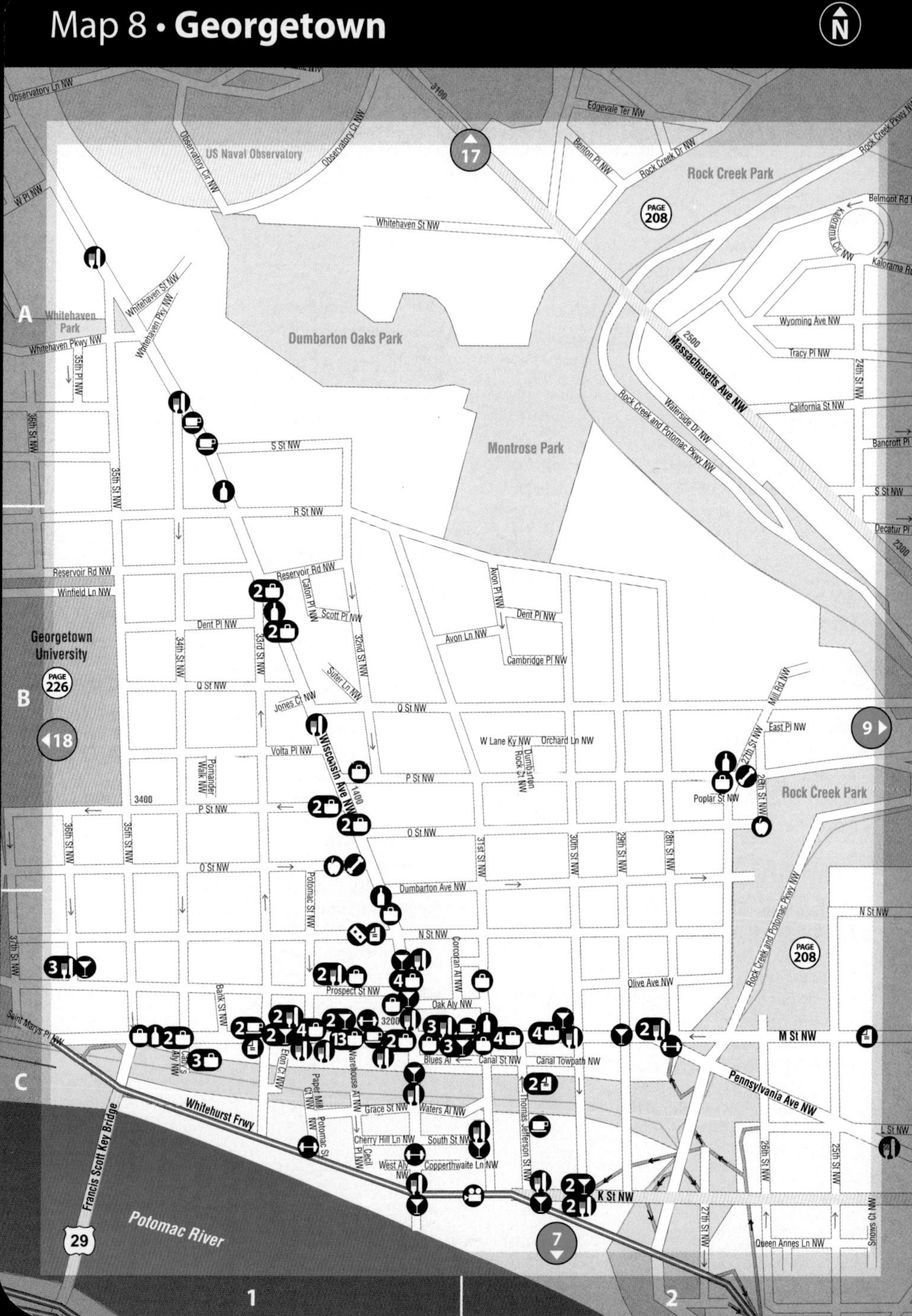

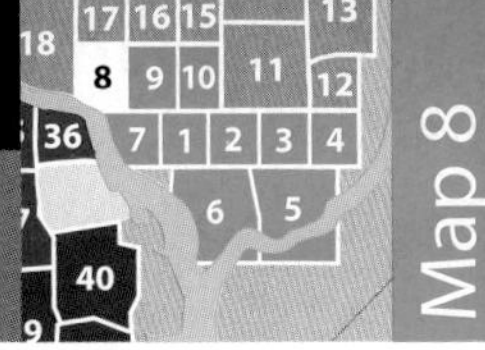

Hands-down, the most comprehensive shopping strips in the city are here (i.e. M Street). Once the sun sets, the human traffic jams don't disperse as Georgetown plays host to a raging nightlife scene. The bars and restaurants roughly fall into three categories: The Tombs and the like for the college crowd, a few joints like Martin's for regular folks, and Nathan's and Farenheit for those annoying few who like to see themselves referred to in print as "glitterati."

Coffee

- **Baked & Wired** • 1052 Thomas Jefferson St NW
- **Café Europa** • 3222 M St NW
- **Starbucks** • 1810 Wisconsin Ave NW
- **Starbucks** • 1855 Wisconsin Ave NW
- **Starbucks** • 3122 M St NW

Copy Shops

- **Copy General (8am-6pm)** • 1055 Thomas Jefferson St NW
- **Kinko's (7am-11pm)** • 3329 M St NW
- **UPS Store (8:30am-6:30pm)** • 3220 N St NW
- **Westend Press (9am-5:30pm)** • 2445 M St NW
- **Zap Copies & Communications (8am-6pm)** • 1052 Thomas Jefferson St NW

Farmer's Markets

- **Georgetown Freshfarm Market** • 3219 O St NW
- **Georgetown Market in Rose Park** • 26th & O Sts NW

Gyms

- **Fitness Co** • 1010 Wisconsin Ave NW
- **Four Seasons Fitness Club** • 2800 Pennsylvania Ave NW
- **Rich Bodies Gym** • 1000 Potomac St NW
- **Washington Sports Clubs** • 3222 M St NW, Ste 140

Liquor Stores

- **Bacchus Wine Cellar** • 1635 Wisconsin Ave NW
- **Dixie Wine & Spirits** • 3429 M St NW
- **Georgetown Wine & Spirits** • 2701 P St NW
- **Potomac Wines and Spirits** • 3100 M St NW
- **Towne Wine & Liquors** • 1326 Wisconsin Ave NW
- **Wagner's Liquor Shop** • 1717 Wisconsin Ave NW

Movie Theaters

- **Loews Georgetown 14** • 3111 K St NW

Nightlife

- **Blues Alley** • 1073 Wisconsin Ave NW
- **Chadwick's** • 3205 K St NW
- **Clyde's** • 3236 M St NW
- **Degrees** • 3100 S St NW
- **Garrett's** • 3003 M St NW
- **The Guards** • 2915 M St NW
- **Martin's Tavern** • 1264 Wisconsin Ave NW
- **Mie N Yu** • 3125 M St NW
- **Modern** • 3287 M St NW
- **Mr Smith's** • 3104 M St NW
- **Old Glory** • 3139 M St NW
- **Rhino Bar & Pumphouse** • 3295 M St NW
- **Riverside Grill** • 3050 K St NW
- **Saloun** • 3239 M St NW
- **Sequoia** • 3000 K St NW
- **The Third Edition Bar** •' 1218 Wisconsin Ave NW
- **Tombs** • 1226 36th St NW
- **Tony and Joe's** • 3000 K St NW

Pet Shops

- **Chichie's Canine Design** • 2614 P St NW
- **Georgetown Pet Gallery** • 3204 O St NW

Restaurants

- **1789** • 1226 36th St NW
- **Aditi** • 3299 M St NW
- **Amma Vegetarian Kitchen** • 3291 M St NW
- **Café Bonaparte** • 1522 Wisconsin Ave NW
- **Café Divan** • 1834 Wisconsin Ave NW
- **Café Milano** • 3251 Prospect St NW
- **Chadwick's** • 3205 K St NW
- **Citronelle** • 3000 M St NW
- **Clyde's** • 3236 M St NW
- **Fahrenheit & Degrees** • 3100 S St NW
- **Filomena Ristorante** • 1063 Wisconsin Ave NW
- **Furin's** • 2805 M St NW
- **J Paul's** • 3218 M St NW
- **La Chaumiere** • 2813 M St NW
- **The Landmark** • 2430 Pennsylvania Ave NW
- **Martin's Tavern** • 1264 Wisconsin NW
- **Morton's of Georgetown** • 3251 Prospect St NW
- **Mr Smith's** • 3104 M St NW
- **Nathan's** • 3150 M St NW
- **Old Glory All-American BBQ** • 3139 M St NW
- **Pizzeria Paradiso** • 3282 M St NW
- **Riverside Grill** • 3050 K St NW
- **Romeo's Café and Pizzeria** • 2132 Wisconsin Ave NW
- **Sequoia** • 3000 K St NW
- **The Third Edition** • 1218 Wisconsin Ave NW
- **The Tombs** • 1226 36th St NW
- **Tony And Joe's Seafood Place** • 3000 K St NW

Shopping

- **Ann Saks** • 3328 M St NW
- **Anthropologie** • 3225 M St NW
- **April Cornell** • 3278 M St NW
- **BCBG** • 3210 M St NW
- **Betsey Johnson** • 1319 Wisconsin Ave NW
- **Beyond Comics 2** • 1419-B Wisconsin Ave NW
- **Blue Mercury** • 3059 M St NW
- **Bo Concepts** • 3342 M St NW
- **Commander Salamander** • 1420 Wisconsin Ave NW
- **Dean and DeLuca** • 3276 M St NW
- **Design Within Reach** • 3307 Cady's Aly NW
- **Diesel** • 1249 Wisconsin Ave NW
- **Express** • 3227 M St NW
- **Georgetown Running Company** • 3401 M St NW
- **Georgetown Tobacco** • 3144 M St NW
- **Georgetown Wine and Spirits** • 2701 P St NW
- **GIA & Co** • 3231 M St NW
- **H&M** • 3223 M St NW
- **The Hattery** • 3233 M St NW
- **Illuminations** • 3323 Cady's Aly NW
- **Intermix** • 3222 M St
- **J Crew** • 3224 M St NW
- **Jaryam** • 1631 Wisconsin Ave NW
- **Jinx Proof Tattoo** • 3289 M St NW
- **Kate Spade** • 3061 M St NW
- **Kenneth Cole** • 1259 Wisconsin Ave NW
- **Ligne Roset** • 3306 M St NW
- **lil' thingamajigs** • 3229 M St NW
- **Lush** • 3066 M St NW
- **MAC** • 3067 M St NW
- **Marvelous Market** • 3217 P St NW
- **Old Print Gallery** • 1220 31st St NW
- **Pottery Barn** • 3077 M St NW
- **Proper Topper** • 3213 P St NW
- **Ralph Lauren Polo Shop** • 3040 M St NW
- **Relish** • 3312 Cady's Aly NW
- **Restoration Hardware** • 1222 Wisconsin Ave NW
- **Revolution Cycles** • 3411 M St NW
- **Sassanova** • 1641 Wisconsin Ave NW
- **Secret Garden** • 3230 M St NW
- **See** • 1261 Wisconsin Ave NW
- **Sephora** • 3065 M St NW
- **The Sharper Image** • 3226 M St NW
- **Sherman Pickey** • 1647 Wisconsin Ave NW
- **Smash** • 3285 1/2 M St NW
- **Smith & Hawken** • 3077 M St NW
- **Sugar** • 1633 Wisconsin Ave NW
- **Talbots** • 3232 M St NW
- **Thomas Sweet Ice Cream** • 3214 P St NW
- **Toka Salon** • 3251 Prospect St NW
- **Urban Outfitters** • 3111 M St NW
- **Victoria's Secret** • 3222 M St NW
- **The White House/Black Market** • 3228 M St NW
- **Zara** • 1234 Wisconsin Ave NW

Video Rental

- **Video Plus** • 3222 N St NW

Map 9 • Dupont Circle / Adams Morgan

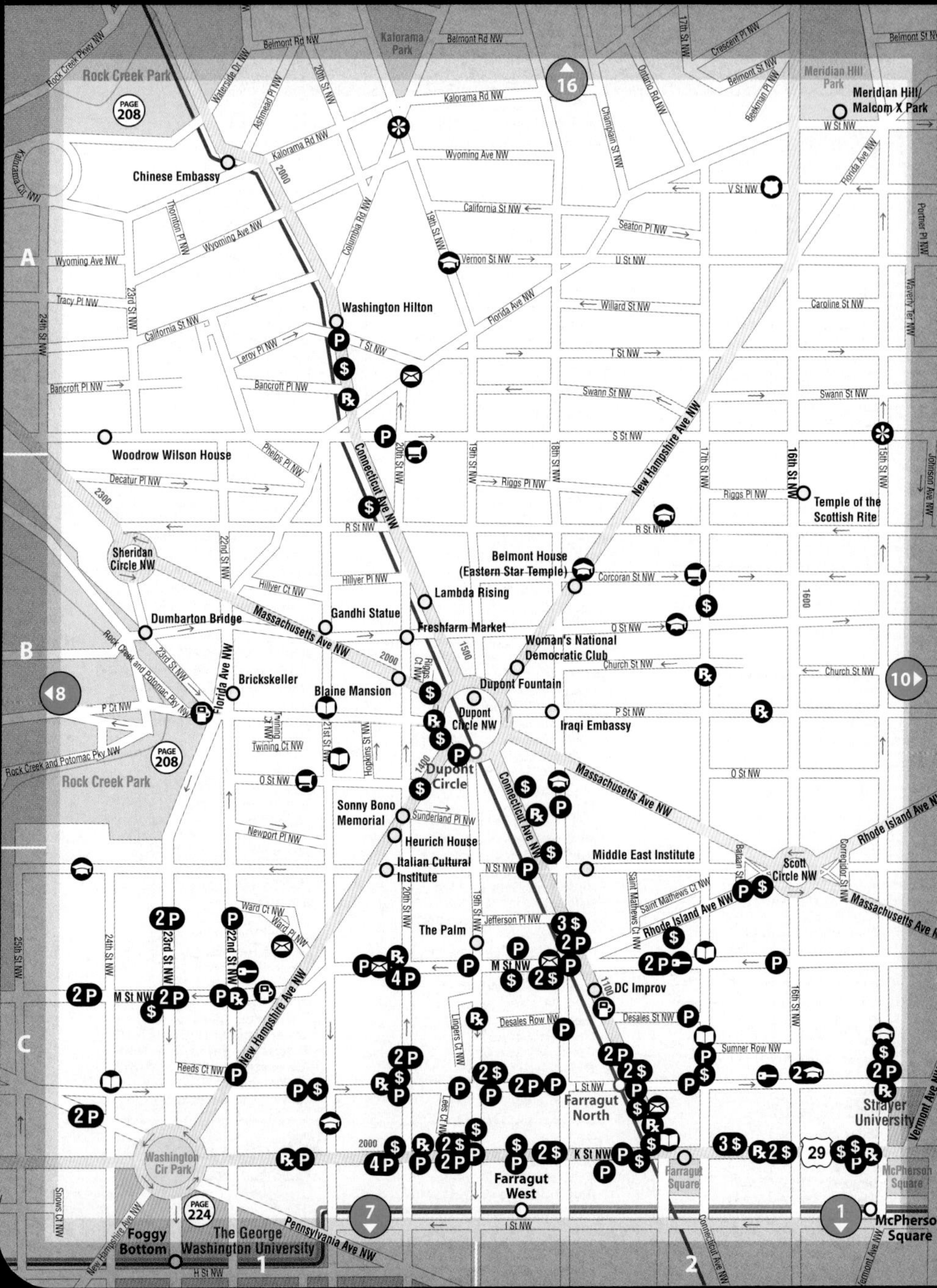

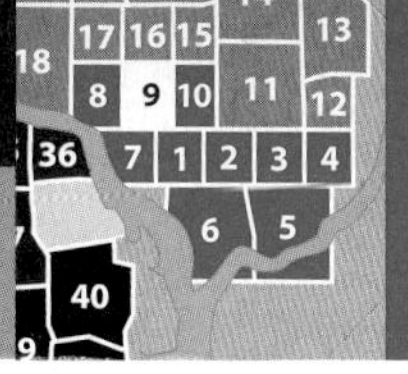

Toto, I don't think we're in Washington anymore. Why, these people aren't corporate-looking and uptight! The district's only section with an undeniable European vibe, Dupont Circle attracts trendsetting hipsters, artsy bohemians and new-age yoga chicks (and dudes). Similar to Greenwich Village, this is a neighborhood where heterosexuals are outnumbered by homosexuals, who are outnumbered by metrosexuals. That said; is it us, or are residents starting to become a little *too* cool for school?

Banks

- **Adams National** • 1501 K St NW
- **Adams National** • 1604 17th St NW
- **Bank of America** • 1801 K St NW
- **Bank of America** • 2101 L St NW
- **Bank of America** • 3 Dupont Cir NW
- **Bank of America (ATM)** • 1612 K St NW
- **BB&T** • 1730 Rhode Island Ave NW
- **BB&T** • 1909 K St NW
- **Chevy Chase** • 1100 17th St NW
- **Chevy Chase** • 1700 K St NW
- **Chevy Chase** • 1800 M St NW
- **Chevy Chase** • 1850 K St NW
- **Chevy Chase (ATM)** • 1050 Connecticut Ave NW
- **Chevy Chase (ATM)** • 1743 Connecticut Ave NW
- **Citibank** • 1000 Connecticut Ave NW
- **Citibank** • 1225 Connecticut Ave NW
- **Eagle Bank** • 1228 Connecticut Ave NW
- **Eagle Bank** • 2001 K St NW
- **Independence Federal Savings** • 1020 19th St NW
- **Independence Federal Savings** • 1229 Connecticut Ave NW
- **M&T Bank** • 1680 K St NW
- **M&T Bank** • 1899 L St NW
- **Mercantile Potomac Bank** • 1629 K St NW
- **PNC** • 1101 15th St NW
- **PNC** • 1800 M St NW
- **PNC** • 1875 Connecticut Ave NW
- **PNC** • 1913 Massachusetts Ave NW
- **PNC** • 1920 L St NW
- **PNC (ATM)** • 1333 New Hampshire Ave NW
- **PNC (ATM)** • 1600 Rhode Island Ave NW
- **Presidential Savings** • 1660 K St NW
- **Sun Trust** • 1111 Connecticut Ave NW
- **Sun Trust** • 1369 Connecticut Ave NW
- **Sun Trust** • 1925 K St NW
- **United Bank** • 1667 K St NW
- **United Bank** • 2301 M St NW
- **Wachovia** • 1100 Connecticut Ave NW
- **Wachovia** • 1300 Connecticut Ave NW
- **Wachovia** • 1510 K St NW
- **Wachovia** • 1800 K St NW
- **Wachovia** • 1850 M St NW
- **Wachovia** • 2000 L St NW

Car Rental

- **Avis** • 1722 M St NW • 202-467-6585
- **Budget** • 1620 L St NW • 202-466-4544
- **Enterprise** • 1221 22nd St NW • 202-872-5790

Community Gardens

Gas Stations

- **Exxon** • 2150 M St NW
- **Mobil** • 2200 P St NW
- **Unocal** • 1150 Connecticut Ave NW

Landmarks

- **Belmont House (Eastern Star Temple)** • 1618 New Hampshire Ave NW
- **Blaine Mansion** • 2000 Massachusetts Ave NW
- **Brickskeller** • 1523 22nd St NW
- **Chinese Embassy** • 2300 Connecticut Ave NW
- **DC Improv** • 1140 Connecticut Ave
- **Dumbarton Bridge** • 23rd St NW & Q St NW
- **Dupont Fountain** • Dupont Cir
- **Farragut Square** • 815 Connecticut Ave NW
- **Freshfarm Market** • 20th St NW near Q St NW
- **Gandhi Statue** • Massachusetts Ave & 21st St NW
- **Heurich House** • 1307 New Hampshire Ave NW
- **Iraqi Embassy** • 1801 P St NW
- **Italian Cultural Institute** • 2025 M St NW
- **Lambda Rising** • 1625 Connecticut Ave NW
- **Meridian Hill/Malcolm X Park** • 15th NW & 16th St NW & W St NW
- **Middle East Institute** • 1761 N St NW
- **The Palm** • 1225 19th St NW
- **Sonny Bono Memorial** • 20th St NW & New Hampshire Ave NW
- **Temple of the Scottish Rite** • 1733 16th St NW
- **Washington Hilton** • 1919 Connecticut Ave NW
- **Woman's National Democratic Club** • 1526 New Hampshire Ave NW
- **Woodrow Wilson House** • 2340 S St NW

Libraries

- **Arthur R Ashe Jr Foreign Policy Library** • 1426 21st St NW
- **Foundation Center** • 1001 Connecticut Ave NW
- **National Geographic Society Library** • 1145 17th St NW
- **Polish Library in Washington** • 1503 21st St NW
- **US Institute of Peace** • 1200 17th St NW # 200
- **West End Library** • 1101 24th St NW

Parking

Pharmacies

- **CVS** • 1025 Connecticut Ave NW
- **CVS** • 1500 K St NW
- **CVS** • 1637 P St NW
- **CVS** • 1990 K St NW
- **CVS** • 2000 L St NW
- **CVS** • 2000 M St NW
- **CVS (24 hrs)** • 6 Dupont Cir NW
- **CVS (24 hrs)** • 2200 M St NW
- **Foer's CARE Pharmacy** • 2141 K St NW
- **Pharmacare** • 1517 17th St NW
- **Rite Aid** • 1034 15th St NW
- **Rite Aid (24 hours)** • 1815 Connecticut Ave NW
- **Stat Script Pharmacy** • 1638 R St NW
- **Tschiffely Pharmacy** • 1145 19th St NW
- **Tschiffely Pharmacy** • 1330 Connecticut Ave NW

Police

- **MPDC 3rd District Station** • 1620 V St NW

Post Offices

- **Farragut Station** • 1800 M St NW
- **Temple Heights Station** • 1921 Florida Ave NW
- **Twentieth St Station** • 2001 M St NW
- **Ward Place Station** • 2121 Ward Pl NW
- **Washington Square Station** • 1050 Connecticut Ave NW

Schools

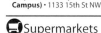

- **Adams Elementary** • 2020 19th St NW
- **Auto Arts Academy** • 1100 16th St NW
- **Emerson Preparatory** • 1324 18th St NW
- **Francis Junior High** • 2425 N St NW
- **Rock Creek International Upper** • 1621 New Hampshire Ave NW
- **Ross Elementary** • 1730 R St NW
- **School for Arts in Learning** • 1100 16th St NW
- **Stevens Elementary** • 1050 21st St NW
- **Strayer University (Washington Campus)** • 1133 15th St NW

Supermarkets

- **Metro IGA Market** • 2130 P St NW
- **Safeway** • 1701 Corcoran St NW
- **Safeway** • 1800 20th St NW

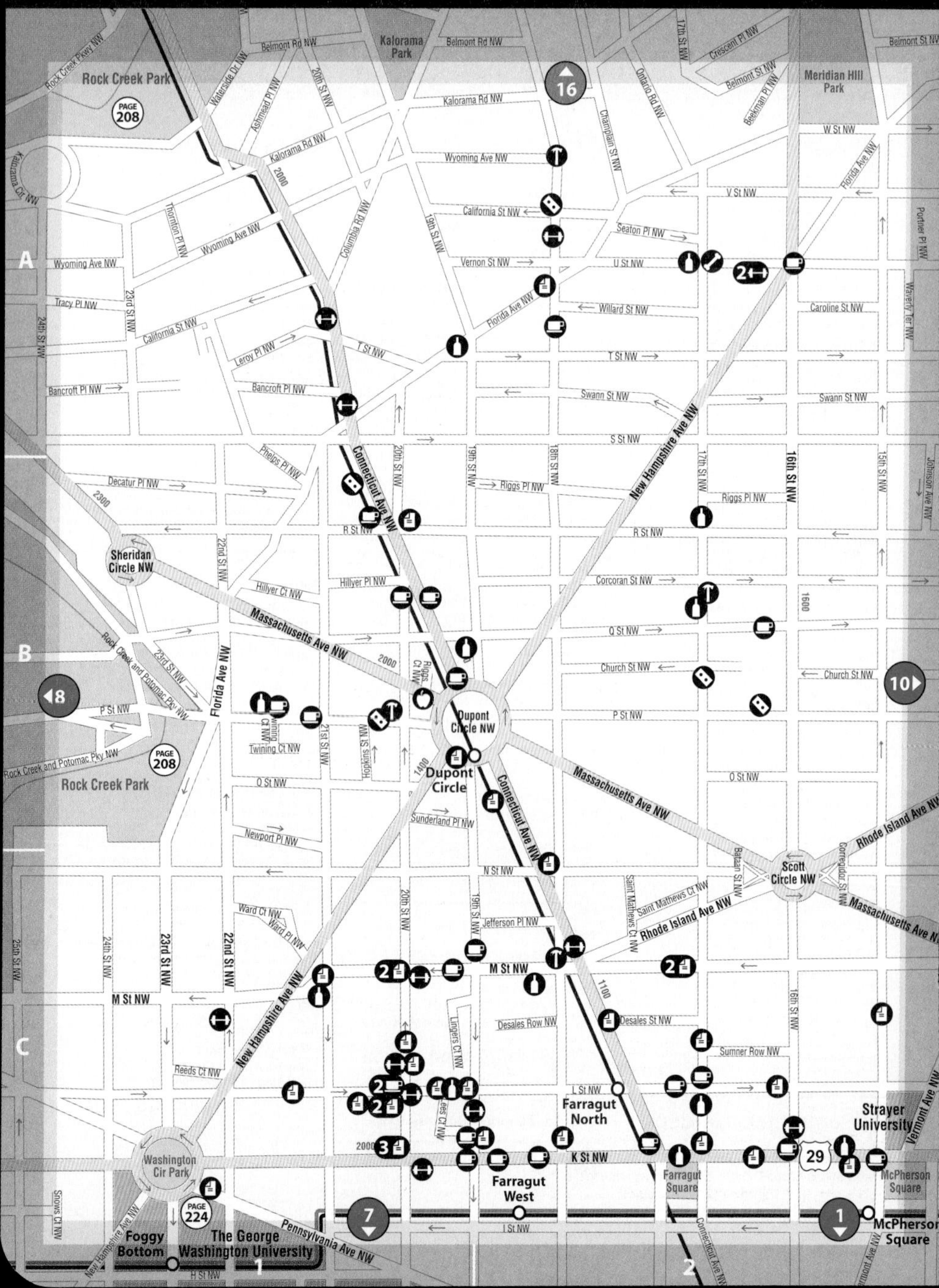

Map 9 • Dupont Circle / Adams Morgan

N

Rock Creek Pkwy NW
Belmont Rd NW
Kalorama Park
Belmont Rd NW
17th St NW
Crescent Pl NW
Belmont St NW
Rock Creek Park
Waterside Dr NW
Ashmead Pl NW
20th St NW
16
Ontario Rd NW
Belmont St NW
Beekman Pl NW
Meridian Hill Park
PAGE 208
Kalorama Rd NW
Champlain St NW
W St NW
Kalorama Rd NW
Kalorama Cir NW
2000
Wyoming Ave NW
Florida Ave NW
V St NW
Thornton Pl NW
Columbia Rd NW
California St NW
19th St NW
Seaton Pl NW
Portner Pl NW
A
Wyoming Ave NW
Wyoming Ave NW
Vernon St NW
U St NW
2
Tracy Pl NW
23rd St NW
Florida Ave NW
Willard St NW
Caroline St NW
24th St NW
California St NW
Waverly Ter NW
Leroy Pl NW
T St NW
T St NW
Bancroft Pl NW
Bancroft Pl NW
Swann St NW
Swann St NW
S St NW
New Hampshire Ave NW
Phelps Pl NW
Connecticut Ave NW
20th St NW
19th St NW
18th St NW
17th St NW
16th St NW
15th St NW
Johnson Ave NW
Decatur Pl NW
Riggs Pl NW
Riggs Pl NW
2300
R St NW
R St NW
Sheridan Circle NW
22nd St NW
Hillyer Pl NW
Corcoran St NW
Hillyer Ct NW
1600
Massachusetts Ave NW
Q St NW
B
Rock Creek and Potomac Pkwy
23rd St NW
2000
Riggs Ct NW
Church St NW
Church St NW
8
Florida Ave NW
10
P St NW
Rock Creek and Potomac Pky NW
Twining Ct NW
21st St NW
Hopkins St NW
Dupont Circle NW
P St NW
Twining Ct NW
Rock Creek and Potomac Pky NW
PAGE 208
Rock Creek Park
1400
Dupont Circle
O St NW
Connecticut Ave NW
Massachusetts Ave NW
O St NW
Sunderland Pl NW
Newport Pl NW
Rhode Island Ave NW
N St NW
Bataan St NW
Scott Circle NW
Corregidor St NW
Saint Mathews Ct NW
Saint Mathews Ct NW
Ward Ct NW
Ward Pl NW
20th St NW
19th St NW
Jefferson Pl NW
Rhode Island Ave NW
Massachusetts Ave NW
25th St NW
24th St NW
23rd St NW
22nd St NW
New Hampshire Ave NW
M St NW
2
1100
M St NW
Lingers Ct NW
Desales Row NW
Desales St NW
16th St NW
C
Sumner Row NW
Reeds Ct NW
2
L St NW
Farragut North
2
Lees Ct NW
Strayer University
Vermont Ave NW
2000
3
K St NW
29
Washington Cir Park
Farragut West
Farragut Square
McPherson Square
PAGE 224
7
1
McPherson Square
Shows Ct NW
New Hampshire Ave NW
Foggy Bottom
The George Washington University
I St NW
Connecticut Ave NW
Pennsylvania Ave NW
Vermont Ave NW
H St NW
1
2

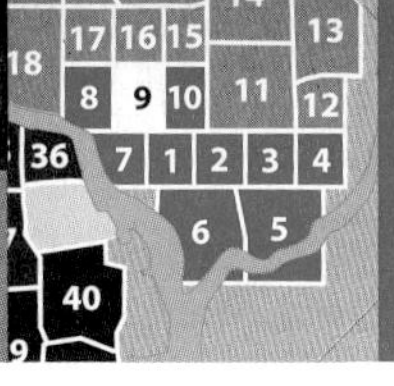

Barnes & Noble and Sam Goody keep out! The entire neighborhood is like a huge consignment shop where one out of every four signs seems to have the word "used" on it. Although the area has been slightly wounded by the Starbucks assault, this is the DC neighborhood where shoppers are most likely to find those one-of-a-kind bargain trinkets that fall in line with their *Sex and the City* ideals.

Coffee

- **Caribou Coffee** • 1101 17th St NW
- **Casey's Coffee** • 2000 L St NW
- **Coffee Espress** • 2001 L St NW
- **Coffee & the Works** • 1627 Connecticut Ave NW
- **Cosí**
  - 1501 K St NW
  - 1875 K St NW
  - 1350 Connecticut Ave NW
  - 1647 20th St NW
  - 1919 M St NW
- **Java Green** • 1020 19th St NW
- **Java House** • 1645 Q St NW
- **Jolt'n Bolt Coffee & Tea House** • 1918 18th St NW
- **LA Café II** • 1819 K St NW
- **Love Café** • 1501 U St NW
- **Soho Tea & Coffee** • 2150 P St NW
- **Starbucks**
  - 2101 P St NW
  - 1205 19th St NW
  - 1600 K St NW
  - 1600 U St NW
  - 1734 L St NW
  - 1001 Connecticut Ave NW
  - 1301 Connecticut Ave NW
  - 1501 Connecticut Ave NW
  - 1700 Connecticut Ave NW
  - 1900 K St NW

Copy Shops

- **AAA Printing & Duplicating (9am-6pm)** • 1353 Connecticut Ave NW
- **ABC Imaging (8am-11pm)** • 1147 20th St NW
- **ABS Complete Printing (8:30am-5pm)** • 1150 Connecticut Ave NW
- **Commercial Duplicating Service (9am-6pm)** • 1920 L St NW
- **Copy Cats (8:30am-5:30pm)** • 1140 17th St NW
- **Copy General (8am-6pm)** • 2000 L St NW
- **Deadline Press (8:30am-5pm)** • 1020 19th St NW
- **Document Technology (24 hours)** • 2000 M St NW
- **Dupont Circle Copy (8:30am-7pm)** • 11 Dupont Cir NW
- **Eagle Printing (8am-5pm)** • 1156 15th St NW
- **Hot-Line Duplicating (10am-5pm)** • 1718 20th St NW
- **Ikon Office Solutions (24 hours)** • 1120 20th St NW
- **Imagenet (24 hours)** • 2000 M St NW
- **Kinko's (7am-11pm)** • 1612 K St NW
- **Kinko's (7am-11pm)** • 2020 K St NW
- **Minuteman Press (9am-5:30pm)** • 2000 K St NW
- **Office Depot (7am-7pm)** • 2000 K St NW
- **Panic Press (9am-5pm)** • 2055 L St NW
- **Park Press (8:30am-6pm)** • 1518 K St NW
- **Press Express Copy & Printing (8am-7pm)** • 1015 18th St NW
- **Printer (9am-5pm)** • 1803 Florida Ave NW
- **Reprographic Technologies (8am-10pm)** • 2000 L St NW
- **Sequential (24 hours)** • 1615 L St NW
- **Sir Speedy Printing (8:30am-5:30pm)** • 1025 17th St NW
- **Sir Speedy Printing (8:30am-5:30pm)** • 1300 Connecticut Ave NW
- **Sir Speedy Printing (8:30am-6pm)** • 2134 L St NW
- **Staples (7am-7pm)** • 1901 L St NW
- **UPS Store (8:30am-6:30pm)** • 1718 M St NW
- **UPS Store (9am-7pm)** • 2100 M St NW
- **UPS Store (9am-7pm)** • 2200 Pennsylvania Ave NW
- **US Printing & Copying (8:30am-6pm)** • 1725 M St NW

Farmer's Markets

- **Dupont Circle Freshfarm** • 1913 Massachusetts Ave NW

Gyms

- **Bally Total Fitness** • 2000 L St NW
- **Capital City Club and Spa** • 1001 16th St NW
- **Curves** • 1710 Rhode Island Ave NW
- **Fitness First** • 1075 19th St
- **Gold's Gym** • 1120 20th St NW
- **Results the Gym** • 1612 U St NW
- **Sports Club/LA** • 1170 22nd St NW
- **Third Power Fitness** • 2007 18th St NW
- **Training For Results** • 1612 U St NW
- **Washington Hilton Sport Club** • 1919 Connecticut Ave NW
- **Washington Sports Club** • 1211 Connecticut Ave NW
- **Washington Sports Club** • 1990 K St NW
- **Washington Sports Club** • 1990 M St NW
- **Washington Sports Club** • 1835 Connecticut Ave NW

Hardware Stores

- **Adams Morgan Hardware** • 2200 18th St NW
- **Candey Hardware** • 1210 18th St NW
- **District True Value Hardware** • 2003 P St NW
- **True Value Hardware** • 1623 17th St NW

Liquor Stores

- **Barmy Wine & Liquor** • 1912 L St NW
- **Bell Liquor & Wine Shoppe** • 1821 M St NW
- **Benmoll Liquors** • 1700 U St NW
- **Berose Liquors** • 1711 17th St NW
- **Cairo Wine & Liquor Store** • 1618 17th St NW
- **Connecticut Avenue Liquors** • 1529 Connecticut Ave NW
- **Downtown Spirits & Deli** • 1522 K St NW
- **Imperial Liquor** • 1050 17th St NW
- **La Salle Liquors** • 1719 K St NW
- **Martin's Wine & Spirits** • 1919 Florida Ave NW
- **State Liquors** • 2159 P St NW
- **Wine Specialists** • 2115 M St NW

Pet Shops

- **Companions Pet Shop** • 1626 U St NW

Video Rental

- **Blockbuster Video** • 1639 P St NW
- **Capitol Video Sales** • 1729 Connecticut Ave NW
- **Capitol Video Sales** • 2028 P St NW
- **The Video Rack** • 1511 17th St Nw
- **Video American of Dupont** • 2104 18th St NW

Map 9 • Dupont Circle / Adams Morgan

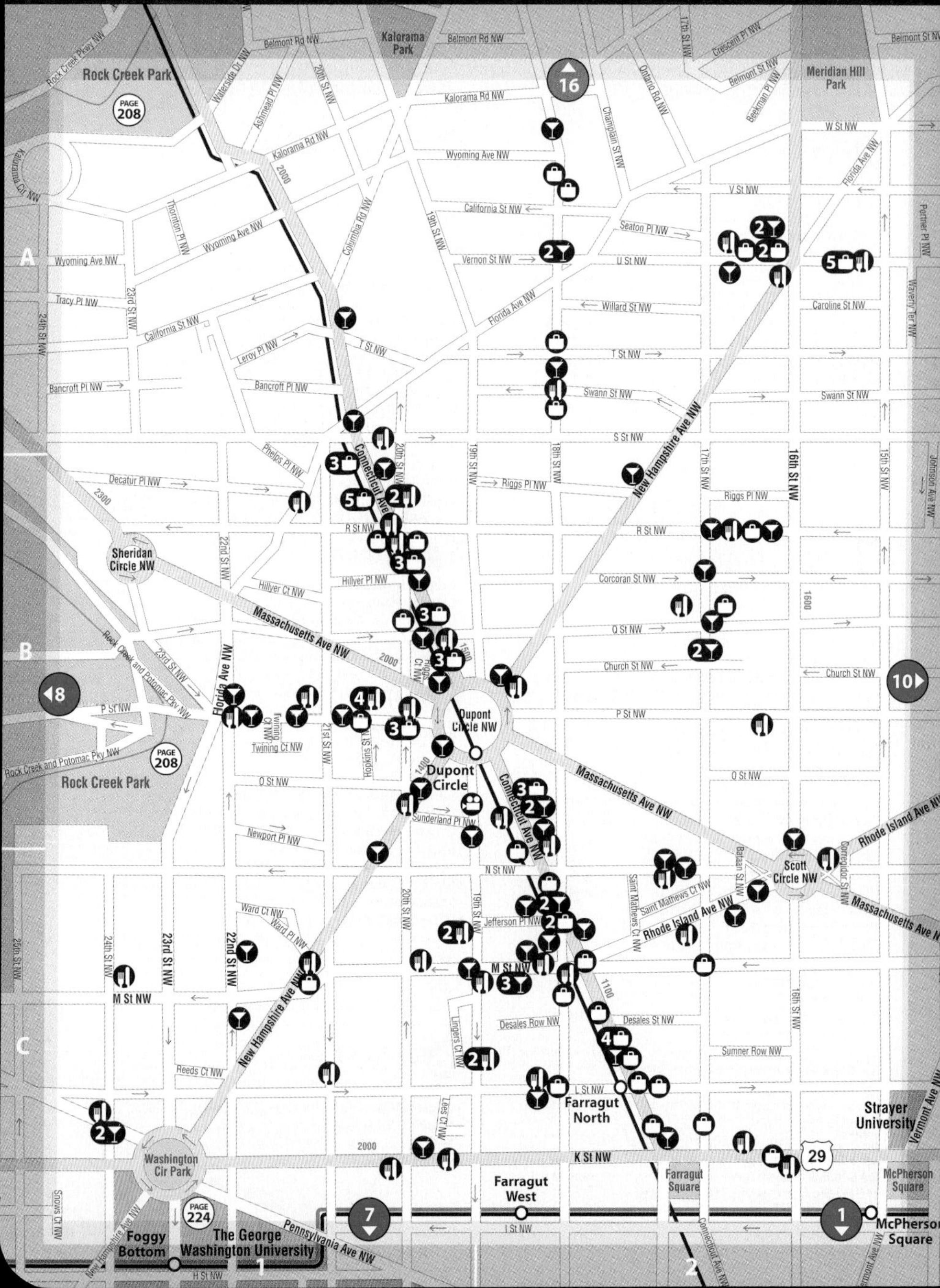

N
Rock Creek Pkwy NW
Rock Creek Park
PAGE 208
Waterside Dr NW
Belmont Rd NW
Kalorama Park
Ashmead Pl NW
20th St NW
Kalorama Rd NW
16
Crescent Pl NW
17th St NW
Ontario Rd NW
Champlain St NW
Belmont St NW
Beekman Pl NW
Meridian Hill Park
W St NW
Kalorama Cir NW
Wyoming Ave NW
2000
California St NW
Columbia Rd NW
19th St NW
V St NW
Florida Ave NW
Seaton Pl NW
Thornton Pl NW
A
Wyoming Ave NW
Vernon St NW
U St NW
Porter Pl NW
Tracy Pl NW
23rd St NW
24th St NW
Willard St NW
Caroline St NW
Waverly Ter NW
California St NW
Leroy Pl NW
T St NW
T St NW
Bancroft Pl NW
Bancroft Pl NW
Swann St NW
Swann St NW
S St NW
Phelps Pl NW
Connecticut Ave NW
18th St NW
New Hampshire Ave NW
16th St NW
15th St NW
Johnson Ave NW
Decatur Pl NW
2300
Riggs Pl NW
Riggs Pl NW
R St NW
R St NW
Sheridan Circle NW
22nd St NW
Hillyer Ct NW
Hillyer Pl NW
Corcoran St NW
1600
Massachusetts Ave NW
Q St NW
Rock Creek and Potomac Pkwy NW
23rd St NW
Florida Ave NW
B
2000
Riggs Ct NW
1500
Church St NW
Church St NW
8
10
P St NW
Twining Ct NW
Twining Ct NW
21st St NW
Hopkins St NW
Dupont Circle NW
P St NW
Rock Creek and Potomac Pkwy NW
PAGE 208
Rock Creek Park
1400
Dupont Circle
O St NW
O St NW
Massachusetts Ave NW
Sunderland Pl NW
Newport Pl NW
Rhode Island Ave NW
Scott Circle NW
Bataan St NW
Corregidor St NW
N St NW
Saint Mathews Ct NW
Ward Ct NW
Ward Pl NW
20th St NW
19th St NW
Jefferson Pl NW
Rhode Island Ave NW
Massachusetts Ave NW
25th St NW
24th St NW
23rd St NW
22nd St NW
M St NW
M St NW
1100
New Hampshire Ave NW
Desales Row NW
Desales St NW
16th St NW
Lingers Ct NW
C
Sumner Row NW
Reeds Ct NW
L St NW
Farragut North
Lees Ct NW
Strayer University
Vermont Ave NW
2000
Washington Cir Park
K St NW
29
Farragut Square
McPherson Square
Snows Ct NW
Farragut West
7
1
McPherson Square
PAGE 224
I St NW
New Hampshire Ave NW
Foggy Bottom
The George Washington University
Pennsylvania Ave NW
Connecticut Ave NW
Vermont Ave NW
H St NW
1
2

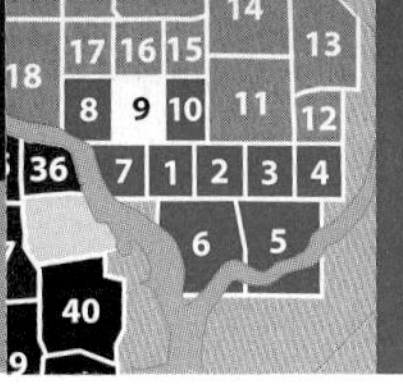

So much to do, so little time. Experience all the flavors of Europe with our suggested itinerary: Dinner: thin-crust pies at Pizza Paradiso (Italian). Movie: an indie flick at Loews 5 (French). Drinks: abbey ales at Brickskellar (Belgian). Dancing: club-style salsa at Café Citron (Spanish). Late night: a drunken stupor at any 18th Street dive out there (Irish).

Movie Theaters

- **Loews Dupont Circle 5** • 1350 19th St NW

Nightlife

- **Aroma** • 2401 Pennsylvania Ave NW
- **Bar Rouge** • 1315 16th St NW
- **Beacon Bar & Grill** • 1615 Rhode Island Ave NW
- **Biddy Mulligan's** • 1500 New Hampshire Ave NW
- **Big Hunt** • 1345 Connecticut Ave NW
- **Bravo Bravo** • 1001 Connecticut Ave NW
- **The Brickskeller** • 1523 22nd St NW
- **Buffalo Billiards** • 1330 19th St NW
- **Café Citron** • 1343 Connecticut Ave NW
- **Café Japone** • 2032 P St NW
- **Camelot** • 1823 M St NW
- **Chaos** • 1603 17th St NW
- **Chi-Cha Lounge** • 1624 U St NW
- **The Childe Harold** • 1610 20th St NW
- **Cloud Dining Lounge** • 1 Dupont Cir
- **Cobalt/30 Degrees** • 1639 R St NW
- **Common Share** • 2003 18th St NW
- **Dragonfly** • 1215 Connecticut Ave NW
- **Eighteenth Street Lounge** • 1212 18th St NW
- **Firefly** • 1310 New Hampshire Ave NW
- **Fireplace** • 2161 P St NW
- **Fox and Hounds Lounge** • 1537 17th St NW
- **Front Page** • 1333 New Hampshire Ave NW
- **Gazuza** • 1629 Connecticut Ave NW
- **Improv** • 1140 Connecticut Ave NW
- **Kramerbooks & Afterwords Café** • 1517 Connecticut Ave NW
- **La Frontera Cantina** • 1633 17th St NW
- **Lauriol Plaza** • 1835 18th St
- **Local 16** • 1602 U St NW
- **Lulu's** • 1217 22nd St NW
- **Madhatter** • 1831 M St NW
- **McClellan's** • 1919 Connecticut Ave NW
- **MCCXXIII** • 1223 Connecticut Ave NW
- **McFadden's** • 2401 Pennsylvania Ave NW
- **Omega DC** • 2122 P St NW
- **Ozio** • 1813 M St NW
- **Recessions** • 1823 L St NW
- **Red** • 1802 Jefferson Pl NW
- **Rumors** • 1900 M St NW
- **Russia House Restaurant and Lounge** • 1800 Connecticut Ave NW
- **Sign of the Whale** • 1825 M St NW
- **Soussi** • 2228 18th St NW
- **Staccato** • 2006 18th St NW
- **Stetson's Famous Bar & Restaurant** • 1610 U St NW
- **Tabard Inn Bar** • 1739 N St NW
- **Tequila Grill** • 1990 K St NW
- **Timberlake's** • 1726 Connecticut Ave NW
- **Topaz Bar** • 1733 N St NW
- **Townhouse Tavern** • 1637 R St NW
- **Trio's Fox & Hounds** • 1533 17th St NW
- **The Wave!** • 1731 New Hampshire Ave NW
- **Zebra Bar and Lounge** • 1170 22nd St NW

Restaurants

- **15 Ria** • 1515 Rhode Island Ave NW
- **Al Tiramisu** • 2014 P St NW
- **Annie's Paramount** • 1609 17th St NW
- **Biddy Mulligan's** • 1500 New Hampshire Ave NW
- **Bistrot du Coin** • 1738 Connecticut Ave NW
- **The Brickskellar** • 1523 22nd St NW
- **Café Citron** • 1343 Connecticut Ave NW
- **Café Luna** • 1633 P St NW
- **Chi-Cha Lounge** • 1624 U St NW
- **Daily Grill** • 1200 18th St NW
- **Food Bar DC** • 1639 R St NW
- **Front Page Restaurant and Grill** • 1333 New Hampshire Ave NW
- **Galileo/Il Laboratorio del Galileo** • 1110 21st St NW
- **I Ricchi** • 1220 19th St NW
- **Johnny's Half Shell** • 2002 P St NW
- **Kramerbooks & Afterwords Café** • 1517 Connecticut Ave NW
- **Lauriol Plaza** • 1835 18th St NW
- **Local 16** • 1602 U St NW
- **Love Café** • 1501 U St NW
- **Luna Grill & Diner** • 1301 Connecticut Ave NW
- **Mackey's Public House** • 1823 L St NW
- **Malaysia Kopitiam** • 1827 M St NW
- **Marcel's** • 2401 Pennsylvania Ave NW
- **McCormick and Schmick's** • 1652 K St NW
- **Meiwah** • 1200 New Hampshire Ave NW
- **Melrose** • 1201 24th St NW
- **Mimi's** • 2120 P St NW
- **Nooshi** • 1120 19th St NW
- **Obelisk** • 2029 P St NW
- **Olives** • 1600 K St NW
- **The Palm** • 1225 19th St NW
- **Pesce** • 2016 P St NW
- **Pizzeria Paradiso** • 2029 P St NW
- **The Prime Rib** • 2020 K St NW
- **Restaurant Nora** • 2132 Florida Ave NW
- **Sam and Harry's** • 1200 19th St NW
- **Sette Osteria** • 1666 Connecticut Ave NW
- **Smith and Wollensky** • 1112 19th St NW
- **Tabard Inn** • 1739 N St NW
- **Teaism** • 2009 R St NW
- **Teatro Goldini** • 1909 K St NW
- **Thaiphoon** • 2011 S St NW
- **Timberlake's** • 1726 Connecticut Ave NW
- **Vidalia** • 1990 M St NW

Shopping

- **Affrica** • 2010 1/2 R St NW
- **Andre Chreky, the Salon Spa** • 1604 K St NW
- **Bang Salon** • 1612 U St NW
- **Bedazzled** • 1507 Connecticut Ave NW
- **Best Cellars** • 1643 Connecticut Ave NW
- **Betsy Fisher** • 1224 Connecticut Ave NW
- **Blue Mercury** • 1619 Connecticut Ave NW
- **Brooks Brothers** • 1201 Connecticut Ave NW
- **Burberry** • 1155 Connecticut Ave NW
- **Cake Love** • 1506 U St NW
- **Comfort One Shoes** • 1621 Connecticut Ave NW
- **Comfort One Shoes** • 1630 Connecticut Ave NW
- **Companions Pet Shop** • 1626 U St Nw
- **Custom Shop Clothiers** • 1033 Connecticut Ave NW
- **Doggie Style** • 1825 18th St NW
- **Downs Engravers & Stationers** • 1746 L St NW
- **Drilling Tennis & Golf** • 1040 17th St NW
- **Filene's Basement** • 1133 Connecticut Ave NW
- **Fufua** • 1642 R St NW
- **The Gap** • 1120 Connecticut Ave NW
- **Ginza** • 1721 Connecticut Ave NW
- **Godiva Chocolatier** • 1143 Connecticut Ave NW
- **The Guitar Shop** • 1216 Connecticut Ave NW
- **Habitat Home Accents & Jewelry** • 1510 U St NW
- **Human Rights Campaign** • 1629 Connecticut Ave NW
- **J Press** • 1801 L St NW
- **Jos A Bank** • 1200 19th St NW
- **The Kid's Closet** • 1226 Connecticut Ave NW
- **Kramerbooks** • 1517 Connecticut Ave NW
- **Kulturas** • 1706 Connecticut Ave NW
- **Lambda Rising Bookstore** • 1625 Connecticut Ave NW
- **Leather Rack** • 1723 Connecticut Ave NW
- **Lucky Brand Dungarees** • 1739 Connecticut Ave NW
- **Marvelous Market** • 1511 Connecticut Ave NW
- **Meeps and Aunt Neensy's** • 1520 U St NW
- **Melody Records** • 1623 Connecticut Ave NW
- **Millennium Decorative Arts** • 1528 U St NW
- **Nana** • 1534 U St NW
- **National Geographic Shop** • 17 & M St NW
- **Newsroom** • 1803 Connecticut Ave NW
- **Pasargad Antique and Fine Persian** • 1217 Connecticut Ave NW
- **Pleasure Palace** • 1710 Connecticut Ave NW
- **Proper Topper** • 1350 Connecticut Ave NW
- **Rizik's** • 1100 Connecticut Ave NW
- **Rock Creek** • 2029 P St NW
- **Second Story Books and Antiques** • 2000 P St NW
- **Secondi** • 1702 Connecticut Ave NW
- **Sisley** • 1666 Connecticut Ave NW
- **Skynear and Co** • 2122 18th St NW
- **Sticky Fingers Bakery** • 1904 18th St NW
- **Tabletop** • 1608 20th St NW
- **The Third Day** • 2001 P St NW
- **Thomas Pink** • 1127 Connecticut Ave NW
- **Tiny Jewel Box** • 1147 Connecticut Ave NW
- **Universal Gear** • 1601 17th St NW
- **Video Americain** • 2104 18th St NW
- **Wild Women Wear Red** • 1512 U St NW
- **Wine Specialists** • 2115 M St NW
- **The Written Word** • 1365 Connecticut Ave NW

Map 10 • Logan Circle / U Street

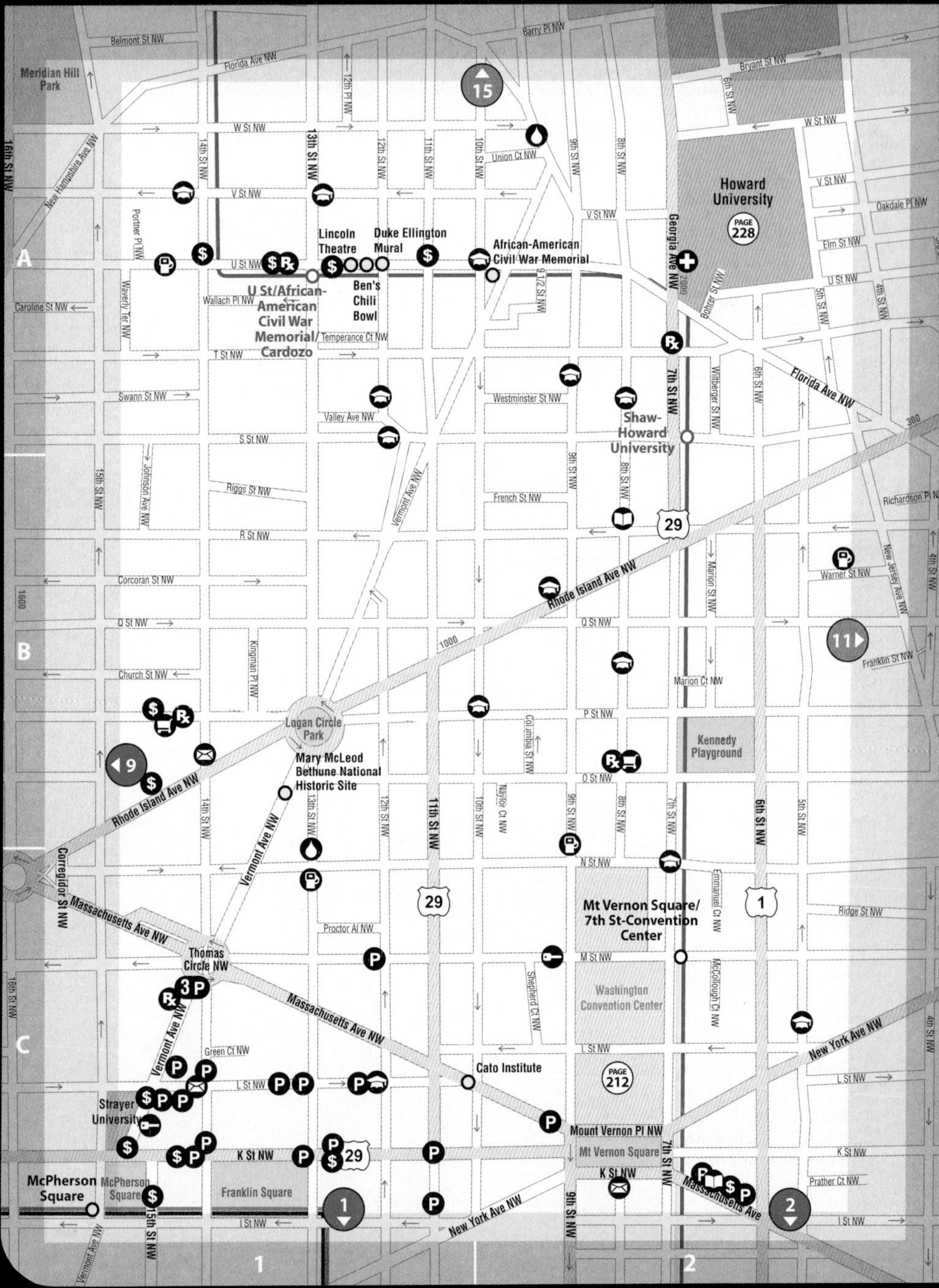

Meridian Hill Park
Belmont St NW
Florida Ave NW
Barry Pl NW
Bryant St NW
12th Pl NW
15
W St NW
Union Ct NW
16th St NW
New Hampshire Ave NW
14th St NW
13th St NW
12th St NW
11th St NW
10th St NW
9th St NW
8th St NW
6th St NW
Howard University
PAGE 228
V St NW
Oakdale Pl NW
Portner Pl NW
Lincoln Theatre
Duke Ellington Mural
African-American Civil War Memorial
Elm St NW
A
U St NW
Georgia Ave NW
2900
Bohrer St NW
U St NW
5th St NW
4th St NW
Caroline St NW
Waverly Ter NW
Wallach Pl NW
U St/African-American Civil War Memorial/Cardozo
Ben's Chili Bowl
9 1/2 St NW
Temperance Ct NW
T St NW
7th St NW
Wiltberger St NW
Florida Ave NW
Swann St NW
Westminster St NW
Valley Ave NW
Shaw-Howard University
300
S St NW
15th St NW
Johnson Ave NW
Riggs St NW
French St NW
Vermont Ave NW
Richardson Pl NW
29
R St NW
Marion St NW
New Jersey Ave NW
Warner St NW
Corcoran St NW
1600
Rhode Island Ave NW
Q St NW
Kingman Pl NW
1000
11
Franklin St NW
B
Church St NW
Marion Ct NW
P St NW
Logan Circle Park
Columbia St NW
Kennedy Playground
9
Mary McLeod Bethune National Historic Site
O St NW
Rhode Island Ave NW
Naylor Ct NW
N St NW
Corregidor St NW
Massachusetts Ave NW
Mt Vernon Square/ 7th St-Convention Center
Emmanuel Ct NW
Ridge St NW
1
Proctor Al NW
Thomas Circle NW
M St NW
Shepherd Ct NW
Washington Convention Center
McCollough Ct NW
C
Green Ct NW
L St NW
Cato Institute
PAGE 212
New York Ave NW
Strayer University
Mount Vernon Pl NW
K St NW
Mt Vernon Square
McPherson Square
Franklin Square
Prather Ct NW
Massachusetts Ave
2
I St NW
New York Ave NW
1
2

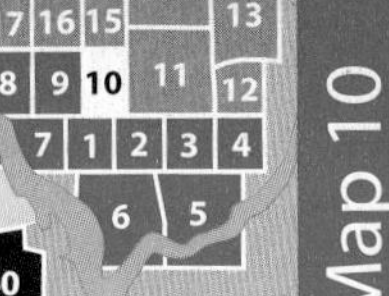

Its hookers-and-crack days long over, this area is a microcosm of DC gentrification. Here you'll find most of the city's hipper restaurants, bars and shops, as well as soaring property values and new buildings advertising "Real New York City-Style Lofts!" The population is very young and vaguely artistic (think hipsters with jobs). Be careful of U Street itself; the muggers haven't disappeared completely.

$ Banks

- **Bank of America** • 1090 Vermont Ave NW
- **Bank of America** • 635 Massachusetts Ave NW
- **BB&T** • 1316 U St NW
- **Chevy Chase** • 925 15th St NW
- **Citibank** • 1000 Vermont Ave NW
- **Eagle Bank** • 1425 K St NW
- **Industrial Bank** • 2000 11th St NW
- **Industrial Bank** • 2000 14th St NW
- **PNC (ATM)** • 1444 Rhode Island Ave NW
- **Sun Trust** • 1250 U St NW
- **Sun Trust** • 1275 K St NW
- **Wachovia** • 1447 P St NW

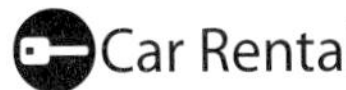

Car Rental

- **Enterprise** • 1029 Vermont Ave NW • 202-393-0900
- **Rent-A-Wreck** • 910 M St NW • 202-408-9828

Car Washes

- **Mr Wash** • 1311 13th St NW
- **Sparkle Car Wash** • 933 Florida Ave NW

Gas Stations

- **Amoco** • 1301 13th St NW
- **Amoco** • 1317 9th St NW
- **Chevron** • 4200 Burroughs Ave NE
- **Mobil** • 1442 U St NW

Hospitals

- **Howard University** • 2041 Georgia Ave NW

o Landmarks

- **African-American Civil War Memorial** • 1000 U St NW
- **Ben's Chili Bowl** • 1213 U St NW
- **Cato Institute** • 1000 Massachusetts Ave NW
- **Duke Ellington Mural** • 1200 U St NW
- **Lincoln Theatre** • 1215 U St NW
- **Mary McLeod Bethune National Historic Site** • 1318 Vermont Ave NW

Libraries

- **Bureau of Alcohol & Tobacco Library** • 650 Massachusetts Ave NW
- **Watha T Daniel Branch Library** • 1701 8th St NW

Parking

Pharmacies

- **CVS** • 1199 Vermont Ave NW
- **CVS** • 1418 P St NW
- **CVS** • 1900 7th St NW
- **Giant Food Pharmacy** • 1414 8th St NW
- **Rite Aid** • 1306 U St NW

Post Offices

- **Martin Luther King Jr Station** • 1400 L St NW
- **Techworld Station** • 800 K St NW

Schools

- **Children's Studio** • 1301 V St NW
- **Cleveland Elementary** • 1825 8th St NW
- **FLOC Learning Center** • 1816 12th St NW
- **Garnet-Patterson Middle** • 2001 10th St NW
- **Garrison Elementary** • 1200 S St NW
- **Immaculate Conception** • 711 N St NW
- **Maya Angelou Public Charter** • 1851 9th St NW
- **Seaton Elementary** • 1503 10th St NW
- **Shaw Junior High** • 925 Rhode Island Ave NW
- **St Augustine** • 1419 V St NW
- **Sunrise Academy** • 1130 6th St NW
- **Thomson Elementary** • 1200 L St NW
- **Ujima Ya Ujamaa** • 1554 8th St NW

Supermarkets

- **Giant Food** • 1414 8th St NW
- **Whole Foods Market** • 1440 P St NW

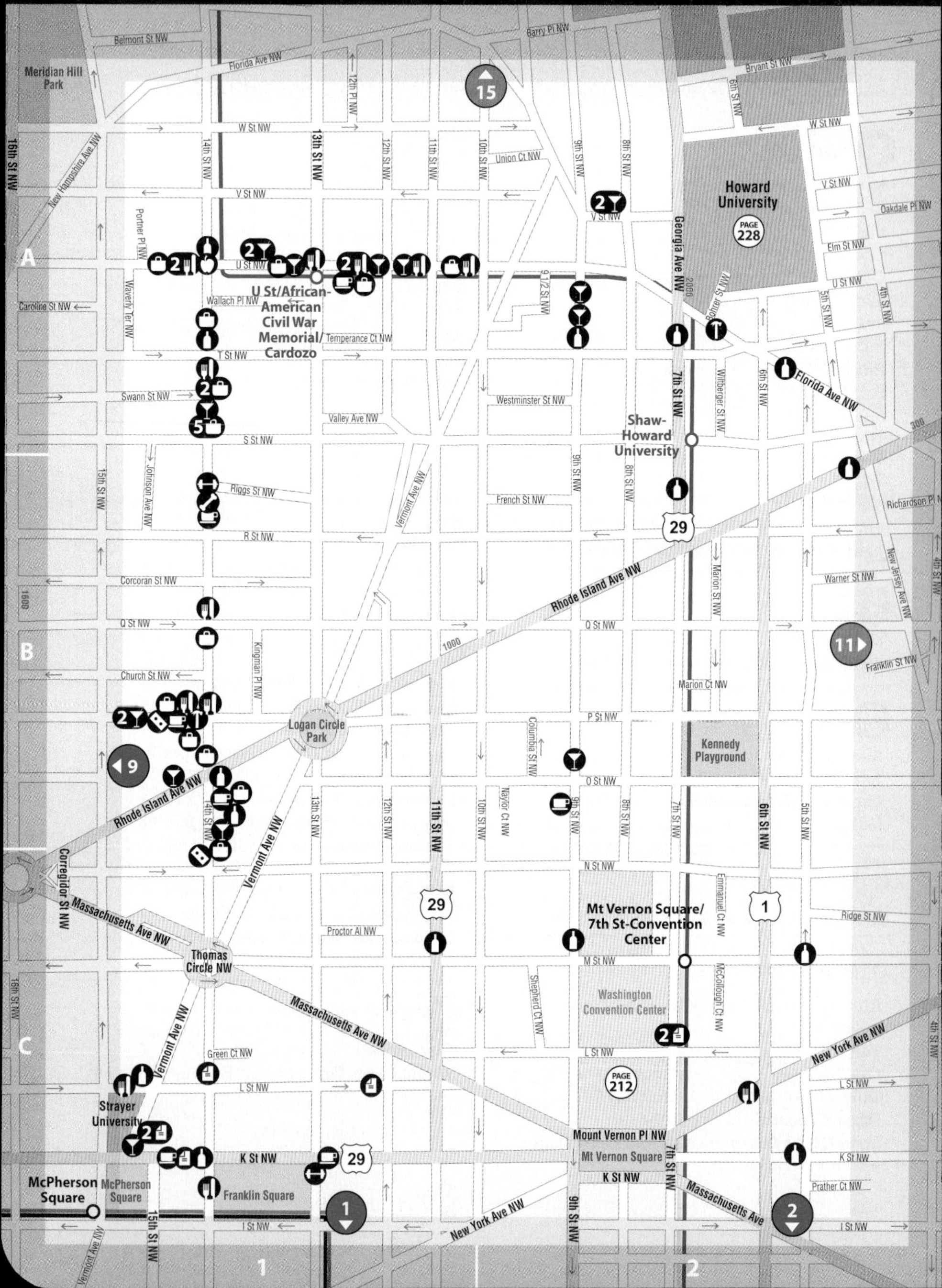

Map 10 • Logan Circle / U Street

N

Meridian Hill Park
Belmont St NW
Florida Ave NW
Barry Pl NW
Bryant St NW
15
W St NW
12th Pl NW
16th St NW
New Hampshire Ave NW
14th St NW
13th St NW
12th St NW
11th St NW
10th St NW
Union Ct NW
9th St NW
8th St NW
Howard University
PAGE 228
6th St NW
V St NW
Oakdale Pl NW
Elm St NW
Portner Pl NW
U St NW
Georgia Ave NW
2000
Bohrer St NW
5th St NW
4th St NW
9 1/2 St NW
Caroline St NW
Waverly Ter NW
Wallach Pl NW
U St/African-American Civil War Memorial/Cardozo
Temperance Ct NW
T St NW
7th St NW
Wiltberger St NW
Florida Ave NW
Swann St NW
Westminster St NW
Valley Ave NW
Shaw-Howard University
300
S St NW
15th St NW
Johnson Ave NW
Riggs St NW
Vermont Ave NW
French St NW
Richardson Pl NW
29
R St NW
Marion St NW
New Jersey Ave NW
Warner St NW
Corcoran St NW
1600
Rhode Island Ave NW
Q St NW
1000
11
Franklin St NW
Kingman Pl NW
Church St NW
Marion Ct NW
P St NW
Logan Circle Park
Columbia St NW
Kennedy Playground
9
O St NW
Naylor Ct NW
N St NW
Corregidor St NW
Massachusetts Ave NW
Mt Vernon Square/ 7th St-Convention Center
Emmanuel Ct NW
1
Ridge St NW
Proctor Al NW
Thomas Circle NW
M St NW
McCollough Ct NW
Shepherd Ct NW
Washington Convention Center
New York Ave NW
Green Ct NW
L St NW
PAGE 212
Strayer University
Mount Vernon Pl NW
K St NW
Mt Vernon Square
McPherson Square
Franklin Square
Prather Ct NW
Massachusetts Ave
I St NW
2
Vermont Ave NW

A
B
C
1
2

Sundries / Entertainment

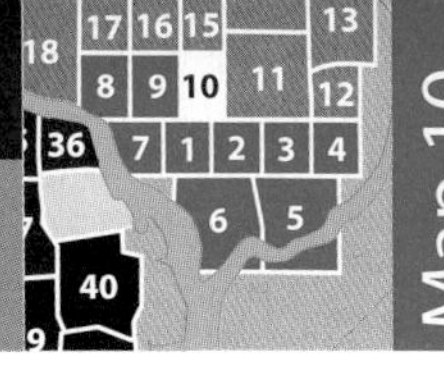

A 14th Street makeover has turned a former prostitutes' catwalk into Whole Foods central. At the same time, U Street has raised from the riot ashes to become boutiqueville. At night, both have some of the best martinis and relaxed bars in the city. Score one of Café Saint-Ex's outdoor tables on a summer night and you're set. Otherwise, check out the jazz at Bohemian Caverns or the bands at the 9:30 Club or Black Cat.

Coffee

- **Azi's Café** • 1336 9th St NW
- **Caribou Coffee** • 1400 14th St NW
- **Cosí** • 1275 K St NW
- **Sparky's Expresso Café** • 1720 14th St NW
- **Starbucks** • 1250 U St NW
- **Starbucks** • 1425 P St NW
- **Starbucks** • 1455 K St NW

Copy Shops

- **Clicks Professional Copy (24 hours)** • 1424 K St NW
- **CPN Technology (9am-5:30pm)** • 1111 7th St NW
- **Instant Copies & Print (9am-6:30pm)** • 1010 Vermont Ave NW
- **Miller Copying Service (9am-6pm)** • 1111 7th St NW
- **Print Express (9am-6pm)** • 1101 14th St NW
- **Sir Speedy Printing (8:30am-5pm)** • 1029 Vermont Ave NW
- **UPS Store (8:30am-7pm)** • 1220 L St NW

Farmer's Markets

- **14th & U Farmers Market** • 14th & U Sts NW

Gyms

- **One World Fitness** • 1738 14th St NW
- **Renaissance Swim & Fitness** • 941 9th St NW

Hardware Stores

- **Best Price Hardware** • 636 Florida Ave NW
- **Logan Hardware** • 1416 P St NW

Liquor Stores

- **A-1 Wine & Liquor** • 1420 K St NW
- **Barrel House** • 1341 14th St NW
- **Best in Liquors** • 1450 P St NW
- **Bestway Liquors** • 2011 14th St NW
- **Beverages Etc** • 1905 9th St NW
- **Continental Liquors** • 1100 Vermont Ave NW
- **District Liquors** • 1211 11th St NW
- **Guilford Liquors** • 446 Rhode Island Ave NW
- **Joe Caplan Liquor** • 1913 7th St Nw
- **Log Cabin Liquors** • 1748 7th St NW
- **Longs Liquors** • 520 Florida Ave NW
- **Modern Liquors** • 1200 9th St NW
- **Paradise Liquor** • 1900 14th St NW
- **S&R Liquors** • 1201 5th St NW
- **S&W Liquors** • 1428 9th St NW
- **Sav-On-Liquors** • 1414 14th St NW
- **Subway Liquors II** • 500 K St NW

Nightlife

- **9:30 Club** • 815 V St NW
- **Bar Nun** • 1326 U St NW
- **Black Cat** • 1811 14th St NW
- **Bohemian Caverns** • 2001 11th St NW
- **Daedalus** • 1010 Vermont Ave NW
- **DC9** • 1940 9th St NW
- **Halo Lounge** • 1435 P St NW
- **Helix Lounge** • 1430 Rhode Island Ave NW
- **Republic Gardens** • 1355 U St NW
- **The Saloon** • 1207 U St NW
- **Titan** • 1337 14th St NW
- **Twins Jazz** • 1344 U St NW

Pet Shops

- **Pet Essentials** • 1722 14th St NW

Restaurants

- **Ben's Chili Bowl** • 1213 U St NW
- **Café Saint-Ex** • 1847 14th St NW
- **Coppi's** • 1414 U St NW
- **DC Coast** • 1401 K St NW
- **Dukem** • 1114 U St NW
- **Georgia Brown's** • 950 15th St NW
- **Logan Tavern** • 1423 P St NW
- **Maggie Moo's** • 1301 U St NW
- **Marrakesh Restaurant** • 617 New York Ave NW
- **Oohhs and Aahhs** • 1005 U St NW
- **Post Pub** • 1422 L St NW
- **Rice** • 1608 14th St NW
- **Saloon** • 1207 U St NW
- **Thai Tanic** • 1236 14th St NW
- **U-topia** • 1418 U St NW

Shopping

- **Blink** • 1431 P St NW
- **Candida's World of Books** • 1541 14th St NW
- **Capitol Records** • 1020 U St NW
- **Garden District** • 1801 14th St NW
- **Go Mama Go!** • 1809 14th St NW
- **Good Wood** • 1428 U St NW
- **Home Rule** • 1807 14th St NW
- **Logan Hardware** • 1416 P St NW
- **Maison 14** • 1325 14th St NW
- **Muleh** • 1831 14th St NW
- **Pink November** • 1231 U St NW
- **Pop** • 1803 14th St NW
- **Pulp** • 1803 14th St NW
- **Reincarnation Furnishings** • 1401 14th St NW
- **Ruff and Ready** • 1908 14th St NW
- **Urban Essentials** • 1330 U St NW
- **Vastu** • 1829 14th St NW

Video Rental

- **Empire Video** • 1435 P St NW
- **Video 2000** • 1320 14th St NW

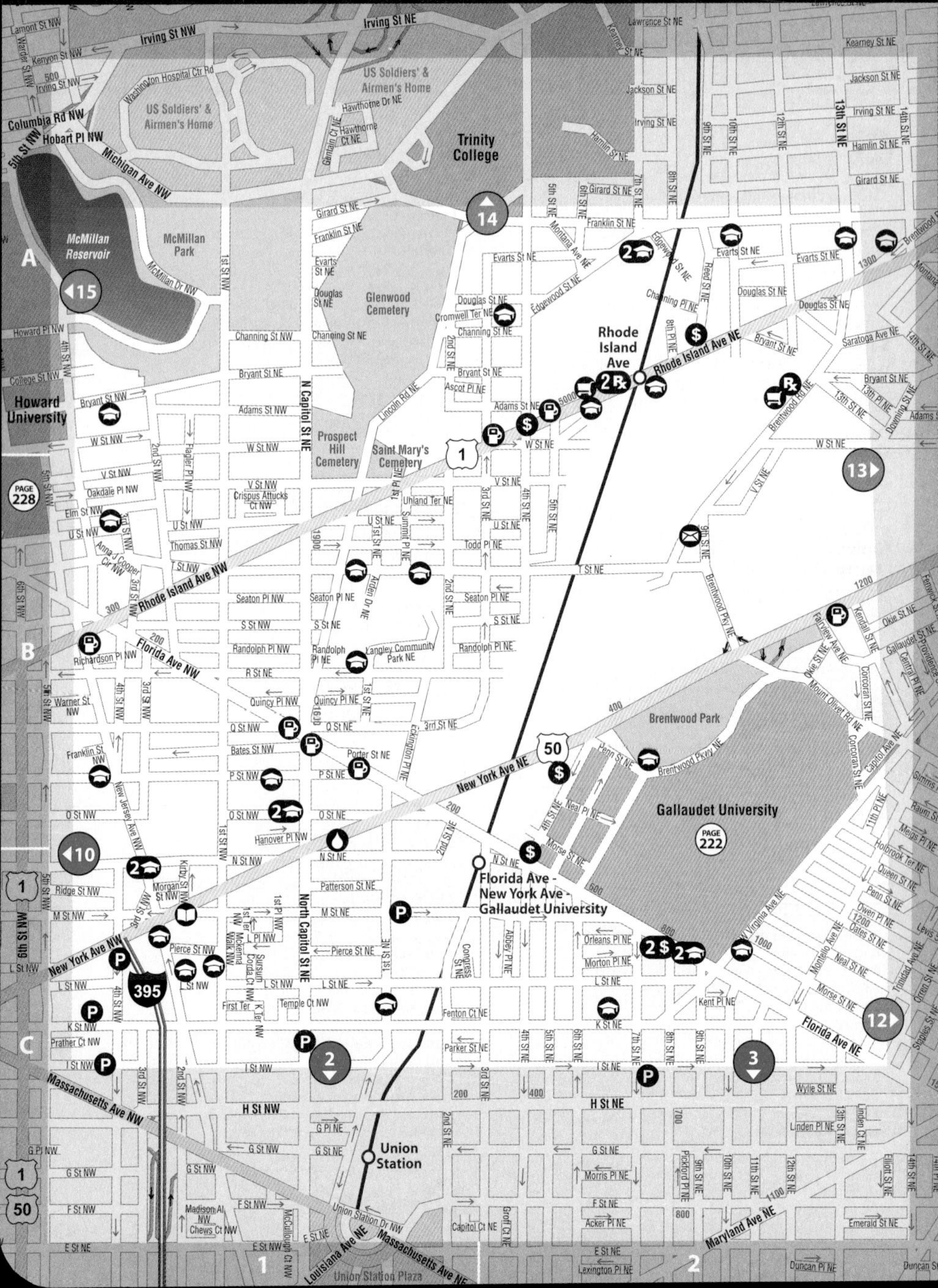

Map 11 • Near Northeast

Trinity College

US Soldiers' & Airmen's Home

McMillan Reservoir

McMillan Park

Glenwood Cemetery

Prospect Hill Cemetery

Saint Mary's Cemetery

Howard University

Rhode Island Ave

Brentwood Park

Gallaudet University

Florida Ave - New York Ave - Gallaudet University

Union Station

Union Station Plaza

Once the second busiest commercial corridor in the city, H Street is slowly starting to recover from the '60s riots. Developers and newcomers are venturing in, while a redevelopment plan is in full swing.

Banks

- **Bank of America** • 915 Rhode Island Ave NE
- **Bank of America (ATM)** • 340 Florida Ave NE
- **PNC** • 1348 4th St NE
- **PNC** • 800 Florida Ave NE
- **PNC (ATM)** • 800 Florida Ave NE
- **Sun Trust** • 410 Rhode Island Ave NE

Car Washes

- **NY Avenue Car Wash** • 39 New York Ave NE

Gas Stations

- **Amoco** • 1231 New York Ave NE
- **Amoco** • 306 Rhode Island Ave NW
- **Amoco** • 400 Rhode Island Ave NE
- **Amoco** • 45 Florida Ave NE
- **Auster** • 22 Florida Ave NW
- **Exxon** • 1 Florida Ave NE
- **Hess** • 1739 New Jersey Ave NW

Libraries

- **Sursum Corda Community Library** • 135 New York Ave NW

Parking

Pharmacies

- **CVS** • 660 Rhode Island Ave NE
- **Giant Food Pharmacy** • 1050 Brentwood Rd NE
- **Safeway** • 514 Rhode Island Ave NE

Post Offices

- **Washington Main Office** • 900 Brentwood Rd NE

Schools

- **Calvary Christian Academy** • 616 Rhode Island Ave NE
- **City Lights** • 62 T St NE
- **Cook Elementary** • 30 P St NW
- **DC Preparatory Academy** • 701 Edgewood St NE
- **Dunbar High** • 1301 New Jersey Ave NW
- **Emery Elementary** • 1720 1st St NE
- **Gage Eckington Elementary** • 2025 3rd St NW
- **Gallaudet University** • 800 Florida Ave NE
- **HD Cooke** • 300 Bryant St NW
- **Holy Name** • 1217 West Virginia Ave NE
- **Holy Redeemer** • 1135 New Jersey Ave NW
- **Hyde Leadership** • 101 T St NE
- **Kendall Demonstration Elementary/Model Secondary** • 800 Florida Ave NE
- **Kennedy Institute Upper** • 680 Rhode Island Ave NE
- **McKinley High** • 151 T St NE
- **Montgomery Elementary** • 421 P St NW
- **Noyes Elementary** • 2725 10th St NE
- **Pre-Engineering Senior High** • 1301 New Jersey Ave NW
- **Shaed Elementary** • 301 Douglas St NE
- **Terrell Center** • 1000 1st St NW
- **Terrell Junior High** • 100 Pierce St NW
- **Tree of Life Community Elementary** • 1401 Brentwood Pkwy NE
- **Walker-Jones Elementary** • 100 L St NW
- **Washington Career High** • 27 O St NW
- **William E Doar Jr Elementary** • 705 Edgewood St NE
- **Wilson Elementary** • 660 K St NE

Supermarkets

- **Giant Food** • 1050 Brentwood Rd NE
- **Safeway** • 514 Rhode Island Ave NE

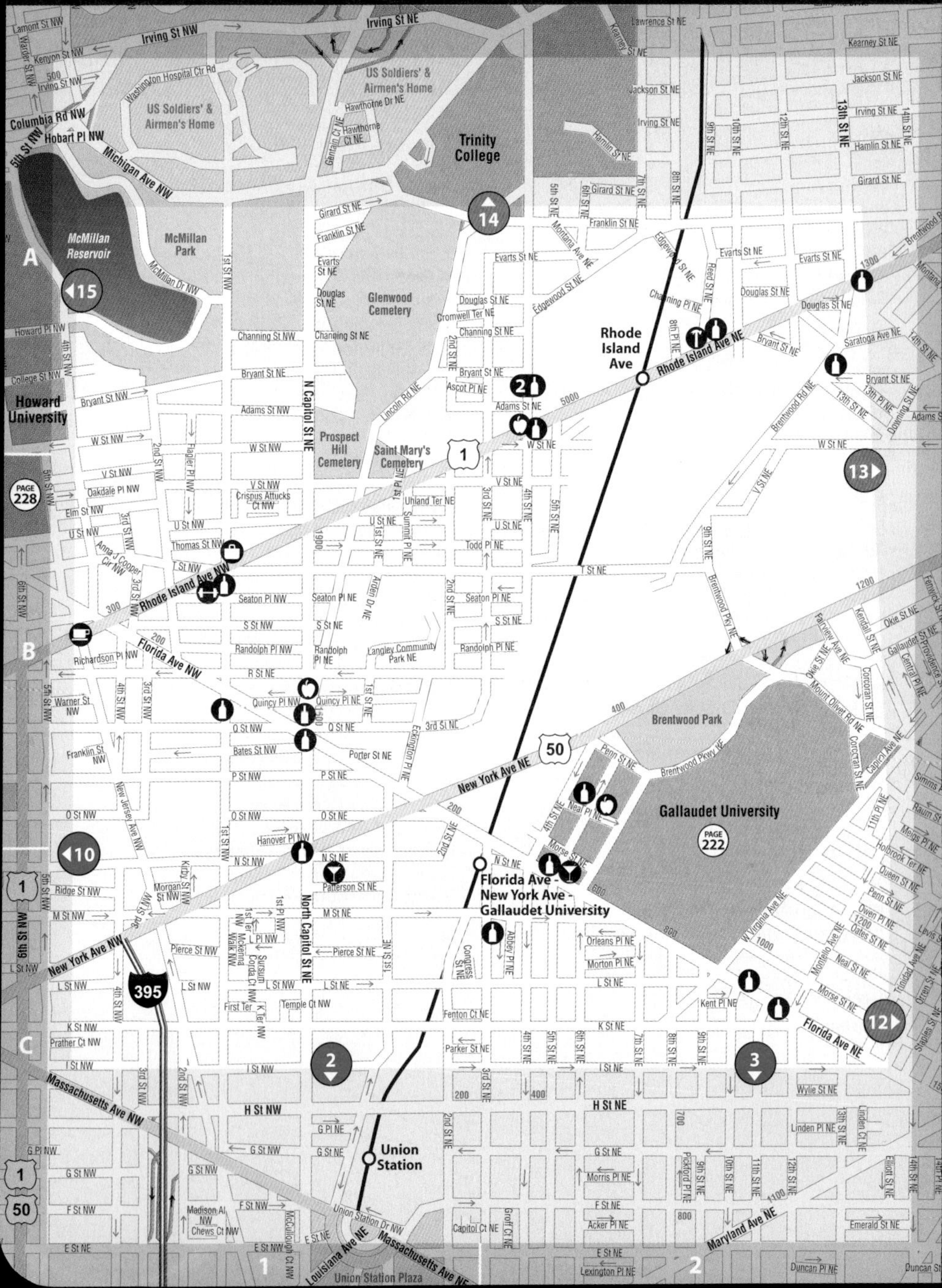

Map 11 • Near Northeast

Sundries / Entertainment

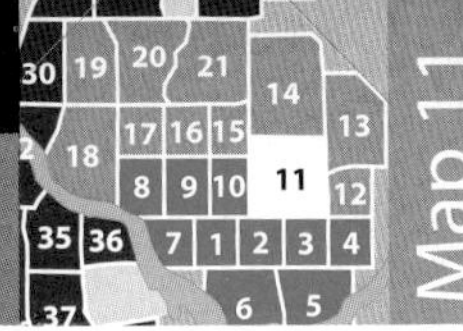

Waiting for revitalization to kick in means traveling to another neighborhood for amenities. That said, a local theater scene is starting to brew around the Atlas Performing Arts Center and H Street Playhouse. We give it four years before the area explodes into the next U Street.

Coffee

- **Dunkin Donuts** • 1739 New Jersey Ave NW

Farmer's Markets

- **DC Farmers Market** • 1309 5th St NE
- **North Capitol Neighborhood Farmers Market** • 1626 N Capitol St NE
- **Rhode Island Flea Market & Farmers Market** • 4th St & Rhode Island Ave NE

Gyms

- **Aerobodies Fitness** • 147 Rhode Island Ave NW

Hardware Stores

- **Home Depot** • 901 Rhode Island Ave NE

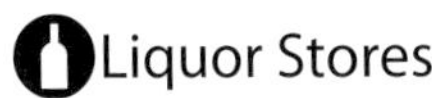

Liquor Stores

- **Big Ben Liquor Store** • 1300 N Capitol St NW
- **Bloomingdale Liquor** • 1836 1st St NW
- **Brentwood Liquors** • 1319 Rhode Island Ave NE
- **Brother's Liquor** • 1140 Florida Ave NE
- **Coast-In Liquors** • 301 Florida Ave NE
- **Edgewood Liquor Store** • 2303 4th St NE
- **J&J Liquor Store** • 1211 Brentwood Rd NE
- **JB Liquorette** • 1000 Florida Ave NE
- **Mac's Wine & Liquor** • 401 Rhode Island Ave NE
- **Northeast Liquors** • 1300 5th St NE
- **Oasis Liquors** • 1179 3rd St NE
- **Rhode Island Subway Liquor** • 914 Rhode Island Ave NE
- **Sosnik's Liquor Store** • 2318 4th St NE
- **Sunset Liquors** • 1627 1st St NW
- **Super Liquors** • 1633 N Capitol St NE
- **Walter Johnson's Liquor Store** • 1542 N Capitol St NW

Nightlife

- **Bud's** • 501 Morse St NE
- **FUR Nightclub** • 33 Patterson St NE

Shopping

- **Windows Café & Market** • 1900 1st St NW

Map 12 • Trinidad

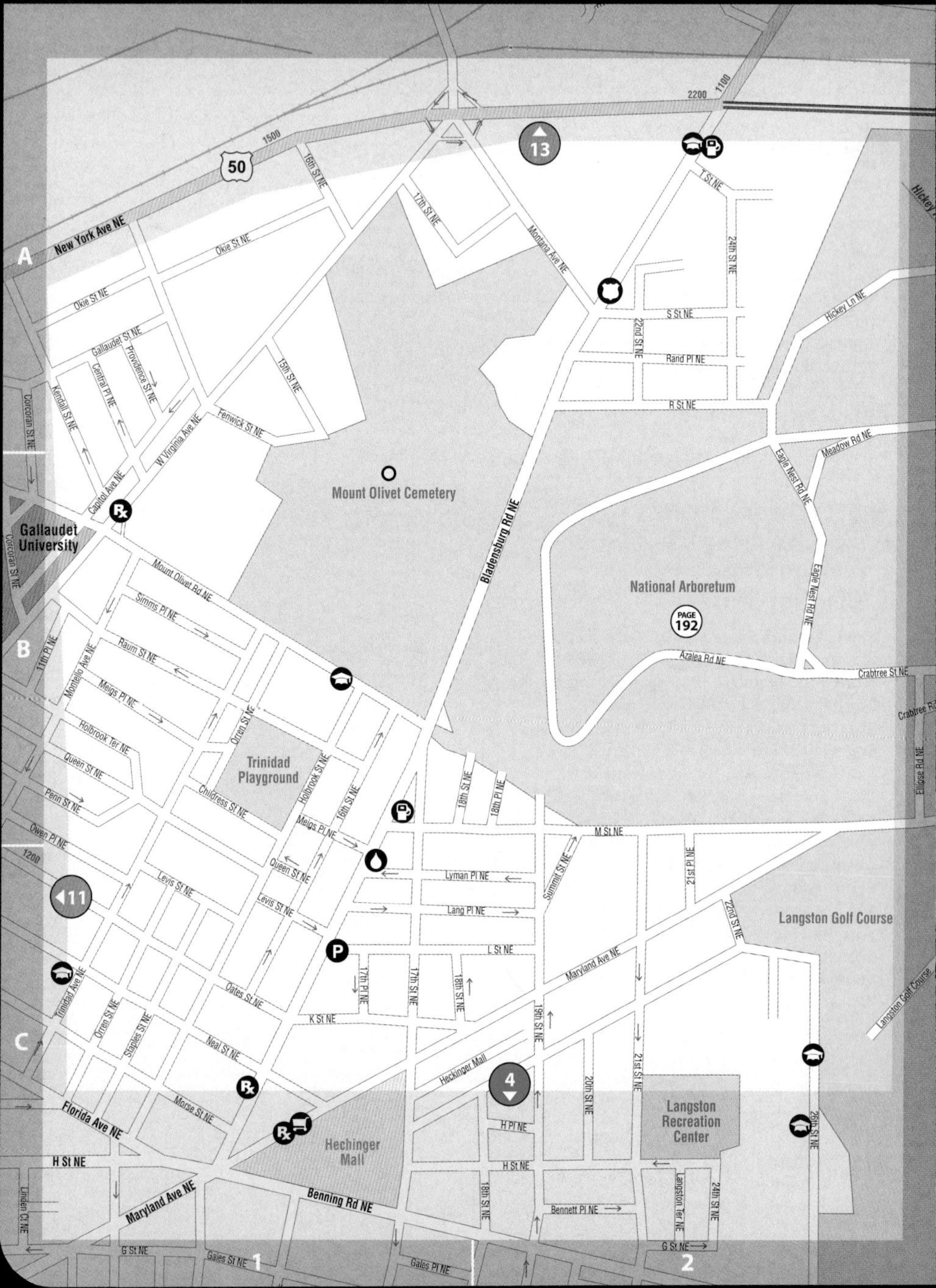

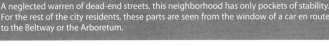

A neglected warren of dead-end streets, this neighborhood has only pockets of stability. For the rest of the city residents, these parts are seen from the window of a car en route to the Beltway or the Arboretum.

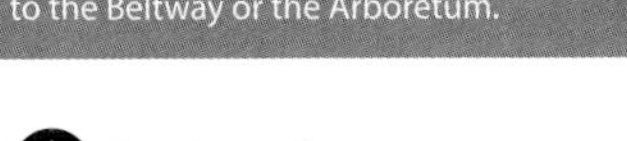

Car Washes

- **Smoke Detail Hand Carwash** • 1161 Bladensburg Rd NE

Gas Stations

- **Amoco** • 1201 Bladensburg Rd NE
- **Exxon** • 1925 Bladensburg Rd NE

Landmarks

- **Mount Olivet Cemetery** • 1300 Bladensberg Rd NW

Parking

Pharmacies

- **CVS** • 845 Bladensburg Rd
- **Mt Olivet CARE Pharmacy** • 1809 West Virginia Ave NE
- **Safeway** • 1601 Maryland Ave NE

Police

- **MPDC 5th District Station** • 1805 Bladensburg Rd NE

Schools

- **Browne Junior High** • 850 26th St NE
- **New School for Enterprise and Development** • 1920 Bladensburg Rd NE
- **Webb Elementary** • 1375 Mount Olive Rd NE
- **Wheatley Elementary (temporarily closed)** • 1299 Neal St NE
- **Young Elementary** • 820 26th St NE

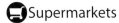

Supermarkets

- **Safeway** • 1601 Maryland Ave NE

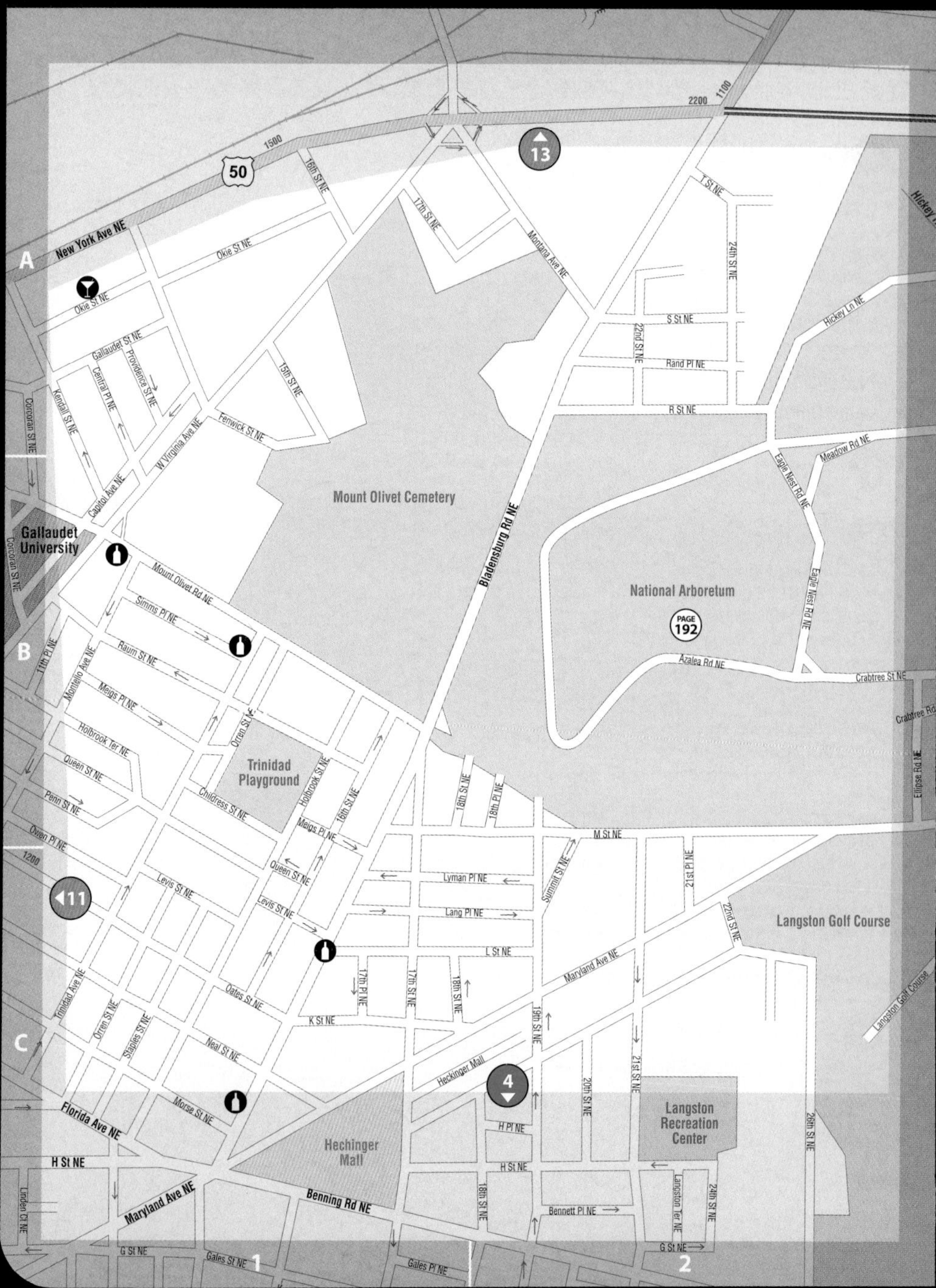

Map 12 • Trinidad

N

Mount Olivet Cemetery
National Arboretum
PAGE 192
Gallaudet University
Trinidad Playground
Langston Golf Course
Langston Recreation Center
Hechinger Mall
13
11
4
50
New York Ave NE
Bladensburg Rd NE
Florida Ave NE
Maryland Ave NE
Benning Rd NE
H St NE
Okie St NE
Gallaudet St NE
Providence St NE
Central Pl NE
Kendall St NE
Capitol Ave NE
W Virginia Ave NE
Fenwick St NE
15th St NE
16th St NE
17th St NE
Montana Ave NE
T St NE
24th St NE
S St NE
22nd St NE
Rand Pl NE
R St NE
Hickey Ln NE
Meadow Rd NE
Eagle Nest Rd NE
Azalea Rd NE
Crabtree St NE
Crabtree Rd
Ellipse Rd NE
Mount Olivet Rd NE
Simms Pl NE
Raum St NE
Meigs Pl NE
Holbrook Ter NE
Queen St NE
Penn St NE
Owen Pl NE
Orren St NE
Montello Ave NE
11th Pl NE
Corcoran St NE
Childress St NE
Holbrook St NE
18th St NE
18th Pl NE
M St NE
Summit St NE
21st Pl NE
Lyman Pl NE
Lang Pl NE
Levis St NE
L St NE
17th Pl NE
Oates St NE
K St NE
19th St NE
21st St NE
22nd St NE
Trinidad Ave NE
Staples St NE
Neal St NE
Morse St NE
Heckinger Mall
20th St NE
H Pl NE
26th St NE
Langston Golf Course
Langston Ter NE
Bennett Pl NE
Linden Ct NE
G St NE
Gales St NE
Gales Pl NE
1500
2200
1100
1200
A
B
C
1
2

Beyond the drivable destination nightclubs, like Dream, there ain't much here to slow down for.

Liquor Stores

- **Acme Liquors** • 1730 Trinidad Ave NE
- **Kovaks Liquors** • 1237 Mount Olivet Rd NE
- **Rose's Liquor** • 830 Bladensburg Rd NE
- **Stanton Liquors** • 1044 Bladensburg Rd NE

Nightlife

- **Dream** • 1350 Okie St NE

Michigan Ave NE
Rhode Island Ave NE
S Dakota Ave NE
Bladensburg Rd NE
New York Ave NE
Franciscan Monastery
Fort Bunker Hill Park
Taft Recreation Center
Barnard Hill Park
Langdon Park
Mount Olivet Cemetery
National Arboretum
PAGE 192

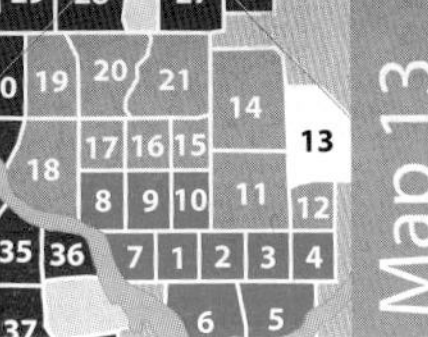

Here's an architecturally diverse little slice of the suburbs within city limits. It's a traditionally African-American middle-class enclave that is diversifying with newcomers from downtown who want more room and yard work.

Banks

- **Industrial Bank** • 2012 Rhode Island Ave NE
- **Wachovia** • 2119 Bladensburg Rd NE

Car Rental

- **A&D Auto Rental** • 2712 Bladensburg Rd NE • 202-832-5300
- **Enterprise** • 1502 Franklin St NE • 202-269-0300
- **Thrifty** • 3210 Rhode Island Ave • 202-636-8470

Car Washes

- **Heaven Sprinkles** • 1923 New York Ave NE
- **Montana Double Car Wash** • 2327 18th St NE

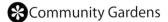

Community Gardens

Gas Stations

- **Amoco** • 2210 Bladensburg Rd NE
- **Exxon** • 2230 New York Ave NE
- **Hess** • 1801 New York Ave NE
- **Shell** • 1765 New York Ave NE
- **Shell** • 1830 Rhode Island Ave NE

Landmarks

- **Franciscan Monastery** • 1400 Quincy St NE

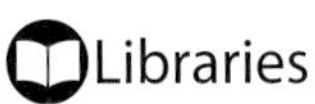

Libraries

- **Woodridge Library** • 1801 Hamlin St NE

Pharmacies

- **Rite Aid** • 1401 Rhode Island Ave NE

Post Offices

- **Woodridge Station** • 2211 Rhode Island Ave NE

Schools

- **Bunker Hill Elementary** • 1401 Michigan Ave NE
- **Burroughs Elementary** • 1820 Monroe St NE
- **Friendship Edison Woodridge Campus** • 2959 Carlton Ave NE
- **Langdon Elementary** • 1900 Evarts St SE
- **Latin American Montessori Bilingual** • 1725 Michigan Ave NE
- **Lincoln Middle** • 1800 Perry St NE
- **Rhema Christian Center** • 1825 Michigan Ave NE
- **Slowe Elementary** • 1404 Jackson St NE
- **St Anselm's Abbey** • 4501 S Dakota Ave NE
- **St Francis de Sales** • 2019 Rhode Island Ave NE
- **Taft** • 1800 Perry St NE

N
Buchanan St NE
Allison St NE
Webster St NE
Varnum Pl NE
Varnum St NE
Michigan Ave NE
Bunker Hill Rd NE
Upshur St NE
Taylor St NE
Shepherd St NE
Ritchie Pl NE
Randolph St NE
Quincy St NE
Perry St NE
Fort Bunker Hill Park
Taft Recreation Center
Otis Pl NE
Otis St NE
Newton St NE
Monroe St NE
Lawrence St NE
Kearney St NE
Jackson St NE
Irving St NE
Fort Pl NE
Fulton Pl NE
Hamlin St NE
Girard St NE
Langdon Park
Franklin St NE
Evarts St NE
Douglas St NE
Channing St NE
Park Ave NE
Saratoga Ave NE
Bryant St NE
Adams St NE
W St NE
V St NE
Rhode Island Ave NE
S Dakota Ave NE
Brentwood Rd NE
Montana Ave NE
Queens Chapel Rd NE
Bladensburg Rd NE
New York Ave NE
Barnard Hill Park
Eastern Ave NE
Myrtle Ave NE
Central Ave NE
Carlton Ave NE
Vista St NE
Mills Ave NE
Woodridge St NE
Thayer St NE
Hoover Rd NE
Chestnut St NE
Walnut St NE
Clinton St NE
Elm St NE
Earl Pl NE
Cherry Rd NE
Berry Rd NE
Yost Pl NE
Banneker Dr NE
Apple Rd NE
31st Pl NE
Ames Pl NE
Fort Lincoln Dr NE
National Arboretum
Hickey Ln NE
Hickey Run
Valley Road NE
Springhouse Rd NE
Conifer Rd
Holly Spring Rd NE
Meadow Rd NE
Mount Olivet Cemetery
T St NE
S St NE
Okie St NE
Fenwick St NE
Kendall St NE
Gallaudet St NE
17th St NE
16th St NE
24th St NE
22nd St NE
Edwin St NE
Lawrence Ave NE
Charles St NE
Adams Pl NE
Lafayette Ave NE
Downing St NE
Downing Pl NE
13th Pl NE
13th St NE
12th St NE
Webster St
Varnum St
Upshur St
Tilden St
Taylor St
Rainier Ave
Russell Ave
Kaywood Dr
Kaywood Pl
28th Pl
Sherwood St NE
Sargent Rd NE
Urell Pl NE
Taussig Pl NE
Sigsbee Pl NE
Oakview Ter NE
Bryant St NE
34th St
Bunker Hill Rd
1
ALT 1
50
14
11
12
PAGE 192
A
B
C
1
2

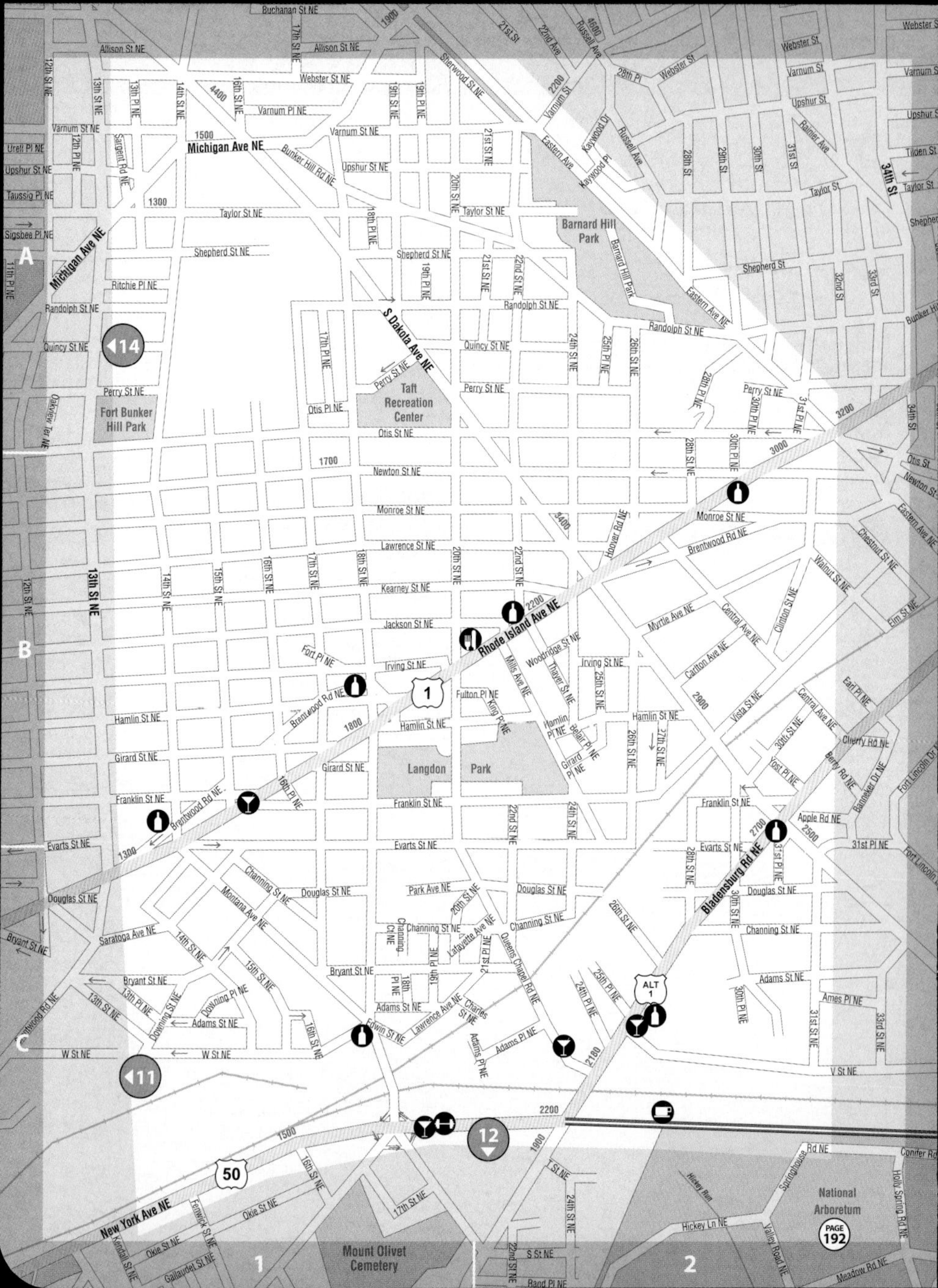

People here came to get away from the urban hubbub. And they did.

Coffee

- **Dunkin' Donuts** • 2420 New York Ave NE

Gyms

- **Mini Health Club** • 1818 New York Ave NE

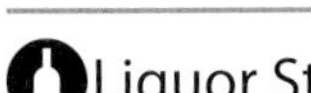

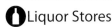

Liquor Stores

- **Good Ole Reliable Liquor** • 1513 Rhode Island Ave NE
- **Montana Liquors** • 1805 Montana Ave NE
- **National Wine & Liquors** • 2310 Rhode Island Ave NE
- **Pal Liquors** • 1905 Brentwood Rd NE
- **Sammy's Liquor** • 2725 Bladensburg Rd NE
- **Stop & Shop Liquors** • 3011 Rhode Island Ave NE
- **Syd's Drive-In Liquor Store** • 2325 Bladensburg Rd NE
- **Woodridge Vet's Liquors** • 1358 Brentwood Rd NE

Nightlife

- **Aqua** • 1818 New York Ave NE
- **Breeze Metro** • 2335 Bladensburg Rd NE
- **DC Tunnel** • 2135 Queens Chapel Rd NE

Restaurants

- **Bamboo Joint Café** • 2062 Rhode Island Ave NE

Map 14 • Catholic U

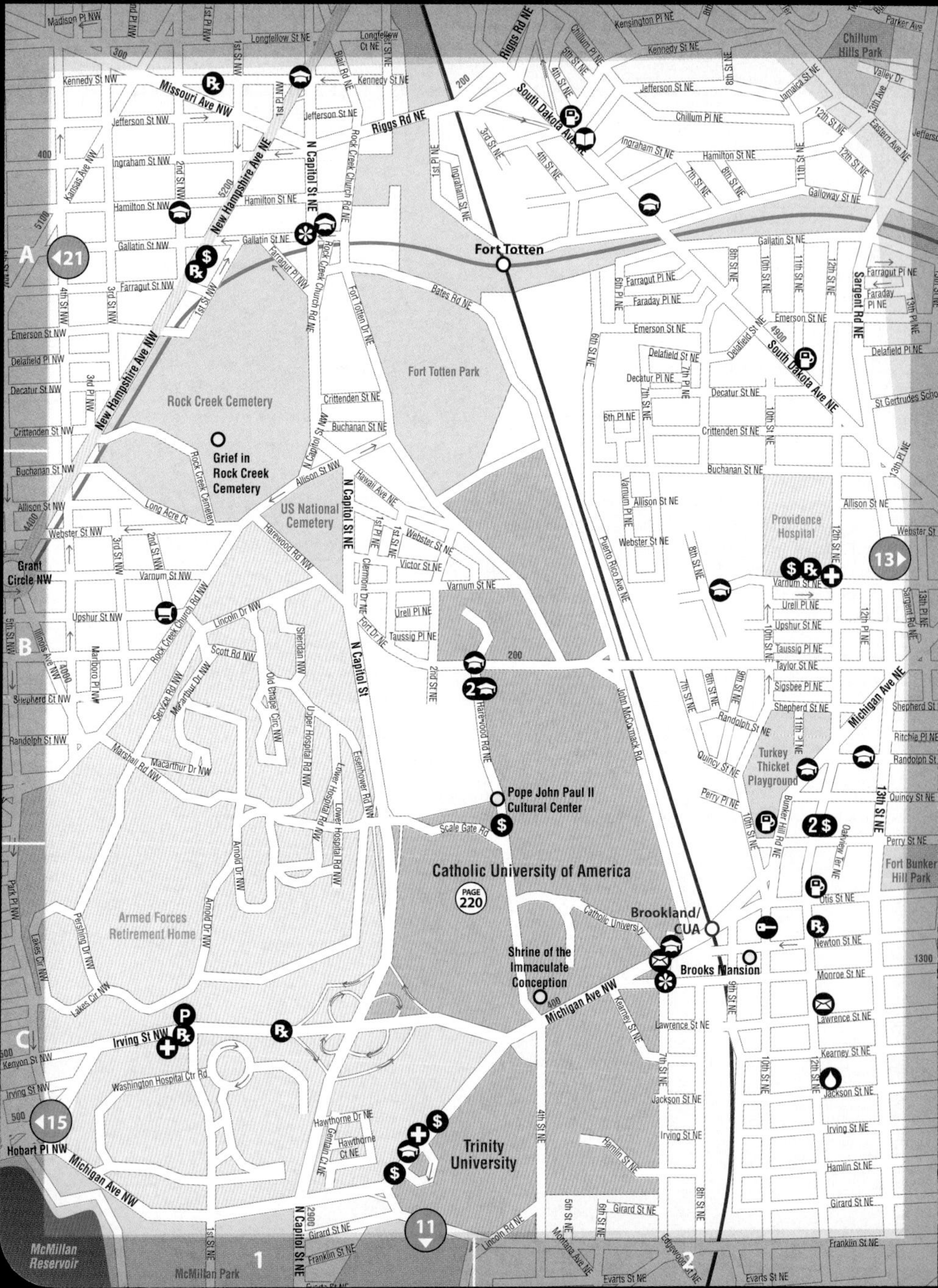

Fort Totten
Fort Totten Park
Rock Creek Cemetery
Grief in Rock Creek Cemetery
US National Cemetery
Armed Forces Retirement Home
Providence Hospital
Turkey Thicket Playground
Fort Bunker Hill Park
Chillum Hills Park
Pope John Paul II Cultural Center
Catholic University of America
PAGE 220
Shrine of the Immaculate Conception
Brookland/ CUA
Brooks Mansion
Trinity University
McMillan Reservoir
McMillan Park
Grant Circle NW

Missouri Ave NW
New Hampshire Ave NE
New Hampshire Ave NW
N Capitol St NE
N Capitol St
Riggs Rd NE
South Dakota Ave NE
Michigan Ave NE
Michigan Ave NW
Rock Creek Church Rd NE
Rock Creek Church Rd NW
Fort Totten Dr NE
Harewood Rd NE
John McCormack Rd
Puerto Rico Ave NE
Sargent Rd NE
13th St NE
Bunker Hill Rd NE
Irving St NW
Kenyon St NW
Hobart Pl NW
Washington Hospital Ctr Rd
Lincoln Rd NE
Montana Ave NE
Edgewood St NE
Eisenhower Rd NW
Marshall Rd NW
Scale Gate Rd
Catholic University
Kansas Ave NW
Illinois Ave NW
Kennedy St NW
Jefferson St NW
Ingraham St NW
Hamilton St NW
Gallatin St NW
Farragut St NW
Emerson St NW
Delafield Pl NW
Decatur St NW
Crittenden St NW
Buchanan St NW
Allison St NW
Webster St NW
Varnum St NW
Upshur St NW
Shepherd St NW
Randolph St NW
Kennedy St NE
Jefferson St NE
Chillum Pl NE
Ingraham St NE
Hamilton St NE
Galloway St NE
Gallatin St NE
Farragut Pl NE
Faraday Pl NE
Emerson St NE
Delafield St NE
Decatur St NE
Crittenden St NE
Buchanan St NE
Allison St NE
Webster St NE
Varnum St NE
Urell Pl NE
Upshur St NE
Taussig Pl NE
Taylor St NE
Sigsbee Pl NE
Shepherd St NE
Randolph St NE
Quincy St NE
Perry Pl NE
Otis St NE
Newton St NE
Monroe St NE
Lawrence St NE
Kearney St NE
Jackson St NE
Irving St NE
Hamlin St NE
Girard St NE
Franklin St NE
Evarts St NE

A
B
C
1
2
21
13
15
11

Essentials

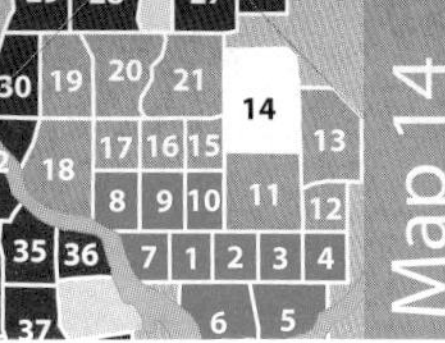

Affectionately called *Little Rome*, Catholic U.'s immediate surroundings (which include more than 60 Catholic institutions) were influenced by 19th century Catholic slaves living on the plantation of Col. Jehiel Brooks (hence the name Brookland). The Basilica of the National Shrine of the Immaculate Conception is the U.S. patronal Catholic church and the largest church in the western hemisphere; convenient for CUA students to take their early morning walks of shame straight into the confessionals.

Banks

- **Chevy Chase** • 210 Michigan Ave NE
- **Chevy Chase (ATM)** • 1150 Varnum St NE
- **Chevy Chase (ATM)** • 3900 Harewood Rd NE
- **Citibank** • 3800 12th St NE
- **PNC** • 3806 12th St NE
- **PNC (ATM)** • 125 Michigan Ave NE
- **Wachovia** • 5005 New Hampshire Ave NW

Car Rental

- **Enterprise** • 3700 10th St NE • 202-635-1104

Car Washes

- **McDonald Custom Car Care** • 3221 12th St NE

Community Gardens

Gas Stations

- **Amoco** • 3701 12th St NE
- **Amoco** • 4925 S Dakota Ave NE
- **Exxon** • 1020 Michigan Ave NE
- **Exxon** • 5501 S Dakota Ave NE

Hospitals

- **Children's National Medical** • 111 Michigan Ave NW
- **Providence** • 1150 Varnum St NE
- **Washington Hospital Center** • 110 Irving St NW

Landmarks

- **Brooks Mansion** • 901 Newton St NE
- **Grief in Rock Creek Cemetery** • Rock Creek Church Rd NW & Webster St NW
- **Pope John Paul II Cultural Center** • 3900 Harewood Rd NE
- **Shrine of the Immaculate Conception** • 400 Michigan Ave NE

Libraries

- **Lamond-Riggs Library** • 5401 S Dakota Ave NE

Parking

Pharmacies

- **CVS** • 128 Kennedy St NW
- **CVS** • 3601 12th St NE
- **Ensign** • 106 Irving St NW
- **New Hampshire CARE Pharmacy** • 5001 New Hampshire Ave NW
- **Washington Hospital Center - Pharmacy** • 20 Irving St NW
- **Wellington Pharmacy** • 1160 Varnum St NE

Post Offices

- **Brookland Station** • 3401 12th St NE
- **Catholic University Cardinal Station** • 620 Michigan Ave NE

Schools

- **Archbishop Carroll** • 4300 Harewood Rd NE
- **Backus Middle** • 5171 S Dakota Ave NE
- **Brookland Elementary** • 1150 Michigan Ave NE
- **Catholic University of America** • 620 Michigan Ave NE
- **JOS-ARZ Academy** • 220 Taylor St NE
- **Maime Lee Elementary** • 100 Gallatin St NE
- **Metropolitan Day** • 1240 Randolph St NE
- **Roots Public Charter** • 15 Kennedy St NW
- **Rudolph Elementary** • 5200 2nd St NW
- **St Anthony** • 12th St NE & Lawrence St NE
- **Trinity University** • 125 Michigan Ave NE
- **Universal Ballet Academy** • 4301 Harewood Rd NE
- **Washington Jesuit Academy** • 900 Varnum St NE

Supermarkets

- **M&S Market** • 213 Upshur St NW

Map 14 • Catholic U

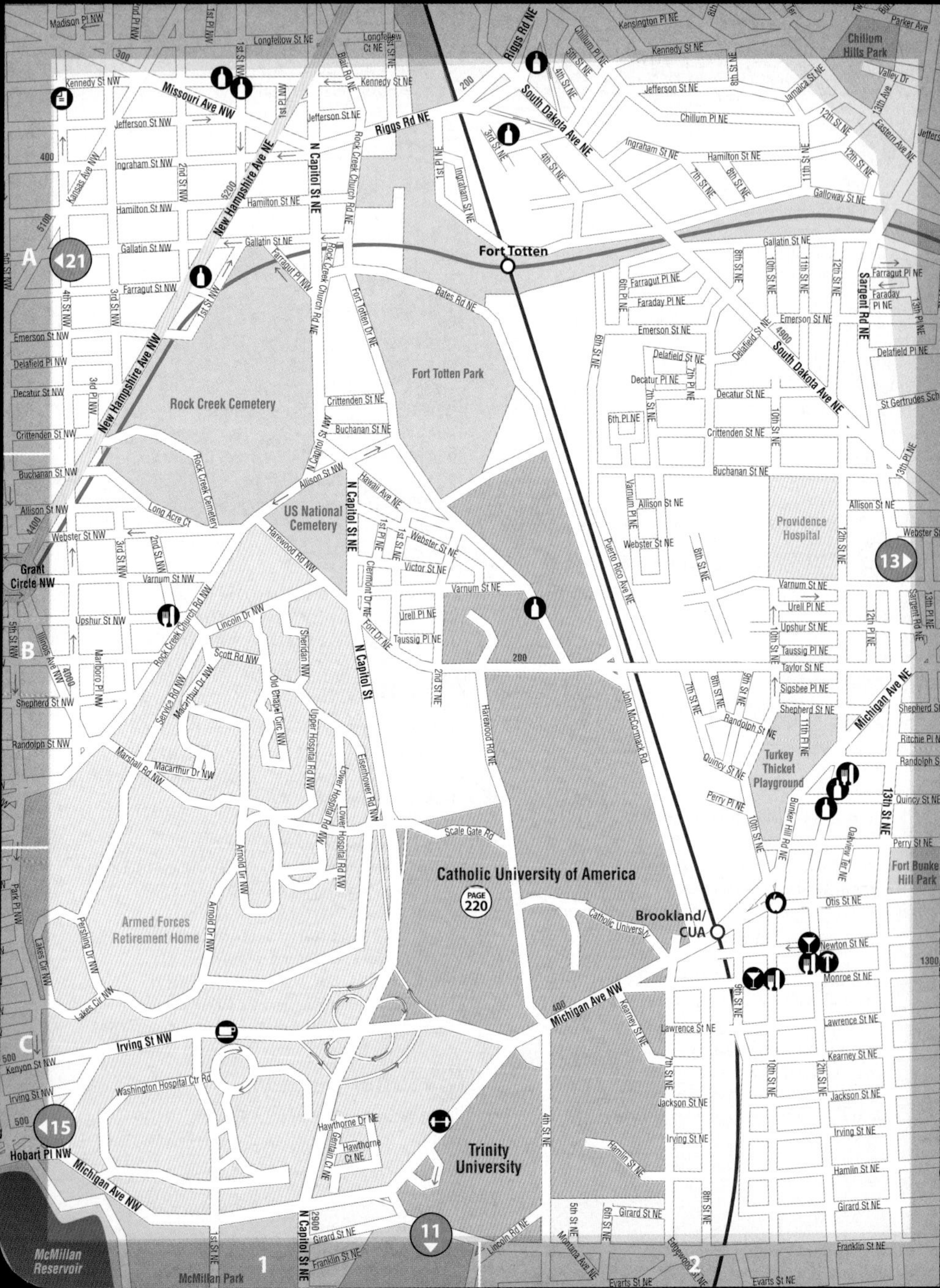

Madison Pl NW
1st Pl NW
2nd Pl NW
Longfellow St NE
Longfellow Ct NE
Riggs Rd NE
Kensington Pl NE
Chillum Pl NE
Kennedy St NE
Parker Ave
Chillum Hills Park
Valley Dr
300
Kennedy St NW
1st St NW
Missouri Ave NW
1st Pl NW
Blair Rd NE
Kennedy St NE
200
5th St NE
4th St NE
South Dakota Ave NE
Jefferson St NE
8th St NE
Jamaica St NE
13th Ave
Jefferson St NW
Jefferson St NE
Riggs Rd NE
3rd St NE
Chillum Pl NE
12th St NE
Eastern Ave NE
Jeffers
400
Kansas Ave NW
Ingraham St NW
2nd St NW
New Hampshire Ave NE
N Capitol St NE
Rock Creek Church Rd NE
1st Pl NE
Ingraham St NE
Ingraham St NE
4th St NE
Hamilton St NE
11th St NE
12th St NE
7th St NE
8th St NE
5200
Galloway St NE
5100
Hamilton St NW
Hamilton St NE
New Hampshire Ave NE
Gallatin St NW
Gallatin St NE
Rock Creek Church Rd NE
Fort Totten
Gallatin St NE
A
21
5th St NW
Farragut Pl NW
8th St NE
10th St NE
11th St NE
12th St NE
Sargent Rd NE
Farragut Pl NE
Farragut Pl NE
Farraday Pl NE
4th St NW
3rd St NW
Farragut St NW
1st St NW
Fort Totten Dr NE
Bates Rd NE
6th Pl NE
Faraday Pl NE
13th Pl NE
Emerson St NW
Emerson St NE
Emerson St NE
4900
Delafield St NE
South Dakota Ave NE
Delafield Pl NW
6th St NE
Delafield St NE
Delafield Pl NE
New Hampshire Ave NW
Fort Totten Park
Decatur St NW
3rd Pl NW
Rock Creek Cemetery
Decatur Pl NE
7th Pl NE
Decatur St NE
Crittenden St NE
7th St NE
St Gertrudes Sch
Crittenden St NW
4th St NE
Buchanan St NE
6th Pl NE
10th St NE
Crittenden St NE
Buchanan St NW
Rock Creek Cemetery
N Capitol St
Allison St NW
Buchanan St NE
13th St NE
Allison St NW
Long Acre Ct
Hawaii Ave NE
Varnum Pl NE
Allison St NE
Allison St NE
4400
US National Cemetery
N Capitol St NE
Providence Hospital
Webster St NW
3rd St NW
2nd St NW
Harewood Rd NW
1st Pl NE
1st St NE
Webster St NE
Puerto Rico Ave NE
Webster St NE
8th St NE
12th St NE
Webster St
13
Grant Circle NW
Victor St NE
Varnum St NW
Clermont Dr NE
Varnum St NE
Varnum St NE
Sargent Rd NE
Urell Pl NE
13th Pl NE
5th St NW
Upshur St NW
Rock Creek Church Rd NW
Lincoln Dr NW
Sheridan NW
Fort Dr NE
Urell Pl NE
Upshur St NE
12th Pl NE
B
Illinois Ave NW
4000
Marlboro Pl NW
Scott Rd NW
Taussig Pl NE
200
Taussig Pl NE
10th St NE
Taylor St NE
Service Rd NW
Macarthur Dr NW
Old Chapel Circ NW
N Capitol St
2nd St NE
Harewood Rd NE
John McCormack Rd
7th St NE
8th St NE
9th St NE
Sigsbee Pl NE
Michigan Ave NE
Shepherd St NW
Shepherd St NE
Shepherd St
Upper Hospital Rd NW
Randolph St NE
11th Pl NE
Ritchie Pl N
Randolph St NW
Eisenhower Rd NW
Lower Hospital Rd NW
Quincy St NE
Turkey Thicket Playground
Randolph S
Marshall Rd NW
Macarthur Dr NW
Perry Pl NE
10th St NE
Bunker Hill Rd NE
13th St NE
Quincy St NE
Scale Gate Rd
Arnold Dr NW
Lower Hospital Rd NW
Oakview Ter NE
Perry St NE
Catholic University of America
PAGE 220
Fort Bunker Hill Park
Park Pl NW
Arnold Dr NW
Otis St NE
Armed Forces Retirement Home
Pershing Dr NW
Catholic University
Brookland/CUA
Newton St NE
Lakes Cir NW
1300
Monroe St NE
9th St NE
Lakes Cir NW
400
Michigan Ave NW
Kearney St NE
Lawrence St NE
Lawrence St NE
C
500
Kenyon St NW
Irving St NW
Kearney St NE
10th St NE
12th St NE
7th St NE
Washington Hospital Ctr Rd
Irving St NW
Jackson St NE
Jackson St NE
500
15
Hawthorne Dr NE
Gentain Ct NE
Hawthorne Ct NE
Irving St NE
Irving St NE
Trinity University
Hobart Pl NW
4th St NE
Hamlin St NE
Hamlin St NE
Michigan Ave NW
8th St NE
Girard St NE
Girard St NE
5th St NE
6th St NE
2900
11
N Capitol St NE
Girard St NE
Lincoln Rd NE
McMillan Reservoir
1st St NE
Franklin St NE
Montana Ave NE
Edgewood St NE
Franklin St NE
1
2
McMillan Park
Evarts St NE
Evarts St NE

Sundries / Entertainment

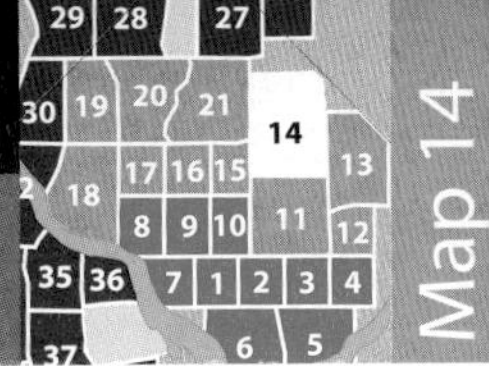

The Catholic theme is so ingrained here, it permeates area bars. At Kelly's Ellis Island you'll encounter a mix of students, priests and racially diverse locals sipping Guinness amidst saintly statues and pictures of the pope. Popular neighborhood tavern Colonel Brooks has a solid draft beer special every day and serves a delightfully tasty burger. There's no profuse reason to travel far for these two bars, but if you do, you'll definitely feel welcomed.

Coffee

- **The Buzz and Authentic Seattle Espresso Bar** • 50 Irving St NW

Copy Shops

- **Quality Printers (10am-6pm)** • 301 Kennedy St NW

Farmer's Markets

- **Historic Brookland Farmer's Market** • 10th St NE & Otis St NE

Gyms

- **Curves** • 212 Michigan Ave NE

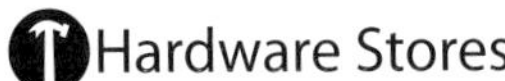

Hardware Stores

- **Brookland True Value** • 3501 12th St NE

Liquor Stores

- **Dakota Liquors** • 5510 3rd St NE
- **Fair Liquors** • 5008 1st St NW
- **Kennedy Liquors** • 5501 1st St NW
- **Michigan Liquor Store Receiver** • 3934 12th St NE
- **Northwest Liquors** • 300 Kennedy St NW
- **Riggs Wine & Liquors** • 5581 S Dakota Ave NE
- **University Wine and Spirits** • 333 Hawaii Ave NE
- **Whelan's Liquors** • 3903 12th St NE

Nightlife

- **Colonel Brooks' Tavern** • 901 Monroe St NE
- **Johnny K's** • 3514 12th St NE

Restaurants

- **Colonel Brooks' Tavern** • 901 Monroe St NE
- **The Hitching Post** • 200 Upshur St NW
- **Kelly's Ellis Island** • 3908 12th St NE
- **Murry and Paul's** • 3513 12th St NE

Map 15 • Columbia Heights

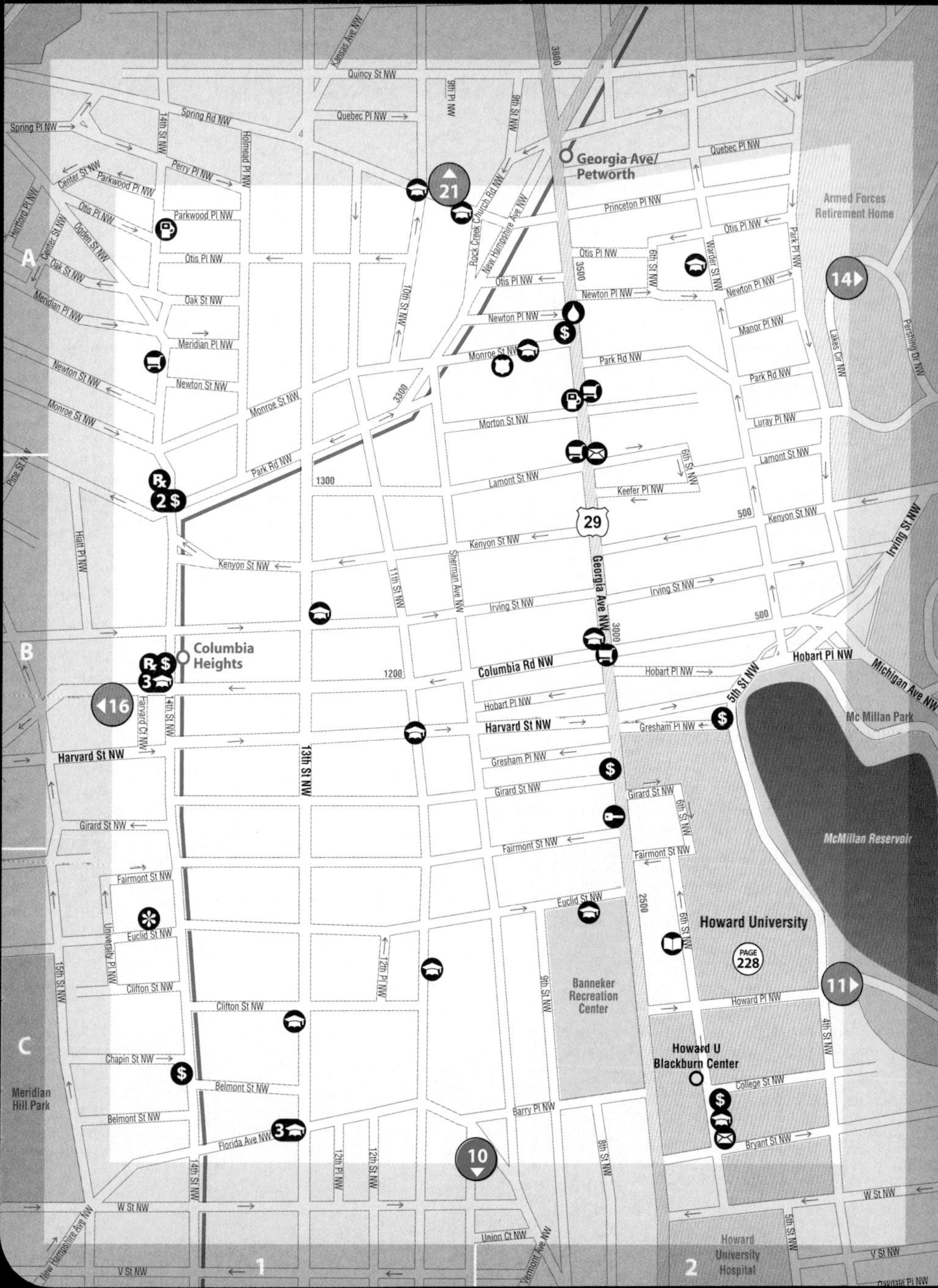

N

Georgia Ave/ Petworth

Columbia Heights

Howard University

PAGE 228

Banneker Recreation Center

Howard U Blackburn Center

Armed Forces Retirement Home

Mc Millan Park

McMillan Reservoir

Meridian Hill Park

Howard University Hospital

21

14

16

11

10

Quincy St NW
Quebec Pl NW
Spring Rd NW
Spring Pl NW
Perry Pl NW
Center St NW
Parkwood Pl NW
Otis Pl NW
Ogden St NW
Oak St NW
Meridian Pl NW
Newton St NW
Monroe St NW
Park Rd NW
Kenyon St NW
Irving St NW
Columbia Rd NW
Hobart Pl NW
Harvard St NW
Gresham Pl NW
Girard St NW
Fairmont St NW
Euclid St NW
Clifton St NW
Chapin St NW
Belmont St NW
Florida Ave NW
Barry Pl NW
W St NW
V St NW
Union Ct NW
Vermont Ave NW
New Hampshire Ave NW
Rock Creek Church Rd NW
Princeton Pl NW
Warder St NW
Newton Pl NW
Manor Pl NW
Luray Pl NW
Lamont St NW
Keefer Pl NW
Morton St NW
Michigan Ave NW
Howard Pl NW
College St NW
Bryant St NW
Lakes Cir NW
Pershing Dr NW
Park Pl NW
Hiatt Pl NW
Harvard Ct NW
University Pl NW
Sherman Ave NW
Georgia Ave NW
Kansas Ave NW
Holmead Pl NW
Hertford Pl NW
Pine St NW
Oakdale Pl NW
14th St NW
15th St NW
13th St NW
12th Pl NW
12th St NW
11th St NW
10th St NW
9th Pl NW
9th St NW
8th St NW
6th St NW
5th St NW
4th St NW

29

3800
3500
3300
3000
2500
1300
1200
500

A
B
C
1
2

Essentials

A new Metro station promised to bring a touch of culture to this long-blighted Latin quarter of town. We haven't seen it yet, but we're not giving up hope. The neighborhood is slowly filling up with non-profit/Peace Corps-type youth, it's very accessible to U Street and Logan Circle, and the construction of long-awaited apartment buildings and an expansive mall is finally nearing completion.

Banks

- **Bank of America** • 2397 6th St NW
- **Bank of America** • 3500 Georgia Ave NW
- **Bank of America** • 511 Gresham Pl NW
- **Bank of America (ATM)** • 2400 14th St
- **Bank of America (ATM)** • 3031 14th St NW
- **PNC** • 3300 14th St NW
- **Wachovia** • 2801 Georgia Ave NW
- **Wachovia** • 3325 14th St NW

Car Rental

- **Enterprise** • 2730 Georgia Ave NW • 202-332-1716

Car Washes

- **Georgia Avenue Car Wash** • 3510 Georgia Ave NW

Community Gardens

Gas Stations

- **Amoco** • 3426 Georgia Ave NW
- **Exxon** • 3540 14th St NW

Landmarks

- **Howard U Blackburn Center** • 2400 6th St NW

Libraries

- **Howard University School of Business Library** • 2600 6th St NW

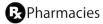

Pharmacies

- **Columbia Heights CARE Pharmacy** • 3316 14th St NW
- **CVS** • 3031 14th St NW

Police

- **MPDC 3rd District Substation** • 750 Park Rd NW

Post Offices

- **Columbia Heights Finance** • 3321 Georgia Ave NW
- **Howard University** • 2400 6th St NW

Schools

- **Banneker High** • 800 Euclid St NW
- **Booker T Washington Public Charter School For Technical** • 1346 Florida Ave NW
- **Bruce-Monroe Elementary** • 3012 Georgia Ave NW
- **Cardozo High** • 1300 Clifton St NW
- **Carlos Rosario High** • 1100 Harvard St NW
- **Cesar Chavez Public Charter School for Public Policy** • 1346 Florida Ave NW
- **DC Bilingual Public Charter** • 1420 Columbia Rd NW
- **EL Haynes Elementary** • 3029 14th St NW
- **Howard University** • 2400 6th St NW
- **Meridian Public Charter** • 1328 Florida Ave NW
- **Meyer Elementary** • 2501 11th St NW
- **Nation House Watoto Shule/Sankofa Fie** • 770 Park Rd NW
- **Next Step/El Proximo Paso** • 1419 Columbia Rd NW
- **Park View Elementary** • 3560 Warder St NW
- **Paul Robeson Center Elementary** • 3700 10th St NW
- **Raymond Elementary** • 915 Spring Rd NW
- **Tubman Elementary** • 3101 13th St NW

Supermarkets

- **Everlasting Life Community Grocery** • 2928 Georgia Ave NW
- **Giant Food** • 3460 14th St NW
- **Murry's Grocery** • 3400 Georgia Ave NW
- **San Cipriano Latin Grocery** • 3304 Georgia Ave NW

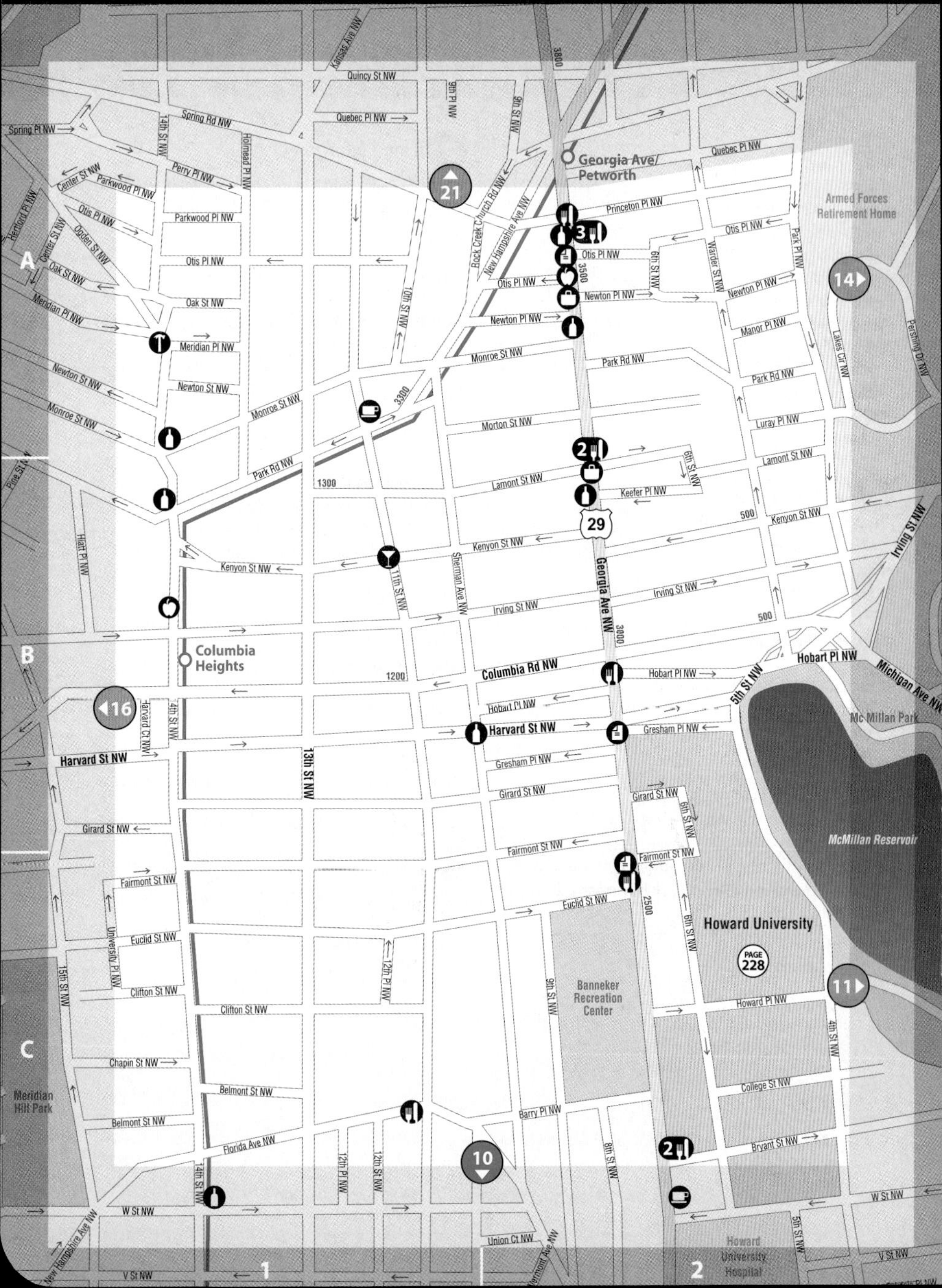

Map 15 • Columbia Heights

N

Georgia Ave/ Petworth

Columbia Heights

Armed Forces Retirement Home

Mc Millan Park

McMillan Reservoir

Howard University

PAGE 228

Banneker Recreation Center

Meridian Hill Park

Howard University Hospital

21

14

16

11

10

29

A

B

C

1

2

Quincy St NW

Quebec Pl NW

Spring Rd NW

Spring Pl NW

Perry Pl NW

Center St NW

Parkwood Pl NW

Hertford Pl NW

Otis Pl NW

Ogden St NW

Oak St NW

Meridian Pl NW

Newton St NW

Monroe St NW

Park Rd NW

Pine St NW

Hiatt Pl NW

Kenyon St NW

Irving St NW

Columbia Rd NW

Harvard St NW

Harvard Ct NW

Girard St NW

Fairmont St NW

Euclid St NW

University Pl NW

Clifton St NW

Chapin St NW

Belmont St NW

Florida Ave NW

W St NW

V St NW

New Hampshire Ave NW

15th St NW

14th St NW

Holmead Pl NW

13th St NW

12th Pl NW

12th St NW

11th St NW

10th St NW

9th Pl NW

9th St NW

8th St NW

Kansas Ave NW

Rock Creek Church Rd NW

Sherman Ave NW

Morton St NW

Lamont St NW

Keefer Pl NW

Hobart Pl NW

Gresham Pl NW

Georgia Ave NW

Princeton Pl NW

Manor Pl NW

Luray Pl NW

Warder St NW

6th St NW

5th St NW

4th St NW

Park Pl NW

Lakes Cir NW

Pershing Dr NW

Michigan Ave NW

Howard Pl NW

College St NW

Barry Pl NW

Bryant St NW

Union Ct NW

Vermont Ave NW

3800

3500

3300

3000

2500

1300

1200

500

Sundries / Entertainment

The pickings are still slim, but a couple of Washington's most secret gems lie within neighborhood lines. Columbia Heights Coffee sits on semi-derelict 11th Street, but serves up the best cup of joe for miles. The unassuming exterior of Wonderland Bar wouldn't have you know it attracts one of the coolest crowds in the city. And the newly resurrected Tivoli Theatre, dedicated exclusively to the Hispanic arts, will be a treasure for years to come.

Coffee

- **Columbia Heights Coffee** • 3416 11th St NW
- **Starbucks** • 2225 Georgia Ave NW

Copy Shops

- **General Services Notary and Copy Services** • 3613 Georgia Ave NW
- **Howard Copy (10am-7pm)** • 2618 Georgia Ave NW
- **Uptown Offices (10am-6pm)** • 2851 Georgia Ave NW

Farmer's Markets

- **Columbia Heights Community Marketplace** • 14th & Irving Sts NW
- **Georgia-Petworth Farmer's Market** • 3600 Georgia Ave NW (corner of New Hampshire Ave)

Hardware Stores

- **Cooper Hardware** • 3459 14th St NW

Liquor Stores

- **CC Liquor** • 3401 14th St NW
- **Florida Liquors** • 2222 14th St NW
- **Giant Liquors** • 3504 Georgia Ave NW
- **Harvard Wine & Liquor Store** • 2901 Sherman Ave NW
- **Lion's Liquor** • 3614 Georgia Ave NW
- **Petworth Liquors** • 3210 Georgia Ave NW
- **Speedy Liquors** • 3328 14th St NW

Nightlife

- **Wonderland Bar and Grill** • 1101 Kenyon St NW

Restaurants

- **Bill's Seafood** • 3601 Georgia Ave NW
- **Brown's Caribbean Bakery** • 3301 Georgia Ave NW
- **Cluck U Chicken** • 2421 Georgia Ave NW
- **Five Guys** • 2301 Georgia Ave NW
- **Florida Ave Grill** • 1100 Florida Ave NW
- **Mario's Pizza** • 3619 Georgia Ave NW
- **Negril** • 2301 Georgia Ave NW
- **Rita's Caribbean Carryout** • 3322 Georgia Ave NW
- **Soul Vegetarian and Exodus Café** • 2606 Georgia Ave NW
- **Temperance** • 3634 Georgia Ave NW

Shopping

- **Mom & Pop's Antiques** • 3534 Georgia Ave NW
- **Planet Chocolate City** • 3225 Georgia Ave NW

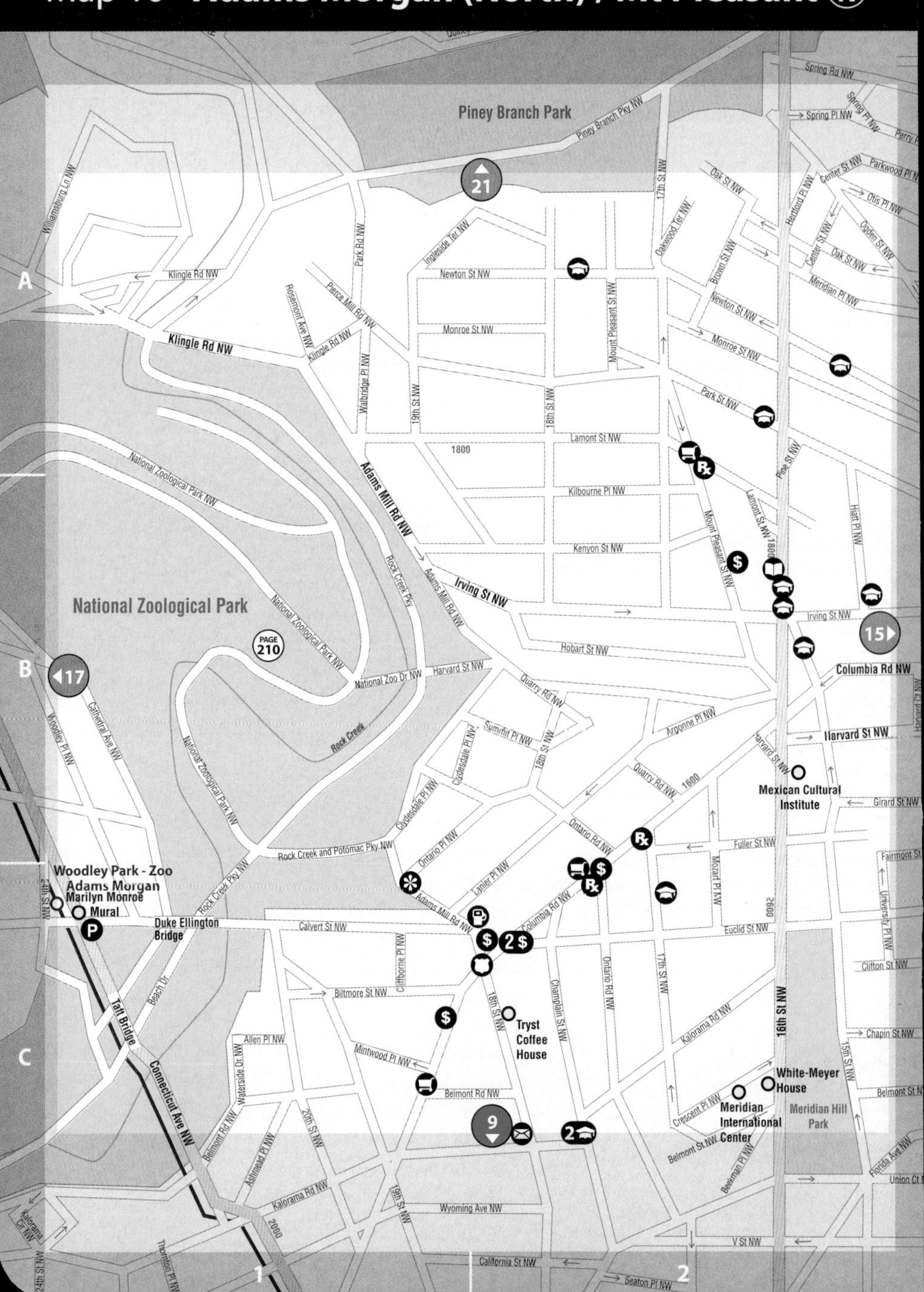
Piney Branch Park
National Zoological Park
PAGE 210
Woodley Park - Zoo
Adams Morgan
Marilyn Monroe Mural
Duke Ellington Bridge
Taft Bridge
Tryst Coffee House
Mexican Cultural Institute
White-Meyer House
Meridian International Center
Meridian Hill Park
Klingle Rd NW
Adams Mill Rd NW
Irving St NW
Columbia Rd NW
Harvard St NW
Connecticut Ave NW
16th St NW
Calvert St NW
Rock Creek and Potomac Pky NW
Rock Creek Pkwy NW
Mount Pleasant St NW
Newton St NW
Monroe St NW
Park St NW
Lamont St NW
Kilbourne Pl NW
Kenyon St NW
Hobart St NW
Euclid St NW
Fuller St NW
Girard St NW
Kalorama Rd NW
Belmont Rd NW
Wyoming Ave NW
California St NW
Florida Ave NW
Piney Branch Pkwy NW
Spring Rd NW
Oak St NW

Essentials

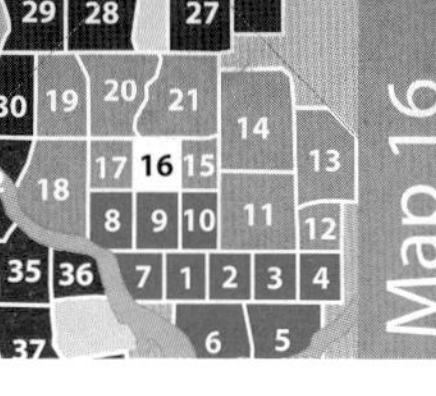

From the Salvadorian community garden to the glut of Ethiopian eats to the frat house scene along 18th street, these two neighborhoods are where different races and ethnicities mix most in DC. Adams Morgan is the nightlife destination, especially for those who may or may not be of drinking age. Mt. Pleasant has fewer offerings, but those that are there are laid-back sanctuaries, set away from the rowdiness to the south.

Banks

- **Bank of America** • 1835 Columbia Rd NW
- **Bank of America** • 3131 Mount Pleasant St NW
- **BB&T** • 1801 Adams Mill Rd NW
- **Citibank** • 1749 1/2 Columbia Rd NW
- **PNC** • 1779 Columbia Rd NW
- **Sun Trust** • 1800 Columbia Rd NW

Community Gardens

Gas Stations

- **Exxon** • 1827 Adams Mill Rd NW

o Landmarks

- **Marilyn Monroe Mural** • Connecticut Ave NW & Calvert St NW
- **Meridian International Center** • 1630 Crescent Pl NW
- **Mexican Cultural Institute** • 2829 16th St NW
- **Tryst Coffee House** • 2459 18th St NW
- **White-Meyer House** • 1624 Crescent Pl NW

Libraries

- **Mt Pleasant Library** • 3160 16th St NW

Parking

Pharmacies

- **CVS** • 1700 Columbia Rd NW
- **Mt Pleasant Care Pharmacy** • 3169 Mount Pleasant St NW
- **Safeway** • 1747 Columbia Rd NW

Police

- **3rd District Latino Liaison Unit** • 1800 Columbia Rd NW

Post Offices

- **Kalorama Station** • 2300 18th St NW

Schools

- **Bancroft Elementary** • 1755 Newton St NW
- **Bell Multicultural High** • 3145 Hiatt Pl NW
- **Capital City Public Charter Elementary** • 3047 15th St NW
- **Cooke Elementary** • 2525 17th St NW
- **DC Alternative Learning Academy** • 3146 16th St NW
- **Elsie Whitlow Stokes Community Freedom** • 1525 Newton St NW
- **Lincoln Middle** • 3101 16th St NW
- **Marie Reed Elementary** • 2200 Champlain St NW
- **Reed Learning Center** • 2200 Champlain St NW
- **Sacred Heart** • 1625 Park Rd NW

Supermarkets

- **Bestway** • 3178 Mt Pleasant St NW
- **Metro IGA** • 1864 Columbia Rd NW
- **Safeway** • 1747 Columbia Rd NW

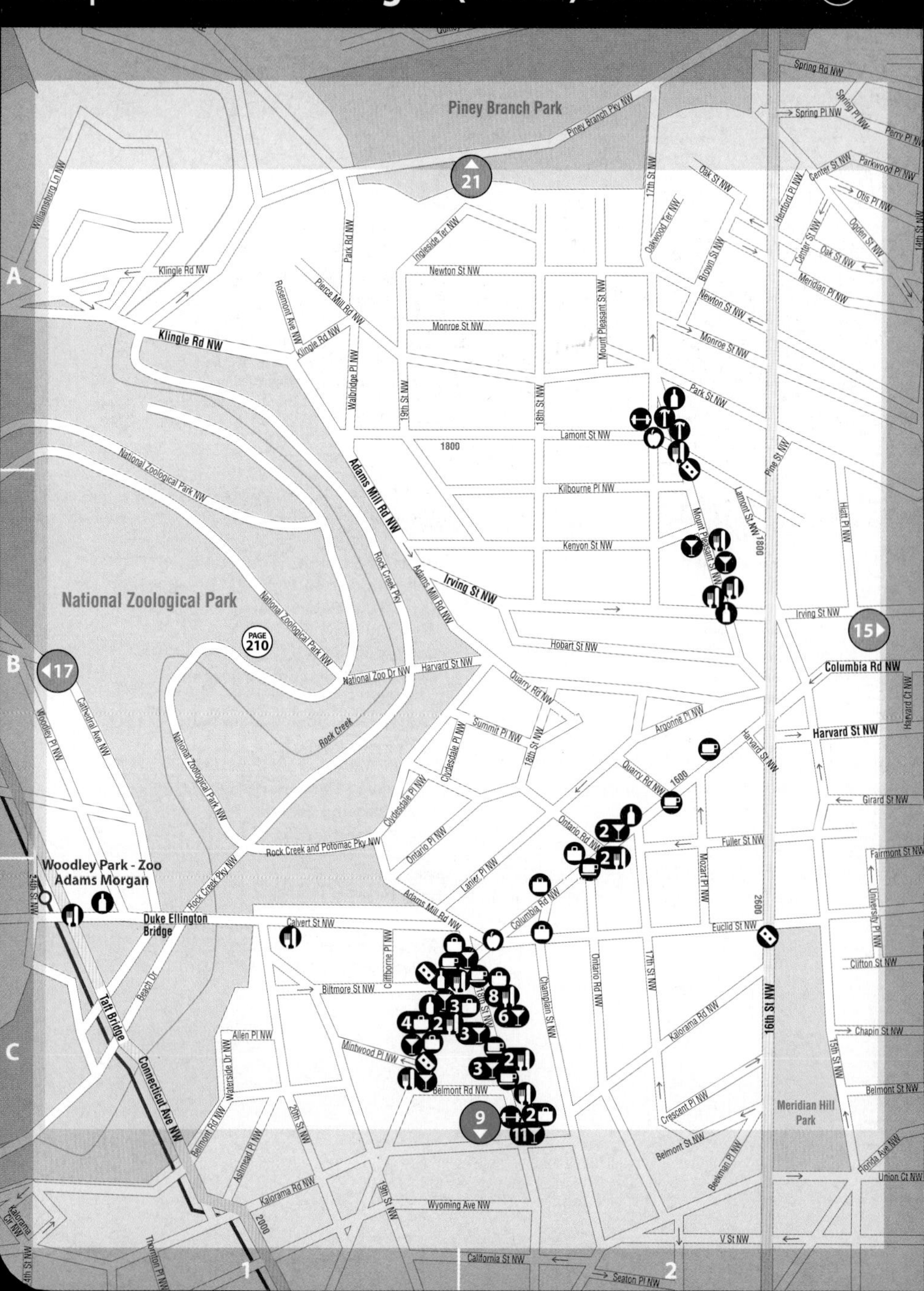
Piney Branch Park
Piney Branch Pkwy NW
21
National Zoological Park
Woodley Park - Zoo
Adams Morgan
Duke Ellington
Bridge
Taft Bridge
Connecticut Ave NW
Klingle Rd NW
Adams Mill Rd NW
Irving St NW
Columbia Rd NW
Harvard St NW
16th St NW
Meridian Hill
Park
Mount Pleasant St NW
Lamont St NW
Kenyon St NW
Kilbourne Pl NW
Park St NW
Newton St NW
Monroe St NW
Hobart St NW
Quarry Rd NW
Calvert St NW
Biltmore St NW
Mintwood Pl NW
Belmont Rd NW
Euclid St NW
Kalorama Rd NW
Wyoming Ave NW
California St NW
Champlain St NW
Ontario Rd NW
17th St NW
18th St NW
19th St NW
Rock Creek
Rock Creek Pkwy NW
Rock Creek and Potomac Pkwy NW
National Zoo Dr NW
PAGE
210
17
15
9
A
B
C
1
2

Sundries / Entertainment

These neighborhoods cater to the drinking crowd. A good day would start with nursing a hangover at the beloved Mt Pleasant institution Dos Gringos. Then, stumble down to wait for a window seat at Tryst, where you can linger over a sandwich. Or save the appetite for a perfectly seasoned steak at Rumba Café. By then you'll be ready for a bar crawl that will, inevitably, end with you shimmying to "Little Red Corvette" at Chief Ike's Mambo Room.

Coffee

- **Café Park Plaza** • 1629 Columbia Rd NW
- **Caribou Coffee** • 2421 18th St NW
- **Crumbs And Coffee** • 1737 Columbia Rd NW
- **Potter's House** • 1658 Columbia Rd NW
- **Queen's Café and Hookah** • 2405 18th St Nw
- **Starbucks** • 1801 Columbia Rd NW
- **Tryst Coffeehouse and Bar** • 2459 18th St NW

Farmer's Markets

- **Adams Morgan** • 18th St & Columbia Rd NW
- **Mt Pleasant Farmers Market** • 17th & Lamont Sts NW

Gyms

- **Curves** • 3220 17th St NW
- **Gold's Gym** • 2318 18th St NW

Hardware Stores

- **Al's Hardware** • 3221 Mt Pleasant St NW
- **Pfeiffer's Hardware** • 3219 Mt Pleasant St NW

Liquor Stores

- **AB Liquor** • 1803 Columbia Rd NW
- **Comet Liquors** • 1815 Columbia Rd NW
- **Lee Irving Liquors** • 3100 Mount Pleasant St NW
- **Metro Liquors** • 1726 Columbia Rd NW
- **Sherry's Wine & Liquor** • 2315 Calvert St NW
- **Sportsman's Wine & Liquors** • 3249 Mount Pleasant St NW

Nightlife

- **Adams Mill Bar and Grill** • 1813 Adams Mill Rd NW
- **Angles Bar & Billiards** • 2339 18th St NW
- **Angry Inch Saloon** • 2450 18th St NW
- **Asylum** • 2471 18th St NW
- **Bedrock Billiards** • 1841 Columbia Rd NW
- **Blue Room Lounge** • 2321 18th St NW
- **Bossa** • 2463 18th St NW
- **Brass Monkey** • 2317 18th St NW
- **Bukom Café** • 2442 18th St NW
- **Café Toulouse** • 2431 18th St NW
- **Chief Ike's Mambo Room** • 1725 Columbia Rd NW
- **Columbia Station** • 2325 18th St NW
- **Cosmo Lounge** • 1725 Columbia Rd NW
- **Crush** • 2323 18th St NW
- **Dan's** • 2315 18th St NW
- **Felix Lounge** • 2406 18th St NW
- **Kokopooli's Pool Hall** • 2305 18th St NW
- **Left Bank** • 2424 18th St NW
- **Madam's Organ** • 2461 18th St NW
- **Pharmacy Bar** • 2337 18th St NW
- **Pharaoh's** • 1817 Columbia Rd NW
- **The Raven** • 3125 Mt Pleasant St NW
- **The Reef** • 2446 18th St NW
- **Rumba Café** • 2443 18th St NW
- **Spy Lounge** • 2406 18th St NW
- **Timehri International** • 2439 18th St NW
- **Toledo Lounge** • 2435 18th St NW
- **Tom Tom** • 2333 18th St
- **Tonic Bar** • 3155 Mt Pleasant St NW
- **Zucchabar** • 1841 Columbia Rd NW

Restaurants

- **Astor Restaurant** • 1829 Columbia Rd NW
- **Bardia's New Orleans Café** • 2412 18th St NW
- **Bukom Café** • 2442 18th St NW
- **Cashion's Eat Place** • 1819 Columbia Rd NW
- **The Diner** • 2438 18th St NW
- **Dos Gringos** • 3116 Mt Pleasant St NW
- **Felix Restaurant & Lounge** • 2406 18th St NW
- **Grill From Ipanema** • 1858 Columbia Rd NW
- **Haydee's** • 3102 Mt Pleasant St NW
- **La Fourchette** • 2429 18th St NW
- **Leftbank** • 2424 18th St NW
- **The Little Fountain Café** • 2339 18th St NW
- **Mama Ayesha's** • 1967 Calvert St NW
- **Marx Café** • 3203 Mt Pleasant St NW
- **Meskerem Ethiopian Restaurant** • 2434 18th St NW
- **Millie & Al's** • 2440 18th St NW
- **Mixtec** • 1729 Columbia Rd NW
- **Pasta Mia** • 1790 Columbia Rd NW
- **Perry's** • 1811 Columbia Rd NW
- **Rumba Café** • 2443 18th St NW
- **Tonic** • 3155 Mt Pleasant St NW
- **Tono Sushi** • 2605 Connecticut Ave NW
- **Tryst** • 2459 18th St NW

Shopping

- **All About Jane** • 2438 1/2 18th St NW
- **Brass Knob** • 2311 18th St NW
- **CD Game Exchange** • 2475 18th St NW
- **City Bikes** • 2501 Champlain St NW
- **Crooked Beat Records** • 2318 18th St NW
- **Design Within Reach** • 1838 Columbia Rd NW
- **Fleet Feet** • 1841 Columbia Rd NW
- **Idle Times Books** • 2467 18th St NW
- **Little Shop of Flowers** • 1812 Adams Mill Rd NW
- **Miss Pixie's Furnishing and What-Not** • 1810 Adams Mill Rd NW
- **Radio Shack** • 1767 Columbia Rd NW
- **Shake Your Booty** • 2439 18th St NW
- **So's Your Mom** • 1831 Columbia Rd NW
- **Trim** • 2700 Ontario Rd NW
- **Yes! Natural Gourmet** • 1825 Columbia Rd NW

Video Rental

- **Blockbuster Video** • 1805 Columbia Rd NW
- **Dorchester Video** • 2480 16th St Nw
- **Lamont Video** • 3171 Mt Pleasant St NW
- **Video King** • 1845 Columbia Rd NW
- **Video Vault** • 113 S Columbus St

Map 17 • Woodley Park / Cleveland Park

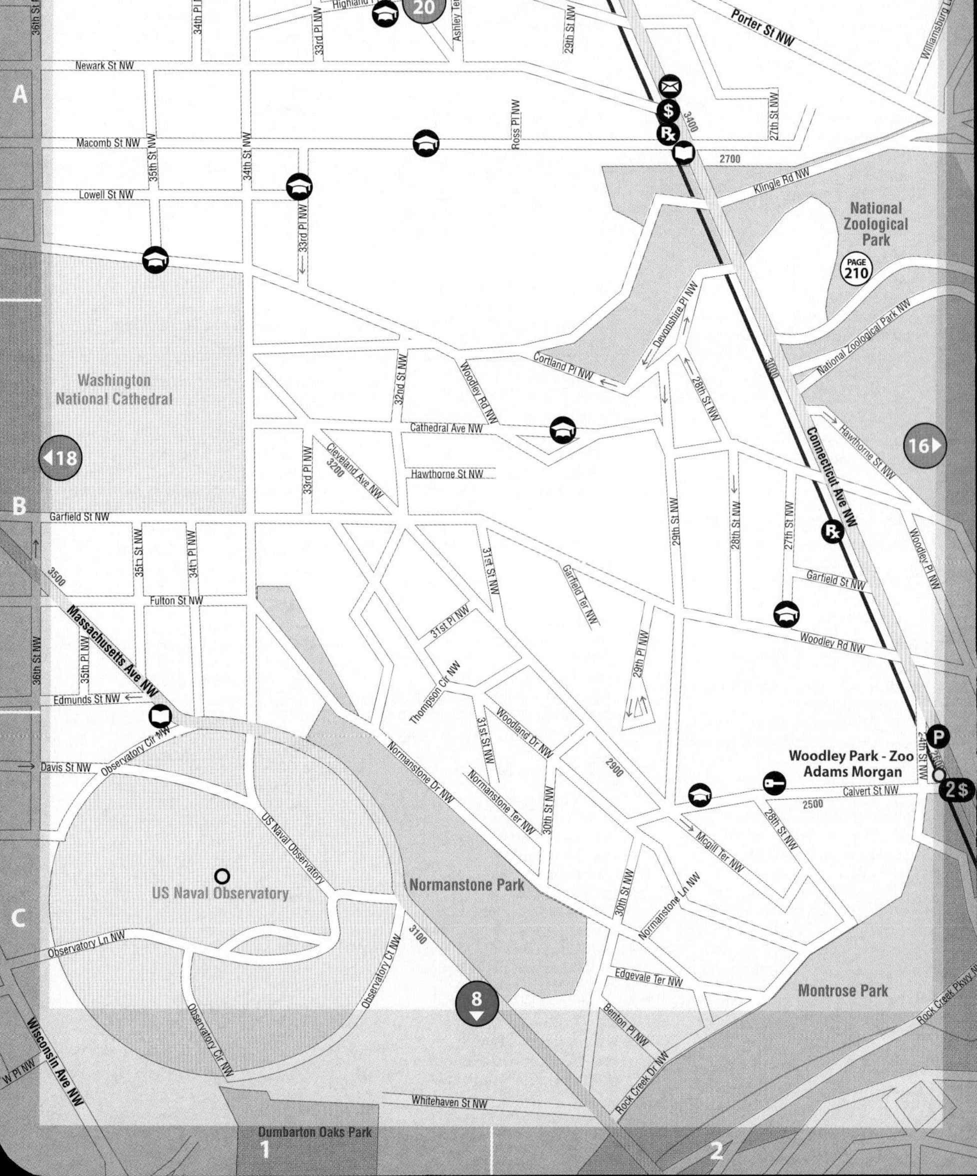

Essentials

Although it sits in the middle of the red line, the Cleveland Park Metro station is the final stop for the cosmopolitan crowd. It's true that area residents more often find themselves traversing the streets of Dupont and Adams Morgan, but this section of town ain't too shabby if you fancy parks, zoos and some distance from all the politicos.

Banks

- **Bank of America** • 2631 Connecticut Ave NW
- **Bank of America** • 3401 Connecticut Ave NW
- **M&T Bank** • 2620 Connecticut Ave NW

Car Rental

- **Enterprise** • 2601 Calvert St NW • 202-232-4443

Landmarks

- **US Naval Observatory** • Massachusetts Ave NW

Libraries

- **Cleveland Park Library** • 3310 Connecticut Ave NW
- **James Melville Gilliss Library** • 3450 Massachusetts Ave NW

Parking

Pharmacies

- **Cathedral CARE Pharmacy** • 3000 Connecticut Ave NW
- **CVS** • 3327 Connecticut Ave NW

Post Offices

- **Cleveland Park Station** • 3430 Connecticut Ave NW

Schools

- **Aidan Montessori** • 2700 27th St NW
- **Beauvoir-The National Cathedral Elementary** • 3500 Woodley Rd NW
- **Eaton Elementary** • 3301 Lowell St NW
- **Maret** • 3000 Cathedral Ave NW
- **National Child Research Center** • 3209 Highland Pl NW
- **Oyster Elementary** • 2801 Calvert St NW
- **Washington International Upper** • 3100 Macomb St NW

Map 17 • Woodley Park / Cleveland Park

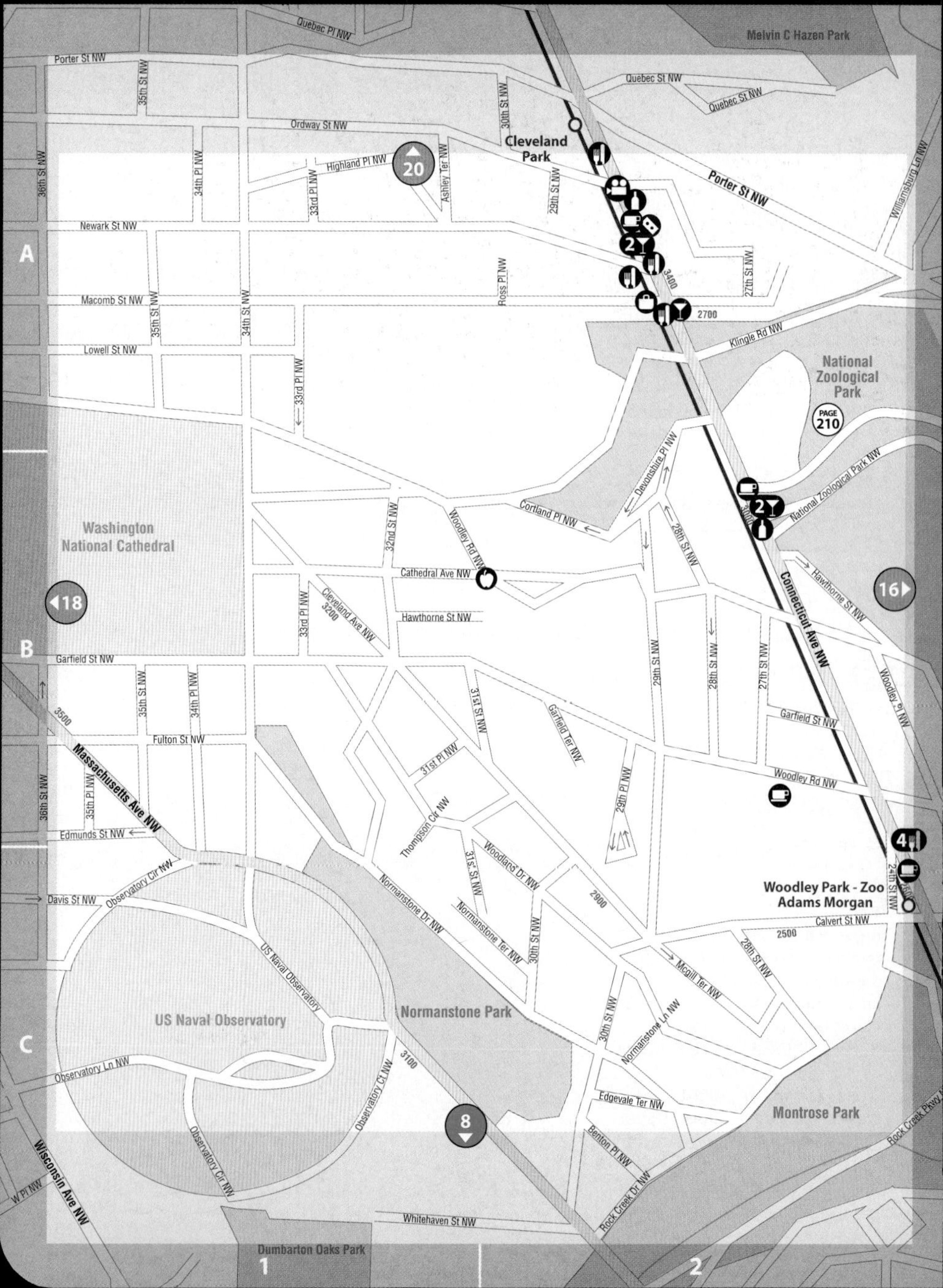

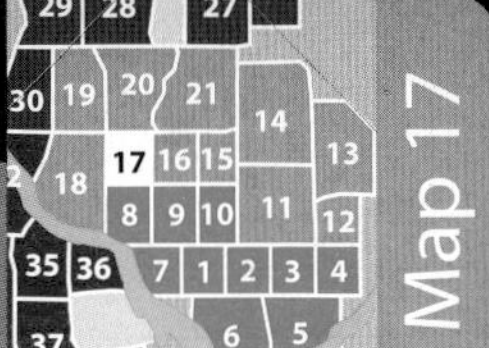

We wouldn't recommend camping out for a week on Connecticut Avenue, but spending a few nights a month here is certainly worth it. The strip's eclectic restaurant offerings cater to a variety of palates, and the dizzying Uptown Theater (featuring only one film a night) is a DC institution. For a true Irish experience, skip party bar 4 Ps and duck into Nanny O'Brien's. The no-frills hole-in-the-wall houses Irish jam sessions every Monday night.

Coffee

- **Café International** • 2633 Connecticut Ave NW
- **Starbucks** • 2660 Woodley Rd NW
- **Starbucks** • 3000 Connecticut Ave NW
- **Starbucks** • 3420 Connecticut Ave NW

Farmer's Markets

- **All Souls Episcopal Church Farmers Market** • Woodley Rd NW & Cathedral Ave NW

Liquor Stores

- **Cathedral Liquors** • 3000 Connecticut Ave NW
- **Cleveland Park Liquor & Wines** • 3423 Connecticut Ave NW

Movie Theaters

- **Cineplex Odeon Uptown** • 3426 Connecticut Ave NW

Nightlife

- **Aroma** • 3417 Connecticut Ave NW
- **Ireland's Four Provinces (4Ps)** • 3412 Connecticut Ave NW
- **Nanny O'Brien's** • 3319 Connecticut Ave NW
- **Oxford Tavern Zoo Bar** • 3000 Connecticut Ave NW

Restaurants

- **Café Paradiso** • 2649 Connecticut Ave NW
- **Ireland's Four Provinces** • 3412 Connecticut Ave NW
- **Lavandou** • 3321 Connecticut Ave NW
- **Lebanese Taverna** • 2641 Connecticut Ave NW
- **Petits Plats** • 2653 Connecticut Ave NW
- **Sake Club** • 2635 Connecticut Ave NW
- **Sorriso** • 3518 Connecticut Ave NW
- **Spices** • 3333A Connecticut Ave NW

Shopping

- **Vace** • 3315 Connecticut Ave NW

Video Rental

- **Potomac Video** • 3418 Connecticut Ave NW

Map 18 • Glover Park / Foxhall

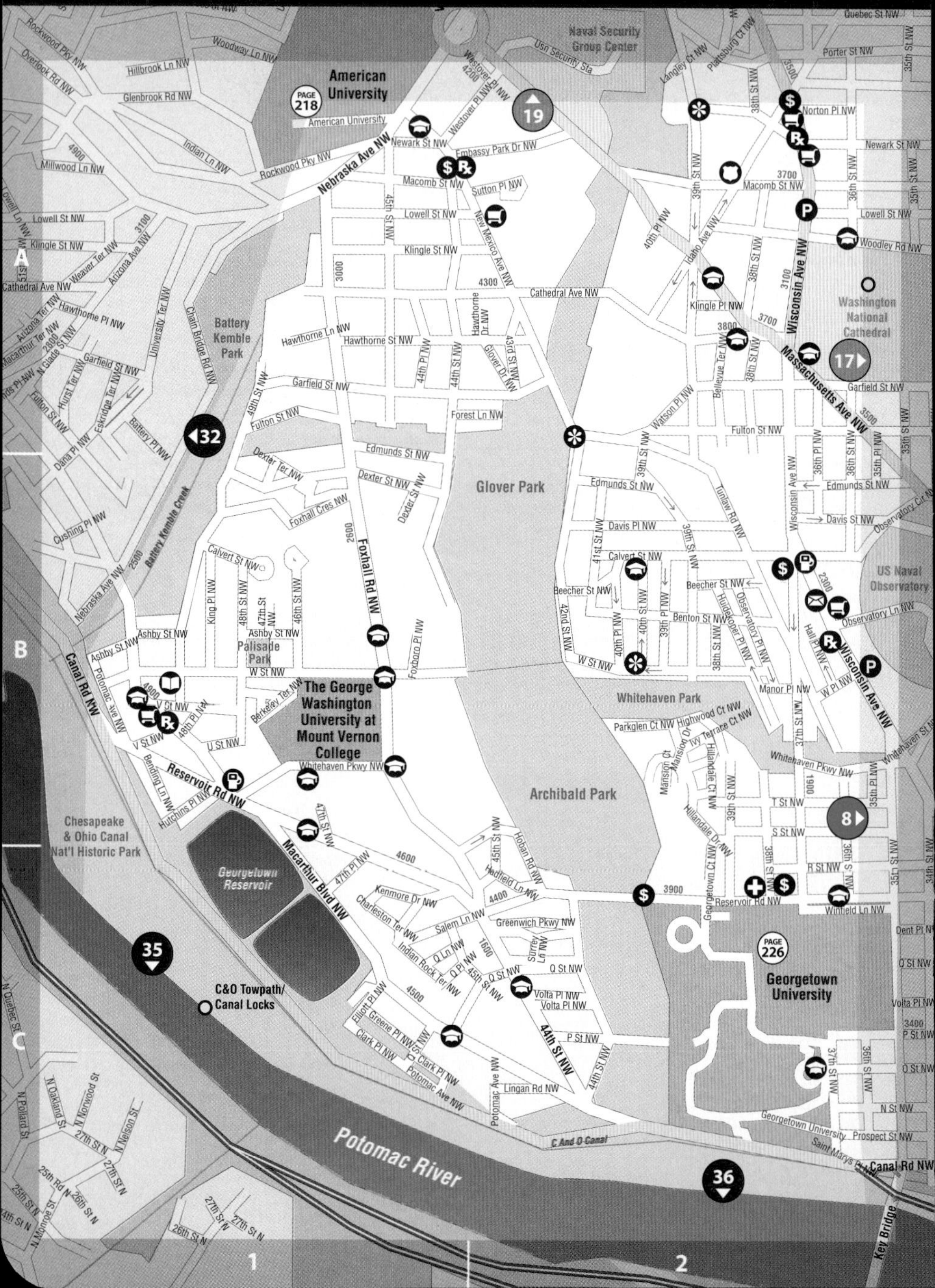

American University
PAGE 218
Naval Security Group Center
Usn Security Sta
19
17
8
32
35
36
Washington National Cathedral
US Naval Observatory
Battery Kemble Park
Glover Park
Palisade Park
The George Washington University at Mount Vernon College
Whitehaven Park
Archibald Park
Chesapeake & Ohio Canal Nat'l Historic Park
Georgetown Reservoir
C&O Towpath/ Canal Locks
Georgetown University
PAGE 226
Potomac River
Key Bridge
Rockwood Pky NW
Overlook Rd NW
Woodway Ln NW
Hillbrook Ln NW
Glenbrook Rd NW
Indian Ln NW
Millwood Ln NW
Lowell Ln NW
Lowell St NW
Klingle St NW
Weaver Ter NW
Arizona Ave NW
Cathedral Ave NW
Arizona Ter NW
Hawthorne Pl NW
Macarthur Ter NW
University Ter NW
Chain Bridge Rd NW
Garfield St NW
N Glade St NW
Hurst Ter NW
Eskridge Ter NW
Battery Pl NW
Fulton St NW
Dana Pl NW
Cushing Pl NW
Battery Kemble Creek
Nebraska Ave NW
Canal Rd NW
Nebraska Ave NW
Newark St NW
Embassy Park Dr NW
Westover Pl NW
Macomb St NW
Sutton Pl NW
New Mexico Ave NW
45th St NW
Klingle St NW
Hawthorne Ln NW
Hawthorne St NW
Hawthorne Dr NW
44th Pl NW
44th St NW
Glover Dr NW
43rd St NW
49th St NW
Forest Ln NW
Edmunds St NW
Dexter Ter NW
Dexter St NW
Foxhall Cres NW
Foxhall Rd NW
Calvert St NW
King Pl NW
48th St NW
47th St NW
46th St NW
Foxboro Pl NW
Ashby St NW
W St NW
V St NW
48th Pl NW
U St NW
Potomac Ave NW
Berkeley Ter NW
Bending Ln NW
Hutchins Pl NW
Reservoir Rd NW
Whitehaven Pkwy NW
47th St NW
Macarthur Blvd NW
47th Pl NW
Kenmore Dr NW
Charleston Ter NW
Hadfield Ln NW
Hoban Rd NW
45th St NW
Salem Ln NW
Greenwich Pkwy NW
Q Ln NW
Q Pl NW
Indian Rock Ter NW
Surrey Ln NW
Q St NW
Volta Pl NW
Elliott Pl NW
Greene Pl NW
Clark Pl NW
P St NW
44th St NW
Potomac Ave NW
Lingan Rd NW
C And O Canal
N Quebec St
N Oakland St
N Norwood St
N Nelson St
N Pollard St
27th St N
25th Rd N
26th St N
25th St N
24th St N
N Monroe St
27th St N
26th St N
Quebec St NW
Porter St NW
Langley Ct NW
Plattsburg Ct NW
38th St NW
Norton Pl NW
Newark St NW
39th St NW
Macomb St NW
Lowell St NW
40th Pl NW
Idaho Ave NW
Woodley Rd NW
Wisconsin Ave NW
Klingle Pl NW
Bellevue Ter NW
38th St NW
Massachusetts Ave NW
Garfield St NW
Watson Pl NW
Fulton St NW
39th St NW
36th Pl NW
36th St NW
35th Pl NW
Edmunds St NW
Tunlaw Rd NW
Davis Pl NW
Davis St NW
Observatory Cir NW
41st St NW
Calvert St NW
Beecher St NW
Huidekoper Pl NW
Observatory Pl NW
Benton St NW
42nd St NW
40th St NW
39th Pl NW
38th St NW
Observatory Ln NW
Hall Pl NW
W Pl NW
Manor Pl NW
37th St NW
Parkglen Ct NW
Highwood Ct NW
Ivy Terrace Ct NW
Mansion Ct
Mansion Dr
Hillandale Ct NW
Hillandale Dr NW
Whitehaven Pkwy NW
Whitehaven St NW
T St NW
S St NW
R St NW
Georgetown Ct NW
Reservoir Rd NW
Winfield Ln NW
Dent Pl NW
O St NW
Volta Pl NW
P St NW
N St NW
Georgetown University
Prospect St NW
Saint Marys Pl NW
Canal Rd NW
35th St NW
34th St NW
A
B
C
1
2

Essentials

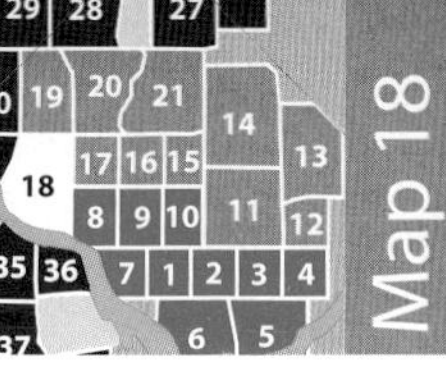

One of the most architecturally diverse areas of the city, this residential stretch is populated largely by Georgetown grad students and gainfully employed 20-somethings who've grown tired of the bar scene but aren't quite ready for Falls Church.

Banks

- **PNC (ATM)** • 3800 Reservoir Rd NW
- **PNC (ATM)** • 4100 Reservoir Rd NW
- **Sun Trust** • 3301 New Mexico Ave NW
- **Sun Trust** • 3440 Wisconsin Ave NW
- **Wachovia** • 3700 Calvert St NW

Community Gardens

Gas Stations

- **Chevron** • 2450 Wisconsin Ave NW
- **Exxon** • 4812 MacArthur Blvd NW

Hospitals

- **Georgetown University** • 3800 Reservoir Rd NW

Landmarks

- **C&O Towpath/Canal Locks** • Along the Potomac River
- **National Cathedral** • Massachusetts Ave NW & Wisconsin Ave NW

Libraries

- **Palisades Library** • 4901 V St NW

Parking

Pharmacies

- **CVS** • 2226 Wisconsin Ave NW
- **CVS** • 4859 MacArthur Blvd
- **Giant Food Pharmacy** • 3406 Wisconsin Ave NW
- **Rite Aid** • 3301 New Mexico Ave NW

Police

- **MPDC 2nd District Station** • 3320 Idaho Ave NW

Post Offices

- **Calvert Station** • 2336 Wisconsin Ave NW

Schools

- **Annunciation** • 3825 Klingle Pl NW
- **Cesar Chavez Public Charter School for Public Policy** • 3855 Massachusetts Ave NW
- **The Field** • 2301 Foxhall Rd NW
- **The George Washington University at Mount Vernon College** • Foxhill Rd NW & W St NW
- **Georgetown Day Lower** • 4530 MacArthur Blvd NW
- **Georgetown University** • 37th St NW & O St NW
- **Lab School of Washington** • 4759 Reservoir Rd NW
- **Mann Elementary** • 4430 Newark St NW
- **National Cathedral** • 3612 Woodley Rd NW
- **Our Lady of Victory** • 4755 Whitehaven Pkwy NW
- **River** • 4880 MacArthur Blvd NW
- **Rock Creek International Lower** • 1550 Foxhall Rd NW
- **St Albans** • 3665 Massachusetts Ave NW
- **St Patrick's Episcopal Day** • 4700 Whitehaven Pkwy NW
- **Stoddert Elementary** • 4001 Calvert St NW
- **Washington International Lower** • 1690 36th St NW

Supermarkets

- **Balducci's** • 3201 New Mexico Ave NW
- **Giant Food** • 3336 Wisconsin Ave NW
- **Safeway** • 4865 MacArthur Blvd NW
- **Whole Foods** • 2323 Wisconsin Ave NW

N

American University
PAGE 218
Naval Security Group Center
Glover Park
Battery Kemble Park
Palisade Park
The George Washington University at Mount Vernon College
Whitehaven Park
Archibald Park
Washington National Cathedral
US Naval Observatory
Chesapeake & Ohio Canal Nat'l Historic Park
Georgetown Reservoir
Georgetown University
PAGE 226
Potomac River
Key Bridge
Nebraska Ave NW
Foxhall Rd NW
Wisconsin Ave NW
Massachusetts Ave NW
Reservoir Rd NW
Macarthur Blvd NW
Canal Rd NW
Cathedral Ave NW
New Mexico Ave NW
44th St NW
Tunlaw Rd NW
Garfield St NW
Fulton St NW
Edmunds St NW
Calvert St NW
W St NW
V St NW
U St NW
Whitehaven Pkwy NW
Prospect St NW
N St NW
C And O Canal
19
17
32
8
35
36
A
B
C
1
2

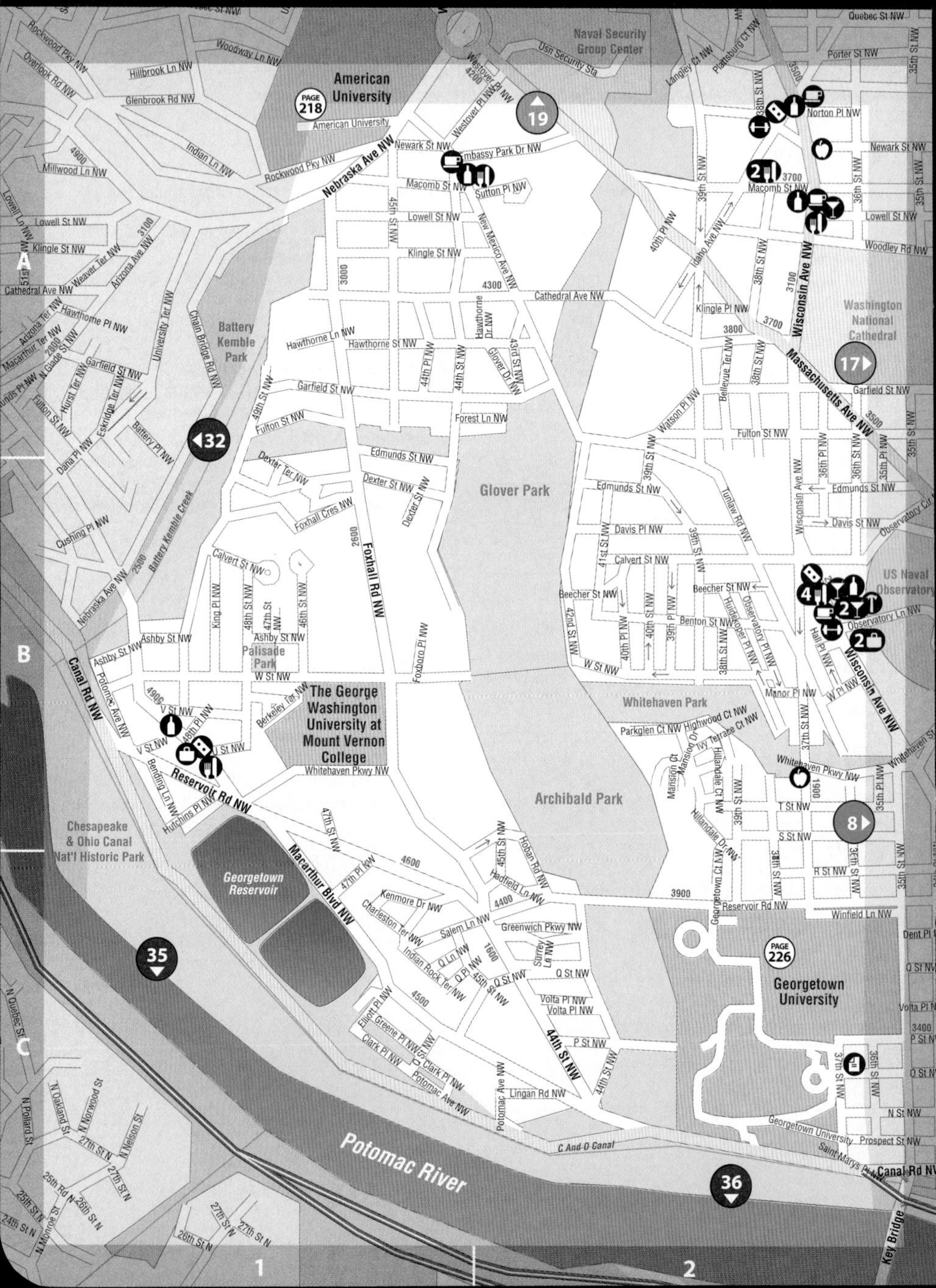

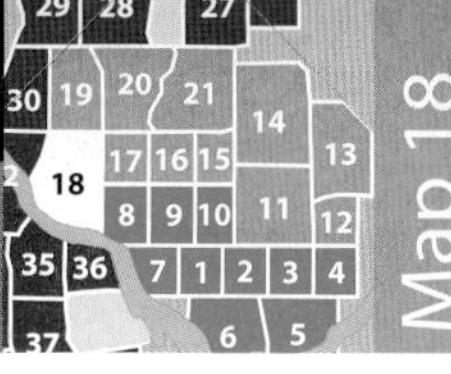

With old neighborhood favorites like the Grog and Tankard and hip newcomers like Bourbon, the stretch of Wisconsin Avenue that runs through this northwest section provides the most vibrancy here. You could be happy eating only 2 Amys' pizza for all eternity. But if your friends insist on some variety, the best sushi place in town, Sushi-Ko, is down the block.

Coffee

- **Foster Brothers Coffee** • 3238 Wisconsin Ave NW
- **Starbucks** • 2302 Wisconsin Ave NW
- **Starbucks** • 3301 New Mexico Ave NW
- **Starbucks** • 3430 Wisconsin Ave NW

Copy Shops

- **UPS Store (8am-7pm)** • 1419 37th St NW

Farmer's Markets

- **New Morning Farm Market** • 37th St NW & Newark St NW
- **New Morning Farm Market** • 37th St & Whitehaven Pwy NW

Gyms

- **Curves** • 3414 Idaho Ave NW
- **Washington Sports Clubs** • 2251 Wisconsin Ave NW

Hardware Stores

- **Glover Park Hardware** • 2251 Wisconsin Ave Nw

Liquor Stores

- **Ace Beverage** • 3301 New Mexico Ave NW
- **Burkas Wine & Liquor Store** • 3500 Wisconsin Ave NW
- **MacArthur Liquors** • 4877 MacArthur Blvd NW
- **Papa's Liquor** • 3703 Macomb St NW
- **Pearson's Liquor & Wine Annex** • 2436 Wisconsin Ave NW

Nightlife

- **Bourbon** • 2348 Wisconsin Ave NW
- **Good Guys Restaurant** • 2311 Wisconsin Ave NW
- **Grog and Tankard** • 2408 Wisconsin Ave NW
- **Zebra Lounge** • 3238 Wisconsin Ave NW

Restaurants

- **2 Amys** • 3715 Macomb St NW
- **Cactus Cantina** • 3300 Wisconsin Ave NW
- **Café Deluxe** • 3228 Wisconsin Ave NW
- **Faccia Luna Trattoria** • 2400 Wisconsin Ave NW
- **Heritage India** • 2400 Wisconsin Ave NW
- **Makoto Restaurant** • 4822 MacArthur Blvd NW
- **Rocklands** • 2418 Wisconsin Ave NW
- **Sushi-Ko** • 2309 Wisconsin Ave NW

Shopping

- **Inga's Once Is Not Enough** • 4830 MacArthur Blvd NW
- **Theodore's** • 2233 Wisconsin Ave NW
- **Treetop Toys** • 3301 New Mexico Ave NW
- **Vespa Washington** • 2233 Wisconsin Ave NW

Video Rental

- **Blockbuster Video** • 2332 Wisconsin Ave NW
- **Potomac Video** • 3408 Idaho Ave NW
- **Potomac Video** • 4828 MacArthur Blvd NW

Friendship Heights
Tenleytown - AU
Tenley Circle NW
Ward Circle NW
Wesley Circle NW
Fort Reno Park
Fort Bayard Park
Muhlenberg Park
Clover Parkway
Naval Security Group Center
American University
Wisconsin Ave NW
Western Ave NW
Connecticut Ave NW
Nebraska Ave NW
Massachusetts Ave NW
River Rd NW
Military Rd NW
Yuma St NW
Grant Rd NW
Murdock Mill Rd NW
Belt Rd NW
Reno Rd NW
Idaho Ave NW
University Ave NW
Legation St NW
Jenifer St NW
Ingomar St NW
Harrison St NW
Garrison St NW
Fessenden St NW
Ellicott St NW
Davenport St NW
Chesapeake St NW
Brandywine St NW
Albemarle St NW
Alton Pl NW
Windom Pl NW
Warren St NW
Veazey St NW
Van Ness St NW
Upton St NW
Tilden St NW
Sedgwick St NW
Rodman St NW
Quebec St NW
Porter St NW
Newark St NW
PAGE 218
29
30
20
18

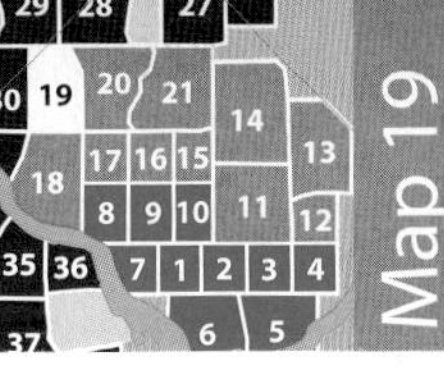

So you want to live in the city, but you really really like the 'burbs? You've found your home! This is a perfectly pleasant area with a feel-good mix of residential, retail, and non-offensive entertainment. It's a good bet you could spend your life in this section of DC and never, ever see a crack pipe.

Banks

- **Bank of America** • 5201 Wisconsin Ave NW
- **BB&T** • 5200 Wisconsin Ave NW
- **Chevy Chase** • 4000 Wisconsin Ave NW
- **Chevy Chase** • 4400 Massachusetts Ave
- **Citibank** • 5001 Wisconsin Ave NW
- **PNC** • 4249 Wisconsin Ave NW
- **PNC** • 5252 Wisconsin Ave NW
- **Sun Trust (ATM)** • 4400 Massachusetts Ave NW

Car Rental

- **Alamoot Rent A Car** • 3314 Wisconsin Ave NW • 800-630-6967
- **Enterprise** • 5220 44th St NW • 202-364-6564

Car Washes

- **Wash & Shine** • 5020 Wisconsin Ave NW

Community Gardens

Gas Stations

- **Exxon** • 4244 Wisconsin Ave NW

Libraries

- **American University Library** • 4400 Massachusetts Ave NW
- **Tenley-Friendship Library** • 4450 Wisconsin Ave NW

Parking

Pharmacies

- **CVS (24 hours)** • 4555 Wisconsin Ave
- **Rodman's Pharmacy** • 5100 Wisconsin Ave NW
- **Safeway** • 4203 Davenport St NW

Post Offices

- **Friendship Station** • 4005 Wisconsin Ave NW

Schools

- **American University** • 4400 Massachusetts Ave NW
- **Deal Junior High** • 3815 Fort Dr NW
- **Georgetown Day Upper** • 4200 Davenport St NW
- **Hearst Elementary** • 3950 37th St NW
- **Janney Elementary** • 4130 Albermarle St NW
- **National Presbyterian** • 4121 Nebraska Ave NW
- **Potomac College** • 4000 Chesapeake St NW
- **Sidwell Friends** • 3825 Wisconsin Ave NW
- **St Ann's Academy** • 4404 Wisconsin Ave NW
- **Wesley Theological Seminary** • 4500 Massachusetts Ave NW
- **Wilson High** • 3950 Chesapeake St NW

Supermarkets

- **Safeway** • 4203 Davenport St NW
- **Whole Foods Market** • 4530 40th St NW

Map 19 • Tenleytown / Friendship Heights

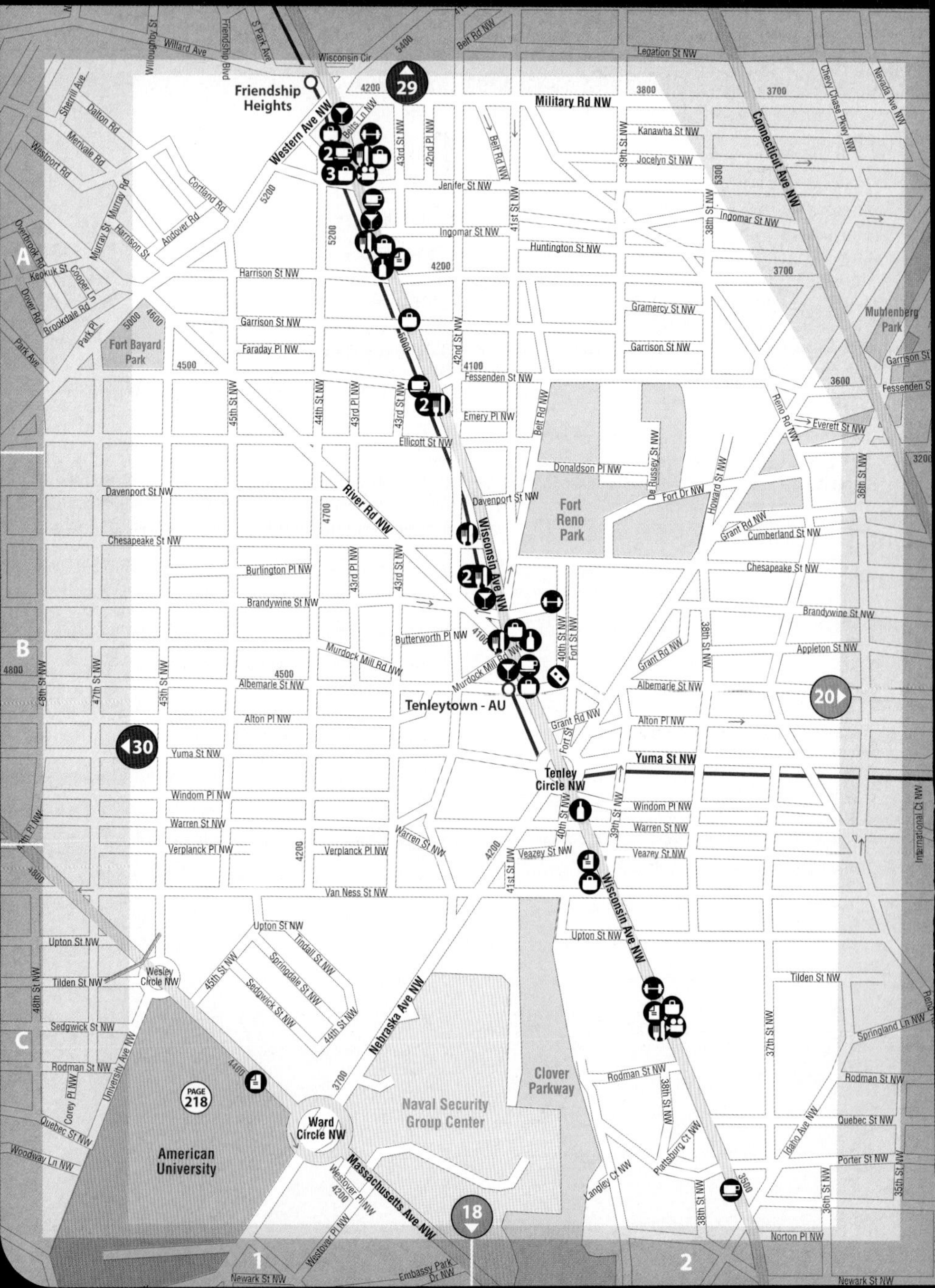

Friendship Heights
Western Ave NW
Wisconsin Cir
Willard Ave
Willoughby St
Friendship Blvd
S Park Ave
Belt Rd NW
Legation St NW
Military Rd NW
Kanawha St NW
Jocelyn St NW
Jenifer St NW
Ingomar St NW
Huntington St NW
Harrison St NW
Gramercy St NW
Garrison St NW
Faraday Pl NW
Fessenden St NW
Emery Pl NW
Ellicott St NW
Everett St NW
Donaldson Pl NW
Davenport St NW
Chesapeake St NW
Burlington Pl NW
Brandywine St NW
Butterworth Pl NW
Murdock Mill Rd NW
Albemarle St NW
Alton Pl NW
Yuma St NW
Windom Pl NW
Warren St NW
Verplanck Pl NW
Veazey St NW
Van Ness St NW
Upton St NW
Tilden St NW
Sedgwick St NW
Rodman St NW
Quebec St NW
Porter St NW
Norton Pl NW
Newark St NW
Woodway Ln NW
Springland Ln NW
Appleton St NW
Cumberland St NW
Grant Rd NW
Fort Dr NW
De Russey St NW
Howard St NW
Reno Rd NW
Connecticut Ave NW
Chevy Chase Pkwy NW
Nevada Ave NW
Sherrill Ave
Dalton Rd
Merivale Rd
Westport Rd
Cortland Rd
Andover Rd
Murray Rd
Murray St
Harrison St
Overbrook Rd
Keokuk St
Cooper Ln
Dover Rd
Brookdale Rd
Park Pl
Park Ave
River Rd NW
Wisconsin Ave NW
Nebraska Ave NW
Massachusetts Ave NW
University Ave NW
Corey Pl NW
Westover Pl NW
Embassy Park Dr NW
Langley Ct NW
Plattsburg Ct NW
Idaho Ave NW
International Ct NW
Tindall St NW
Springdale St NW
Sedgwick St NW
45th St NW
44th St NW
43rd Pl NW
43rd St NW
42nd Pl NW
42nd St NW
41st St NW
40th St NW
39th St NW
38th St NW
37th St NW
36th St NW
35th St NW
47th St NW
48th St NW
Fort St
Fort Bayard Park
Fort Reno Park
Muhlenberg Park
Tenleytown - AU
Tenley Circle NW
Wesley Circle NW
Ward Circle NW
Clover Parkway
Naval Security Group Center
American University
PAGE 218
29
30
20
18
A
B
C
1
2

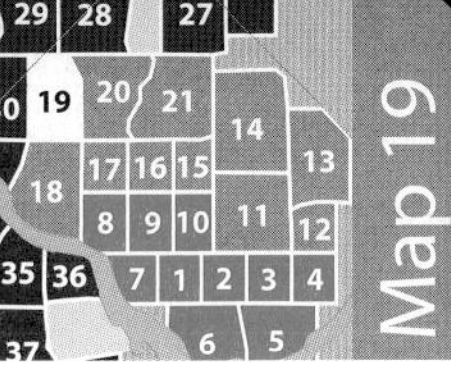

Easy, if bland, living here. There are lots of bright, friendly restaurants with menus heavy on the portobello mushrooms and Herbs D'Provence. K's New York Deli, one of the city's only full-scale Jewish delis, is a rare exception.

Coffee

- **Connie's Café** • 4224 Fessenden St NW
- **Cosí** • 5252 Wisconsin Ave NW
- **L Lounge** • 3515 Wisconsin Ave NW
- **Mazza Café** • 5300 Wisconsin Ave Nw
- **Starbucks** • 4513 Wisconsin Ave NW
- **Starbucks** • 5335 Wisconsin Ave NW

Copy Shops

- **Kinko's (6am-11pm)** • 5225 Wisconsin Ave NW
- **Kwik Kopy Printing (8am-6pm)** • 4000 Wisconsin Ave NW
- **UPS Store (8:30am-7:30pm)** • 4410 Massachusetts Ave NW
- **UPS Store (8:30am-7pm)** • 4200 Wisconsin Ave NW

Gyms

- **Sport & Health Clubs** • 4000 Wisconsin Ave NW
- **Sport & Health Clubs** • 4001 Brandywine St NW
- **Washington Sports Clubs** • 5345 Wisconsin Ave NW

Liquor Stores

- **Paul's Wine & Liquors** • 5205 Wisconsin Ave NW
- **Tenley Mini Market** • 4326 Wisconsin Ave NW
- **Tenley Wine & Liquors** • 4525 Wisconsin Ave NW

Movie Theaters

- **AMC Mazza Gallerie 7** • 5300 Wisconsin Ave NW
- **Cineplex Odeon Wisconsin Avenue Cinemas** • 4000 Wisconsin Ave NW

Nightlife

- **Chadwick's** • 5247 Wisconsin Ave NW
- **Guapo's** • 4515 Wisconsin Ave NW
- **Maggianos** • 5333 Wisconsin Ave NW
- **Malt Shop** • 4611 Wisconsin Ave NW

Restaurants

- **4912 Thai Cuisine** • 4912 Wisconsin Ave NW
- **Bambule** • 5225 Wisconsin Ave
- **Café Ole** • 4000 Wisconsin Ave NW
- **Guapos Mexican Cuisine & Cantina** • 4515 Wisconsin Ave NW
- **K's New York Deli** • 4620 Wisconsin Ave NW
- **Maggiano's Little Italy** • 5333 Wisconsin Ave NW
- **Matisse** • 4934 Wisconsin Ave NW
- **Murasaki** • 4620 Wisconsin Ave NW
- **Steak 'n Egg Kitchen** • 4700 Wisconsin Ave NW

Shopping

- **Borders Books & Music** • 5333 Wisconsin Ave NW
- **The Container Store** • 4500 Wisconsin Ave NW
- **Elizabeth Arden Red Door Salon & Spa** • 5225 Wisconsin Ave NW
- **Georgette Klinger** • 5345 Wisconsin Ave NW
- **Hudson Trail Outfitters** • 4530 Wisconsin Ave NW
- **Johnson's Florist & Garden Centers** • 4200 Wisconsin Ave NW
- **Neiman Marcus** • 5300 Wisconsin Ave NW
- **Pottery Barn** • 5335 Wisconsin Ave NW
- **Roche Bobois** • 5301 Wisconsin Ave NW
- **Rodman's** • 5100 Wisconsin Ave NW
- **Serenity Day Spa** • 4000 Wisconsin Ave NW

Video Rental

- **Hollywood Video** • 4530 40th St NW

N

Northampton St NW
Mckinley St NW
Morrison St NW
Livingston St NW
Legation St NW
39th St NW
3800
3700
3200
Kanawha St NW
Jocelyn St NW
5300
38th St NW
Ingomar St NW
Ingomar Pl NW
Huntington St NW
3700
Gramercy St NW
Garrison St NW
Broad Branch Rd NW
Chevy Chase Pkwy NW
Nebraska Ave NW
5400
Livingston St NW
Legation St NW
30th Pl NW
30th St NW
31st St NW
Mckinley Pl NW
Mckinley St NW
Kanawha St NW
29th St NW
Newlands St NW
5500
St. Johns College
Monk Dr NW
St. Johns College
Oregon Ave NW
2600
28
Military Rd NW
Jocelyn St NW
29th St NW
28th St NW
27th St NW
Jenifer St NW
Rock Creek Park Golf Course
Beach Dr NW
Glover Rd NW
Rock Creek Park Nature Center
Ross Dr NW
Grant Rd NW
Rock Creek Park
PAGE 208
Chappell Rd NW
Muhlenberg Park
Linnean Ter NW
34th St NW
33rd St NW
Harrison St NW
Broad Branch Ter NW
Garrison St NW
Fessenden St NW
Fessenden St NW
3600
Reno Rd NW
Everett St NW
30th Pl NW
30th St NW
2900
De Russey St NW
Fort Dr NW
Howard St NW
Fort Reno Park
3200
32nd St NW
Ellicott St NW
Linnean Ave NW
Ellicott Ter NW
36th St NW
Connecticut Ave NW
Davenport St NW
Grant Rd NW
Cumberland St NW
Grant Rd NW
Chesapeake St NW
Gates Rd NW
Chesterfield Pl NW
29th Pl NW
Chesapeake St NW
Chesapeake St NW
Ridge Rd NW
Brandywine St NW
Grant Rd NW
38th St NW
Appleton St NW
Appleton St NW
31st St NW
4500
29th St NW
Allendale Pl NW
28th St NW
Albemarle St NW
3500
4500
32nd St NW
2900
3800
Alton Pl NW
19
35th St NW
Audubon Ter NW
21
Yuma St NW
Soapstone Valley Park
39th St NW
Windom Pl NW
Windom Pl NW
Warren St NW
Van Ness - UDC
Veazey St NW
UDC Van Ness Campus
Veazey Ter NW
Lenore Ln NW
Linnean Ave NW
Chesapeake St NW
Van Ness St NW
4200
4100
Upton St NW
International Dr NW
Upton St NW
Tilden Pl NW
Tilden St NW
28th Pl NW
Spring Of Freedom St NW
Tilden St NW
Broad Branch Rd NW
Beach Dr NW
4200
Varnum St NW
Mathewson Dr NW
Trumbull Ter NW
1900
Taylor St NW
Shepherd St NW
Randolph St NW
Quincy St NW
Piney Branch Park
Wisconsin Ave NW
Springland Ln NW
37th St NW
Reno Rd NW
Sedgwick St NW
29th St NW
Shoemaker St NW
Tilden St NW
Rock Creek Park
Rodman St NW
38th St NW
Idaho Ave NW
Melvin C Hazen Park
Rowland Pl NW
33rd Pl NW
Rodman St NW
Quebec St NW
Platsburg Ct NW
Porter St NW
35th St NW
3500
Ordway St NW
38th St NW
Cleveland Park
Quebec St NW
17
Williamsburg Ln NW
Norton Pl NW
Highland Pl NW
34th Pl NW
34th St NW
Ashley Ter NW
30th St NW
29th St NW
Porter St NW
39th St NW
36th St NW
Newark St NW
33rd Pl NW
Ross Pl NW
27th St NW
Macomb St NW
Lowell St NW
35th St NW
33rd St NW
Klingle Rd NW
Klingle Rd NW
Woodley Rd NW
38th St NW
Washington National Cathedral
Cleveland Ave NW
32nd St NW
Woodley Rd NW
Cortland Pl NW
Devonshire Pl NW
28th St NW
National Zoological Park NW
National Zoological Park NW
Rock Creek and Potomac Pky NW
Park Rd NW
Rosemont Ave NW
Pierce Mill Rd NW
Ingleside Ter NW
Walbridge Pl NW
19th St NW
18th St NW
Newton St NW
Monroe St NW
Lamont St NW
Kenyon St NW
Klingle Pl NW
Bladen Ter NW
Argyle Ter NW
A
B
C
1
2

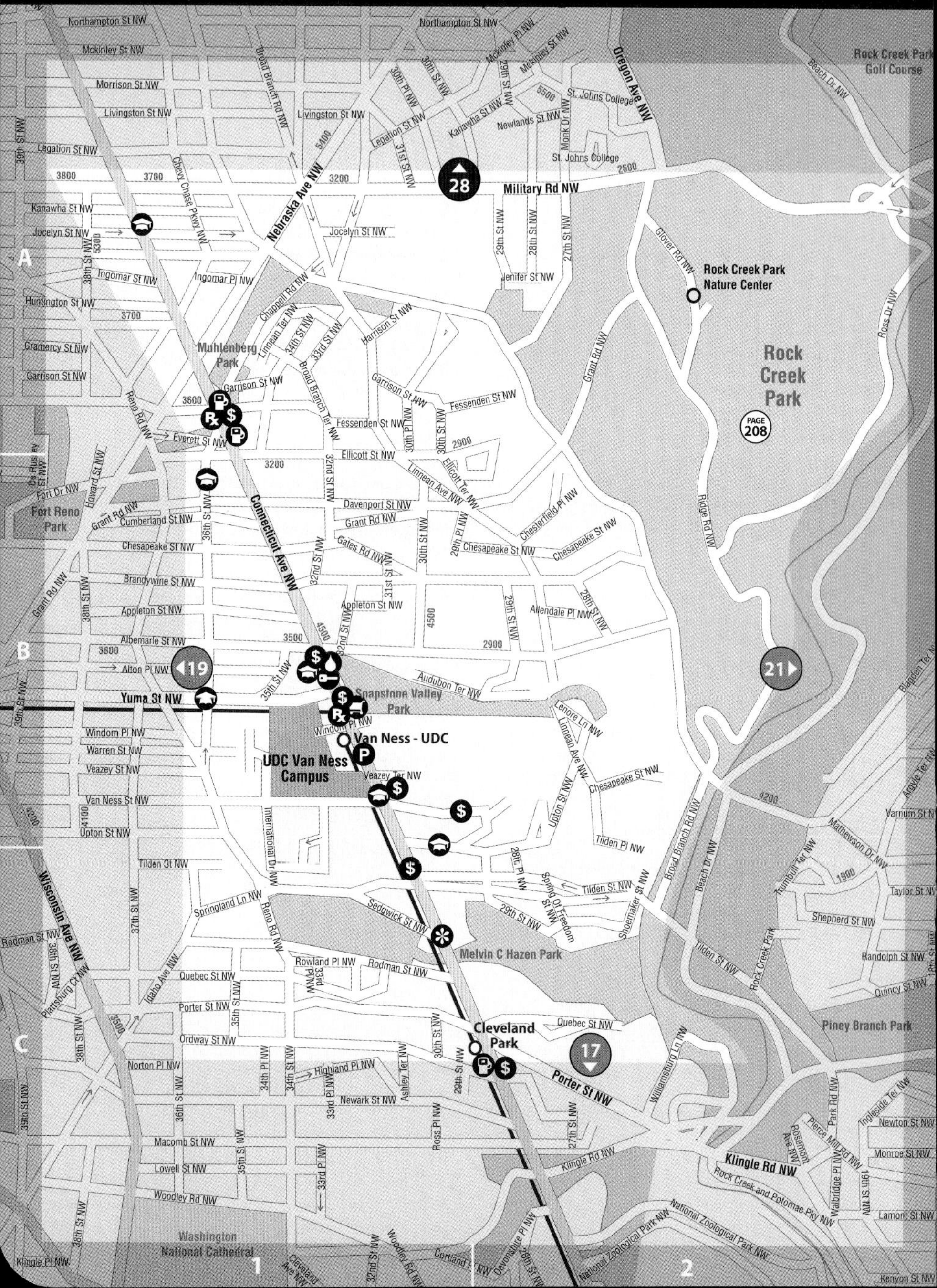

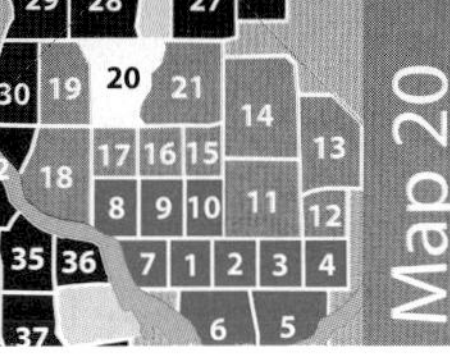

Self-satisfied liberals unite! These blocks are dominated by well-meaning professionals who carry their own bags to the organic market, shun fancy restaurants for Vietnamese, and endure one-sided leftist debates at Politics & Prose. But don't get too radical; they like their coffeehouses grunge-free.

Banks

- **Bank of America** • 4201 Connecticut Ave NW
- **Chevy Chase** • 3519 Connecticut Ave NW
- **Chevy Chase** • 4455 Connecticut Ave NW
- **PNC** • 4000 Connecticut Ave NW
- **PNC (ATM)** • 3003 Van Ness St NW
- **Sun Trust** • 5000 Connecticut Ave NW
- **Wachovia** • 4340 Connecticut Ave NW

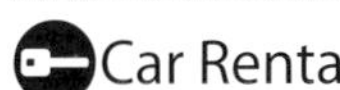

Car Rental

- **Avis** • 4400 Connecticut Ave NW • 202-686-5149

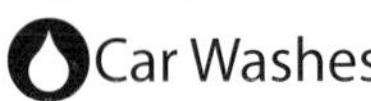

Car Washes

- **Connecticut Avenue Brushless** • 4432 Connecticut Ave NW

Community Gardens

Gas Stations

- **Amoco** • 5001 Connecticut Ave NW
- **Exxon** • 3535 Connecticut Ave NW
- **Sunoco** • 4940 Connecticut Ave NW

Landmarks

- **Rock Creek Park Nature Center** • 5200 Glover Rd NW

Parking

Pharmacies

- **CVS** • 4309 Connecticut Ave NW
- **CVS** • 5013 Connecticut Ave NW

Schools

- **Auguste Montessori** • 3600 Ellicott St NW
- **Edmund Burke** • 2955 Upton St NW
- **Franklin Montessori School Forest Hills Campus** • 4473 Connecticut Ave NW
- **Montessori School of Chevy Chase** • 5312 Connecticut Ave NW
- **Murch Elementary** • 4810 36th St NW
- **Sheridan** • 4400 36th St NW
- **University of the District of Columbia** • 4200 Connecticut Ave NW

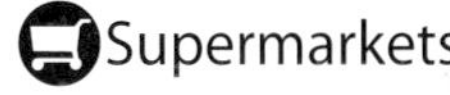

Supermarkets

- **Giant Food** • 4303 Connecticut Ave NW

Map 20 • Cleveland Park / Upper Connecticut

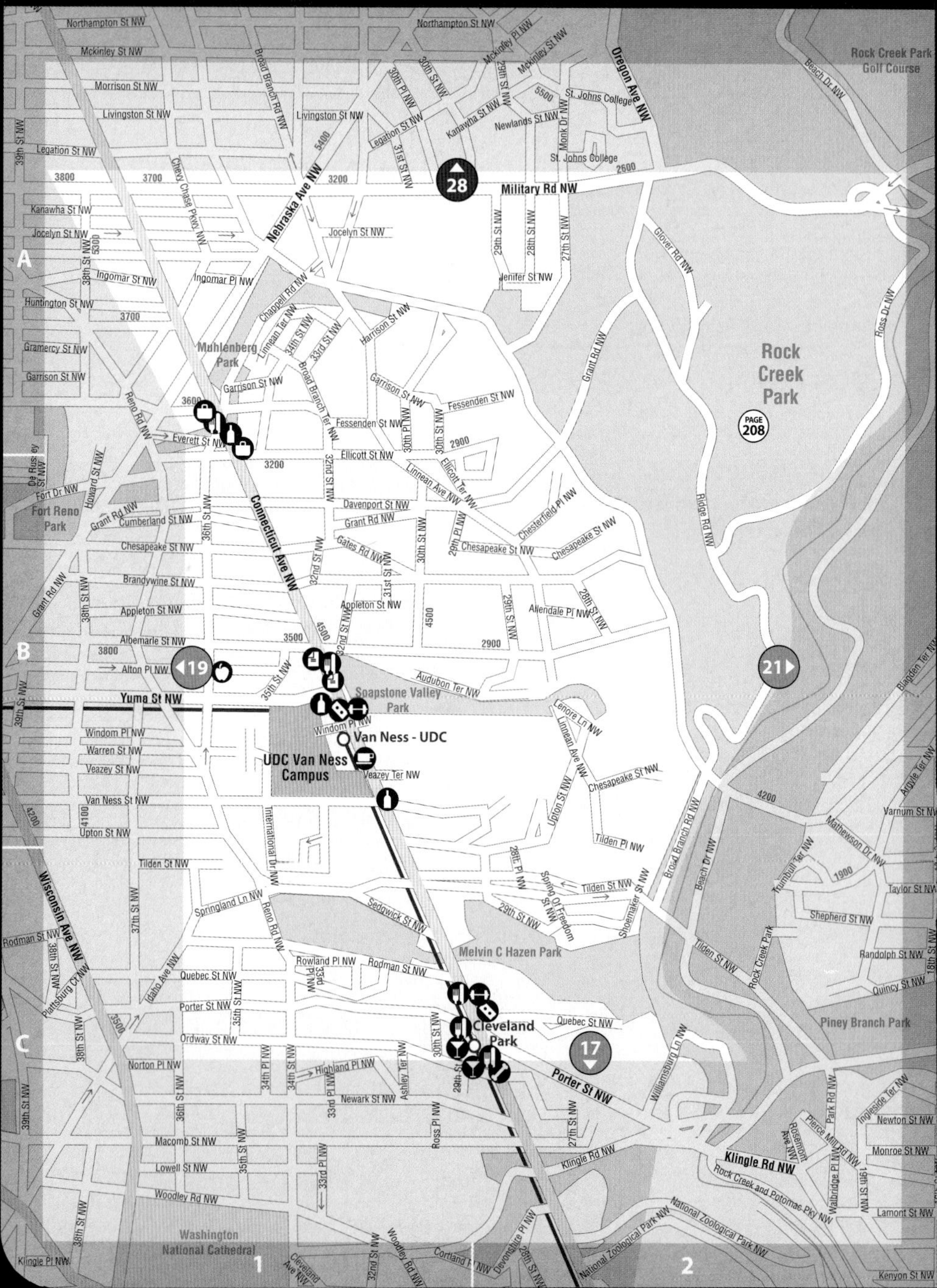

Luckily, liberals tend to have adventuresome palates. Outside of Virginia's immigrant neighborhoods, this area has the best sampling of worldly menus. Delhi Dhaba, Indique, and Sala Thai are all worth the trek.

Coffee

- **Sirius Coffee Company** • 4250 Connecticut Ave Nw

Copy Shops

- **Office Depot (8am-7pm)** • 4455 Connecticut Ave NW
- **UPS Store (9am-6pm)** • 4401 Connecticut Ave NW

Farmer's Markets

- **New Morning Farm Market** • 36th St NW & Alton Pl NW

Gyms

- **City Fitness Gym** • 3525 Connecticut Ave NW
- **Gold's Gym** • 4310 Connecticut Ave NW

Liquor Stores

- **Calvert Woodley Liquors** • 4339 Connecticut Ave NW
- **Sheffield Wine & Liquor Shoppe** • 5025 Connecticut Ave NW
- **Van Ness Liquors** • 4201 Connecticut Ave NW

Nightlife

- **Atomic Billiards** • 3427 Connecticut Ave NW
- **Park Bench Pub** • 3433 Connecticut Ave NW

Pet Shops

- **Petco** • 3505 Connecticut Ave NW

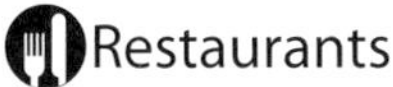

Restaurants

- **Buck's Fishing & Camping** • 5031 Connecticut Ave NW
- **Delhi Dhaba** • 4455 Connecticut Ave NW
- **Indique** • 3512 Connecticut Ave NW
- **Palena** • 3529 Connecticut Ave NW
- **Sala Thai** • 3507 Connecticut Ave NW

Shopping

- **Marvelous Market** • 5035 Connecticut Ave NW
- **Politics & Prose** • 5015 Connecticut Ave NW

Video Rental

- **Blockbuster Video** • 3519 Connecticut Ave NW
- **Video Warehouse** • 4300 Connecticut Ave NW

Rock Creek Park Golf Course
Rock Creek Park
PAGE 208
William Fitzgerald Tennis Stadium
Piney Branch Park
Georgia Ave-Petworth
US Soldiers' & Airmen's Home
Military Rd NW
Missouri Ave NW
16th St
13th St NW
Georgia Ave NW
Colorado Ave NW
Iowa Ave NW
Arkansas Ave NW
Illinois Ave NW
Kansas Ave NW
New Hampshire Ave NW
Grant Circle NW
Piney Branch Pky NW
Rock Creek Ford Rd NW
Klingle Rd NW
Adams Mill Rd NW
Rock Creek and Potomac Pky
Beach Dr NW
Ridge Rd NW
Glover Rd NW
Broad Branch Rd NW
Rock Creek
Blagden Ave NW
Bladgen Ter NW
Mathewson Dr NW
Crestwood Dr NW
Spring Rd NW
Special Ed. Ctr
Sheridan St NW
Somerset Pl NW
Rittenhouse St NW
Quintana Pl NW
Peabody St NW
Oglethorpe St NW
Nicholson St NW
Madison St NW
Kennedy St NW
Jefferson St NW
Ingraham St NW
Hamilton St NW
Gallatin St NW
Farragut St NW
Emerson St NW
Delafield Pl NW
Decatur St NW
Crittenden St NW
Buchanan St NW
Allison St NW
Webster St NW
Varnum St NW
Upshur St NW
Taylor St NW
Shepherd St NW
Randolph St NW
Quincy St NW
Quebec Pl NW
Princeton Pl NW
Otis Pl NW
Newton Pl NW
Park Rd NW
Morton St NW
Lamont St NW
Kilbourne Pl NW
Keefer Pl NW
Kenyon St NW
27
14
15
16
20
A
B
C
1
2

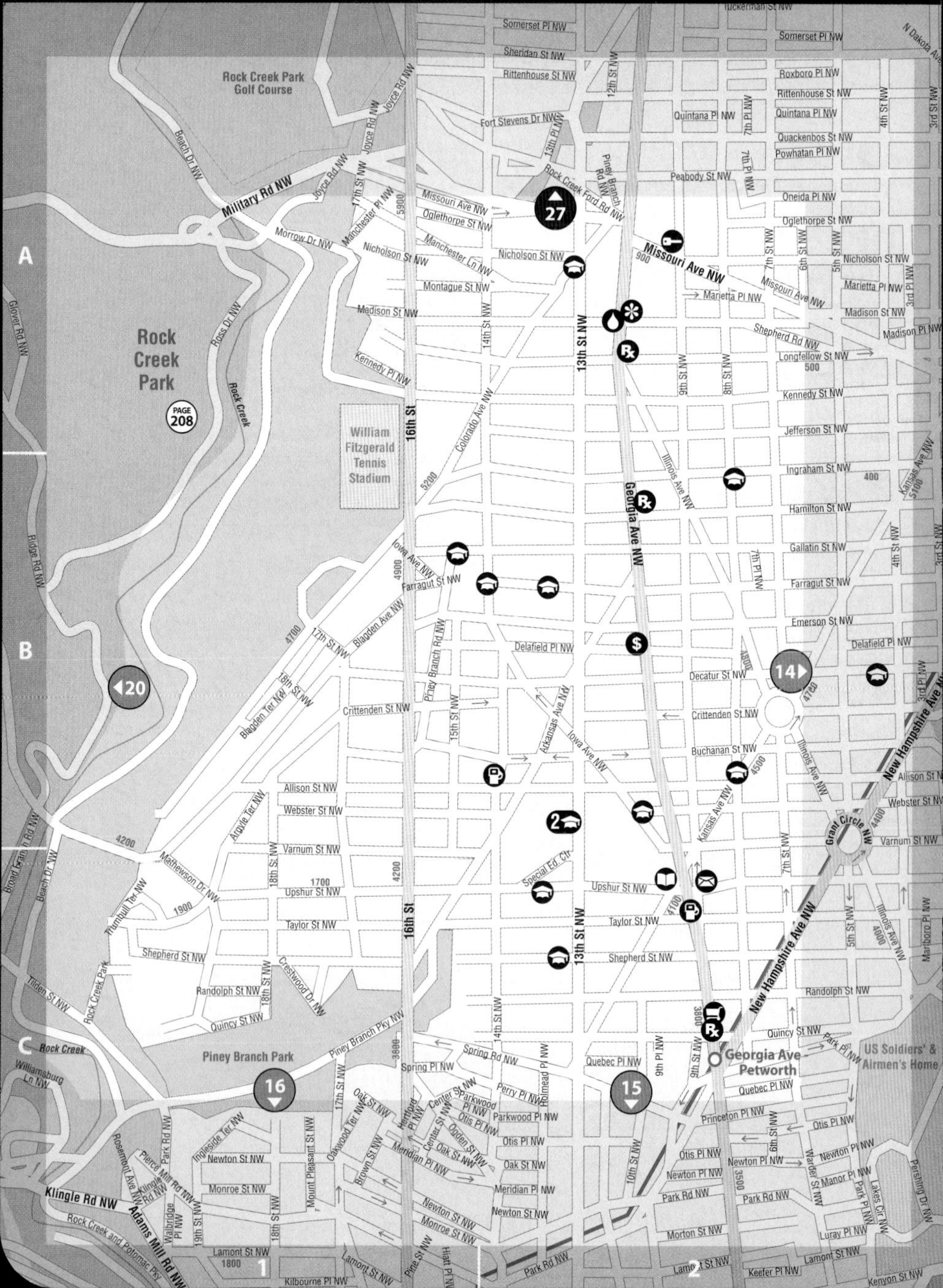

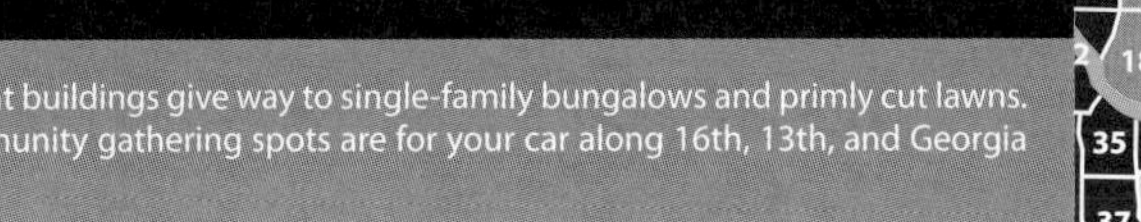

High-rise apartment buildings give way to single-family bungalows and primly cut lawns. The only real community gathering spots are for your car along 16th, 13th, and Georgia at rush hour.

Banks

- **Industrial Bank** • 4812 Georgia Ave NW

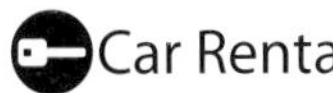

Car Rental

- **Enterprise** • 927 Missouri Ave NW • 202-726-6600

Car Washes

- **Car Wash Express** • 5758 Georgia Ave NW

Community Gardens

Gas Stations

- **Exxon** • 4501 14th St NW
- **Shell** • 4140 Georgia Ave NW

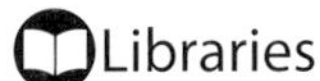

Libraries

- **Petworth Library** • 4200 Kansas Ave NW

Pharmacies

- **CVS** • 5227 Georgia Ave NW
- **Rite Aid** • 5600 Georgia Ave NW
- **Safeway** • 3830 Georgia Ave NW

Post Offices

- **Petworth Station** • 4211 9th St NW

Schools

- **The Academy for Ideal Education Lower** • 1501 Gallatin St NW
- **Barnard Elementary** • 430 Decatur St NW
- **Brightwood Elementary** • 1300 Nicholson St NW
- **British School of Washington** • 4715 16th St NW
- **Clark Elementary** • 4501 Kansas Ave NW
- **Community Academy** • 1300 Allison St NW
- **Ideal Learning Center** • 1501 Gallatin St NW
- **Kennedy Institute Lower** • 801 Buchanan St NW
- **Kingsbury Day** • 5000 14th St NW
- **Macfarland Middle** • 4400 Iowa Ave NW
- **Parkmont** • 4842 16th St
- **Paul Junior High** • 5800 8th St NW
- **Powell Elementary** • 1350 Upshur St NW
- **Roosevelt High** • 4301 13th St NW
- **Sharpe Health** • 4300 13th St NW
- **St Gabriel** • 510 Webster St NW
- **Tots Developmental** • 1317 Shepherd St NW
- **Truesdell Elementary** • 800 Ingraham St NW
- **West Elementary** • 1338 Farragut St NW

Supermarkets

- **Safeway** • 3830 Georgia Ave NW

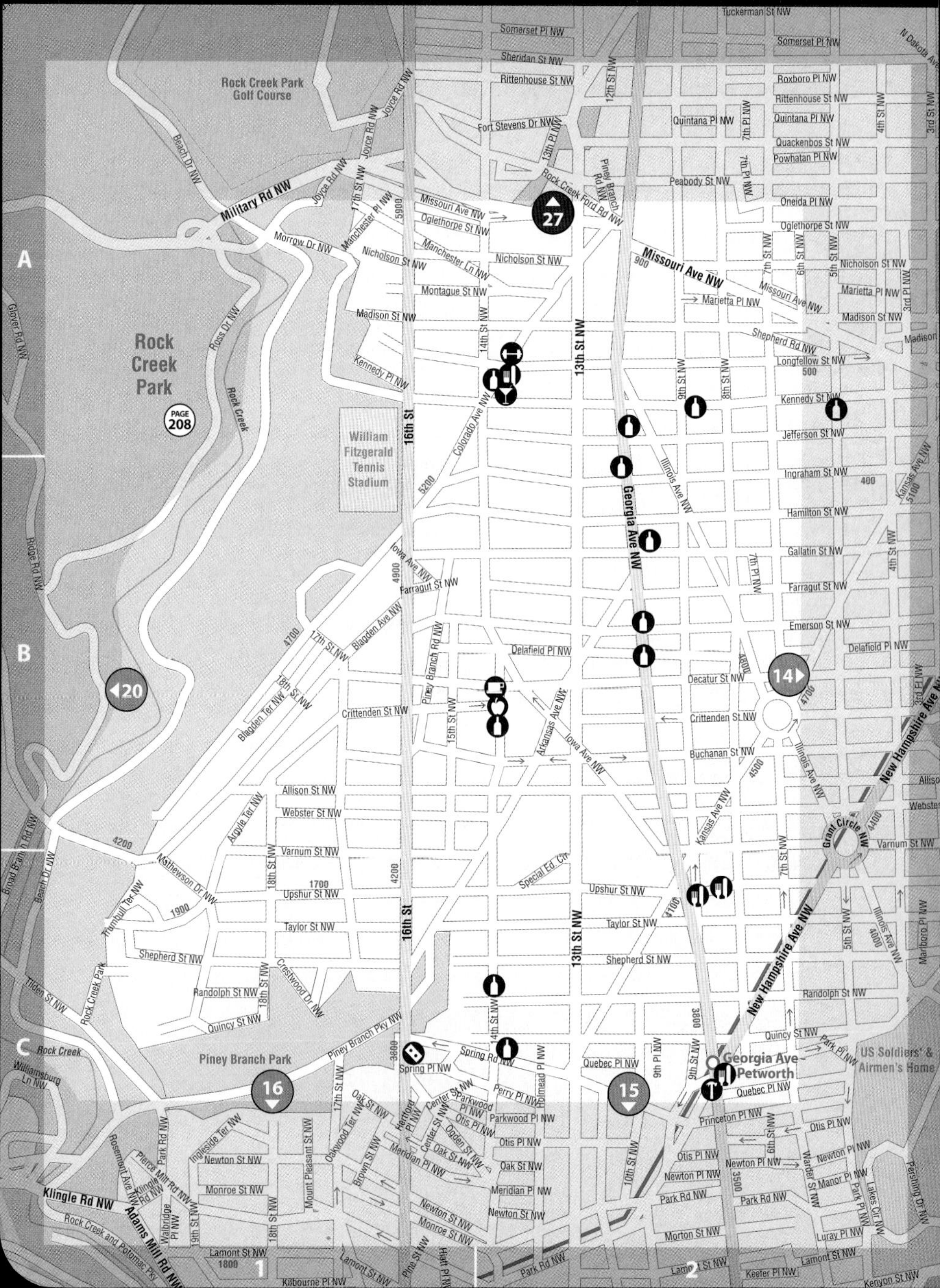

A
B
C
1
2

Rock Creek Park Golf Course
Rock Creek Park
PAGE 208
William Fitzgerald Tennis Stadium
Piney Branch Park
US Soldiers' & Airmen's Home
Georgia Ave Petworth
27
20
14
16
15

Military Rd NW
Missouri Ave NW
16th St
13th St NW
Georgia Ave NW
New Hampshire Ave NW
Grant Circle NW
Piney Branch Pky NW
Klingle Rd NW
Adams Mill Rd NW
Rock Creek and Potomac Pky
Beach Dr NW
Ridge Rd NW
Glover Rd NW
Ross Dr NW
Joyce Rd NW
Morrow Dr NW
Colorado Ave NW
Iowa Ave NW
Arkansas Ave NW
Kansas Ave NW
Illinois Ave NW
Blagden Ave NW
Rock Creek Ford Rd NW
Tuckerman St NW
Somerset Pl NW
Sheridan St NW
Rittenhouse St NW
Fort Stevens Dr NW
Quintana Pl NW
Quackenbos St NW
Powhatan Pl NW
Peabody St NW
Oneida Pl NW
Oglethorpe St NW
Nicholson St NW
Marietta Pl NW
Madison St NW
Montague St NW
Kennedy St NW
Longfellow St NW
Jefferson St NW
Ingraham St NW
Hamilton St NW
Gallatin St NW
Farragut St NW
Emerson St NW
Delafield Pl NW
Decatur St NW
Crittenden St NW
Buchanan St NW
Allison St NW
Webster St NW
Varnum St NW
Upshur St NW
Taylor St NW
Shepherd St NW
Randolph St NW
Quincy St NW
Spring Rd NW
Quebec Pl NW
Princeton Pl NW
Otis Pl NW
Newton Pl NW
Park Rd NW
Morton St NW
Lamont St NW
Kilbourne Pl NW
Kenyon St NW
Keefer Pl NW

Colorado Kitchen is worth a trip, as are Domku and Sweet Mango Café. Otherwise, the offerings here are few and far between and a car is essential to get to them or, better yet, to drive elsewhere.

Coffee

- **Mocha Hut** • 4706 14th St NW

Farmer's Markets

- **14th St Heights Community Market** • 14th & Crittenden Sts NW

Gyms

- **Curves** • 5521 Colorado Ave NW

Hardware Stores

- **Capitol Locksmith** • 3655 Georgia Ave NW

Liquor Stores

- **Colony Liquor & Groceries** • 4901 Georgia Ave NW
- **Colorado Liquor Store** • 5514 Colorado Ave NW
- **Decatur Liquors** • 4704 14th St NW
- **Hamilton Wine & Liquor Store** • 5205 Georgia Ave NW
- **Herman's Liquor Store** • 3712 14th St NW
- **J-B Liquors** • 3914 14th St NW
- **Jefferson Liquor Store** • 5307 Georgia Ave NW
- **LA Casa Morata** • 5421 Georgia Ave NW
- **Rocket Liquors** • 900 Kennedy St NW
- **Target Liquor** • 500 Kennedy St NW
- **Three Way Liquor Store** • 4823 Georgia Ave NW

Nightlife

- **Twins Lounge** • 5516 Colorado Ave NW

Restaurants

- **China American Inn** • 845 Upshur St NW
- **Colorado Kitchen** • 5515 Colorado Ave NW
- **Domku** • 821 Upshur St NW
- **Sweet Mango Café** • 3701 New Hampshire Ave NW

Video Rental

- **Woodner Video** • 3636 16th St NW

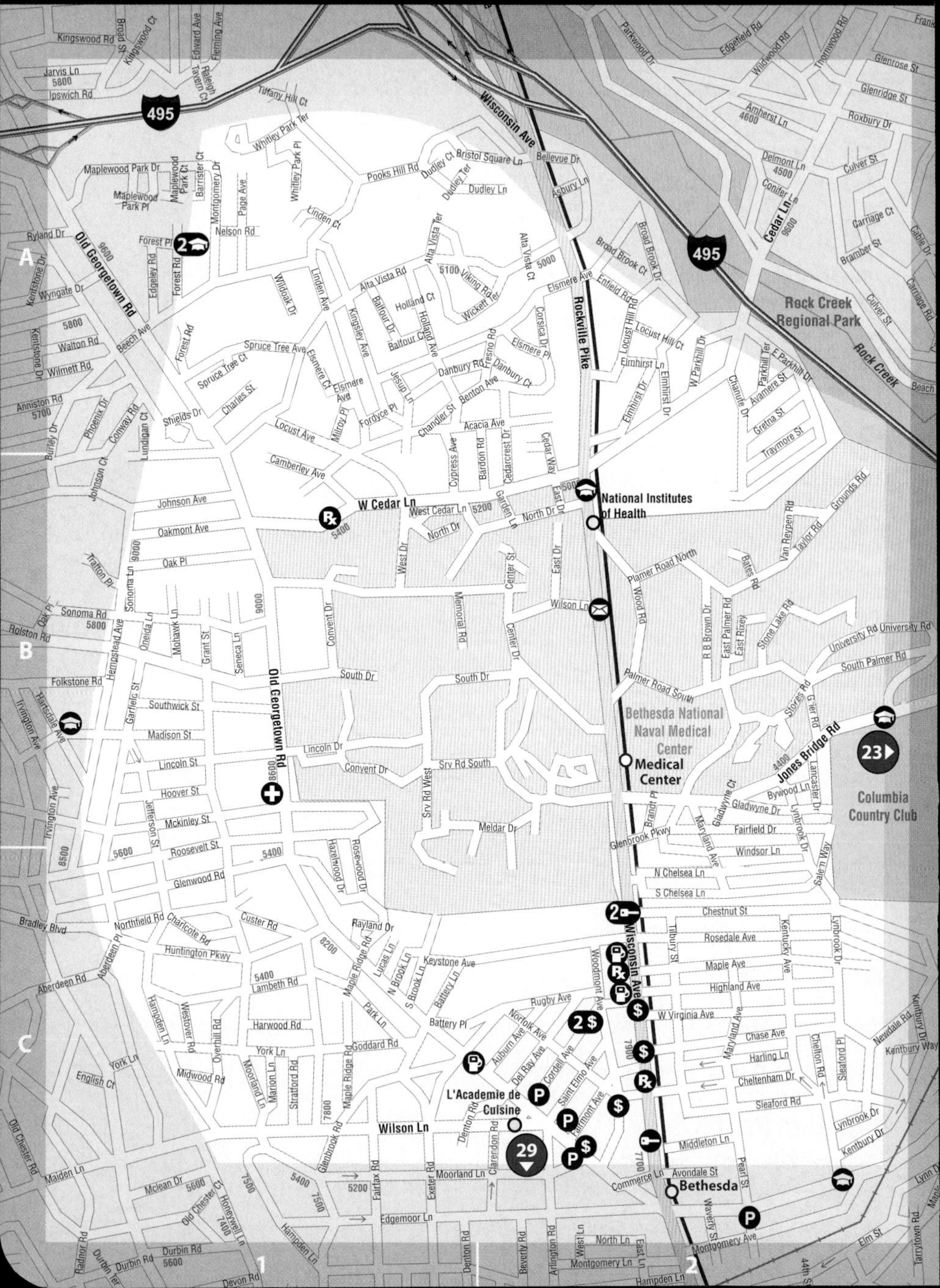

Map 22 • Downtown Bethesda

N

495

Wisconsin Ave

Rockville Pike

Old Georgetown Rd

W Cedar Ln

National Institutes of Health

Bethesda National Naval Medical Center

Medical Center

Jones Bridge Rd

Rock Creek Regional Park

Rock Creek

Columbia Country Club

23

L'Academie de Cuisine

29

Wilson Ln

Bethesda

Bradley Blvd

Montgomery Ave

A

B

C

1

2

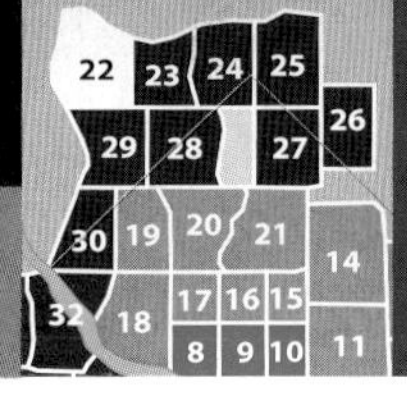

Downtown Bethesda is really its own city rather than a neighborhood. It's got the hotels, shopping, business and traffic to make it feel urban enough for upper-middle-class folks who don't like the hassle of a real city. An influx of younger residents are now making the area a little more lively.

Banks

- **Chevy Chase** • 4825 Cordell Ave
- **Chevy Chase** • 7700 Old Georgetown Rd
- **Citibank** • 8001 Wisconsin Ave
- **Eagle Bank** • 7815 Woodmont Ave
- **Sun Trust (ATM)** • 4836 Cordell Ave
- **Wachovia** • 7901 Wisconsin Ave

Car Rental

- **Budget** • 8400 Wisconsin Ave • 301-816-6000
- **Enterprise** • 7725 Wisconsin Ave • 301-907-7780
- **Sears Rent A Car & Truck** • 8400 Wisconsin Ave • 301-816-6050

Gas Stations

- **Amoco** • 8101 Wisconsin Ave
- **Exxon** • 7975 Old Georgetown Rd
- **Texaco** • 8240 Wisconsin Ave

Hospitals

- **Suburban** • 8600 Old Georgetown Rd

Landmarks

- **L'Academie de Cuisine** • 5021 Wilson Ln
- **National Institutes of Health** • 9000 Rockville Pike

Parking

Pharmacies

- **CVS (24 hours)** • 7809 Wisconsin Ave
- **Foer's CARE Pharmacy** • 8218 Wisconsin Ave
- **Village Green CARE Apothecary** • 5415 W Cedar Ln

Post Offices

- **National Naval Med Center** • 8901 Rockville Pike

Schools

- **Bethesda-Chevy Chase High** • 4301 East West Hwy
- **Bradley Hills Elementary** • 8701 Hartsdale Ave
- **French International** • 9600 Forest Rd
- **Lycee Rochambeau** • 9600 Forest Rd
- **Stone Ridge** • 9101 Rockville Pike
- **Uniformed Services University** • 4301 Jones Bridge Rd

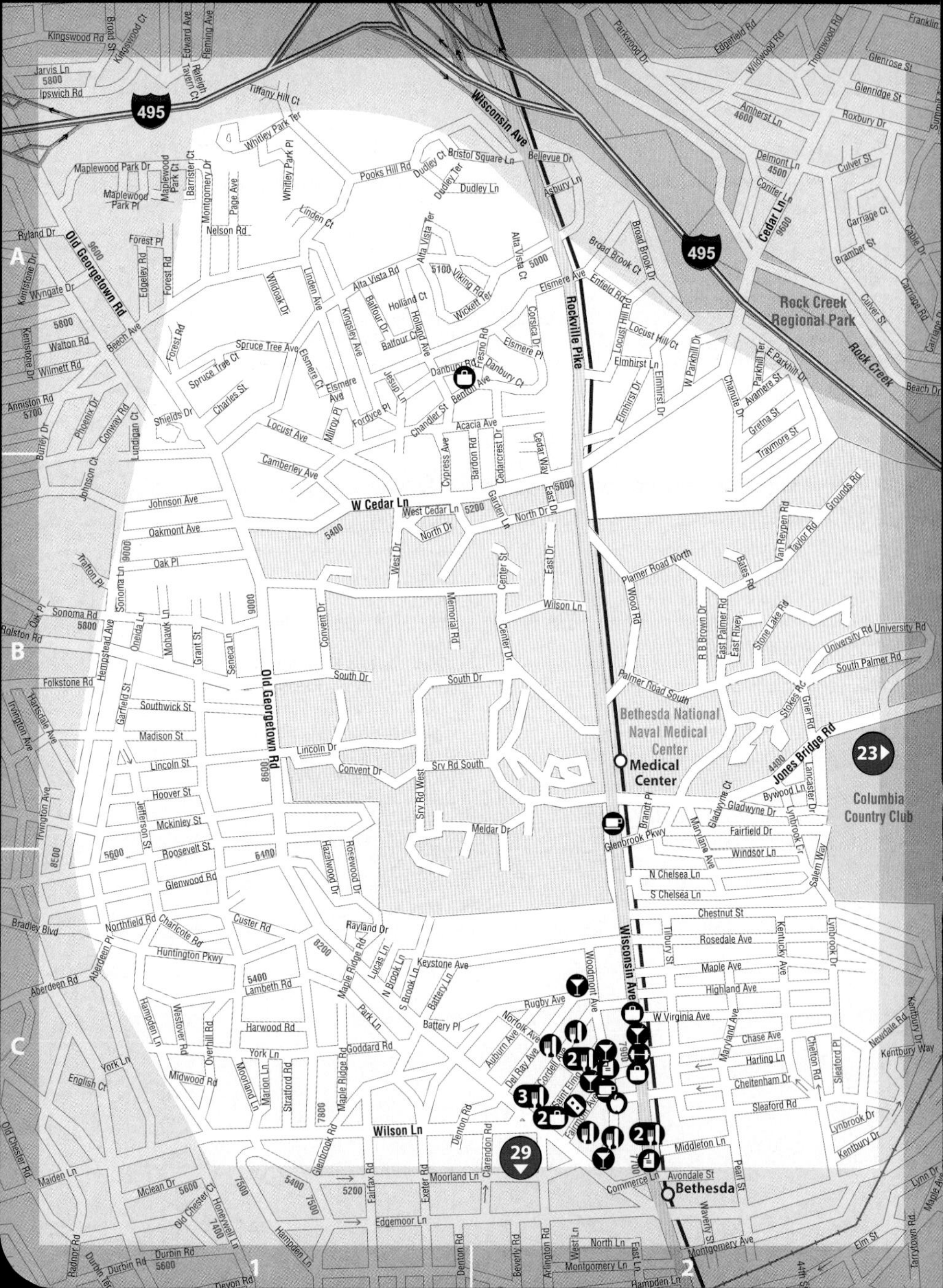

Map 22 • Downtown Bethesda

N

495

Wisconsin Ave

Rockville Pike

Old Georgetown Rd

Cedar Ln

Rock Creek Regional Park

Rock Creek

W Cedar Ln

Bethesda National Naval Medical Center

Medical Center

Jones Bridge Rd

Columbia Country Club

23

Glenbrook Pkwy

Palmer Road South

Plamer Road North

Wilson Ln

Woodmont Ave

Bethesda

29

Montgomery Ave

Bradley Blvd

Kingswood Rd

Jarvis Ln

Ipswich Rd

Tiffany Hill Ct

Whitley Park Ter

Pooks Hill Rd

Bristol Square Ln

Dudley Ln

Maplewood Park Dr

Nelson Rd

Linden Ct

Alta Vista Rd

Elmsere Ave

Broad Brook Ct

Spruce Tree Ave

Beech Ave

Locust Ave

Acacia Ave

Camberley Ave

Johnson Ave

Oakmont Ave

Oak Pl

Sonoma Rd

Folkstone Rd

Southwick St

Madison St

Lincoln St

Hoover St

Mckinley St

Roosevelt St

Glenwood Rd

Northfield Rd

Custer Rd

Huntington Pkwy

Keystone Ave

Lambeth Rd

Rugby Ave

Battery Pl

Harwood Rd

York Ln

Goddard Rd

Midwood Rd

W Virginia Ave

Chase Ave

Harling Ln

Cheltenham Dr

Sleaford Rd

Middleton Ln

Avondale St

Commerce Ln

Moorland Ln

Edgemoor Ln

Chestnut St

Rosedale Ave

Maple Ave

Highland Ave

N Chelsea Ln

S Chelsea Ln

Fairfield Dr

Windsor Ln

Gladwyne Dr

University Rd

South Palmer Rd

Meldar Dr

South Dr

Convent Dr

Srv Rd South

Lincoln Dr

North Dr

Wilson Ln

Durbin Rd

North Ln

Montgomery Ln

Hampden Ln

1

2

A

B

C

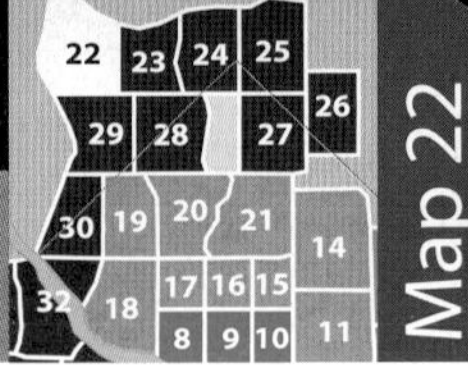

Several new apartment buildings have injected some life into the social scene here. The offerings are surprisingly diverse—fancy restaurants share the street with sports bars and comic book stores. The smoking ban has dampened the drinking crowds a bit, giving you an indication (in case the baby strollers didn't tip you off) of who's still running the show in Bethesda.

- **Dunkin' Donuts** • 8901 Wisconsin Ave
- **Starbucks** • 7700 Norfolk Ave

- **Reprographic Technologies (7:30am-6:30pm)** • 7902 Woodmont Ave
- **Spectrum Printing (8:30am-6pm)** • 7700 Wisconsin Ave

- **Bethesda Farmers Market** • Norfolk & Woodmont Aves

- **Fitness First** • 7900 Wisconsin Ave NW

- **Black's Bar & Kitchen** • 7750 Woodmont Ave
- **Rock Bottom Brewery** • 7900 Norfolk Ave
- **Saphire** • 7940 Wisconsin Ave
- **South Beach Café** • 7904 Woodmont Ave
- **Yacht Club of Bethesda** • 8111 Woodmont Ave

- **Bacchus** • 7945 Norfolk Ave
- **Black's Bar & Kitchen** • 7750 Woodmont Ave
- **Buon Giorno** • 8003 Norfolk Ave
- **Faryab** • 4917 Cordell Ave
- **Grapeseed** • 4865 Cordell Ave
- **Haandi** • 4904 Fairmont Ave
- **Matuba** • 4918 Cordell Ave
- **Olazzo** • 7921 Norfolk Ave
- **The Original Pancake House** • 7700 Wisconsin Ave
- **Tako Grill** • 7756 Wisconsin Ave
- **Tragara** • 4935 Cordell Ave

- **Crate & Barrel** • Westfield Shoppingtown Montgomery, Benton Ave & Fresno Rd
- **Daisy Too** • 4940 St Elmo Ave
- **Ranger Surplus** • 8008 Wisconsin Ave
- **Second Story Books & Antiques** • 4914 Fairmont Ave
- **Zelaya** • 4940 St Elmo Ave

Video Rental

- **Version Francaise (French only)** • 4930 St Elmo Ave

Map 23 • Kensington

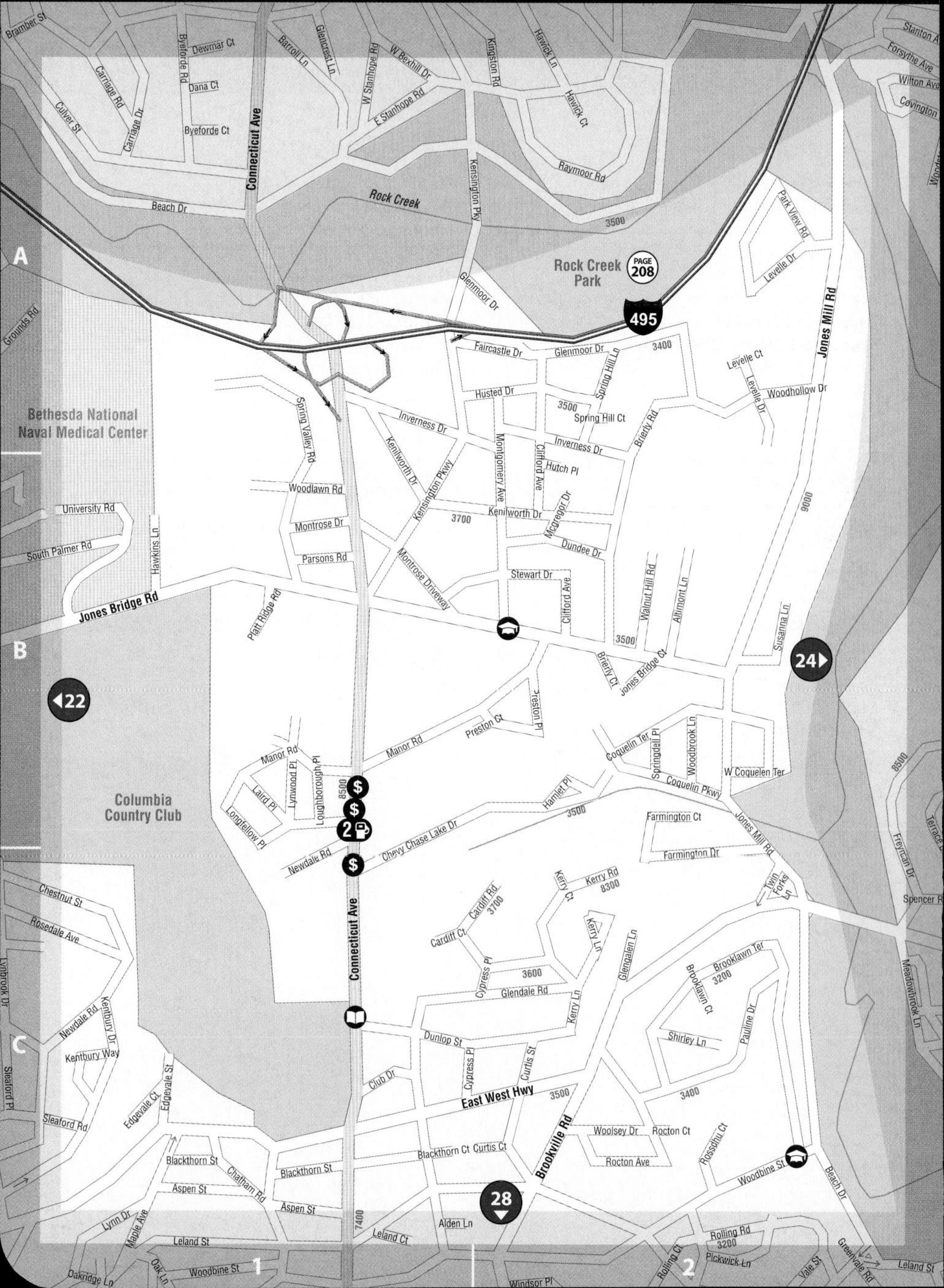

Rock Creek Park
PAGE 208
495
Bethesda National Naval Medical Center
Columbia Country Club
Connecticut Ave
Jones Bridge Rd
Jones Mill Rd
East West Hwy
Brookville Rd
Rock Creek
Kensington Pkwy
Beach Dr
24
22
28

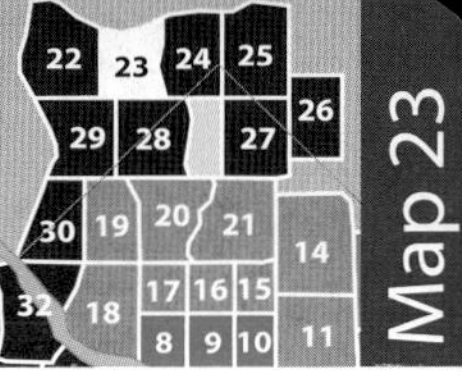

You might as well be on location at a Smith & Hawken catalog shoot. The fussy homes and landscaping here make it a sought-after suburb for those who don't mind driving everywhere and can't afford the more prestigious Chevy Chase address.

Banks

- **Chevy Chase** • 8401 Connecticut Ave
- **Chevy Chase (ATM)** • 8531 Connecticut Ave
- **Sun Trust** • 8510 Connecticut Ave

Gas Stations

- **Citgo** • 8505 Connecticut Ave
- **Sunoco** • 8500 Connecticut Ave

Libraries

- **Chevy Chase Library** • 8005 Connecticut Ave

Schools

- **Lycee Rochambeau** • 3200 Woodbine St
- **North Chevy Chase Elementary** • 3700 Jones Bridge Rd

N
Rock Creek
Rock Creek Park
PAGE 208
495
Bethesda National Naval Medical Center
Columbia Country Club
Connecticut Ave
Jones Bridge Rd
Jones Mill Rd
East West Hwy
Brookville Rd
Kensington Pkwy
Beach Dr
Manor Rd
Chevy Chase Lake Dr
Coquelin Pkwy
Spring Valley Rd
Woodlawn Rd
Montrose Dr
Parsons Rd
Montrose Driveway
Kenilworth Dr
Inverness Dr
Montgomery Ave
Clifford Ave
Hutch Pl
Mcgregor Dr
Dundee Dr
Stewart Dr
Walnut Hill Rd
Altimont Ln
Brierly Rd
Spring Hill Ct
Spring Hill Ln
Glenmoor Dr
Faircastle Dr
Husted Dr
Park View Rd
Levelle Dr
Levelle Ct
Woodhollow Dr
Susanna Ln
Brierly Ct
Jones Bridge Ct
Preston Ct
Preston Pl
Coquelin Ter
Springdell Pl
Woodbrook Ln
W Coquelen Ter
Hamlet Pl
Farmington Ct
Farmington Dr
Twin Forks Ln
Kerry Ct
Kerry Rd
Kerry Ln
Cardiff Ct
Cardiff Rd
Cypress Pl
Glendale Rd
Glengalen Ln
Brooklawn Ter
Brooklawn Ct
Shirley Ln
Pauline Dr
Dunlop St
Curtis St
Club Dr
Woolsey Dr
Rocton Ct
Rocton Ave
Rossdhu Ct
Woodbine St
Blackthorn Ct
Curtis Ct
Blackthorn St
Chatham Rd
Aspen St
Alden Ln
Leland Ct
Leland St
Rolling Rd
Rolling Ct
Pickwick Ln
Vale St
Greenvale Rd
Windsor Pl
Oakridge Ln
Oak Ln
Lynn Dr
Maple Ave
Edgevale Ct
Edgevale St
Sleaford Rd
Sleaford Pl
Kentbury Way
Kentbury Dr
Newdale Rd
Rosedale Ave
Chestnut St
Lynbrook Dr
Manor Rd
Lynwood Pl
Laird Pl
Loughborough Pl
Longfellow Pl
Platt Ridge Rd
Hawkins Ln
University Rd
South Palmer Rd
Grounds Rd
Beach Dr
Culver St
Carriage Rd
Carriage Dr
Byeforde Rd
Dewmar Ct
Dana Ct
Byeforde Ct
Barroll Ln
Glencrest Ln
W Stanhope Rd
E Stanhope Rd
W Bexhill Dr
Kingston Rd
Hawick Ln
Hawick Ct
Raymoor Rd
Glenmoor Dr
Brambar St
Stanton Av
Forsythe Ave
Wilton Ave
Covington
Frederick Dr
Spencer Rd
Meadowbrook Ln
Leland St
3500
3400
3700
9000
8500
8300
3600
3200
7400
A
B
C
1
2
22
24
28

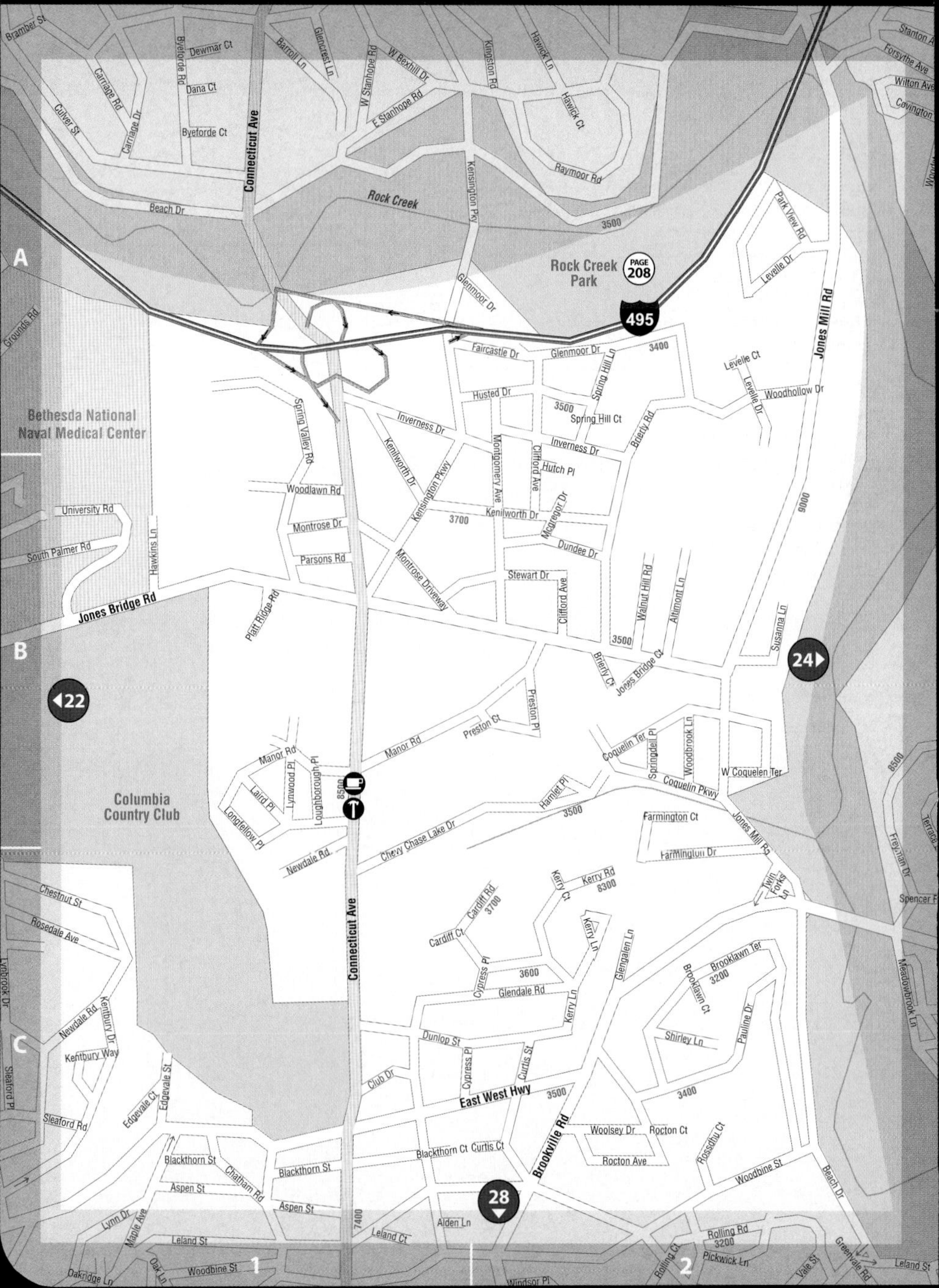

Good thing there's HBO.

Coffee

- **Starbucks** • 8542 Connecticut Ave

Hardware Stores

- **Thomas W Perry** • 8513 Connecticut Ave

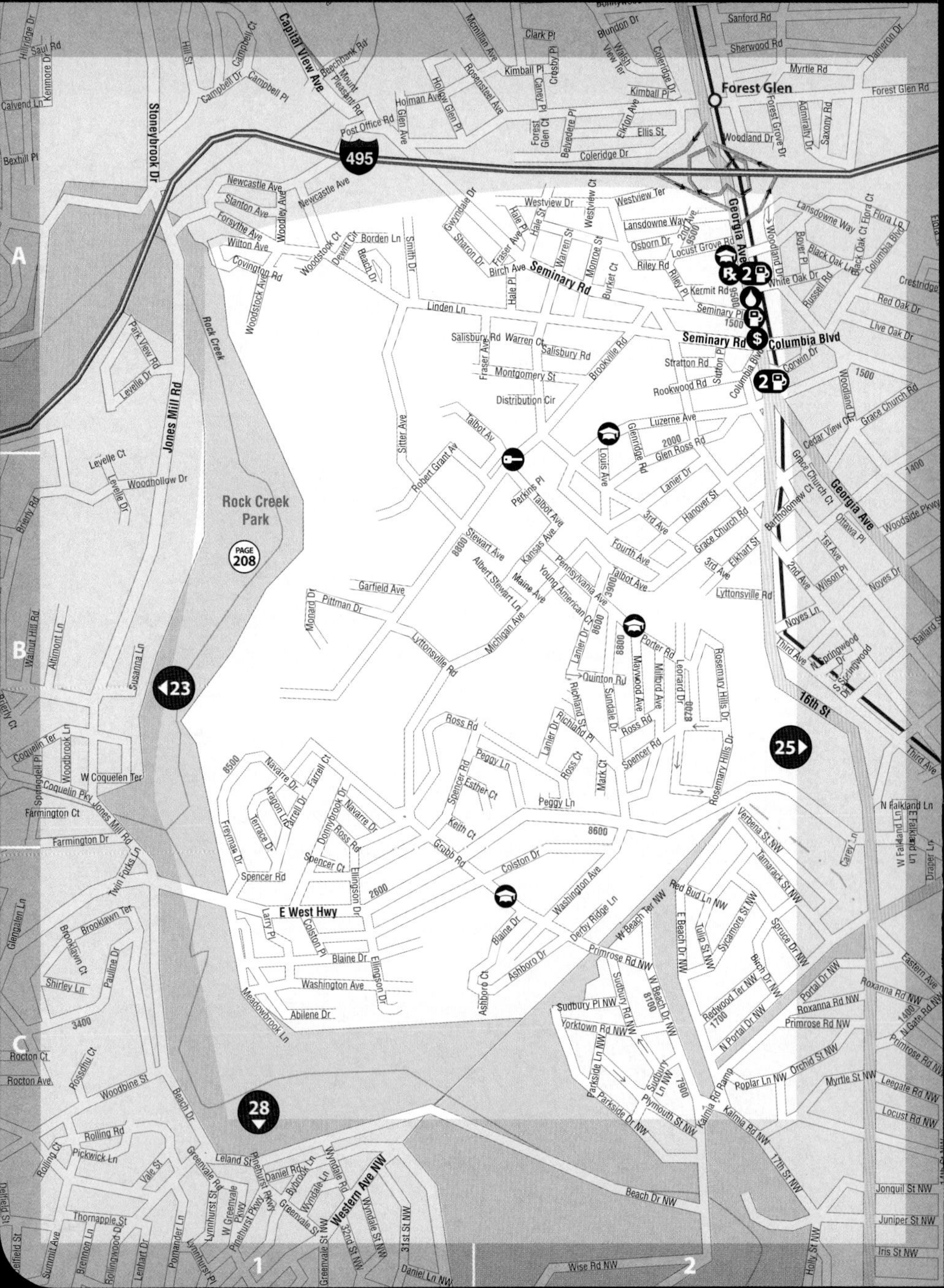

Map 24 • Upper Rock Creek Park

Forest Glen
495
Capital View Ave
Stoneybrook Dr
Jones Mill Rd
Rock Creek
Rock Creek Park
PAGE 208
Seminary Rd
Columbia Blvd
Georgia Ave
16th St
Linden Ln
Lyttonsville Rd
E West Hwy
Beach Dr NW
Western Ave NW
Sanford Rd
Sherwood Rd
Myrtle Rd
Forest Glen Rd
Woodland Dr
Coleridge Dr
Newcastle Ave
Stanton Ave
Forsythe Ave
Wilton Ave
Covington Rd
Woodstock Ave
Borden Ln
Smith Dr
Westview Dr
Lansdowne Way
Osborn Dr
Riley Rd
Kermit Rd
Salisbury Rd
Montgomery St
Distribution Cir
Talbot Av
Robert Grant Av
Luzerne Ave
Glen Ross Rd
Lanier Dr
Hanover St
Grace Church Rd
Fourth Ave
Talbot Ave
Pennsylvania Ave
Kansas Ave
Stewart Ave
Garfield Ave
Pittman Dr
Michigan Ave
Porter Rd
Quinton Rd
Maywood Ave
Milford Ave
Rosemary Hills Dr
Ross Rd
Spencer Rd
Peggy Ln
Grubb Rd
Colston Dr
Washington Ave
Derby Ridge Ln
Blaine Dr
Ashboro Dr
Abilene Dr
Meadowbrook Ln
Verbena St NW
Tamarack St NW
Red Bud Ln NW
Primrose Rd NW
Sudbury Rd NW
Yorktown Rd NW
Parkside Dr NW
Plymouth St NW
Kalmia Rd NW
17th St NW
Portal Dr NW
Roxanna Rd NW
Myrtle St NW
Locust Rd NW
Jonquil St NW
Juniper St NW
Iris St NW
Wise Rd NW
Daniel Ln NW
Leland St
Rolling Rd
Pickwick Ln
Thornapple St
Woodbine St
Rocton Ave
Rocton Ct
Farmington Dr
Coquelin Pky
Twin Forks Ln
Brooklawn Ter
Shirley Ln
Pauline Dr
Woodhollow Dr
Levelle Ct
Park View Rd
Jones Mill Rd
23
25
28
A
B
C
1
2

A mix of residential, schools, and industrial with zero attraction for outsiders.

Banks

- **Citibank** • 9400 Georgia Ave

Car Rental

- **Enterprise** • 9151 Brookville Rd • 301-565-4000

Car Washes

- **Montgomery Hills Car Wash** • 9500 Georgia Ave

Gas Stations

- **Chevron** • 9475 Georgia Ave
- **Citgo** • 9501 Georgia Ave
- **Exxon** • 9331 Georgia Ave
- **Exxon** • 9336 Georgia Ave
- **Shell** • 9510 Georgia Ave

Pharmacies

- **CVS** • 9520 Georgia Ave

Schools

- **Calvary Lutheran** • 9545 Georgia Ave
- **Rock Creek Forest Elementary** • 8330 Grubb Rd
- **Rosemary Hills Elementary** • 2111 Porter Rd
- **Woodlin Elementary** • 2101 Luzerne Ave

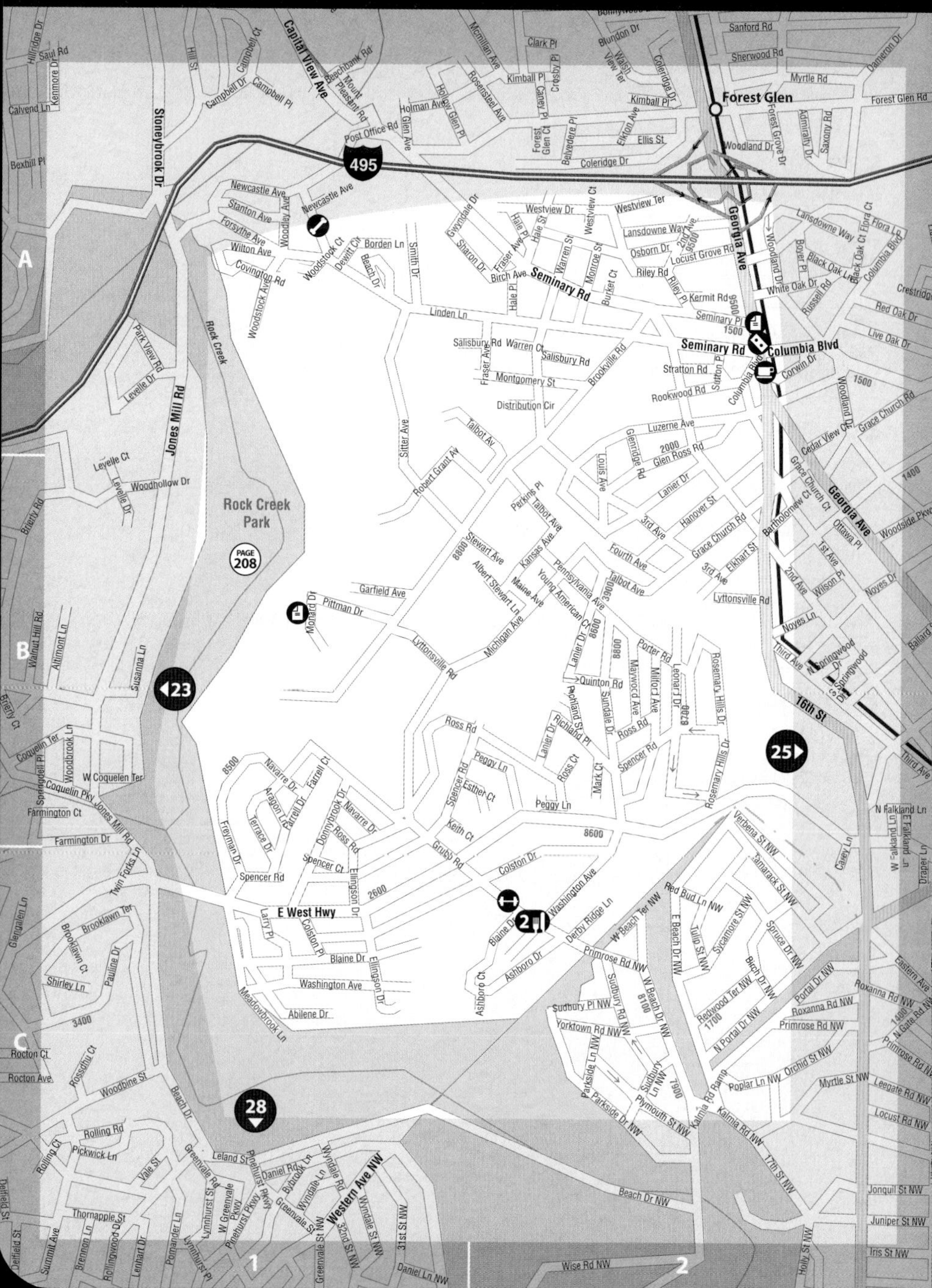

Map 24 • Upper Rock Creek Park

Forest Glen
Sanford Rd
Sherwood Rd
Myrtle Rd
Forest Glen Rd
Dameron Dr
Woodland Dr
Forest Grove Dr
Admiralty Dr
Saxony Rd
Bonnywood Dr
Blundon Dr
Clark Pl
Walsh View Ter
Coleridge Dr
Kimball Pl
Crosby Pl
Caney Pl
Elkton Ave
Ellis St
Forest Glen Ct
Belvedere Pl
Coleridge Dr
Mcmillan Ave
Rosensteel Ave
Hollow Glen Pl
Holman Ave
Glen Ave
Post Office Rd
Capital View Ave
Beechbank Rd
Mount Pleasant Rd
Campbell Ct
Campbell Dr
Campbell Pl
Hill St
Hillridge Dr
Saul Rd
Kenmore Dr
Calvend Ln
Bexhill Pl
Stoneybrook Dr
495
Newcastle Ave
Stanton Ave
Forsythe Ave
Wilton Ave
Woodley Ave
Covington Rd
Woodstock Ave
Woodstock Ct
Dewitt Cir
Borden Ln
Beach Dr
Smith Dr
Gwyndale Dr
Sharon Dr
Fraser Ave
Hale Pl
Hale St
Birch Ave
Seminary Rd
Westview Dr
Westview Ct
Warren St
Monroe St
Burket Ct
Westview Ter
Lansdowne Way
Osborn Dr
2nd Ave
9500
Locust Grove Rd
Riley Rd
Riley Pl
Kermit Rd
Georgia Ave
Seminary Pl
1500
Seminary Rd
Columbia Blvd
Stratton Rd
Sutton Pl
Corwin Dr
Rookwood Rd
Lansdowne Way
Flora Ln
Boyer Pl
Black Oak Ln
Black Oak Ct
Columbia Blvd
White Oak Dr
Russell Rd
Crestridge
Red Oak Dr
Live Oak Dr
Woodland Dr
Grace Church Rd
Cedar View Ct
1400
Linden Ln
Salisbury Rd
Warren Ct
Salisbury Rd
Fraser Ave
Montgomery St
Brookville Rd
Distribution Cir
Park View Rd
Levelle Dr
Rock Creek
Jones Mill Rd
Talbot Av
Sitter Ave
Robert Grant Av
Luzerne Ave
Glenridge Rd
Louis Ave
2000
Glen Ross Rd
Lanier Dr
Hanover St
Grace Church Rd
Grace Church Ct
Bartholomew Ct
Georgia Ave
Woodside Pkwy
Ottawa Pl
1st Ave
Wilson Pl
2nd Ave
Noyes Dr
Noyes Ln
Ballard
Levelle Ct
Levelle Dr
Woodhollow Dr
Brierly Rd
Rock Creek Park
PAGE 208
Perkins Pl
Talbot Ave
3rd Ave
Fourth Ave
Elkhart St
3rd Ave
Lyttonsville Rd
8800
Stewart Ave
Kansas Ave
Albert Stewart Ln
Maine Ave
Young American Ct
Pennsylvania Ave
3900
Talbot Ave
Garfield Ave
Monard Dr
Pittman Dr
Lyttonsville Rd
Michigan Ave
8600
Lanier Dr
8800
Porter Rd
Maywood Ave
Milford Ave
Leonard Dr
8700
Rosemary Hills Dr
Quinton Rd
Richland St
Sundale Dr
Ross Rd
Spencer Rd
Richland Pl
Lanier Dr
Ross Ct
Mark Ct
Rosemary Hills Dr
Third Ave
N Springwood Dr
S Springwood Dr
16th St
Walnut Hill Rd
Altimont Ln
Susanna Ln
23
Brierly Ct
Coquelin Ter
Woodbrook Ln
W Coquelen Ter
Spangdell Pl
Coquelin Pky
Jones Mill Rd
Farmington Ct
Farmington Dr
Ross Rd
Peggy Ln
Spencer Rd
Esther Ct
Peggy Ln
8500
Navarre Dr
Farrell Ct
Aragon Ln
Farrell Dr
Terrace Dr
Donnybrook Dr
Navarre Dr
Ross Rd
Keith Ct
8600
Freyman Dr
Spencer Ct
Ellingson Dr
Grubb Rd
Colston Dr
Spencer Rd
2600
Washington Ave
Twin Forks Ln
25
N Falkland Ln
E Falkland Ln
W Falkland Ln
Carey Ln
Draper Ln
Verbena St NW
Tamarack St NW
Red Bud Ln NW
Sycamore St NW
Tulip St NW
Spruce Dr NW
Birch Dr NW
E West Hwy
Larry Pl
Colston Pl
Blaine Dr
Derby Ridge Ln
W Beach Ter NW
E Beach Dr NW
Blaine Dr
Ellingson Dr
Ashboro Dr
Primrose Rd NW
Redwood Ter NW
1700
Portal Dr NW
N Portal Dr NW
Roxanna Rd NW
Primrose Rd NW
Eastern Ave
Roxanna Rd NW
1400
N Gate Rd NW
Primrose St NW
Glengalen Ln
Brooklawn Ter
Brooklawn Ct
Pauline Dr
Washington Ave
Ellingson Dr
Ashboro Ct
Sudbury Rd NW
W Beach Dr NW
8100
Sudbury Pl NW
Yorktown Rd NW
Shirley Ln
Abilene Dr
Meadowbrook Ln
3400
Rocton Ct
Rossdhu Ct
Rocton Ave
Woodbine St
Beach Dr
Parkside Ln NW
Parkside Dr NW
Sudbury Ln NW
Plymouth St NW
7900
Kalmia Rd Ramp
Kalmia Rd NW
Poplar Ln NW
Orchid St NW
Myrtle St NW
Leegate Rd NW
Locust Rd NW
28
Rolling Rd
Rolling Ct
Pickwick Ln
Vale St
Leland St
Greenvale Rd
Pinehurst Pkwy
Daniel Rd
Bybrook Ln
Wyndale Ln
Wyndale Rd
Western Ave NW
17th St NW
Beach Dr NW
Jonquil St NW
Juniper St NW
Iris St NW
Holly St NW
Delfield St
Summit Ave
Thornapple St
Brennon Ln
Rollingwood Dr
Lenhart Dr
Pomander Ln
Lynnhurst St
W Greenvale Pkwy
Pinehurst Pkwy
Lynnhurst Pl
Greenvale St
Greenvale St NW
32nd St NW
Wyndale St NW
31st St NW
Daniel Ln NW
Wise Rd NW
A
B
C
1
2

If you're in the mood for excitement, just hope your car doesn't stall.

• **Dunkin' Donuts** • 9328 Georgia Ave

• **Allied Printing (9am-6pm)** • 8844 Monard Dr
• **Staples (7am-9pm)** • 9440 Georgia Ave

• **Rock Creek Sport Club** • 8325 Grubb Rd

• **Cat Practice** • 2816 Linden Ln

• **Parkway Deli** • 8317 Grubb Rd
• **redDog Café** • 8301A Grubb Rd

• **BIGG Wolf Movie Discounters** • 9421 Georgia Ave

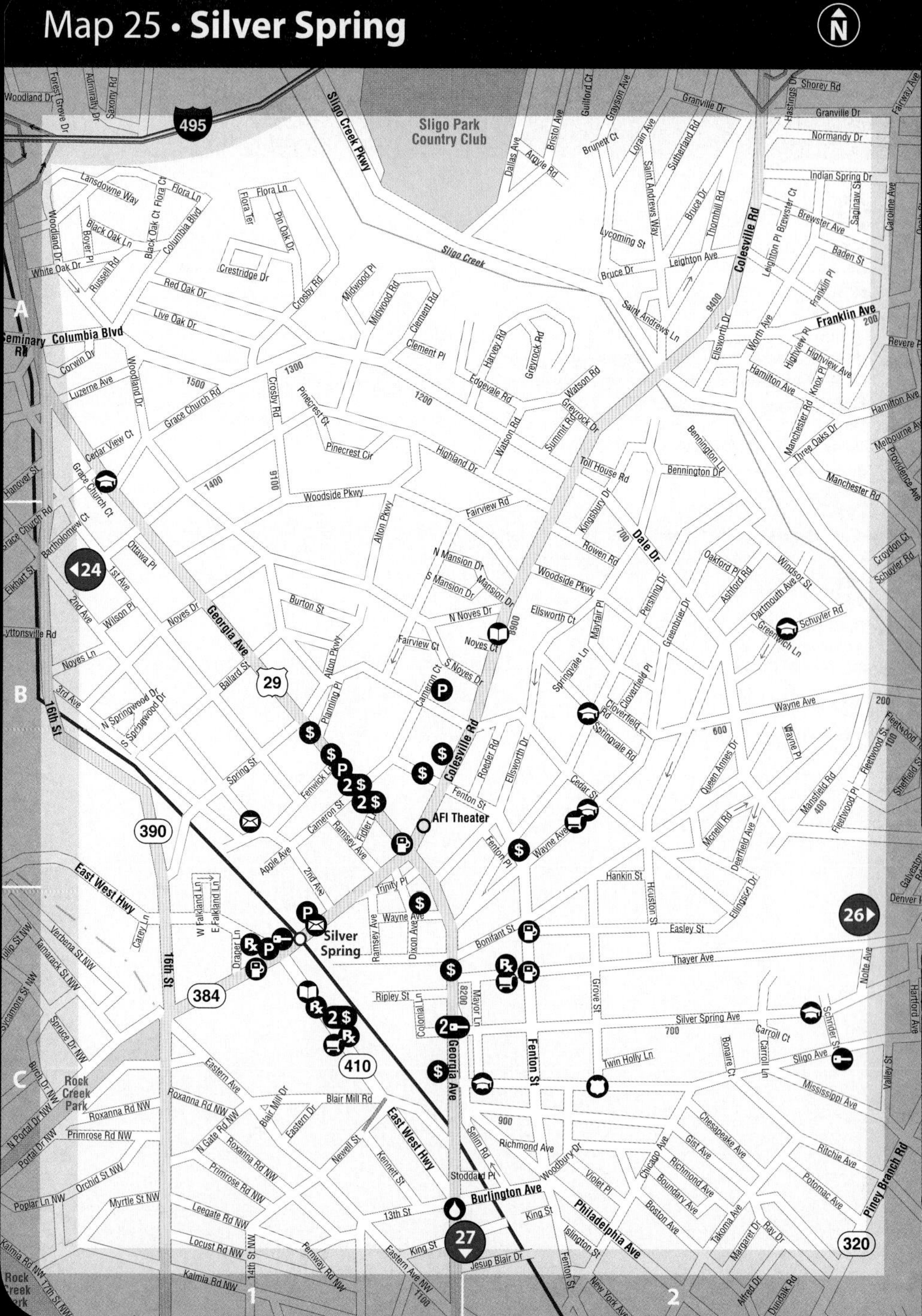
N
Sligo Park Country Club
Sligo Creek Pkwy
Sligo Creek
495
Colesville Rd
Georgia Ave
29
390
384
410
320
16th St
East West Hwy
Philadelphia Ave
Burlington Ave
Franklin Ave
Dale Dr
Woodside Pkwy
Wayne Ave
Fenton St
AFI Theater
Silver Spring
Rock Creek Park
Piney Branch Rd
24
26
27
A
B
C
1
2

Essentials

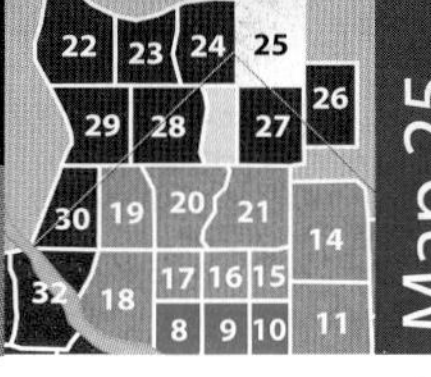

Some call downtown Silver Spring cute, others call it corny. Both descriptions are accurate. With Rockwellesque storefronts mixed with Red Lobsteresque restaurants, this "city" plays heavily to its target audience: people who value community and predictability. To its credit, the neighborhood does boast an ethnically diverse population and a number of restaurants reflect this. But dinner/movie/late night cup of coffee is the typical Friday night lineup.

Banks

- **Adams National** • 8121 Georgia Ave
- **Bank of America** • 8511 Georgia Ave
- **Bank of America** • 8788 Georgia Ave
- **BB&T** • 1100 Wayne Ave
- **Chevy Chase** • 8315 Georgia Ave
- **Chevy Chase** • 8676 Georgia Ave
- **Chevy Chase (ATM)** • 1280 East West Hwy
- **Eagle Bank** • 8677 Georgia Ave
- **M&T Bank** • 8737 Colesville Rd
- **Provident Bank** • 8730 Georgia Ave
- **Sun Trust** • 1286 East West Hwy
- **Sun Trust** • 8700 Georgia Ave
- **United Bank** • 8630 Fenton St
- **Wachovia** • 8701 Georgia Ave

Car Rental

- **Budget** • 619 Sligo Ave •
- **Enterprise** • 8208 Georgia Ave • 301-563-6500
- **Enterprise** • 8401 Colesville Rd • 301-495-4120
- **Hertz** • 8203 Georgia Ave • 301-588-0608

Car Washes

- **Mr Wash** • 7996 Georgia Ave

Gas Stations

- **Citgo** • 8333 Fenton St
- **Crown** • 8600 Georgia Ave
- **Exxon** • 8301 Fenton St
- **Exxon** • 8384 Colesville Rd

Landmarks

- **AFI Theater** • 8633 Colesville Rd

Libraries

- **NOAA Central Library** • 1315 East West Hwy
- **Silver Spring Library** • 8901 Colesville Rd

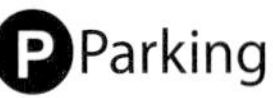

Parking

Pharmacies

- **CVS (24 hours)** • 1290 East West Hwy
- **Giant Food Pharmacy** • 1280 East West Hwy
- **Rite Aid** • 1411 East West Hwy
- **Safeway** • 909 Thayer Ave

Police

- **3rd District - Silver Spring** • 801 Sligo Ave

Post Offices

- **Silver Spring Finance Centre** • 8455 Colesville Rd
- **Silver Spring Main Office** • 8616 2nd Ave

Schools

- **Chelsea** • 711 Pershing Dr
- **East Silver Spring Elementary** • 631 Silver Spring Ave
- **Grace Episcopal Day** • 9115 Georgia Ave
- **Sligo Creek Elementary** • 500 Schuyler Rd
- **St Michael's Elementary** • 824 Wayne Ave
- **The Nora** • 955 Sligo Ave

Supermarkets

- **Giant Food** • 1280 East West Hwy
- **Safeway** • 909 Thayer Ave
- **Whole Foods Market** • 833 Wayne Ave

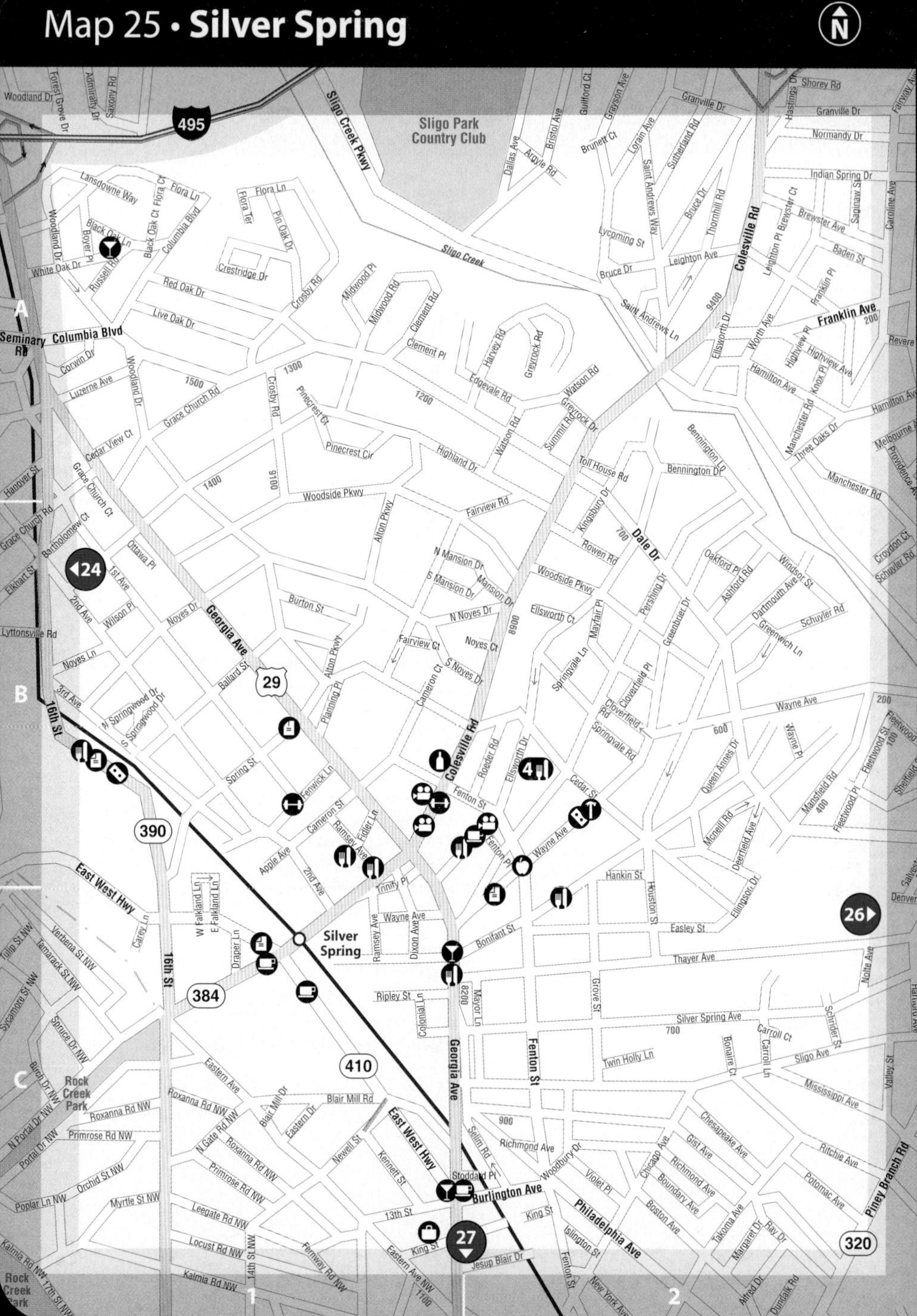

N
495
Sligo Park Country Club
Sligo Creek Pkwy
Sligo Creek
Woodland Dr
Forest Grove Dr
Admiralty Dr
Saxony Rd
Lansdowne Way
Flora Ln
Flora Ct
Flora Ter
Columbia Blvd
Black Oak Ln
Black Oak Ct
Bower Pl
Russell Rd
White Oak Dr
Crestridge Dr
Pin Oak Dr
Red Oak Dr
Live Oak Dr
Crosby Rd
Midwood Pl
Midwood Rd
Clement Rd
Clement Pl
Dallas Ave
Argyle Rd
Bristol Ave
Guilford Ct
Grayson Ave
Brunett Ct
Lorain Ave
Saint Andrews Way
Sutherland Rd
Bruce Dr
Thornhill Rd
Lycoming St
Leighton Ave
Saint Andrews Ln
Ellsworth Dr
Colesville Rd
9400
Shorey Rd
Granville Dr
Hastings Dr
Normandy Dr
Indian Spring Dr
Brewster Ct
Brewster Ave
Saginaw St
Caroline Ave
Baden St
Leighton Pl
Franklin Pl
Franklin Ave
200
Worth Ave
Highview Pl
Highview Ave
Hamilton Ave
Knox Pl
Manchester Rd
Three Oaks Dr
Melbourne Ave
Providence Ave
Reverie
Fairway Ave
A
Seminary Rd
Columbia Blvd
Corwin Dr
Luzerne Ave
1500
Grace Church Rd
1300
Pinecrest Ct
Pinecrest Cir
1200
Edgevale Rd
Harvey Rd
Greyrock Rd
Watson Rd
Summit Rd
Greyrock Dr
Highland Dr
Toll House Rd
Bennington Ln
Bennington Dr
Cedar View Ct
Grace Church Ct
Hanover St
Grace Church Rd
Bartholomew Ct
1400
9100
Woodside Pkwy
Fairview Rd
Alton Pkwy
Kingsbury Dr
700
Dale Dr
Rowen Rd
Oakford Pl
Ashford Rd
Windsor St
Croydon Ct
Schuyler Rd
24
Elkhart St
Ottawa Pl
1st Ave
2nd Ave
Wilson Pl
Noyes Dr
Georgia Ave
N Mansion Dr
S Mansion Dr
Mansion Dr
Woodside Pkwy
Burton St
N Noyes Dr
Ellsworth Ct
Mayfair Pl
Pershing Dr
Dartmouth Ave
Schuyler Rd
Greenwich Ln
Lyttonsville Rd
Noyes Ln
8900
Fairview Ct
Noyes Ct
S Noyes Dr
Springvale Ln
Greenbriar Dr
Cloverfield Pl
Cloverfield Rd
B
3rd Ave
16th St
N Springwood Dr
S Springwood Dr
Ballard St
29
Planning Pl
Cameron Ct
Colesville Rd
Roeder Rd
Ellsworth Dr
Springvale Rd
Wayne Ave
200
600
Wayne Pl
Fleetwood St
Sheffield
Queen Annes Dr
Spring St
Fenwick Ln
Fenton St
Cedar St
4
Mansfield Rd
400
Fleetwood Pl
390
Cameron St
Ramsey Ave
Fidler Ln
Fenton Pl
Wayne Ave
Mcneill Rd
Deerfield Ave
Apple Ave
2nd Ave
Trinity Pl
Hankin St
Houston St
Ellingsor Dr
East West Hwy
W Falkland Ln
E Falkland Ln
Carey Ln
Draper Ln
16th St
Silver Spring
Ramsey Ave
Wayne Ave
Dixon Ave
Bonifant St
Easley St
26
Denver
Galveston
Tulip St NW
Verbena St NW
Tamarack St NW
Sycamore St NW
384
Thayer Ave
Ripley St
Colonial Ln
8200
Mayor Ln
Grove St
Nolte Ave
Hartford Ave
Spruce Dr NW
Silver Spring Ave
700
Carroll Ct
Schrider St
Georgia Ave
Fenton St
Carroll Ln
Bonaire Ct
Twin Holly Ln
Sligo Ave
Valley St
410
Eastern Ave
Birch Dr NW
C
Rock Creek Park
Blair Mill Dr
Blair Mill Rd
Roxanna Rd NW
Eastern Dr
East West Hwy
Mississippi Ave
N Portal Dr NW
Primrose Rd NW
N Gate Rd NW
Roxanna Rd NW
Newell St
Kennett St
900
Selim Rd
Richmond Ave
Woodbury Dr
Chesapeake Ave
Gist Ave
Ritchie Ave
Piney Branch Rd
Portal Dr NW
Orchid St NW
Primrose Rd NW
Stoddard Pl
Violet Pl
Chicago Ave
Richmond Ave
Boundary Ave
Potomac Ave
Poplar Ln NW
Myrtle St NW
Burlington Ave
Philadelphia Ave
Leegate Rd NW
13th St
King St
Boston Ave
Takoma Ave
Margaret Dr
Ray Dr
320
14th St NW
Locust Rd NW
Fernway Rd
27
King St
Jesup Blair Dr
Islington St
Fenton St
Kalmia Rd NW
17th St NW
Kalmia Rd NW
Eastern Ave NW
1100
New York Ave
Alfred Dr
Dundalk Rd
Rock Creek Park
1
2

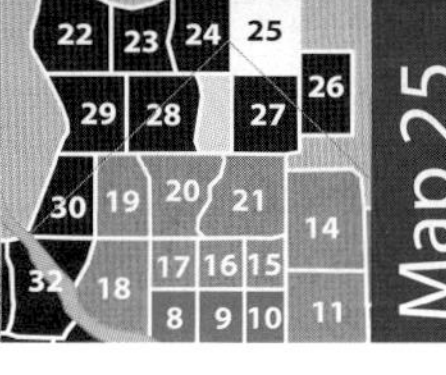

Playing obscure indie flicks as well as timeless gems, the American Film Institute Theater is the reason to come to Silver Spring. Hell, it's the reason to move to Silver Spring. While in town you can take advantage of a number of pre-flick eateries of big-city caliber. Our picks are Bombay Gaylord and Roger Miller Restaurant. Small caveat to alcoholics: Silver Spring bars are few and far between.

Coffee

- **Caribou Coffee** • 1316 East West Hwy
- **Mayorga Coffee Factory** • 8040 Georgia Ave
- **Starbucks** • 8399 Colesville Rd
- **Starbucks** • 915 Ellsworth Dr

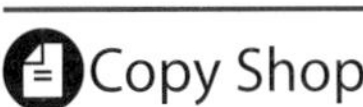

Copy Shops

- **ABC Imaging (8am-6pm)** • 1300 Spring St
- **Copy Connection (8:30am-6pm)** • 962 Wayne Ave
- **Kinko's (24 hours)** • 1407 East West Hwy
- **UPS Store (9am-7pm)** • 8639 16th St

Farmer's Markets

- **Silver Spring Farmer's Market** • Fenton St & Wayne Ave

Gyms

- **Curves** • 1320 Fenwick Ln
- **Gold's Gym** • 8661 Colesville Rd

Hardware Stores

- **Strosniders Hardware Store** • 815 Wayne Ave

Liquor Stores

- **Silver Spring Liquor Store** • 8715 Colesville Rd

Movie Theaters

- **AFI Silver Theater** • 8633 Colesville Rd
- **AMC City Place 10** • 8661 Colesville Rd
- **The Majestic 20** • 900 Ellsworth Dr

Nightlife

- **Mayorga** • 8040 Georgia Ave
- **Quarry House Tavern** • 8401 Georgia Ave

Restaurants

- **Austin Grill** • 919 Ellsworth Dr
- **Bombay Gaylord** • 8401 Georgia Ave
- **Cubano's** • 1201 Fidler Ln
- **Eggspectation** • 923 Ellsworth Dr
- **El Aguila** • 8649 16th St
- **Lebanese Taverna** • 933 Ellsworth Dr
- **Mi Rancho** • 8701 Ramsey Ave
- **Potbelly Sandwich Works** • 917 Ellsworth Dr
- **Roger Miller Restaurant** • 941 Bonifant St
- **Romano's Macaroni Grill** • 931 Ellsworth Dr

Shopping

- **Kingsbury Chocolates** • 1017 King St

Video Rental

- **Blockbuster Video** • 8601 16th St
- **Hollywood Video** • 825 Wayne Ave

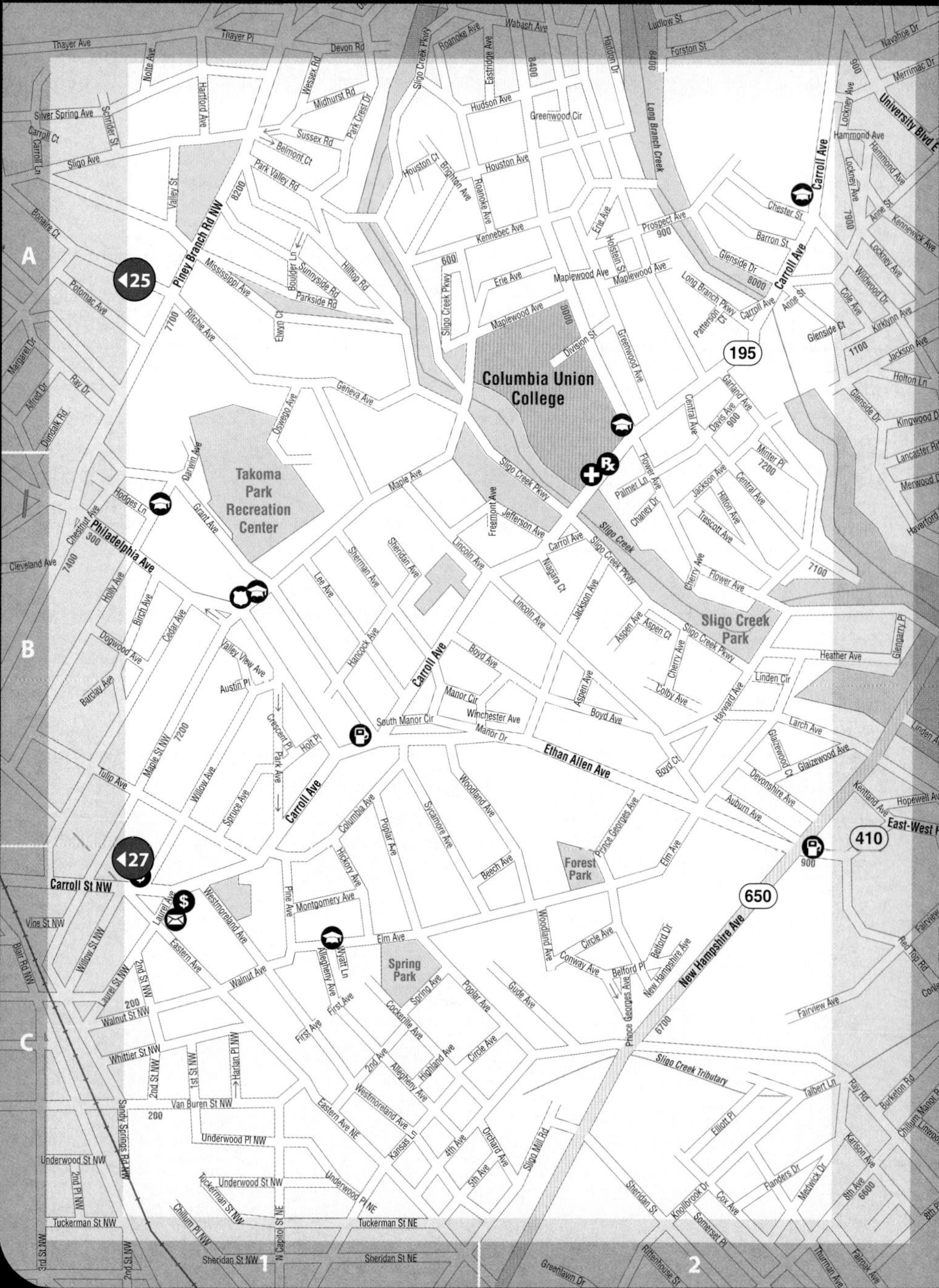

Map 26 • Takoma Park

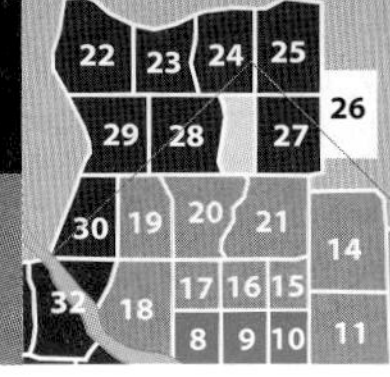

Everybody here likes to call themselves residents of "The People's Republic of Takoma Park," thanks to their liberal ways—it's a designated nuclear-free zone. They are, for the most part, sincere left-wingers. But these well-off suburbanites do have bigger houses and more video stores than most proletariats.

Banks

- **Bank of America** • 6950 Carroll Ave
- **Sun Trust** • 6931 Laurel Ave

Gas Stations

- **Amoco** • 920 East West Hwy
- **Citgo** • 7224 Carroll Ave

Hospitals

- **Washington Adventist** • 7600 Carroll Ave

Pharmacies

- **Washington Adventist Family Pharmacy** • 7610 Carroll Ave

Police

- **Takoma Park Police Dept** • 7500 Maple Ave

Post Offices

- **Takoma Park** • 6909 Laurel Ave

Schools

- **Columbia Union College** • 7600 Flower Ave
- **John Nevins Andrews** • 117 Elm Ave
- **Piney Branch Elementary** • 7510 Maple Ave
- **Takoma Academy** • 8120 Carroll Ave
- **Takoma Park Elementary** • 7511 Holly Ave

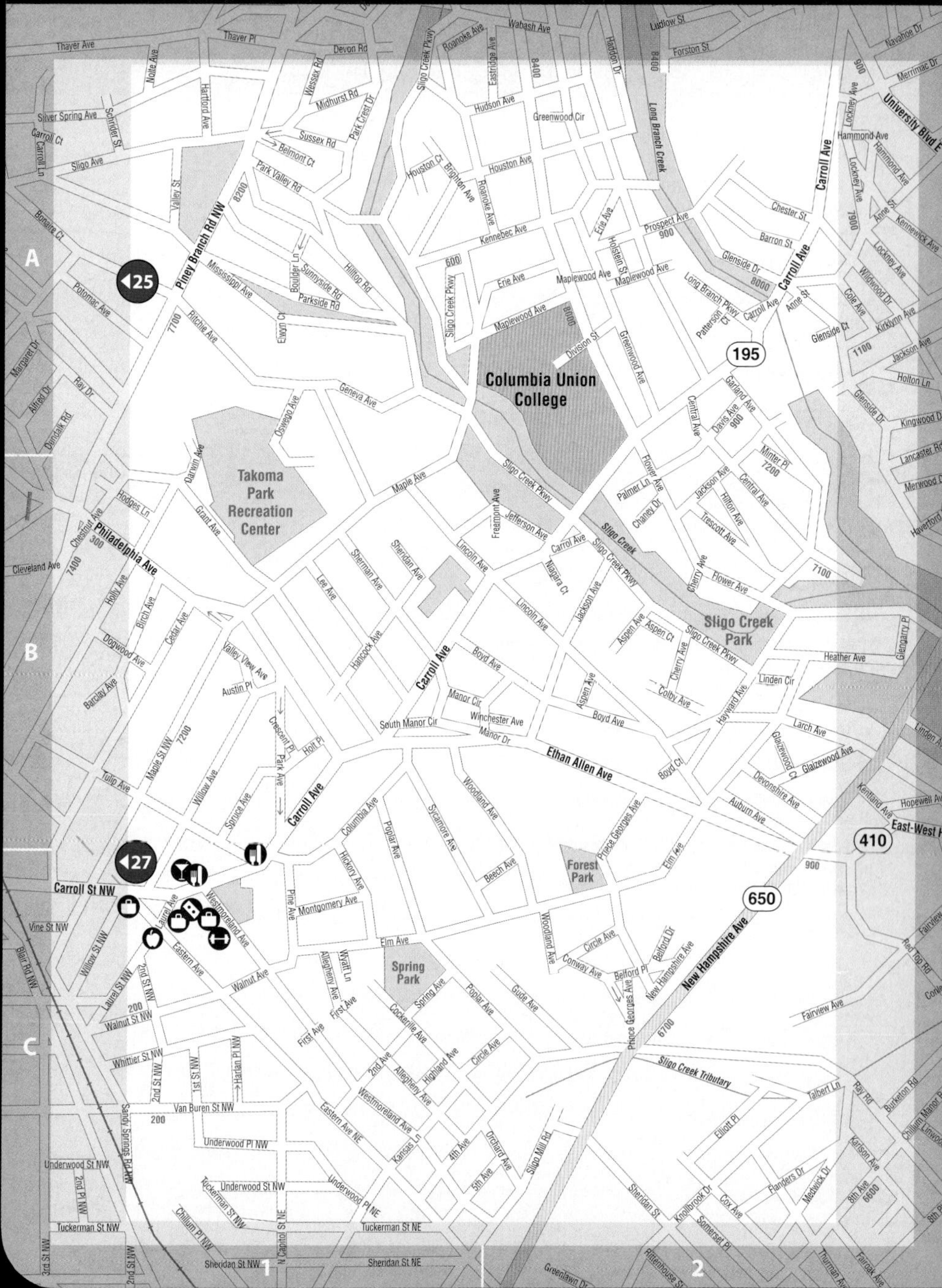

Map 26 • Takoma Park

N

A
B
C
1
2

◀25
◀27

Columbia Union College
Takoma Park Recreation Center
Sligo Creek Park
Forest Park
Spring Park

195
410
650

Long Branch Creek
Sligo Creek
Sligo Creek Tributary

Thayer Ave
Thayer Pl
Devon Rd
Wabash Ave
Ludlow St
Forston St
Navahoe Dr
Merrimac Dr
University Blvd E
Nolte Ave
Hartford Ave
Wessex Rd
Midhurst Rd
Roanoke Ave
Eastridge Ave
Sligo Creek Pkwy
Haddon Dr
Silver Spring Ave
Schrider St
Carroll Ct
Carroll Ln
Sligo Ave
Sussex Rd
Park Crest Dr
Belmont Ct
Park Valley Rd
Hudson Ave
Greenwood Cir
Houston Ct
Brighton Ave
Houston Ave
Hammond Ave
Lockney Ave
Carroll Ave
Chester St
Barron St
Glenside Dr
Anne St
Kennewick Ave
Bonaire Ct
Valley St
Piney Branch Rd NW
Mississippi Ave
Boulder Ln
Sunnyside Rd
Hilltop Rd
Parkside Rd
Kennebec Ave
Erie Ave
Holstein St
Prospect Ave
Maplewood Ave
Long Branch Pkwy
Patterson Ct
Cole Ave
Wildwood Dr
Kirklynn Ave
Glenside Ct
Jackson Ave
Holton Ln
Potomac Ave
Elwyn Ct
Ritchie Ave
Division St
Greenwood Ave
Garland Ave
Davis Ave
Central Ave
Kingwood Dr
Lancaster Rd
Merwood Dr
Haverford
Margaret Dr
Alfred Dr
Ray Dr
Dundalk Rd
Geneva Ave
Oswego Ave
Darwin Ave
Maple Ave
Fremont Ave
Jefferson Ave
Minter Pl
Flower Ave
Palmer Ln
Chaney Dr
Hilton Ave
Trescott Ave
Hodges Ln
Chestnut Ave
Philadelphia Ave
Grant Ave
Sherman Ave
Sheridan Ave
Lincoln Ave
Carrol Ave
Niagara Ct
Cherry Ave
Cleveland Ave
Holly Ave
Birch Ave
Cedar Ave
Lee Ave
Aspen Ave
Aspen Ct
Glengarry Pl
Heather Ave
Dogwood Ave
Valley View Ave
Hancock Ave
Boyd Ave
Linden Cir
Barclay Ave
Austin Pl
Manor Cir
Winchester Ave
Colby Ave
Hayward Ave
Larch Ave
Linden Ave
Crescent Pl
Holt Pl
South Manor Cir
Manor Dr
Ethan Allen Ave
Glaizewood Ct
Glaizewood Ave
Maple St NW
Park Ave
Boyd Ct
Devonshire Ave
Kentland Ave
Hopewell Ave
East-West Hwy
Tulip Ave
Willow Ave
Spruce Ave
Columbia Ave
Poplar Ave
Sycamore Ave
Woodland Ave
Prince Georges Ave
Auburn Ave
Hickory Ave
Beech Ave
Elm Ave
Carroll St NW
Vine St NW
Laurel Ave
Westmoreland Ave
Pine Ave
Montgomery Ave
Fairview Ave
Red Top Rd
Blair Rd NW
Willow St NW
Eastern Ave
Walnut Ave
Allegheny Ave
Wyatt Ln
Conway Ave
Circle Ave
Belford Dr
Belford Pl
New Hampshire Ave
Laurel St NW
2nd St NW
First Ave
Spring Ave
Gude Ave
Walnut St NW
Cockerille Ave
Whittier St NW
Harlan Pl NW
1st St NW
2nd Ave
Highland Ave
Talbert Ln
Ray Rd
Burketon Rd
Chillum Manor Rd
Van Buren St NW
Sandy Springs Rd NW
Eastern Ave NE
Underwood Pl NW
Kansas Ln
4th Ave
Orchard Ave
Sligo Mill Rd
Elliott Pl
Karlson Ave
Underwood St NW
2nd Pl NW
Tuckerman St NW
5th Ave
Underwood Pl NE
Sheridan St
Knollbrook Dr
Cox Ave
Flanders Dr
Medwick Dr
8th Ave
Chillum Pl NW
N Capitol St
Tuckerman St NE
Somerset Pl
3rd St NW
Sheridan St NW
Sheridan St NE
Greenlawn Dr
Rittenhouse St
Thurman Ave
Fairoak Ave

900
8400
8200
7700
8000
600
1100
7200
7400
300
7100
200
6700
6600

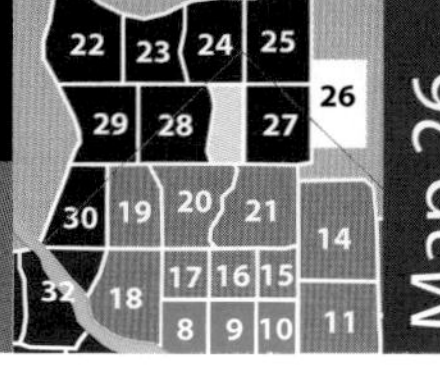

If you're into organic markets and independent shops that sell homemade crafts and tie-dye, endure the long metro ride to spend a few hours here. Once the sun starts setting, catch a train back. It is, after all, a suburb…

Farmer's Markets

- **Takoma Park Farmers Market** • Laurel & Eastern Aves

Gyms

- **Curves** • 7008 Westmoreland Ave

Nightlife

- **Taliano's** • 7001 Carroll Ave

Restaurants

- **Mark's Kitchen** • 7006 Carroll Ave
- **Savory** • 7071 Carroll Ave

Shopping

- **Dan the Music Man** • 6855 Eastern Ave
- **Polly Sue's** • 6915 Laurel Ave
- **Takoma Underground** • 7014 Westmoreland Ave

Video Rental

- **Video American Takoma Park** • 6937 Laurel Ave

N

Walter Reed Army Medical Center
Battleground National Military Cemetery
Rock Creek Golf Course
Fort Slocum Park

16th St NW
Georgia Ave NW
Alaska Ave NW
Piney Branch Rd NW
Eastern Ave NW
Blair Rd
Chestnut St NW
Philadelphia Ave
Carroll St NW
Cedar St NW
Missouri Ave NW
13th St NW
N Dakota Ave NW
Burlington Ave
Kalmia Rd NW
Jonquil St NW
Juniper St NW
Iris St NW
Hemlock St NW
Holly St NW
Geranium St NW
Floral St NW
Fern St NW
North Rd
Elder St NW
Dogwood St NW
Dahlia St NW
Highland Ave NW
Butternut St NW
Aspen St NW
Whittier Pl NW
Whittier St NW
Venable Pl NW
Van Buren St NW
Underwood St NW
Tewkesbury Pl NW
Tuckerman St NW
Somerset Pl NW
Sheridan St NW
Roxboro Pl NW
Rittenhouse St NW
Quintana Pl NW
Quackenbos St NW
Powhatan Pl NW
Peabody St NW
Oneida Pl NW
Oglethorpe St NW
Nicholson St NW
Rock Creek Ford Rd NW
Fort Stevens Dr NW
Luzon Ave NW
Main Dr NW
Sherrill Dr NW
Joyce Rd NW
Manchester Ln NW
Sandy Springs Rd NW
Laurel Ave
Takoma Ave
New York Ave
Albany Ave
Brashear Ave
Baltimore Ave
Cleveland Ave
Tulip Ave
Spring Pl NW
Locust Rd NW
Leegate Rd NW
Primrose Rd NW
Fern Pl NW
Floral Pl NW
Brummel Ct NW
Shepherd Rd
Walnut St NW
Vine St NW
Maple St NW

29
25
26
21
PAGE 208

A
B
C
1
2

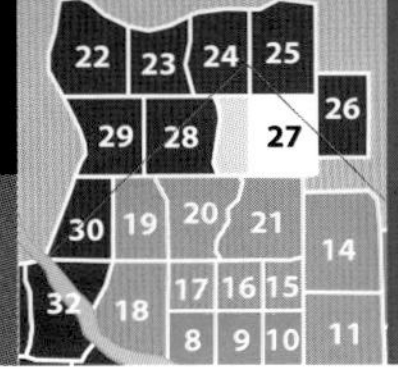

DC's beloved military hospital has now closed its doors for good. We can thank DC's not-so-beloved Secretary of Defense, Donald Rumsfeld.

Banks

- **Chevy Chase (ATM)** • 7600 Takoma Ave
- **Independence Federal Savings** • 7901 Eastern Ave
- **M&T Bank** • 6434 Georgia Ave NW
- **PNC** • 7601 Georgia Ave NW
- **Sun Trust** • 6422 Georgia Ave NW

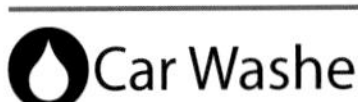

Car Washes

- **Mr Gee's Car Wash** • 6315 Georgia Ave NW

Community Gardens

Gas Stations

- **Amoco** • 6300 Georgia Ave NW
- **Amoco** • 6401 Georgia Ave NW
- **Amoco** • 7000 Blair Rd NW
- **Amoco** • 7605 Georgia Ave NW
- **Exxon** • 6350 Georgia Ave NW
- **Exxon** • 7401 Georgia Ave NW
- **Shell** • 6419 Georgia Ave NW
- **Texaco** • 2300 Columbia Pike

o Landmarks

- **Battleground National Military Cemetery** • 6625 Georgia Ave NW
- **Walter Reed Army Medical Center** • 6900 Georgia Ave NW

Libraries

- **Juanita E Thornton Library** • 7420 Georgia Ave NW
- **Takoma Park Library** • 416 Cedar St NW

Pharmacies

- **CVS** • 110 Carroll Ave NW
- **CVS** • 6514 Georgia Ave NW
- **CVS (24 hrs)** • 6514 Georgia Ave NW
- **Medicine Shoppe** • 7814 Eastern Ave NW
- **Phamily CARE Pharmacy** • 6323 Georgia Ave NW
- **Safeway** • 6500 Piney Branch Rd NW

Police

- **MPDC 4th District Station** • 6001 Georgia Ave NW

Post Offices

- **Brightwood Station** • 6323 Georgia Ave NW
- **Walter Reed Station** • 6800 Georgia Ave NW

Schools

- **A-T Seban Mesut** • 5924 Georgia Ave NW
- **Academia de la Recta Porta** • 7614 Georgia Ave NW
- **Coolidge High** • 6315 5th St NW
- **Jewish Primary Day School of the Nation's Capital** • 6045 16th St NW
- **Lowell** • 1460 Kalmia Rd NW
- **Montgomery College (Takoma Park Campus)** • 7600 Takoma Ave
- **Nativity Catholic Academy** • 6008 Georgia Ave NW
- **Shepherd Elementary** • 7800 14th St NW
- **Strayer University (Takoma Park Campus)** • 6830 Laurel St NW
- **Takoma** • 7010 Piney Branch Rd NW
- **Takoma Park Middle** • 7611 Piney Branch Rd NW
- **The Bridges Academy** • 6119 Georgia Ave NW
- **Washington Theological Union** • 6896 Laurel St NW
- **Whittier Elementary** • 6201 5th St NW

Supermarkets

- **Safeway** • 6500 Piney Branch Rd NW

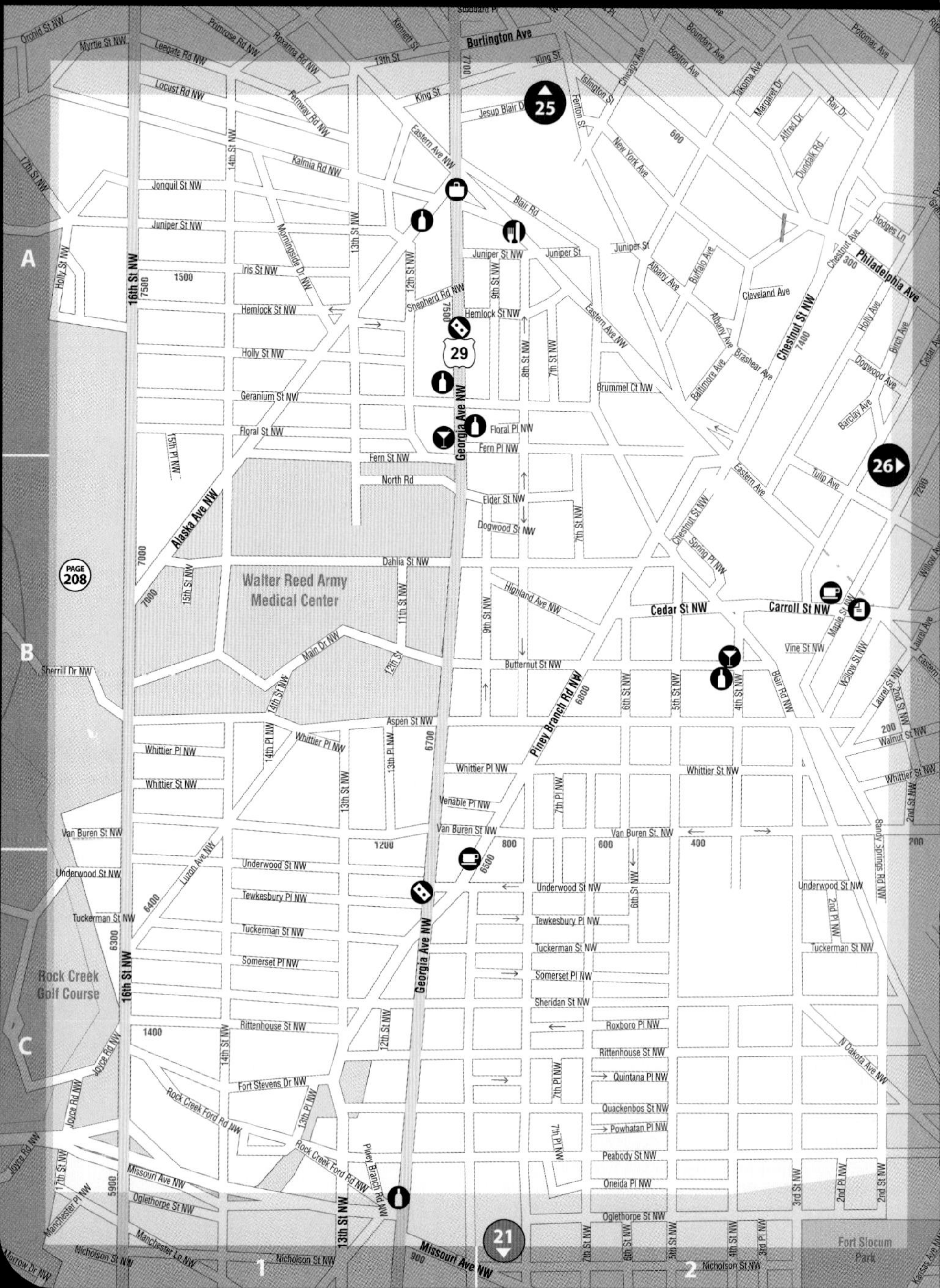

Map 27 • Walter Reed

Walter Reed Army Medical Center

Rock Creek Golf Course

Fort Slocum Park

16th St NW
Georgia Ave NW
Alaska Ave NW
Piney Branch Rd NW
Blair Rd
Eastern Ave NW
Philadelphia Ave
Chestnut St NW
Cedar St NW
Carroll St NW
Missouri Ave NW
Burlington Ave
N Dakota Ave NW
Rock Creek Ford Rd NW
Sandy Springs Rd NW

25
26
21
PAGE 208

Sundries / Entertainment

The back roads are pleasantly sleepy for the families who live here, while the major road that cuts through caters to commuters, who use it as a speedway from the beltway to downtown. If you like your food fast and your banks drive-through, then by all means spend an afternoon here.

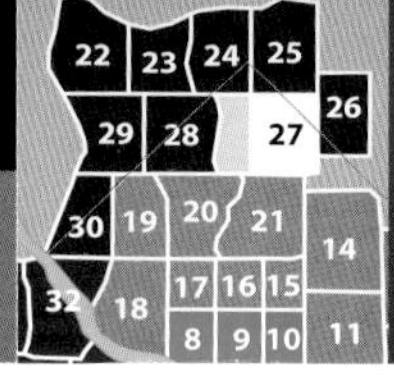

Coffee

- **Savory Takoma Metro** • 314 Carroll St NW
- **Starbucks** • 6500 Piney Branch Rd NW

Copy Shops

- **Community Printing (8am-5pm)** • 6979 Maple St NW

Liquor Stores

- **Brightwood Liquor Store** • 5916 Georgia Ave NW
- **Cork'n Bottle Liquors** • 7421 Georgia Ave NW
- **Mayfair Liquor** • 7312 Georgia Ave NW
- **Morris Miller Liquors** • 7804 Alaska Ave NW
- **S&S Liquors** • 6925 4th St NW

Nightlife

- **Charlie's** • 7307 Georgia Ave NW
- **Takoma Station Tavern** • 6914 4th St NW

Restaurants

- **Blair Mansion Inn/Murder Mystery Dinner Theatre** • 7711 Eastern Ave

Shopping

- **KB News Emporium** • 7898 Georgia Ave

Video Rental

- **Blockbuster Video** • 6428 Georgia Ave NW
- **Royce's** • 7445 Georgia Ave NW

Columbia Country Club
Chevy Chase Country Club
Rock Creek Park
Pinehurst Parkway
Pinehurst Circle NW
Chevy Chase Circle NW
Avalon Theatre
Little Forest Park
Muhlenberg Park
Connecticut Ave NW
Western Ave NW
Brookville Rd
Utah Ave NW
Nebraska Ave NW
Oregon Ave NW
Broad Branch Rd NW
Military Rd NW
Chevy Chase Pkwy NW
PAGE 208
23
24
29
20
A
B
C
1
2

Essentials

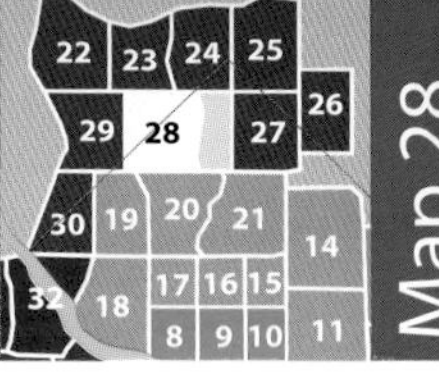

You'll have to have a bank account on par with the comedian of the same name if you want to settle here, the poshest of the city's Maryland suburbs. (Don't bother debating the point with Bethesda folks.)

Banks

- **Chevy Chase** • 5714 Connecticut Ave NW
- **Citibank** • 5700 Connecticut Ave NW
- **M&T Bank** • 5630 Connecticut Ave NW
- **PNC** • 5530 Connecticut Ave NW
- **Wachovia** • 5701 Connecticut Ave NW

Gas Stations

- **Exxon** • 5521 Connecticut Ave NW

Landmarks

- **Avalon Theatre** • 5612 Connecticut Ave NW

Libraries

- **Chevy Chase Library** • 5625 Connecticut Ave NW

Pharmacies

- **Brookville CARE Pharmacy** • 7025 Brookville Rd
- **Chevy Chase Pharmacy** • 3812 Northampton St NW
- **CVS** • 5550 Connecticut Ave NW
- **Safeway** • 5545 Connecticut Ave NW

Police

- **Chevy Chase Village Police** • 5906 Connecticut Ave NW

Post Offices

- **Chevy Chase Branch** • 5910 Connecticut Ave NW
- **Northwest Station** • 5636 Connecticut Ave NW

Schools

- **Blessed Sacrament Elementary** • 5841 Chevy Chase Pkwy NW
- **Chevy Chase Elementary** • 4015 Rosemary St
- **Episcopal Center for Children** • 5901 Utah Ave NW
- **Lafayette Elementary** • 5701 Broad Branch Rd NW
- **St John's College High** • 2607 Military Rd NW

Supermarkets

- **Magruder's** • 5626 Connecticut Ave NW
- **Safeway** • 5545 Connecticut Ave NW

Map 28 • Chevy Chase

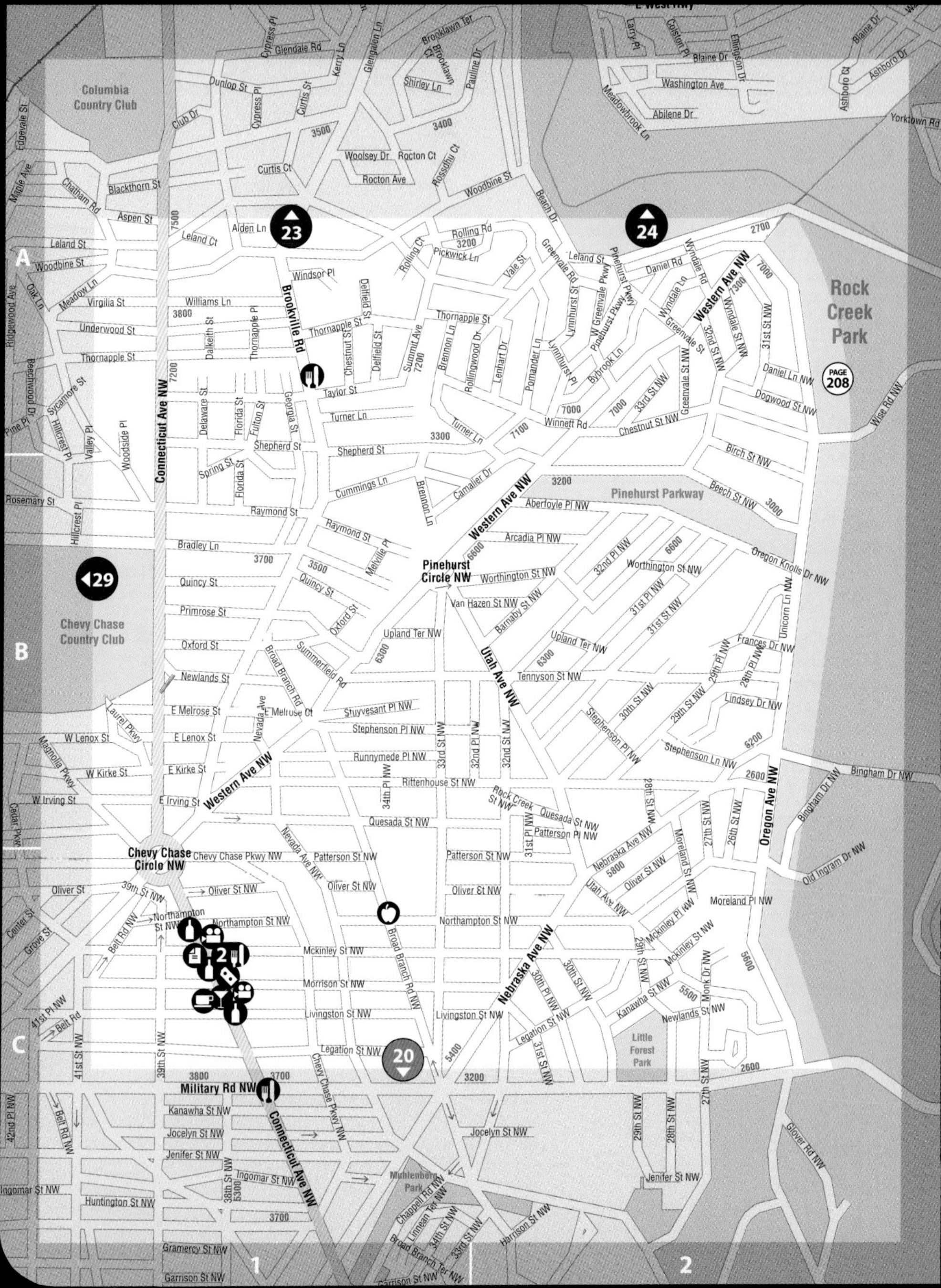

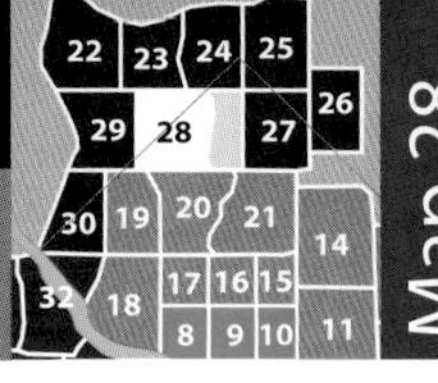

Connecticut Avenue is where the locals go to mingle with riff-raff. Magruder's is one of several pre-Whole Foods gourmet shops with precious produce, and the liquor stores have impressive wine collections. But the family atmosphere here is lighter than Wisconsin Avenue's high-end retail to the west. Here, you can get a bagel in peace or order a milkshake at American City Diner and slurp it down while watching a lousy projection of an old Hitchcock flick.

Coffee

- **Starbucks** • 5500 Connecticut Ave NW

Copy Shops

- **UPS Store (8:45am-6:30pm)** • 5505 Connecticut Ave NW

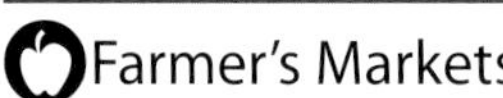

Farmer's Markets

- **Chevy Chase Farmer's Market** • Broad Branch Rd NW & Northampton St NW

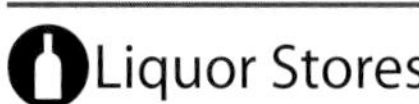

Liquor Stores

- **Chevy Chase Wine & Spirits** • 5544 Connecticut Ave NW
- **Circle Liquors of Chevy Chase** • 5501 Connecticut Ave NW
- **Magruder's Produce** • 5626 Connecticut Ave NW

Movie Theaters

- **American City Movie Diner** • 5532 Connecticut Ave NW
- **Avalon Theatre** • 5612 Connecticut Ave NW

Nightlife

- **Chevy Chase Lounge** • 5510 Connecticut Ave NW

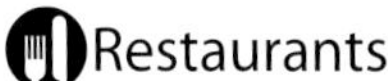

Restaurants

- **American City Diner of Washington** • 5332 Connecticut Ave NW
- **Arucola** • 5534 Connecticut Ave NW
- **Bread & Chocolate** • 5542 Connecticut Ave NW
- **La Ferme** • 7101 Brookville Rd

Video Rental

- **Potomac Video** • 5536 Connecticut Ave NW

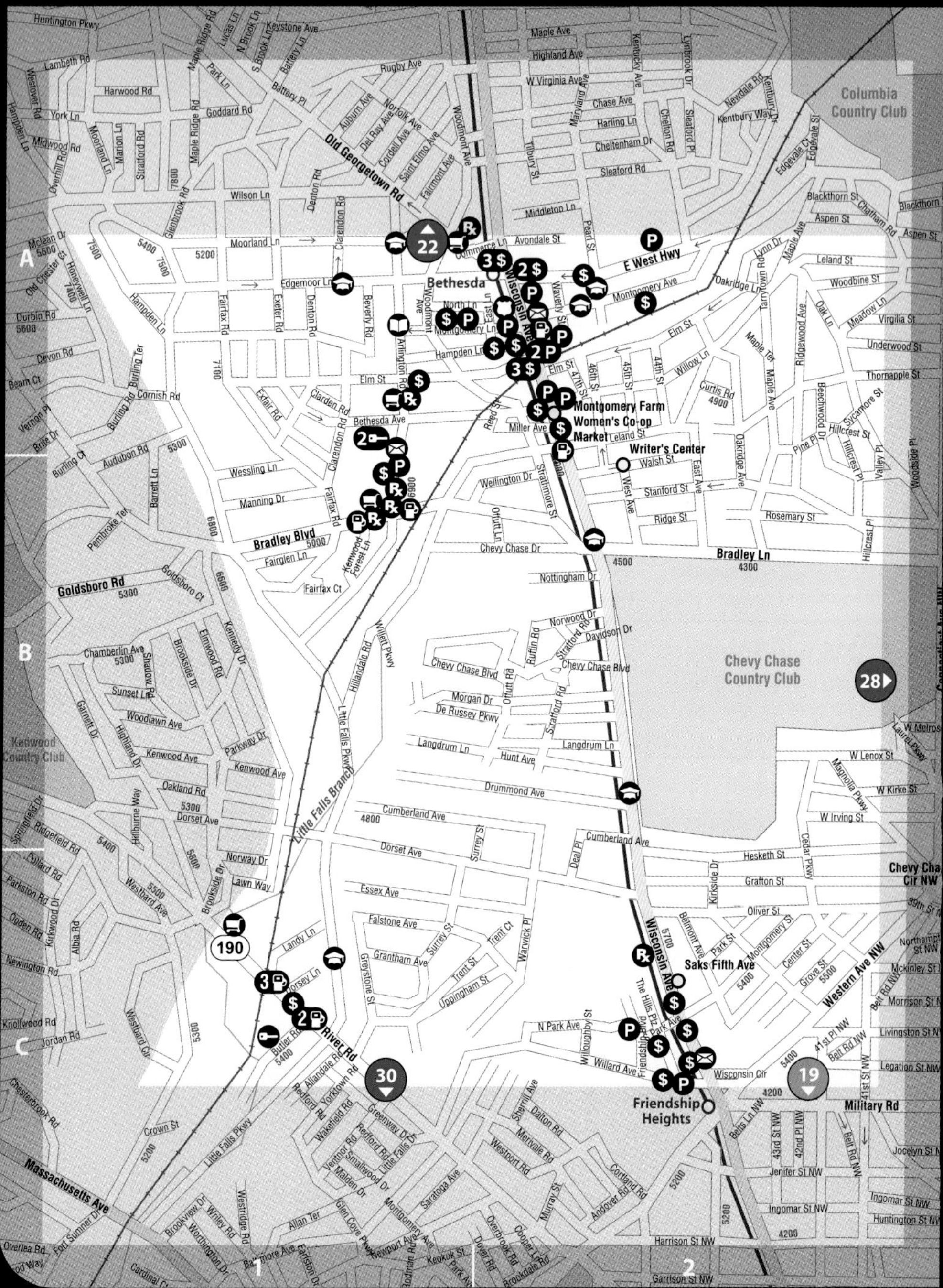

Map 29 • Bethesda / Chevy Chase Business

Bethesda

Montgomery Farm Women's Co-op Market

Writer's Center

Saks Fifth Ave

Friendship Heights

Columbia Country Club

Chevy Chase Country Club

Kenwood Country Club

Wisconsin Ave

E West Hwy

Old Georgetown Rd

Bradley Blvd

Bradley Ln

Goldsboro Rd

River Rd

Massachusetts Ave

Western Ave NW

Military Rd

Little Falls Branch

Little Falls Pkwy

Chevy Chase Cir NW

22

28

30

19

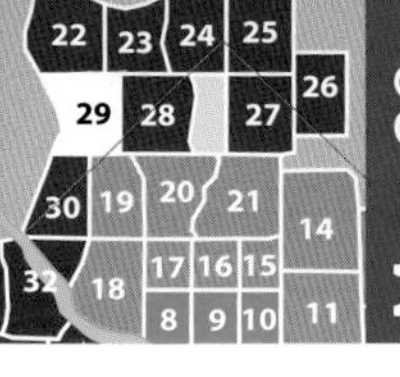

They may not let you in their country club, but if you have a credit card they'll let you in their stores. Downtown Bethesda (Map 22) is really part of the same area and will give you a few more options. You'll need them.

Banks

- **Bank of America** • 4411 S Park Ave
- **Bank of America** • 5135 River Rd
- **Bank of America** • 7316 Wisconsin Ave
- **BB&T** • 4719 Hampden Ln
- **Chevy Chase** • 4708 Bethesda Ave
- **Chevy Chase** • 5476 Wisconsin Ave
- **Chevy Chase** • 7501 Wisconsin Ave
- **Chevy Chase (ATM)** • 7142 Arlington Rd
- **Chevy Chase (ATM)** • 7500 Old Georgetown Rd
- **Independence Federal Savings** • 5530 Wisconsin Ave
- **M&T Bank** • 4800 Hampden Ln
- **Mellon Bank** • 2 Bethesda Metro Ctr
- **Mercantile Potomac Bank** • 4424 Montgomery Ave
- **PNC** • 7235 Wisconsin Ave
- **Presidential Savings** • 4520 East West Hwy
- **Provident Bank** • 5416 Wisconsin Ave
- **Provident Bank** • 7508 Wisconsin Ave
- **Sandy Spring** • 7126 Wisconsin Ave
- **Sun Trust** • 4455 Willard Ave
- **Sun Trust** • 7500 Wisconsin Ave
- **United Bank** • 7250 Wisconsin Ave
- **United Bank** • 7535 Old Georgetown Rd
- **Wachovia** • 6921 Arlington Rd

Car Rental

- **Budget** • 4932 Bethesda Ave •
- **Rent-A-Wreck** • 5455 Butler Rd • 301-654-2252
- **Sears Rent A Car** • 4932 Bethesda Ave • 301-816-6050

Gas Stations

- **Chevron** • 5001 Bradley Blvd
- **Citgo** • 4972 Bradley Blvd
- **Citgo** • 5054 River Rd
- **Exxon** • 5143 River Rd
- **Exxon** • 7100 Wisconsin Ave
- **Exxon** • 7340 Wisconsin Ave
- **Getty** • 5151 River Rd
- **Mobil** • 5201 River Rd
- **Shell** • 5110 River Rd

Landmarks

- **Montgomery Farm Women's Co-op Market** • 7155 Wisconsin Ave
- **Saks Fifth Avenue** • 5555 Wisconsin Ave
- **Writer's Center** • 4508 Walsh St

Libraries

- **Bethesda Library** • 7400 Arlington Rd

Parking

Pharmacies

- **Bradley CARE Drugs/Braden's Pharmacy** • 6900 Arlington Rd
- **CVS (24 hours)** • 6917 Arlington Rd
- **Giant Food Pharmacy** • 7142 Arlington Rd
- **Medical CARE Pharmacy of Chevy Chase** • 5530 Wisconsin Ave
- **Safeway** • 5000 Bradley Blvd
- **Safeway** • 7625 Old Georgetown Rd

Police

- **2nd District - Bethesda** • 7359 Wisconsin Ave

Post Offices

- **Bethesda** • 7400 Wisconsin Ave
- **Bethesda Chevy Chase** • 7001 Arlington Rd
- **Friendship Heights Station** • 5530 Wisconsin Ave

Schools

- **Bethesda Elementary** • 7600 Arlington Rd
- **Concord Hill** • 6050 Wisconsin Ave
- **DeVry University (Bethesda Center)** • 4550 Montgomery Ave
- **Oneness Family** • 6701 Wisconsin Ave
- **Our Lady of Lourdes** • 7500 Pearl St
- **Sidwell Friends Lower** • 5100 Edgemoor Ln
- **Washington Episcopal** • 5600 Little Falls Pkwy

Supermarkets

- **Giant Food** • 7142 Arlington Rd
- **Safeway** • 5000 Bradley Blvd
- **Safeway** • 7625 Old Georgetown Rd
- **Whole Foods Market** • 5269 River Rd

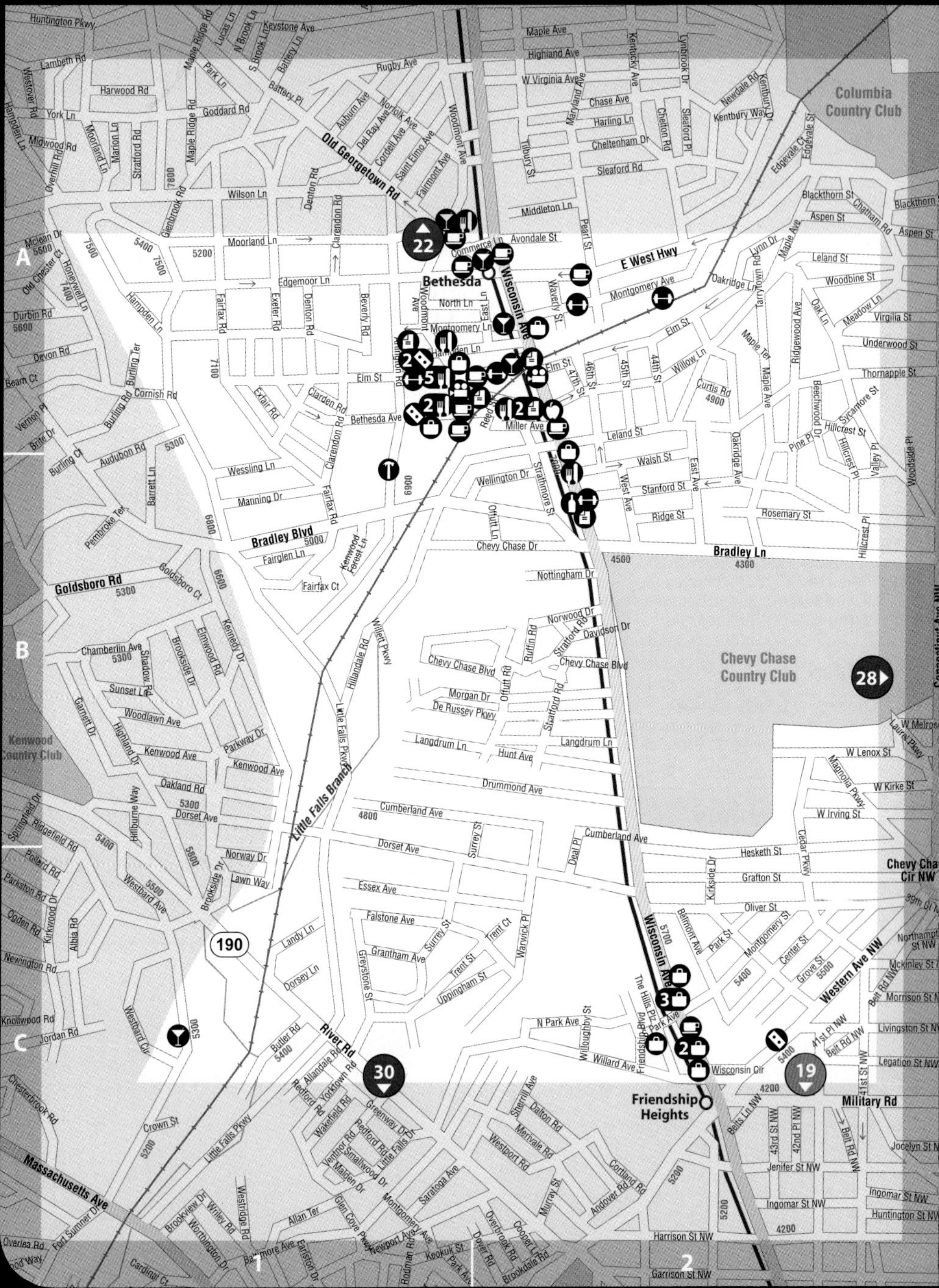
N
Huntington Pkwy
Keystone Ave
Lucas Ln
N Brook Ln
S Brook Ln
Battery Ln
Battery Pl
Maple Ridge Rd
Park Ln
Lambeth Rd
Westover Rd
Harwood Rd
Rugby Ave
Hampden Ln
York Ln
Goddard Rd
Auburn Ave
Norfolk Ave
Dal Ray Ave
Cordell Ave
Saint Elmo Ave
Fairmont Ave
Woodmont Ave
Midwood Rd
Moorland Ln
Marion Ln
Stratford Rd
Maple Ridge Rd
Old Georgetown Rd
Overhill Rd
Glenbrook Rd
7800
Wilson Ln
Denton Rd
Clarendon Rd
Maple Ave
Highland Ave
W Virginia Ave
Maryland Ave
Kentucky Ave
Lynbrook Dr
Chase Ave
Harling Ln
Cheltenham Dr
Chelton Rd
Seaford Pl
Seaford Rd
Tilbury St
Newdale Rd
Kentbury Dr
Kentbury Way
Edgevale Ct
Edgevale St
Columbia Country Club
Blackthorn St
Aspen St
Chatham Rd
Middleton Ln
Pearl St
Mclean Dr
5600
Old Chester Ct
Honeywell Ln
7500
5400
7500
5200
Moorland Ln
Commerce Ln
Avondale St
22
Bethesda
Wisconsin Ave
E West Hwy
Lynn Dr
Maple Ave
Leland St
Woodbine St
Edgemoor Ln
Hampden Ln
Fairfax Rd
Exeter Rd
Denton Rd
Beverly Rd
Woodmont Ave
North Ln
East Ln
Waverly St
Montgomery Ave
Oakridge Ln
Tarrytown Rd
Durbin Rd
5600
7400
Montgomery Ln
Hampden Ln
Arlington Rd
Elm St
Meadow Ln
Virgilia St
Oak Ln
Ridgewood Ave
Maple Ter
Maple Ave
Willow Ln
Underwood St
Devon Rd
Burling Ter
7100
Elm St
47th St
46th St
45th St
44th St
Thornapple St
Beam Ct
Cornish Rd
Exfair Rd
Clarden Rd
Bethesda Ave
Reed St
Miller Ave
Curtis Rd
4900
Beechwood Dr
Sycamore St
Vernon Pl
Burling Rd
Brite Dr
Hillcrest St
Oakridge Ave
Leland St
Pine Pl
Hillcrest Pl
Valley Pl
Woodside Pl
Burling Ct
Audubon Rd
5300
Wessling Ln
Clarendon Rd
Walsh St
East Ave
Barrett Ln
6900
Wellington Dr
Strathmore St
West Ave
Stanford St
Manning Dr
Fairfax Rd
Ridge St
Rosemary St
Pembroke Ter
6800
Bradley Blvd
5000
Kenwood Forest Ln
Offutt Ln
Chevy Chase Dr
Bradley Ln
4500
4300
Hillcrest Pl
Fairglen Ln
Goldsboro Rd
5300
Goldsboro Ct
6600
Fairfax Ct
Nottingham Dr
Norwood Dr
Stratford Rd
Davidson Dr
Ruffin Rd
Kennedy Dr
Willett Pkwy
Chevy Chase Blvd
Offutt Rd
Chevy Chase Blvd
Chevy Chase Country Club
28
B
Chamberlin Ave
5300
Shadow Rd
Brookside Dr
Elmwood Rd
Hillandale Rd
Morgan Dr
De Russey Pkwy
Stratford Rd
Sunset Ln
Garrett Dr
Woodlawn Ave
Little Falls Pkwy
W Melrose
Laurel Pkwy
Kenwood Country Club
Highland Dr
Kenwood Ave
Parkway Dr
Langdrum Ln
Hunt Ave
Langdrum Ln
W Lenox St
Kenwood Ave
Magnolia Pkwy
Oakland Rd
Drummond Ave
W Kirke St
Hillburne Way
5300
Dorset Ave
Little Falls Branch
Cumberland Ave
4800
W Irving St
Springfield Dr
Ridgefield Rd
5400
5800
Surrey St
Cumberland Ave
Cedar Pkwy
Dorset Ave
Deal Pl
Pollard Rd
Norway Dr
Hesketh St
Chevy Chase Cir NW
Parkston Rd
5500
Westbard Ave
Lawn Way
Brookside Dr
Essex Ave
Kirkside Dr
Grafton St
Kirkwood Dr
39th St
Ogden Rd
Oliver St
Falstone Ave
Trent Ct
Warwick Pl
5700
Belmont Ave
Park St
Montgomery St
Center St
Northampton St NW
Albia Rd
190
Landy Ln
Surrey St
Grantham Ave
Greystone St
5500
Grove St
Newington Rd
Trent St
Dorsey Ln
Uppingham St
5400
Western Ave NW
Mckinley St
Belt Rd NW
The Hills Plz
3
Morrison St NW
Knollwood Rd
Jordan Rd
Westbard Cir
5300
N Park Ave
Willoughby St
Park Ave
Friendship Blvd
41st Pl NW
Livingston St NW
C
Butler Rd
5400
River Rd
Willard Ave
2
Belt Rd NW
Legation St NW
Chesterbrook Rd
Allandale Rd
Redford Rd
Yorktown Rd
30
Wisconsin Cir
5400
19
4200
41st St NW
Military Rd
Friendship Heights
Betts Ln NW
Crown St
Wakefield Rd
Greenway Dr
Sherrill Ave
Dalton Rd
Merivale Rd
Westport Rd
5200
Little Falls Pkwy
Ventnor Rd
Redford Rd
Little Falls
Smallwood Dr
Malden Dr
43rd St NW
42nd Pl NW
Belt Rd NW
Jocelyn St NW
Massachusetts Ave
Saratoga Ave
Cortland Rd
Andover Rd
Murray St
Jenifer St NW
Fort Sumner Dr
Brookview Dr
Wriley Rd
Westridge Rd
Allan Ter
Glen Cove Pkwy
Montgomery Ave
Overbrook Rd
Cooper Ln
5200
Ingomar St NW
Ingomar St NW
Huntington St NW
Overlea Rd
Worthington Dr
Baltimore Ave
Earlston Dr
Newport Ave
Rodman Rd
Keokuk St
Park Ave
Dover Rd
Brookdale Rd
4200
Harrison St NW
Cardinal Ct
1
2
Garrison St NW

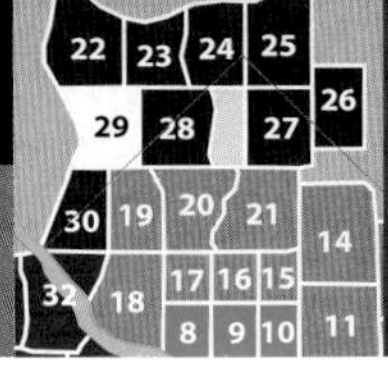

Wisconsin Avenue is a capitalist's dream. But if you're after anything other than high-end mall shopping, it won't be yours. The restaurants tend to be chains and there are plenty of Starbucks to keep you peppy for the next purchase.

Coffee

- **Caribou Coffee** • 7629 Old Georgetown Rd
- **Cosí** • 7251 Woodmont Ave
- **Dunkin' Donuts** • 4810 Bethesda Ave
- **Kudo Beans Café** • 7501 Wisconsin Ave
- **On Time Café** • 4801 Edgemoor Ln
- **Quartermaine Coffee Roasters** • 4817 Bethesda Ave
- **Starbucks** • 4520 East West Hwy
- **Starbucks** • 5454 Wisconsin Ave
- **Starbucks** • 7140 Wisconsin Ave

Copy Shops

- **ABC Imaging (8am-6pm)** • 7315 Wisconsin Ave
- **Best Impressions (8am-5:30pm)** • 4710 Bethesda Ave
- **Kinko's (24 hours)** • 4809 Bethesda Ave
- **Print 1 Printing & Copying (8am-5:30pm)** • 4710 Bethesda Ave
- **Staples (8am-9pm)** • 6800 Wisconsin Ave
- **UPS Store (9am-6pm)** • 4938 Hampden Ln

Farmer's Markets

- **Montgomery Farm Women's Co-op Market** • 7155 Wisconsin Ave

Gyms

- **Bethesda Sport & Health Club** • 4400 Montgomery Ave
- **Curves** • 6831 Wisconsin Ave
- **Fit Inc** • 4963 Elm St
- **Metro Fitness** • 4550 Montgomery Ave
- **Washington Sports Clubs** • 4903 Elm St

Hardware Stores

- **Strosniders Hardware Store** • 6930 Arlington Rd

Liquor Stores

- **Chevy Chase Liquors** • 6831 Wisconsin Ave

Movie Theaters

- **Landmark Bethesda Row Cinema** • 7235 Woodmont Ave
- **Regal Bethesda 10** • 7272 Wisconsin Ave

Nightlife

- **Barking Dog** • 4723 Elm St
- **Flanagan's** • 7637 Old Georgetown Rd
- **Strike Bethesda** • 5353 Westbard Ave
- **Tommy Joe's** • 4714 Montgomery Ln
- **Uncle Jed's Roadhouse** • 7525 Old Georgetown Rd

Restaurants

- **Gifford's** • 7237 Woodmont Ave
- **Green Papaya** • 4922 Elm St
- **Hinode** • 4914 Hampden Ln
- **Jaleo** • 7271 Woodmont Ave
- **Outback Steakhouse** • 7720 Woodmont Ave
- **Persimmon** • 7003 Wisconsin Ave
- **Raku** • 7240 Woodmont Ave
- **Ri-Ra Irish Restaurant Pub** • 4931 Elm St
- **Rio Grande** • 4870 Bethesda Ave
- **Tara Thai** • 4828 Bethesda Ave
- **Thyme Square** • 4735 Bethesda Ave

Shopping

- **Chicos** • 5418 Wisconsin Ave
- **Gianni Versace** • 5454 Wisconsin Ave
- **Marvelous Market** • 4832 Bethesda Ave
- **Mustard Seed** • 7349 Wisconsin Ave
- **Parvizian Masterpieces** • 7034 Wisconsin Ave
- **Relish** • 5454 Wisconsin Ave
- **Saks Fifth Avenue** • 5555 Wisconsin Ave
- **Saks Jandel** • 5510 Wisconsin Ave
- **Sylene** • 4407 S Park Ave
- **Tickled Pink** • 7259 Woodmont Ave
- **Tiffany & Co** • 5500 Wisconsin Ave

Video Rental

- **Blockbuster Video** • 4860 Bethesda Ave
- **Blockbuster Video** • 5440 Western Ave
- **Hollywood Video** • 4920 Hampden Ln

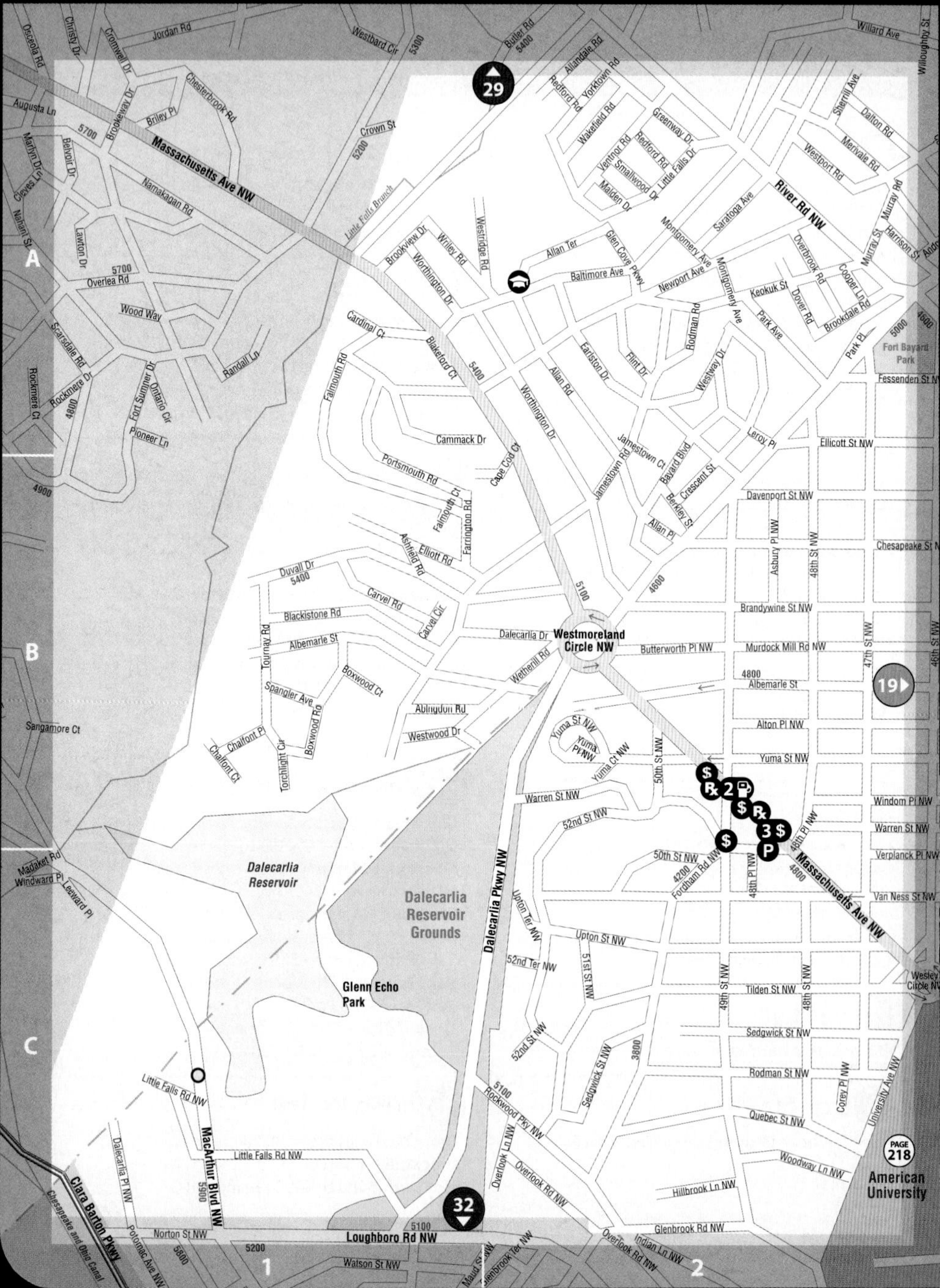

Map 30 • Westmoreland Circle

N

29

A

B

C

19

32

1

2

PAGE 218

American University

Westmoreland Circle NW

Massachusetts Ave NW

River Rd NW

Dalecarlia Pkwy NW

MacArthur Blvd NW

Loughboro Rd NW

Clara Barton Pkwy

Chesapeake and Ohio Canal

Dalecarlia Reservoir

Dalecarlia Reservoir Grounds

Glenn Echo Park

Fort Bayard Park

Wesley Circle NW

Little Falls Branch

Osceola Rd
Christy Dr
Cromwell Dr
Jordan Rd
Westbard Cir
5300
Butler Rd
5400
Willard Ave
Willoughby St
Allandale Rd
Yorktown Rd
Redford Rd
Augusta Ln
Brookeway Dr
Chesterbrook Rd
Briley Pl
Crown St
5200
5700
Marlyn Dr
Belvoir Dr
Cleves Ln
Nahant St
Namakagan Rd
Lawton Dr
Overlea Rd
Wood Way
Scarsdale Rd
Rockmere Dr
Rockmere Ct
4800
Fort Sumner Dr
Ontario Cir
Pioneer Ln
Randall Ln
4900
Wakefield Rd
Greenway Dr
Ventnor Rd
Redford Rd
Smallwood Dr
Little Falls Dr
Malden Dr
Sherrill Ave
Dalton Rd
Merivale Rd
Westport Rd
Murray Rd
Harrison St
Andover
Saratoga Ave
Montgomery Ave
Glen Cove Pkwy
Allan Ter
Baltimore Ave
Newport Ave
Keokuk St
Overbrook Rd
Cooper Ln
Dover Rd
Brookdale Rd
Murray St
5000
4600
Park Ave
Park Pl
Brookview Dr
Wriley Rd
Westridge Rd
Worthington Dr
Cardinal Ct
Blakeford Ct
5400
Falmouth Rd
Rodman Rd
Earlston Dr
Flint Dr
Westway Dr
Allan Rd
Worthington Dr
Fessenden St NW
Cammack Dr
Cape Cod Ct
Portsmouth Rd
Falmouth Ct
Farrington Rd
Jamestown Rd
Jamestown Ct
Bayard Blvd
Crescent St
Berkley St
Allan Pl
Leroy Pl
Ellicott St NW
Davenport St NW
Asbury Pl NW
48th St NW
Chesapeake St NW
Ashfield Rd
Elliott Rd
Duvall Dr
5400
Carvel Rd
Carvel Cir
Blackistone Rd
Tournay Rd
Albemarle St
4600
5100
Brandywine St NW
47th St NW
46th St NW
Dalecarlia Dr
Butterworth Pl NW
Murdock Mill Rd NW
4800
Albemarle St
Wetherill Rd
Boxwood Ct
Spangler Ave
Boxwood Rd
Abingdon Rd
Westwood Dr
Alton Pl NW
Sangamore Ct
Chalfont Pl
Chalfont Ct
Torchlight Cir
Yuma St NW
Yuma Pl NW
Yuma Ct NW
50th St NW
Yuma St NW
Warren St NW
52nd St NW
Windom Pl NW
Warren St NW
48th Pl NW
Verplanck Pl NW
50th St NW
4200
Fordham Rd NW
48th Pl NW
4800
Van Ness St NW
Madaket Rd
Windward Pl
Leeward Pl
Upton Ter NW
Upton St NW
52nd Ter NW
51st St NW
49th St NW
Tilden St NW
48th St NW
52nd St NW
Sedgwick St NW
Sedgwick St NW
3800
Rodman St NW
Corey Pl NW
University Ave NW
Little Falls Rd NW
5100
Rockwood Pky NW
Quebec St NW
Overlook Ln NW
Overlook Rd NW
Woodway Ln NW
Little Falls Rd NW
Dalecarlia Pl NW
5900
Hillbrook Ln NW
5100
Glenbrook Rd NW
Norton St NW
5200
Potomac Ave NW
5000
Watson St NW
Maud St NW
Glenbrook Ter NW
Overlook Rd NW
Indian Ln NW

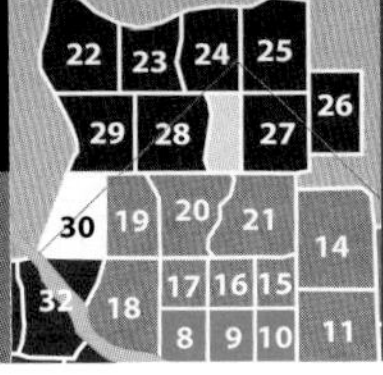

This 'hood is entirely residential and hidden among some of the city's most picturesque parkland. Big names who like their privacy reside here. They are not the types who party with paparazzi. They like the fact that there is really nothing to do here.

Banks

- **Bank of America** • 4301 49th St NW
- **Bank of America (ATM)** • 4851 Massachusetts Ave NW
- **Chevy Chase** • 4860 Massachusetts Ave NW
- **PNC** • 4835 Massachusetts Ave NW
- **United Bank** • 4900 Massachusetts Ave NW
- **Wachovia** • 4841 Massachusetts Ave NW

Gas Stations

- **Exxon** • 4861 Massachusetts Ave NW
- **Exxon** • 4866 Massachusetts Ave NW

Parking

Pharmacies

- **Center CARE Pharmacy** • 4900 Massachusetts Ave NW
- **CVS** • 4851 Massachusetts Ave NW

Schools

- **Westbrook Elementary** • 5110 Allan Ter

Map 30 • Westmoreland Circle

See "Essentials."

Coffee

• **Starbucks** • 4820 Massachusetts Ave NW

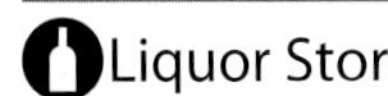

Liquor Stores

• **Wagshal's Delicatessen** •
4855 Massachusetts Ave NW

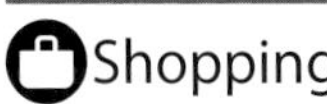

Shopping

• **Crate & Barrel** • 4820 Massachusetts Ave NW

Map 31 • Chesterbrook

Residents of Falls Church say they would rather live here because it's nicer. God help us for saying this, but we'd prefer Falls Church.

Schools

• **Jamestown Elementary** • 3700 N Delaware St

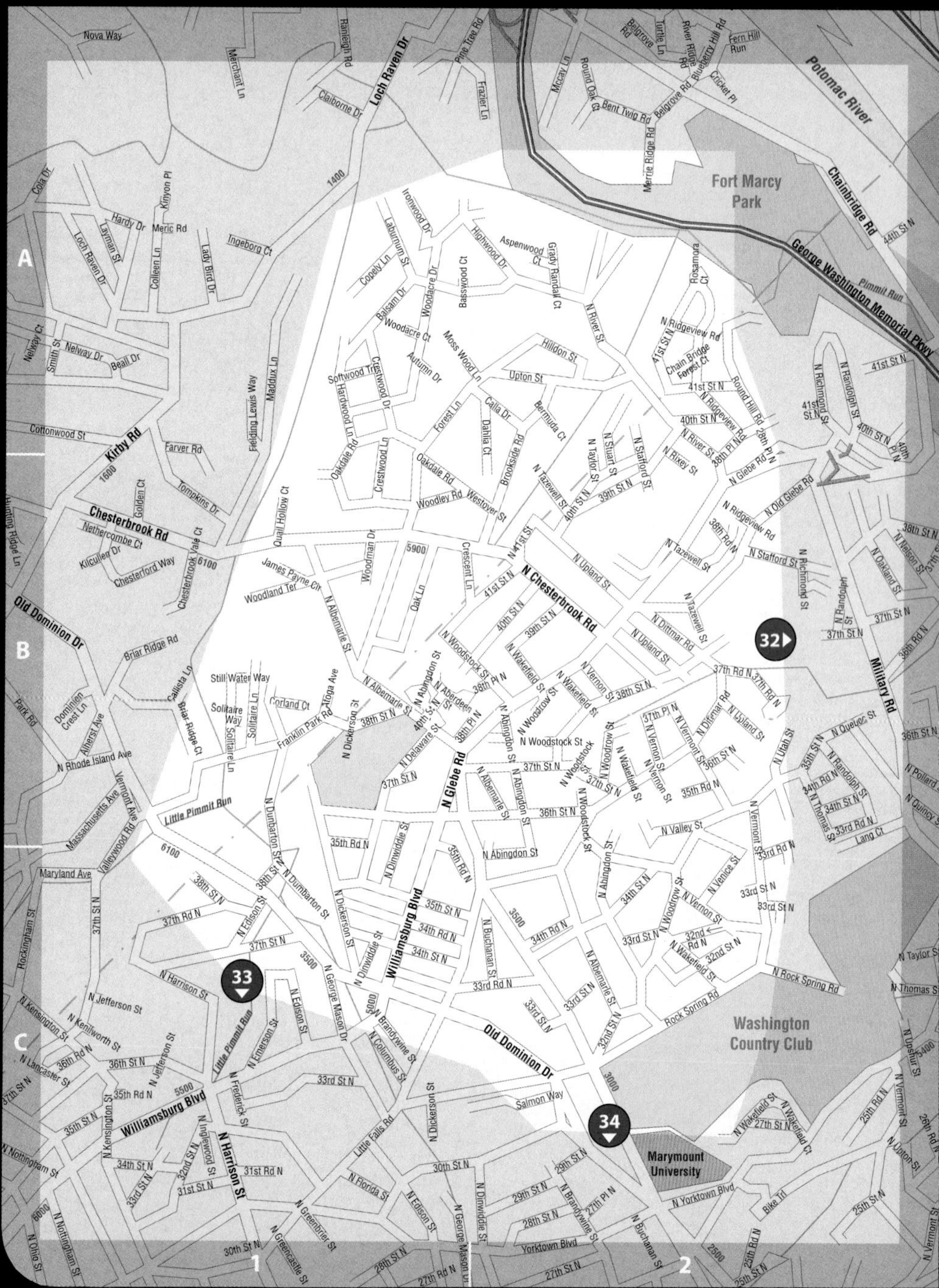

Map 31 • Chesterbrook

N

Potomac River
Fort Marcy Park
Chainbridge Rd
George Washington Memorial Pkwy
Pimmit Run
Washington Country Club
Marymount University
Military Rd
Old Dominion Dr
N Chesterbrook Rd
Chesterbrook Rd
Kirby Rd
Loch Raven Dr
N Glebe Rd
Williamsburg Blvd
N Harrison St
Little Pimmit Run
N Rhode Island Ave
Nova Way
Raleigh Rd
Merchant Ln
Claiborne Dr
Pine Tree Rd
Frazier Ln
Belgrove Rd
Turtle Ln
River Ridge Rd
Blueberry Hill Rd
Fern Hill Run
Mccay Ln
Round Oak Ct
Bent Twig Rd
Cricket Pl
Merrie Ridge Rd
44th St N
Cola Dr
Kinyon Pl
Hardy Dr
Meric Rd
Layman St
Loch Raven Dr
Colleen Ln
Lady Bird Dr
Ingeborg Ct
Ironwood Dr
Laburnum St
Highwood Dr
Aspenwood Ct
Grady Randall Ct
Rosamora Ct
Copely Ln
Woodacre Dr
Basswood Ct
Balsam Dr
Woodacre Ct
N River St
N Ridgeview Rd
Nelway Ct
Smith St
Nelway Dr
Beall Dr
Maddux Ln
Fielding Lewis Way
Moss Wood Ln
Hilldon St
41st St N
Chain Bridge Forest Ct
Round Hill Rd
N Richmond St
N Randolph St
Softwood Trl
Autumn Dr
Upton St
Hardwood Ln
Crestwood Dr
Forest Ln
Calla Dr
Bermuda Ct
41st St N
40th St N
N Ridgeview Rd
28th Pl N
40th St N
40th Pl N
Cottonwood St
Farver Rd
Oakdale Rd
Crestwood Ln
Dahlia Ct
Brookside Rd
N Taylor St
N Stuart St
N Stafford St
N River St
N Rixey St
38th Pl N
N Glebe Rd
1600
Tompkins Dr
Golden Ct
Oakdale Rd
Woodley Rd
Westover St
N Tazewell St
40th St N
39th St N
N Old Glebe Rd
Hunting Ridge Ln
Nethercombe Ct
Quail Hollow Ct
N 41st St
N Ridgeview Rd
38th Rd N
38th St N
N Nelson St
Kilcullen Dr
Chesterford Way
Chesterbrook Vale Ct
6100
5900
Woodman Dr
Crescent Ln
N Upland St
N Tazewell St
N Stafford St
N Oakland St
James Payne Cir
Woodland Ter
N Albemarle St
Oak Ln
41st St N
N Richmond St
N Randolph St
37th St N
Briar Ridge Rd
40th St N
39th St N
N Tazewell St
N Dittmar Rd
37th St N
36th Rd N
N Woodstock St
N Wakefield St
N Upland St
32
Still Water Way
Callista Ln
N Albemarle St
N Abingdon St
N Aberdeen St
38th Pl N
N Vernon St
38th St N
37th Rd N
Dominion Crest Ln
Park Rd
Alherst Ave
Solitaire Way
Solitaire Ln
Corland Ct
Atoga Ave
Briar Ridge Ct
Franklin Park Rd
N Dickerson St
38th St N
40th St N
38th Pl N
N Wakefield St
N Woodrow St
37th Pl N
N Vermont St
N Dittmar Rd
N Upland St
N Queens St
36th St N
N Delaware St
N Abingdon St
N Woodstock St
N Vernon St
36th St N
N Utah St
35th St N
N Randolph St
N Pollard St
Massachusetts Ave
Vermont Ave
37th St N
N Albemarle St
N Abingdon St
37th St N
N Woodstock St
37th St N
N Wakefield St
35th Rd N
34th Rd N
N Thomas St
34th St N
33rd Rd N
Lang Ct
N Quincy St
Valleywood Rd
Little Pimmit Run
N Dumbarton St
36th St N
N Woodstock St
N Valley St
N Vermont St
33rd Rd N
35th Rd N
N Dinwiddie St
35th Rd N
N Abingdon St
6100
Maryland Ave
38th St N
N Edison St
N Dumbarton St
N Dickerson St
35th St N
N Abingdon St
34th St N
N Woodrow St
N Venice St
33rd St N
33rd St N
Rockingham St
37th St N
37th Rd N
N Edison St
37th St N
34th Rd N
34th St N
N Buchanan St
3500
34th Rd N
N Vernon St
32nd Rd N
33rd St N
32nd St N
N Wakefield St
N Taylor St
N Harrison St
3500
N George Mason Dr
N Dinwiddie St
33rd Rd N
N Albemarle St
N Rock Spring Rd
N Thomas St
33
N Jefferson St
N Edison St
5000
N Brandywine St
33rd St N
33rd St N
Rock Spring Rd
N Kensington St
N Kenilworth St
N Emerson St
N Columbus St
32nd St N
N Upshur St
5400
N Lancaster St
36th Rd N
36th St N
N Jefferson St
33rd St N
3000
37th St N
35th Rd N
5500
N Frederick St
N Dickerson St
Salmon Way
N Wakefield St
27th St N
N Wakefield Ct
25th Rd N
N Vermont St
26th Rd N
35th St N
N Kensington St
N Inglewood St
Little Falls Rd
34
N Nottingham St
34th St N
32nd St N
31st Rd N
30th St N
29th St N
N Upton St
33rd St N
31st St N
N Florida St
N Edison St
N George Mason Dr
N Dinwiddie St
29th St N
N Brandywine St
27th Pl N
N Yorktown Blvd
Bike Trl
25th St N
6000
N Nottingham St
N Greenbrier St
28th St N
N Ohio St
30th St N
N Greencastle St
28th St N
27th Rd N
Yorktown Blvd
27th St N
N Buchanan St
2500
25th Rd N
25th St N
N Vermont St

A
B
C
1
2

If you're searching for nightlife, we suggest you move a bit south to Ballston, in which case we'd be able to help you; or a bit west to McLean, in which case you'd have your own restaurant selections, thank you very much.

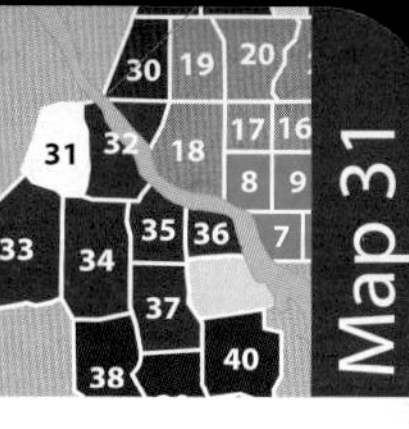

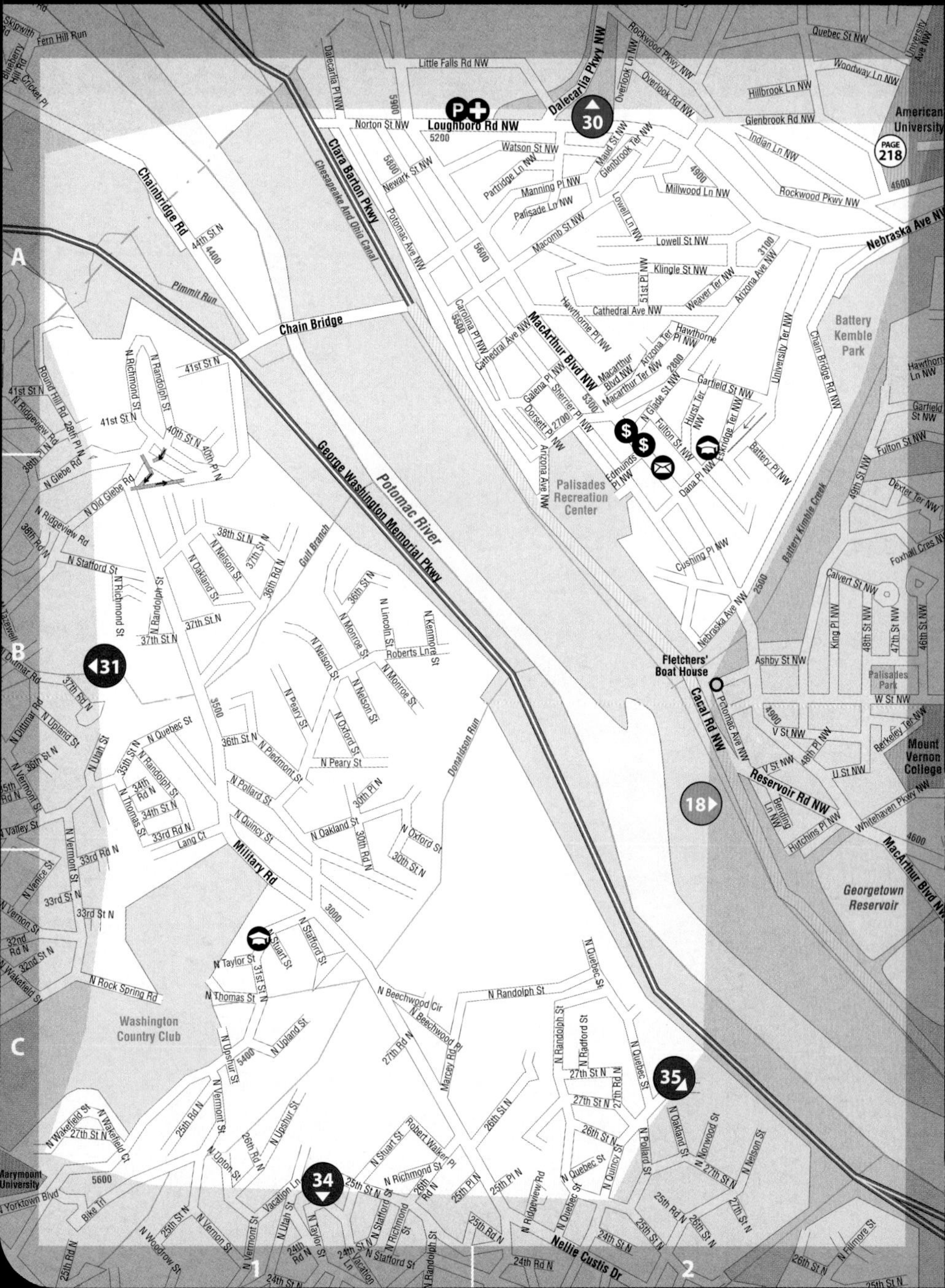

Map 32 • Cherrydale / Palisades

Here are two pretty and sleepy residential neighborhoods that line the Potomac and surround the region's favorite baby mill, Sibley Memorial Hospital.

Banks

- **Citibank** • 5250 MacArthur Blvd NW
- **Wachovia** • 5201 MacArthur Blvd NW

Hospitals

- **Sibley Memorial** • 5255 Loughboro Rd NW

Landmarks

- **Fletchers' Boat House** • 4940 Canal Rd NW

Parking

Post Offices

- **Palisades Station** • 5136 MacArthur Blvd NW

Schools

- **Key Elementary** • 5001 Dana Pl NW
- **Taylor Elementary** • 2600 N Stuart St

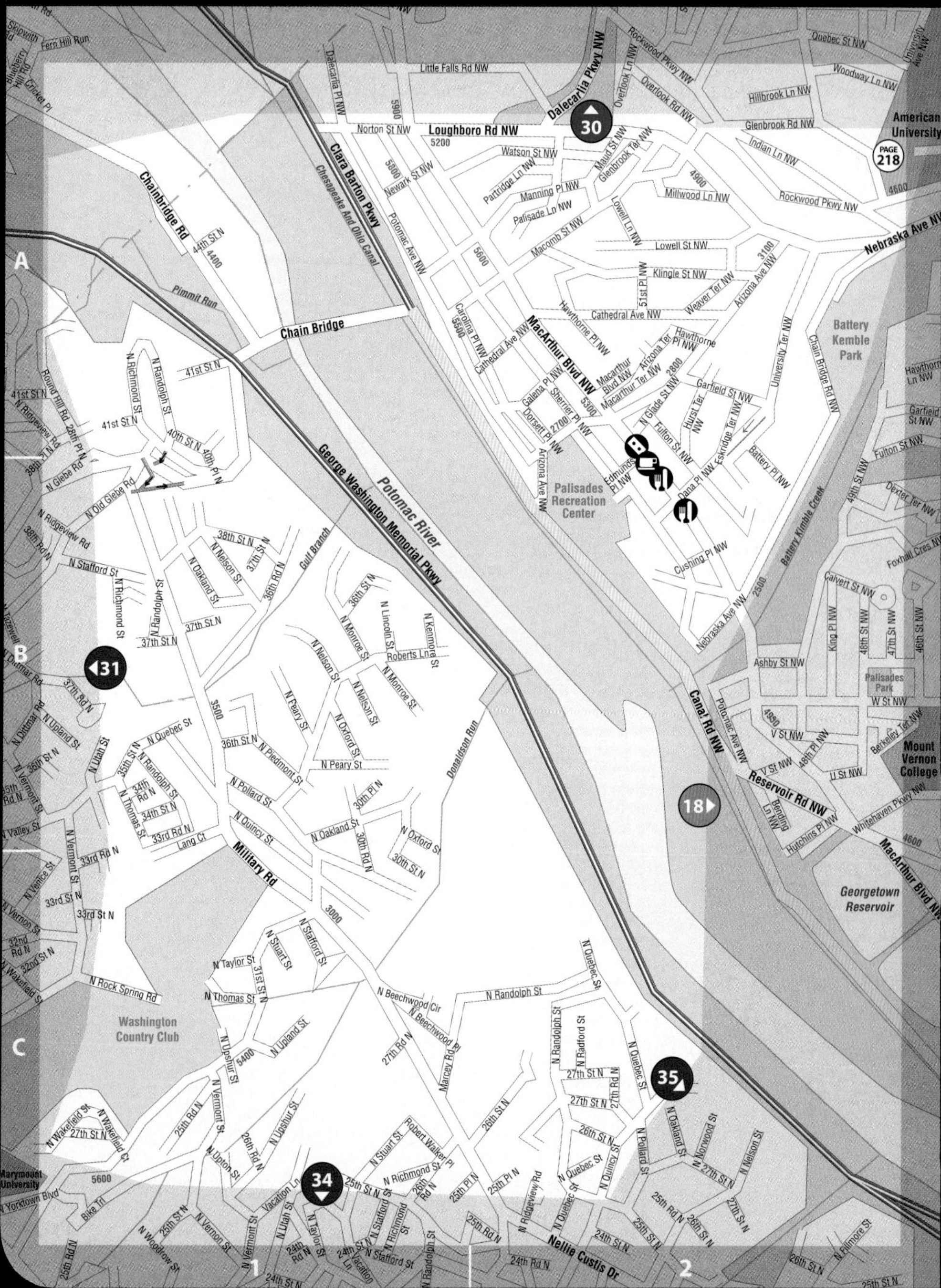

N

Fern Hill Run
Blueberry Hill Rd
Cricket Pl
Dalecarlia Pl NW
Little Falls Rd NW
Dalecarlia Pkwy NW
Rockwood Pkwy NW
Overlook Ln NW
Overlook Rd NW
Quebec St NW
University Ave NW
Woodway Ln NW
Hillbrook Ln NW
Glenbrook Rd NW
Indian Ln NW
American University
PAGE 218
Rockwood Pkwy NW
4600
Millwood Ln NW
4900
30
5900
Norton St NW
Loughboro Rd NW
5200
Watson St NW
Maud St NW
Glenbrook Ter NW
Clara Barton Pkwy
Chesapeake And Ohio Canal
5800
Newark St NW
Partridge Ln NW
Manning Pl NW
Palisade Ln NW
Macomb St NW
Lowell Ln NW
Lowell St NW
Nebraska Ave NW
Potomac Ave NW
5600
Chainbridge Rd
44th St N
4400
Pimmit Run
3100
Klingle St NW
51st Pl NW
Weaver Ter NW
Arizona Ave NW
Cathedral Ave NW
Chain Bridge
Carolina Pl NW
5500
Cathedral Ave NW
MacArthur Blvd NW
Hawthorne Pl NW
Arizona Ter
Hawthorne Pl NW
University Ter NW
Chain Bridge Rd NW
Battery Kemble Park
Hawthorne Ln NW
N Richmond St
N Randolph St
41st St N
Round Hill Rd
41st St N
N Ridgeview Rd
28th Pl N
41st St N
40th St N
40th Pl N
38th Pl N
N Glebe Rd
N Old Glebe Rd
Macarthur Blvd NW
Macarthur Ter NW
2800
Galena Pl NW
Sherrier Pl NW
5300
Dorsett Pl NW
2700
N Glade St NW
Garfield St NW
Hurst Ter NW
Fulton St NW
Eskridge Ter NW
Garfield St NW
Fulton St NW
Battery Pl NW
Edmunds Pl NW
Dana Pl NW
49th St NW
Dexter Ter NW
Arizona Ave NW
Palisades Recreation Center
George Washington Memorial Pkwy
Potomac River
Battery Kimble Creek
Foxhall Cres NW
N Ridgeview Rd
38th Rd N
N Stafford St
N Richmond St
38th St N
N Nelson St
37th St N
N Oakland St
36th Rd N
Gulf Branch
36th St N
N Randolph St
37th St N
37th St N
N Monroe St
N Lincoln St
N Kenmore St
Roberts Ln
Cushing Pl NW
Calvert St NW
Nebraska Ave NW
2500
King Pl NW
48th St NW
47th St NW
46th St NW
Ashby St NW
Palisades Park
W St NW
B
31
Dittmar Rd
37th Rd N
N Nelson St
N Monroe St
N Peary St
N Nelson St
N Oxford St
Donaldson Run
Canal Rd NW
Potomac Ave NW
4950
V St NW
48th Pl NW
Berkeley Ter NW
Mount Vernon College
N Dittmar Rd
N Upland St
36th St N
N Utah St
N Quebec St
3500
35th St N
36th St N
N Piedmont St
N Peary St
N Vermont St
34th Rd N
N Randolph St
N Thomas St
34th St N
33rd Rd N
N Pollard St
30th Pl N
V St NW
Reservoir Rd NW
U St NW
Whitehaven Pkwy NW
18
Bending Ln NW
Hutchins Pl NW
N Valley St
Lang Ct
N Quincy St
N Oakland St
30th Rd N
N Oxford St
30th St N
4600
MacArthur Blvd NW
N Vermont St
33rd Rd N
Military Rd
Georgetown Reservoir
N Venice St
33rd St N
33rd St N
N Vernon St
32nd Rd N
32nd St N
N Wakefield St
3000
N Stafford St
N Stuart St
N Taylor St
31st St N
N Quebec St
N Rock Spring Rd
N Thomas St
N Beechwood Cir
N Randolph St
N Beechwood Pl
Washington Country Club
N Upland St
N Upshur St
5400
27th Rd N
Marcey Rd
N Randolph St
N Radford St
N Quebec St
C
27th St N
27th Rd N
35
27th St N
N Vermont St
25th Rd N
N Upshur St
26th St N
N Oakland St
N Norwood St
N Wakefield St
27th St N
N Wakefield Ct
26th Rd N
Robert Walker Pl
N Stuart St
26th St N
N Pollard St
N Nelson St
27th St N
N Upton St
N Richmond St
N Quebec St
Marymount University
5600
34
25th St N
26th Rd N
25th Pl N
25th Pl N
N Ridgeview Rd
N Quincy St
25th Rd N
26th St N
27th St N
N Yorktown Blvd
Bike Trl
Vacation Ln
N Quebec St
25th St N
N Filmore St
N Woodrow St
25th St N
N Vernon St
N Vermont St
N Utah St
N Taylor St
N Stafford St
N Richmond St
25th Rd N
24th St N
Nellie Custis Dr
25th Rd N
24th Rd N
24th St N
24th St N
N Stafford St
N Randolph St
24th Rd N
26th St N
25th St N
1
2

Wait for the delivery at one of the few neighborhood spots along MacArthur Boulevard.

• **Starbucks** • 5185 MacArthur Blvd NW

• **Bambu** • 5101 Macarthur Blvd NW
• **Starland Café** • 5125 MacArthur Blvd NW

• **Potomac Video** • 5185 MacArthur Blvd NW

Map 33 • Falls Church

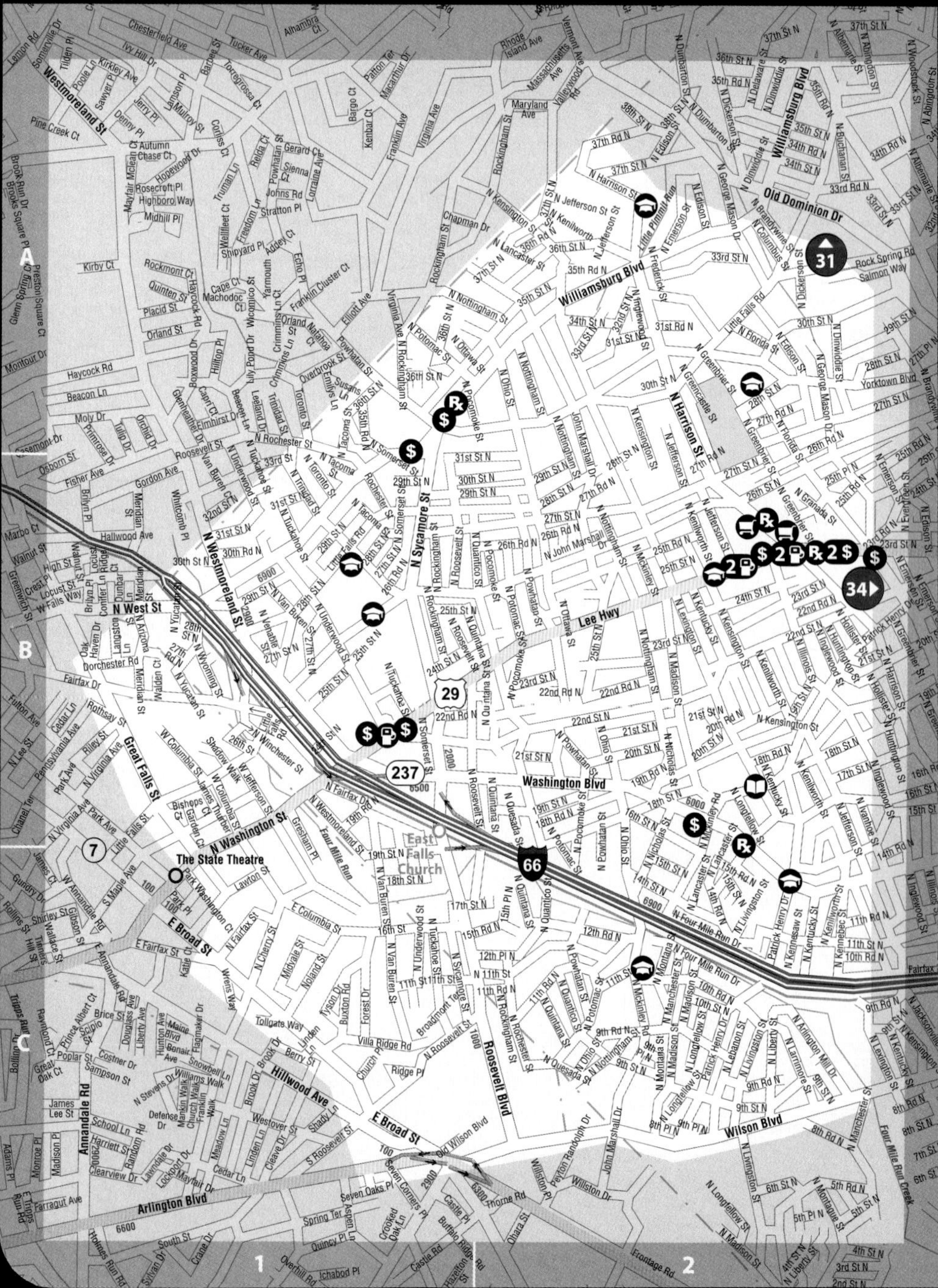

A
B
C
1
2

31
34

Westmoreland St
Chesterfield Ave
Tucker Ave
Alhambra Ct
Rhode Island Ave
Massachusetts Ave
Vermont Ave
Valleywood Rd
Maryland Ave
N Dumbarton St
36th St N
37th St N
37th Rd N
38th St N
N Harrison St
Little Pimmit Run
N Jefferson St
N Kenilworth St
N Edison St
N Emerson St
Williamsburg Blvd
Old Dominion Dr
Rock Spring Rd
Salmon Way
33rd St N
33rd Rd N
34th St N
34th Rd N
35th St N
35th Rd N
N George Mason Dr
N Dinwiddie St
N Dickerson St
N Delaware St
N Brandywine St
N Columbus St
N Buchanan St
N Albemarle St
N Abingdon St
N Woodstock St
Kirby Ct
Rockmont Ct
Quinten St
Placid St
Orland St
Haycock Rd
Beacon Ln
Moly Dr
Osborn St
Fisher Ave
Gordon Ave
Hallwood Ave
Roosevelt St
N Rochester St
N Somerset St
N Sycamore St
N Rockingham St
N Roosevelt St
N Quintana St
N Quantico St
N Pocomoke St
N Potomac St
N Ottawa St
N Ohio St
N Nottingham St
John Marshall Dr
N Kensington St
N Jefferson St
N Harrison St
N Greenbrier St
N Florida St
N Granada St
Yorktown Blvd
N Westmoreland St
N Tuckahoe St
N Underwood St
N Van Buren St
N Tacoma St
N Toronto St
Little Falls Rd
Lee Hwy
29
22nd Rd N
22nd St N
21st St N
20th St N
19th St N
18th St N
17th St N
16th St N
15th St N
14th St N
12th Rd N
11th St N
10th Rd N
9th St N
N Washington St
N West St
Great Falls St
Fairfax Dr
Dorchester Rd
Rothsay St
The State Theatre
Park Ave
N Virginia Ave
7
237
N Fairfax Dr
Four Mile Run
East Falls Church
66
Washington Blvd
N McKinley Rd
N Nicholas St
N Lancaster St
N Longfellow St
N Livingston St
Patrick Henry Dr
N Kennesaw St
N Kentucky St
N Kennebec St
N Four Mile Run Dr
N Montana St
N Manchester St
N Madison St
N Liberty St
N Larrimore St
N Arlington Mill Dr
Wilson Blvd
E Broad St
E Columbia St
E Fairfax St
Roosevelt Blvd
Hillwood Ave
Annandale Rd
Arlington Blvd
Old Wilson Blvd
Seven Corners Pl
Thorne Rd
Willston Dr
Peyton Randolph Dr
John Marshall Dr
Ridge Pl
Villa Ridge Rd
Tollgate Way
Broadmont Ter
Forest Dr
Buxton Rd
Noland St
Midvale St
N Cherry St
Wrens Way
Shady Ln
Westover St
Cedar Ln
Mayfair Dr
Lockport Dr
Spring Ter
Aspen Ln
Quincy Pl
Castle Pl
Buffalo Ridge Rd
Ohara St
Frontage Rd
Four Mile Run Creek
N Jacksonville St
N Lexington St
N Manchester St
N Montague St
5th St N
6th St N
4th St N
3rd St N
2nd St N
Fairfax Dr
Tripps Run
Farragut Ave
Adams Pl
Monroe Pl
Madison Pl
James Lee St
School Ln
Harriett St
Random Rd
Clearview Dr
Poplar St
Sampson St
Great Oak Ct
Costner Dr
Brice St
Douglass Ave
Liberty Ave
Hunton Ave
Maine Blvd
Bolling Rd
Haycock Rd
Montour Dr
Glenn Spring Ct
Preston Square Ct
Brook Run Dr
Brooks Square Pl
Pine Creek Ct
Lemon Rd
Tilden Pl
Kirkley Ave
Ivy Hill Dr
Barbee St
Torregrossa Ct
Patton Ter
Macarthur Dr
Virginia Ave
Franklin Ave
Kenbar Ct
Bargo Ct
Elliott Ave
Chapman Dr
Rockingham St
Walnut St
High St
Crest Pl
Locust St
W Falls Way
Greenwich St
Marbo Ct
Cedar Ln
Fulton Ave
N Lee St
Pennsylvania Ave
Riley St
Chanel Ter
James Ct
Gundry Dr
Rollins St
Shirley St
Gibson St
Wallace St
Timber Hill St
S Maple Ave
W Annandale Rd
Park Washington Ct
Park Pl
Lawton St
Gresham Pl
Bishops Ct
Garden Ct
James Thurber Ct
W Columbia St
W Jefferson St
Shadow Walk
N Winchester St
W Broad St
Meridian St
Little Falls St
N Yucatan St
N Wyoming St
N Arizona St
Haven Dr
Oak St
Langston Blvd
Dunbar Ct
Berry St
Linden Ln
Tyson Dr
Church Pl
Cleave Dr
Meadow Ln
Lawndale Dr
Defense Dr
Hillwood Ave
N Stevens Dr
Williams Walk
Snowbell Ln
Hagmaker Dr
Mankin Walk
Church Walk
Franklin Walk
Brook Dr
Seven Oaks Pl
Crooked Oak Ln
Hazelton St
Castle Rd
Ichabod Pl
Overhill Rd
Sylvan Dr
Crane Dr
Holmes Run Rd
South St
6600
6900
6500
6300
6000
2900
2000
1000
100
300
E Tripps Run Rd

Embroiled in a civil war of sorts, Falls Church is being pulled in different directions by urban professionals stymied with Arlington envy, and old guard recalcitrants ready to reenact Pickett's charge to preserve the Commonwealth. What's left is a neighborhood struggling for identity, with trendy fusion restaurants occupying the same blocks as strip mall bars that specialize in $1.75 bottles of Bud.

Banks

- **Bank of America** • 5226 Lee Hwy
- **BB&T** • 5515 Lee Hwy
- **BB&T** • 6745 Lee Hwy
- **Sun Trust** • 6711 Lee Hwy
- **United Bank** • 5335 Lee Hwy
- **United Bank** • 6402 Williamsburg Blvd
- **Virginia Commerce** • 5350 Lee Hwy
- **Virginia Commerce** • 6500 Williamsburg Blvd
- **Wachovia** • 1701 N McKinley Rd

Gas Stations

- **Amoco** • 5601 Lee Hwy
- **Chevron** • 5618 Lee Hwy
- **Citgo** • 5510 Lee Hwy
- **Exxon** • 6730 Lee Hwy
- **Sunoco** • 5501 Lee Hwy

Landmarks

- **The State Theatre** • 220 N Washington St

Libraries

- **Westover Library** • 1800 N Lexington St

Pharmacies

- **CVS** • 5402 Lee Hwy
- **CVS** • 6404 Williamsburg Blvd
- **Harris Teeter Pharmacy** • 2425 N Harrison St
- **Rite Aid** • 5841 N Washington Blvd
- **Safeway** • 2500 N Harrison St

Schools

- **Bishop O'Connell** • 6600 Little Falls Rd
- **McKinley Elementary** • 1030 N McKinley Rd
- **Rivendell** • 5700 Lee Hwy
- **Swanson Middle** • 5800 N Washington Blvd
- **Tuckahoe Elementary** • 6550 26th St N
- **Williamsburg Middle** • 3600 N Harrison St
- **Yorktown High** • 5201 28th St N

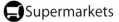

Supermarkets

- **Harris Teeter** • 2425 N Harrison St
- **Safeway** • 2500 N Harrison St

N
A
B
C
1
2
31
34
2
7
29
237
66
East Falls Church
Westmoreland St
N Westmoreland St
Williamsburg Blvd
Old Dominion Dr
N Harrison St
N Sycamore St
Lee Hwy
Washington Blvd
N Washington St
Great Falls St
E Broad St
Hillwood Ave
Roosevelt Blvd
Wilson Blvd
Arlington Blvd
Annandale Rd
N West St
Four Mile Run
N Four Mile Run Dr
Four Mile Run Creek
Little Pimmit Run
Chesterfield Ave
Tucker Ave
Rhode Island Ave
Vermont Ave
Massachusetts Ave
Maryland Ave
Virginia Ave
Franklin Ave
Rockingham St
Chapman Dr
N Kensington St
N Jefferson St
N Edison St
N George Mason Dr
Rock Spring Rd
Salmon Way
Little Falls Rd
N Dinwiddie St
Yorktown Blvd
N Nottingham St
N Ohio St
John Marshall Dr
N Powhatan St
N Quintana St
N Roosevelt St
N Tuckahoe St
N Underwood St
N Van Buren St
N Fairfax Dr
N Kentucky St
N Kenilworth St
N Lexington St
N Madison St
N Illinois St
N Inglewood St
Patrick Henry Dr
N Livingston St
N Manchester St
N Lancaster St
N McKinley Rd
N Longfellow St
N Arlington Mill Dr
Park Ave
S Maple Ave
E Columbia St
W Columbia St
Haycock Rd
Gordon Ave
Roosevelt St
N Rochester St
Fisher Ave
Hallwood Ave
Fairfax Dr
Dorchester Rd
Rothsay St
Tollgate Way
Villa Ridge Rd
Ridge Pl
Seven Corners Pl
Seven Oaks Pl
Thorne Rd
Williston Dr
Peyton Randolph Dr
Frontage Rd
Farragut Ave
Sampson St
Poplar St
Westover St
Broadmont Ter
Forest Dr
Buxton Rd
Lawton St
Gresham Pl
Kirby Ct
Orland St
Placid St
Beacon Ln
Osborn St
Pine Creek Ct
Montour Dr
37th St N
36th St N
35th St N
34th St N
33rd St N
31st St N
30th St N
29th St N
28th St N
27th St N
26th St N
25th St N
24th St N
23rd St N
22nd St N
21st St N
20th St N
19th St N
18th St N
17th St N
16th St N
15th St N
14th St N
12th St N
11th St N
10th St N
9th St N
8th St N
6th St N
5th St N
4th St N
3rd St N

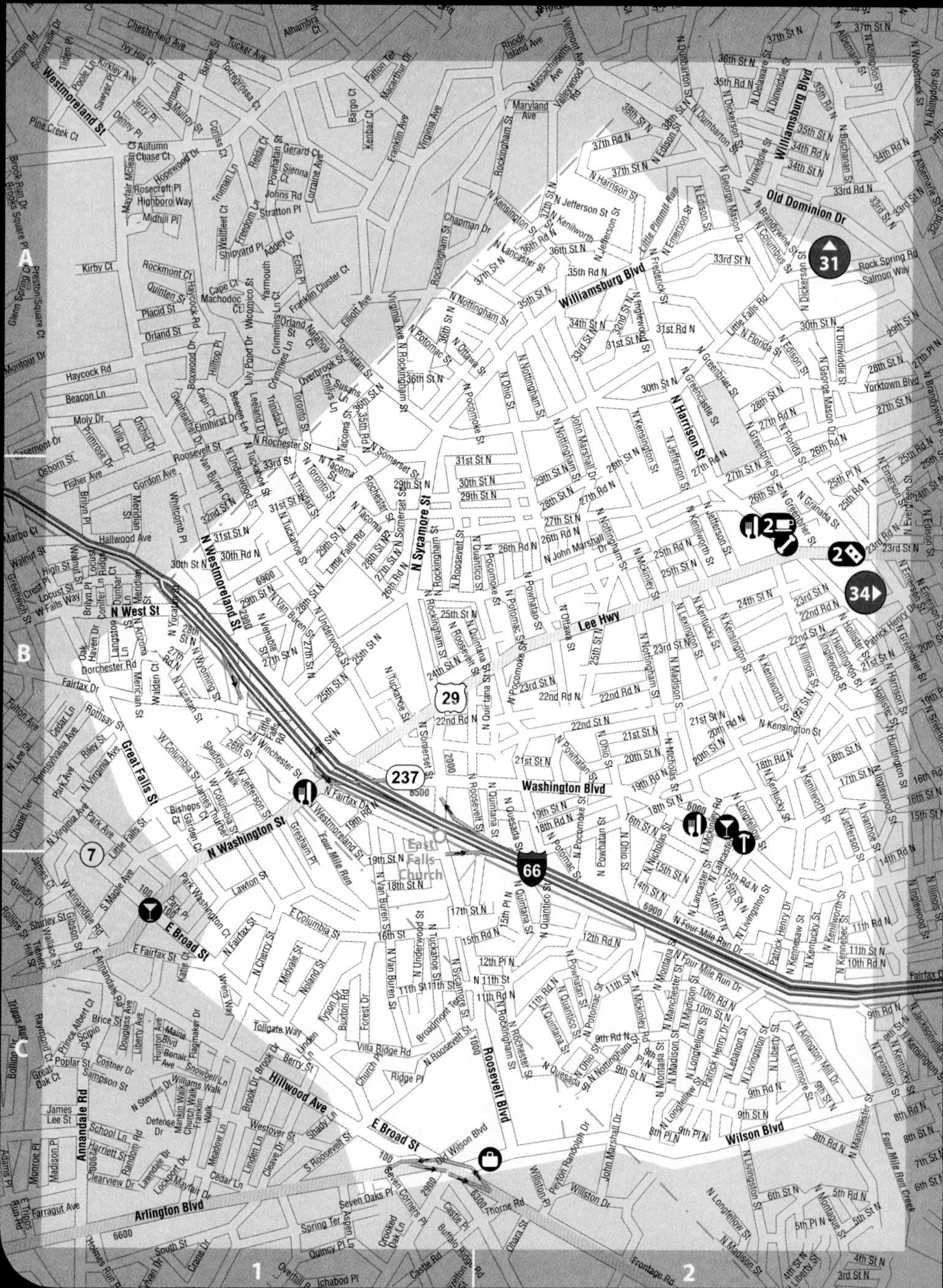

Sundries / Entertainment

A capacious music venue without the grunge mentality of U Street, the State Theatre serves up a solid assortment of bills causing people from (gasp!) other parts of town to visit. After the show grab a pint at Ireland's Four Provinces across the street. Before complaining that this bar reeks of the suburbs, remember that your other option is probably a bar that reeks of the sticks.

Coffee

- **Starbucks** • 2441 N Harrison St
- **Starbucks** • 2500 N Harrison St

Hardware Stores

- **Ayer's True Value** • 5853 N Washington Blvd

Nightlife

- **Ireland's Four Provinces** • 105 W Broad St
- **Lost Dog Café** • 5876 Washington Blvd

Pet Shops

- **Dogma** • 2445 N Harrison St

Restaurants

- **La Cote d'Or Café** • 6876 Lee Hwy
- **Lebanese Taverna** • 5900 Washington Blvd
- **Taqueria Poblano** • 2503 N Harrison St

Shopping

- **Eden Supermarket** • 6763 Wilson Blvd

Video Rental

- **Blockbuster Video** • 5400 Lee Hwy
- **Hollywood Video** • 5401 Lee Hwy

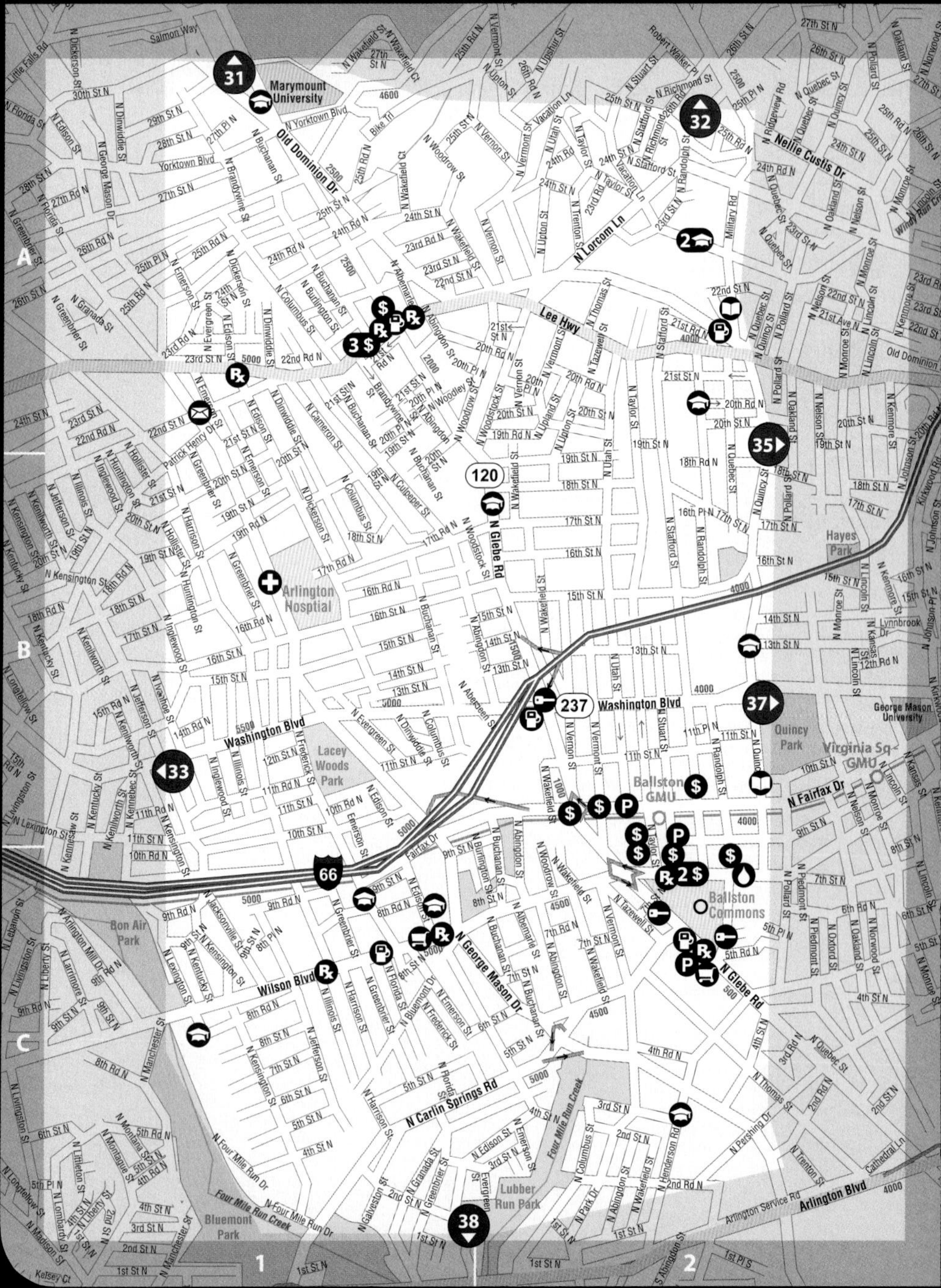

Map 34 • Ballston

Essentials

If the yuppies live in Clarendon, then their yuppies-in-training live in neighboring Ballston. Not quite as lah-dee-dah but aspiring to get there, Ballston seems to spit out a new high rise building every other month. It will be interesting to see if gentrification wipes away the long-rooted Peruvian/Salvadorian culture in this quarter as it did in Clarendon. We hope not.

Banks

- **Alliance Bank** • 4501 N Fairfax Dr
- **Bank of America** • 4201 Wilson Blvd
- **BB&T** • 4707 Lee Hwy
- **BB&T** • 920 N Taylor St
- **Chevy Chase** • 4238 Wilson Blvd
- **Chevy Chase** • 4700 Lee Hwy
- **Citibank** • 1010 N Glebe Rd
- **PNC (ATM)** • 850 N Randolph St
- **Presidential Savings** • 901 N Stuart St
- **Sun Trust** • 4710 Lee Hwy
- **Sun Trust** • 900 N Taylor St
- **Wachovia** • 1011 N Stafford St
- **Wachovia** • 2213 N Glebe Rd

Car Rental

- **Enterprise** • 1211 N Glebe Rd • 703-248-7180
- **Enterprise** • 601 N Randolph St • 703-312-7900
- **Enterprise** • 700 N Glebe Rd • 703-243-5404

Car Washes

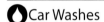

- **Shell Car Wash** • 4030 Wilson Blvd

Gas Stations

- **Exxon** • 4035 Old Dominion Dr
- **Exxon** • 4746 Lee Hwy
- **Exxon** • 660 N Glebe Rd
- **Sunoco** • 4601 Washington Blvd
- **Texaco** • 5201 Wilson Blvd

Hospitals

- **Virginia Hospital Center, Arlington** • 1701 N George Mason Dr

Landmarks

- **Ballston Commons** • 4238 Wilson Blvd

Libraries

- **Arlington Central Library** • 1015 N Quincy St
- **Cherrydale Library** • 2190 Military Rd

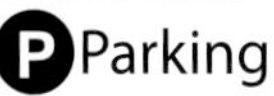

Parking

Pharmacies

- **CVS** • 4238 Wilson Blvd
- **CVS** • 4709 Lee Hwy
- **Harris Teeter Pharmacy** • 600 N Glebe Rd
- **Medicine Shoppe** • 5513 Wilson Blvd
- **Preston's CARE Pharmacy** • 5101 Lee Hwy
- **Rite Aid** • 4720B Lee Hwy
- **Safeway** • 5101 Wilson Blvd

Post Offices

- **North Station** • 2200 N George Mason Dr

Schools

- **Arlington Traditional** • 855 N Edison St
- **Ashlawn Elementary** • 5950 N 8th Rd
- **Barrett Elementary** • 4401 N Henderson Rd
- **Glebe Elementary** • 1770 N Glebe St
- **H-B Woodlawn** • 4100 Vacation Ln
- **Marymount University** • 2807 N Glebe Rd
- **St Agnes Elementary** • 2024 N Randolph St
- **St Ann Elementary** • 980 N Frederick St
- **Stratford Program** • 4102 N Vacation Ln
- **Washington Lee High** • 1300 N Quincy St

Supermarkets

- **Harris Teeter** • 600 N Glebe Rd
- **Safeway** • 5101 Wilson Blvd

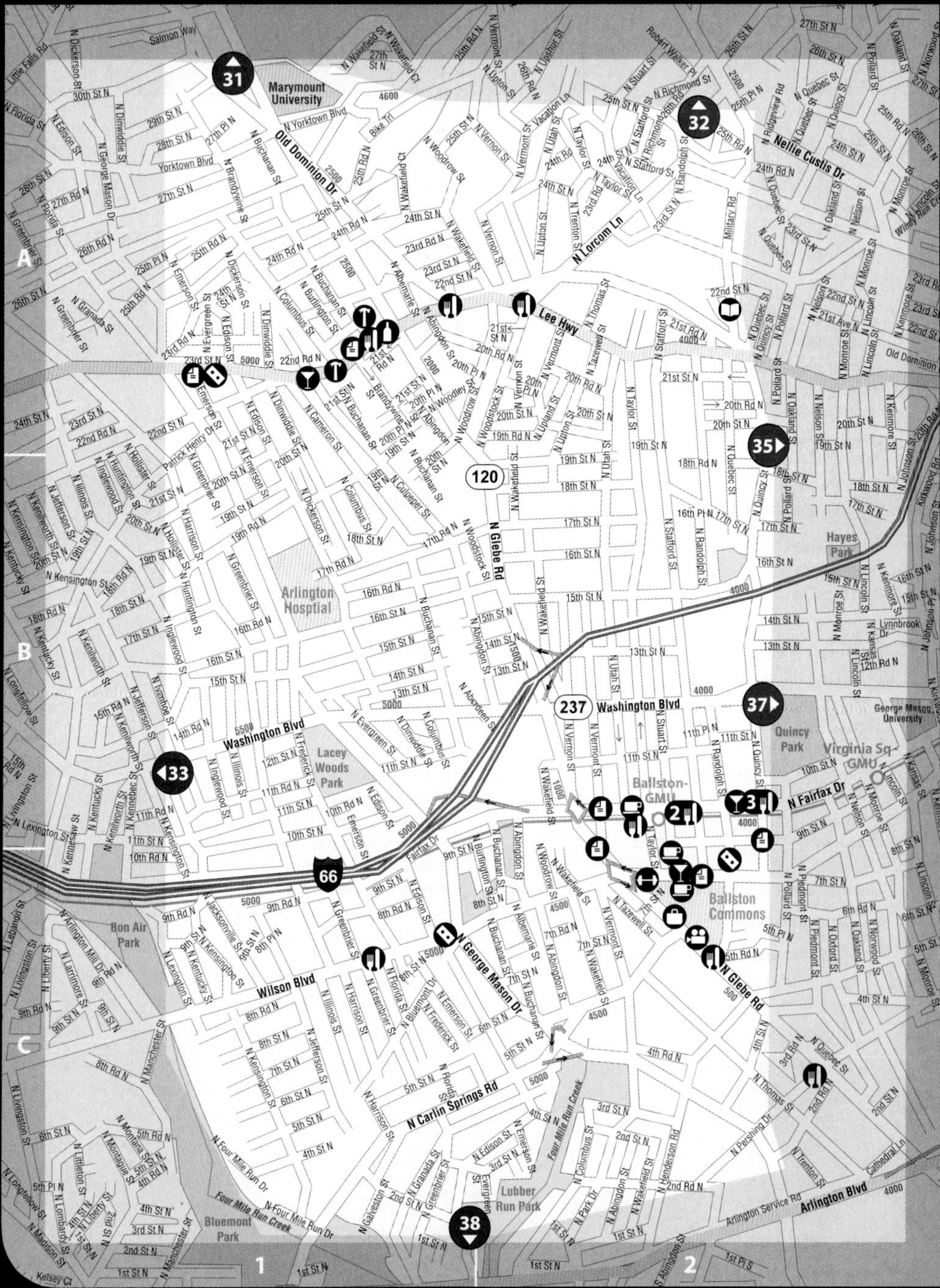
N
31
32
33
35
37
38
Marymount University
Old Dominion Dr
N Yorktown Blvd
Yorktown Blvd
Lee Hwy
N Lorcom Ln
Nellie Custis Dr
Military Rd
N Glebe Rd
120
237
Washington Blvd
N Fairfax Dr
Wilson Blvd
N George Mason Dr
N Carlin Springs Rd
Arlington Blvd
Arlington Service Rd
66
Arlington Hospital
Lacey Woods Park
Hayes Park
Quincy Park
George Mason University
Virginia Sq-GMU
Ballston-GMU
Ballston Commons
Bon Air Park
Bluemont Park
Lubber Run Park
Four Mile Run Creek
N Four Mile Run Dr
Salmon Way
Little Falls Rd
N Pershing Dr
Cathedral Ln
A
B
C
1
2

Sundries / Entertainment

About twice a year Ballston plays host to some of the best street festivals in Northern Virginia, so keep an eye out for these little-known gems. Otherwise, the Ballston Commons Mall isn't exactly Pentagon City, but it does house a conveniently located movie theater and the only mall-bar we would ever recommend: Rock Bottom Brewery. (Apologies to the also-popular Bailey's sports pub, which to us resembles a poorly lit appliance section of Sears.)

Coffee

- **Cosí** • 4250 Fairfax Dr
- **Starbucks** • 4238 Wilson Blvd
- **Starbucks** • 901 N Stuart St

Copy Shops

- **Copy & Convenience (9am-5:30pm)** • 2219 N Columbus St
- **Kinko's (6am-11pm)** • 4501 N Fairfax Dr
- **Minuteman Press (8:30am-5pm)** • 4001 N 9th St
- **Print Time (10am-7pm)** • 5137 Lee Hwy
- **Staples (7am-9pm)** • 910 N Glebe Rd
- **UPS Store (8am-7pm)** • 4201 Wilson Blvd

Gyms

- **Sport & Health Clubs** • 4328 Wilson Blvd

Hardware Stores

- **Arlington Bill's Hardware** • 2213 N Buchanan St
- **Bill's True Value Hardware** • 4756 Lee Hwy

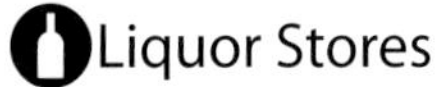

Liquor Stores

- **Virginia ABC** • 4709 Lee Hwy

Movie Theaters

- **Regal Ballston Common 12** • 671 N Glebe Rd

Nightlife

- **Bailey's Pub and Grille** • 4234 Wilson Blvd
- **Carpool** • 4000 N Fairfax Dr
- **Cowboy Café** • 4792 Lee Hwy
- **Rock Bottom Brewery** • 4238 Wilson Blvd

Restaurants

- **Café Parisien Express** • 4520 Lee Hwy
- **Café Tirolo** • 4001 N Fairfax Dr
- **Crisp & Juicy** • 4540 Lee Hwy
- **El Paso Café** • 4235 N Pershing Dr
- **Flat Top Grill** • 4245 N Fairfax Dr
- **Layalina** • 5216 Wilson Blvd
- **Metro 29 Diner** • 4711 Lee Hwy
- **Rio Grande Café** • 4301 N Fairfax Dr
- **Rocklands** • 4000 Fairfax Dr
- **Tara Thai** • 4001 Fairfax Dr
- **Tutto Bene** • 501 N Randolph St

Shopping

- **Pottery Barn** • Balston Commons, 2700 Clarendon Blvd

Video Rental

- **Dollar Video** • 5133 Lee Hwy
- **Top Video** • 850 N Randolph St
- **Video 95** • 5011 Wilson Blvd

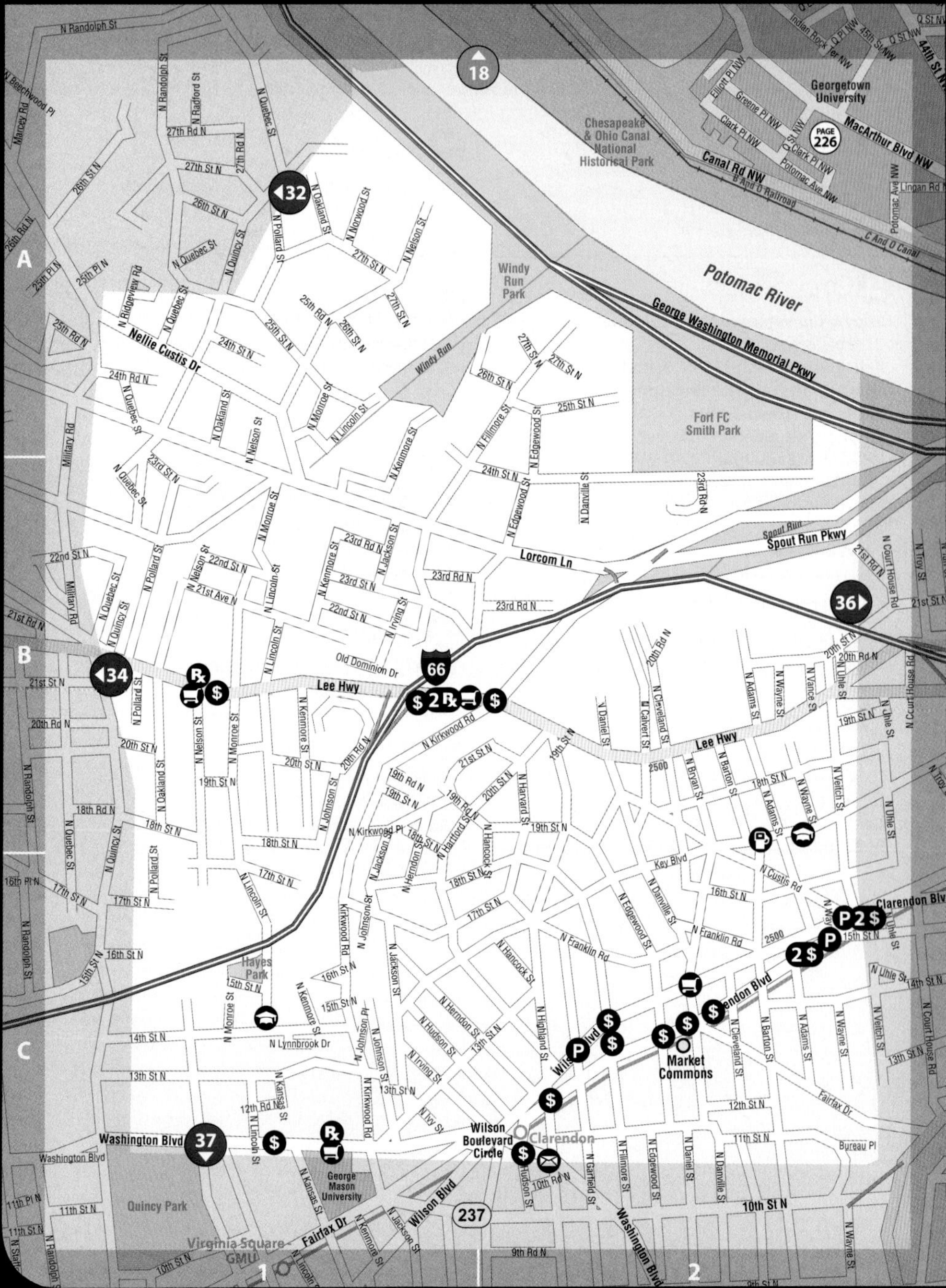

Map 35 • Clarendon

N Randolph St
N Quebec St
N Radford St
27th Rd N
27th St N
26th St N
26th St N
N Quincy St
N Pollard St
N Oakland St
N Norwood St
N Nelson St
27th St N
25th Rd N
26th St N
25th St N
24th St N
Nellie Custis Dr
N Ridgeview Rd
25th Rd N
25th Pl N
26th Rd N
Marcey Rd
N Beechwood Pl
24th Rd N
Military Rd
N Monroe St
N Lincoln St
N Kenmore St
Windy Run
Windy Run Park
Chesapeake & Ohio Canal National Historical Park
Georgetown University
MacArthur Blvd NW
Canal Rd NW
Potomac River
George Washington Memorial Pkwy
Fort FC Smith Park
N Fillmore St
N Edgewood St
25th St N
24th St N
N Danville St
23rd Rd N
Spout Run Pkwy
Lorcom Ln
23rd Rd N
23rd St N
22nd St N
N Irving St
N Jackson St
22nd St N
21st Ave N
N Quincy St
21st Rd N
Old Dominion Dr
Lee Hwy
21st St N
20th Rd N
20th St N
19th St N
18th Rd N
18th St N
17th St N
16th St N
15th St N
Hayes Park
N Kirkwood Rd
19th St N
N Harvard St
N Hancock St
Key Blvd
N Custis Rd
16th St N
N Franklin Rd
Clarendon Blvd
Wilson Blvd
Market Commons
14th St N
N Lynnbrook Dr
13th St N
12th Rd N
Washington Blvd
Quincy Park
George Mason University
Wilson Boulevard Circle
Clarendon
10th Rd N
10th St N
Fairfax Dr
Virginia Square-GMU
Washington Blvd
12th St N
11th St N
Bureau Pl
N Veitch St
N Wayne St
N Uhle St
N Court House Rd
21st St N
20th Rd N
19th St N
15th St N
14th St N
13th St N
9th Rd N

Essentials

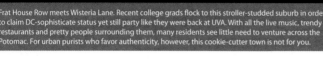

Frat House Row meets Wisteria Lane. Recent college grads flock to this stroller-studded suburb in order to claim DC-sophisticate status yet still party like they were back at UVA. With all the live music, trendy restaurants and pretty people surrounding them, many residents see little need to venture across the Potomac. For urban purists who favor authenticity, however, this cookie-cutter town is not for you.

Banks

- **BB&T** • 2200 Wilson Blvd
- **Chevy Chase** • 3141 Lee Hwy
- **Chevy Chase (ATM)** • 2700 Clarendon Blvd
- **Chevy Chase (ATM)** • 2800 Clarendon Blvd
- **Chevy Chase (ATM)** • 3115 Lee Hwy
- **Chevy Chase (ATM)** • 3450 Washington Blvd
- **PNC** • 2601 Clarendon Blvd
- **PNC (ATM)** • 1303 N Filmore St
- **PNC (ATM)** • 2201 Wilson Blvd
- **PNC (ATM)** • 3100 Clarendon Blvd
- **Sun Trust** • 3713 Lee Hwy
- **Sun Trust (ATM)** • 2250 Clarendon Blvd
- **Virginia Commerce** • 2930 Wilson Blvd
- **Wachovia** • 2200 Clarendon Blvd
- **Wachovia** • 3140 Washington Blvd

Gas Stations

- **Exxon** • 2410 Lee Hwy

Landmarks

- **Market Commons** • 2690 Clarendon Blvd

Parking

Pharmacies

- **CVS (24 hours)** • 3133 Lee Hwy
- **Eckerd's** • 3130 Lee Hwy
- **Giant Food Pharmacy** • 3450 Washington Blvd
- **Safeway** • 3713 Lee Hwy

Post Offices

- **Arlington Main Office** • 3118 Washington Blvd

Schools

- **Arlington Science Focus** • 1501 N Lincoln St
- **Francis Scott Key Elementary** • 2300 Key Blvd

Supermarkets

- **Giant Food** • 3115 Lee Hwy
- **Giant Food** • 3450 Washington Blvd
- **Safeway** • 3713 Lee Hwy
- **Whole Foods Market** • 2700 Wilson Blvd

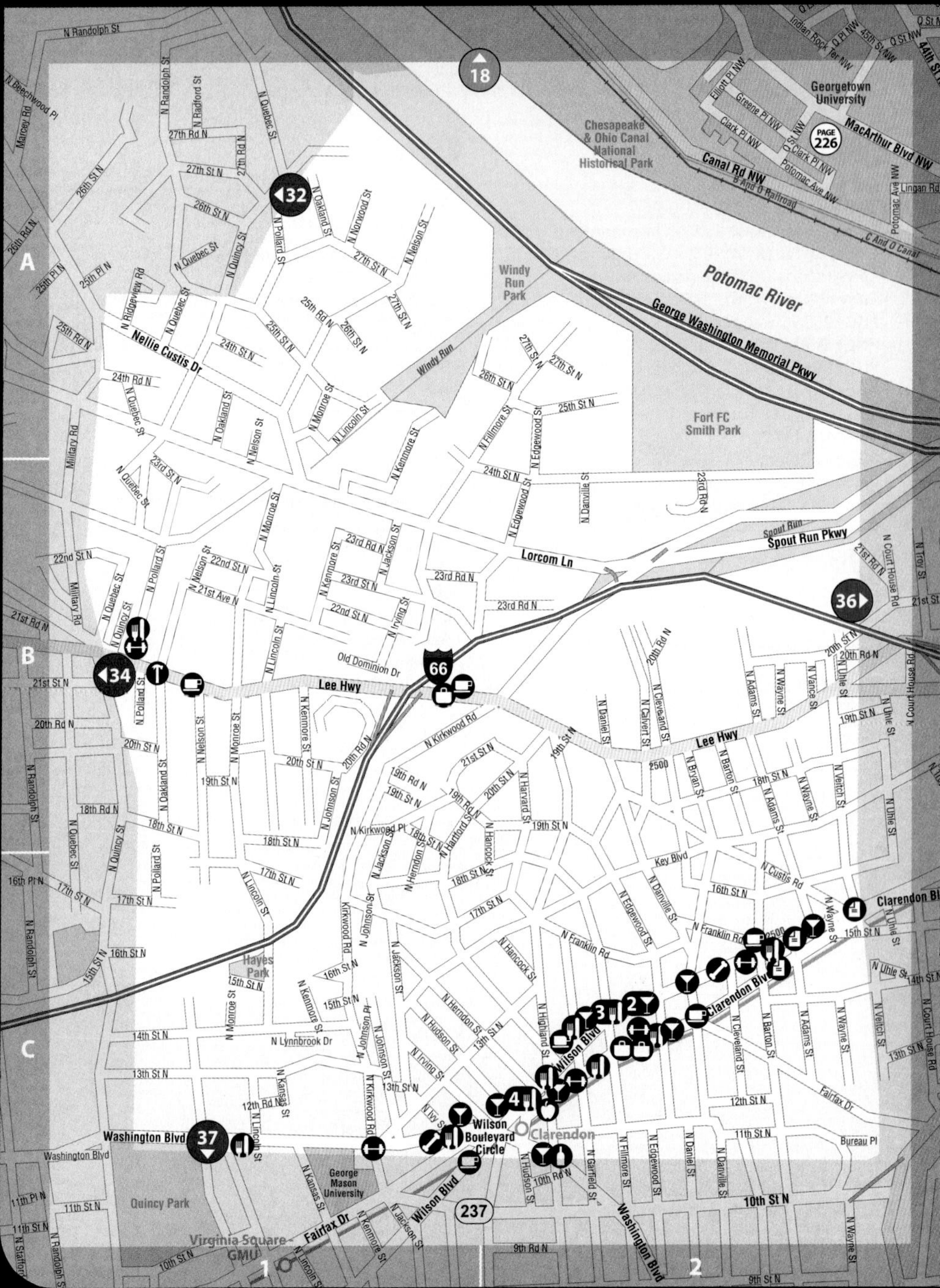
N
A
B
C
1
2
18
32
34
36
37
PAGE 226
66
237
Georgetown University
Chesapeake & Ohio Canal National Historical Park
Potomac River
George Washington Memorial Pkwy
MacArthur Blvd NW
Canal Rd NW
B And O Railroad
C And O Canal
Potomac Ave NW
Lingan Rd
Indian Rock Ter NW
Q Pl NW
45th St NW
Q St NW
44th St
Elliott Pl NW
Greene Pl NW
Clark Pl NW
Q St NW
Windy Run Park
Windy Run
Fort FC Smith Park
Spout Run
Spout Run Pkwy
Lorcom Ln
Lee Hwy
Old Dominion Dr
Nellie Custis Dr
Military Rd
N Randolph St
N Radford St
N Quebec St
N Quincy St
N Pollard St
N Oakland St
N Norwood St
N Nelson St
N Monroe St
N Lincoln St
N Kenmore St
N Jackson St
N Irving St
N Fillmore St
N Edgewood St
N Danville St
N Ridgeview Rd
N Beechwood Pl
Marcey Rd
27th Rd N
27th St N
26th St N
26th Rd N
25th Pl N
25th Rd N
25th St N
24th St N
24th Rd N
23rd St N
23rd Rd N
22nd St N
21st Ave N
21st Rd N
21st St N
20th Rd N
20th St N
19th St N
19th Rd N
18th Rd N
18th St N
17th St N
16th Pl N
16th St N
15th St N
14th St N
13th St N
12th Rd N
12th St N
11th Pl N
11th St N
10th St N
10th Rd N
9th Rd N
9th St N
N Kirkwood Rd
N Kirkwood Pl
Kirkwood Rd
N Johnson St
N Harvard St
N Hartford St
N Hancock St
N Herndon St
N Hudson St
N Highland St
N Ivy St
N Kansas St
N Garfield St
N Daniel St
N Calvert St
N Cleveland St
N Bryan St
N Barton St
N Adams St
N Wayne St
N Vance St
N Uhle St
N Veitch St
N Court House Rd
N Troy St
N Custis Rd
N Franklin Rd
Key Blvd
Clarendon Blvd
Wilson Blvd
Wilson Boulevard Circle
Clarendon
Fairfax Dr
Washington Blvd
Bureau Pl
N Lynnbrook Dr
N Stafford St
Hayes Park
Quincy Park
George Mason University
Virginia Square - GMU
2500

For those with significant others, head out at dusk and enjoy moderately-priced sidewalk dining at Mexicali Blues. Then stroll over to Harry's Tap Room — one of the only suburban Virginia restaurant/bars that can make you feel Washington cosmo-chic (at $7.50 a drink, it better). If you're without a partner, wait 'til ten o'clock and hit up one of the area's half-dozen singles bars; Meet someone, hook up a few times and follow instructions above.

Coffee

- **Hot Shotz** • 3018 Wilson Blvd
- **Java Shack** • 2507 N Franklin Rd
- **Murky Coffee** • 3211 N Wilson Blvd
- **Starbucks** • 2690 Clarendon Blvd
- **Starbucks** • 3125 Lee Hwy
- **Starbucks** • 3713 Lee Hwy

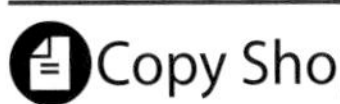

Copy Shops

- **Kinko's (24 hours)** • 2300 Clarendon Blvd
- **Southeastern Printing & Litho (8:30am-5pm)** • 2401 Wilson Blvd
- **UPS Store (9am-7pm)** • 2200 Wilson Blvd

Farmer's Markets

- **Claredon Farmers Market** • Clarendon Blvd & N Highland St

Gyms

- **Arlington Sport & Health Club** • 1122 N Kirkwood Rd
- **Curves** • 2105 N Pollard St
- **Curves** • 2529 Wilson Blvd
- **Studio Body Logic** • 3017 Clarendon Blvd
- **Washington Sports Clubs** • 2800 Clarendon Blvd

Hardware Stores

- **Cherrydale Hardware & Garden** • 3805 Lee Hwy
- **Virginia Hardware** • 2915 Wilson Blvd

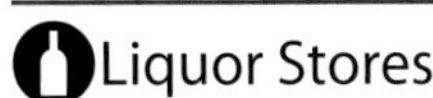

Liquor Stores

- **Virginia ABC** • 1039 N Highland St

Nightlife

- **Clarendon Ballroom** • 3185 Wilson Blvd
- **Clarendon Grill** • 1101 N Highland St
- **Galaxy Hut** • 2711 Wilson Blvd
- **Harry's Tap Room** • 2800 Clarendon Blvd
- **Iota** • 2832 Wilson Blvd
- **Mister Days** • 3100 Clarendon Blvd
- **Molly Malone's** • 3207 Washington Blvd
- **Whitlow's on Wilson** • 2854 Wilson Blvd

Pet Shops

- **AKA Spot** • 2622 Wilson Blvd
- **Petco** • 3200 Washington Blvd

Restaurants

- **Aegean Taverna** • 2950 Clarendon Blvd
- **Boulevard Woodgrill** • 2901 Wilson Blvd
- **Café Dalat** • 3143 Wilson Blvd
- **Delhi Dhaba Indian Café & Carryout** • 2424 Wilson Blvd
- **Faccia Luna Trattoria** • 2909 Wilson Blvd
- **Hard Times Café** • 3028 Wilson Blvd
- **Harry's Tap Room** • 2800 Clarendon Blvd
- **Hope Key** • 3131 Wilson Blvd
- **Lazy Sundae** • 2925 Wilson Blvd
- **Mexicali Blues** • 2933 Wilson Blvd
- **Minh's Restaurant** • 2500 Wilson Blvd
- **Pica Deli Gourmet and Wines** • 3471 N Washington Blvd
- **Portabellos** • 2109 N Pollard St
- **Queen Bee** • 3181 Wilson Blvd
- **Silver Diner** • 3200 Wilson Blvd

Shopping

- **Orvis Company Store** • 2879 Clarendon Blvd
- **The Container Store** • 2800 Clarendon Blvd
- **The Italian store** • 3123 Lee Hwy

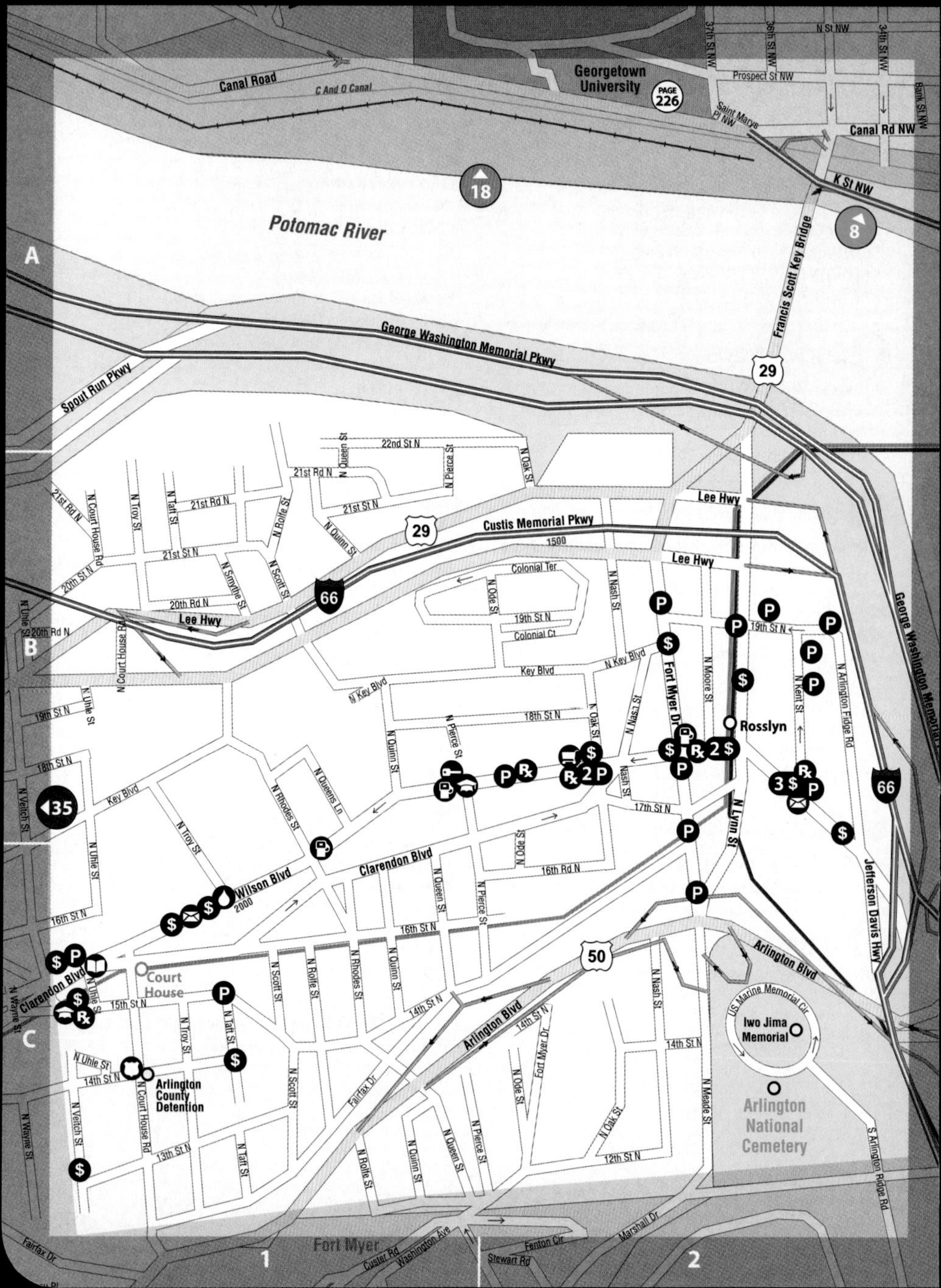

N
Canal Road
C And O Canal
Georgetown University
PAGE 226
37th St NW
36th St NW
N St NW
34th St NW
Prospect St NW
Bank St NW
Saint Marys Pl NW
Canal Rd NW
K St NW
18
8
Potomac River
Francis Scott Key Bridge
George Washington Memorial Pkwy
Spout Run Pkwy
29
22nd St N
N Queen St
N Pierce St
N Oak St
21st Rd N
21st St N
21st Rd N
N Court House Rd
N Troy St
N Taft St
N Rolfe St
N Quinn St
Custis Memorial Pkwy
Lee Hwy
1500
20th St N
21st St N
N Smythe St
N Scott St
Colonial Ter
N Ode St
N Nash St
20th Rd N
66
Lee Hwy
N Uhle St
20th Rd N
19th St N
Colonial Ct
19th St N
Key Blvd
N Key Blvd
Fort Myer Dr
N Moore St
N Kent St
N Arlington Ridge Rd
George Washington Memorial
N Key Blvd
N Uhle St
19th St N
18th St N
N Nash St
Rosslyn
N Quinn St
N Pierce St
N Oak St
2
18th St N
Key Blvd
N Veitch St
35
N Queens Ln
N Rhodes St
N Troy St
Nash St
17th St N
3
N Lynn St
66
N Uhle St
N Ode St
16th Rd N
Jefferson Davis Hwy
Clarendon Blvd
Wilson Blvd
2000
N Queen St
N Pierce St
16th St N
16th St N
50
Arlington Blvd
Clarendon Blvd
N Uhle St
Court House
N Wayne St
15th St N
N Scott St
N Rolfe St
N Rhodes St
N Quinn St
N Nash St
14th St N
US Marine Memorial Cir
Iwo Jima Memorial
N Troy St
N Taft St
Arlington Blvd
14th St N
N Uhle St
14th St N
Arlington County Detention
N Court House Rd
N Veitch St
N Scott St
Fairfax Dr
N Ode St
Fort Myer Dr
N Meade St
Arlington National Cemetery
N Wayne St
N Oak St
S Arlington Ridge Rd
13th St N
N Taft St
N Rolfe St
N Quinn St
N Queen St
N Pierce St
12th St N
Marshall Dr
Fairfax Dr
Fort Myer
Custer Rd
Washington Ave
Fenton Cir
Stewart Rd
A
B
C
1
2

Essentials

Welcome to the concrete jungle. You should never be at a loss for parking in Rosslyn, where garages outnumber grass blades. This is one of the least life-affirming neighborhoods in the city, but the upshot is that greener and greater neighborhoods are easily accessible. You just have to leave Rossyln to get there.

Banks

- **Bank of America** • 1700 N Moore St
- **Bank of America** • 2111 Wilson Blvd
- **BB&T** • 1901 Ft Myer Dr
- **Chevy Chase** • 1100 Wilson Blvd
- **Chevy Chase (ATM)** • 1611 N Kent St
- **PNC** • 1801 N Lynn St
- **PNC** • 2050 Wilson Blvd
- **PNC (ATM)** • 1100 Wilson Blvd
- **PNC (ATM)** • 1320 N Veitch St
- **PNC (ATM)** • 1401 N Taft St
- **Presidential Savings** • 1700 N Moore St
- **Sun Trust** • 1000 Wilson Blvd
- **Sun Trust** • 2121 15th St N
- **Wachovia** • 1300 Wilson Blvd
- **Wachovia** • 2026 Wilson Blvd
- **Wachovia (ATM)** • 1500 Wilson Blvd

Car Rental

- **Enterprise** • 1560 Wilson Blvd • 703-528-6466

Car Washes

- **Car Cleaning & Restoration** • 2000 Wilson Blvd

Gas Stations

- **Amoco** • 1625 Wilson Blvd
- **Chevron** • 1830 N Ft Myer Dr
- **Exxon** • 1824 Wilson Blvd

o Landmarks

- **Arlington County Detention Facility (Jail)** • 1425 N Courthouse Rd
- **Arlington National Cemetery** • Arlington National Cemetery
- **Iwo Jima Memorial** • Marshall Dr

Libraries

- **Arlington Public Library Information & Referral Office** • 2100 Clarendon Blvd

Parking

Pharmacies

- **CVS** • 1100 Wilson Blvd
- **CVS** • 1555 Wilson Blvd
- **CVS** • 2121 15th St N
- **Rite Aid** • 1700 N Moore St
- **Safeway** • 1525 Wilson Blvd

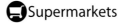

Police

- **Arlington County Police Department** • 1425 N Courthouse Rd

Post Offices

- **Court House Station** • 2043 Wilson Blvd
- **Rosslyn Station** • 1101 Wilson Blvd, Ste 1

Schools

- **Nottingham Elementary (Temporary Location)** • 1601 Wilson Blvd
- **Strayer University (Arlington Campus)** • 2121 15th St N

Supermarkets

- **Safeway** • 1525 Wilson Blvd

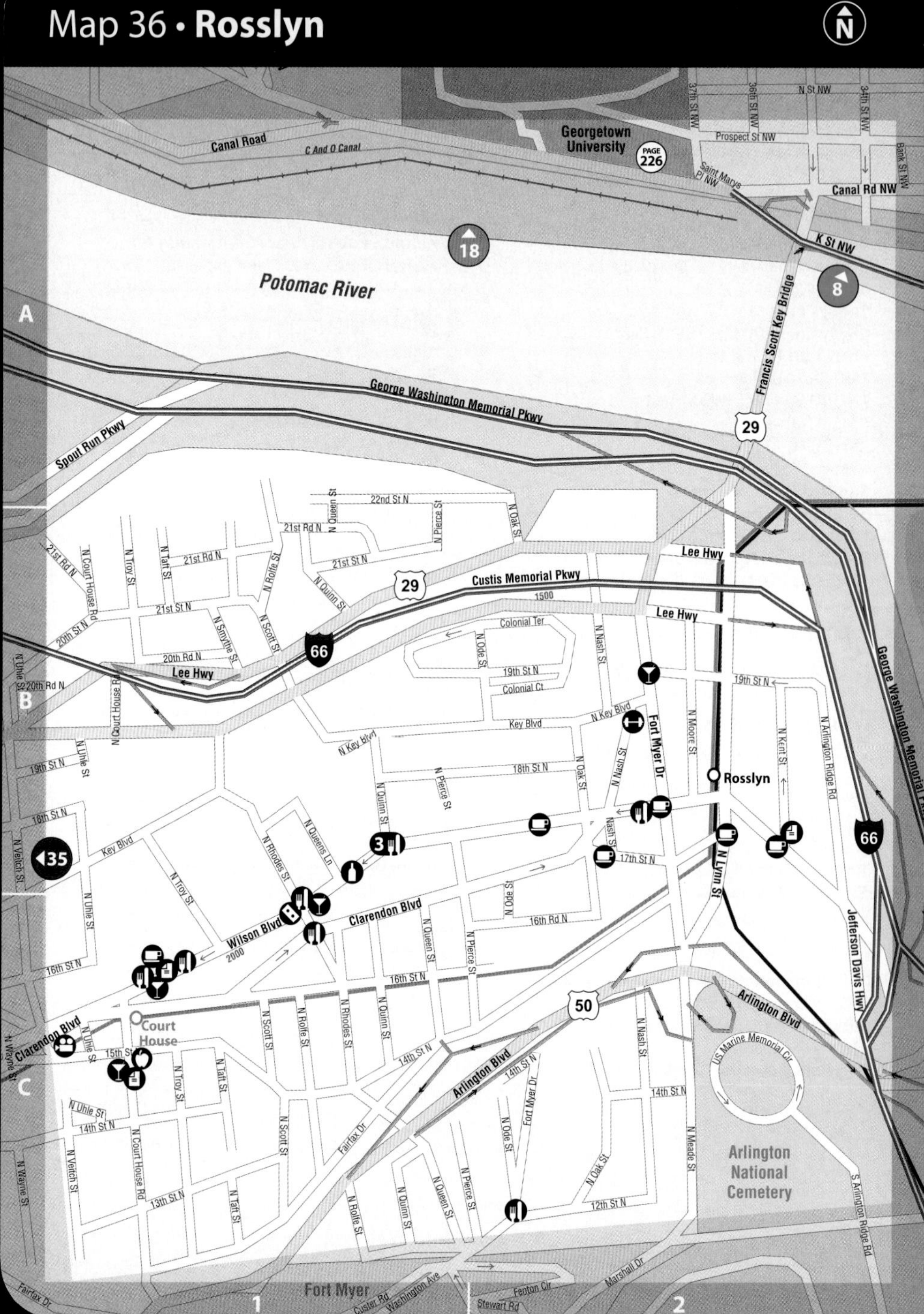
N
Georgetown University
PAGE 226
Canal Road
C And O Canal
37th St NW
36th St NW
35th St NW
34th St NW
N St NW
Prospect St NW
Bank St NW
Saint Marys Pl NW
Canal Rd NW
K St NW
18
8
Potomac River
A
Francis Scott Key Bridge
George Washington Memorial Pkwy
29
Spout Run Pkwy
22nd St N
21st Rd N
21st St N
21st Rd N
21st St N
20th Rd N
20th St N
20th Rd N
N Queen St
N Pierce St
N Oak St
N Court House Rd
N Troy St
N Taft St
N Rolfe St
N Quinn St
N Smythe St
N Scott St
N Uhle St
Custis Memorial Pkwy
1500
Lee Hwy
66
Colonial Ter
N Ode St
19th St N
Colonial Ct
Key Blvd
N Key Blvd
N Nash St
Fort Myer Dr
N Moore St
19th St N
N Kent St
N Arlington Ridge Rd
George Washington Memorial Pkwy
B
19th St N
18th St N
N Pierce St
N Oak St
Rosslyn
18th St N
N Veitch St
35
Key Blvd
N Rhodes St
N Queens Ln
N Troy St
3
Nash St
17th St N
N Lynn St
Jefferson Davis Hwy
Wilson Blvd
2000
Clarendon Blvd
N Ode St
16th Rd N
N Queen St
N Pierce St
16th St N
16th St N
50
Arlington Blvd
Court House
Clarendon Blvd
N Uhle St
15th St N
N Wayne St
N Scott St
N Rolfe St
N Rhodes St
N Quinn St
14th St N
N Nash St
US Marine Memorial Cir
C
N Troy St
N Taft St
N Uhle St
14th St N
N Scott St
Fairfax Dr
Arlington Blvd
14th St N
Fort Myer Dr
N Ode St
14th St N
N Meade St
Arlington National Cemetery
N Veitch St
N Court House Rd
13th St N
N Taft St
N Rolfe St
N Quinn St
N Queen St
N Pierce St
N Oak St
12th St N
S Arlington Ridge Rd
N Wayne St
Fairfax Dr
Fort Myer
Custer Rd
Washington Ave
Stewart Rd
Fenton Cir
Marshall Dr
1
2

The fast food and lunch joints tend to cater to the working stiffs who head home after 5, but there are markets and dry cleaners and the like to serve those who actually live here. If you're after any real shopping or nightlife, hike a few blocks to Clarendon or across the bridge to Georgetown.

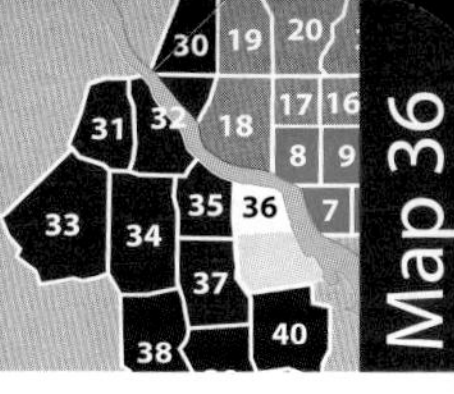

Coffee

- **Coffee Express** • 1100 Wilson Blvd
- **Coffee Express** • 1300 Wilson Blvd
- **Cosí** • 2050 Wilson Blvd
- **Starbucks** • 1501 N 17th St
- **Starbucks** • 1525 Wilson Blvd
- **Starbucks** • 1735 N Lynn St

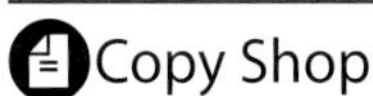

Copy Shops

- **Minuteman Press (8:30am-5pm)** • 1601 N Kent St
- **Office Depot (8am-8pm)** • 1515 N Courthouse Rd
- **USA Print & Copy (8am-5pm)** • 2044 Wilson Blvd

Farmer's Markets

- **Arlington County Farmer's Market** • N 14th St & N Courthouse Rd

Gyms

- **Gold's Gym** • 1830 N Nash St

Liquor Stores

- **Virginia ABC** • 1731 Wilson Blvd

Movie Theaters

- **AMC Courthouse Plaza 8** • 2150 Clarendon Blvd

Nightlife

- **Continental** • 1911 Ft Myer Dr
- **Ireland's Four Courts** • 2051 Wilson Blvd
- **Rhodeside Grill** • 1836 Wilson Blvd
- **Summers Grill and Sports Pub** • 1520 N Courthouse Rd

Restaurants

- **Gua-Rapo** • 2039 Wilson Blvd
- **Guajillo** • 1727 Wilson Blvd
- **Il Radicchio** • 1801 Clarendon Blvd
- **Ireland's Four Courts** • 2051 Wilson Blvd
- **Mezza9** • 1325 Wilson Blvd
- **Quarter Deck Restaurant** • 1200 Ft Myer Dr
- **Ray's the Steaks** • 1725 Wilson Blvd
- **Rhodeside Grill** • 1836 Wilson Blvd
- **Village Bistro** • 1723 Wilson Blvd

Video Rental

- **Hollywood Video** • 1900 Wilson Blvd

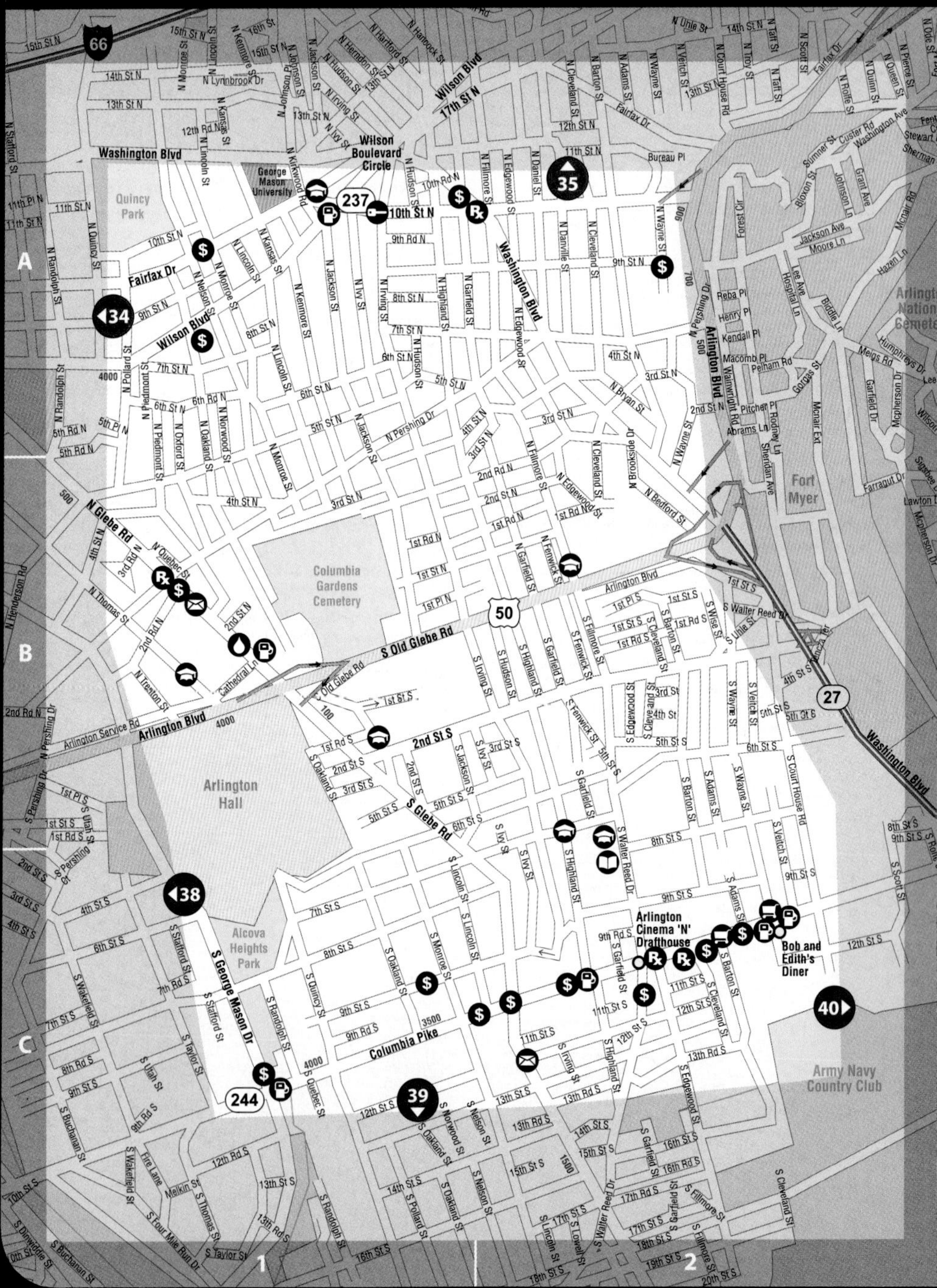

Quincy Park
George Mason University
Wilson Boulevard Circle
Columbia Gardens Cemetery
Arlington Hall
Alcova Heights Park
Arlington Cinema 'N' Drafthouse
Bob and Edith's Diner
Army Navy Country Club
Fort Myer
Arlington National Cemetery

Washington Blvd
Wilson Blvd
Arlington Blvd
S Old Glebe Rd
N Glebe Rd
S Glebe Rd
Columbia Pike
S George Mason Dr
Fairfax Dr
10th St N
2nd St S

34 35 38 39 40

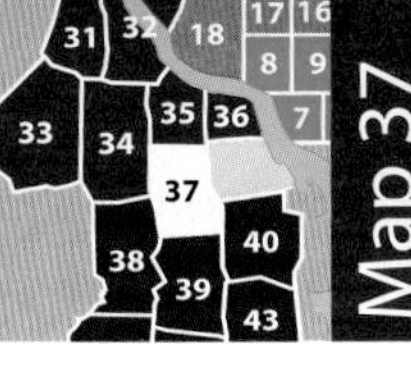

Straightforward military base complete with muscle cars, drab apartment buildings and aging neighborhoods with scraggly lawns. The next Fort Meyer battle will involve a well-funded army of imperialist yuppies spreading gentrification.

Banks

- **Bank of America** • 3401 Columbia Pike
- **Bank of America** • 3625 Fairfax Dr
- **BB&T** • 1100 S Walter Reed Dr
- **BB&T** • 3001 N Washington Blvd
- **Chevy Chase** • 3532 Columbia Pike
- **Chevy Chase** • 901 N Nelson St
- **Chevy Chase (ATM)** • 2411 Columbia Pike
- **Chevy Chase (ATM)** • 2515 Columbia Pike
- **Sun Trust** • 249 N Glebe Rd
- **Sun Trust** • 3108 Columbia Pike
- **United Bank** • 2300 S 9th St
- **United Bank** • 3801 Wilson Blvd
- **Wachovia** • 951 S George Mason Dr

Car Rental

- **Avis** • 3206 10th St N • 703-516-4202

Car Washes

- **Mr Wash** • 101 N Glebe Rd

Gas Stations

- **Chevron** • 67 N Glebe Rd
- **Citgo** • 2324 Columbia Pike
- **Hess** • 3299 Wilson Blvd
- **Mobil** • 3100 Columbia Pike
- **Shell** • 4211 Columbia Pike

Landmarks

- **Arlington Cinema 'N' Drafthouse** • 2903 Columbia Pike
- **Bob & Edith's Diner** • 2310 Columbia Pike

Libraries

- **Columbia Pike Library** • 816 S Walter Reed Dr

Pharmacies

- **CVS** • 256 N Glebe Rd
- **CVS** • 2601 Columbia Tpke
- **CVS** • 2900 N 10th St
- **Eckerd's** • 2820 Columbia Pike

Post Offices

- **Buckingham Station** • 235 N Glebe Rd
- **South Station** • 1210 S Glebe Rd

Schools

- **Henry Elementary** • 701 S Highland St
- **Jefferson Middle** • 125 S Old Gebe Rd
- **Long Branch Elementary** • 33 N Fillmore St
- **St Charles** • 3299 N Fairfax Dr
- **St Thomas More Cathedral** • 105 N Thomas St
- **Technical Education & Career Center** • 816 S Walter Reed Dr

Supermarkets

- **Giant Food** • 2515 Columbia Pike
- **Safeway** • 2303 Columbia Pike

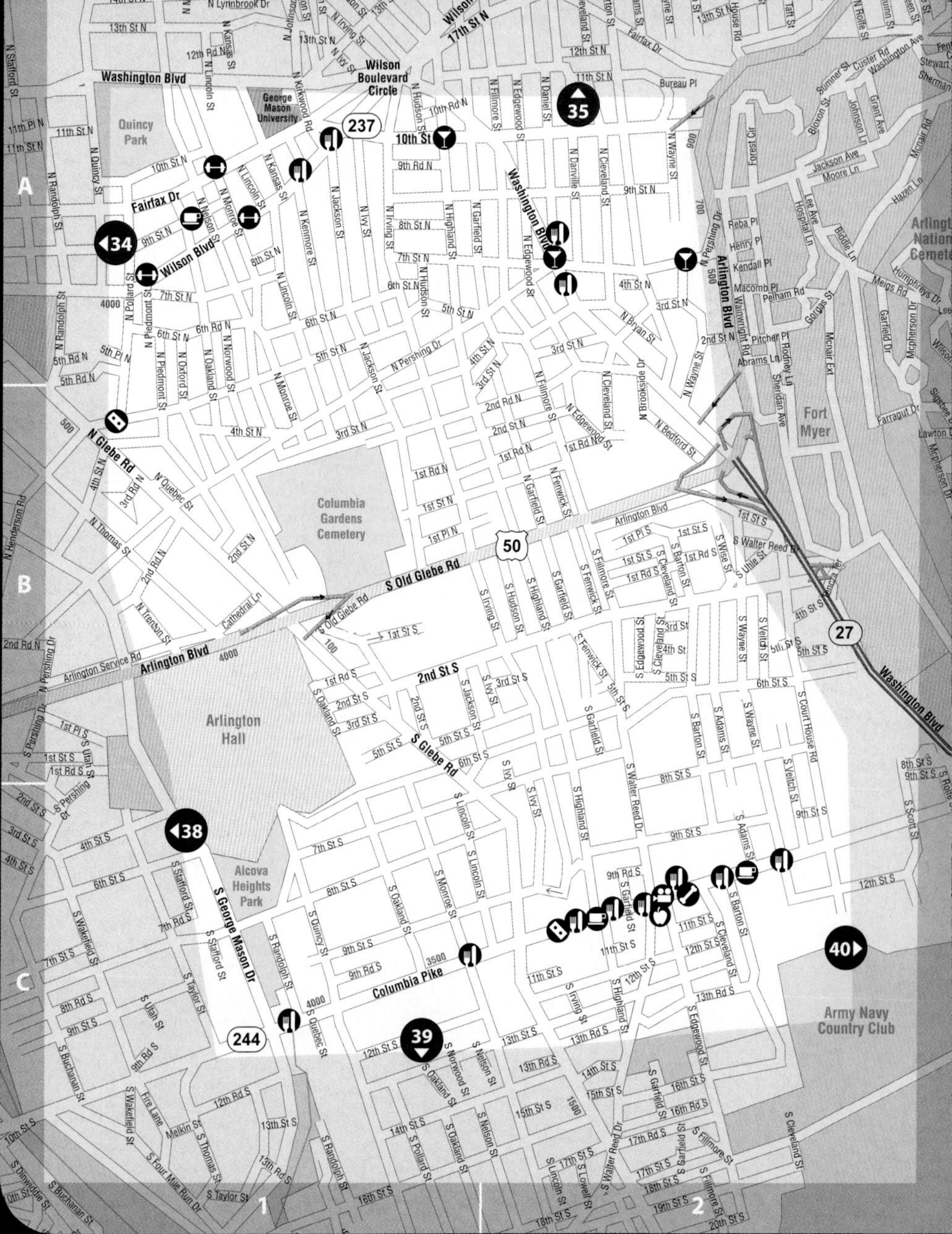
Wilson Boulevard Circle
Washington Blvd
Wilson Blvd
Arlington Blvd
Columbia Pike
S Old Glebe Rd
S George Mason Dr
N Glebe Rd
Quincy Park
George Mason University
Columbia Gardens Cemetery
Arlington Hall
Alcova Heights Park
Fort Myer
Army Navy Country Club
Arlington National Cemetery

People love Bob & Edith's Diner, Rincome, and the slow pace of Rappahannock Coffee. Others just come when they're in the market for a crew cut. However, many of the local businesses are being torn down and transformed into upscale markets and condos, and the area's circus of clownish locals is being replaced by Cirque de Soleil snobs. The rise of Tallula/fall of Whitey's is a perfect example.

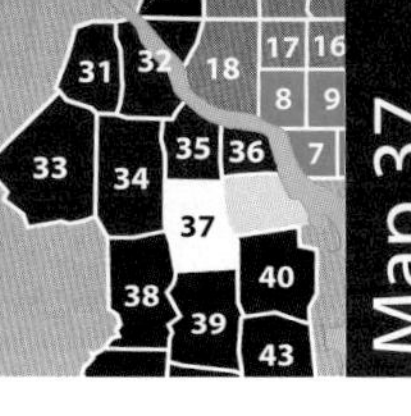

Coffee

- **Dunkin' Donuts** • 3100 Columbia Pike
- **Rappahannock Coffee & Roasting** • 2406 Columbia Pike
- **Starbucks** • 901 N Nelson St

Farmer's Markets

- **Columbia Pike Farmer's Market** • Columbia Pike & S Walter Reed Dr

Gyms

- **Aerobic Workout** • 954 N Monroe St
- **Curves** • 3528 Wilson Blvd
- **Gold's Gym** • 3910 Wilson Blvd

Movie Theaters

- **Cinema 'N' Draft House** • 2903 Columbia Pike

Nightlife

- **Jay's Saloon** • 3114 N 10th St
- **Royal Lee Bar and Grill** • 2211 N Pershing Dr
- **Tallula** • 2761 Washington Blvd

Pet Shops

- **Birds 'N' Things** • 2628 Columbia Pike

Restaurants

- **Atilla's** • 2705 Columbia Pike
- **Bob & Edith's Diner** • 2310 Columbia Pike
- **The Broiler** • 3601 Columbia Pike
- **El Charrito Caminante** • 2710 N Washington Blvd
- **El Pollo Rico** • 932 N Kenmore St
- **Manee Thai** • 2500 Columbia Pike
- **Mario's Pizza House** • 3322 Wilson Blvd
- **Matuba** • 2915 Columbia Pike
- **Mrs Chen's Kitchen** • 3101 Columbia Pike
- **Pan American Bakery** • 4113 Columbia Pike
- **Rincome Thai Cuisine** • 3030 Columbia Pike
- **Tallula Restaurant** • 2761 Washington Blvd

Video Rental

- **Hollywood Video** • 3263 Columbia Pike
- **Video Warehouse** • 3411 5th St S

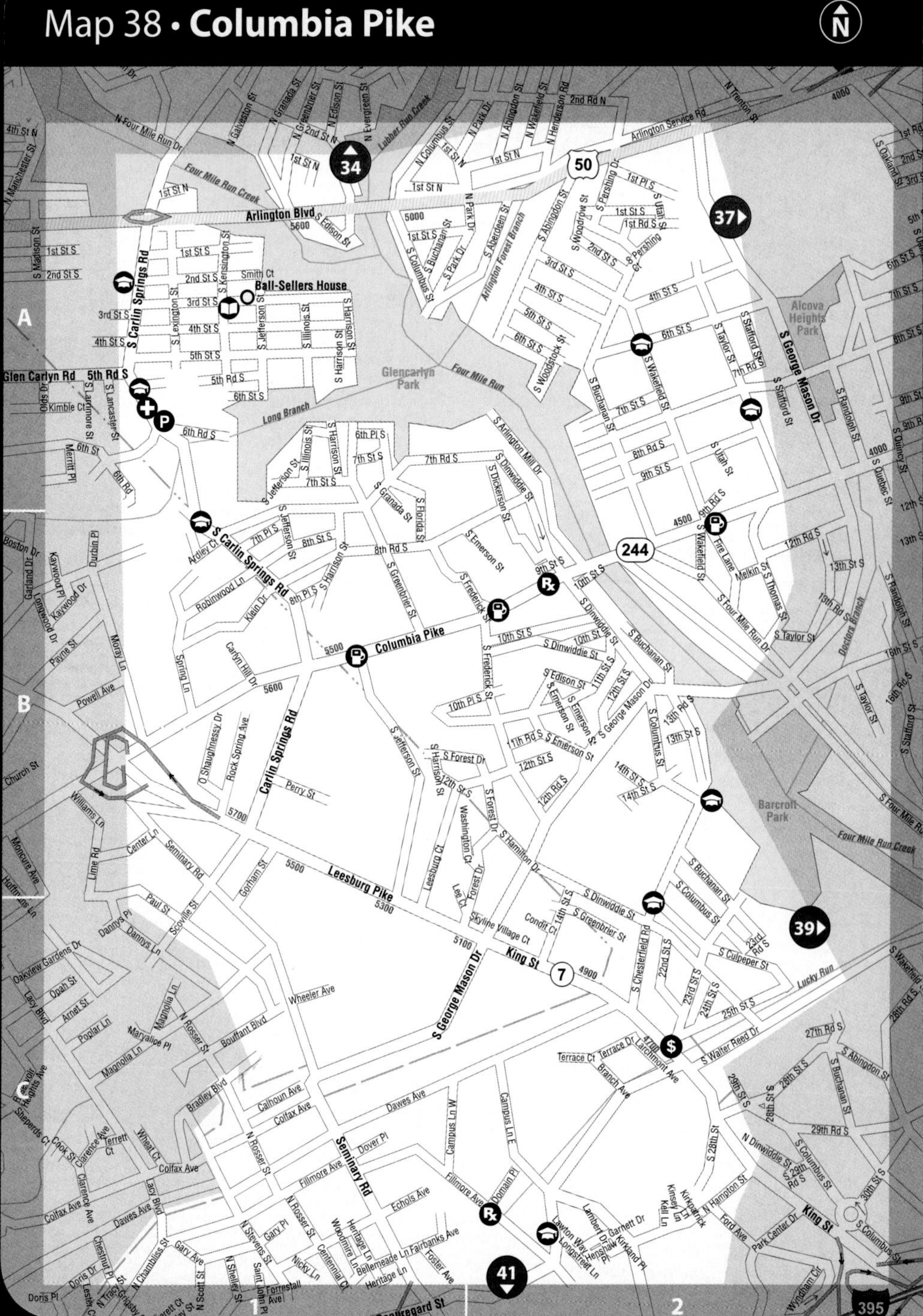
N
34
37
39
41
50
244
7
395
A
B
C
1
2
Arlington Blvd
5600
5000
Four Mile Run Creek
N Four Mile Run Dr
Lubber Run Creek
Arlington Service Rd
2nd Rd N
N Trenton St
4000
1st St N
N Galveston St
N Granada St
N Greenbrier St
N Edison St
N Evergreen St
N 2nd St N
N Columbus St
N Park Dr
N Abingdon St
N Wakefield St
N Henderson Rd
N Park Dr
S Edison St
S Columbus St
S Buchanan St
S Park Dr
S Aberdeen St
Arlington Forest Branch
S Abingdon St
S Woodrow St
S Pershing Dr
S Uhle St
1st Pl S
1st St S
1st Rd S
2nd St S
3rd St S
4th St S
5th St S
6th St S
S Woodstock St
Ball-Sellers House
Smith Ct
S Carlin Springs Rd
S Kensington St
S Lexington St
S Jefferson St
S Illinois St
S Harrison St
4th St S
5th St S
5th Rd S
6th St S
Glen Carlyn Rd
5th Rd S
Olds Dr
Kimble Ct
S Lamore St
S Lancaster St
Merritt Pl
6th St
6th Rd
6th Rd S
Long Branch
Glencarlyn Park
Four Mile Run
S Manchester St
S Madison St
4th St N
Alcova Heights Park
S George Mason Dr
S Taylor St
S Stafford St
7th Rd S
S Wakefield St
S Buchanan St
7th St S
8th Rd S
9th St S
S Utah St
S Randolph St
S Quincy St
S Quebec St
4000
4500
9th Rd S
Fire Lane
12th Rd S
13th St S
Melkin St
S Thomas St
S Four Mile Run Dr
13th Rd S
Doctors Branch
S Taylor St
16th St S
16th Rd S
S Stafford St
6th Pl S
6th St S
7th St S
7th Rd S
S Arlington Mill Dr
S Dinwiddie St
S Dickerson St
S Granada St
S Florida St
S Jefferson St
7th Pl S
8th St S
8th Rd S
8th Pl S
S Emerson St
S Frederick St
S Greenbrier St
9th St S
10th St S
Ardley Ct
Robinwood Ln
Klein Dr
Boston Dr
Garland Dr
Kaywood Pl
Kaywood Dr
Durbin Pl
Longwood Dr
Payne St
Moray Ln
Powell Ave
Spring Ln
Carlyn Hill Dr
Columbia Pike
5500
5600
10th St S
S Dinwiddie St
10th Pl S
S Edison St
11th St S
12th St S
S Emerson St
S George Mason Dr
S Columbus St
13th Rd S
13th St S
S Buchanan St
14th St S
14th St S
11th Rd S
12th St S
12th Rd S
S Forest Dr
S Jefferson St
S Harrison St
12th St S
Washington Ct
S Forest Dr
S Hamilton Dr
Leesburg Ct
Lea Ct
Forest Dr
O Shaughnessy Dr
Rock Spring Ave
Carlin Springs Rd
Perry St
5700
Church St
Williams Ln
Moncure Ave
Lime Rd
Center Ln
Seminary Rd
Gorham St
Leesburg Pike
5500
5300
Paul St
Scoville St
Dannys Pl
Dannys Ln
Barcroft Park
Four Mile Run Creek
S Four Mile Run Dr
S Buchanan St
S Columbus St
S Dinwiddie St
14th St S
S Greenbrier St
Condit Ct
Skyline Village Ct
S Chesterfield Rd
22nd St S
23rd St S
24th St S
25th St S
23rd Rd S
S Culpeper St
Lucky Run
S Wakefield St
28th Rd S
5100
King St
4900
S George Mason Dr
Oakview Gardens Dr
Opah St
Lacy Blvd
Arnet St
Poplar Ln
Magnolia Ln
Maryalice Pl
N Rosser St
Bouffant Blvd
Wheeler Ave
S Walter Reed Dr
27th Rd S
Terrace Ct
Terrace Dr
Larchmont Ave
Branch Ave
S Abingdon St
28th St S
S Buchanan St
29th St S
26th St S
29th Rd S
N Dinwiddie St
S Columbus St
29th Rd S
30th St S
Bradley Blvd
Calhoun Ave
Colfax Ave
Dawes Ave
Campus Ln W
Campus Ln E
S 28th St
N Rosser St
Seminary Rd
Dover Pl
Fillmore Ave
Fillmore Ave
Domain Pl
Echols Ave
Colfax Ave
Clarence Ave
Terrett Ct
Cook St
Wheat Ct
Sheperds Ct
Lacy Blvd
Dawes Ave
Gary Pl
N Rosser St
Heritage Ln
Woodmire Ln
Bellemeade Ln
Fairbanks Ave
Foster Ave
Heritage Ln
Centennial Ct
Nicky Ln
N Stevens St
Saint John Pl
Forrestall Ave
N Shelley St
N Scott St
Gary Ave
N Chambliss St
N Tracy St
Chestnut Pl
Doris Dr
Lester Ct
Doris Pl
Beauregard St
Lawton Way
Longstreet Ln
Lambert Dr
Henshaw Pl
Garnett Dr
Kirkland Pl
Kinsey Ln
Keill Ln
Kirkpatrick Ln
N Hampton St
Ford Ave
Park Center Dr
King St
S Columbus St
Windham Ct
4700

Essentials

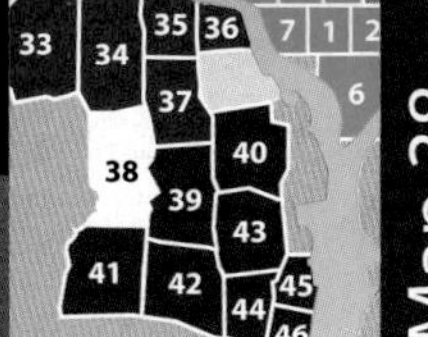

Gentrification meets immigration along this thoroughfare in transition. New condos replace old strip malls, and the sidewalks struggle for identity as the scent of pupusas, pad Thai, and poured concrete fill the air.

Banks

- **Wachovia** • 4651 King St

Gas Stations

- **Amoco** • 4625 Columbia Pike
- **Mobil** • 5200 Columbia Pike
- **Shell** • 5511 Columbia Pike

Hospitals

- **Northern Virginia Community** • 601 S Carlin Springs Rd

Landmarks

- **Ball-Sellers House** • 5620 Third St S

Libraries

- **Glencarlyn Public Library** • 300 S Kensington St

Parking

Pharmacies

- **Allied Pharmacy** • 5100 Fillmore Ave
- **CVS** • 5017 Columbia Pike

Schools

- **Barcroft Elementary** • 625 S Wakefield St
- **Campbell Elementary** • 737 S Carlin Springs
- **Carlin Springs Elementary** • 5995 5th Rd S
- **Claremont Immersion** • 4700 S Chesterfield Rd
- **Kenmore Middle** • 200 S Carlin Springs Rd
- **Northern Virginia Community College (Alexandria Campus)** • 3001 N Beauregard St
- **Our Savior Lutheran** • 825 S Taylor St
- **Wakefield High** • 4901 S Chesterfield Rd

Map 38 • Columbia Pike

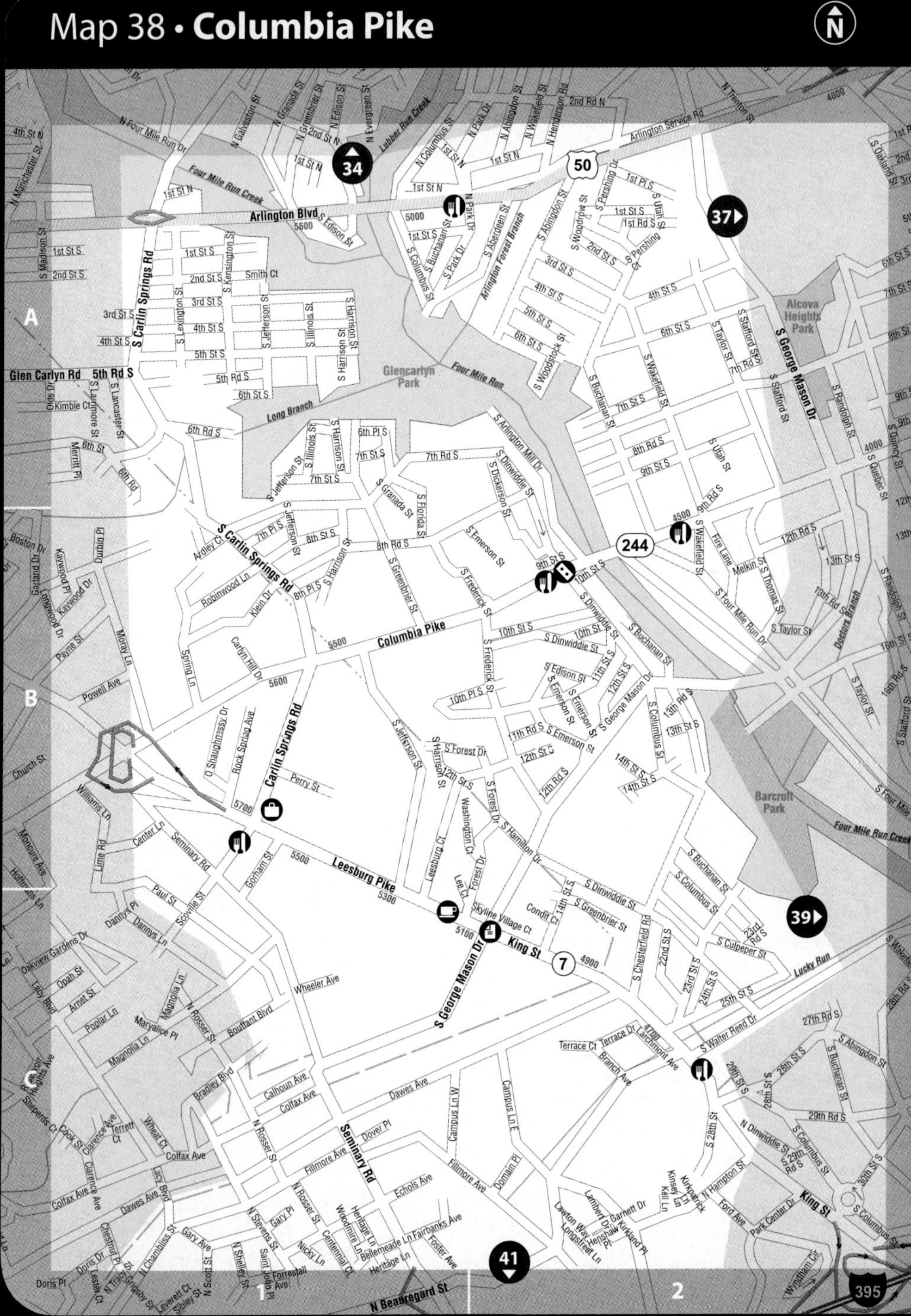

Other than a couple of beloved local chains like Bob & Edith's and Five Guys, there's little of interest.

Coffee

• **Starbucks** • 5115 Leesburg Pike

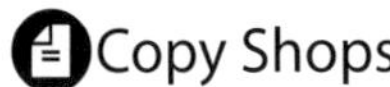

Copy Shops

• **Kwik Kopy Printing (9am-5pm)** • 5100 Leesburg Pike

Restaurants

• **Andy's Carry-Out** • 5033 Columbia Pike
• **Athens Restaurant** • 3541 Carlin Springs Rd
• **Atlacatl** • 4701 Columbia Pike
• **Crystal Thai** • 4819 Arlington Blvd
• **Five Guys** • 4626 King St

Shopping

• **REI** • 3509 Carlin Springs Rd

Video Rental

• **Tum Videos** • 5001 Columbia Pike

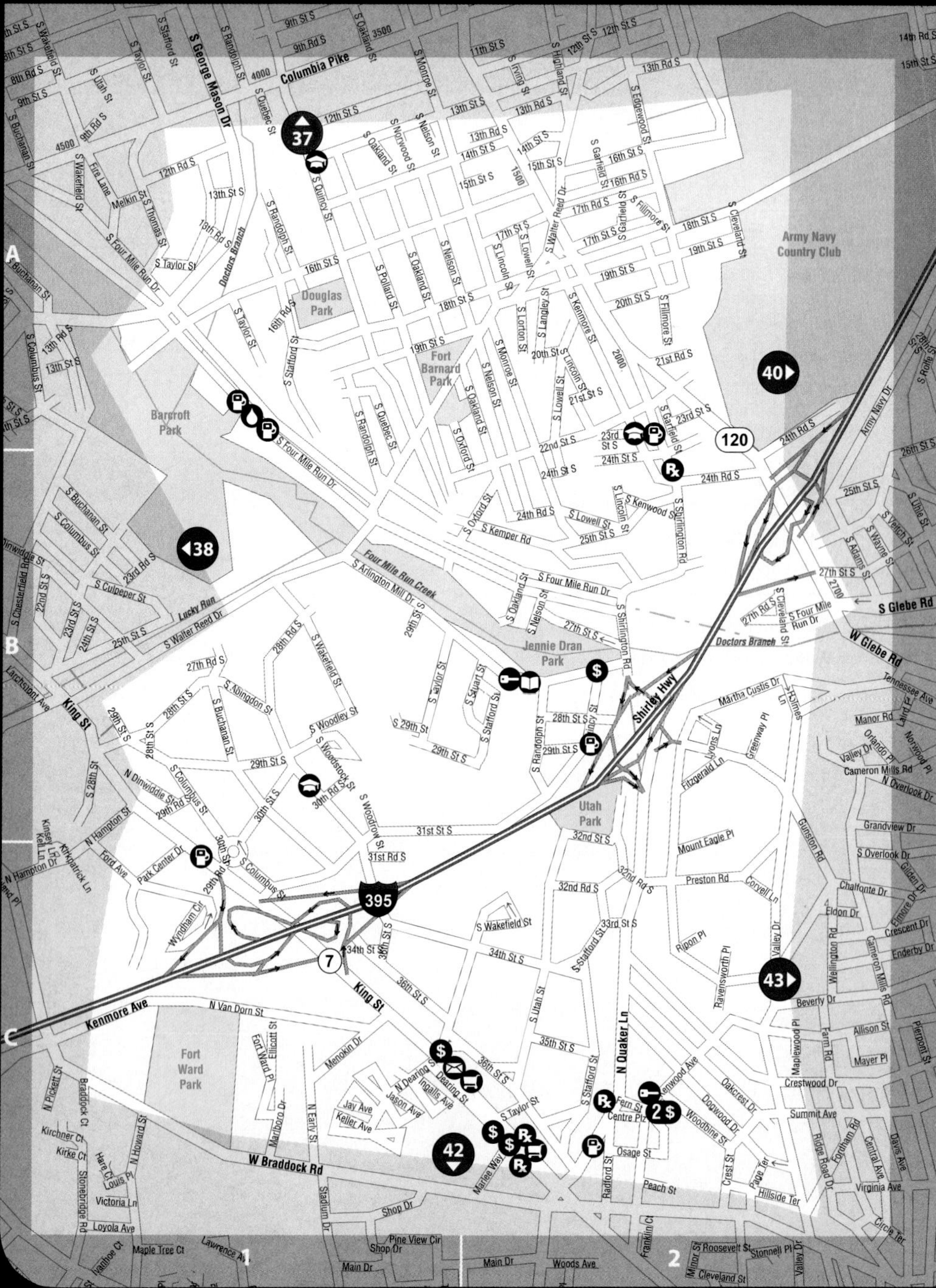

Map 39 • Shirlington

37
38
40
42
43

A
B
C
1
2

Columbia Pike
4000
4500
3500
1500
2000
2700
S George Mason Dr
Army Navy Country Club
Douglas Park
Fort Barnard Park
Barcroft Park
Four Mile Run Creek
S Four Mile Run Dr
Doctors Branch
Lucky Run
Jennie Dran Park
Utah Park
Fort Ward Park
Shirley Hwy
395
120
7
King St
Kenmore Ave
N Van Dorn St
W Braddock Rd
N Quaker Ln
S Glebe Rd
W Glebe Rd
Army Navy Dr
S Walter Reed Dr
S Arlington Mill Dr
S Shirlington Rd
9th St S
9th Rd S
8th Rd S
11th St S
12th St S
12th Rd S
13th St S
13th Rd S
14th St S
15th St S
16th St S
16th Rd S
17th St S
17th Rd S
18th St S
19th St S
19th Rd S
20th St S
21st St S
21st Rd S
22nd St S
23rd St S
23rd Rd S
24th St S
24th Rd S
25th St S
26th St S
27th St S
27th Rd S
28th St S
28th Rd S
29th St S
29th Rd S
30th St S
30th Rd S
31st St S
31st Rd S
32nd St S
32nd Rd S
33rd St S
34th St S
35th St S
36th St S
S Wakefield St
S Utah St
S Taylor St
S Stafford St
S Randolph St
S Quebec St
S Quincy St
S Oakland St
S Monroe St
S Nelson St
S Norwood St
S Pollard St
S Oxford St
S Lincoln St
S Lowell St
S Lorton St
S Langley St
S Kenmore St
S Irving St
S Highland St
S Garfield St
S Fillmore St
S Edgewood St
S Cleveland St
S Kenwood St
S Kemper Rd
S Buchanan St
S Columbus St
S Thomas St
S Chesterfield Rd
S Culpeper St
S Abingdon St
S Woodley St
S Woodstock St
S Woodrow St
S Dinwiddie St
S Adams St
S Wayne St
S Veitch St
S Uhle St
S Rolfe St
Fire Lane
Melkin St
Park Center Dr
Wyndham Cir
Ford Ave
N Hampton Dr
N Dinwiddie St
Kirkpatrick Ln
Kell Ln
Kinsey Ln
N Pickett St
Braddock Ct
Kirchner Ct
Kirke Ct
N Howard St
Hare Ct
Louis Pl
Stonebridge Rd
Victoria Ln
Loyola Ave
Maple Tree Ct
Lawrence Ave
Ivanhoe Ct
Ellicott St
Fort Ward Pl
Marlboro Dr
N Early St
Stadium Dr
Menokin Dr
Jay Ave
Keller Ave
Jason Ave
Ingalls Ave
N Dearing St
Dearing St
Marlee Way
Shop Dr
Pine View Cir
Main Dr
Woods Ave
Franklin Ct
Minor St
Roosevelt St
Stonnell Pl
Cleveland St
Valley Dr
Radford St
Osage St
Fern St
Centre Plz
Peach St
Crest St
Page Ter
Hillside Ter
Woodbine St
Dogwood Dr
Oakcrest Dr
Kenwood Ave
Martha Custis Dr
Holmes Ln
Lyons Ln
Greenway Pl
Fitzgerald Ln
Mount Eagle Pl
Preston Rd
Corvell Ln
Ripon Pl
Ravensworth Pl
Gunston Rd
Maplewood Pl
Beverly Dr
Farm Rd
Crestwood Dr
Summit Ave
Ridge Road Dr
Fordham Rd
Central Ave
Davis Ave
Virginia Ave
Circle Ter
Allison St
Mayer Pl
Pierpont St
Wellington Rd
Cameron Mills Rd
Enderby Dr
Crescent Dr
Elmore Dr
Eldon Dr
Chalfonte Dr
Glidden Dr
S Overlook Dr
Grandview Dr
N Overlook Dr
Valley Dr
Orlando Pl
Norwood Pl
Manor Rd
Laird Pl
Tennessee Ave
S Taylor St
Centre Plz

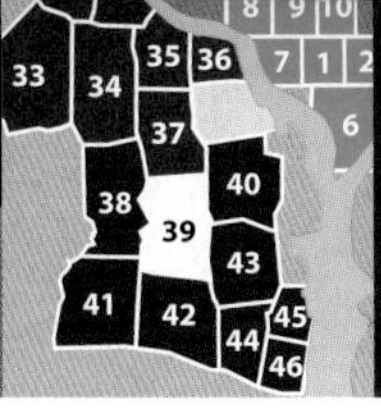

Originally considered the rough side of the tracks, this area has finally caught up with the Association of Northern Virginia Yuppies movement. However, don't expect to meet the man/woman of your dreams here: there are zero singles bars. But it's a great first date spot with that person you met last week in Clarendon.

Banks

- **BB&T** • 2700 S Quincy St
- **Burke & Herbert** • 1705 Fern St
- **Chevy Chase** • 3690 King St
- **Sun Trust** • 3610 King St
- **Wachovia** • 1711 Fern St
- **Wachovia** • 3624 King St

Car Rental

- **Enterprise** • 1575 Kenwood Ave • 703-647-1216
- **Enterprise** • 2778 S Arlington Mill Dr • 703-820-7100

Car Washes

- **David's Car Wash** • 4148 S Four Mile Run Dr

Gas Stations

- **Exxon** • 2316 S Shirlington Rd
- **Exxon** • 4368 King St
- **Mobil** • 4154 S Four Mile Run Dr
- **Shell** • 1333 N Quaker Ln
- **Shell** • 2817 S Quincy St
- **Shell** • 4060 S Four Mile Run Dr

Libraries

- **Shirlington Library** • 2786 S Arlington Mill Dr

Pharmacies

- **CVS** • 1521 N Quaker Ln
- **Green Valley** • 2415 S Shirlington Rd
- **Rite Aid** • 3614 King St
- **Safeway** • 3526 King St

Post Offices

- **Park Fairfax Station** • 3682 King St

Schools

- **Abingdon Elementary** • 3035 S Abingdon St
- **Drew Model Elementary** • 3500 S 23 St
- **Randolph Elementary** • 1306 S Quincy St

Supermarkets

- **Giant Food** • 3680 King St
- **Safeway** • 3526 King St

N

Columbia Pike
S George Mason Dr
S Four Mile Run Dr
Doctors Branch
Douglas Park
Fort Barnard Park
Barcroft Park
Army Navy Country Club
Four Mile Run Creek
S Arlington Mill Dr
Lucky Run
S Walter Reed Dr
Jennie Dean Park
Shirley Hwy
S Shirlington Rd
King St
S Glebe Rd
W Glebe Rd
Utah Park
Fort Ward Park
Kenmore Ave
N Van Dorn St
W Braddock Rd
N Quaker Ln
Valley Dr
Gunston Rd
S Four Mile Run Dr
S Kemper Rd
S Kenwood St
Martha Custis Dr
Mount Eagle Pl
Preston Rd
Fitzgerald Ln
Greenway Pl
Ravensworth Pl
Maplewood Pl
Oakcrest Dr
Dogwood Dr
Woodbine St
Kenwood Ave
Fern St
Centre Plz
Osage St
Peach St
Hillside Ter
Crestwood Dr
Summit Ave
Virginia Ave
Beverly Dr
Allison St
Mayer Pl
Menokin Dr
Dearing St
Ingalls Ave
Jason Ave
Jay Ave
Keller Ave
Marlboro Dr
N Early St
Stadium Dr
Shop Dr
Pine View Cir
Main Dr
Woods Ave
Maple Tree Ct
Loyola Ave
Victoria Ln
Stonebridge Rd
Braddock Ct
N Pickett St
N Howard St
Kirchner Ct
Kirke Ct
Hare Ct
Louis Pl
Fort Ward Pl
Ellicott St
Wyndham Cir
Park Center Dr
Ford Ave
N Hampton Dr
Kirkpatrick Ln
Kinsey Ln
Kell Ln
N Dinwiddie St
S Columbus St
S Buchanan St
S Abingdon St
S Woodley St
S Woodstock St
S Woodrow St
S Wakefield St
S Taylor St
S Stuart St
S Stafford St
S Randolph St
S Quincy St
20th Ct S
29th St S
30th Rd S
31st St S
31st Rd S
32nd St S
32nd Rd S
33rd St S
34th St S
35th St S
36th St S
S Utah St
Radford St
Crest St
Page Ter
Franklin Ct
Roosevelt St
Stonnell Pl
Lawrence Ave
Mariee Way

37
38
40
42
43
120
395
7
A
B
C
1
2

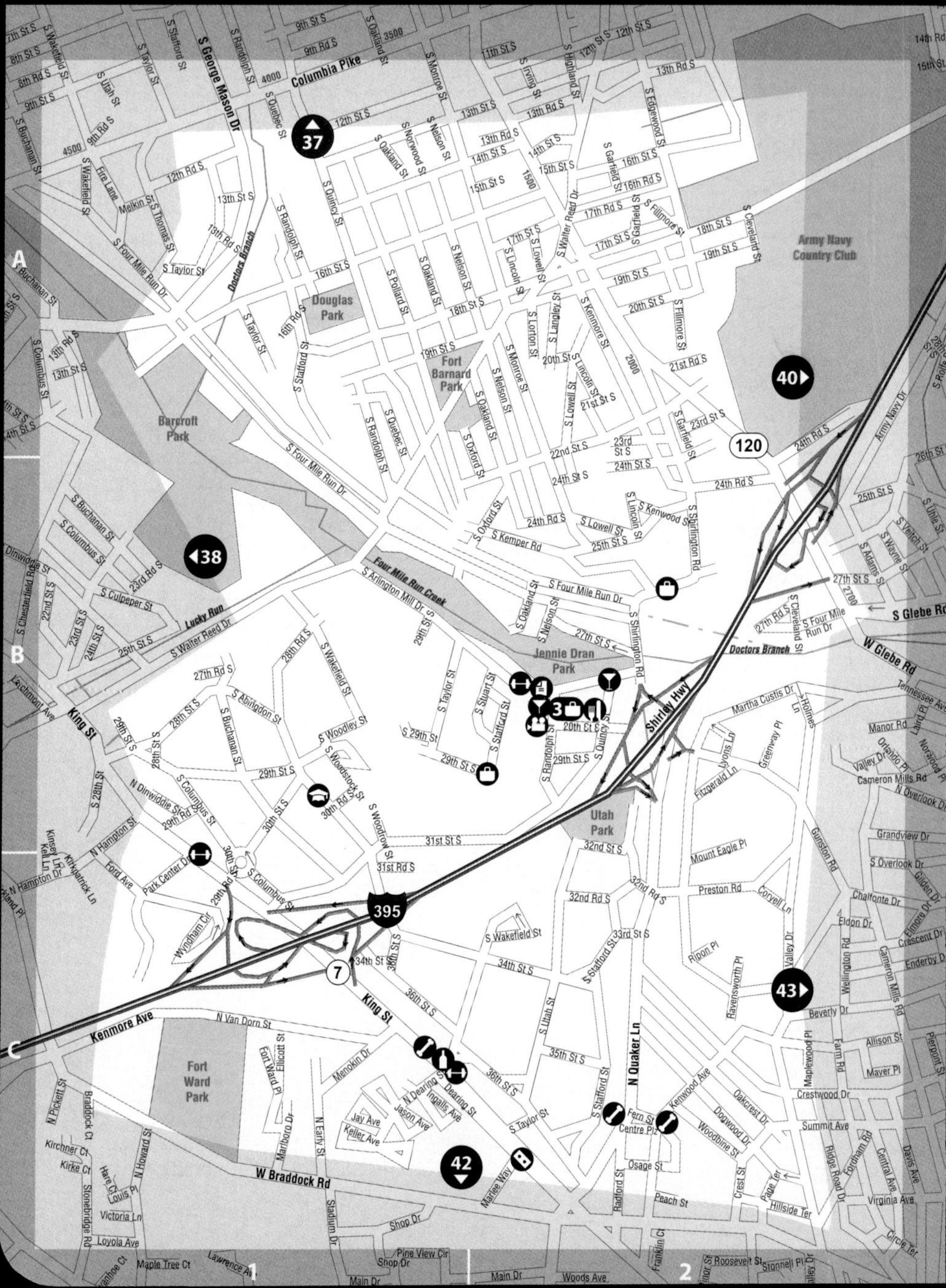

The Curious Grape not only stocks a terrific selection of vino and cheese, but the staff offers free tastings and mini wine-education courses. Ask them about the wine dinners, too. Catch a newly-released art flick at Odeon Shirlington 7, and stop in for dinner at Guapo's, considered by many to be the best Mexican restaurant in the area.

Coffee

- **Starbucks** • 3690 Q King St

Copy Shops

- **UPS Store (9am-7pm)** • 2776 S Arlington Mill Dr

Gyms

- **Center Club** • 4300 King St
- **Curves** • 2772 S Arlington Mill Dr
- **Washington Sports Clubs** • 3654 King St

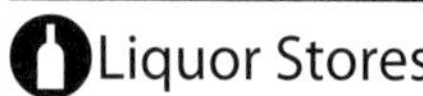

Liquor Stores

- **Virginia ABC** • 3678 King St

Movie Theaters

- **Cineplex Odeon Shirlington 7** • 2772 S Randolph St

Nightlife

- **The Bungalow, Billiards & Brew Co** • 2766 S Arlington Mill Dr
- **Capitol City Brewing Company** • 2700 S Quincy St
- **Guapo's** • 4028 S 28th St

Pet Shops

- **For Pet's Sake** • 1537 N Quaker Ln
- **One Good Tern** • 1710 Fern St
- **Pro Feed** • 3690 King St

Restaurants

- **Carlyle Grande Café** • 4000 28th St S

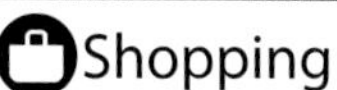

Shopping

- **Best Buns Bread Co** • 4010 28th St S
- **Books a Million** • 4201 28th St S
- **Carlyle Grande Café** • 4000 28th St S
- **The Curious Grape** • 4056 28th St S
- **Washington Golf Centers** • 2625 Shirlington Rd

Video Rental

- **Blockbuster Video** • 3610 King St

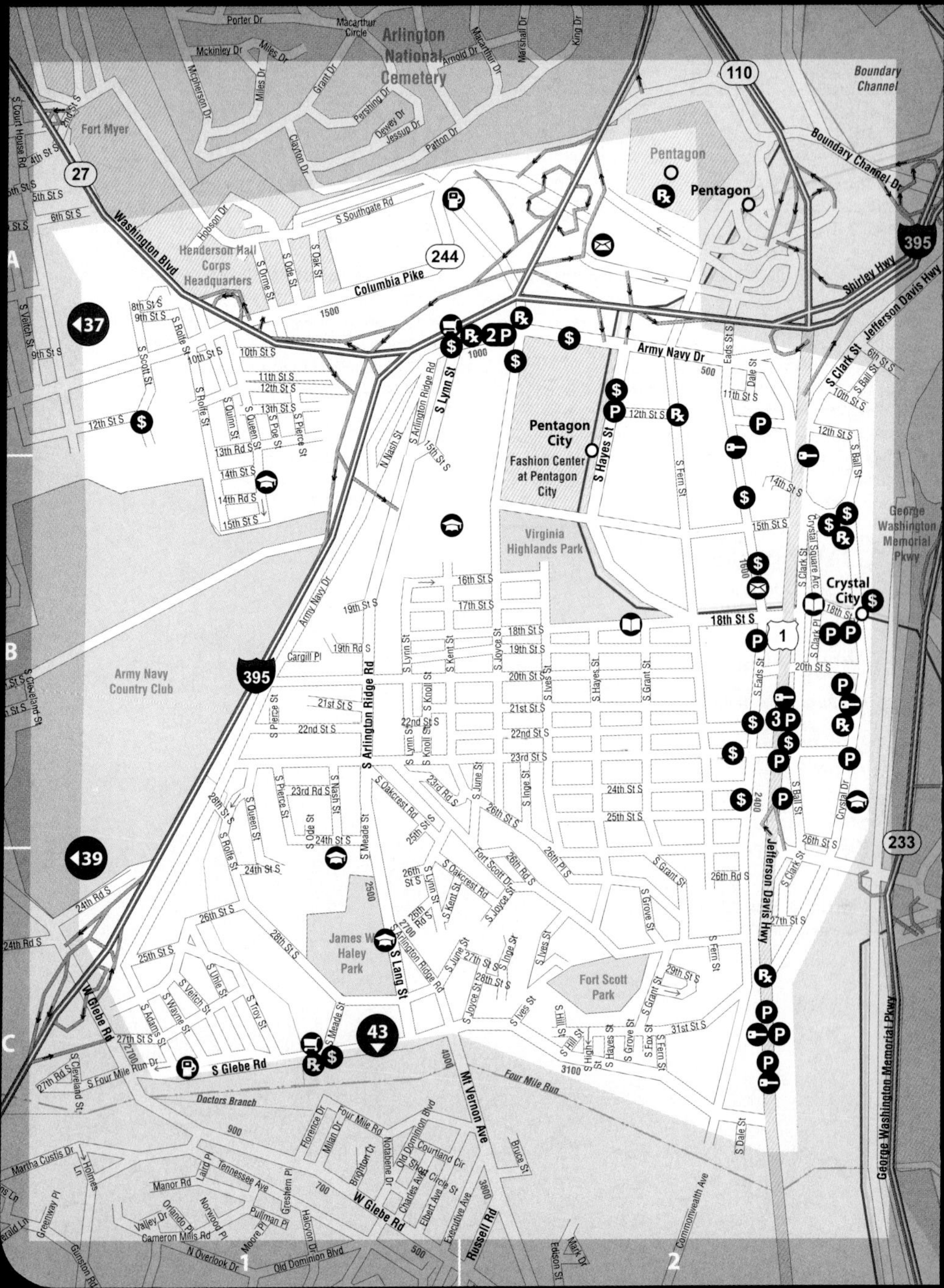

Map 40 • Pentagon City

Porter Dr
Macarthur Circle
Arlington National Cemetery
Mckinley Dr
Miles Dr
Arnold Dr
Macarthur Dr
Marshall Dr
King Dr
110
Boundary Channel
Mcpherson Dr
Grant Dr
Pershing Dr
Dewey Dr
Jessup Dr
Patton Dr
Clayton Dr
Fort Myer
S Court House Rd
2nd St S
4th St S
5th St S
6th St S
27
Pentagon
Boundary Channel Dr
Washington Blvd
S Southgate Rd
Hobson Dr
Henderson Hall Corps Headquarters
S Orme St
S Ode St
S Oak St
244
Columbia Pike
1500
395
Shirley Hwy
Jefferson Davis Hwy
37
S Veitch St
8th St S
9th St S
S Rolfe St
S Scott St
9th St S
10th St S
11th St S
12th St S
13th St S
13th Rd S
14th St S
14th Rd S
15th St S
S Quinn St
S Queen St
S Poe St
S Pierce St
2 P
1000
S Lynn St
S Arlington Ridge Rd
N Nash St
15th St S
Army Navy Dr
500
Eads St S
Dale St
11th St S
S Clark St
6th St S
S Ball St
10th St S
12th St S
Pentagon City
Fashion Center at Pentagon City
S Hayes St
S Fern St
14th St S
15th St S
1600
Crystal Square Arc
Virginia Highlands Park
George Washington Memorial Pkwy
Crystal City
16th St S
17th St S
18th St S
19th St S
19th Rd S
Cargill Pl
20th St S
21st St S
22nd St S
23rd St S
23rd Rd S
24th St S
25th St S
26th St S
26th Rd S
27th St S
28th St S
29th St S
31st St S
Army Navy Country Club
S Cleveland St
S Arlington Ridge Rd
S Kent St
S Joyce St
S Ives St
S Grant St
S Knoll St
S Lynn St
S June St
S Inge St
S Eads St
S Clark Pl
S Ball St
Crystal Dr
3 P
2400
233
S Oakcrest Rd
S Nash St
S Meade St
S Ode St
S Queen St
S Rolfe St
28th St S
24th Rd S
39
Fort Scott Dr
26th Pl S
S Grove St
2500
2700
James W Haley Park
S Lang St
Fort Scott Park
S Fern St
S Hill St
S High St
S Fox St
24th Rd S
25th St S
W Glebe Rd
S Uhle St
S Veitch St
S Wayne St
S Adams St
S Troy St
43
S Glebe Rd
S Four Mile Run Dr
27th Rd S
4000
3100
S Dale St
Four Mile Run
Doctors Branch
900
Florence Dr
Milan Dr
Four Mile Run Dr
Old Dominion Blvd
Mt Vernon Ave
Bruce St
Martha Custis Dr
Holmes Ln
Laird Pl
Tennessee Ave
Manor Rd
Gresham Pl
Brighton Ct
Notabene Dr
Courtland Cir
Charles Ave
Elbert Ave
Executive Ave
Commonwealth Ave
700
W Glebe Rd
3600
Greenway Pl
Orlando Pl
Norwood Pl
Pullman Pl
Valley Dr
Moore Pl
Cameron Mills Rd
Halcyon Dr
Russell Rd
Edison St
Mark Dr
N Overlook Dr
Old Dominion Blvd
500
Gunston Rd
1
2
A
B
C

Imagine *Blade Runner* without Harrison Ford. The Pentagon is a scary version of a possible future, with its vast underground corridors filled with uniformed workers bustling to and from military posts. Weird, and best to avoid.

Banks

- **Bank of America** • 1101 S Joyce St
- **Bank of America** • 1425 S Eads St
- **Bank of America (ATM)** • 900 Army Navy Dr
- **BB&T** • 2113 Crystal Plz Arc
- **BB&T** • 2221 S Eads St
- **BB&T** • 2947 S Glebe Rd
- **Burke & Herbert** • 500 23rd St S
- **Chevy Chase** • 1100 S Hayes St
- **Chevy Chase** • 1621 Crystal Sq Arc
- **Chevy Chase** • 2901 S Glebe Rd
- **PNC (ATM)** • 1301 S Scott St
- **PNC (ATM)** • 1600 S Eads St
- **Wachovia** • 1755 Jefferson Davis Hwy
- **Wachovia** • 251 18th St S
- **Wachovia (ATM)** • 1615 Crystal Sq Arc

Car Rental

- **Alamo** • 2780 Jefferson Davis Hwy • 703-684-0086
- **Budget** • 1200 S Eads St • 703-351-7500
- **Dollar** • 2600 Jefferson Davis Hwy • 866-434-2226
- **Enterprise** • 2020 Jefferson Davis Hwy • 703-553-7744
- **Enterprise** • 2121 Crystal Dr • 703-553-2930
- **Rent-A-Wreck** • 901 S Clark St • 703-413-7100

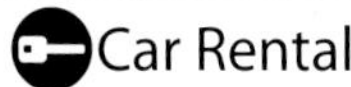

Gas Stations

- **Citgo** • 801 S Joyce St
- **Exxon** • 2720 S Glebe Rd

Landmarks

- **Pentagon** • Boundary Channel Dr

Libraries

- **Arlington County Aurora Hills Library** • 735 18th St S
- **U S Patent & Trademark Library** • 2021 S Clark Pl

Parking

Pharmacies

- **Costco Wholesale Pharmacy** • 1200 S Fern St
- **CVS** • 2400 Jefferson Davis Hwy
- **CVS** • The Pentagon
- **Eckerd's** • 1301 Joyce St
- **Giant Food Pharmacy** • 2901 S Glebe Rd
- **Harris Teeter Pharmacy** • 900 Army Navy Dr
- **Rite Aid** • 1667 Crystal Sq Arc
- **Rite Aid** • 2120 Crystal Plz Arc

Post Offices

- **Eads Station** • 1720 S Eads St
- **Pentagon Branch** • 9998 The Pentagon

Schools

- **DeVry University (Arlington Campus)** • 2450 Crystal Dr
- **Gunston Middle** • 2700 S Lang St
- **Hoffman-Boston Elementary** • 1415 S Queen St
- **Oakridge Elementary** • 1414 24th St

Supermarkets

- **Giant Food** • 2901 S Glebe Rd
- **Harris Teeter** • 900 Army Navy Dr

Map 40 • Pentagon City

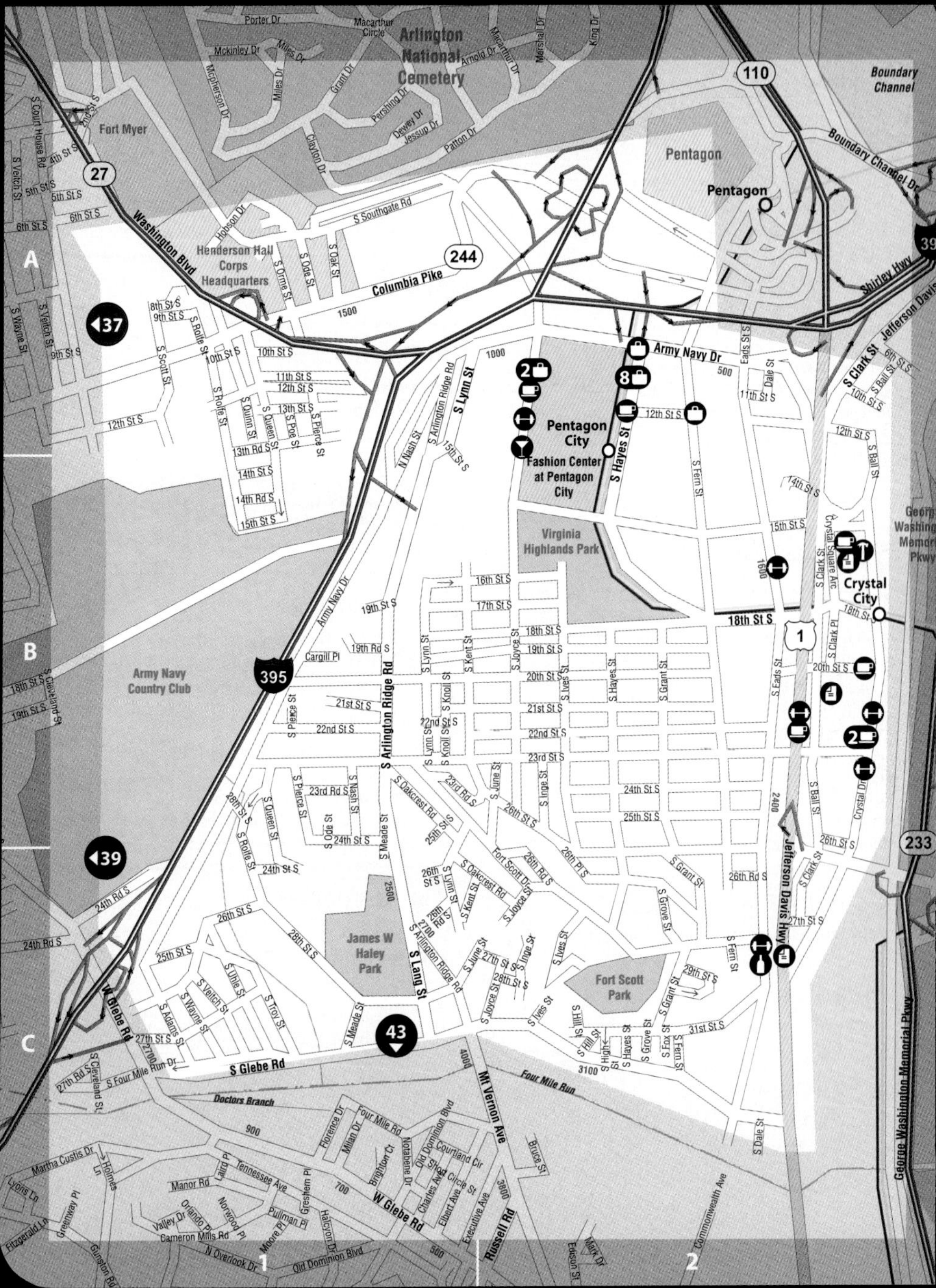

Arlington National Cemetery
Fort Myer
Henderson Hall Corps Headquarters
Pentagon
Boundary Channel
Pentagon City
Fashion Center at Pentagon City
Virginia Highlands Park
Crystal City
Army Navy Country Club
James W Haley Park
Fort Scott Park
Four Mile Run
Doctors Branch
George Washington Memorial Pkwy

Washington Blvd
Columbia Pike
Army Navy Dr
S Hayes St
S Lynn St
S Arlington Ridge Rd
18th St S
Jefferson Davis Hwy
S Glebe Rd
W Glebe Rd
Mt Vernon Ave
Russell Rd
Shirley Hwy
Boundary Channel Dr
S Lang St
Commonwealth Ave

27
110
244
395
1
233
37
39
43

A
B
C
1
2

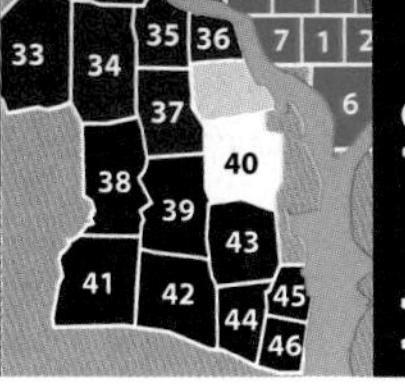

The Fashion Center at Pentagon City is the only traditional mall that's accessible by Metro. So if you really miss a good food court meal, take the yellow or blue line straight here.

Coffee

- **Coffee Company** • 2143 Crystal Plz Arc
- **Dunkin Donuts** • 1687 Crystal Sq Arc
- **Starbucks** • 1100 S Hayes St
- **Starbucks** • 1101 S Joyce St
- **Starbucks** • 1201 S Hayes St
- **Starbucks** • 1649 Crystal Sq Arc
- **Starbucks** • 1700 Jefferson Davis Hwy
- **Starbucks** • 2231 Crystal Dr

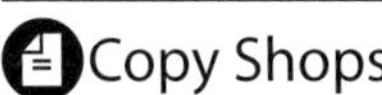

Copy Shops

- **Crystal City Copy (8am-5:30pm)** • 2341 Jefferson Davis Hwy
- **Kinko's (24 hours)** • 1601 Crystal Sq Arc
- **Minuteman Press (8:30am-5:30pm)** • 2187 Crystal Plz Arc

Gyms

- **Bally Total Fitness** • 1201 S Joyce St
- **Beyond Fitness** • 1600 S Eads St
- **Crystal Park Sport & Health** • 2231 Crystal Dr
- **Curves** • 2345 Crystal Dr
- **Gateway Sport & Health** • 1235 Jefferson Davis Hwy
- **Gold's Gym** • 2955 S Glebe Rd

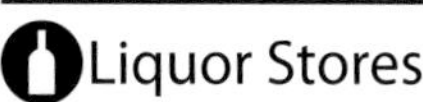

Hardware Stores

- **Crystal City Hardware** • 1612 Crystal Sq Arc

Liquor Stores

- **Virginia ABC** • 2955 S Glebe Rd

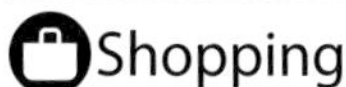

Nightlife

- **Sine Irish Pub** • 1301 S Joyce St

Shopping

- **Abercrombie & Fitch** • 1101 S Hayes St
- **BCBG** • 1100 S Hayes St
- **bebe** • 1100 S Hayes St
- **Costco** • 1200 S Fern St
- **Eddie Bauer** • 1100 S Hayes St
- **Elizabeth Arden Red Door Salon & Spa** • 1101 S Joyce St
- **Jean Machine** • 1100 S Hayes St
- **Kenneth Cole** • 1100 S Hayes St
- **Macy's** • 1000 S Hayes St
- **Williams-Sonoma** • 1100 S Hayes St

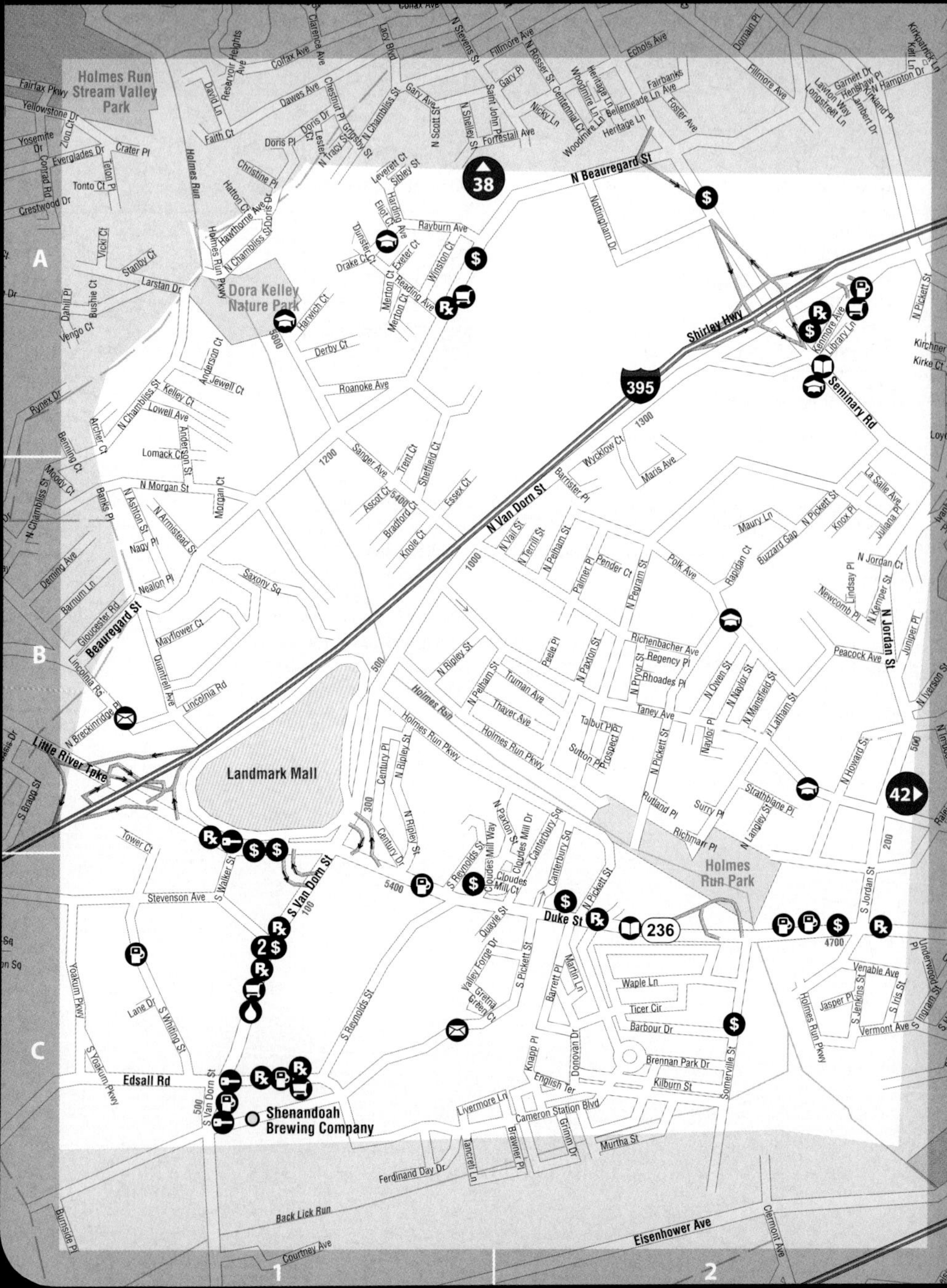

N
Holmes Run Stream Valley Park
Dora Kelley Nature Park
Landmark Mall
Holmes Run Park
Shenandoah Brewing Company
N Beauregard St
Shirley Hwy
395
Seminary Rd
N Van Dorn St
S Van Dorn St
Duke St
236
Little River Tpke
Beauregard St
Edsall Rd
Eisenhower Ave
Back Lick Run
Holmes Run Pkwy
N Jordan St
38
42
A
B
C
1
2

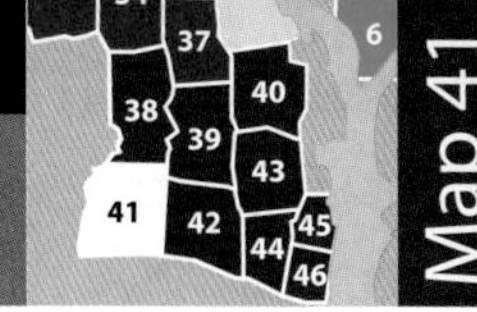

Whoever named this neighborhood must have loved irony. The area takes its name from the 1960s-built (and 1990s-renovated) Landmark Mall, but there are surprisingly few landmarks in this nondescript residential area. Unless you consider highway entrances and exits noteworthy.

Banks

- **Bank of America (ATM)** • 5801 Duke St
- **BB&T** • 233 S Van Dorn St
- **BB&T** • 4999 Seminary Rd
- **Burke & Herbert** • 155 N Paxton St
- **Provident Bank** • 231 S Van Dorn St
- **Sun Trust** • 1460 N Beauregard St
- **Sun Trust** • 4616 Kenmore Ave
- **Sun Trust** • 5701 Duke St
- **Virginia Commerce** • 5140 Duke St
- **Virginia Commerce (ATM)** • 185 Somervelle St
- **Wachovia** • 4601 Duke St

Car Rental

- **Avis** • 6001 Duke St • 703-256-4335
- **Enterprise** • 512 S Van Dorn St • 703-823-5700
- **Enterprise** • 5800 Edsall Rd • 703-658-0010

Car Washes

- **Mr Wash** • 420 S Van Dorn St

Gas Stations

- **Exxon** • 4550 Kenmore Ave
- **Exxon** • 4657 Duke St
- **Exxon** • 501 S Van Dorn St
- **Mobil** • 190 S Whiting St
- **Shell** • 4670 Duke St
- **Shell** • 5740 Edsall Rd
- **Sunoco** • 5412 Duke St

Landmarks

- **Shenandoah Brewing Company** • 652 S Pickett St

Libraries

- **Alexandria Charles E Beatley Jr Central Library** • 5005 Duke St
- **Ellen Coolidge Burke Branch Library** • 4701 Seminary Rd

Pharmacies

- **CVS** • 1462 Beauregard St
- **CVS** • 259 S Van Dorn St
- **CVS** • 4606 Kenmore Ave
- **CVS** • 5801 Duke St
- **CVS (24 hours)** • 5101 Duke St
- **Giant Pharmacy** • 5730 Edsall Rd
- **Rite Aid** • 4515 Duke St
- **Safeway** • 299 S Van Dorn St

Post Offices

- **Lincolnia Station** • 6137 Lincolnia Rd
- **Trade Center Station** • 340 S Pickett St

Schools

- **Francis C Hammond Middle** • 4646 Seminary Rd
- **James K Polk Elementary** • 5000 Polk Ave
- **John Adams Elementary** • 5651 Rayburn Ave
- **Patrick Henry Elementary** • 4643 Taney Ave
- **William Ramsey Elementary** • 5700 Sanger Ave

Supermarkets

- **Giant Food** • 1476 N Beauregard St
- **Giant Food** • 5730 Edsall Rd
- **Magruders** • 4604 Kenmore Ave
- **Safeway** • 299 S Van Dorn St

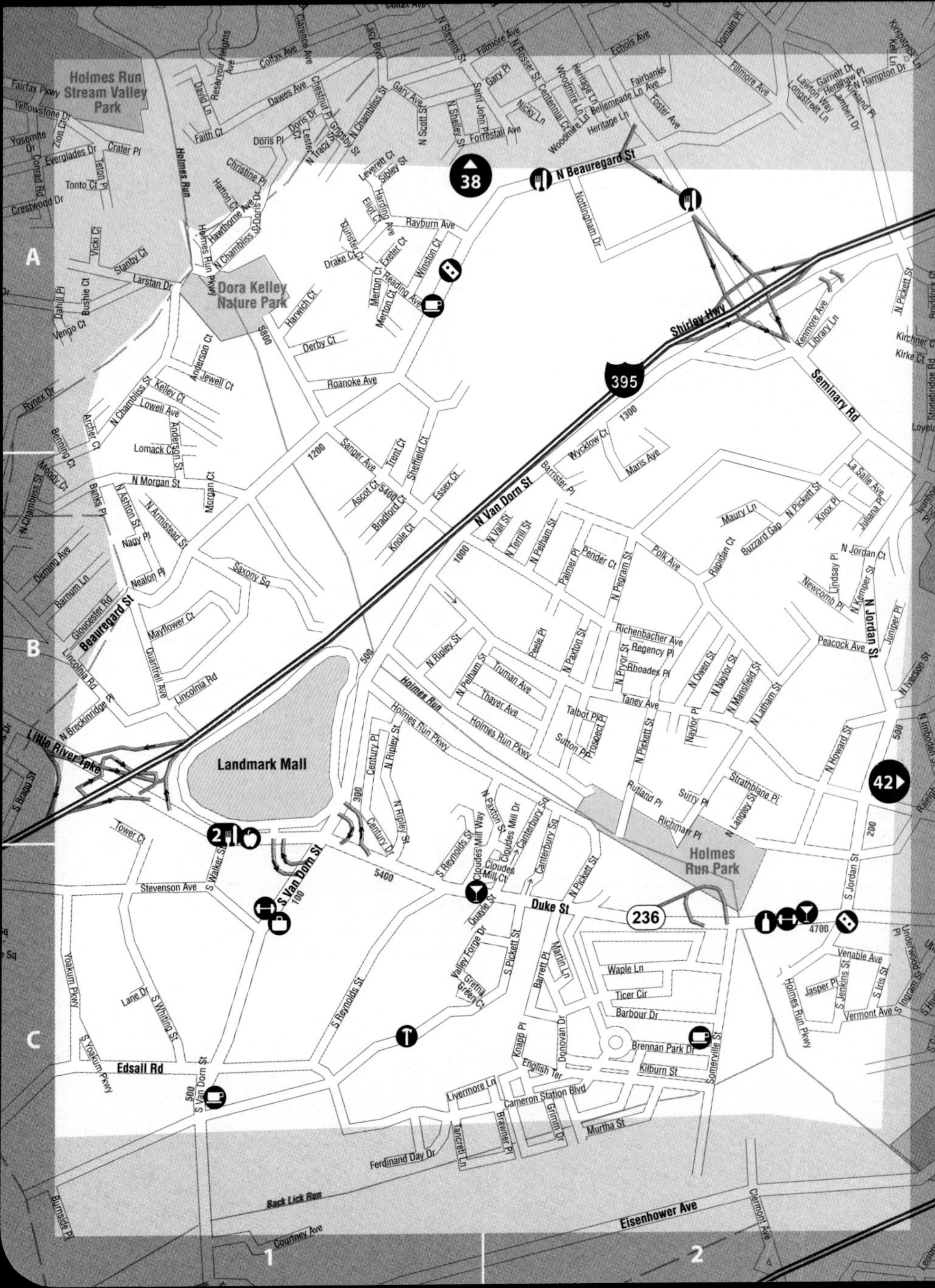

A
B
C
1
2

Holmes Run Stream Valley Park
Dora Kelley Nature Park
Landmark Mall
Holmes Run Park

38
42
395
236

Colfax Ave
Fairfax Pkwy
Yellowstone Dr
Yosemite Dr
Zion Ct
Everglades Dr
Crater Pl
Conrad Rd
Teton Pl
Tonto Ct
Crestwood Dr
Reservoir Heights Ave
David Ln
Faith Ct
Dawes Ave
Clarence Ave
Chestnut Pl
Doris Pl
Doris Dr
Lester Ct
N Tracy St
Grigsby St
N Chambliss St
Lacy Blvd
Gary Ave
N Scott St
N Shelley St
Saint John Pl
Forrestall Ave
N Stevens St
Fillmore Ave
Gary Pl
N Rosser St
Nicky Ln
Centennial Ct
Woodmire Ln
Heritage Ln
Bellemeade Ln
Fairbanks Ave
Echols Ave
Foster Ave
Domain Pl
Kirkpatrick Ln
Kell Ln
Garnett Dr
Henshaw Pl
Lawton Way
Longstreet Ln
Kirkland Pl
Lambert Dr
N Hampton Dr
Christine Pl
Hatton Ct
Hawthorne Ave
Holmes Run
Holmes Run Pkwy
Vicki Ct
Stanby Ct
Larstan Dr
Dahill Pl
Bushie Ct
Vengo Ct
Leverett Ct
Sibley St
Harding Ave
Eliot Ct
Rayburn Ave
Dunster Ct
Drake Ct
Exeter Ct
Winston Ct
Merton Ct
Reading Ave
Harwich Ct
Derby Ct
Roanoke Ave
N Beauregard St
Nottingham Dr
Shirley Hwy
Kenmore Ave
Library Ln
N Pickett St
Kirchner Ct
Kirke Ct
Seminary Rd
Rynex Dr
Anderson Ct
Jewell Ct
N Chambliss St
Kelley Ct
Lowell Ave
Anderson St
Archer Ct
Benning Ct
Lomack Ct
Moody Ct
N Morgan St
Morgan Ct
Banks Pl
N Ashton St
N Armistead St
Nagy Pl
Deming Ave
Barnum Ln
Nealon Pl
Saxony Sq
Gloucester Rd
Beauregard St
Mayflower Ct
Quantrell Ave
Lincolnia Rd
N Breckinridge Pl
Little River Tpke
S Bragg St
Sanger Ave
Trent Ct
Sheffield Ct
Ascot Ct
Bradford Ct
Essex Ct
Knole Ct
N Van Dorn St
Wycklow Ct
Maris Ave
Barrister Pl
N Vail St
N Terrill St
N Pelham St
Palmer Pl
Pender Ct
N Pegram St
Polk Ave
Rapidan Ct
Maury Ln
Buzzard Gap
La Salle Ave
Knox Pl
Juliana Pl
N Jordan Ct
Lindsay Pl
N Kemper St
Newcomb Pl
N Jordan St
Juniper Pl
Peacock Ave
N Iverson St
N Ripley St
Truman Ave
Thayer Ave
Peele Pl
N Paxton St
Richenbacher Ave
Regency Pl
N Pryor St
Rhoades Pl
N Owen St
N Naylor St
N Mansfield St
N Latham St
Taney Ave
Talbot Pl
Prospect Pl
Sutton Pl
N Pickett St
Naylor Pl
N Howard St
Holmes Run Pkwy
Century Ln
Century Dr
Rutland Pl
Surry Pl
Strathblane Pl
Richmarr Pl
N Langley St
Tower Ct
S Walker St
S Van Dorn St
Stevenson Ave
S Reynolds St
Cloudes Mill Way
Cloudes Mill Dr
Cloudes Mill Ct
N Paxton St
Canterbury Sq
Quayle St
Duke St
S Pickett St
S Jordan St
Underwood Pl
Venable Ave
Holmes Run Pkwy
Jasper Pl
S Jenkins St
S Iris St
S Ingram St
Vermont Ave
Yoakum Pkwy
S Yoakum Pkwy
Lane Dr
S Whiting St
Valley Forge Dr
Gretna Green Ct
Barrett Pl
Martin Ln
Waple Ln
Ticer Cir
Barbour Dr
Brennan Park Dr
Somerville St
Knapp Pl
Donovan Dr
English Ter
Kilburn St
Edsall Rd
Livermore Ln
Cameron Station Blvd
Grimm Dr
Murtha St
Tancreti Ln
Brawner Pl
Ferdinand Day Dr
Back Lick Run
Eisenhower Ave
Clermont Ave
Burnside Pl
Courtney Ave

5800
1300
1200
5400
1000
500
300
100
5400
4700
500
200
500

Drive to Dunkin' Donuts. Get coffee. Drive back onto highway. You've done Landmark.

Coffee

- **Cameron Perks** • 4911 Brenman Park Dr
- **Dunkin' Donuts** • 504 S Van Dorn St
- **Starbucks** • 1462 N Beauregard St

Farmer's Markets

- **Northern Neck Vegetable Growers Association Farmers Market** • 5801 Duke St

---

Gyms

- **Curves** • 4613 Duke St
- **Fitness First** • 255 S Van Dorn St

Hardware Stores

- **Home Depot** • 400 S Pickett St

Liquor Stores

- **Virginia ABC** • 4647 Duke St

Nightlife

- **Mango Mike's** • 4580 Duke St
- **Shooter McGee's** • 5239 Duke St

Restaurants

- **Clyde's** • 1700 N Beauregard St
- **Finn & Porter** • 5000 Seminary Rd
- **Ruby Tuesday** • 5801 Duke St
- **The American Café** • 5801 Duke St

Shopping

- **BJ's Wholesale Club** • 101 S Van Dorn St

Video Rental

- **Blockbuster Video** • 1480 N Beauregard St
- **Video Palace** • 8 S Jordan St

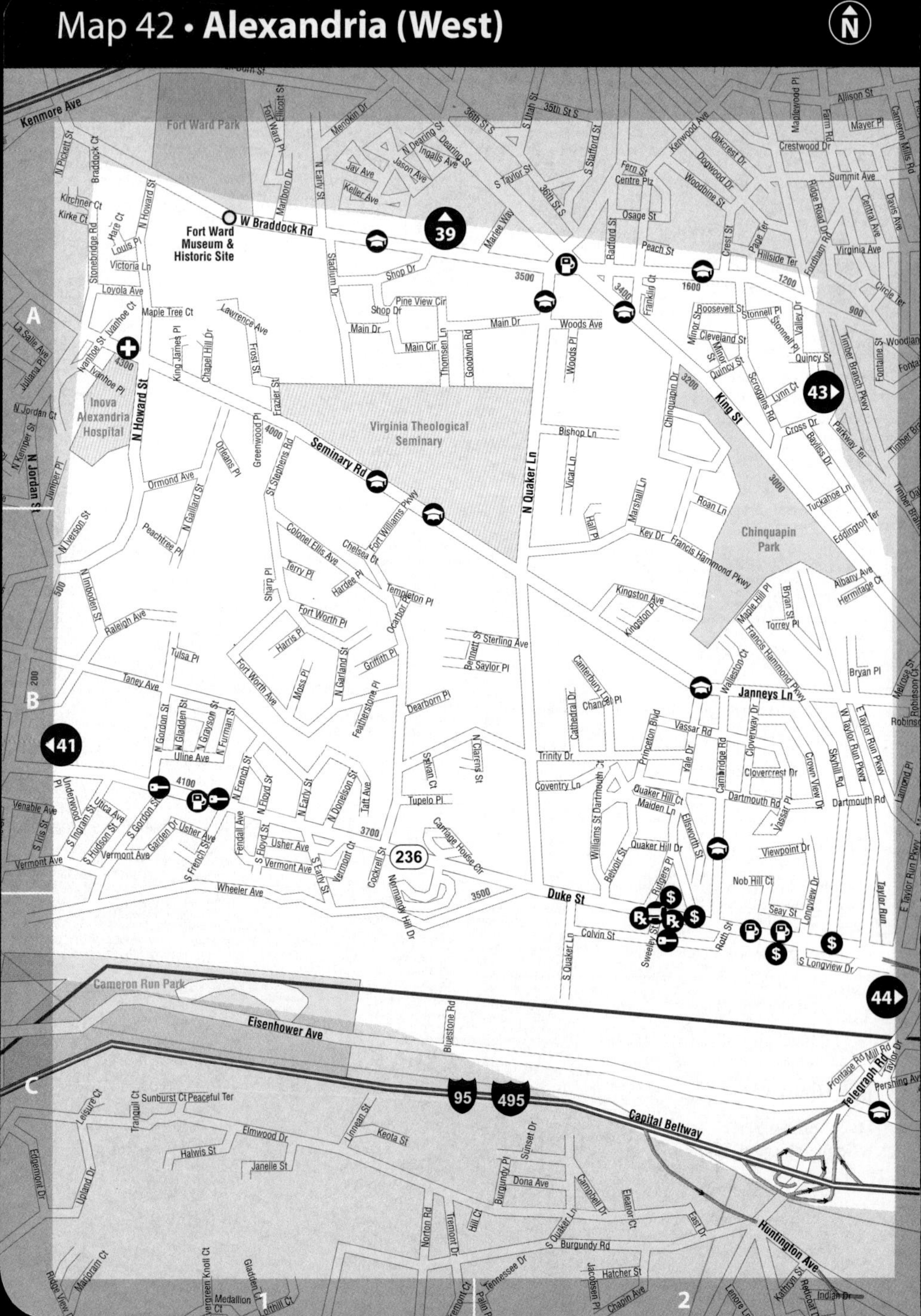

Fort Ward Park
Fort Ward Museum & Historic Site
W Braddock Rd
Kenmore Ave
Seminary Rd
Virginia Theological Seminary
Inova Alexandria Hospital
N Howard St
N Quaker Ln
King St
Chinquapin Park
Francis Hammond Pkwy
Janneys Ln
Duke St
Wheeler Ave
Cameron Run Park
Eisenhower Ave
Capital Beltway
Telegraph Rd
Huntington Ave
S Quaker Ln
Burgundy Rd
39
41
43
44
236
95
495
A
B
C
1
2

Pleasant and suburban, there are many reasons a family would relocate to a neighborhood like this. There's just little reason why anybody else would.

Banks

- **Bank of America** • 2747 Duke St
- **Burke & Herbert (ATM)** • 2836 Duke St
- **Chevy Chase** • 3131 Duke St
- **Sun Trust** • 3101 Duke St

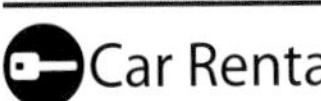

Car Rental

- **Enterprise** • 4213 Duke St • 703-212-4700
- **Hertz** • 16 Sweeley St • 703-751-1250
- **Rent For Less** • 4105 Duke St • 703-370-5666

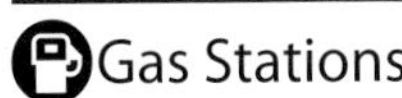

Gas Stations

- **Crown** • 4109 Duke St
- **Mobil** • 2838 Duke St
- **Mobil** • 3500 King St
- **Shell** • 2922 Duke St

Hospitals

- **Inova Alexandria** • 4320 Seminary Rd

Landmarks

- **Fort Ward Museum and Historic Site** • 4301 W Braddock Rd

Pharmacies

- **CVS (24 hours)** • 3130 Duke St
- **Giant Food Pharmacy** • 3131 Duke St

Schools

- **Bishop Ireton High** • 201 Cambridge Rd
- **Blessed Sacrement** • 1417 W Braddock Rd
- **Douglas MacArthur Elementary** • 1101 Janneys Ln
- **Episcopal High** • 1200 N Quaker Ln
- **Minnie Howard** • 3801 W Braddock Rd
- **Strayer University (Alexandria Campus)** • 2730 Eisenhower Ave
- **TC Williams High** • 3330 King St
- **Thornton Friends** • 3830 Seminary Rd
- **Virginia Theological Seminary** • 3737 Seminary Rd

Supermarkets

- **Giant Food** • 3131 Duke St

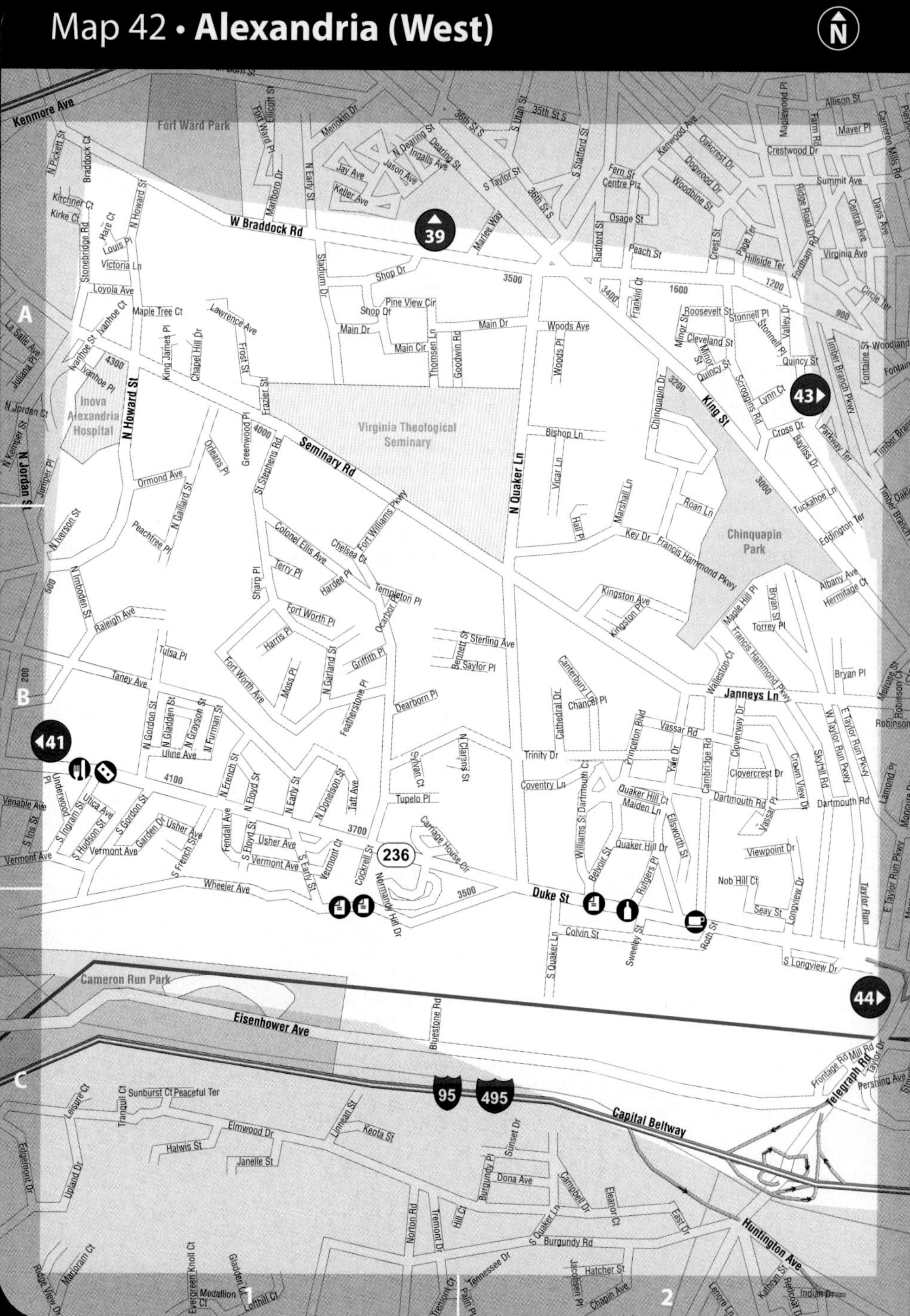

Kenmore Ave
Fort Ward Park
W Braddock Rd
39
Seminary Rd
Virginia Theological Seminary
N Quaker Ln
King St
Chinquapin Park
Francis Hammond Pkwy
Janneys Ln
Inova Alexandria Hospital
N Howard St
N Jordan St
Duke St
236
41
43
44
Cameron Run Park
Eisenhower Ave
95
495
Capital Beltway
Telegraph Rd
Huntington Ave
A
B
C
1
2

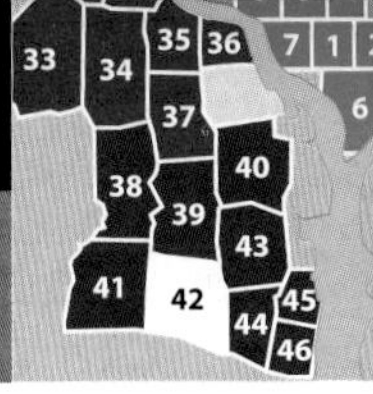

The area is in transition, so shopping is somewhat sparse, but a few good restaurants do exist. Check out Tempo, which mixes Northern Italian and French cuisines.

Coffee

- **Dunkin' Donuts** • 3050 Duke St

Copy Shops

- **Global Printing (8am-5pm)** • 3670 Wheeler Ave
- **Graphic Images (8am-6pm)** • 3660 Wheeler Ave
- **UPS Store (9am-7pm)** • 3213 Duke St

Liquor Stores

- **Virginia ABC** • 3161 Duke St

Restaurants

- **Tempo Restaurant** • 4321 Duke St

Video Rental

- **Blockbuster Video** • 4349 Duke St

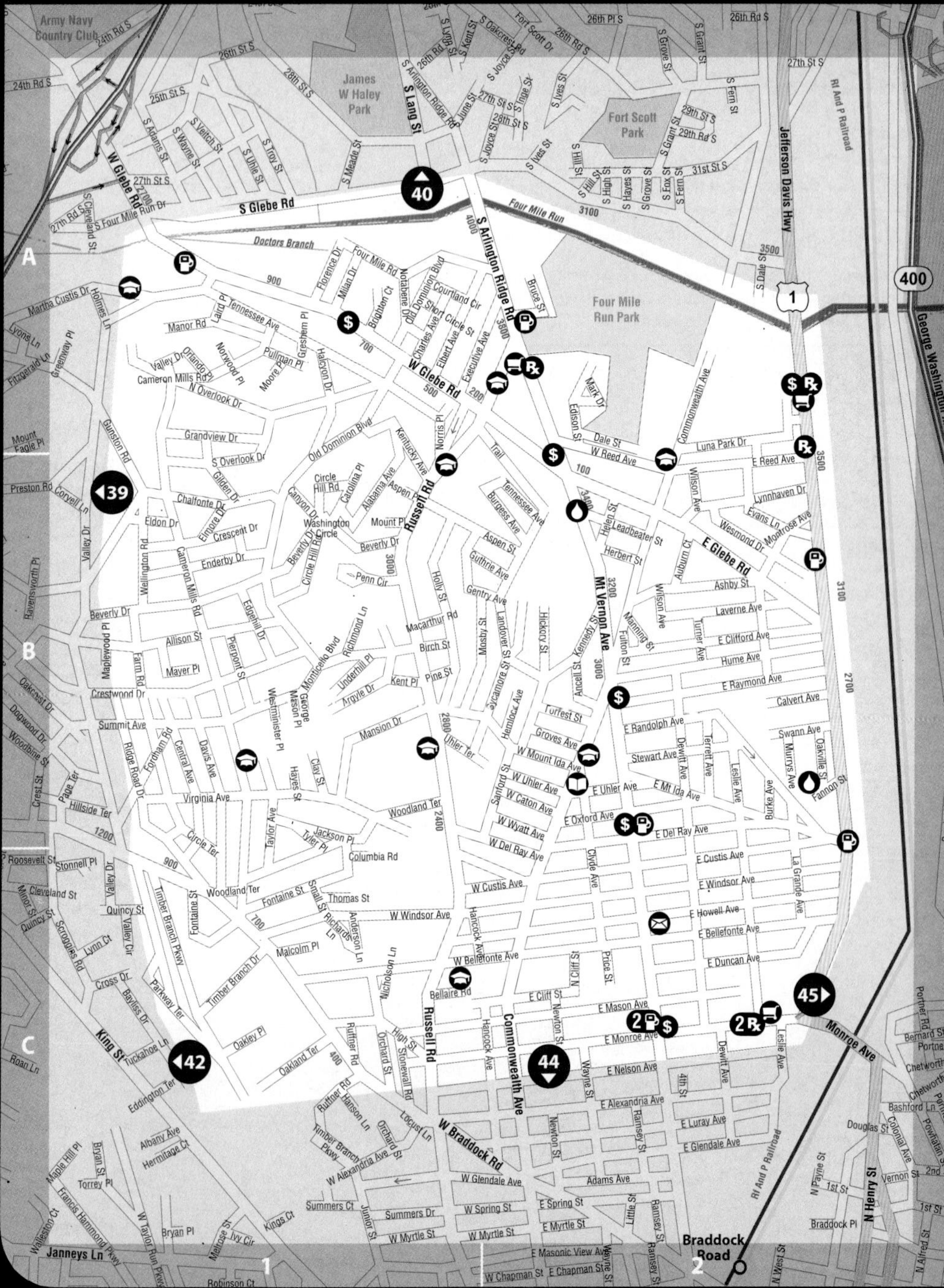
N
Army Navy Country Club
James W Haley Park
Fort Scott Park
Four Mile Run Park
Four Mile Run
Doctors Branch
S Glebe Rd
W Glebe Rd
E Glebe Rd
S Arlington Ridge Rd
Jefferson Davis Hwy
Rf And P Railroad
George Washington
Mt Vernon Ave
Russell Rd
Commonwealth Ave
W Braddock Rd
Monroe Ave
King St
N Henry St
Braddock Road
Martha Custis Dr
Tennessee Ave
Manor Rd
Valley Dr
Cameron Mills Rd
N Overlook Dr
Grandview Dr
S Overlook Dr
Gunston Rd
Preston Rd
Corvell Ln
Chalfonte Dr
Eldon Dr
Crescent Dr
Enderby Dr
Wellington Rd
Beverly Dr
Allison St
Mayer Pl
Crestwood Dr
Summit Ave
Virginia Ave
Woodland Ter
Mansion Dr
Monticello Blvd
Old Dominion Blvd
Circle Hill Rd
Washington Circle
Penn Cir
Macarthur Rd
Birch St
Kent Pl
Pine St
Argyle Dr
Underhill Pl
Holly St
Mosby St
Hickory St
Kennedy St
Leadbeater St
Herbert St
Ashby St
Laverne Ave
E Clifford Ave
Hume Ave
E Raymond Ave
Calvert Ave
E Randolph Ave
Swann Ave
Stewart Ave
W Mount Ida Ave
E Uhler Ave
E Mt Ida Ave
W Uhler Ave
W Caton Ave
W Wyatt Ave
E Oxford Ave
E Del Ray Ave
W Del Ray Ave
E Custis Ave
W Custis Ave
E Windsor Ave
W Windsor Ave
E Howell Ave
E Bellefonte Ave
W Bellefonte Ave
E Duncan Ave
E Cliff St
E Mason Ave
E Monroe Ave
E Nelson Ave
E Alexandria Ave
E Luray Ave
E Glendale Ave
W Glendale Ave
Adams Ave
W Spring St
E Spring St
W Myrtle St
E Myrtle St
E Masonic View Ave
W Chapman St
E Chapman St
Janneys Ln
Timber Branch Pkwy
Oakley Pl
Oakland Ter
Luna Park Dr
W Reed Ave
E Reed Ave
Lynnhaven Dr
Evans Ln
Wesmond Dr
Montrose Ave
Commonwealth Ave
Dale St
Edison St
Mark Dr
Bruce St
S Lang St
S Meade St
27th St S
26th St S
S Four Mile Run Dr
29th St S
31st St S
1
400
40
39
42
44
45
A
B
C
1
2

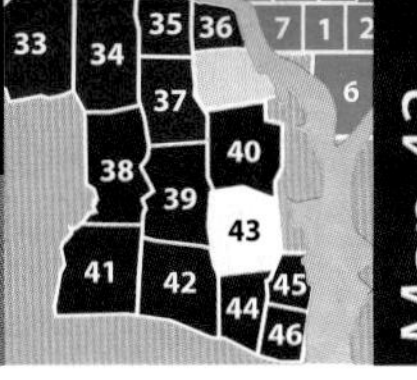

For the most part, this is the low-rent section of Alexandria, although there are a fair number of semi-luxe apartments on the outskirts toward Crystal City. Crime is fairly high here, so be careful.

Banks

- **Bank of America (ATM)** • 600 N Glebe Rd
- **Burke & Herbert** • 306 E Monroe Ave
- **Provident Bank** • 3801 Jefferson Davis Hwy
- **Sun Trust** • 2809 Mount Vernon Ave
- **Virginia Commerce** • 2401 Mt Vernon Ave
- **Wachovia** • 3506 Mount Vernon Ave

Car Washes

- **Mr Wash** • 3407 Mount Vernon Ave
- **Nab Auto Appearance Salon** • 2414 Oakville St

Gas Stations

- **Citgo** • 1015 W Glebe Rd
- **Citgo** • 2312 Mount Vernon Ave
- **Crown** • 3216 Jefferson Davis Hwy
- **Exxon** • 1601 Mount Vernon Ave
- **Exxon** • 2300 Jefferson Davis Hwy
- **Exxon** • 4001 Mount Vernon Ave
- **Shell** • 1600 Mount Vernon Ave

Libraries

- **Alexandria James M Duncan Branch Library** • 2501 Commonwealth Ave

Pharmacies

- **CVS** • 3811 Mount Vernon Ave
- **CVS** • 415 Monroe Ave
- **Giant Pharmacy** • 425 East Monroe Ave
- **Shopper's Pharmacy** • 3801 Jefferson Davis Hwy
- **Target** • 3101 Jefferson Davis Hwy

Post Offices

- **Potomac Station Finance** • 1908 Mount Vernon Ave

Schools

- **Alexandria Country Day** • 2400 Russell Rd
- **Charles Barrett Elementary** • 1115 Martha Custis Dr
- **Cora Kelly Elementary** • 3600 Commonwealth Ave
- **George Mason Elementary** • 2601 Cameron Mills Rd
- **Grace Episcopal** • 3601 Russell Rd
- **Immanuel Lutheran** • 109 Belleaire Rd
- **Mount Vernon Elementary** • 2601 Commonwealth Ave
- **St Rita** • 3801 Russell Rd

Supermarkets

- **Giant Food** • 425 E Monroe Ave
- **My Organic Market** • 3831 Mount Vernon Ave
- **Shoppers Food Warehouse** • 3801 Jefferson Davis Hwy

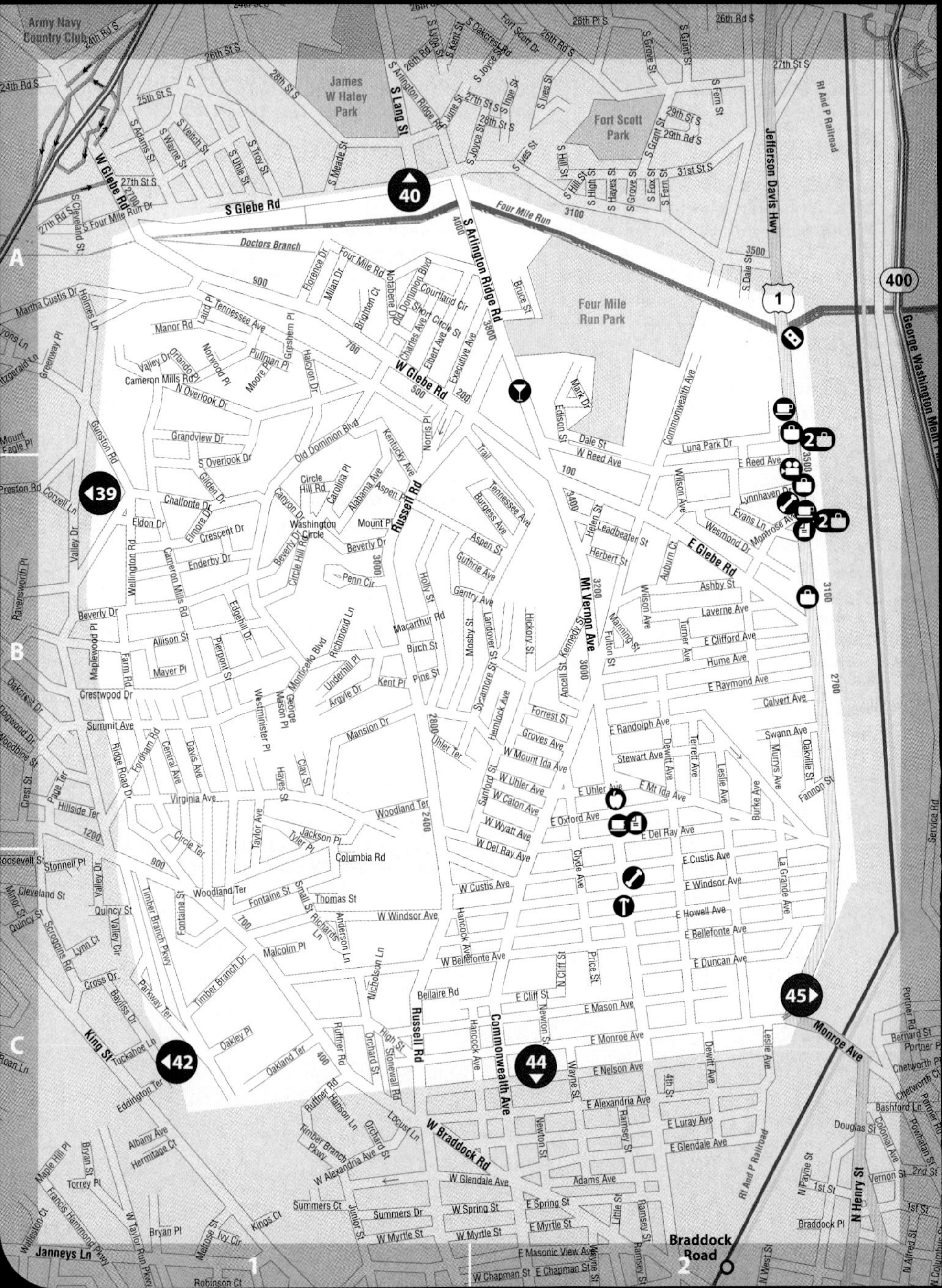
N
Army Navy Country Club
24th Rd S
26th St S
28th St S
25th St S
James W Haley Park
S Lang St
S Arlington Ridge Rd
26th Rd S
S Lynn St
S Kent St
S Oakcrest Rd
Fort Scott Dr
26th Rd S
26th Pl S
26th Rd S
S Grove St
S Grant St
27th St S
S Fern St
Rf And P Railroad
S Joyce St
S June St
27th St S
S Inge St
S Ives St
28th St S
Fort Scott Park
29th St S
29th Rd S
S Adams St
S Veitch St
S Wayne St
S Uhle St
S Troy St
S Meade St
S Ives St
S Hill St
S High St
S Hayes St
S Grove St
S Fox St
S Fern St
31st St S
Jefferson Davis Hwy
W Glebe Rd
27th St S
S Cleveland St
27th Rd S
S Four Mile Run Dr
2700
40
S Glebe Rd
Four Mile Run
3100
4000
Doctors Branch
Four Mile Rd
Florence Dr
Milan Dr
Notabene Dr
Old Dominion Blvd
Courtland Cir
Bruce St
3500
S Dale St
A
400
1
900
Martha Custis Dr
Holmes Ln
Tennessee Ave
Brighton Ct
Short Circle St
Charles Ave
Elbert Ave
Executive Ave
3800
Four Mile Run Park
George Washington Mem Pkwy
Manor Rd
Laird Pl
Gresham Pl
700
Pullman Pl
Valley Dr
Orlando Pl
Norwood Pl
Moore Pl
Halcyon Dr
W Glebe Rd
500
200
Cameron Mills Rd
N Overlook Dr
Mark Dr
Edison St
Commonwealth Ave
Mount Eagle Pl
Gunston Rd
Grandview Dr
Old Dominion Blvd
Kentucky Ave
Norris Pl
Dale St
W Reed Ave
Luna Park Dr
E Reed Ave
S Overlook Dr
Trail
100
Wilson Ave
3500
39
Preston Rd
Corvell Ln
Gilden Dr
Circle Hill Rd
Carolina Pl
Alabama Ave
Aspen Pl
Russell Rd
Tennessee Ave
Burgess Ave
3400
Helen St
Lynnhaven Dr
Chalfonte Dr
Canyon Dr
Evans Ln
Eldon Dr
Elmore Dr
Crescent Dr
Washington Circle
Mount Pl
Leadbeater St
Wesmond Dr
Montrose Ave
Valley Dr
Wellington Rd
Beverly Dr
Aspen St
Herbert St
Auburn Ct
E Glebe Rd
Cameron Mills Rd
Enderby Dr
Circle Hill Rd
3000
Guthrie Ave
Mt Vernon Ave
Ravensworth Pl
Penn Cir
Holly St
Gentry Ave
3200
Wilson Ave
Ashby St
3100
Beverly Dr
Edgehill Dr
Richmond Ln
Hickory St
Manning St
Laverne Ave
Maplewood Pl
Macarthur Rd
Mosby St
Landover St
Kennedy St
B
Allison St
Pierpont St
Monticello Blvd
Birch St
Fulton St
Turner Ave
E Clifford Ave
Farm Rd
Mayer Pl
Underhill Pl
Pine St
Sycamore St
Ancell St
3000
Hume Ave
Crestwood Dr
Argyle Dr
Kent Pl
E Raymond Ave
2700
Oakcrest Dr
George Mason Pl
Westminster Pl
Hemlock Ave
Forrest St
Calvert Ave
Summit Ave
Mansion Dr
2800
E Randolph Ave
Dogwood Dr
Ridge Road Dr
Fordham Rd
Central Ave
Davis Ave
Uhler Ter
Groves Ave
Swann Ave
Woodbine St
W Mount Ida Ave
Stewart Ave
Dewitt Ave
Terrett Ave
Leslie Ave
Murrys Ave
Oakville St
Clay St
Hayes St
Sanford St
W Uhler Ave
Burke Ave
Crest St
Page Ter
E Uhler Ave
E Mt Ida Ave
Fannon St
Virginia Ave
W Caton Ave
Hillside Ter
Woodland Ter
2400
E Oxford Ave
Taylor Ave
W Wyatt Ave
Service Rd
1200
Jackson Pl
E Del Ray Ave
Tyler Pl
W Del Ray Ave
Circle Ter
Columbia Rd
Clyde Ave
E Custis Ave
Roosevelt St
Stonnell Pl
900
La Grande Ave
Valley Dr
Woodland Ter
W Custis Ave
E Windsor Ave
Minor St
Cleveland St
Timber Branch Pkwy
Fontaine St
Fontaine St
Small St
Thomas St
Quincy St
Quincy St
Valley Cir
Richards Ln
Anderson Ln
W Windsor Ave
E Howell Ave
Scroggins Rd
700
Hancock Ave
E Bellefonte Ave
Lynn Ct
Malcolm Pl
Nicholson Ln
W Bellefonte Ave
N Cliff St
Price St
E Duncan Ave
Cross Dr
Timber Branch Dr
Bayliss Dr
Parkway Ter
Bellaire Rd
E Cliff St
45
Portner Rd
E Mason Ave
Newton St
Russell Rd
Commonwealth Ave
Ruffner Rd
Orchard St
High St
Stonewall Rd
Hancock Ave
Oakley Pl
E Monroe Ave
Monroe Ave
Bernard St
Portner Pl
C
King St
Tuckahoe Ln
Roan Ln
42
Oakland Ter
400
44
Wayne St
E Nelson Ave
Dewitt Ave
Leslie Ave
Chetworth Pl
Chetworth Ct
Eddington Ter
Ruffner Rd
Hanson Ln
Locust Ln
E Alexandria Ave
4th St
Bashford Ln
Portner Rd
Timber Branch Pkwy
Orchard St
W Braddock Rd
Ramsey St
Newton St
E Luray Ave
Douglas St
Colonial Ave
Albany Ave
Hermitage Ct
W Alexandria Ave
E Glendale Ave
Rf And P Railroad
Powhatan St
Maple Hill Pl
Bryan St
Torrey Pl
W Glendale Ave
Adams Ave
N Payne St
1st St
N Henry St
Vernon St
2nd St
Francis Hammond Pkwy
Summers Ct
Junior St
Summers Dr
W Spring St
E Spring St
Little St
Ramsey St
1st St
Walleston Ct
Kings Ct
Melrose St
Ivy Cir
Bryan Pl
W Taylor Run Pkwy
W Myrtle St
W Myrtle St
E Myrtle St
Braddock Pl
Braddock Road
Janneys Ln
E Masonic View Ave
Wayne St
Ramsey St
West St
N Alfred St
N Columbus St
1
2
Robinson Ct
W Chapman St
E Chapman St

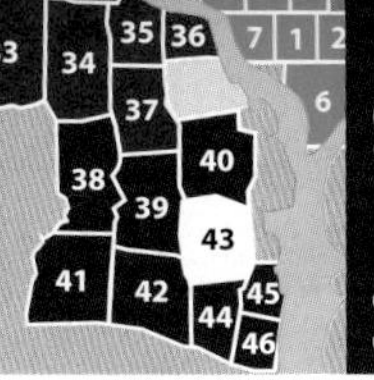

Potomac Yard, which houses the Regal Potomac Yard 16, is the biggest draw in the area with large, clean, box stores including Target, Barnes & Noble, Sports Authority, and Old Navy. Locals and non-locals alike flock here to shop.

Coffee

- **Dunkin' Donuts** • 3325 Jefferson Davis Hwy
- **St Elmo's Coffee Pub** • 2300 Mount Vernon Ave
- **Starbucks** • 3825 Jefferson Davis Hwy

Copy Shops

- **Staples (7am-9pm)** • 3301 Jefferson Davis Hwy
- **UPS Store (9am-7pm)** • 2308 Mount Vernon Ave

Farmer's Markets

- **Del Ray Farmer's Market** • Mt Vernon & Oxford Aves

Hardware Stores

- **Executive Lock & Key** • 2003 Mount Vernon Ave

Movie Theaters

- **Regal Potamic Yard 16** • 3575 Jefferson Davis Hwy

Nightlife

- **Birchmere** • 3701 Mt Vernon Ave

Pet Shops

- **Hydrant Dog Bakery** • 2101 Mount Vernon Ave
- **Petsmart** • 3351 Jefferson Davis Hwy

Shopping

- **Barnes & Noble** • 3651 Jefferson Davis Hwy
- **Best Buy** • 3401 Jefferson Davis Hwy
- **Old Navy** • 3621 Jefferson Davis Hwy
- **PETsMART** • 3351 Jefferson Davis Hwy
- **Sports Authority** • 3701 Jefferson Davis Hwy
- **Staples** • 3301 Jefferson Davis Hwy
- **Target** • 3101 Jefferson Davis Hwy

Video Rental

- **Hollywood Video** • 3925 Jefferson Davis Hwy

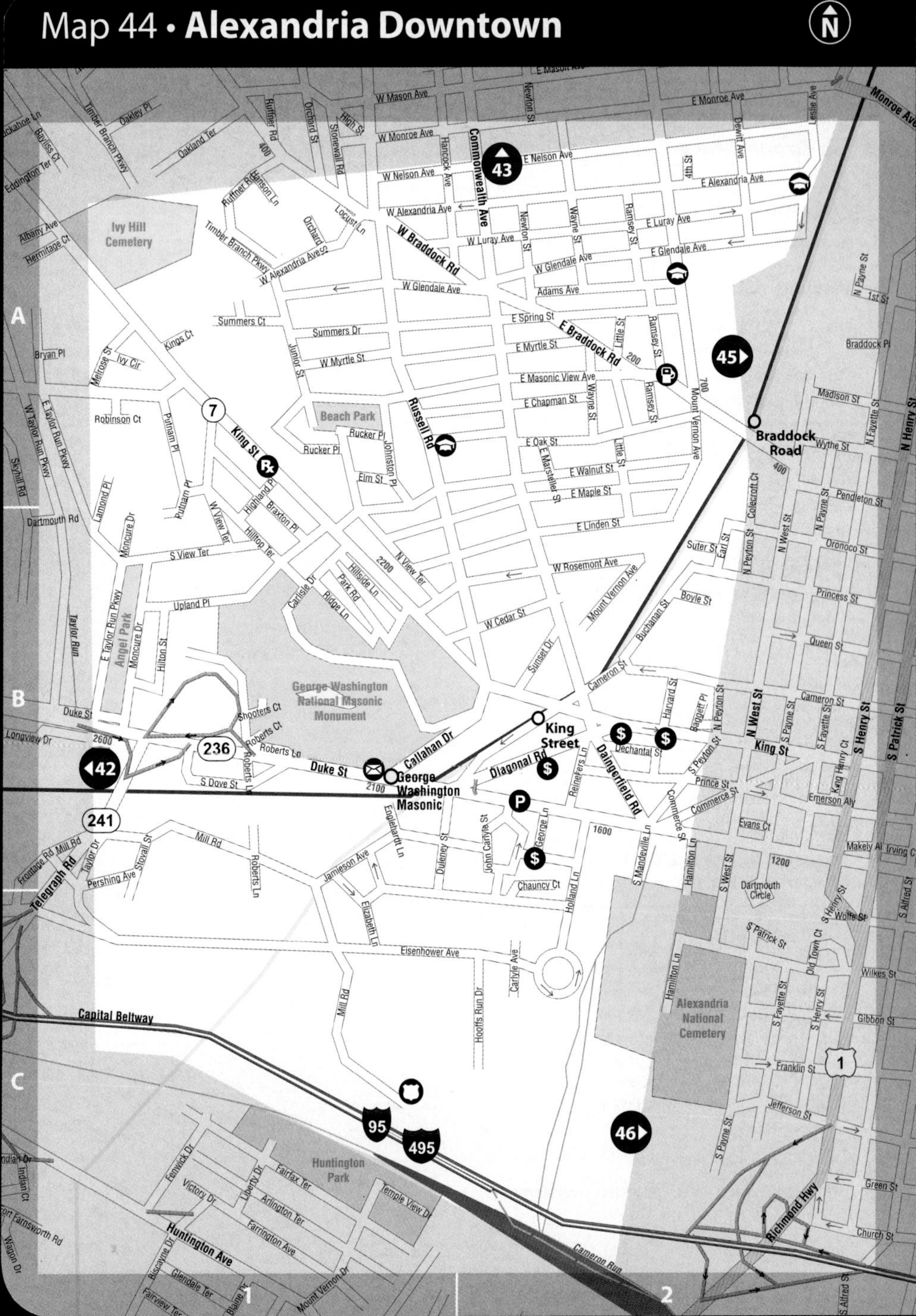

Map 44 • Alexandria Downtown
N
A
B
C
1
2
43
45
46
42
Ivy Hill Cemetery
Beach Park
George Washington National Masonic Monument
Angel Park
Huntington Park
Alexandria National Cemetery
Braddock Road
King Street
George Washington Masonic
Capital Beltway
Cameron Run
Richmond Hwy
95
495
1
7
236
241
King St
Duke St
Commonwealth Ave
W Braddock Rd
E Braddock Rd
Russell Rd
Mount Vernon Ave
Diagonal Rd
Daingerfield Rd
Callahan Dr
Eisenhower Ave
Telegraph Rd
Huntington Ave
N West St
S Henry St
N Henry St
S Patrick St
Monroe Ave
E Monroe Ave
W Monroe Ave
W Mason Ave
E Nelson Ave
W Nelson Ave
E Alexandria Ave
W Alexandria Ave
E Luray Ave
W Luray Ave
E Glendale Ave
W Glendale Ave
Adams Ave
E Spring St
E Myrtle St
W Myrtle St
E Masonic View Ave
E Chapman St
E Oak St
E Walnut St
E Maple St
E Linden St
W Rosemont Ave
W Cedar St
Summers Ct
Summers Dr
Rucker Pl
Elm St
Kings Ct
Bryan Pl
Ivy Cir
Robinson Ct
S View Ter
Upland Pl
Shooters Ct
Roberts Ct
Roberts Ln
S Dove St
Mill Rd
Pershing Ave
Jamieson Ave
Chauncy Ct
Dechantal St
Prince St
Commerce St
Emerson Aly
Evans Ct
Makely Al
Irving Ct
Dartmouth Circle
Wolfe St
Wilkes St
Gibbon St
Franklin St
Jefferson St
Green St
Church St
Cameron St
Queen St
Princess St
Oronoco St
Pendleton St
Wythe St
Madison St
Braddock Pl
1st St
Suter St
Boyle St
Buchanan St
Sunset Dr
Hooffs Run Dr
Carlyle Ave
Holland Ln
S Mandeville Ln
Hamilton Ln
Dulaney St
John Carlyle St
George Ln
Elizabeth Ln
Reinekers Ln
Harvard St
Baggett Pl
N Peyton St
S Peyton St
N Payne St
S Payne St
S Fayette St
N Fayette St
S West St
Old Town Ct
King Henry Ct
S Alfred St
Colecroft Ct
Earl St
Little St
Ramsey St
Wayne St
Newton St
Hancock Ave
Dewitt Ave
Leslie Ave
4th St
Junior St
Johnston Pl
Carlisle Dr
Ridge Ln
Park Rd
Hillside Ln
N View Ter
W View Ter
Hilltop Ter
Braxton Pl
Highland Pl
Putnam Pl
Moncure Dr
Lamond Pl
Melrose St
E Taylor Run Pkwy
W Taylor Run Pkwy
Taylor Run
Skyhill Rd
Dartmouth Rd
Albany Ave
Hermitage Ct
Eddington Ter
Bayliss Ct
Oakland Ter
Oakley Pl
Timber Branch Pkwy
Ruffner Rd
Hanson Ln
Orchard St
Stonewall Rd
High St
Locust Ln
Hilton St
Longview Dr
Duke St
Frontage Rd
Taylor Dr
Stovall St
Roberts Ln
Engleharddt Ln
Mill Rd
Fenwick Dr
Victory Dr
Liberty Dr
Fairfax Ter
Arlington Ter
Farrington Ave
Temple View Dr
Biscayne Dr
Glendale Ter
Fairview Ter
Blaine Dr
Mount Vernon Dr
Indian Dr
Indian Ct
Farnsworth Rd
Wagon Dr
2600
2100
2200
1600
1200
400
200
700

Essentials

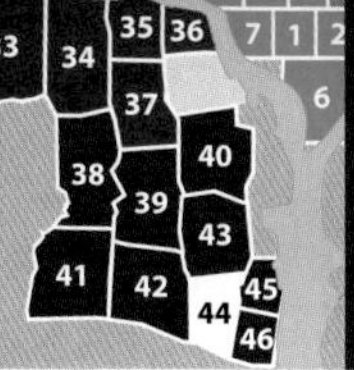

The Metro entrance to Alexandria is inauspicious with its anonymous office buildings. Don't turn back. You're a cobblestone's throw away from the action. Point the compass southeast and walk.

Banks

- **BB&T** • 1717 King St
- **Burke & Herbert** • 1775 Jamieson Ave
- **PNC** • 1700 Diagonal Rd
- **Sun Trust** • 1650 King St

Gas Stations

- **Mobil** • 317 E Braddock Rd

Landmarks

- **George Washington Masonic National Memorial** • 101 Callahan Dr

Parking

Police

- **Alexandria Police Dept** • 2003 Mill Rd

Post Offices

- **Memorial Station** • 2226 Duke St

Schools

- **Commonwealth Academy** • 1321 Leslie Ave
- **George Washington Middle** • 1005 Mt Vernon Ave
- **Maury Elementary** • 600 Russell Rd

Map 44 • Alexandria Downtown

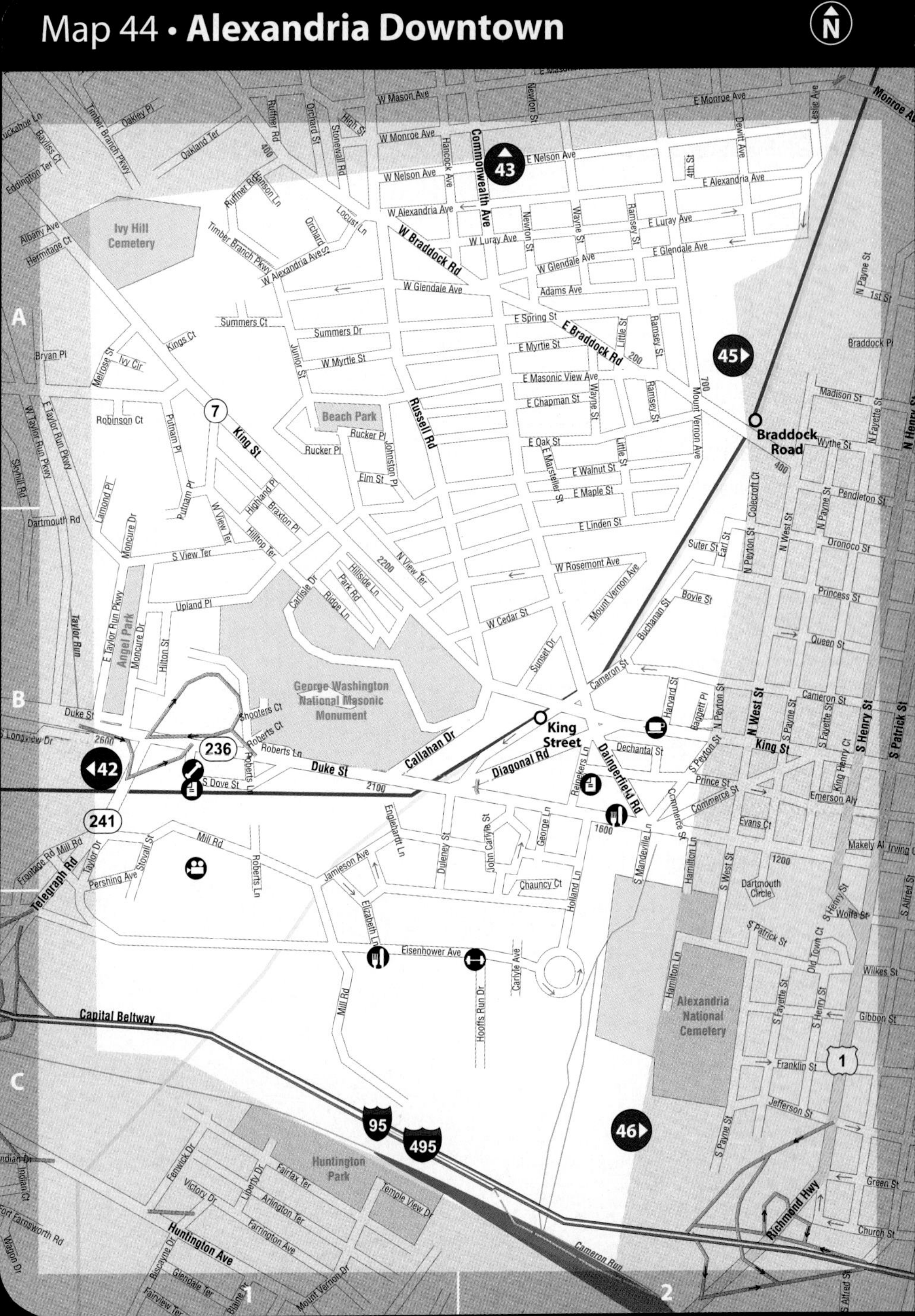

The Table Talk has great food and a charming ambiance.

Coffee

- **Café Aurora** • 1630 King St

Copy Shops

- **ABC Imaging (8:30am-6:30pm)** • 225 Reinekers Ln
- **Carriage Trade Publications (9am-5:30pm)** • 2393 S Dove St

Gyms

- **Jungle's Gym Fitness** • 305 Hooffs Run Dr

Movie Theaters

- **AMC Hoffman Center 22** • 206 Swamp Fox Rd

Pet Shops

- **Petsage** • 2391 S Dove St

Restaurants

- **Café Old Towne** • 2111 Eisenhower Ave
- **Table Talk** • 1623 Duke St

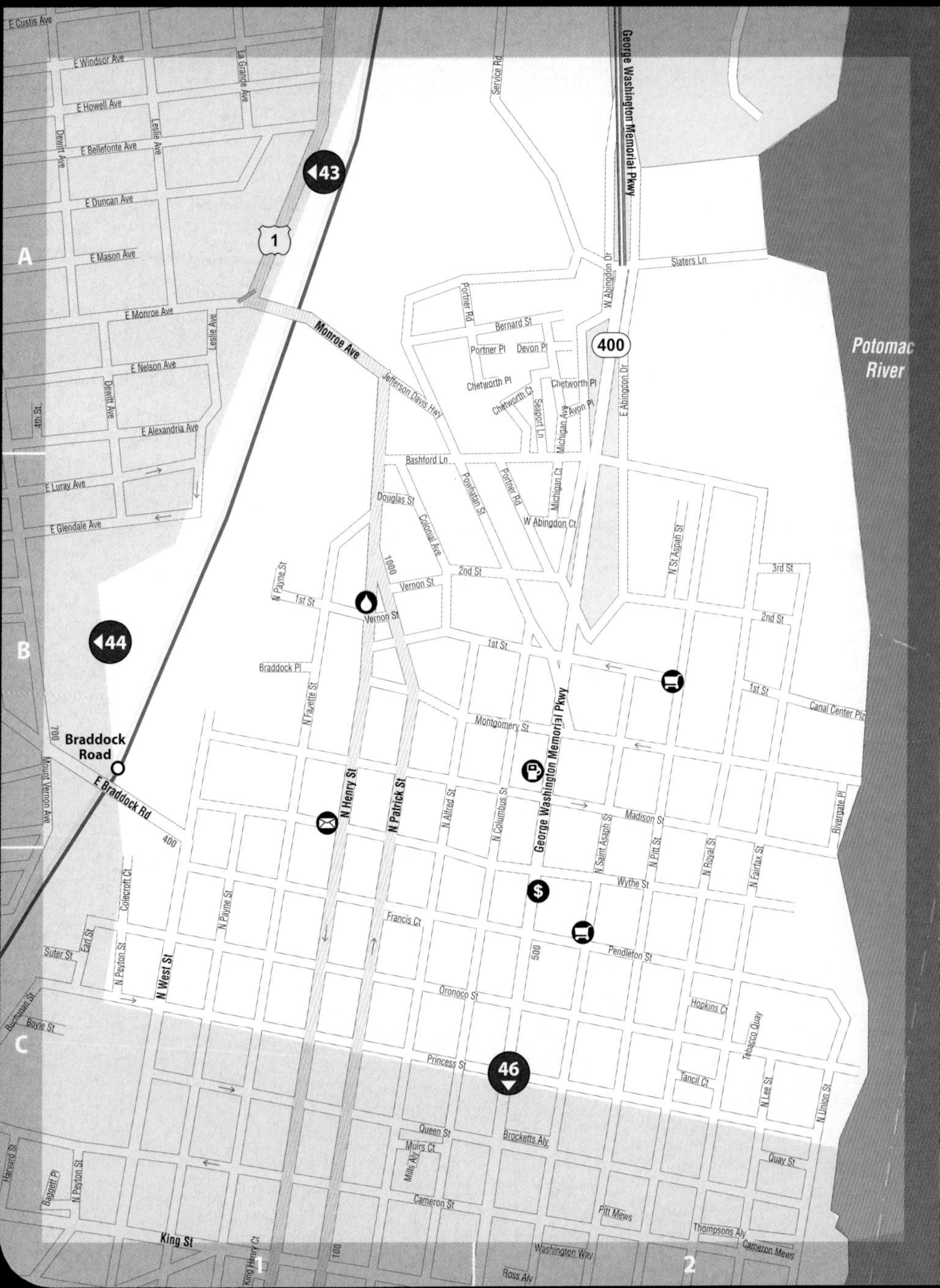

Map 45 • Old Town (North)

N

E Custis Ave
E Windsor Ave
La Grande Ave
E Howell Ave
Leslie Ave
Dewitt Ave
E Bellefonte Ave
43
E Duncan Ave
1
A
E Mason Ave
E Monroe Ave
Leslie Ave
E Nelson Ave
Dewitt Ave
4th St
E Alexandria Ave
E Luray Ave
E Glendale Ave
Service Rd
George Washington Memorial Pkwy
Slaters Ln
W Abingdon Dr
Portner Rd
Bernard St
Monroe Ave
400
Portner Pl
Devon Pl
Potomac River
Jefferson Davis Hwy
Chetworth Pl
Chetworth Ct
Chetworth Pl
Avon Pl
Seaport Ln
Michigan Ave
E Abingdon Dr
Bashford Ln
Powhatan St
Portner Rd
Michigan Ct
Douglas St
Colonial Ave
W Abingdon Ct
N St Asaph St
1000
2nd St
3rd St
N Payne St
Vernon St
1st St
Vernon St
2nd St
B
44
1st St
Braddock Pl
N Fayette St
1st St
Canal Center Plz
700
Montgomery St
Braddock Road
Mount Vernon Ave
E Braddock Rd
N Henry St
N Patrick St
N Alfred St
N Columbus St
George Washington Memorial Pkwy
Madison St
Rivergate Pl
400
N Saint Asaph St
N Pitt St
N Royal St
N Fairfax St
Colecroft Ct
N Payne St
Wythe St
Francis Ct
Earl St
Suter St
N Peyton St
N West St
500
Pendleton St
Oronoco St
Hopkins Ct
Buchanan St
Boyle St
C
Tobacco Quay
Princess St
46
Tancil Ct
N Lee St
N Union St
Queen St
Brocketts Aly
Muirs Ct
Mills Aly
Quay St
Harvard St
Baggett Pl
N Peyton St
Cameron St
Pitt Mews
Thompsons Aly
King St
King Henry Ct
100
Washington Way
Cameron Mews
Ross Aly
1
2

Essentials

The upper area of Old Town is not much more than offices and homes. It is prime real estate for both, given the proximity to the heart of Old Town. But if you're in for a day or night trip, don't bother.

Banks

• **Chevy Chase** • 697 N Washington St

Car Washes

• **Yates's Car Wash** • 1018 N Henry St

Gas Stations

• **Exxon** • 834 N Washington St

Post Offices

• **Alexandria Main Office** • 1100 Wythe St

Supermarkets

• **Giant Food** • 530 1st St
• **Trader Joe's** • 612 N St Asaph St

Map 45 • Old Town (North)

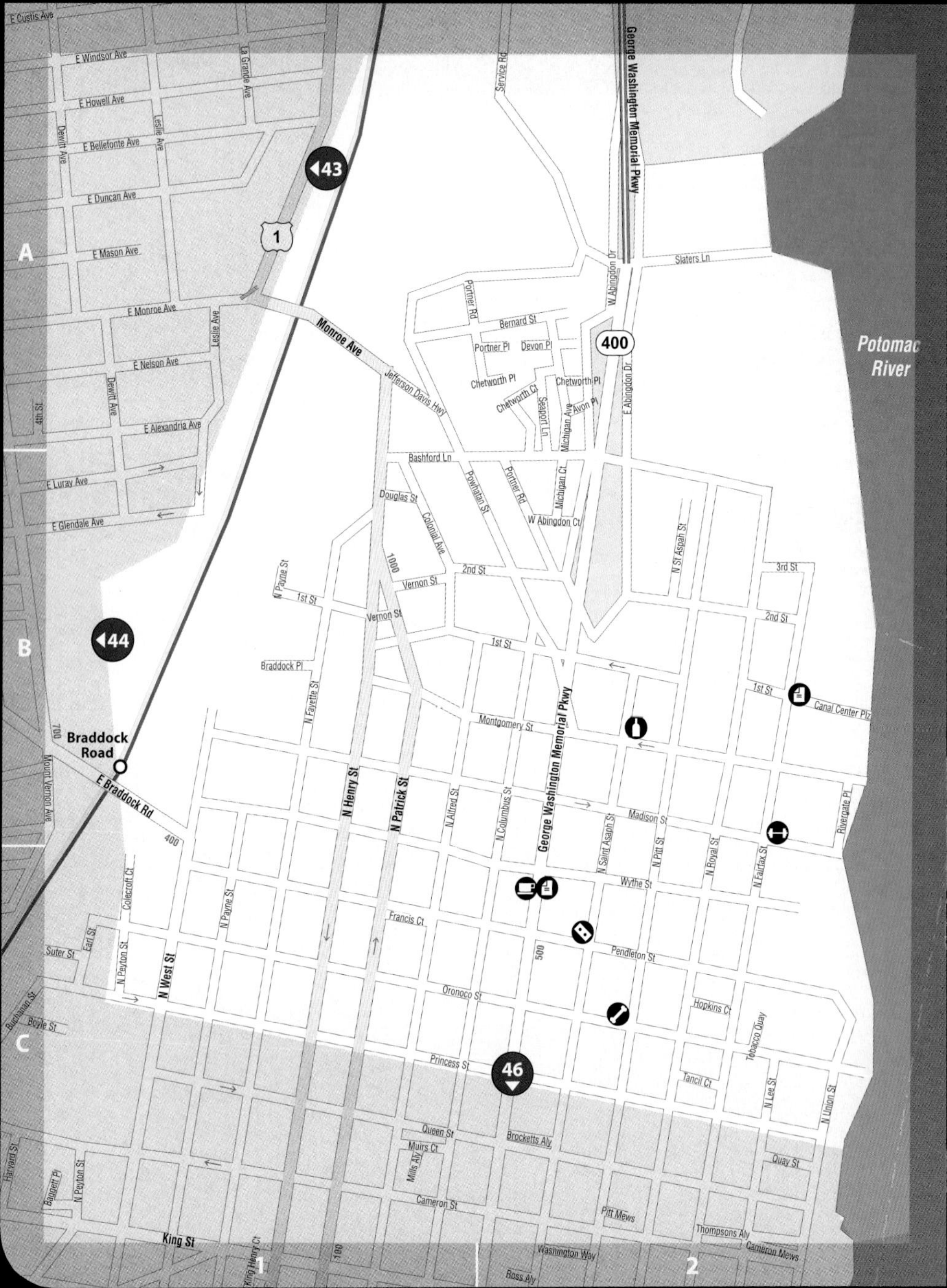

N

E Custis Ave
E Windsor Ave
La Grande Ave
E Howell Ave
Leslie Ave
Dewitt Ave
E Bellefonte Ave
43
E Duncan Ave
1
A
E Mason Ave
Service Rd
George Washington Memorial Pkwy
Slaters Ln
W Abingdon Dr
Portner Rd
Bernard St
E Monroe Ave
Leslie Ave
Monroe Ave
400
Portner Pl
Devon Pl
Potomac River
E Nelson Ave
Dewitt Ave
Jefferson Davis Hwy
Chetworth Pl
Chetworth Pl
Chetworth Ct
Seaport Ln
Michigan Ave
Avon Pl
E Abingdon Dr
4th St
E Alexandria Ave
Bashford Ln
E Luray Ave
Powhatan St
Portner Rd
Michigan Ct
Douglas St
E Glendale Ave
Colonial Ave
W Abingdon Ct
N St Asaph St
1000
N Payne St
2nd St
3rd St
Vernon St
1st St
Vernon St
2nd St
B
44
1st St
Braddock Pl
N Fayette St
1st St
Canal Center Plz
700
Braddock Road
Montgomery St
George Washington Memorial Pkwy
Mount Vernon Ave
E Braddock Rd
N Henry St
N Patrick St
N Alfred St
N Columbus St
Madison St
Rivergate Pl
N Saint Asaph St
N Pitt St
N Royal St
N Fairfax St
400
Colecroft Ct
N Payne St
Wythe St
Francis Ct
Earl St
Suter St
N Peyton St
N West St
500
Pendleton St
Oronoco St
Hopkins Ct
Tobacco Quay
Buchanan St
Boyle St
C
Princess St
46
Tancil Ct
N Lee St
N Union St
Queen St
Brocketts Aly
Muirs Ct
Mills Aly
Harvard St
Baggett Pl
N Peyton St
Quay St
Cameron St
Pitt Mews
Thompsons Aly
King St
King Henry Ct
100
Washington Way
Cameron Mews
1
2
Ross Aly

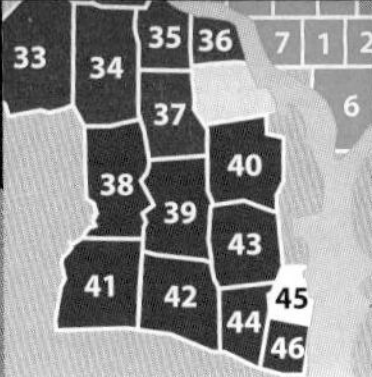

Southside 815 is a casual neighborhood bar/Creole restaurant where you'll often encounter locals on the sidewalk patio devouring beer and wings.

Coffee

• **Starbucks** • 683 N Washington St

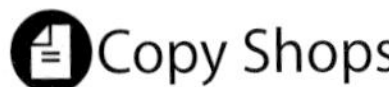

Copy Shops

• **Kinko's (24 hours)** • 685 N Washington St
• **Kwik Kopy Printing (8:30am-5pm)** • 99 Canal Center Plz

Gyms

• **Old Town Sport & Health Club** • 209 Madison St

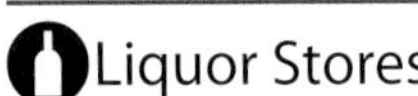

Liquor Stores

• **Virginia ABC** • 901 N St Asaph St

Pet Shops

• **Olde Towne School For Dogs** • 529 Oronoco St

Video Rental

• **Blockbuster Video** • 602 N St Asaph St

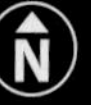

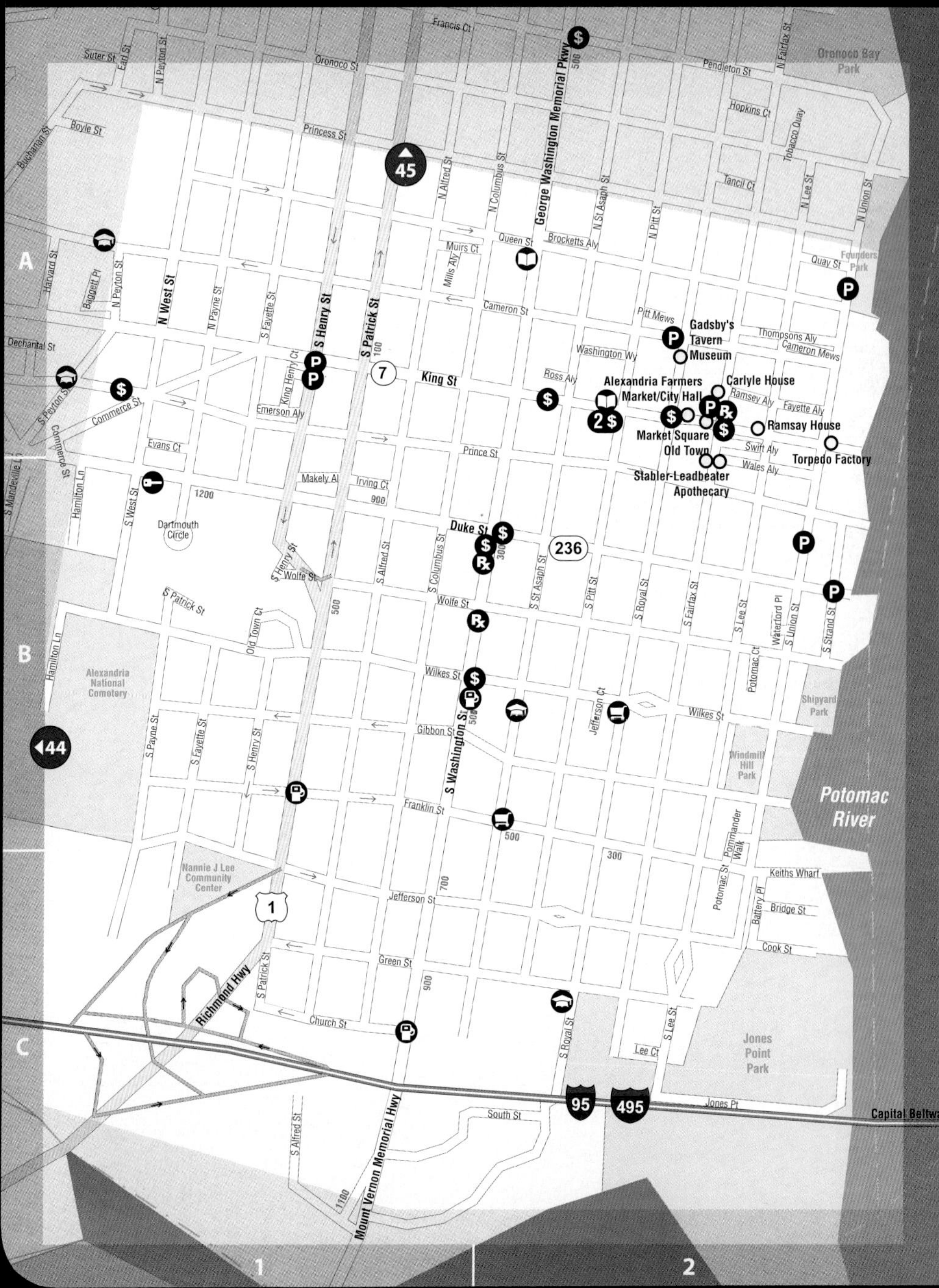

N
Francis Ct
Suter St
Earl St
N Peyton St
Oronoco St
George Washington Memorial Pkwy
Pendleton St
N Fairfax St
Oronoco Bay Park
Hopkins Ct
Tobacco Quay
Boyle St
Buchanan St
Princess St
45
N Alfred St
N Columbus St
N St Asaph St
Tancil Ct
N Lee St
N Union St
N Pitt St
Queen St
Brocketts Aly
Muirs Ct
Mills Aly
Quay St
Founders Park
A
Harvard St
Baggett Pl
N Peyton St
N West St
N Payne St
S Fayette St
S Henry St
S Patrick St
Cameron St
Pitt Mews
Gadsby's Tavern Museum
Thompsons Aly
Cameron Mews
Dechantal St
Washington Wy
King Henry Ct
7
King St
Ross Aly
Alexandria Farmers Market/City Hall
Carlyle House
Ramsey Aly
Fayette Aly
S Peyton St
Commerce St
Emerson Aly
Market Square
Ramsay House
Old Town
Swift Aly
Evans Ct
Prince St
Wales Aly
Torpedo Factory
Stabler-Leadbeater Apothecary
Commerce St
S Mandeville Ln
Hamilton Ln
S West St
1200
Makely Al
Irving Ct
900
Dartmouth Circle
Duke St
236
S Henry St
Wolfe St
S Alfred St
S Columbus St
S St Asaph St
S Pitt St
S Royal St
S Fairfax St
S Lee St
Waterford Pl
S Union St
S Strand St
S Patrick St
Wolfe St
Old Town Ct
500
B
Hamilton Ln
Alexandria National Cemetery
Wilkes St
Potomac Ct
Shipyard Park
Jefferson Ct
Wilkes St
S Washington St
Gibbon St
44
S Payne St
S Fayette St
S Henry St
Windmill Hill Park
Potomac River
Franklin St
500
Pommander Walk
300
Nannie J Lee Community Center
Keiths Wharf
700
Potomac St
Jefferson St
Battery Pl
Bridge St
1
Cook St
Richmond Hwy
S Patrick St
Green St
900
Church St
S Royal St
S Lee St
Lee Ct
Jones Point Park
C
95
495
Jones Pt
Capital Beltwa
South St
S Alfred St
Mount Vernon Memorial Hwy
1100
1
2

If you're 25 and cool, you live in Dupont; If you're 35 and cool, you live in Old Town. Situated on the water and peppered with shops, boutiques and enough cobblestone to make you think you're in Tuscany, the Colonial District is, perhaps, the Washington area's oldest and most precious neighborhood. Although residents are upwardly mobile, they're devoid of the holier-than-thou attitude possessed by their Brooks Brothers kinfolk from Georgetown.

Banks

- **Bank of America** • 600 N Washington St
- **BB&T** • 300 S Washington St
- **Burke & Herbert** • 117 S Fairfax St
- **Burke & Herbert** • 621 King St
- **Chevy Chase** • 500 S Washington St
- **PNC** • 411 King St
- **Sun Trust** • 515 King St
- **United Bank** • 301 S Washington St
- **Virginia Commerce** • 1414 Prince St
- **Virginia Commerce** • 506 King St

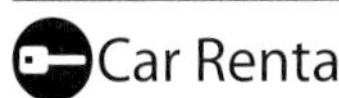

Car Rental

- **Thrifty** • 1306 Duke St • 703-684-2068

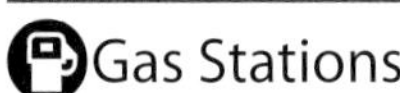

Gas Stations

- **Exxon** • 501 S Washington St
- **Exxon** • 700 S Patrick St
- **Mobil** • 1001 S Washington St

Landmarks

- **Alexandria Farmer's Market** • 301 King St
- **Alexandria City Hall** • 301 King St
- **Carlyle House** • 121 N Fairfax St
- **Gadsby's Tavern Museum** • 134 N Royal St
- **Market Square Old Town** • 301 King St
- **Ramsay House** • 221 King St
- **Stabler-Leadbeater Apothecary** • 105 S Fairfax St
- **Torpedo Factory** • 201 N Union St

Libraries

- **Alexandria Kate Waller Barrett Branch Library** • 717 Queen St
- **Alexandria Law Library** • 520 King St, Room L-34

Parking

Pharmacies

- **Alexandria Medical Arts Pharmacy** • 315 S Washington St
- **CVS** • 326 King St
- **CVS** • 433 S Washington St

Schools

- **Jefferson-Houston Elementary** • 1501 Cameron St
- **Lyles-Crouch Elementary** • 530 S St Asaph St
- **St Coletta** • 207 S Peyton St
- **St Mary** • 400 Green St

Supermarkets

- **Balducci's** • 600 Franklin Ave
- **Safeway** • 500 S Royal St

N
Francis Ct
Suter St
Earl St
N Peyton St
Oronoco St
George Washington Memorial Pkwy
Pendleton St
N Fairfax St
Oronoco Bay Park
Boyle St
Buchanan St
Princess St
Hopkins Ct
Tobacco Quay
45
N Alfred St
N Columbus St
N St Asaph St
N Pitt St
Tancil Ct
N Lee St
N Union St
Queen St
Brocketts Aly
Muirs Ct
Mills Aly
Quay St
Founders Park
A
Harvard St
Baggett Pl
N Peyton St
N West St
N Payne St
S Fayette St
S Henry St
S Patrick St
Cameron St
Pitt Mews
Thompsons Aly
Cameron Mews
Dechantal St
Washington Wy
King Henry Ct
7
King St
Ross Aly
Ramsey Aly
Fayette Aly
S Peyton St
Commerce St
Emerson Aly
Swift Aly
Wales Aly
Evans Ct
Prince St
Commerce St
S Mandeville Ln
Hamilton Ln
S West St
1200
Makely Al
Irving Ct
900
Duke St
Dartmouth Circle
236
S Henry St
Wolfe St
S Alfred St
S Columbus St
S St Asaph St
S Pitt St
S Royal St
S Fairfax St
S Lee St
Waterford Pl
S Union St
S Strand St
S Patrick St
Old Town Ct
Wolfe St
500
Potomac Ct
B
Hamilton Ln
Alexandria National Cemetery
Wilkes St
Jefferson Ct
Wilkes St
Shipyard Park
44
S Payne St
S Fayette St
S Henry St
Gibbon St
S Washington St
Windmill Hill Park
Potomac River
Franklin St
Pommander Walk
500
300
Nannie J Lee Community Center
Jefferson St
700
Keiths Wharf
1
Potomac St
Battery Pl
Bridge St
Cook St
S Patrick St
Green St
Richmond Hwy
900
Church St
S Royal St
S Lee St
C
Lee Ct
Jones Point Park
95
495
Jones Pt
Capital Beltway
South St
S Alfred St
Mount Vernon Memorial Hwy
1100
1
2

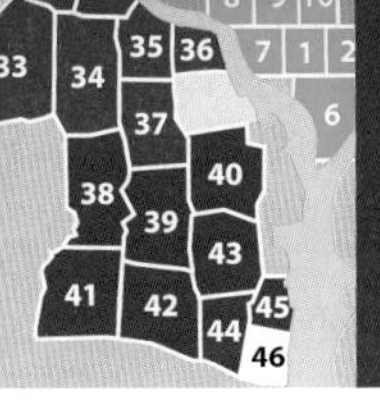

Voted by The Washington Post as the "Best Place to Bring a First Date" the last two years in a row, Old Town is its own little island of entertainment. Be sure to hit up the enormously popular happy hour at Café Salsa before landing on the dance floor a little later on. Vermillion adds a NYC-chic lounge option to the Alexandria mix, and 219 Restaurant brings the Acadian flair of Bourbon Street to King Street.

Coffee

- **Cosí** • 700 King St
- **Et Cetera** • 212 Queen St
- **Firehook Bakery & Coffee House** • 105 S Union St
- **Firehook Bakery & Coffee House** • 214 N Fayette St
- **Misha's** • 102 S Patrick St
- **Old Town Coffee Tea & Spice** • 215 S Union St
- **Perk Up** • 829 S Washington St
- **Starbucks** • 100 S Union St
- **Starbucks** • 510 King St
- **Uptowner Café** • 1609 King St

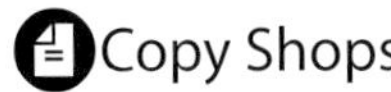

Copy Shops

- **Insty-Prints (8:30am-5:30pm)** • 1421 Prince St
- **Office Depot (8am-7pm)** • 200 N Washington St
- **UPS Store (8am-8pm)** • 107 S West St

Farmer's Markets

- **Alexandria City Farmer's Market** • 301 King St

Movie Theaters

- **Old Town Theater** • 815 1/2 King St

Nightlife

- **Café Salsa** • 808 King St
- **Founders' Brewing Company** • 607 King St
- **Hard Times Café** • 1404 King St
- **Laughing Lizzard Lounge** • 1324 King St
- **Murphy's** • 713 King St
- **Rock It Grill** • 1319 King St
- **South Austin Grill** • 801 King St
- **State Theatre** • 220 N Washington St
- **Tiffany Tavern** • 1116 King St
- **Vermillion** • 1120 King St

Pet Shops

- **Fetch** • 101 S St Asaph St

Restaurants

- **219 Restaurant** • 219 King St
- **China King Restaurant** • 701 King St
- **Faccia Luna Trattoria** • 823 S Washington St
- **The Grille** • 116 S Alfred St
- **Il Porto** • 121 King St
- **Portner's** • 109 S St Asaph St
- **Restaurant Eve** • 110 S Pitt St
- **Southside 815** • 815 S Washington St
- **The Warehouse** • 214 King St

Shopping

- **Blink** • 1303 King St
- **Comfort One Shoes** • 201 King St
- **Hysteria** • 125 S Fairfax St
- **La Cuisine** • 323 Cameron St
- **My Place in Tuscany** • 1127 King St
- **P&C Art** • 212 King St
- **Tickled Pink** • 103 S St Asaph St
- **The Torpedo Factory** • 105 N Union St

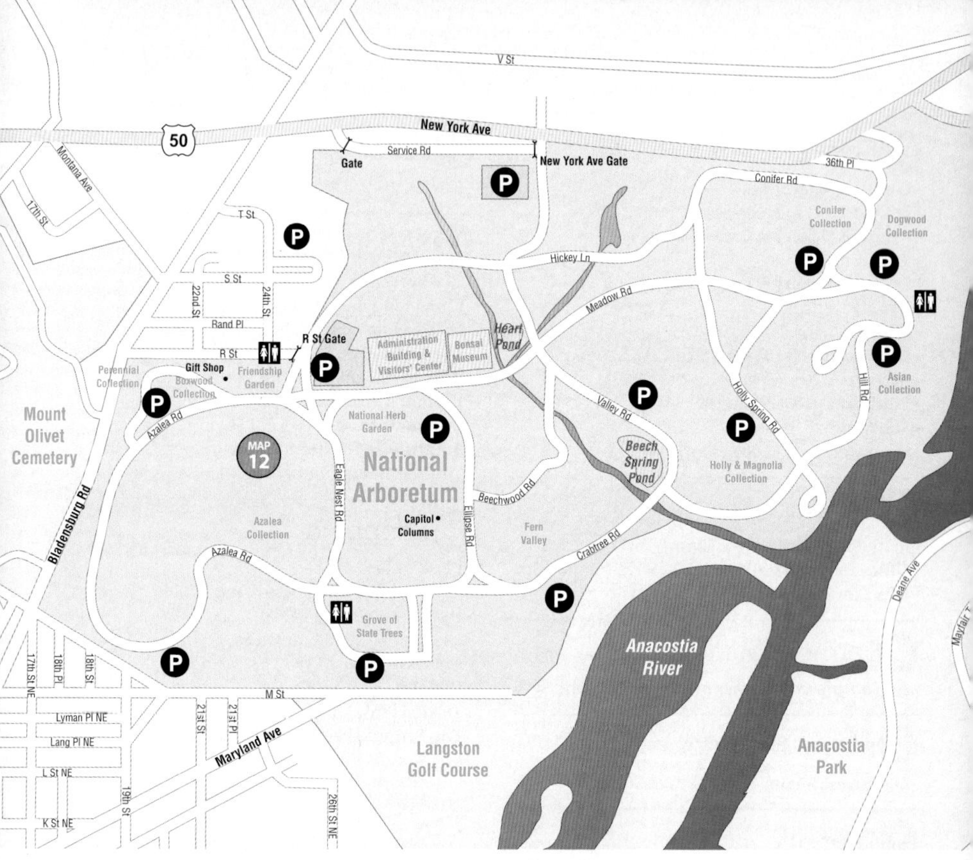

General Information

NFT Map:	12
Address:	3501 New York Ave NE Washington, DC 20002
Phone:	202-245-2726
Website:	www.usna.usda.gov
Hours:	Daily: 8 am-5 pm, except Dec 25th
Admission:	Free

Overview

The 446 acres of greenery and 9.5 miles of paved roads that make up the National Arboretum are, hands down, the nicest acres in the area for walking, running, or riding bikes. The Arboretum's biggest draw—besides escaping the day-to-day hustle and bustle of city life—is the National Bonsai and Penjing Museum, where you'll find over 150 miniature trees (some hundreds of years old). A rock garden, koi pond, and ikebana exhibit (the Japanese art of flower arranging) surround the museum, and are enough to clear anyone's head—unless they have allergies.

Other major attractions depend on the season. Late April sees thousands of azaleas burst into bloom, and different species continue flowering through July. The World Bonsai Convention hits the Arboretum at the end of May, and the dogwoods bloom in March and continue to flower through June. In short, there's always something to see, and there's always a reason to come back. Check the website's "What's Blooming" page to see what's coming up, changing color, or showing off.

While flowers may bloom and fade, the view of the Anacostia flowing quietly behind the Dogwood Collection is here to stay. As are the 22 Corinthian columns planted in a grassy field near the entrance, open to the sky. Originally part of the Capitol Building, these columns are probably the closest thing America has to the Parthenon.

If you want to mix education with pleasure, visit the Economic Botany Herbarium—a collection of over 650,000 dried plant specimens for classification studies of agriculture, medicine, science, and education. The volunteer staff also breeds plants for other locales throughout the country in a controlled greenhouse.

The National Bonsai Collection and Penjing Museum is open 10 am-3:30 pm. The Arbor House Gift Shop is open from March 1 through mid-December; weekday hours are 10 am-3:30 pm and weekend hours are 10 am-5 pm.

Activities

The paved roads serve as excellent biking and jogging paths. Picnicking is allowed in designated areas. The Arbor Café is located next to the Administration Building and is open Friday through Sunday. Fishing, fires, and flower picking are all prohibited, and pets must be kept on leashes. The Arboretum offers public education programs including lectures, workshops, demonstrations, and plant, flower, and art exhibitions.

A 48-passenger open-air tram runs through the park with a 40-minute, non-stop, narrated tour covering the Arboretum's history, mission, and current highlights. Tram services are available on weekends from mid-April through October: $4 adults, $3 seniors, $2 kids 4-16 years old, and free for kids 4 and under.

The Full Moon Hikes, available during the spring and fall, take participants on a five-mile moonlit trek through the grounds, with curators providing horticultural facts along the way. Hikes cost $12 general admission, $10 for Friends of the National Arboretum. You'll need to register early as there is limited space and tours fill up quickly (as in, we called at the beginning of April to book a tour in May, and we were already too late). Twilight Tours cost $7 ($5 for FONA), and are slower-paced opportunities to explore the Arboretum after closing time. Pre-registration is required for both activities; call 202-245-5898 to make your reservation, or find the mail-in form online.

How to Get There—Driving

From northwest Washington, follow New York Avenue east to the intersection of Bladensburg Road. Turn right onto Bladensburg Road and drive four blocks to R Street. Make a left on R Street and continue two blocks to the Arboretum gates.

Parking

Large free parking lots are located near the Grove of State Trees, near the R Street entrance, and near the New York Avenue entrance. Smaller lots are scattered throughout the grounds close to most of the major collections. Several of the parking areas have recently been expanded, and a free shuttle through the park runs continuously during summer months.

How to Get There—Mass Transit

The X6 Metrobus provides a direct shuttle from Union Station on weekends and holidays, except December 25th. The bus leaves every 40 minutes from 7:55 am to 4:35 pm and the fare is $1.25 one-way (35¢ with rail transfer). On weekdays, the closest Metro subway stop is Stadium Armory Station on the Blue and Orange lines. Transfer to Metrobus B-2, get off on Bladensburg Road, and walk two blocks to R Street. Make a right on R Street and continue two more blocks to the Arboretum gates.

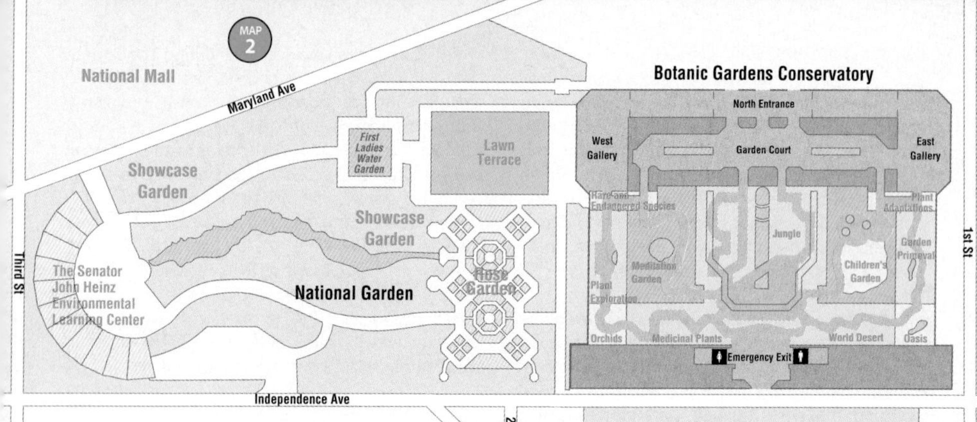

General Information

NFT Map:	2
Address:	100 Maryland Ave SW Washington, DC 20024
Phone:	202-225-8333
Website:	www.usbg.gov
Hours:	10 am-5 pm every day, including holidays
Admission:	Free

Overview

One minute, you're staring up at the U.S. Capitol—the symbol of the world's most powerful city; the next minute you're trudging through a jungle, surrounded by Jurassic trees and carnivorous plants. Known as Washington's "Secret Garden," the U.S. Botanic Garden is one of the nation's oldest botanical gardens and home to 26,000 different specimens. The refurbished Conservatory features a 24-foot high mezzanine level allowing visitors to gaze downward onto a canopied rainforest. Its distinctive glass façade now houses advanced environmental control systems that allow orchid buds to bloom in the same building as desert brush and nearly 4,000 other living plants. If you're looking for a particular organism but don't know where to start, you can tap into USBG's massive computer database and search by common name, scientific name, or geographic location.

The USBG offers classes, exhibits, lectures, and symposia throughout the year. Visit during the week and you might be lucky enough to land on a tour (schedules vary, so be sure to check the website for up-to-date event listings). Set to open in summer 2006 is the National Garden, a three-acre plot of land located just west of the Conservatory. The Garden will feature an Environmental Learning Center, lecture hall, library, and various specialty gardens showcasing the unusual, useful, and ornamental plants that flourish in the mid-Atlantic region. Bartholdi Park, located across Independence Avenue from the Conservatory, was created in 1932 and named for sculptor Frederic Auguste Bartholdi. In addition to creating the aptly-named Bartholdi Fountain in the center of the park, he also designed the Statue of Liberty. The park is open daily from dawn until dusk.

How to Get There—Mass Transit

Taking public transportation is highly recommended, as there is limited metered parking near the USBG. By Metro, take the Blue or Orange line to Federal Center SW or Capitol South stations. If you're using the Metro Bus, take the 30, 32, 34, 35, or 36 to Independence Avenue and First Street, SW.

General Information

NFT Map: 5
Location: 225 7th St SE
Washington, DC 20003
Phone: 202-544-0083
Website: www.easternmarket.net
Hours: Tues-Fri: 10 am-6 pm; Sat: 8 am-6 pm; Sun: 8 am-4 pm.

Overview

Eastern Market is as unpretentious as DC gets. Leave your Hill lapel pin and the Georgetown classism behind, 'cause here you'll only spill bacon grease on 'em. The 16,500-square-foot indoor market has barely changed since it opened in 1873. Even now, as it sits at the center of a newly yuppified neighborhood and enjoys its status as a member of the *National Register of Historic Places*, it remains a working market for working people.

Join the line at Market Lunch in South Hall to be abused by over-stressed workers doling out pancakes, pork, and killer crab cakes. You need to order quickly because the line is usually long and the staff's patience is not—don't even think about paying with plastic.

On weekends, locals and day-trippers jam in to bid for fresh produce, bread, fish, cheese, and chicken. On the sidewalks outside, artists, farmers, and charlatans hawk their wares. Antique and collectibles vendors fill the playground behind Hines Junior High School with piles of trinkets, textiles, and trash. If you're dating someone with blue hair, Eastern Market is the perfect place to buy them some funky topaz earrings, or a watercolor painting with glitter.

Market 5 Gallery

202-543-7293; www.market5gallery.org

The non-profit arts organization Market 5 dominates the North Hall. The group hosts art fairs and sponsors Saturday performances. Artists, musicians, and artisans have always been a part of the traditional "marketplace," and the Saturday festival on the gallery's North Plaza was begun in 1978 to bring the tradition back to Eastern Market.

Market 5 is also an art gallery that gives classes in the arts for the Capitol Hill community. Hours: Tues-Fri: 11 am-5 pm; Sat-Sun: 8 am-5 pm.

How to Get There—Driving

Parking is scarce, but if you must: from the south, take I-395 across the 14th Street Bridge, bear right over the bridge onto Eisenhower (SW) Expressway; exit at 6th Street SE, the first exit beyond South Capitol Street. At the bottom of the ramp, continue one block and turn left on 7th Street SE. The next major intersection with a traffic light is Pennsylvania Avenue. You'll see Hines School on the opposite corner.

From the west, take I-66 to Rosslyn, Virginia, and Route 110 to I-395 N, then follow the directions above.

From the north, take Baltimore-Washington Parkway and I-295, exiting at Pennsylvania Avenue (East). A U-turn can be made at the second light to head westbound on Pennsylvania to 7th Street SE, where you need to make a right.

From the east, take either Route 50 or I-495 to I-295, and follow the directions above.

Parking

Diagonal parking is available on 7th Street, on the alley sides of the Market, and there's some curb parking in the Capitol Hill neighborhood. On weekends, it's best to take the Metro.

How to Get There—Mass Transit

Take the Blue or Orange Metro Lines to the Eastern Market station and walk north out of the station along 7th Street SE.

Montrose Park
Dumbarton Oaks
Oak Hill Cemetery
Georgetown University
PAGE 226
Georgetown Recreation Center
MAP 8
The Tombs
Old Stone House
C&O Canal Path
Potomac River
Massachusetts Av
Waterside Dr
S St NW
R St NW
Reservoir Rd NW
Winfield Ln NW
Dent Pl NW
Q St NW
Volta Pl NW
P St NW
O St NW
N St NW
Prospect St NW
M St NW
Canal Rd
Water St NW
Grace St NW
South St NW
K St
Wisconsin Ave NW
Caton Pl NW
32nd St NW
Avon Pl NW
Dem Pl NW
Avon Ln NW
Cambridge Pl
West Ln Ky NW
East Pl NW
Poplar St NW
Dumbarton St NW
31st St NW
30th St NW
29th St NW
28th St NW
27th St NW
26th St NW
37th St NW
36th St NW
35th St NW
34th St NW
33rd St NW
Potomac St NW
Bank St NW
Congress St NW
Oak Aly NW
Blues Aly NW
Thomas Jefferson St NW
Cecil Pl NW
Pennsylvania Av
L St NW
K St NW
Queen Annes Ln
29

Overview

NFT Map: 8

Like a socialite fleeing the masses, Georgetown hides in a metro-inaccessible western corner of northwest Washington. Here it retains its cobblestone charm and snooty superiority despite the mall-ization of its main drags. The tourists and suburbanites mob stretches of M Street and Wisconsin Avenue on pleasant weekend days, but the Georgetown residents are either current or future (calling all Georgetown students) owners of the city's priciest real estate.

At night, the neighborhood sheds its good breeding to become a boisterous, if not diverse, nightlife scene. The crush of restaurants and bars swing open to welcome college partiers or the better-coiffed see-and-be-seen crowd.

Don't waste your time sitting in a cab on the popular blocks of M Street. Traffic crawls and you can waste precious partying/shopping time as you ask the cab driver to explain the taxicab map (DC's Rosetta Stone). Cut your losses and walk—it's only a few blocks and will save you time and frustration.

Despite the area's highbrow reputation for elite schools and garden-lined historical houses, Georgetown's proximity to the Potomac makes it prone to unruly flooding. Turn on the news after the next big thunderstorm. The local networks send out camera crews and pretty young women who wear pastel L.L. Bean raincoats and talk into microphones. Invariably, a group of privileged neighborhood children shout at the TV cameras as they ride their bicycles through the bubbling, knee-deep water, not realizing that it is saturated with their own excrement.

History

Georgetown was formed in 1751, and the neighborhood's access to the Potomac River was a big draw to the shipping community.

After the Civil War, the area became a haven for freed slaves seeking financial freedom. But a devastating flood in 1890 forced the Canal Company into bankruptcy and triggered an economic depression. By the end of World War I, Georgetown had become a total slum. In the 1930s, New Deal government officials rediscovered the convenience and charm beneath the grime, and with their help, Georgetown began its physical rehab and social climb back to its current grandeur.

Attractions

Georgetown hosts the city's most compact collection of historic, retail, gastronomic, and nightlife draws. The Old Stone House, built in 1765, is the oldest surviving building on its original lot in the federal city, and predates the city of DC itself. The rumored-to-be-haunted-house and its gardens are both publicly strollable. The C&O Canal Path is a 180-mile leaf-shrouded park that runs alongside a murky, but historically interesting, canal. The canal was originally a water highway that linked the rapidly growing west to the east and allowed farmers to ship their goods to market. The canal path is now more of a runner and biker highway. Locals use it to work off the one-too-manys they imbibed at bars like Georgetown University's esteemed The Tombs. For a more relaxing respite, Dumbarton Oaks is a Federal-style 19th century mansion surrounded by sublime gardens.

For a complete list of stores and restaurants in Georgetown, consult the comprehensive Georgetown website: www.georgetowndc.com. For a selection of our favorite Georgetown bars, restaurants, and shopping venues, see Map 8.

How to Get There—Driving

M Street NW can be reached from the Francis Scott Key Bridge, Canal Road NW, and Pennsylvania Avenue.

Parking

Street parking in Georgetown is a pain. A paid garage is your best bet. There are several in the area with reasonable hourly and daily rates. See map for locations.

How to Get There—Mass Transit

Metrobus routes 30, 32, 34, 35, or 36 marked "Friendship Heights" run west on Pennsylvania Avenue. Buses cost $1.20 one-way and only accept exact change or a bus pass.

There is no metro stop in Georgetown, but on a pleasant day, if you're equipped with good walking shoes, the Foggy Bottom-GWU stop on the Orange and Blue lines is a ten minute walk from the east end of the neighborhood. The Rosslyn stop on the same line is a ten-minute walk from Georgetown's west end.

The Georgetown Metro Connection serves all Metrobus stops in Georgetown and operates express service between Georgetown and Foggy Bottom-GWU, Rosslyn, and Dupont Circle Metro stations. The bus leaves the metro stations every ten minutes daily and costs $1 one-way. Shuttle Hours: Mon-Thurs: 7 am -12 am; Fri: 7 am-2 am; Sat: 8 am -2 am; Sun: 8 am-12 am.

The Monuments / Potomac Park / Tidal Basin

The Ellipse
Bolivar
23rd St
22nd St
21st St
20th St
19th St
18th St
17th St
15th St
Haupt Fountains
Einstein
Jose Artigas
2nd Division Monument
Constitution Ave
German American
Friendship Garden
Vietnam Veterans Memorial
The 56 Signers of the Declaration of Independence Memorial
Henry Bacon Dr
The Three Servicemen
Vietnam Women's Memorial
Ticket Kiosk
Arts of Peace
Reflecting Pool
WWII Memorial
Washington Monument
Arts of War
Lincoln Memorial
Constitution Gardens
MAP 1
Daniel French Dr
Korean War Veterans Memorial
John Paul Jones Memorial
MAP 7
WWII Memorial
Independence Ave
John Ericsson Memorial
Independence Ave
Kutz Bridge
Japanese Lantern
E Basin Dr
West Potomac Park
W Basin Dr
Ohio Dr
Tidal Basin
Japanese Pagoda
FDR Memorial Park
Potomac River
Jefferson Memorial
Ohio Dr
East Basin Dr
Lady Bird Johnson Park
395
Cuban Friendship Urn
Lyndon B Johnson Memorial Grove
MAP 6
Washington Memorial Pkwy
George Mason Memorial Bridge
Ohio Dr
East Potomac Park
Navy & Marine Memorial
Rochambeau Bridge
Arland D Williams Jr Memorial Bridge
Buckeye Dr
Lagoon

General Information

NFT Maps: 1, 6, and 7
Website: www.nps.gov
Phone: 202-426-6841

Overview

If there's one thing DC loves more than a free museum, it's a commemorative lawn ornament. The District is packed with monuments, statues, plaques, and fountains. This is especially apparent while strolling through Potomac Park, where you'll find the Lincoln, FDR, Jefferson, and Washington memorials, as well as tributes to those who served in WWI, WWII, the Korean War, and Vietnam, all within walking distance of one another.

Presidential Monuments

The tall, unadorned monument commemmorating America's first president is as recognizable a landmark as the White House or the Capitol.

Had the Washington Monument been built in Europe, it would, most likely, squirt water from several places, have 12 pairs of ornately sculpted angel wings fluttering from its sides, and feature a large, bronze pair of breasts over the entranceway. But the simplicity and straightforwardness of the building is a tribute to the gravitas, fortitude, and simple elegance of the man it represents.

Entry to the Washington Monument is free, although your ticket is only valid during a specified entry time. Free tickets are distributed on a first-come, first-served basis at the kiosk on the Washington Monument grounds (at 15th Street and Madison Drive). Advance reservations can be made online at reservations.nps.gov. The ticket kiosk is open daily from 8 am until 4:30 pm (closed December 25th), and tickets usually run out early in the day. If you plan on visiting the monument, make it your first stop.

While many visitors use the monument as a vantage point from which to view the surrounding city, the tall structure itself is really as impressive as the view it affords. The exterior walls are constructed of white marble from Maryland; the interior walls are lined with granite from Maine. Construction began in 1848 and was only one-third complete when the Civil War broke out—hence the change in stone color a third of the way up. Construction resumed after the war, but by then, the color of stone in the quarry had changed. Today, the Washington Monument remains the tallest and most revered structure in DC, giving it alpha-monument status and deflecting the exploding metropolitan population out into surrounding farmland instead of upward into the city sky.

The Lincoln Memorial, which stands in front of the reflecting pool across from the Washington Monument, was designed to look like a Greek Temple. The 36 pillars represent the 36 states that existed at the time of Lincoln's death. The larger-than-life-sized sculpture of honest Abe inside underscores the man's great physical and political stature. Visiting the monument is free, and the structure is open to the public year-round.

Tidal Basin

The Tidal Basin was constructed in the late 1800s as a swimming hole in the middle of the park. It's no longer a place for a refreshing dip. Besides the questionable cleanliness of this urban pond, the ample federal security forces in the neighborhood are likely the strictest lifeguards in the country. If you're set on dipping a toe in the water, join the tourists and rent a paddle boat. For two weeks every spring, cherry blossoms bloom around the basin and throughout the parks. The original trees were a gift from Japan in 1912, and their bloom inspires an annual Japanese-influenced festival to kick off the spring. The domed Jefferson Memorial, easily the most elegant memorial of them all, resides on the basin's edge.

East Potomac Park

East Potomac Park is a rather run-of-the-mill park. Yeah, sure, it's got a golf course, tennis courts, swimming pool, basketball court, baseball field, hiking trails, and a playground. But we've become spoiled and these amenities feel like necessities, not luxuries.

A five-piece sculpture titled *The Awakening* can be found on the very southern tip of East Potomac Park at Hains Point (not pictured on the map). This aluminum depiction of a 100-foot giant emerging from the ground is, like the park it's in, more fun, less epic. You'll need to drive or bike out there because there's no public transportation for miles.

How to Get There—Driving

I-66 and I-395 run to the parks from the south. I-495, New York Avenue, Rock Creek Parkway, George Washington Memorial Parkway, and the Cabin John Parkway will get you there from the north. I-66, Route 50, and Route 29 run to the parks from the west. Routes 50, 1, and 4 are the way to go from the east.

Parking

Public parking is available along the Basin but, depending on the time of day, it's likely to be hard to find a spot. You'll end up driving around and around in circles and eventually parking far out and walking long distances.

How to Get There—Mass Transit

The Foggy Bottom, Metro Center, Federal Triangle, Smithsonian, and L'Enfant Plaza stops on the Orange and Blue Lines are all within walking distance of various monuments and parks. Metro Center is also a Red Line Stop. L'Enfant Plaza is also on the Green and Yellow Lines.

General Information

NFT Maps:	1 & 2
National Mall Website:	www.nps.gov/nama
National Mall Phone:	202-426-6841
Smithsonian Website:	www.si.edu
Smithsonian Phone:	202-633-1000
U.S. Capitol Website:	www.aoc.gov
House of Reps:	www.house.gov
Senate:	www.senate.gov
Capitol Switchboard:	202-224-2131
Capitol Tour Info:	202-225-6827

National Mall

Washington DC's National Mall represents the American dream, where a melting pot of foreigners and locals gather for leisurely picnics or heated protests—without having to do any of the yard work! The layout for the sprawling grass lawn was designed by Frenchman Pierre L'Enfant in the late 18th century as an open promenade. Despite the explosive growth of the surrounding city, the mall has remained true to L'Enfant's vision. Its eminent strollability is a magnet to hordes of fanny-packed tourists, and its renowned marble monuments attract travel-weary schoolchildren from all over the world. The iconic marble memorials to Washington, Jefferson, Lincoln, and FDR are close by, along with the somber Vietnam and Korean War memorials, and the newly unveiled WWII memorial. On any given day, there's also likely to be a kite festival, political rally, or spirited Frisbee game underway.

Smithsonian Institution

The Smithsonian Institution is made up of 16 different museums, some of them nowhere near the mall (one is in NYC), and a zoo. But the primary museums are mostly clustered around the mall—here you'll find the Air and Space Museum, the Natural History Museum, and the Hirshhorn. The Smithsonian Information Center in the Castle is the

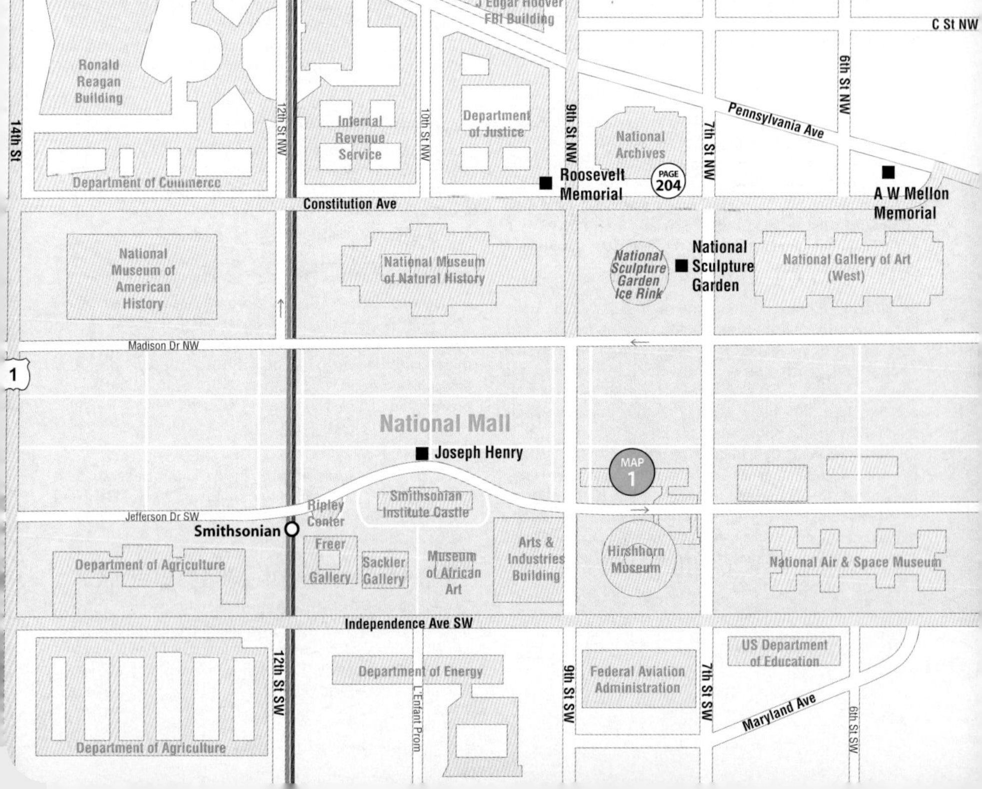

best orientation point if you plan to become one of the 24 million visitors who check out one of its DC properties this year.

Like the country it caters to, the Smithsonian collection reflects a hodgepodge of experiences and backgrounds: between its museums on the Mall, the institution's got the Hope Diamond, Japanese scrolls, and even Archie Bunker's chair. Though there is serious art at the the National Gallery, the Hirshhorn, and several of the smaller museums, the "most popular" distinction goes to the Air and Space Museum, for its sheer wowza! factor of dangling airplanes and shuttles. A close runner-up is the National History Museum, known both affectionately and derisively as "America's Attic." Besides Archie's chair, it accommodates Dorothy's ruby slippers, Muhammad Ali's gloves, George Washington's uniform, Julia Childs' entire kitchen, and Adlai Stevenson's briefcase. Fortunately the National Gallery provides a welcome counterpoint to all this kitsch…

Smithsonian Institution Building (The Castle)
The first building of what has become the Smithsonian empire was the Castle, built in 1855. The Castle was, for a time, the only Smithsonian building, housing all aspects of the institution's operations (including an apartment for the first Secretary of the Smithsonian, Joseph Henry). It now serves as the seat of the Smithsonian's administrative offices, as well as a general information center. The beauty and stature of the building make it a good point of orientation for mall visitors. (www.si.edu/visit/infocenter/sicastle, 202-633-1000)

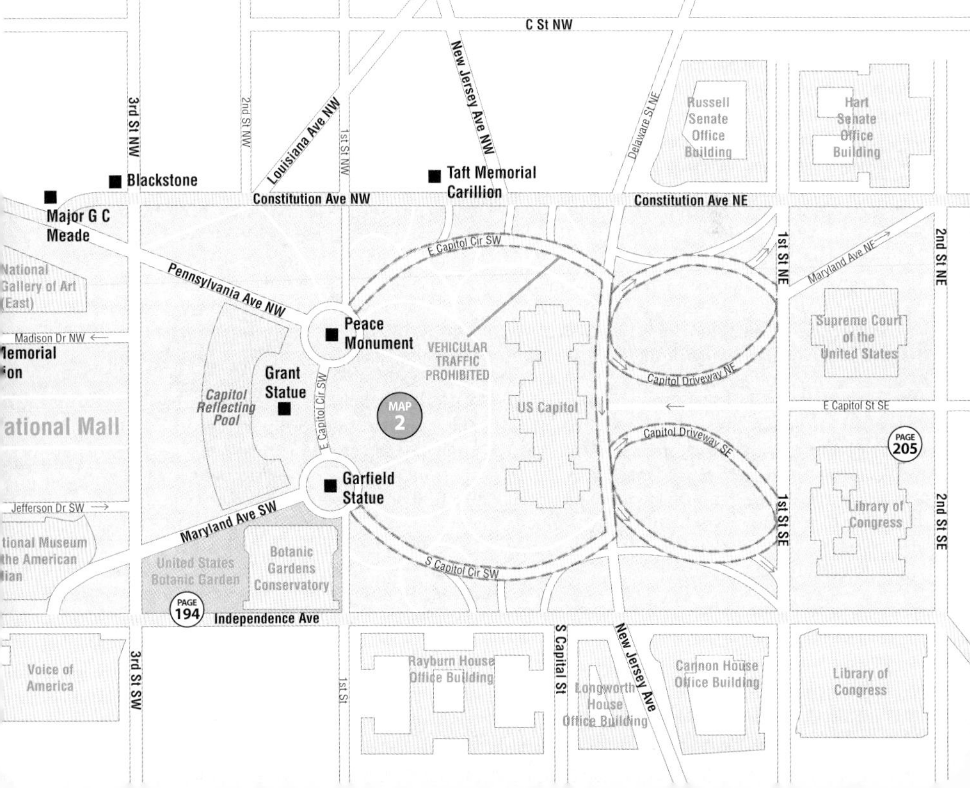

The National Museum of the American Indian
This new museum opened on the National Mall in September, 2004. Upon entering, visitors are greeted by the Welcome Wall—a projection of hundreds of written and spoken words meaning "welcome" in native languages throughout the Americas. Hours: Mon-Sun: 10:30 am-5:30 pm. (4th St & Independence Ave, SW; www.americanindian.si.edu)

National Air and Space Museum
This museum maintains the largest collection of historic aircraft and spacecraft in the world. Hundreds of artifacts are on display, including the original Wright 1903 airplane, the Spirit of St. Louis, the Apollo 11 command module, and a lunar rock sample that visitors can touch. Hours: 10 am-5:30 pm (6th St & Independence Ave, SW; www.nasm.si.edu)

The National Gallery of Art
The National Gallery's two wings house a collection of art as impressive as any similar institution in the country. Everything else about Washington might get you overcooked on Greek Revival architecture, but the National Gallery shows in rich detail how DC is actually one of the key places in the world to visit for art. The Gallery houses everything from Byzantine art to some of today's leading artists, including Andy Goldsworthy's brilliant new work *Roof*, permanently on display on the ground floor of the East Wing. There is also a small sculpture garden next to the West Wing, which houses a mini "greatest hits" of post-WWII large-format sculpture—highly recommended. Hours: (galleries & garden) Mon-Sat: 10 am-5 pm ; Sunday: 11 am-6 pm. Note: the Sculpture Garden is open until 9 pm on Fridays during the summer. (Between 3rd St NW & 7th St NW at Constitution Ave; www.nga.org)

Hirshhorn Museum and Sculpture Garden
Conceived as the nation's museum of modern and contemporary art, the Hirshhorn has over 11,500 pieces of internationally significant art, including ample space for large-scale installation works. Hours: Mon-Sun: 10 am-5:30 pm. Sculpture Garden Hours: 7:30 am-dusk. (7th St & Independence Ave, SW; hirshhorn.si.edu)

Arts and Industries Building
The second-oldest Smithsonian building is not in the best shape. In 2004, conditions deteriorated to a point where "diapers" had to be installed on the roof to catch falling debris and the building was closed for renovations. The good news is that a new roof is being installed, and the building will be eventually restored to its former glory. In the meantime, visitors can still access the Discovery Theater, a live performance venue for children. It is temporarily located behind the Smithsonian Castle. (900 Jefferson Dr, SW; www.si.edu/ai).

National Museum of African Art
The National Museum of African Art is the only museum in the United States devoted exclusively to the display and study of traditional and contemporary arts of sub-Sahara Africa. The museum displays everything from ceramics, textiles, furniture, and tools to masks, figures, and musical instruments. Hours: Mon-Sun: 10 am-5:30 pm. (950 Independence Ave, SW; www.nmafa.si.edu)

Freer and Sackler Galleries
These twin galleries are connected via an underground passageway and house a world-renowned Asian art collection. When it opened in 1923, the Freer Gallery was the first Smithsonian museum dedicated to the fine arts. The Sackler Gallery opened in 1987. The Freer is home to one of the most extensive collections of art by American artist James McNeil Whistler. While you won't find the famous picture of his mother here, you'll find some of his other works, including his portraits and the famous Peacock Room. (Freer Gallery: Jefferson Dr & 12th St, SW; Sackler Gallery: 1050 Independence Ave; www.asia.si.edu)

National Museum of American History
This museum's mission is to collect, care for, and study the objects that reflect the experience of the American people. What better place for the Declaration of Independence Desk, Dizzy Gillespie's trumpet, or Eli Whitney's cotton gin? Two of our favorites are the original Kermit the Frog puppet and Prince's guitar. This museum is a pack rat's dream. Hours: Mon-Sun: 10 am-5:30 pm. (14th St & Constitution Ave, NW; americanhistory.si.edu)

National Museum of Natural History
Visitors come far and wide to catch a glimpse of the 45.5-carat Hope Diamond, but there's more to this museum than one rock. The National Museum of Natural History has an impressive collection of dinosaur and mammal fossils, an insect zoo (check out the daily tarantula feeding!), and an amazing array of stuffed animals (courtesy of taxidermy, not FAO Schwartz). If you're really into rocks, check out the gem collection, which includes meteorites and the Logan Sapphire; at 423 carats, it is the largest publicly displayed sapphire in the country. Hours: Mon-Sun: 10 am-5:30 pm. (10th St & Constitution Ave, NW, www.mnh.si.edu)

US Capitol
The US Capitol is located on Capitol Hill, between 1st and 3rd Streets and between Constitution Avenue NE and Independence Avenue SE. Big white dome. Hard to miss.

Home to the House of Representatives and the Senate, this icon is both a history museum and a functioning office where Hillary Clinton, Ted Kennedy, and Liddy Dole are working stiffs. It's also DC's orientation point. Every city address is based on where it lies in relation to the Capitol. After hours, drunken Hill staffers use it as a compass to get themselves home.

Construction began on the Capitol in 1793 and was more or less finished by 1813. The Capitol was burned by the British In 1814, during the War of 1812, but rain saved the structure from complete collapse. Restoration and expansion followed, the result being the building that all Americans recognize today (probably thanks to *Independence Day*). If you've ever wondered who the lady on top of the dome is, she's no-one in particular. She represents freedom, and was sculpted by Thomas Crawford.

The District of Columbia gets one representative in the House based on population but, like Guam and American Samoa, receives no representation in the Senate because it isn't a state. Hence the local "Taxation without Representation" license plates.

The Capitol is closed New Year's Day, Thanksgiving, and Christmas. Every other day, the public is welcome to explore the annals of the government. Tours are free (unless you count taxes, in which case they're only free if you're a foreigner). Passes are available beginning at 9 am and distributed on a first come, first served basis. Passes are not offered in advance, and distribution is limited to one pass per person. The much anticipated visitors' center is scheduled to be finished sometime in 2006. Hours: Mon-Sat: 9:30 am-4:30 pm.

How to Get There—Driving

From the south, I-66 and I-395 will take you straight to the Mall. I-495, New York Avenue, Rock Creek Parkway, George Washington Memorial Parkway, and the Cabin John Parkway will get you there from the north. From the west, I-66, US Route 50, and 29 will take you to the mall. US Routes 50, 1, and 4 will have you mall-bound from the east.

Parking

There is some handicapped parking at the nearby Lincoln and FDR memorials; otherwise you're dealing with regular street parking, which usually has a maximum time allocation of three hours. There are parking garages located close to the mall, but be prepared to pay a hefty fee for the convenience.

How to Get There—Mass Transit

Take the Orange and Blue Lines to Federal Triangle, Smithsonian and Federal Center SW; the Yellow and Green Lines to Archives/Navy Memorial; the Red Line to Union Station and Judiciary Square; and the Yellow, Green, Blue, and Orange Lines to L'Enfant Plaza.

General Information

NFT Map:	2
DC Address:	700 Pennsylvania Ave NW Washington, DC 20408
MD Address:	8601 Adelphi Rd College Park, MD 20740-6001
Phone:	866-272-6272
Website:	www.archives.gov www.nara.gov
DC Hours:	Mon-Sun: 10 am-5:30 pm (winter); 10 am-7 pm (spring); 10 am-9 pm (summer)
College Park Hours:	Mon, Wed: 8:45 am-5 pm; Tues, Thurs, Fri: 9:45 am-9 pm; Sat: 8:45 am-4:45 pm

Overview

The National Archives is not just for scholars. It's for (dare we say the word) tourists, too. The DC branch (built in 1935, in the standard massive-stone-building-with-lots-of-columns style of the times) holds an impressive collection of our country's most important artifacts, including original documents of the Constitution, the Declaration of Independence, the Bill of Rights, and the Louisiana Purchase. But the National Archives isn't all about old papers either. (We're tearing down *all* those nasty misconceptions!) The building also has on display important historical photographs and memorabilia—like the rifle that shot JFK. Since the guided tour is a bit dull, we advise striking off on your own and poking around at your own pace.

The DC branch is also a must-stop if you're at all interested in the booming hobby of genealogy, as it's probably the nation's top repository of information on who served in the military and where. They've got pension records and the like dating back to the Revolutionary War. The organization also offers free workshops to help you navigate through all they have to offer. It's a great place to research what Grandpa did in World War II—or to just scam on cute grad students working on their theses.

More serious students of US history will find the much newer Archives II building (built in the mid 1990s) to be a nerd's paradise. Located in College Park, Maryland, the building is airy, high-tech, and staffed by friendly, helpful employees who generally know a hell of a lot more about what you're researching than you do. It's here that you'll find post-WWII documents, all of the presidential memoirs, a fascinating collection of WWII film footage (perhaps explaining the unusually high number of Japanese and Russian professors), as well as the infamous Nixon Tapes. The official website offers a great overview of what they've got and where to find it.

Admission to the archives is free at both locations. Leave your Swiss Army knife at home if you don't want to lose it, as security at the National Archives rivals BWI's. And if it's your first time visiting, you'll need to spend an hour or so getting a research card.

How to Get There—Mass Transit

The best way to get to the DC branch is by Metro: take the Yellow or Green Lines to the Archives/Navy Memorial stop. A shuttle bus between the two branches leaves every hour between 8 am and 5 pm.

How to Get There—Driving

To get to College Park from I-495, take Exit 28B to New Hampshire Avenue (Route 650) South. Then take a left at the second light onto Adelphi Road. Follow Adelphi Road for a couple of miles and you'll see the sign for Archives II on the left. If you're leaving from downtown DC, expect about a 45-minute drive. The National Archives and Records Administration's website claims that visitor parking is limited, but we've never had any problems.

If you're driving to the DC branch, keep in mind that parking is street-only.

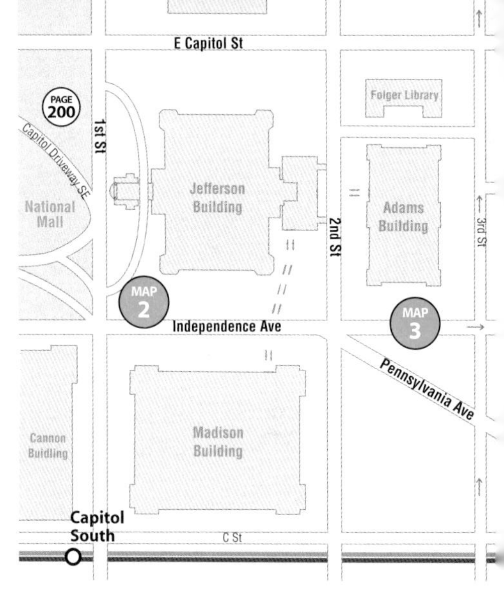

General Information

NFT Maps:	2, 3
Address:	101 Independence Ave SE Washington, DC 20540
Phone:	202-707-5000
Website:	www.loc.gov
Hours:	James Madison Building: Mon-Fri: 8:30 am-9:30 pm; Sat: 8:30 am-6:30 pm Thomas Jefferson Building: Mon-Sat: 10 am-5:30 pm John Adams Building: Mon, Wed, Thurs: 8:30 am-9:30 pm; Tues, Fri, Sat: 8:30 am-5:30 pm

Overview

The Library of Congress doesn't own every book ever published. It IS, however, the largest library in the world. The collection includes more than 128 million items packed on 532 miles of bookshelves in a three-building complex: the Thomas Jefferson Building opened in 1897 and is home to the soaring stained glass Great Hall; the John Adams Building was built in 1939; and the James Madison Building was constructed in 1980. All three buildings are clustered together on Capitol Hill. The Declaration of Independence, the Constitution, a Gutenberg Bible, and the Giant Bible of Mainz are on permanent display.

Sounds like a bibliophile's dream, right? Harsh reality: this is no lending library. The Library of Congress, despite being a great asset to the American public, can't be used like your neighborhood library, or a local bookstore. The Library's mission is to serve as a reference library and educational resource for our government *leaders*, not for us plebeians. In the Library of Congress, children can't run between non-fiction aisles clutching ice cream sandwiches as their mothers discuss ergonomic spatulas on their cell phones. To do more than merely wander through the ornate sections, you have to be older than 18 and register at the Reader Registration Station. The Visitors' Center offers information, a short introductory film, and free guided tours.

The Library has two theaters—the Coolidge Auditorium, located in the Thomas Jefferson Building, and the tiny Mary Pickford Theater in the Madison Building. Built in 1924, the 511-seat Coolidge Auditorium still hosts regular concerts and is known for its remarkable acoustics. Admission to all events is free, however reservations must be made through TicketMaster (two ticket limit per customer), which charges a $2 handling fee. The 64-seat Mary Pickford Theater screens films ranging from those of Pickford's era to modern films. Admission is free, but reservations are required. Visit the Library's website for movie and show times.

History

The Library of Congress was first established in 1800, when the seat of government moved from Philadelphia to DC, and President John Adams approved legislation to create a Congressional law library. The first acquisition consisted of 740 volumes and three maps from London. 14 years later, the British army invaded the city and burned the Capitol building, including the amassed 3,000 volumes that made up the Library of Congress at the time. Thomas Jefferson offered to sell his personal library to Congress to restore its lost collection. Jefferson's 6,487 volumes, which were then the largest and finest collection of books in the country, were purchased for $23,940 (the equivalent of 958 copies of *The Da Vinci Code*). Jefferson's collection, which included works on architecture, science, literature, geography, and art, greatly expanded the Library's previously legal collection.

It was in 1870, under the leadership of librarian Ainsworth Spofford, that the collection outgrew its home. The copyright law of 1870 required all copyright applicants to send the Library of Congress two free copies of their book. The Library was flooded with pamphlets, manuscripts, photographs, and books, and eventually—16 years later—Congress authorized the construction of a new building for all their books.

How to Get There—Mass Transit

The two metro stops closest to the Library are Capitol South (Orange/Blue Lines) and Union Station (Red Line). Capitol South is located a block south of the Thomas Jefferson building, across Independence Avenue. From Union Station, walk south on 1st Street, NE towards the Capitol (it's hard to miss). You'll pass the Supreme Court on your way to the Thomas Jefferson building, which will be on the east side of 1st Street—about a 15 minute walk from Union Station.

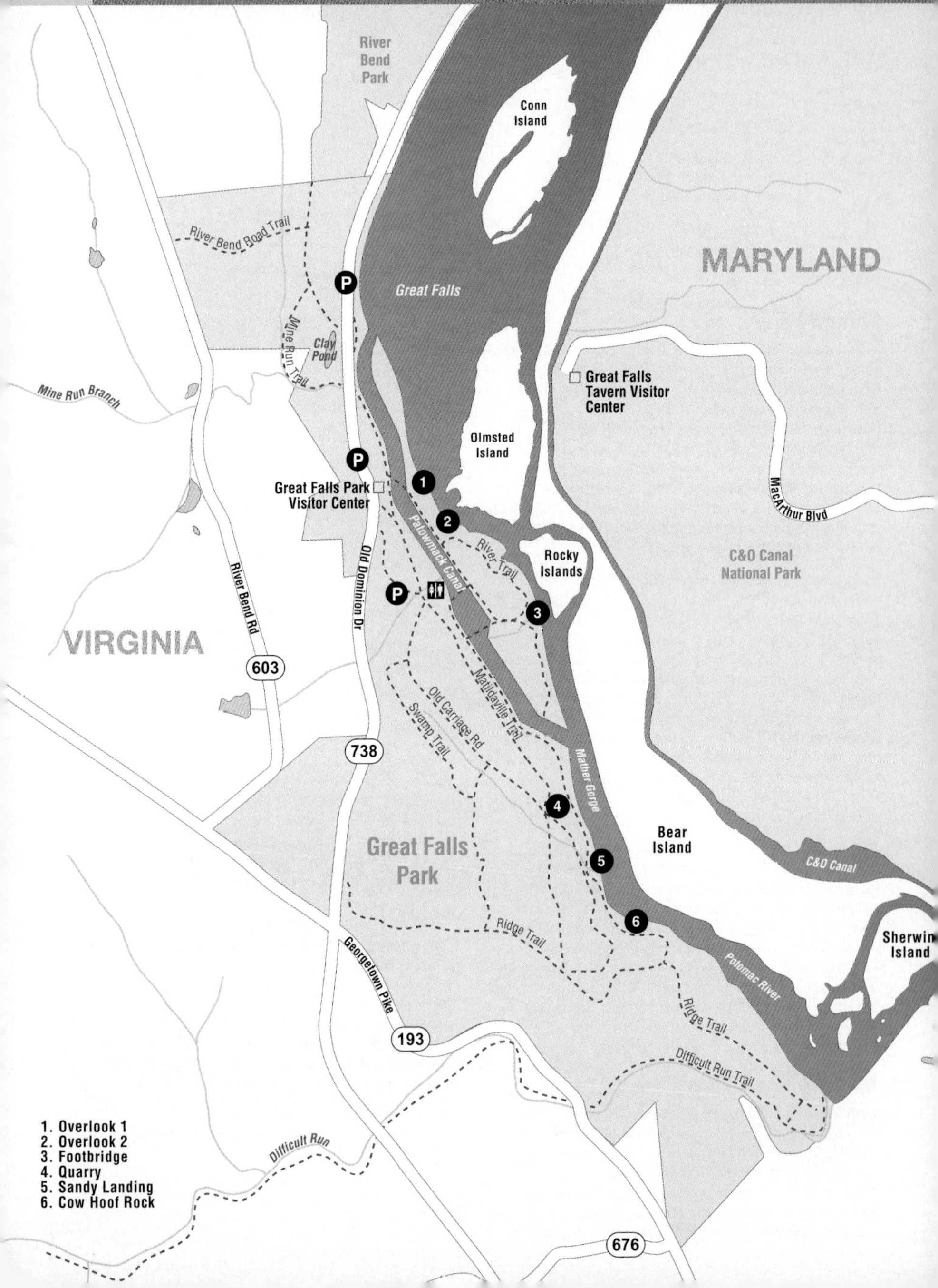

1. Overlook 1
2. Overlook 2
3. Footbridge
4. Quarry
5. Sandy Landing
6. Cow Hoof Rock

General Information

Address: 9200 Old Dominion Dr
McLean, VA 22101
Phone: 703-285-2965
Website: www.nps.gov/gwmp/grfa
Fees: Annual Park Pass: $20
Vehicle: $5 for 3 days
Individual: $3 for 3 days (entering by means other than vehicle - e.g. foot, bike)
All passes valid on both sides of the falls.
Open: 7 am-dusk year-round, closed Christmas

Overview

The aptly named Great Falls Park is 14 miles upriver from Washington, DC, where the Potomac River cracks into cascading rapids and 20-foot waterfalls. The river drops 76 feet in elevation over a distance of less than a mile and narrows from almost 1,000 feet to 100 feet as it gushes through the narrow Mather Gorge. It's the steepest and most spectacular fall line rapid of any eastern river. You can check out the falls from either Virginia, where the viewing area expands into a massive park, or Maryland, where there are fewer amenities but you can get there with two wheels; the Maryland side of the falls is technically in the C&O Canal National Historical Park.

History

The Great Falls weren't always so admired. In the mid-1700s, they presented a near impossible obstacle for navigating the Potomac. One of the most significant engineering feats of the 18th century in the US was the development of a system of canals that lifted and lowered riverboats for over 200 miles of the river. The remains of the Patowmack Canal, one the system's largest and most difficult to create, can still be seen in the park today.

John McLean and Steven Elkins purchased the land surrounding Great Falls and built an amusement park there in the early 1900s that was wildly popular with tourists. Visitors traveled from Georgetown by trolley to take a spin on the wooden carousel. However, time and constant flood damage dampened the thrills until it was eventually closed. Today the land is under the authority and protection of the National Park Service.

Activities

Picnic areas with tables and grills are available on a first-come, first-served basis and ground fires are strictly prohibited. Unfortunately, there are no covered picnic tables in the event of inclement weather, so check the forecast before packing your basket. If you forget your picnic, there is a basic concession stand (open seasonally) located in the Visitor Center courtyard on the Maryland side.

If it's sweat-breaking activity you're after, a scenic, sometimes rocky, bike-riding trail extends between the Maryland side of the falls and downtown Washington. Hiking trails of various length and difficulty wind along the river, and horseback riding, bird watching, rock climbing, fishing, whitewater rafting, and kayaking can be enjoyed at locations throughout the park.

If you plan on rock climbing, registration is not necessary, however there are voluntary sign-in sheets located in the visitor center courtyard and the Lower Parking Lot. If fishing is more your speed, a Virginia or Maryland fishing license is required for anglers over 16 years of age. Whitewater boating is recommended only for experienced boaters and, not surprisingly, you're only allowed to launch your craft *below* the falls.

Stop by the visitor center (open daily from 10 am-4 pm) on the Virginia side of the park or check out the National Park Service website for more information. www.nps.gov/gwmp/grfa/faqs/activities.htm

How to Get There—Driving

From I-495, take Exit 44, Route 193 W (Georgetown Pike). Turn right at Old Dominion Drive (approximately 4 1/2 miles). Drive for 1 mile to the entrance station. Parking, falls overlooks, and the visitor center are all centrally located.

To get to the visitor center on the Maryland side, take I-495 to Exit 41/MacArthur Boulevard E towards Route 189. Follow MacArthur Road all the way to the visitor center.

There is no public transportation available near the park.

Parks & Places • **Rock Creek Park**

General Information

NFT Maps:	20, 21, 23, 24, and 28
Website:	www.nps.gov/rocr
Visitor Information:	202-895-6070

Overview

If tourists have taken over the National Mall, at least locals still have Rock Creek Park to call their own. This 1,754-acre forest doesn't even make it onto many tourist maps—which may explain its popularity with people who live here. You can bike a full mile without breaking for fanny-packers, or go for a jog without worrying about traffic. The park, which stretches from Georgetown to the Maryland state line, is one of the largest forested urban parks in the country. There are three visitors' centers in the park: the Nature Center and Planetarium, Pierce Mill, and the Old Stone House. A paved bike and running path twists alongside the creek that gives the park its name. Dozens of more secluded, rocky paths break off from the path, one of which gained notoriety in 2002 when the body of federal intern/Congressional paramour Chandra Levy was discovered nearby. The park actually has one of the lowest crime rates in the city—but it's an urban park, nevertheless, so lugging along a cell phone or a hiking partner ain't a bad idea.

History

In 1866, federal officials proposed cordoning off some of the forest area as a presidential retreat. By the time Congress took up the plan in 1890, the vision had been democratized and the forest became a public park.

The oldest house in Washington, appropriately named "Old Stone House," is in Rock Creek Park. Now a colonial museum with an English garden, Old Stone House is located on M Street in Georgetown, between 30th and 31st Streets. Pierce Mill, a gristmill where corn and wheat were ground into flour using water power from Rock Creek, was built in the 1820s and is located over the bridge on Tilden Street. (Pierce Mill has been indefinitely closed to the public for repairs, but the Pierce Barn remains open.) There are also remains of several Civil War earthen fortifications in the park, including Fort Stevens, the only Civil War battle site in DC.

Activities

There are more than 30 picnic areas spread throughout the park, all of which can be reserved in advance for parties of up to 100 people (202-673-7646). A large field located at 16th and Kennedy Streets has several areas suitable for soccer, football, volleyball, and field hockey. Fields can be reserved ahead of time (202-673-7749). The Rock Creek Tennis Center has 15 clay and ten hard-surface tennis courts that must be reserved, in person, for a small fee (202-722-5949). The outdoor courts are open from April through November, and five heated indoor courts open during winter months. Three clay courts located off Park Road, east of Pierce Mill, can also be reserved in person, May through September.

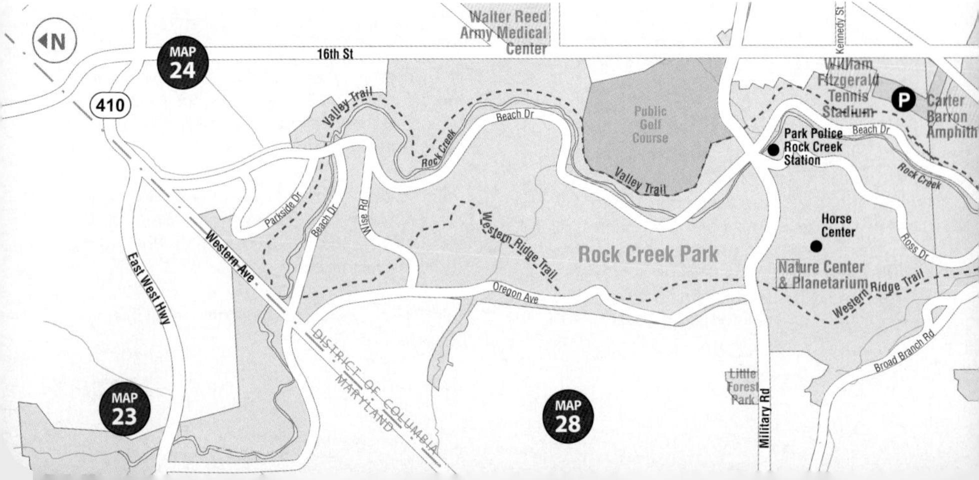

An extensive network of hiking trails runs through Rock Creek Park and the surrounding areas. Blue-blazed paths maintained by the Potomac Appalachian Trail Club run along the east side of the creek, and green-blazed trails follow the park's western ridge. Tan-blazed trails connect the two systems. The paved path for bikers and rollerbladers runs from the Lincoln Memorial, through the park, and into Maryland. Memorial Bridge connects the path to the Mount Vernon Trail in Virginia. Beach Drive between Military and Broad Branch Roads is closed to cars on weekends and on major holidays, giving bikers free range. However, bikes are still not permitted on horse or foot trails at any time. If you're willing to ditch the bike for another kind of ride, horseback riding lessons and guided trail rides are also available at the Rock Creek Park Horse Center (202-362-0117), located next door to the Nature Center.

At the Rock Creek Nature Center, 5200 Glover Rd, NW, you'll find the Planetarium, which features after school shows for children on Wednesdays at 4 pm and weekends at 1 pm and 4 pm. The park also hosts outdoor Shakespeare performances at the Carter Barron Amphitheater (16th St & Colorado Ave, 202-426-0486) on summer evenings. Nature Center Hours: Wed-Sun: 9 am-5 pm. Closed on national holidays.

How to Get There—Driving

To get to the Nature Center from downtown DC, take the Rock Creek/Potomac Parkway north to Beach Drive. Exit onto Beach Drive N and follow it to Broad Branch Road. Make a left and then a right onto Glover Road, and follow the signs to the Nature Center. Note: the Parkway is one-way going south on weekdays from 6:45 am-9:45 am. During this time you can take 16th Street to Military Road W, then turn left on Glover Road. The Parkway is one-way going north from 3:45 pm-6:30 pm; take Glover Road to Military Road east, then head south on 16th Street toward downtown DC. If all you're looking to do is get into the park, consult the map below—the place is so huge that no matter where you live, you're probably close to some branch of it.

Parking

Expansive parking lots are located next to the Nature Center and Planetarium. There are parking lots dotted throughout the park but, depending on your destination, you might be better off looking for street parking in nearby neighborhoods.

How to Get There—Mass Transit

Take the Red Metro line to either the Friendship Heights or Fort Totten Metro stops to get to the Nature Center. Transfer to the E2 bus line, which runs along Military/ Missouri/ Riggs Road between the two stations. Get off at the intersection of Glover (also called Oregon) and Military Roads and walk south on the trail up the hill to the Nature Center.

Check the map, though; the park covers so much ground in the DC Metro area that getting there may be easier than you think. There's certainly no need to start your visit at the Nature Center. If you live anywhere from Adams Morgan to way out in Kensington, the park might be only a jog or a quick bike ride away.

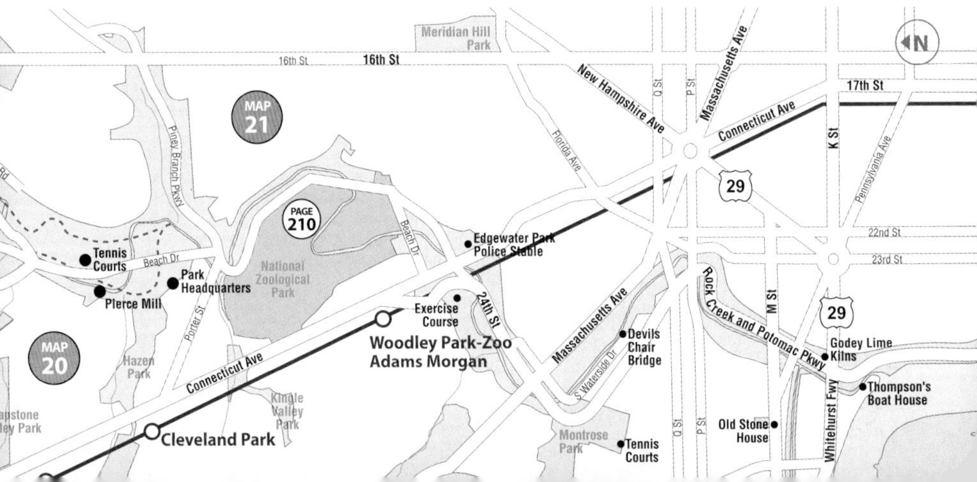

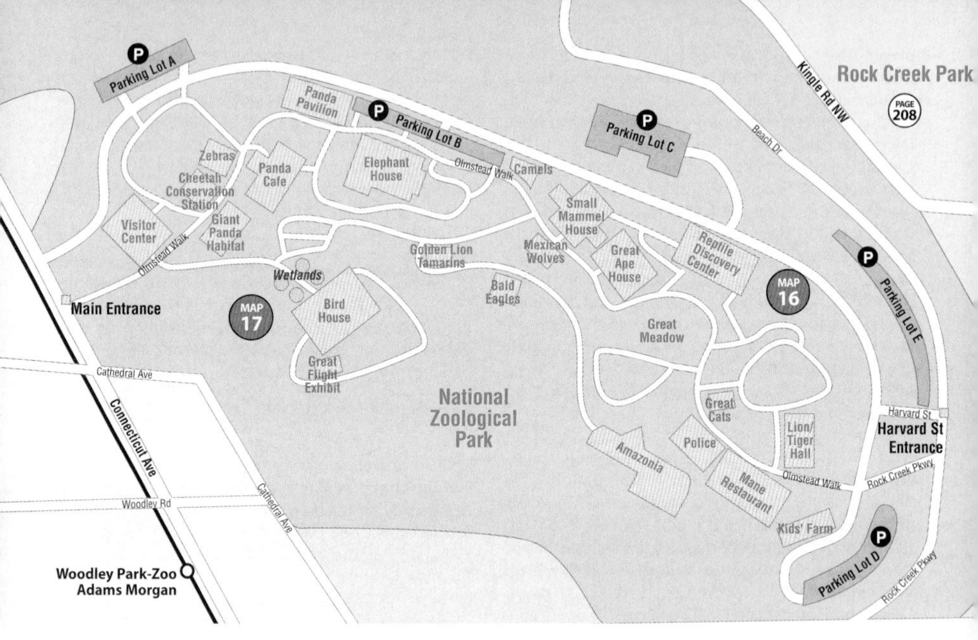

General Information

NFT Maps:	16 & 17
Address:	3001 Connecticut Ave NW Washington, DC 20008
Phone:	202-673-4800
Website:	www.natzoo.si.edu
Hours:	6 am-8 pm Apr 6-Oct 25; 6 am-6 pm the rest of the year. (Closed Christmas Day)
Admission:	Free

Overview

Nestled in Rock Creek Park, the National Zoological Park is a branch of the Smithsonian Institute (read: it should be taken very seriously). With 2,700 animals of 435 different species, there are more pampered foreign residents living in the National Zoo than on Embassy Row. The unofficial city mascots, giant pandas Tian Tian and Mei Xiang, are on what seems to be a permanent loan from China. The animal enclosures mimic natural habitats, and most exhibits strive to entertain while slipping in as much educational value as possible for all of those visiting school children.

The zoo is a favorite jogging route for area residents—especially on winter snow days when Olmsted walk is known to be one of the few regularly plowed paths in the city. In the spring and summer, the zoo is packed with students and campers on field trips in the mornings and early afternoons. If you want to avoid them, try going before 10 am or after 2 pm. The animals tend to be more active at these times anyway, and lines to see the popular exhibits and animals are usually shorter.

Parking

Enter the zoo from Connecticut Avenue, Harvard Street, or Rock Creek Parkway. Because parking on zoo grounds is limited, public transportation is recommended. If you're set on driving, parking at the zoo costs $7 for the first four hours, $12 for more than four hours. Lots fill early in the day during the summer, so plan to arrive by 9:30 am at the latest if you're going to be parking.

How to Get There—Mass Transit

By Metro, take the Red Line to the Woodley Park/Zoo/Adams-Morgan stop or the Cleveland Park stop; the zoo entrance lies halfway between these stops and both are a short stroll away. It's an uphill walk from Woodley Park, while the walk from Cleveland Park is fairly flat.

From the Woodley Park/Zoo/Adams-Morgan stop, walk north (to your left as you face Connecticut Avenue—away from the McDonalds and the CVS), and the zoo is about three blocks from the stop. From the Cleveland Park stop, walk south toward the greater number of shops and restaurants that line Connecticut Avenue (away from the 7-11 and the Exxon station).

If you prefer above-ground mass transit, Metrobus lines L1 and L2 stop at the zoo's Connecticut Avenue entrance. L4 and H4 stop at the zoo's Harvard Street entrance.

General Information

Address: 4368 Chantilly Shopping Ctr
Chantilly, VA 20153
Phone: 703-378-0910
Website: www.dullesexpo.com

Overview

Dulles Expo Center should really just knock off the last two letter of "Dulles" and be done with it. "Dull" is the reigning word here—it accurately describes the area (Chantilly); the spaces in the Center itself (two separate low-slung, charmless rectangles); and most of the exhibits, exhibitors, and exhibitees. Pray to whatever gods you believe in that if you have to attend a show or convention in DC, it'll be at the Washington Convention Center. Dulles Expo's only saving grace is that it has the best convention center parking in the universe—immediately outside the two buildings. Other than that...

A cab from Dulles to the Expo Center will cost about $20. A taxi from Reagan National Airport costs approximately $45. If you really want to fly into Baltimore-Washington International Airport, be prepared to cough up $85 for your 1.5-hour schlep.

Hotels

The Expo Center has an on-site Holiday Inn and several hotels within walking distance. Certain hotels have specials for specific conventions, so ask when you book. Or browse hotel-specific websites such as hotels.com and pricerighthotels.com.

- **Comfort Suites Chantilly-Dulles Airport,** 13980 Metrotech Dr, 703-263-2007
- **Fairfield Inn Dulles Chantilly South,** 3960 Corsair Ct, 703-435-1111
- **Hampton Inn-Dulles South,** 4050 Westfax Dr, 703-818-8200
- **Homestead Village,** 4505 Brookfield Coroporate Dr, 703-263-3361
- **Holiday Inn Select,** 4335 Chantilly Shopping Ctr, 703-815-6060
- **Courtyard by Marriott,** 3935 Centerview Dr, 703-709-7100
- **Sierra Suites,** 4506 Brookfield Corporate Dr, 703-263-7200
- **Staybridge Suites,** 3860 Centerview Dr, 703-435-8090
- **TownePlace Suites by Marriott,** 14036 Thunderbolt Pl, 703-709-0453
- **Westfields Marriott,** 14750 Conference Center Dr, 703-818-0300
- **Wingate Inn Dulles Airport,** 3940 Centerview Dr, 571-203-0999

How to Get There—Driving

From Washington DC, travel west on Constitution Avenue, and follow the signs to I-66 W to Virginia. Remain on I-66 W for about 25 miles until exit 53B, Route 28 N (Dulles Airport). Drive three miles north on Route 28, and then turn right onto Willard Road. Take the second left off into the Chantilly Shopping Center. From there, follow the signs to the Expo Center.

From Dulles Airport, follow exit signs for Washington DC. Stay towards the right for about one mile, and take Route 28 S towards Centerville. Drive six miles and pass over Route 50. At the first light past Route 50, make a left on Willard Road. Follow signs to the Expo Center.

Better yet, don't go at all.

Parking

The Dulles Expo and Conference Center has 2,400 parking spaces on-site! (When their website has to brag about parking, you know we're not just being cynical about this place). If you arrive in your RV, you'll have to find a campsite for the night, as campers, RVs, trucks, and oversized vehicles will be ticketed if parked overnight.

How to Get There—Mass Transit

There is no public transportation to the Dulles Expo and Conference Center. Remember, this is America.

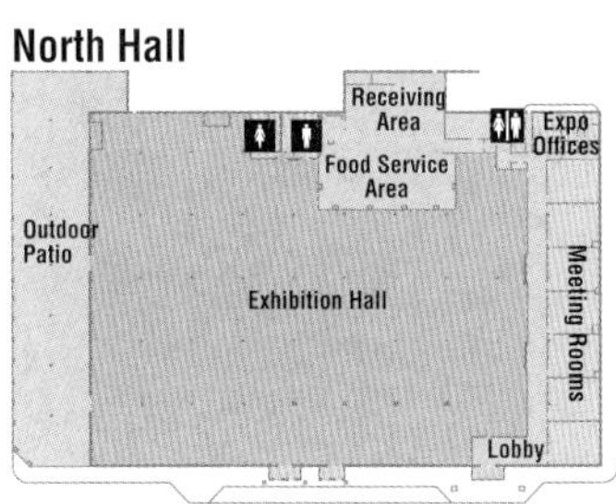

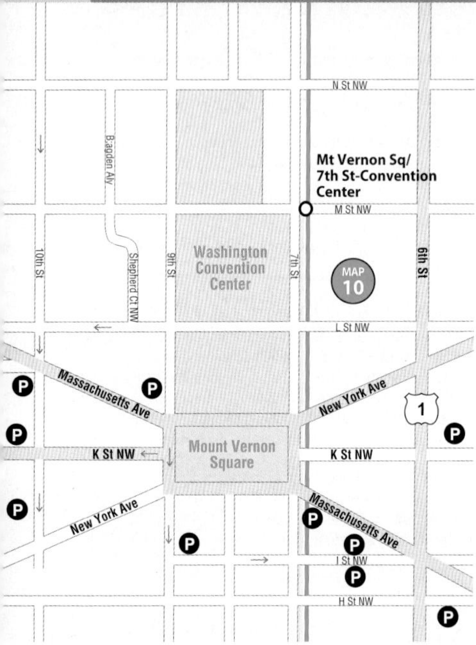

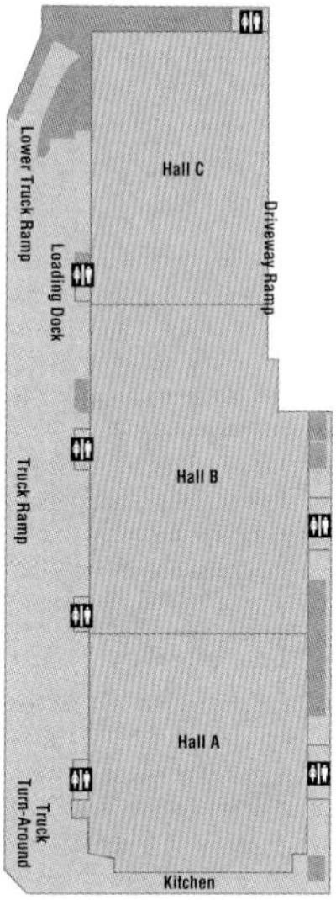

N St NW
Blagden Aly
Mt Vernon Sq/
7th St-Convention
Center
M St NW
10th St
Shepherd Ct NW
9th St
Washington
Convention
Center
7th St
MAP
10
6th St
L St NW
Massachusetts Ave
New York Ave
1
Mount Vernon
Square
K St NW
K St NW
New York Ave
Massachusetts Ave
I St NW
H St NW
P

Lower Truck Ramp
Loading Dock
Hall C
Driveway Ramp
Hall B
Truck Ramp
Hall A
Truck
Turn-Around
Kitchen

LOWER LEVEL

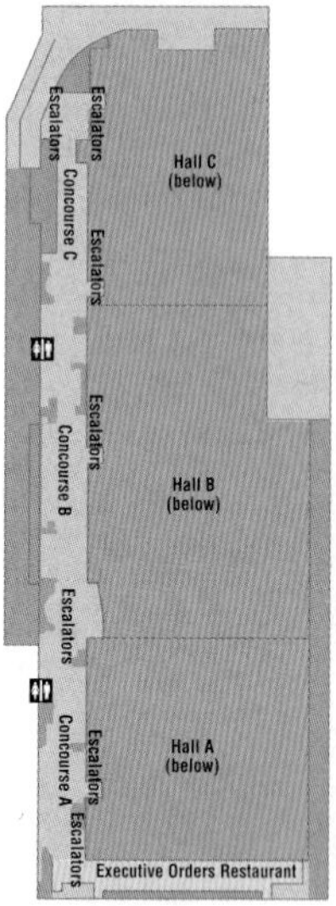

Escalators
Escalators
Concourse C
Escalators
Hall C
(below)
Escalators
Concourse B
Hall B
(below)
Escalators
Escalators
Concourse A
Escalators
Hall A
(below)
Executive Orders Restaurant

CONCOURSE A,B & C

N Street
M Street
9th Street
7th Street
Escalators
152B 152A 151B 151A 150B 150A
155 154B 154A 153 148 149A 149B
160 146C 147B 144C
159B 144B
159A 146B 147A 144A
158B 145B 143C
158A 146A 145A 143B
157 143A
156 140B 142
140A 141
Escalators
L Street
103B 103A 102B 102A 101
Escalators
Escalators
Escalators
Mount Vernon Place

STREET LEVEL

Up to
Docks
Truck
Ramp
Drive-In
Ramp
Escalators
Hall E
Truck Ramp
Escalators
Concourse
Open to Below
Hall D
Compactor
Loading Docks
Drive-In Ramp
Truck Ramp
Escalators
Food
Court
210
209C 209B 209A
Escalators
204A 204B 204C
205
206 207A 207B 208B 208A
203B 203A 202B 202A 201
Concourse
Concourse
Open to Below

LEVEL TWO

Café
Hall E
(below)
Hall D
(below)
Service Corridor
Service
Corridor
Service Corridor
Ballroom A
Ballroom B
Ballroom C
306
305
304
303
302
301
Escalators
Escalators
Pre-Function

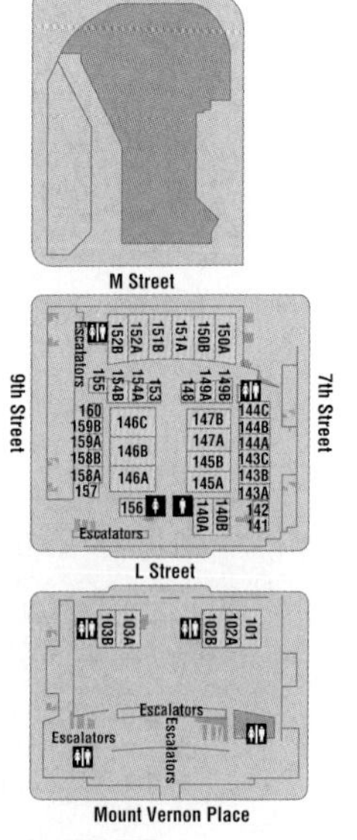

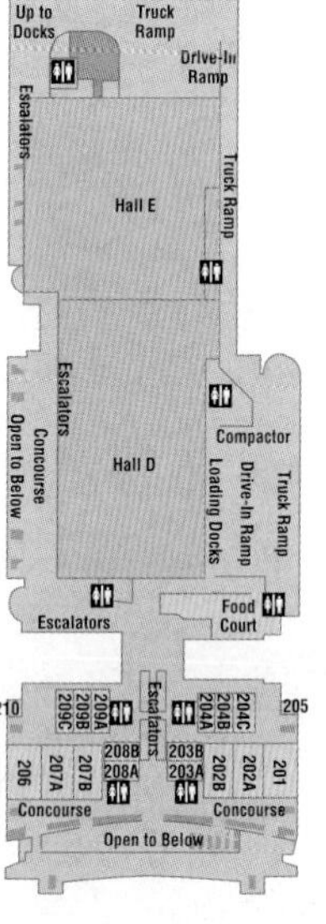

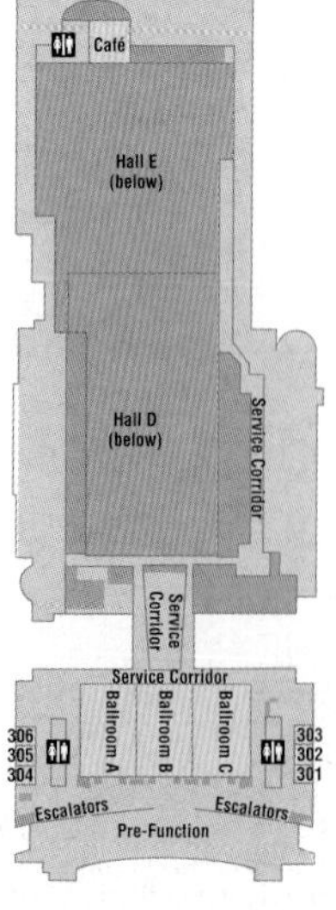

LEVEL THREE

General Information

NFT Map: 10
Address: 801 Mt Vernon Pl NW
Washington, DC 20001
Phone: 800-368-9000 or 202-249-3000
Website: www.dcconvention.com

Overview

The Washington Convention Center is a white and glass 2.3 million-square-foot mammoth covering six city blocks, from 7th Street to 9th Street and N Street to Mount Vernon Place. The building is the largest in DC and has the distinction of being the largest excavation site in the Western Hemisphere; 2 million tons of earth was removed during construction. Whether exhibiting or attending, you'd be well advised to wear comfy shoes to traverse the 700,000 square feet of exhibit space, 125,000 square feet of meeting space, and 40,000 square feet of retail space. The center hosts everything from small seminars for 80 participants to giant expos that welcome 35,000 attendees.

Along with the MCI Center, the Convention Center is a pillar of revitalization for this previously seedy neighborhood. Thanks to that success, conventioneers have many more amenities to choose from in the area. The City Museum is across the street and a string of shops, restaurants, and nightlife beckon nearby. Nevertheless, occasional panhandlers still canvass the area, hoping to profit from pedestrians with open maps making their way toward the Convention Center. The fastest and cheapest way to the Convention Center is to keep that map folded in your coat pocket and follow the platinum blonde in the plastic cowboy hat pasted with event-related bumper stickers.

If you're flying in for a convention, a cab from BWI or Dulles will cost you more than $70 to downtown DC. From Reagan, it should be no more than $15.

Hotels

If you know which hotel you want to stay in, give them a call and ask if they have any special rates for the dates you'll be attending. If you're not with any particular rewards program and don't care where you stay, try the official Washington tourism website at www.washington.org or hotel-specific websites such as www.hotels.com and www.pricerighthotels.com.

- **Renaissance Hotel** • 999 9th St NW, 202-898-9000
- **Henley Park** • 926 Massachusetts Ave NW, 202-638-5200
- **Courtyard Marriott Convention Center** • 900 F St NW, 202-638-4600
- **Morrison Clark Inn** • 1101 11th St NW, 202-898-1200
- **Marriott Metro Center** • 775 12th St NW, 202-737-2200
- **Four Points by Sheraton** • 1201 K St NW, 202-289-7600
- **Hamilton Crowne Plaza** • 1001 14th St NW, 202-682-0111
- **Hilton Garden Inn** • 815 14th St NW, 202-783-7800
- **Hotel Sofitel** • 806 15th St NW, 202-737-8800
- **Washington Plaza** • 10 Thomas Cir NW, 202-842-1300
- **Holiday Inn Downtown** • 1155 14th St NW, 202-737-1200
- **Wyndham Washington, DC** • 1400 M St NW, 202-429-1700
- **The Madison** • 1177 15th St NW, 202-862-1600
- **Hotel Helix** • 1430 Rhode Island Ave NW, 202-462-9001
- **Homewood Suites by Hilton** • 1475 Massachusetts Ave NW, 202-265-8000
- **Capitol Hilton** • 1001 16th St NW, 202-393-1000
- **Holiday Inn Central** • 1501 Rhode Island Ave NW, 202-483-2000
- **Comfort Inn** • 1201 13th St NW, 202-682-5300
- **Grand Hyatt Washington** • 1000 H St NW, 202-582-1234

Eating

You'll find a number of restaurants located in the Convention Center and dozens more within easy walking distance. Executive Orders, located on the L1 Concourse, offers selections from Foggy Bottom Grill, Wolfgang Puck Express, Seafood by Phillips, Subculture, Bello Pronto, Mr. Thoi's Fine Asian Cuisine, and Latin American Cuisine. Located on Level Two off the L Street Bridge, the Supreme Court is a retail food court offering Wolfgang Puck Express, Quizno's, and Foggy Bottom Grill.

The Lobby Café, located by the main entrance, sells coffee and deluxe pastries to help exhibitors and attendees wake up in the mornings. Within each exhibit hall, there are also permanent and portable outlets/carts serving everything from coffee to Tex-Mex.

Parking

The center does not have its own parking facility, and there are about 100 metered parking spaces close to the convention center, so you'll be pretty fortunate if you manage to snag one. Otherwise, be prepared to pay for one of the many parking lots within a three-block radius of the center.

How to Get There—Mass Transit

The closest Metro stop is Mt Vernon Sq/7th St-Convention Center on the Yellow or Green Lines.

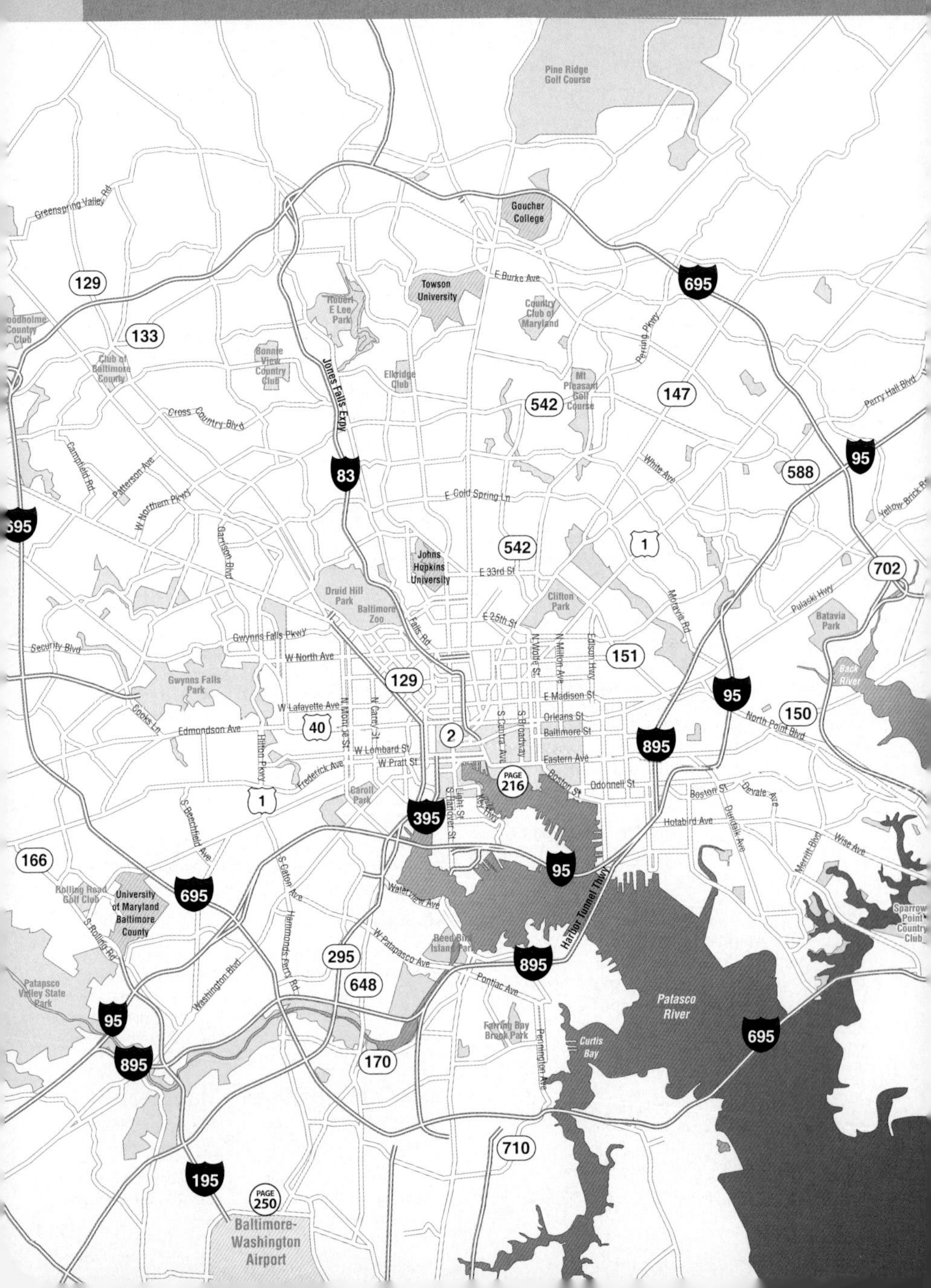

Pine Ridge Golf Course
Goucher College
Towson University
Robert E Lee Park
Country Club of Maryland
Bonnie View Country Club
Club of Baltimore County
Elkridge Club
Mt Pleasant Golf Course
Johns Hopkins University
Druid Hill Park
Baltimore Zoo
Clifton Park
Batavia Park
Back River
Gwynns Falls Park
Carroll Park
Rolling Road Golf Club
University of Maryland Baltimore County
Patapsco Valley State Park
Reed Bird Island Park
Farring Bay Brook Park
Patasco River
Curtis Bay
Sparrows Point Country Club
Baltimore-Washington Airport
PAGE 216
PAGE 250
Greenspring Valley Rd
Cross Country Blvd
Campfield Rd
Patterson Ave
W Northern Pkwy
Garrison Blvd
Jones Falls Expy
E Burke Ave
Perring Pkwy
White Ave
E Cold Spring Ln
E 33rd St
E 25th St
Perry Hall Blvd
Yellow Brick Rd
Pulaski Hwy
Moravia Rd
Security Blvd
Gwynns Falls Pkwy
W North Ave
Falls Rd
N Wolfe St
N Milton Ave
Edison Hwy
E Madison St
Orleans St
Baltimore St
Eastern Ave
Boston St
Odonnell St
North Point Blvd
Devale Ave
Dundalk Ave
Hotabird Ave
Merritt Blvd
Wise Ave
W Lafayette Ave
N Monroe St
N Carey St
Edmondson Ave
Cooks Ln
Hilton Pkwy
W Lombard St
W Pratt St
Frederick Ave
S Central Ave
S Broadway
Light St
S Hanover St
Key Hwy
S Beechfield Ave
S Caton Ave
Hammonds Ferry Rd
Waterview Ave
W Patapsco Ave
Harbor Tunnel Thwy
Pontiac Ave
Pennington Ave
S Rolling Rd
Washington Blvd
129
133
695
83
542
147
95
588
1
702
151
150
895
40
2
129
395
166
295
648
170
710
195

Overview

Think of Baltimore as DC's scruffy, boho kid brother—the guy who may not have gone to The Right School, but is a hell of a lot more fun at family reunions. After decades of urban decay and years as one the murder capitals of the nation, Baltimore's making one heck of a comeback—both jobs and people have been flooding back into town over the last five years. With real estate prices a fraction of DC's (you can get a 19th-century townhouse in Bawlmer for about the same price as an efficiency in Adams Morgan), more and more Washingtonians are moving north—and the bustling, quirky nightlife and just-plain-good neighbors usually make them glad they moved.

Getting There

Take I-295 N to Baltimore City past Oriole Park at Camden Yards. 295 will become Russell Street and then Paca Street. Make a right onto Pratt Street. Follow Pratt Street six blocks to the Inner Harbor, which will be on your right. The Visitor Center is located along the Inner Harbor's west wall (near Light Street).

Attractions

Harborplace

200 E Pratt St, 410-332-4191; www.harborplace.com

One of Baltimore's most well-known attractions is Harborplace, owned by the Rouse Company (i.e. it looks exactly the same as New York's South Street Seaport, Boston's Faneuil Hall, New Orleans' Riverwalk Marketplace, etc). The outdoor mall's retail stores and chain restaurants circle the harbor. Since most residents only hang at Harborplace when they're showing off their oily waterfront to out-of-towners, Harborplace becomes a mob of tourists and DC day-trippers on sunny weekends. Shop hours: Mon-Sat: 10 am-9 pm; Sun: 10 am-7 pm.

National Aquarium in Baltimore

501 E Pratt St, 410-576-3800; www.aqua.org

Baltimore's aquarium is certainly the the city's most popular tourist attraction. Entry isn't cheap, and there's bound to be a line to get in, but attractions like the Tropical Rain Forest (complete with piranhas and poisonous frogs) and the dolphin show make it worth all the hassle. Admission costs $17.95 for adults, $10.95 for kids (3-11), and $16.95 for seniors (65+). Tickets often sell out, but you can buy advance tickets through Ticketmaster. Aquarium hours: Sun-Thurs: 9 am-5 pm; Fri: 9 am-8 pm.

Maryland Science Center

601 Light St; 410-685-5225; www.mdsci.org

The Maryland Science Center is one of the oldest scientific institutions in the country (it traces its history back to 1797) and features a variety of exhibits for both adults and kids, from dinosaur fossils to an IMAX theater. The center is usually open from 10 am to 6 pm daily, although hours change by season; admission prices range from $14 to $19.50, depending on what exhibits you'd like to visit. Admission for children costs between $9.50 to $13.50, and admission for members is always free.

Babe Ruth Birthplace and Museum

216 Emory St, 410-727-1539; www.baberuthmuseum.com

Visit the place where Babe was really a babe. The Sultan of Swat was born in this historic building, which has been transformed into a shrine to Babe, as well as to Baltimore's Colts and Orioles and Johnny Unitas (famed quarterback for the Colts). Admission costs $6 for adults and $3 for children 16 and under. Hours: Mon-Sun: 10 am-5 pm.

The Baltimore Zoo

978 Druid Park Lake Dr, 410-396-7102; www.baltimorezoo.org

Located in Druid Hill Park, the zoo allows you to come face-to-face with over 2,200 exotic mammals, birds, and reptiles amid a wooded 180-acre setting. Kids can enjoy the number-one-rated children's zoo, while adults can look forward to the zoo's spring beer and wine festival, Brew at the Zoo. (Plan on hearing lots of jokes about polar beer, penguinness, and giraffes of wine.) Admission to the zoo costs $15 for adults, $10 for the kiddies, and $12 for the grannies, but parking is always free! The zoo is open daily, Mar-Dec 10 am-4:30 pm.

Lexington Market

400 W Lexington St, 410-685-6169; www.lexingtonmarket.com

Baltimore's Lexington Market is the world's largest continuously running market. Founded in 1782, the market continues to be a rowdy place of commerce, with over 140 vendors selling and displaying foods of all types. The market is famous for its top-quality fresh meats, seafood, poultry, groceries, specialty items, and prepared foods for take-out and on-site consumption. Visit the market during the Chocolate Festival and the Preakness Crab Derby (yes, they actually race crabs). During "Lunch with the Elephants," held annually in the spring, a herd of elephants from the Ringling Bros. and Barnum & Bailey Circus marches from the Baltimore Arena to the market, where they proceed to eat the world's largest stand-up vegetarian buffet. Market hours: Mon-Sat: 8:30 am-6 pm.

National Museum of Dentistry

31 S Greene St, 410-706-0600; www.dentalmuseum.org

After munching on goodies at the Lexington Market, swing on by the National Museum of Dentistry to learn about all the cavities you just got. This Smithsonian affiliate offers interactive exhibits—and the gift shop sells chocolate toothbrushes (Reason enough to check it out!). Plaque got you gloomy? Edgar Allan Poe's grave is just down the street. Admission to the museum costs $4.50 for adults and $2.50 for kids, students, and seniors. Hours: Wed-Sat: 10 am to 4 pm; Sun: 10 am-1 pm.

The Power Plant

601 E Pratt St, 410-752-5444

Once upon a time, the Power Plant was an honest-to-goodness power plant. In 1998, it was converted into a full-fledged mall. Guess retail's just a different kinda community fuel. Inside the Power Plant, you'll find Barnes & Noble, ESPN Zone, Gold's Gym, and the Hard Rock Café.

Power Plant Live!

Market Pl & Water St, 410-727- 5483; www.powerplantlive.com

Located a block away from the Power Plant, Power Plant Live! is a dining and entertainment megaplex. You can have a full night without leaving the indoor/outdoor complex. Dinner, dancing, comedy, and stiff drinks are served up by eight bars and seven restaurants. Because of an arena liquor license, you can take your drink from one establishment to the next. During the summer, check out the free outdoor concerts. Past headliners include the Soundtrack of Our Lives, Aimee Mann, Elvis Costello, and the Wildflowers.

American Visionary Art Museum

800 Key Hwy, 410-244-1900; www.avam.org

The Visionary Art Museum exhibits works from self-taught, intuitive artists, whose backgrounds range from housewives to homeless. The museum is also home to Baltimore's newest outdoor sculptural landmark—the Giant Whirligig. Standing tall at an imposing 55 feet, this multicolored, wind-powered sculpture was created by 76-year-old mechanic, farmer, and artist, Vollis Simpson. Every spring, the museum hosts a race of human-powered works of art designed to travel on land, through mud, and over deep harbor waters. Museum hours: Tues-Sun: 10 am to 6 pm. Admission costs $11 for adults and $7 for students, seniors, and children.

Pagoda at Patterson Park

www.pattersonpark.com

One of the most striking structures in Baltimore's Patterson Park is the newly renovated Pagoda. Originally built in 1891, the Pagoda was designed as a people's lookout tower. From the 60-foot-high octagonal tower, you can see downtown, the suburbs, and the harbor. Pagoda Hours: Sun: 12 pm-6 pm; Mon: 6 pm-8 pm, May-Oct.

Camden Yards

There's more to Camden Yards than just Cal Ripken. At the turn of the century, Camden Yard was a bustling freight and passenger railroad terminal. For decades, Camden Station served as a major facility for the Baltimore and Ohio Railroad (that's the B&O Railroad for Monopoly fans). The Yards were once home to thousands of commuters, and now they're home to thousands of fans who come out to see their beloved Orioles play.

Where to Drink

- **Bohager's**, 701 South Eden St (off map), 410-363-7220.
- **Club Charles**, 1724 N Charles St, 410-727-8815.
- **Cross Street Market**, 1065 S Charles St.
- **The Horse You Came In On**, 1626 Thames St, 410-327-8111.

Where to Eat

- **Bertha's**, 734 S Broadway, 410-327-5795.
- **Boccaccio Restaurant**, 925 Eastern Ave, 410-234-1322.
- **Faidley's Seafood**, Lexington Market, 203 N Paca St, 410-727-4898.
- **Helen's Garden**, 2908 O' Donnell St, 410-276-2233.
- **Jimmy's**, 801 S Broadway, 410-327-3273.
- **John Steven Ltd**, 1800 Thames St, 410-327-5561.
- **Joy America Cafe**, American Visionary Art Museum, 800 Key Hwy, 410-244-6500.
- **Matsuri**, 1105 S Charles St, 410-752-8561.
- **Obrycki's Crab House**, 1727 E Pratt St, 410-732-6399.
- **Rusty Scupper**, 402 Key Hwy, 410-727-3678.
- **Vespa**, 1117-21 S Charles St, 410-385-0355.
- **Ze Mean Bean**, 1739 Fleet St, 410-675-5999.

Where to Eat—Off Map

- **Brass Elephant**, 924 N Charles St, 410-547-8480.
- **Café Hon**, 1002 W 36th St, 410-243-1230.
- **Ikaros**, 4805 Eastern Ave, 410-633-3750.
- **Tapas Teatro**, 1711 N Charles St, 410-332-0110.

Where to Shop

- **The Antique Man,** 1806 Fleet St, 410-732-0932.
- **A Cook's Table,** 717 Light St, 410-539-8600.
- **Mystery Loves Company**, 1730 Fleet St, 410-276-6708.
- **Sound Garden**, 1616 Thames St, 410-563-9011.

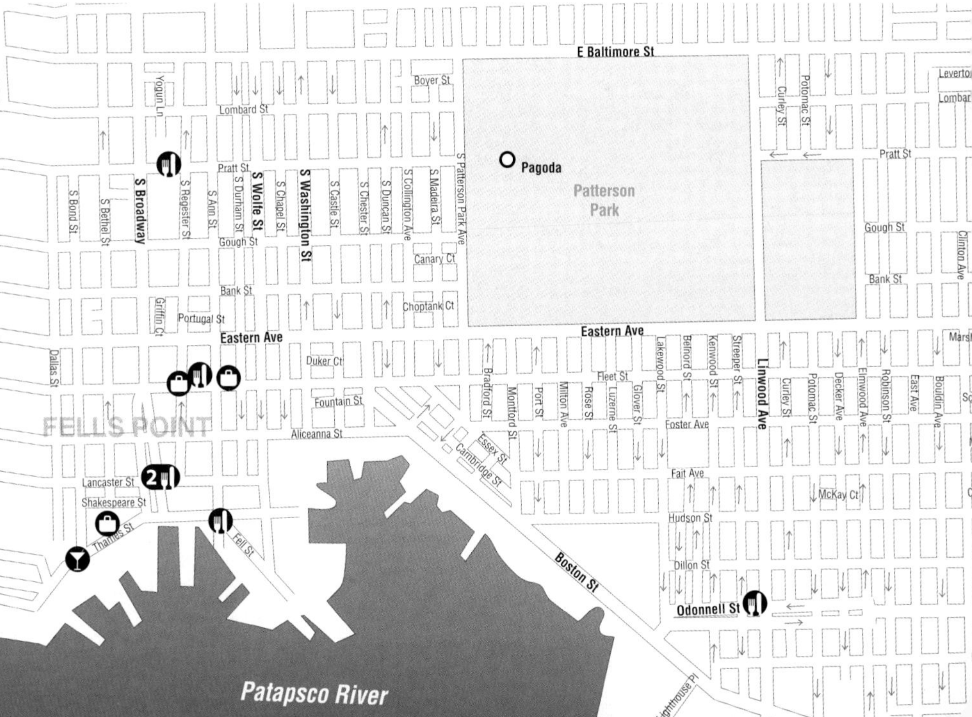

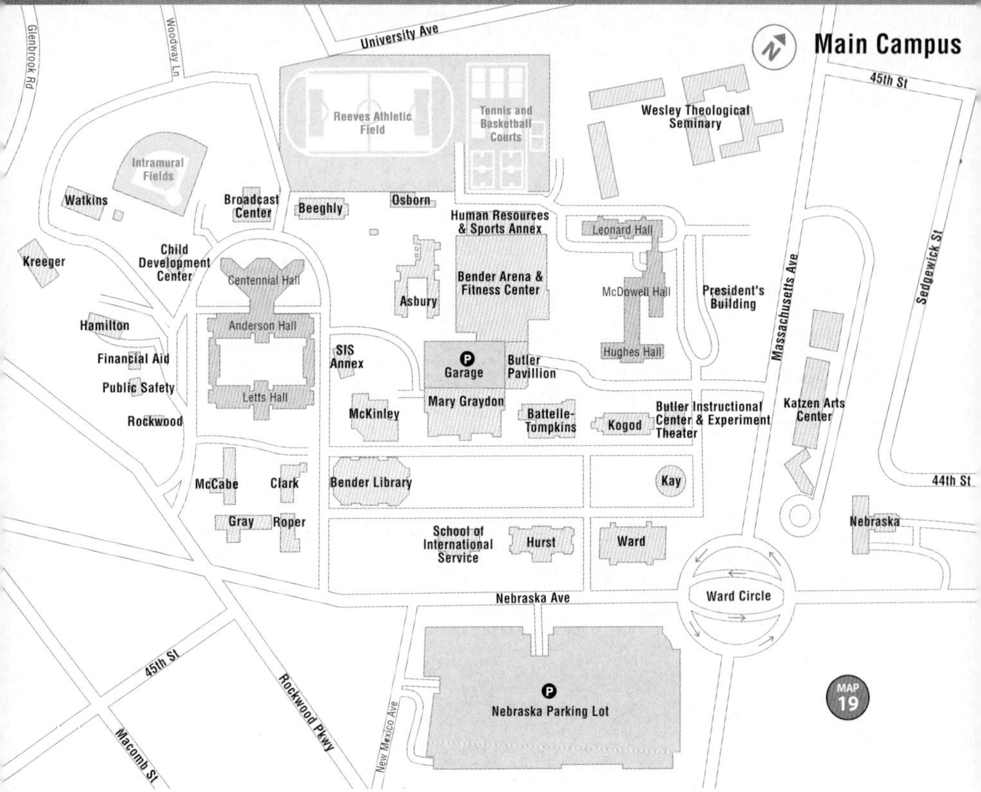

Main Campus
University Ave
Glenbrook Rd
Woodway Ln
45th St
Reeves Athletic Field
Tennis and Basketball Courts
Wesley Theological Seminary
Intramural Fields
Watkins
Broadcast Center
Beeghly
Osborn
Human Resources & Sports Annex
Leonard Hall
Kreeger
Child Development Center
Centennial Hall
Asbury
Bender Arena & Fitness Center
McDowell Hall
President's Building
Massachusetts Ave
Sedgewick St
Hamilton
Anderson Hall
Financial Aid
SIS Annex
Garage
Butler Pavillion
Hughes Hall
Public Safety
Letts Hall
Mary Graydon
Rockwood
McKinley
Battelle-Tompkins
Kogod
Butler Instructional Center & Experiment Theater
Katzen Arts Center
McCabe
Clark
Bender Library
Kay
44th St
Gray
Roper
School of International Service
Hurst
Ward
Nebraska
Ward Circle
Nebraska Ave
45th St
Rockwood Pkwy
Macomb St
New Mexico Ave
Nebraska Parking Lot
MAP 19

Tenley Campus
42nd St
Dunblane House
Constitution Building
Federal Hall
Yuma St
Warren St
Congressional Hall
Capital Hall
Nebraska Ave

WCL Campus
50th St
WCL 4910
Yuma St
49th St
Massachusetts Ave
Washington College of Law
Fordham Rd
48th St
Windham St
48th St

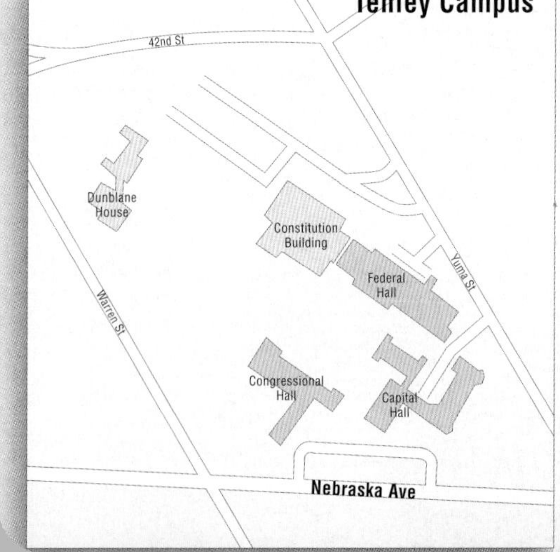

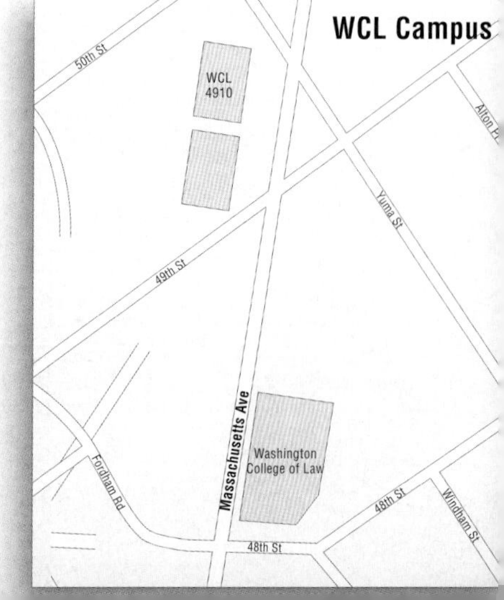

General Information

NFT Map: 19
Main Campus: 4400 Massachusetts Ave NW
Washington, DC 20016
Phone: 202-885-1000
Website: www.american.edu

Overview

American University began as an idea in the mind of George Washington, who envisioned a great "national university" in the nation's capital. If Washington rode the Tenleytown shuttle to campus today, he'd have to be impressed. Though it may seem as if much of the AU student body hails from Long Island, New Jersey, or the Philly suburbs, in fact the school has over 11,000 students from more than 150 countries. This diversity, along with being located in the nation's capitol, makes AU a popular place to study public policy and international affairs. With no Wednesday classes and a heavy internship focus, AU has become a foreign affairs, NGO, and Hill staffer factory. AU students brag that while Georgetown's stuffed shirts end up at DC think tanks, *their* grads actually go out and get their hands dirty. Indeed, it's often the school's idealistic crowd that most resents the "brat pack" contingent of diplomat kids and OPEC heirs, who enroll more out of interest in DC's nightlife than the university's serious-minded pursuits.

Nestled in tony upper northwest DC, AU's leafy quad gives it a classic liberal arts school look. But its picturesque campus doesn't lack for intrigue: work on the Manhattan Project started out in AU's McKinley building, because its unusual architecture ensured that any mishap would cause the building to self-implode and therefore limit any widespread repercussions.

Tuition

In the 2005-2006 academic year, undergraduate tuition for students living on campus amounted to $27,552, with room and board an additional $10,750. Graduate student tuition, fees, and expenses vary by college.

Sports

AU's Eagles play a nice range of NCAA Division I men's and women's sports, including basketball, cross-country, soccer, swimming and diving, tennis, and track and field. Male-exclusive sports include golf and wrestling, while women play field hockey, volleyball, and lacrosse. The men's basketball team wins every year, but can have trouble drumming up fan interest; it's a running joke that mid-season you'll find more students waiting for AU's shuttle than in Bender Arena. A few years ago, the Eagles left the Colonial Athletic Association to join the Patriot League in hopes of winning the league championship and an automatic bid to the NCAA tourney. So far, the Eagles have watched Holy Cross and Bucknell go to the Big Dance.

The American Outdoor Tennis Courts have been the site of several championship wins for the women's and men's tennis teams. Reeves Field won "Soccer Field of the Year" from the Sports Turf Managers' Association, and has also hosted professional practices of the Barcelona and Uruguay national soccer teams.

Culture on Campus

AU operates its wildly wonkish and popular radio station, WAMU 88.5 FM, broadcasting NPR programs as well as locally produced shows like Kojo Nnamdi and Diane Rehm. Bender Arena has hosted a number of high-profile events including the Smashing Pumpkins, Bob Dylan, and heavy-metal vet Archbishop Desmond Tutu. The Katzen Arts Center at AU opened in late '05, bringing all of AU's arts programs under one roof, including its Watkins collection of over 4,400 modern works of Washington-area art.

Department Contact Information

Undergraduate Admissions 202-885-6000
Graduate Affairs & Admissions 202-885-6064
College of Arts & Sciences 202-885-2453
Kogod School of Business 202-885-1900
School of Communication 202-885-2060
School of International Service 202-885-1600
School of Public Affairs 202-885-2940
Washington College of Law 202-274-4000
Washington College of Law Library .. 202-274-4350
Student Services 202-885-3310
Athletic Department 202-885-3000
University Library 202-885-3232

Catholic University of America

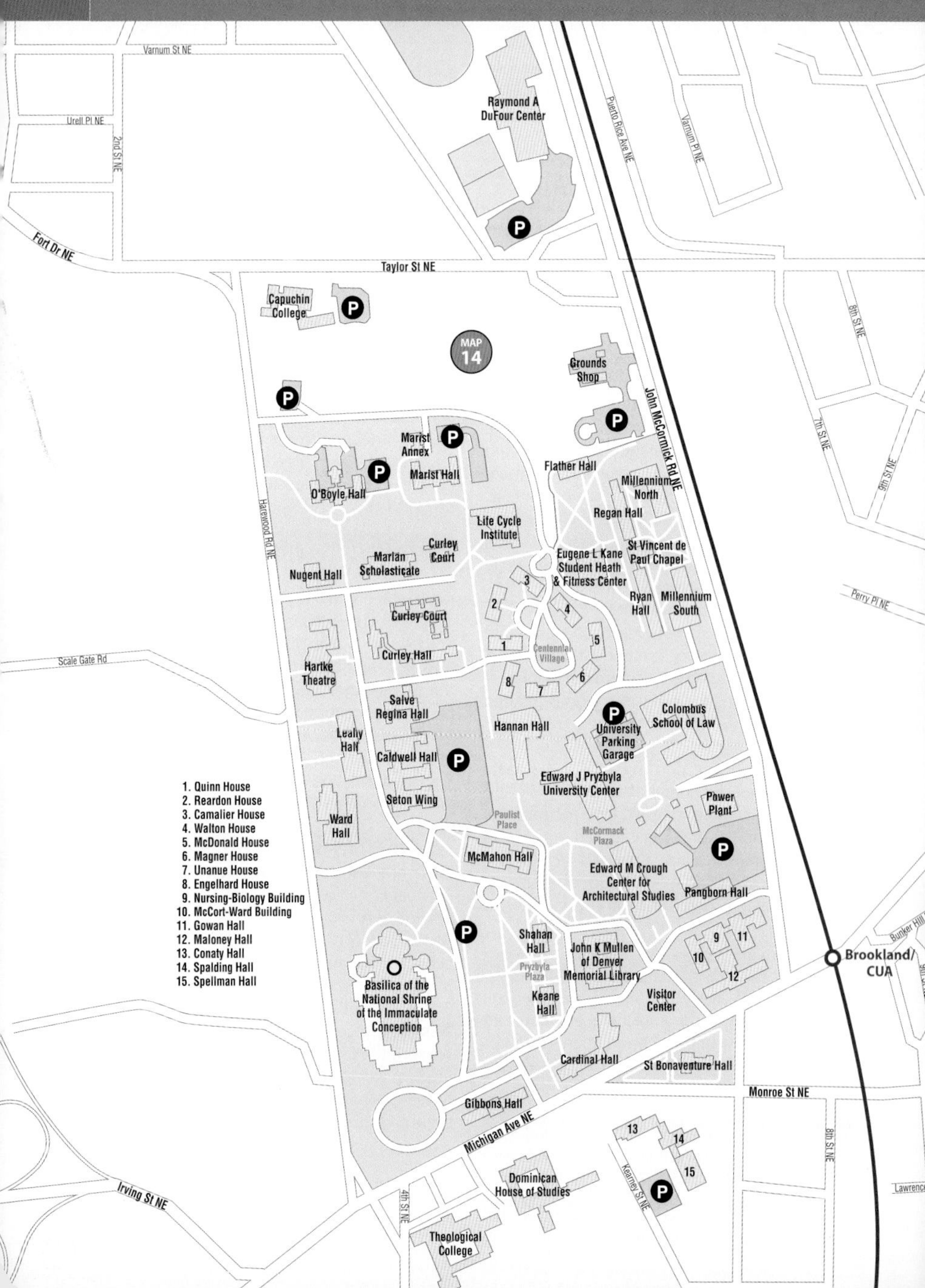

Varnum St NE
Urell Pl NE
2nd St NE
Fort Dr NE
Raymond A DuFour Center
Puerto Rico Ave NE
Varnum Pl NE
Taylor St NE
Capuchin College
MAP 14
Grounds Shop
John McCormick Rd NE
8th St NE
7th St NE
9th St NE
Perry Pl NE
Marist Annex
Marist Hall
O'Boyle Hall
Flather Hall
Millennium North
Regan Hall
Harewood Rd NE
Life Cycle Institute
Curley Court
Marian Scholasticate
Nugent Hall
Eugene L Kane Student Heath & Fitness Center
St Vincent de Paul Chapel
Ryan Hall
Millennium South
Curley Court
Curley Hall
Centennial Village
Scale Gate Rd
Hartke Theatre
Salve Regina Hall
Hannan Hall
University Parking Garage
Colombus School of Law
Leahy Hall
Caldwell Hall
Seton Wing
Edward J Pryzbyla University Center
Power Plant
Ward Hall
Paulist Place
McCormack Plaza
McMahon Hall
Edward M Crough Center for Architectural Studies
Pangborn Hall
Shahan Hall
John K Mullen of Denver Memorial Library
Pryzbyla Plaza
Keane Hall
Visitor Center
Basilica of the National Shrine of the Immaculate Conception
Brookland/ CUA
Bunker Hill
Cardinal Hall
St Bonaventure Hall
Monroe St NE
Gibbons Hall
Michigan Ave NE
Irving St NE
4th St NE
Kearney St NE
Dominican House of Studies
Theological College
Lawrence
1. Quinn House
2. Reardon House
3. Camalier House
4. Walton House
5. McDonald House
6. Magner House
7. Unanue House
8. Engelhard House
9. Nursing-Biology Building
10. McCort-Ward Building
11. Gowan Hall
12. Maloney Hall
13. Conaty Hall
14. Spalding Hall
15. Spellman Hall

Catholic University of America

General Information

NFT Map: 14
Address: 620 Michigan Ave NE
Washington, DC 20064
Phone: 202-319-5000
Website: www.cua.edu

Overview

Lesser known than its Washington rivals but equal in academic distinction, CUA was established in 1887 as a graduate research institution where the Roman Catholic Church could do its thinking. It remains the only American university founded with a papal charter. With a board of trustees still brimming with US cardinals and bishops, the school is considered the national university of the Catholic Church.

That said, CUA is by no means a seminary. Nearly fifteen percent of its 2,900 undergraduates represent religions other than Catholicism, and although shadowed by the colossal Basilica of the National Shrine of the Immaculate Conception (the largest church in America), the laissez-faire campus lacks an in-your-face-piousness to which other orthodox colleges subscribe. Comprising 193 acres, the campus is the largest and arguably the most beautiful of the DC universities. Prominent alums include Susan Sarandon, Ed McMahon, Jon Voight, Brian Cashman (GM of the New York Yankees), and Maureen Dowd.

Though mostly religious, CUA's student body sometimes tries hard to prove otherwise. "Catholic U: Don't Let the Name Fool You" has been a longstanding motto of a ruddy-faced breed of students that knows how to put the "Irish" in Irish Catholic. With a flourishing party scene, CUA is well-represented among the DC drinking establishment. And no, Mr. Joel, Catholic girls do not always start much too late.

Tuition

Tuition for the 2005-2006 school year cost $24,800, with an additional $9,400 for room and board. Add some books here and some travel there, and the final price tag reads $38,700. Even the pope needs to eat.

Sports

Formerly a member of NCAA's Division I, the Catholic Cardinals (as in the little red bird, not the man with the incense and the big hat) downshifted into Division III during the 1970s. Of all the school's sports, men's basketball reigns supreme. Winner of the 2000-01 Division-III National Championship, the team reeled off five consecutive Sweet Sixteen seasons before the streak ground to a halt last year. The women's squad, which posted a 20-win season last year, is also a powerhouse within CUA's Capital Athletic Conference. And although the Catholic football team stumbled over the last few seasons, it dominated the gridiron during the nineties, ranking as high as number ten in the nation.

Culture on Campus

Boasting an extraordinary music program—one of the tops in the country—CUA's Benjamin T. Rome School of Music continuously churns out gem after gem. Thanks to a recent grant, CUA music students study with some of the most renowned composers, directors, and musicians working on Broadway today. The school stages over 200 musicals, operas, chamber concerts, and orchestral and choral performances throughout the academic year. For listings, including Department of Drama productions, visit performingarts.cua.edu.

Department Contact Information

Undergraduate Admissions 202-319-5305
Graduate Admissions 202-319-5057
Athletics............................ 202-319-5610
The Benjamin T. Rome
School of Music 202-319-5414
The Columbus School of Law........ 202-319-5151
Conferences and Summer Programs. 202-319-5291
Hartke Theatre Box Office 202-319-5367
Metropolitan College 202-319-5794
The National Catholic School
of Social Service.................. 202-319-5458
Public Affairs......................... 202-319-5600
The School of Arts and Sciences
(undergrad) 202-319-5114
The School of Arts and Sciences (grad) 202-319-5251
The School of Canon Law........... 202-319-5492
The School of Engineering 202-319-5160
The School of Library
and Information Science........... 202-319-5085
The School of Nursing............... 202-319-5400
The School of Philosophy 202-319-5259
The School of Theology
and Religious Studies.............. 202-319-5683
Summer Sessions 202-319-5257

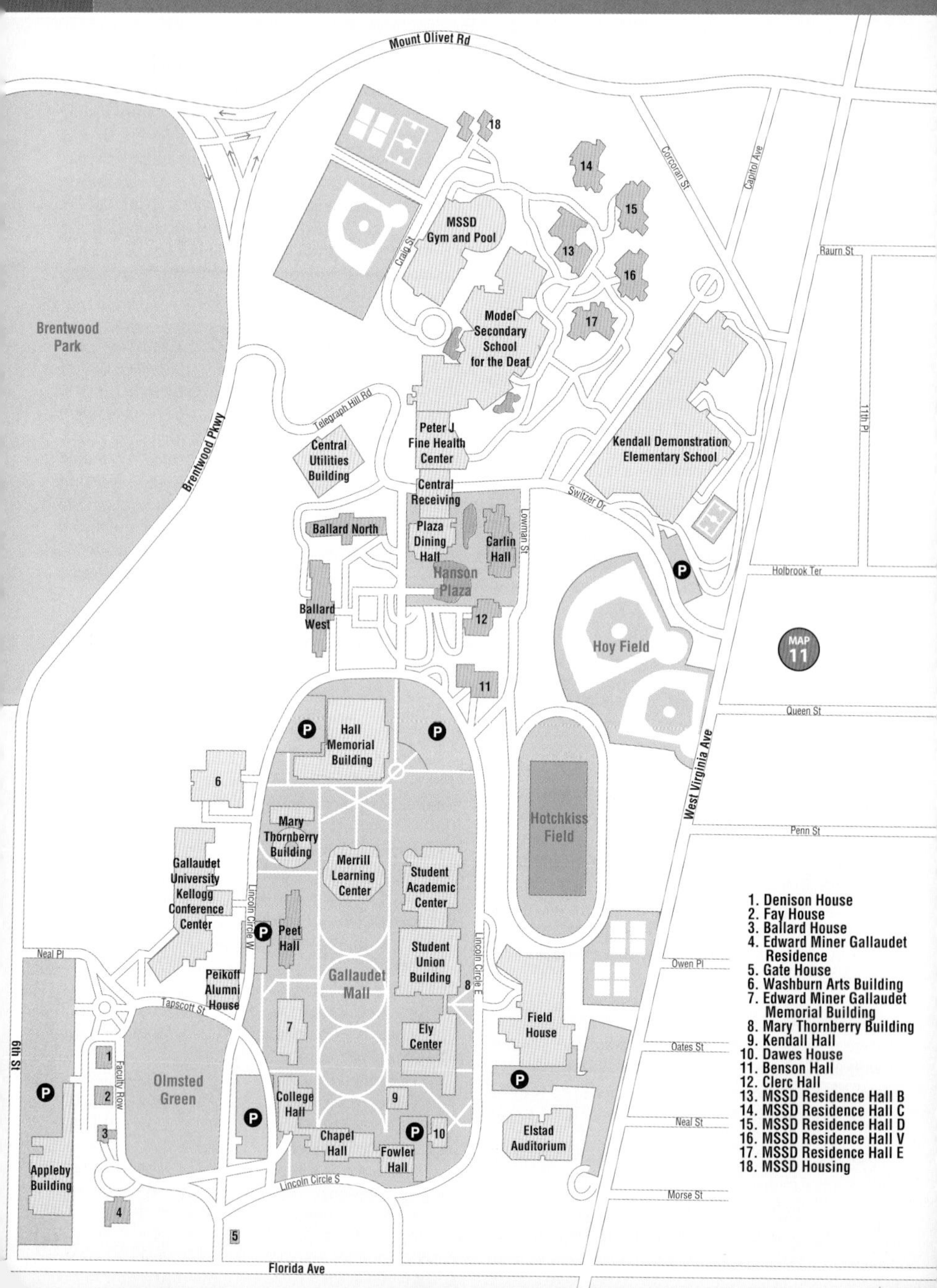

1. Denison House
2. Fay House
3. Ballard House
4. Edward Miner Gallaudet Residence
5. Gate House
6. Washburn Arts Building
7. Edward Miner Gallaudet Memorial Building
8. Mary Thornberry Building
9. Kendall Hall
10. Dawes House
11. Benson Hall
12. Clerc Hall
13. MSSD Residence Hall B
14. MSSD Residence Hall C
15. MSSD Residence Hall D
16. MSSD Residence Hall V
17. MSSD Residence Hall E
18. MSSD Housing

General Information

NFT Map: 11
Address: 800 Florida Ave NE
Washington, DC 20002
Phone: 202-651-5050
Website: www.gallaudet.edu

Overview

Gallaudet is the premier university for the deaf and hearing-impaired, and the only university in the world where deaf students and those without hearing problems mingle. It is a campus where English and American Sign Language (ASL) coexist. Students can choose from more than 40 majors and all aspects of the school, including classes and workshops, are designed to accommodate deaf students. Even the hearing students, who make up about 5% of each entering class, must always communicate through visual communication.

Thomas Hopkins Gallaudet co-founded the American School for the Deaf in Hartford, CT, in 1817 as the first such school in the country. Forty years later, his youngest son, Dr. Edward Minor Gallaudet, established a school for the deaf in DC. In 1864, that school became the world's first and only liberal arts university for the deaf. In 1988, I. King Jordan, the University's first deaf president was appointed after students, backed by a number of alumni, faculty, and staff, shut down the campus, demanding that a deaf president be appointed.

Tuition

In the 2004-2005 academic year, tuition for U.S. residents was $9,630 for undergraduate and $10,600 for graduate programs. For international students tuition was $19,260 and $21,200 respectively. Room and board for both programs was $8,270.

Sports

The birth of the football huddle took place at Gallaudet. Legend has it that prior to the 1890s, football players stood around discussing their plays out of earshot of the other team. This posed a problem for Gallaudet's team; they communicated through signing and opposing teams could see the plays that were being called. Paul Hubbard, a star football player at the university, is credited with coming up with the huddle to prevent prying eyes from discovering plays.

Gallaudet also boasts 14 NCAA Division III teams, and several intramural sports teams.

In the summer, Gallaudet runs popular one-week sports camps, where teens from all over the US, as well as the local area, stay on campus and participate in basketball and volleyball activities. Check the website for details.

Culture on Campus

Gallaudet's Dance Company performs modern, tap, jazz, and other dance styles incorporating ASL. Gallaudet also produces several theater productions every year, all of which are signed with vocal interpretation. The school is smack in the middle of a neighborhood quickly transitioning from rough to trendy. Check out the nearby theaters, coffeehouses, and farmer's market before gentrification smoothes out the hard edges.

Department Contact Information

Admissions: 800-995-0550
Graduate School and
Professional Programs: 800-995-0513
College of Liberal Arts, Sciences
and Technologies: 202-651-5470
Center for ASL Literacy: 202-651-5778
Financial Aid: 202-651-5299
Gallaudet Library: 202-651-5231
Registrar: 202-651-5393
Visitors Center: 202-651-5050

The George Washington University

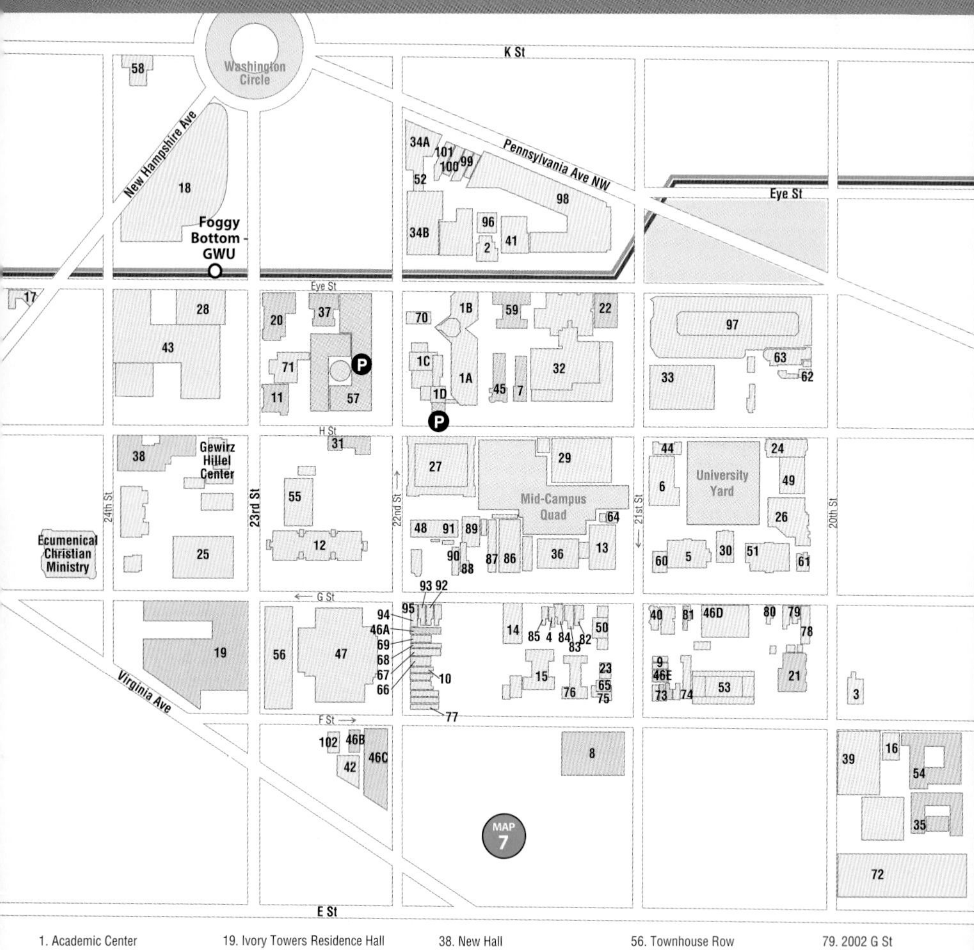

1. Academic Center
   A. Phillips Hall
   B. Rome Hall
   C. Smith Hall of Art
   D. Visitor Center
2. John Quincy Adams House
3. Alumni House
4. Hortense Amsterdam House
5. Bell Hall
6. Corcoran Hall
7. Crawford Hall
8. Dakota
9. Davis-Hodgkins House
10. Abba Eban House
11. Fulbright Hall
12. Funger Hall
13. Hall of Government
14. GSEHD
15. Guthridge Hall
16. The George Washington University Club
17. The George Washington University Inn
18. Hospital, GW
19. Ivory Towers Residence Hall
20. Kennedy Onassis Hall
21. Key Hall
22. Lafayette Hall
23. Lenthall Houses
24. Lerner Hall
25. Lerner Family Health and Wellness Center
26. Jacob Burns Library (Law)
27. Melvin Gelman Library (University)
28. Paul Himmelfarb Health Sciences Library (Medical)
29. Lisner Auditorium
30. Lisner Hall
31. Madison Hall
32. Marvin Center
33. Media & Public Affairs
34. Medical Faculty Associates
   A. H. B. Burns Memorial Bldg
   B. Ambulatory Care Center
35. Mitchell Hall
36. Monroe Hall
37. Munson Hall
38. New Hall
39. Old Main
40. Quigley's
41. Rice Hall
42. Riverside Towers Hall
43. Ross Hall
44. Samson Hall
45. Schenley Hall
46. Scholars Village Townhouses
   A. 619 22nd St
   B. 2208 F St
   C. 520-526 22nd St
   D. 2028 G St
   E. 605-607 21st St
47. Smith Center
48. Staughton Hall
49. Stockton Hall
50. Strong Hall
51. Stuart Hall
52. Student Health Service
53. Support Building
54. Thurston Hall
55. Tompkins Hall of Engineering
56. Townhouse Row
57. University Garage
58. Warwick Bldg
59. The West End
60. Woodhull House
61. 700 20th St
62. 812 20th St
63. 814 20th St
64. 714 21st St
65. 600 21st St
66. 609 22nd St
67. 613 22nd St
68. 615 22nd St
69. 617 22nd St
70. 837 22nd St
71. 817 23rd St
72. 1957 E St
73. 2033-37 F St
74. 2031 F St
75. 2101 F St
76. 2109 F St
77. 2147 F St
78. 2000 G St
79. 2002 G St
80. 2008 G St
81. 2030 G St
82. 2106 G St
83. 2108 G St
84. 2112 G St
85. 2114 G St
86. 2125 G St
87. 2127 G St
88. 2129 G St
89. 2129 G St (rear)
90. 2131 G St
91. 2131 G St (rear)
92. 2136 G St
93. 2138 G St
94. 2140 G St
95. 2142 G St
96. 2129-33 Eye St (rear)
97. 2000 Pennsylvania Ave NW
98. 2100 Pennsylvania Ave NW
99. 2136 Pennsylvania Ave NW
100. 2140 Pennsylvania Ave NW
101. 2142 Pennsylvania Ave NW
102. Newman Catholic Center

General Information

NFT Map: 7
Address: 2121 Eye St NW
Washington, DC 20052
Phone: 202-994-1000
Website: www.gwu.edu

Overview

Once considered nothing more than a second-rate commuter school for graduate and law students, GW, like the city it inhabits, has enjoyed a massive boom in popularity over the past ten years. The school has more than 9,000 full-time undergraduate students and more than 5,000 graduate students stomping around Foggy Bottom in search of wisdom and love. The school recently wrapped up some of its large-scale construction projects and unveiled new academic buildings, a renovated fitness center, and a television studio where they currently film CNN's Crossfire. The GW "campus," for lack of a better word, now stretches its tentacles far into Foggy Bottom, leaving some neighbors none too pleased.

Unlike their counterparts over at Georgetown (who smugly refer to GW as a school for the Georgetown waitlist), GW students understand the meaning of having a life outside of academics. They love their city environs; they seem surprisingly street-smart; they take full advantage of government and congressional internships; and they venture farther afield when it comes to socializing. (Tuesday nights being the exception, when local bar McFadden's is invaded by what seems to be the entire student body.) But GW students aren't all play—the libraries, which stay open 24 hours, are never empty, and each year students are selected to be Rhodes, Truman, Marshall, and Fulbright scholars.

While many undergraduates hail from similar upper-middle class backgrounds, 139 foreign countries are represented in the student body. Collectively, students have a motley appearance, further differentiating them from the Lacoste poster children of Georgetown. Tuition-wise, GW is the city's most expensive school, and with the deep pockets comes more than a few pompous attitudes. Bigshot alums include J Edgar Hoover, Jackie O, Kenneth Starr, General Colin Powell, as well as four presidential children.

Tuition

Tuition for the 2005-2006 school year cost $36,370, with an additional $10,500 for room and board. Add on personal expenses and books, for a whopping yearly total of $49,350.

Athletics

The university's fight song, "Hail to the buff, hail to the blue, hail to the buff and blue," provides hours of double-entendre fun for the students and it seems to work for the athletes too. The university's 22 NCAA Division I teams, known as the fighting Colonials, usually place well in their A-10 conference, especially in basketball: last season, the women's basketball team went to the NCAA Tournament for the 12th time, and the men's team won the first Atlantic Ten Men's Basketball Championship since 1976.

Culture on Campus

The Robert H and Clarice Smith Hall of Art is a modern facility that features five floors dedicated to the study and practice of art. Students participate annually in two major shows, and faculty members also display their art on campus.

The Department of Theatre and Dance produces two dance concerts, three plays, and one musical each year. These productions are performed either in the 435-seat Dorothy Betts Marvin Theatre, or the 1,490-seat Lisner Auditorium (don't miss the Dimock Gallery of Fine Art on the first floor). If you're unaffiliated with the university, tickets to performances will probably cost between $15 and $30. For more information on performances presented by the Theatre and Dance Department, call 202-994-6178.

For information on tickets for the Dorothy Betts Marvin Theatre, call 202-994-7411. For information on tickets for the Lisner Auditorium, call 202-994-6800.

Department Contact Information

Undergraduate Admissions: 202-994-6040
Athletics: 202-994-6650
Campus Bookstore: 202-994-6870
College of Arts & Science: 202-994-6210
Elliot School of International Affairs: 202-994-3002
Financial Aid: 202-994-6620
Gelman Library:......................... 202-994-6558
Graduate School of Education: 202-994-2194
Law School:............................ 202-994-6288
Registrar: 202-994-4900
School of Business:..................... 202-994-8252
School of Medicine :..................... 202-994-3501
Student Activities Center: 202-994-6555
University Police (emergency):........... 202-994-6111
University Police (non-emergency):...... 202-994-6110
Visitor Center:.......................... 202-994-6602

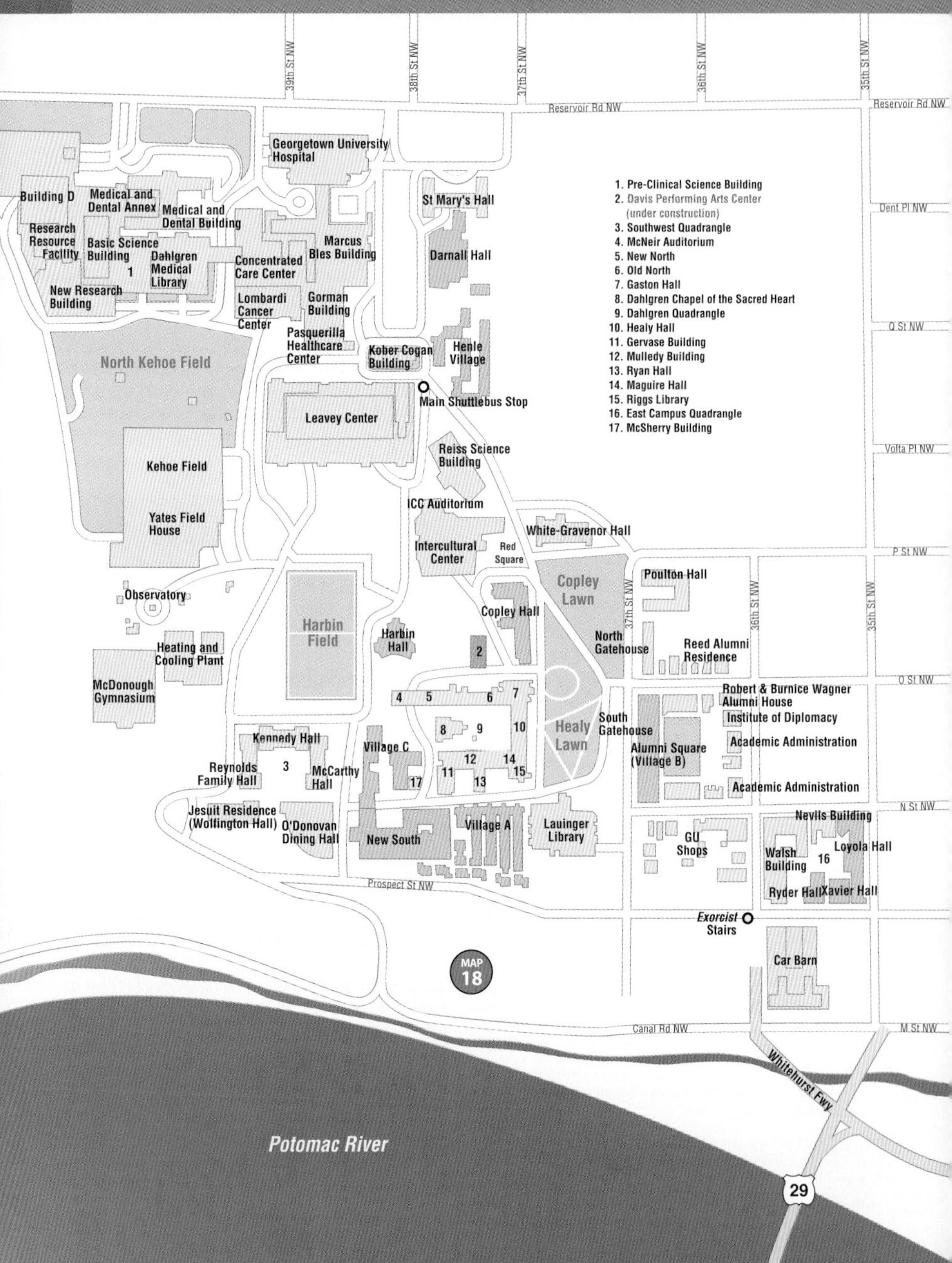

39th St NW
38th St NW
37th St NW
36th St NW
35th St NW
Reservoir Rd NW
Dent Pl NW
Q St NW
Volta Pl NW
P St NW
O St NW
N St NW
M St NW
Prospect St NW
Canal Rd NW
Whitehurst Fwy
Georgetown University Hospital
Building D
Medical and Dental Annex
Medical and Dental Building
Research Resource Facility
Basic Science Building
Dahlgren Medical Library
Concentrated Care Center
Marcus Bles Building
St Mary's Hall
Darnall Hall
New Research Building
Lombardi Cancer Center
Gorman Building
Pasquerilla Healthcare Center
Kober Cogan Building
Henle Village
North Kehoe Field
Main Shuttlebus Stop
Leavey Center
Reiss Science Building
Kehoe Field
Yates Field House
ICC Auditorium
White-Gravenor Hall
Intercultural Center
Red Square
Copley Lawn
Poulton Hall
Observatory
Harbin Field
Harbin Hall
Copley Hall
North Gatehouse
Reed Alumni Residence
Heating and Cooling Plant
McDonough Gymnasium
Robert & Burnice Wagner Alumni House
Institute of Diplomacy
Healy Lawn
South Gatehouse
Academic Administration
Kennedy Hall
Village C
Alumni Square (Village B)
Reynolds Family Hall
McCarthy Hall
Academic Administration
Jesuit Residence (Wolfington Hall)
O'Donovan Dining Hall
New South
Village A
Lauinger Library
GU Shops
Nevils Building
Loyola Hall
Walsh Building
Ryder Hall
Xavier Hall
Exorcist Stairs
Car Barn
MAP 18
Potomac River
29
1. Pre-Clinical Science Building
2. Davis Performing Arts Center (under construction)
3. Southwest Quadrangle
4. McNeir Auditorium
5. New North
6. Old North
7. Gaston Hall
8. Dahlgren Chapel of the Sacred Heart
9. Dahlgren Quadrangle
10. Healy Hall
11. Gervase Building
12. Mulledy Building
13. Ryan Hall
14. Maguire Hall
15. Riggs Library
16. East Campus Quadrangle
17. McSherry Building

General Information

NFT Map: 18
Main Campus: 37th & O Sts NW
Washington, DC 20057
Phone: 202-687-0100
Website: www.georgetown.edu

Overview

Georgetown University was founded the same year the US Constitution took effect, making the school not only the nation's oldest Catholic and Jesuit university, but also about the same age as most of the neighborhood's socialites. But seriously, Georgetown is the most prestigious college in town, and a "feeder school" for the federal government and foreign-policy community. Alumni include former president Bill Clinton, Supreme Court Justice Antonin Scalia, and broadcast journalist/Kennedy heir/California First Lady Maria Shriver. The campus sets the tone for the neighborhood around it—beautiful, old, distinguished, and snooty.

Georgetown's history is long and sometimes spooky. According to campus rumor, the attic of Healy Hall is haunted by the ghost of a priest who died while winding the clock in the building's famous spire. During the Civil War, the university's buildings became bunkers and hospitals for the Yankee troops. Once the war ended, the school adopted blue and gray as its official colors to symbolize the reunification of North and South. More recently, it became part of Hollywood history by providing the setting for a scene from *The Exorcist*, a novel by alum William Peter Blatty. The creepy "*Exorcist* stairs" can be found on campus at the junction of Prospect and 36th Streets.

Tuition

In the 2005-2006 academic year, undergraduate tuition for full-time students cost $31,656. The average room and board costs were an additional $10,739. With books, travel, and other fees, the average total cost of attendance was $45,850. Tuition fees vary by school and the graduate division.

Sports

The university's teams are known as the Hoyas because, the story goes, a student well-versed in Greek and Latin started cheering "Hoya Saxa!" which translates to "What Rocks!" The cheer proved popular and the term "Hoyas" was adopted for all Georgetown teams. Since it was difficult to find an animal that represented "what," the mascot became a bulldog.

Georgetown is renowned for its baseball and basketball teams. (This is where Patrick Ewing got his start.) It also offers men's crew, football, golf, lacrosse, sailing, soccer, swimming/diving, tennis, and track. Women's sports include basketball, crew, field hockey, golf, lacrosse, sailing, soccer, swimming/diving, tennis, track, and volleyball. For tickets to all Georgetown athletic events, call 202-687-HOYA. Georgetown also offers intramural sports including volleyball, flag football, racquetball, basketball, ultimate Frisbee, arm wrestling, table tennis, softball, and floor hockey.

Culture on Campus

Although best known for its more philistine programs—government, law, and medicine—Georgetown has an extensive arts program within its Department of Art, Music, and Theater. Students can major in studio arts, art history, or performing arts. Extracurricular-wise, Georgetown has two theater troupes, an improv group, two a cappella singing groups, an orchestra, and a band. There are also six art galleries around campus devoted to the best of student offerings.

Department Contact Information

Undergraduate Admissions 202-687-3600
Graduate Admissions 202-687-5568
Georgetown Law Center 202-662-9000
McDonough School of Business 202-687-3851
Edmund A. Walsh School
of Foreign Service 202-687-5696
Georgetown University
Medical Center 202-687-5100
School of Nursing & Health Studies .. 202-687-2681
Department of Athletics............. 202-687-2435

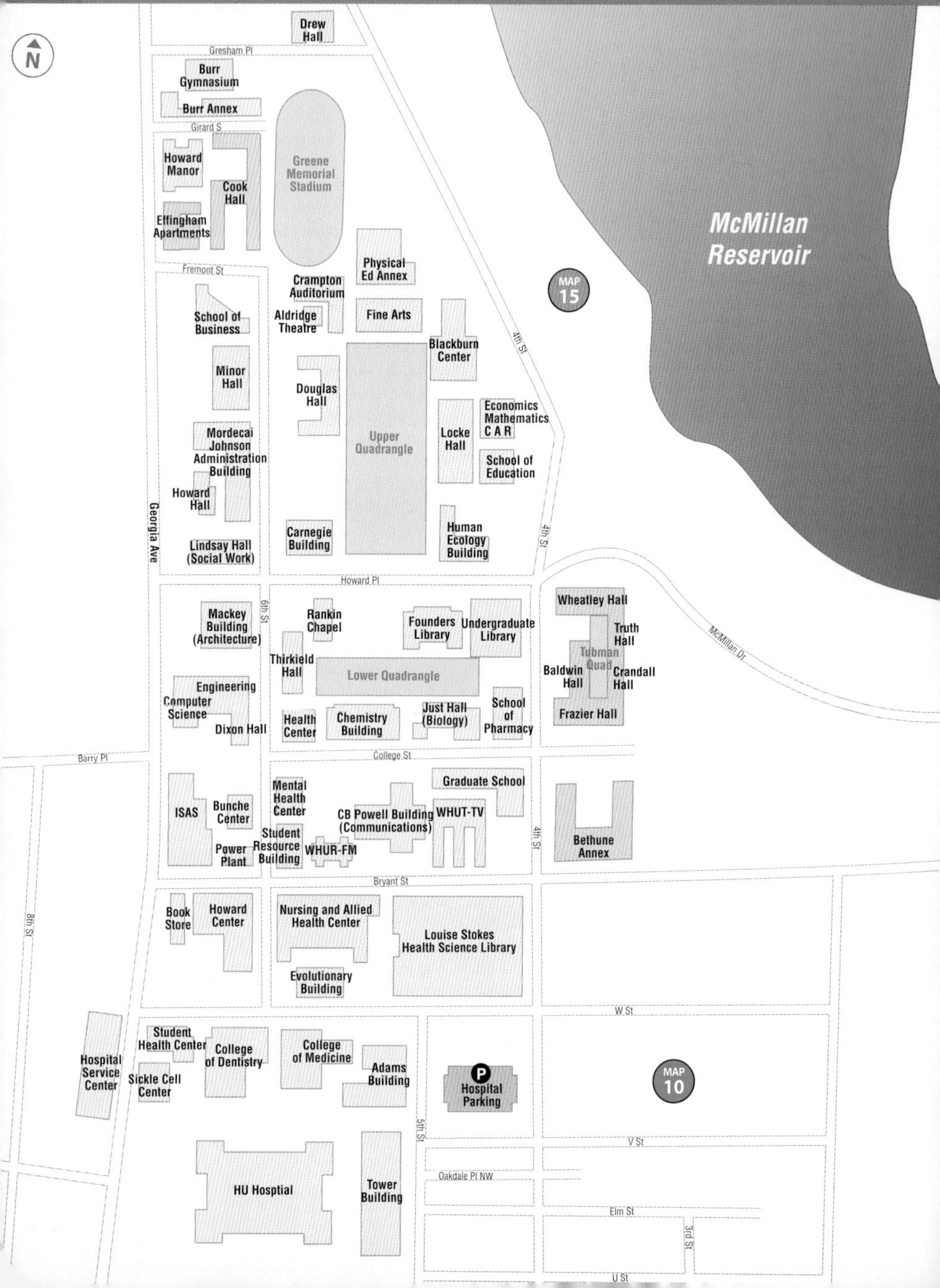

N
Drew Hall
Gresham Pl
Burr Gymnasium
Burr Annex
Girard S
Howard Manor
Cook Hall
Effingham Apartments
Greene Memorial Stadium
McMillan Reservoir
Fremont St
Physical Ed Annex
Crampton Auditorium
MAP 15
School of Business
Aldridge Theatre
Fine Arts
Blackburn Center
4th St
Minor Hall
Douglas Hall
Locke Hall
Economics Mathematics C A R
Upper Quadrangle
Mordecai Johnson Administration Building
School of Education
Howard Hall
Georgia Ave
Lindsay Hall (Social Work)
Carnegie Building
Human Ecology Building
Howard Pl
Wheatley Hall
Mackey Building (Architecture)
6th St
Rankin Chapel
Founders Library
Undergraduate Library
Truth Hall
Thirkield Hall
Tubman Quad
McMillan Dr
Lower Quadrangle
Baldwin Hall
Crandall Hall
Engineering
Computer Science
Dixon Hall
Health Center
Chemistry Building
Just Hall (Biology)
School of Pharmacy
Frazier Hall
Barry Pl
College St
Mental Health Center
Graduate School
ISAS
Bunche Center
CB Powell Building (Communications)
WHUT-TV
Student Resource Building
Power Plant
WHUR-FM
Bethune Annex
Bryant St
Book Store
Howard Center
Nursing and Allied Health Center
Louise Stokes Health Science Library
8th St
Evolutionary Building
W St
Student Health Center
College of Dentistry
College of Medicine
Adams Building
Hospital Service Center
Sickle Cell Center
P
Hospital Parking
MAP 10
5th St
V St
Oakdale Pl NW
HU Hosptial
Tower Building
Elm St
3rd St
U St

General Information

NFT Maps: 10 & 15
Main Campus: 2400 Sixth St NW
Washington, DC 20059
Phone: 202-806-6100
Website: www.howard.edu

Overview

Founded in 1866 as a theological seminary for African-American ministers, Howard University remains an African-American institute (although no longer a seminary) to this day, and has long been a dominant intellectual, cultural, and physical presence in the District. Distinguished Howard alum include novelist Zora Neale Hurston, Supreme Court Justice Thurgood Marshall, Nobel Laureate Toni Morrison, and mayor Shirley Franklin, the first female mayor of Atlanta.

Howard University once occupied a lone single-frame building and now has five campuses spanning more than 260 acres. The library system houses the largest collection of African-American literature in the nation. Despite its large physical size, Howard is a relatively small school with roughly 7,000 undergraduate students and almost 11,000 students total.

Its main campus is located just minutes away from the Capitol and the White House on "the hilltop," one of the highest elevation points in the city. The campus leads right into U Street, one of the premier catwalks of the city. The area was once the city's center of jazz and African-American nightlife before falling on rough times. But now it's back and considered the hippest of areas, with avant-garde fashion, deluxe condos, and over-priced everything.

Tuition

In the 2004-2005 academic year, undergraduate tuition for students living off-campus cost $6,150 per semester. Room and board averaged around $5,570. Graduate tuition, fees, and expenses vary by school and department.

Sports

Howard is a member of the Mid-Eastern Athletic Conference and participates in the NCAA's Division I. The last noteworthy sports achievement dates way back to 2003, when the women's cross-country team ran away with the MEAC championship trophy. Other teams have a less than stellar record. The male basketball team ranked 319th out of 326 teams in 2004. But losing (a lot) hasn't hurt their popularity on campus. Games still draw crowds. Intercollegiate men's sports include basketball, cross-country, soccer, tennis, football, swimming, wrestling, and track. Women's sports include basketball, tennis, cross-country, track, volleyball, and swimming.

Culture on Campus

The Howard University Gallery of Art offers rotating exhibitions of national and international artists, as well as a permanent collection of African artifacts, Renaissance and Baroque paintings, European prints, and contemporary art.

The Department of Theatre Arts produces dance and drama performances throughout the school year in the Ira Aldridge Theater, which also hosts visiting professional theater troupes. Student tickets cost $7.50 and general admission costs $15. The season always brings in a decidedly diverse bag of productions: last year, the theater staged Sartre's "No Exit," the musical "Into the Woods", and a "Rasta/Reggae Play Reading Series." Other fine arts majors are offered through the Department of Art and the Department of Music. The university also has several bands and choirs, which perform regularly.

Howard University Television, WHUT-TV, is the only African-American-owned public television station in the country. It has been operating for 29 years and reaches half a million households in the Washington metropolitan area. Howard University also runs commercial radio station WHUR-FM (96.3).

Department Contact Information

Admissions 202-806-2755
College of Arts & Sciences 202-806-6700
School of Business 202-806-1500
School of Communications 202-806-7690
School of Dentistry 202-806-0440
School of Divinity 202-806-0500
School of Education 202-806-7340
School of Engineering, Architecture,
and Computer Sciences 202-806-6565
Graduate School of Arts & Sciences 202-806-6800
School of Law 202-806-8000
College of Medicine 202-806-6270
College of Pharmacy, Nursing, and
Allied Health Sciences 202-806-5431
School of Social Work 202-806-7300
Student Affairs 202-806-2100
Athletic Department 202-806-7140
Founders Library 202-806-7234

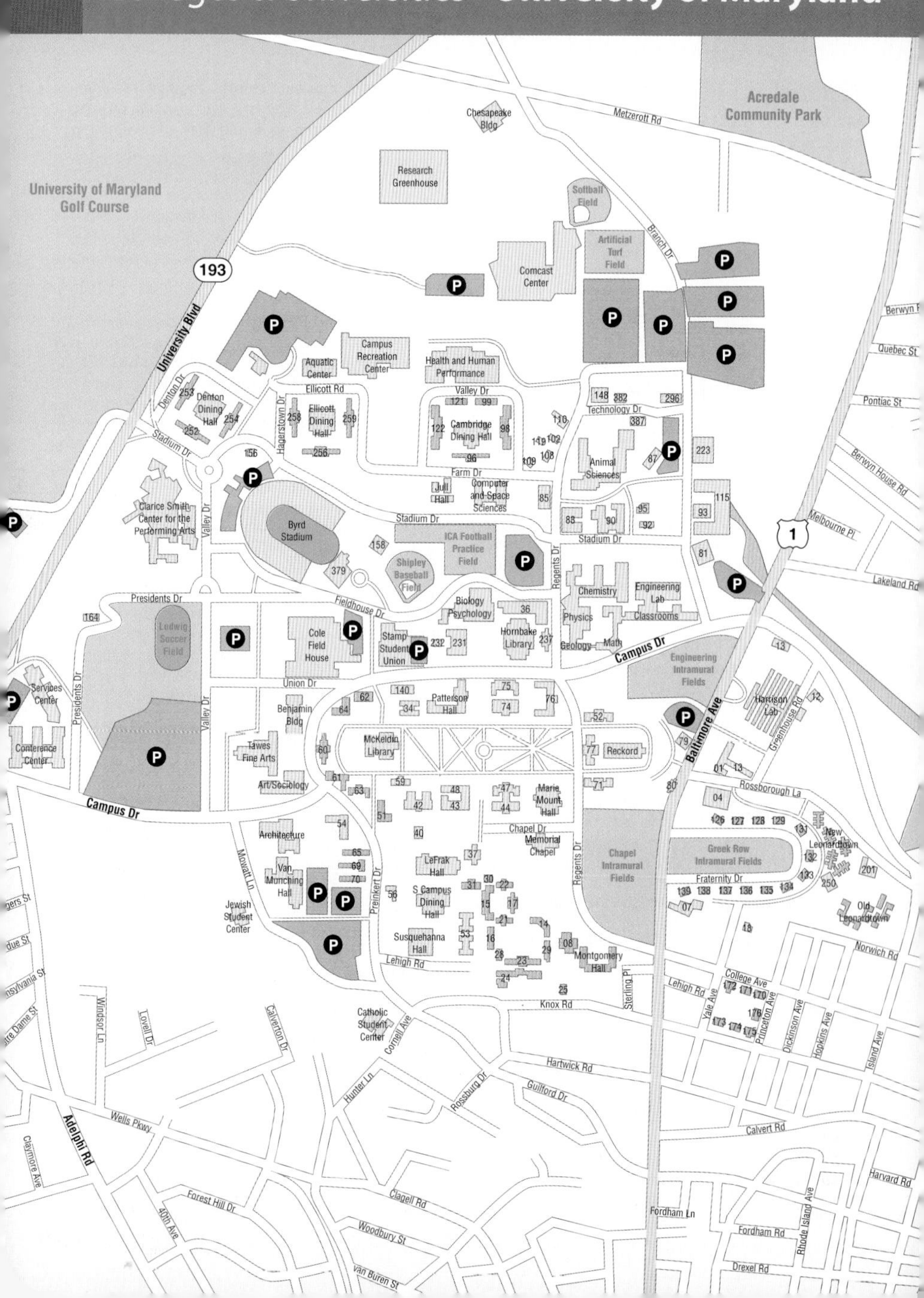
University of Maryland Golf Course
Acredale Community Park
Chesapeake Bldg
Metzerott Rd
Research Greenhouse
Softball Field
Artificial Turf Field
Branch Dr
Comcast Center
193
University Blvd
Campus Recreation Center
Aquatic Center
Health and Human Performance
Ellicott Rd
Valley Dr
Denton Dr
Denton Dining Hall
Ellicott Dining Hall
Cambridge Dining Hall
Technology Dr
Animal Sciences
Stadium Dr
Hagerstown Dr
Farm Dr
Juli Hall
Computer and Space Sciences
Clarice Smith Center for the Performing Arts
Byrd Stadium
ICA Football Practice Field
Shipley Baseball Field
Regents Dr
Chemistry
Physics
Geology
Math
Engineering Lab Classrooms
Presidents Dr
Fieldhouse Dr
Biology Psychology
Hornbake Library
Ludwig Soccer Field
Cole Field House
Stamp Student Union
Campus Dr
Engineering Intramural Fields
Services Center
Conference Center
Union Dr
Benjamin Bldg
Patterson Hall
Tawes Fine Arts
McKeldin Library
Reckord
Harrison Lab
Greenhouse Rd
Baltimore Ave
Art/Sociology
Marie Mount Hall
Rossborough La
Architecture
Chapel Dr
Memorial Chapel
Chapel Intramural Fields
Greek Row Intramural Fields
New Leonardtown
Old Leonardtown
Fraternity Dr
Mowatt Ln
Van Munching Hall
LeFrak Hall
S Campus Dining Hall
Preinkert Dr
Jewish Student Center
Susquehanna Hall
Montgomery Hall
Lehigh Rd
Knox Rd
Sterling Pl
College Ave
Yale Ave
Princeton Ave
Dickinson Ave
Hopkins Ave
Norwich Rd
Catholic Student Center
Cornell Ave
Windsor Ln
Lovell Dr
Calverton Dr
Hartwick Rd
Guilford Dr
Rossburg Dr
Hunter Ln
Wells Pkwy
Adelphi Rd
Calvert Rd
Claymore Ave
Forest Hill Dr
Clagett Rd
40th Ave
Woodbury St
Fordham Ln
Fordham Rd
Van Buren St
Drexel Rd
Harvard Rd
Rhode Island Ave
Island Ave
Berwyn Rd
Quebec St
Pontiac St
Berwyn House Rd
Melbourne Pl
Lakeland Rd
1
P

General Information

Address: College Park, MD 20742
Phone: 301-405-1000
Website: www.umd.edu

Overview

University of Maryland's gargantuan size masks its humble beginnings. First chartered as a small agricultural college in March of 1856, the full public university now has almost 35,000 students roaming its 1,500 acres. Between the 13 colleges, 111 undergraduate majors, study abroad programs, and Honors programs, there's enough excitement and intellectual rigor to keep the brightest Marylanders interested. And for students who've been surrounded by pastoral green quads for so long it makes them want to gag, the school's very own Metro Stop will shuttle them into the vast city that awaits to the south.

Tuition

Undergraduate tuition for the 2004•2005 school year cost $7,410 for in state residents, and $18,710 for non-residents. Room and board averaged around $7,791.

Sports

While there's never been a real dearth of Terrapin pride, it's only sky•rocketed in recent years. An ACC basketball championship win over the Duke Blue Devils, victory at college football's Gator Bowl, and a 2003 NCAA men's basketball Championship win have strengthened Marylanders' love of their winning teams. With 27 Varsity sports teams competing at UMD, the athletic program is widely recognized as one of the best in the country for both men's and women's sports, and the Terps are one of only six schools to have won a national championship in both football and men's basketball.

Culture on Campus

The Clarice Smith Performing Arts Center hosts high profile performers and ensembles. Past guests have included Yo-Yo Ma, the Woolly Mammoth Theater Company, and the Maryland Opera Studio. The Center is also home of the UM symphony orchestra and jazz band. Tickets are usually free or, at most, five bucks for students. You don't have to be affiliated with the university to attend events—just be prepared to shell out up to $30 if you're not a student, faculty member, or staff. 301-405-2787; www.claricesmithcenter.umd.edu.

Department Contact Information

Campus Information: 301-405-1000
Undergraduate Admissions:............. 301-314-8385
Graduate Admissions:.................. 301-405-0376
Bookstore:............................ 301-314-7848
Registrar: 301-314-8249
Bursar:............................... 301-314-9000
Athletic Department:.................. 800-462-8377
Ticket Office:........................ 301-314-7070
Clark School of Engineering:.......... 301-405-3855
College of Education: 301-405-2344
School of Architecture:............... 301-405-6284
School of Public Affairs: 301-405-6330
Smith School of Business: 301-405-2286
Art and Humanities:................... 301-405-2108
Behavioral and Social Sciences:....... 301-405-1697
Life Sciences: 301-405-2071

Building Listings

1 - Central Heating Plant
4 - Ritchie Coliseum
5 - Service Building Annex
7 - Pocomoke Building
8 - Annapolis Hall
12 - Plant Operations & Maintenance Complex
13 - Shuttle Bus Facility
14 - Harford Hall
15 - Calvert Hall
16 - Baltimore Hall
17 - Cecil Hall
18 - Police Substation
21 - Prince George's Hall
22 - Kent Hall
23 - Washington Hall
24 - Allegany Hall
25 - Charles Hall
28 - Howard Hall
29 - Frederick Hall
30 - Talbot Hall
34 - Jimenez Hall
36 - Plant Science
37 - Shoemaker Building
40 - Morrill Hall
42 - Tydings Hall
43 - Taliaferro Hall
44 - Skinner Building
47 - Woods Hall
48 - Francis Scott Key Hall
51 - Worcester Hall
52 - Mitchell Building Registration Office
53 - Dance Building
54 - Preinkert Field House
59 - Journalism Building
60 - Anne Arundel Hall
61 - Queen Anne's Hall
62 - St. Mary's Hall
63 - Somerset Hall
64 - Dorchester Hall
65 - Carroll Hall
66 - West Education Annex
69 - Wicomico Hall
70 - Caroline Hall
71 - Lee Building
74 - Holzapfel Hall
75 - Shriver Laboratory
76 - Symons Hall
77 - Main Administration
79 - Visitors Center
80 - Rossborough Inn
81 - Wind Tunnel Building
83 - JM Patterson Building
85 - Institute for Physical Science & Technology
87 - Central Animal Resources Facility
90 - Chemical and Nuclear Engineering Building
93 - Engineering Annex
96 - Cambridge Hall
98 - Centreville Hall
99 - Bel Air Hall
102 - Agriculture Shed
108 - Horse Barn
109 - Sheep Barn
110 - Cattle Barn
115 - AV Williams
119 - Blacksmith Shop
121 - Performing Arts Center, Clarice Smith
122 - Cumberland Hall
126 - Kappa Alpha Fraternity
127 - Sigma Alpha Mu Fraternity
128 - Delta Tau Delta Fraternity
129 - Sigma Alpha Epsilon Fraternity
131 - Beta Theta Pi Fraternity
132 - Phi Sigma Kappa Fraternity
133 - Pi Kappa Phi Fraternity
134 - Chi Omega Sorority
135 - Sigma Kappa Sorority
136 - Alpha Epsilon Phi Sorority
137 - Zeta Tau Alpha Sorority
138 - Sigma Phi Epsilon Fraternity
139 - Zeta Beta Tau Fraternity
140 - Health Center
148 - Manufacturing Building
156 - Apiary
158 - Varsity Sports Teamhouse
170 - Alpha Delta Pi Sorority
171 - Phi Kappa Tau Fraternity
172 - Alpha Chi Omega Sorority
173 - Delta Phi Epsilon Sorority
174 - Phi Sigma Sigma Sorority
175 - Delta Gamma Sorority
176 - Alpha Phi Sorority
201 - Leonardtown office building
223 - Energy Research
231 - Microbiology Building
232 - Nyumburu Cultural Center
237 - Geology Building
250 - Leonardtown community center
252 - Denton Hall
253 - Easton Hall
254 - Elkton Hall
256 - Ellicott Hall
258 - Hagerstown Hall
259 - LaPlata Hall
296 - Agriculture/Life Science Surge Building
379 - Football Team Building
382 - Neutral Buoyancy Research Facility
387 - Tap Building

General Information

Address: 1600 FedEx Wy
Landover, MD 20785
Redskins Website: www.redskins.com
FedEx Field Website:
www.fedex.com/us/sports/fedexfield/
Stadium Admin: 301-276-6000
Ticket Office: 301-276-6050

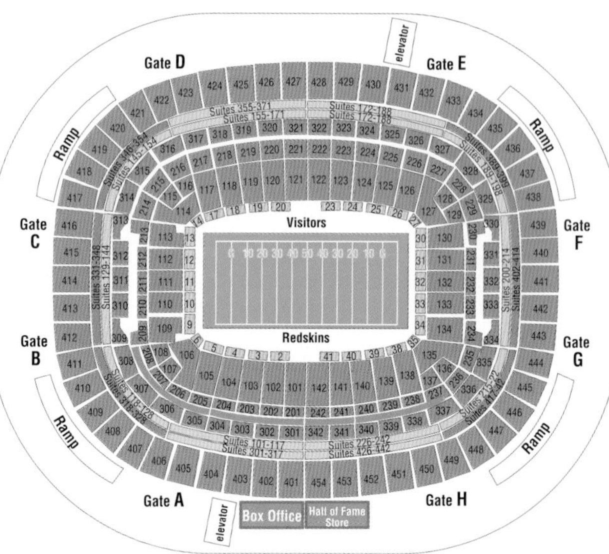

Overview

No city is more infatuated with its football team than Washington is with the Redskins…in the *off*-season, that is. Summer after summer, the team's front office puts together a line-up it claims will march straight to the Super Bowl, and year after year, the beloved 'Skins fall flat on their faces. Part of the problem is Daniel Snyder, the team's unpopular owner, who knows football like Paris Hilton knows rodeo, yet insists on dropping megadimes on washed-up players whom he deems messianic. (We think Deion Sanders may still be collecting Redskins paychecks.)

Alas, the upcoming season will mark the first time in the last several years that nothing will be expected from the team; at least it's nice to know there won't be any disappointments. Mediocre quarterback Patrick Ramsey and ill-suited running back Clinton Portis will captain a joke of an offense, and the team's freshly depleted defense will be of no consolation. Although second-time skipper Joe Gibbs could be elected mayor of this town, many fans see him as too old-school to coach in this, the era of the prima donna (Leon can't do everything). Let's just pray we aren't cheering "go Ravens" by mid-October.

The stadium itself is a diamond in the middle of a very large rough known as Landover, Maryland. During the late 1980s, then-owner Jack Kent Cooke envisioned a new and sensational stadium, settling on a site deep in the Maryland suburbs just inside the Washington Beltway. Although Cooke didn't live to see the $300 million project completed, Jack Kent Cooke Stadium officially opened its gates September 14, 1997 (Snyder sold the naming rights to FedEx shortly after purchasing the team in 1999). The colossal structure is equipped to hold more than 90,000 fans, good for tops in the NFL.

How to Get There—Driving

Take E Capitol Street (Central Avenue) to Harry Truman north, then take a right onto Lottsford Road. Follow Lottsford to Arena Drive and you're there. Keep your eyes peeled for the many signs that will direct you to the field.

Parking

FedEx Field provides off-stadium parking that can cost as much as $25, with a free shuttle ride to the stadium. The team did their damnedest to prevent fans from parking for free at the nearby Landover Mall and walking to the game, but a Prince George's County judge overturned a county policy restricting pedestrian movement in the area. So you can pay up for convenience or exercise your civic rights to park free and schlep.

How to Get There—Mass Transit

Take the Orange Line to the Landover stop or the Blue Line to the Addison Road, Morgan Boulevard, or Largo Town Center stops—all are close by. Five-dollar round-trip shuttle buses depart from these stations for FedEx Field every 15 minutes, from two hours before the game until two hours after.

How to Get Tickets

If you enjoy the prospect of languishing in a years-long line, join the Redskins season ticket waiting list by visiting www.redskins.com/tickets. If you're just looking for individual game tickets, call 301-276-6050.

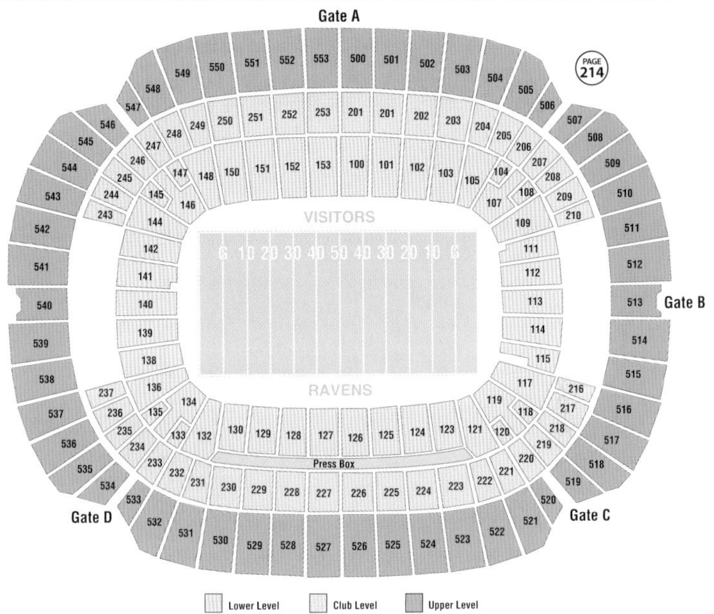

PAGE 214

General Information

Address: 1101 Russell St, Baltimore, MD 21230
Phone: 410-261-7283
Website: www.baltimoreravens.com

Overview

Dominating Baltimore's skyline from I-95, M&T Bank Stadium is a menacing structure to say the least. Its team, the "Bol'more" Ravens, flew into town 10 years ago via Cleveland and wasted no time in capturing the 2001 Super Bowl title. Former MVP Ray Lewis and future MVP Terrell Suggs anchor a potent defense that last year ranked 4th in its conference. On the other hand, the Ravens' lackluster offense—occasionally without star running back/cocaine pusher Jamal Lewis—would have a hard time scoring points against the DC Divas, the District's all-female team.

In Baltimore, as is customary with most NFL cities, the name of the game, or *pre-game*, is tailgating. For 1 pm games, the festivities usually commence at about 9 am. The parking lots slowly swell with inebriated men fashioning O-linemen bellies, confirming Baltimore's reputation as a football town. Outsiders need not be afraid, however, because unlike fans in nearby cities (read: Philadelphia), Ravens fans are gracious hosts and typically welcome others to the party. Once inside the stadium, expect to pay through the nose for food—though the Maryland crab cakes are definitely worth the high price, and the stadium's hot dogs are pretty damn good, too. After the game, Pickles and Sliders, two sports bars on nearby Washington Boulevard, are where weary DC travelers head to quench their thirst.

How to Get There—Driving

Take I-95 N towards Baltimore. Take Exit 52 to Russell Street (heading north) and the stadium is on the right.

Parking

M&T Bank provides parking, for which you need to buy a permit ahead of time. Otherwise, there are 15,000 spaces-worth of public parking nearby.

How to Get There—Mass Transit

The MTA Light Rail provides service directly to the new Hamburg Street Light Rail stop, operational only on game days. Trains run every 17 minutes from Hunt Valley and Cromwell Station/Glen Burnie, and every 34 minutes from Penn Station and BWI. Be sure to leave early to beat the crowds on game days. You can also take the 3, 7, 10, 14, 17, 19/19A, 27, or 31 buses that all stop within walking distance of the stadium.

How to Get Tickets

To purchase tickets, visit the Ravens' website, or call 410-261-7283. Tickets can also be purchased through Ticketmaster (www.ticketmaster.com).

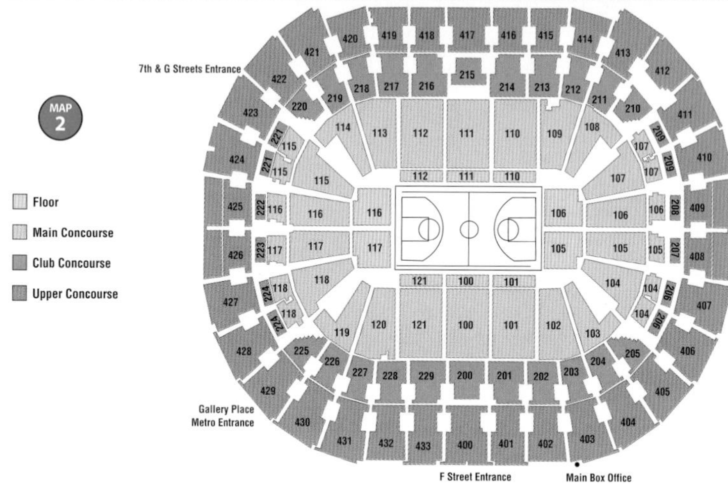

General Information

NFT Map: 2
Address: 601 F St NW
Washington, DC 20004
MCI Center Phone: 202-628-3200
MCI Center Website: www.mcicenter.com
Wizards Phone: 202-661-5100
Wizards Website: www.washingtonwizards.com
Capitals Phone: 202-266-2200
Capitals Website: www.washingtoncaps.com
Mystics Phone: 202-661-5000
Mystics Website www.washingtonmystics.com
Georgetown Basketball Phone: 202-687-4692
Georgetown Basketball Website: www.guhoyas.com

Overview

In 1997, DC's new MCI Center reversed a decades-old trend of arenas planting roots in the suburbs by bringing it all back to the 'hood. The block-sized complex (which includes a 20,000-seat stadium as well as bars, restaurants, and stores) is now the centerpiece of downtown's gentrification juggernaut.

In addition to the Caps and the artists-formerly-known-as-the-Bullets, the MCI Center is also home to the Washington Mystics, who boast the largest fan base in the WNBA. The Georgetown Hoyas basketball team hoops it up in the arena as well. Beyond the ballers, MCI Center hosts big-name concerts from the likes of Cher, Britney, and Madonna, circuses (both Ringling and Cirque de Soleil have performed here), and all sorts of other events.

How to Get There—Driving

From downtown, turn left onto 7th Street from either Constitution Avenue or New York Avenue. The MCI Center is on the northeast corner of F and 7th.

Parking

You're on your own. There's a lot of parking around but, unless you're a season ticket holder, it's not supplied by the MCI Center. Garage prices vary, but you should expect to spend about $20 for the night.

How to Get There—Mass Transit

MCI Center is accessible by the Metro's Red, Yellow, and Green Lines; get off at the Gallery Place-Chinatown stop.

How to Get Tickets

Tickets for all MCI Center events are available through the Ticketmaster website at www.ticketmaster.com (with the inevitable Ticketmaster markup, of course), or by calling 703-573-7328. Wizards tickets range from $12 to $310 for an individual game. Assuming there's actually a hockey season, Caps tickets will run you $10 to $230. (You'd think all that cash would keep the greedy icemen happy.) Mystics tickets range from $8 to $85, and Hoyas tickets are between $5 and $22.50. All teams offer season and multi-game ticket packages. Check out individual team websites for prices.

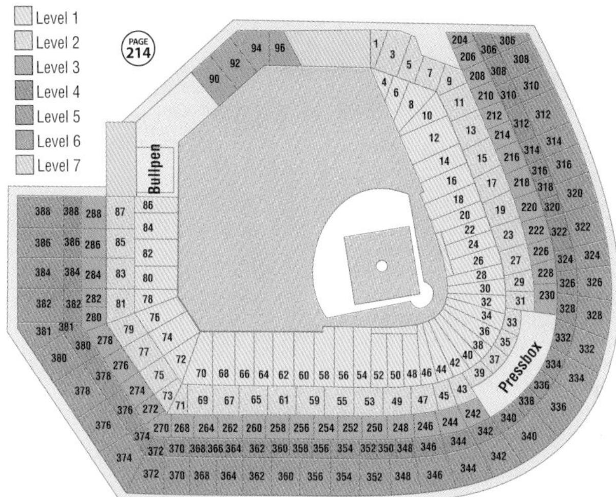

General Information

Address: 333 W Camden St
Baltimore, MD 21201
Website: www.theorioles.com
Phone: 888-848-2473

Overview

Oriole Park at Camden Yards opened in 1992, launching a "traditional" trend in stadium design that continues to this day. In the face of dozens of corporations eager to smear their names across the park, the Orioles have refused to budge. All brick and history, the Yards stand downtown on a former railroad center, two blocks from Babe Ruth's birthplace. Center field sits atop the site where the Bambino's father ran a bar. The goods include double-decker bullpens, a sunken, asymmetrical field, and "Boog's BBQ," run by ex-Oriole Boog Powell, who is known to occasionally man the grill himself.

The Birds, unlike their stadium, haven't been much to look at in recent years. But this, like everything about Baltimore, is changing; new additions, such as shortstop and 2002 American League MVP Miguel Tejada, Cubs slugger/accused 'roider Sammy Sosa, catcher Javy Lopez, pitcher Sidney Ponson, returning first baseman/Viagra shill Rafael Palmeiro, and manager Lee Mazzilli, have Baltimore looking stronger in the Yanks/Sox-dominated American League East. Meanwhile, DC's successful wooing of the Montreal Expos (aka Washington Nationals) to the city may mean a hefty loss of revenue for the Orioles. Stay tuned.

How to Get There—Driving

Take MD 295 (B-W Pkwy/Russell St) to downtown Baltimore, which gets very congested on game days. You can also take I-95 North to Exits 53 (I-395), 52 (Russell St), or 52 (Washington Blvd) and follow signs to the park.

Parking

Parking at Camden Yards is reserved, but there are several public garages nearby. Prices range from $3 to $6.

How to Get There—Mass Transit

Take the MARC from Union Station in DC to Camden Station in Baltimore. It takes about an hour and ten minutes, costs $7, and the last train leaves at 6:30 pm. To return from a night game, the 701 MTA bus will get you home in 50 minutes for free with your Baltimore-bound MARC ticket.

The weekends are another story. Your only choice here is the 703 MTA bus, which runs from Greenbelt Metro Station to Camden Yards for $9.

How to Get Tickets

Orioles tickets can be purchased on their website, or by calling 888-848-2473. Individual game tickets range from $9 to $55. Group and season tickets are also available.

Robert F Kennedy Memorial Stadium

General Information

NFT Map: 4
Address: 2400 E Capitol St SE, Washington, DC 20003
Websites: www.dcunited.com
www.dcsec.com
Phone: 202-547-9077

Overview

After 34 years, Major League Baseball has returned to DC and, unlike the football squad that left for RFK's prettier, younger sister, the well-traveled hearts of the Washington Nationals club (formerly the Montreal Expos) have fallen for the old stadium. The players like the view from home plate because the dark background brings out the ball. The owners like the crowds. The baseball-starved fans like everything, especially the stands that bounce when the crowd gets rowdy. The only ones that don't like anything are the Baltimore Orioles, who have lost some of their fans. This isn't RFK Stadium's first foray into hosting the nation's favorite pastime. The Washington Senators (of "Damn Yankees" fame) also played there 1962 until 1971, when they moved to Arlington, Texas and became the Rangers.

The stadium is a local favorite for sentimental reasons. From the 1961 to 1996 seasons, football legends like Joe Gibbs, John Riggins, Joe Theisman, Vince Lombardi, Art Monk, and George Allen patrolled the RFK gridiron and sidelines. The Redskins played in five Super Bowls during that time, and brought home three titles to show for it. RFK hosted football back when the sport was still a game, without ridiculous fireworks, blaring music, and overpriced beer. When the Redskins franchise abandoned RFK for a bigger, swankier stadium in Maryland, they left behind much more than empty seats and an antiquated scoreboard.

RFK Stadium is now home to DC United, DC's increasingly popular Major League Soccer team. United has put together an impressive resume in a short period of time, winning the MLS Cup Championship in 1996, 1997, 1999 and 2004. In a league where most fans support individual players from their respective countries, DC United offers a solid team and fledgling fan base comprised of people who cheer not only for where they are from, but for where they are now.

MAP 4

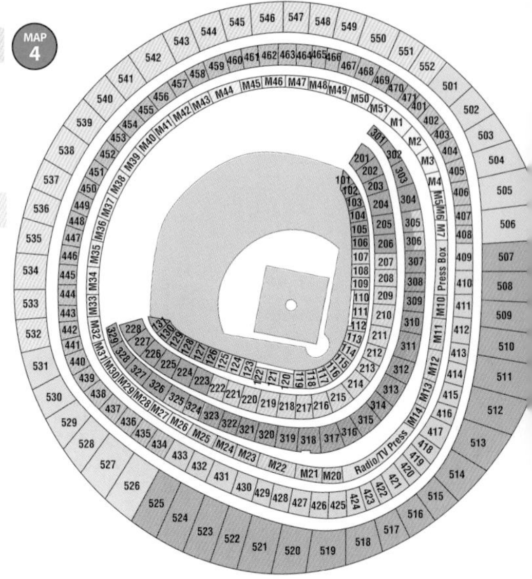

How to Get There—Driving

Follow Constitution Avenue east past the Capitol to Maryland Avenue. Turn left on Maryland and go two blocks to Stanton Square. At Stanton Square, turn right onto Massachusetts Avenue. Go around Lincoln Park to E Capitol Street and turn right.

Parking

Stadium parking costs between $3 and $10, depending on the event you're attending.

How to Get There—Mass Transit

Take the Metro to the Stadium-Armory Station on the Blue and Orange Lines.

How to Get Tickets

For United tickets, call 703-478-6600. All RFK events, including United soccer matches and Nationals' games, can be purchased through Ticketmaster (202-397-7328, www.ticketmaster.com). Tickets to Nationals' games range from $7 to $45.

General Information

Washington Area Bicyclist Association: www.waba.org
Bike Washington: www.bikewashington.org
Bike the Sites Bicycle Tours: www.bikethesites.com
C&O Canal Towpath: www.nps.gov/choh
Capitol Crescent Trail: www.cctrail.org
Mount Vernon Trail: www.nps.gov/gwmp/mvt.html

Overview

A bike in DC is as necessary as a political affiliation. The city tries to satisfy the needs of its mountain and road bikers alike with plenty of multi-terrain trails, a few good urban commuting routes, and one massive citywide bike ride in the fall. When it comes to bikes onboard mass transit, the Metrobus and Metrorail have lenient policies that also help when a bike route, or your energy, dead-ends.

While commuting by bike is doable, it can get rather dicey. Bike lanes don't really exist in much of DC, and state law mandates that cyclists have to follow traffic laws—so plan on mixing it up with the cars on your way to work. Even though DC residents are an honest bunch, it's a good idea to keep your bike locked whenever it's out of your sight. For more information regarding bicycle commuting, check out the Washington Area Bicyclist Association website. The site also provides information about the annual "Bike DC."

Bike Trails

The **Chesapeake and Ohio (C&O) Canal** is probably the city's most popular bike route. The trail spans over 184 miles, and most of it is unpaved, so it's not a trail for the weak of butt. The trail begins in Georgetown and follows the route of the Potomac River from DC to Cumberland, Maryland. Biking is permitted only on the towpath. Campsites are located from Swains Lock to Seneca for bikers following the full length of the trail. But be warned: because the first 20 miles are the most heavily used, conditions within the Beltway are significantly better than those outside of it. The towpath sometimes floods, so its best to check the website, www.nps.gov/choh, for possible closures before breaking out the wheels.

The **Capital Crescent Trail** is a "rail trail"—a bike trail converted from abandoned or unused railroad tracks. The trail spans 11 miles between Georgetown and Silver Spring, Maryland. On the trail's first seven miles, from Georgetown to Bethesda, you'll encounter gentle terrain and ten foot-wide asphalt paths. On weekdays, the trail is used predominantly by commuters, and on weekends it gets crowded with recreational cyclists, rollerbladers, joggers, and dogs. Check out www.cctrail.org.

The **Mount Vernon Trail** offers a wide range of scenic views of the Potomac River and national monuments to ensure an inspiring and patriotic ride. The 18.5-mile trail stretches from Roosevelt Island through Old Town Alexandria to George Washington's house in Mount Vernon. To find out more about these and other bike trails, check out the Bike Washington web site.

Bikes and Mass Transit

If you need a break while riding in the city, you can hop off your bike and take it on a bus or on Metrorail for free. All DC buses are equipped with racks to carry up to two bikes per bus. You can also ride the Metrorail with your wheels on weekends, and during non-rush hour times on weekdays (that means no bikes from 7 am-10 am and from 4 pm-7 pm). Also be sure to use elevators when accessing the Metrorail—blocking the stairs and escalators with your bulky bike makes officials and non-biking commuters testy.

Bike Shops

- **A&A Discount Bicycles** (sales, repair, and rental) • 1034 33rd St NW • 202-337-0254 • Map 18
- **Better Bikes** (rental and delivery) • 202-293-2080 • www.betterbikesinc.com
- **Bicycle Pro Shop** (sales, repair, and rental) • 3403 M St NW • 202-337-0311 www.bicycleproshop.com • Map 18
- **Big Wheel Bikes** (sales, repair, and rental) • 1034 33rd St NW • 202-337-0254 • www.bigwheelbikes.com • Map 18
- **Capitol Hill Bikes** (sales, repair, and rental) • 709 8th St SE • 202-544-4234 • www.capitolhillbikes.com • Map 5
- **City Bikes** (sales, repair, and rental) • 2501 Champlain St NW • 202-265-1564 • www.citybikes.com • Map 16
- **District Hardware/The Bike Shop** (sales and repair) • 2003 P St NW • 202-659-8686 • Map 9
- **Hudson Trail Outfitters** (sales and repair) • 4530 Wisconsin Ave NW • 202-363-9810 • www.hudsontrail.com • Map 19
- **Revolution Cycles** (sales, repair, and rental) • 3411 M St NW • 202-965-3601 • www.revolutioncycles.com • Map 18

General Information

DC Department of Parks and Recreation: www.dc.gov
Washington Area Roadskaters (WAR): www.skatedc.org

Overview

DC supports a surprisingly thriving skating scene, thanks in a large part to the non-profit inline skater's group WAR (www.skatedc.org). Popular places where skaters meet up include the White House, whose traffic-free roadway and easy Metro access contribute to its popularity; Rock Creek Park, which is closed to cars on weekends; and East Potomac Park, whose 3.2-mile Ohio Drive loop was recently repaved. For more information about skating in DC, check out WAR's website.

Indoor Skating

If the weather is grim, or if you want to put in some good practice on predictably level terrain, check out **Franconia Roller Skating Center** in Alexandria. Hours: Sat-Thurs: 7 pm-10 pm; Fri: 7 pm-11 pm; Sat: 10 am-4 pm; 703-971-3334. Other rinks in DC's suburbs include **Wheels Skating Center**, 1200 Odenton Rd, MD (410-674-9661); and **Rockville Skating Center**, 1632 E Gude Dr, Rockville, MD (301-340-7767)

Skate Parks

After years of hostile restrictions and citations against skaters grinding away outside government buildings, a skate park was finally built in the Shaw neighborhood in 2003. It's free and located on the corner of 11th Street and Rhode Island Avenue. 202-282-0758 - Map10.

Other outdoor skate parks in the DC area include:

Alexandria Skate Park • 3540 Wheeler Ave, Alexandria • 703-838-4343/4344 • Map 42

The Powhatan Springs Park • 6020 Wilson Blvd, Arlington, VA • 703-533-1839 • Map 33
A 15,000-square-foot park, featuring 8'- and 6'-deep bowls and 4' and 6' half-pipes.

Ice-Skating

Finding natural outdoor ice thick enough to support skating can be difficult in DC. But during particularly cold winters, the National Parks Service allows ice-skaters out onto the C&O Canal (the ice has to be more than three inches thick, so it's got to be *really* cold). The National Park Service hotline provides information on skate-safe areas: 301-767-3707.

Skating at the **National Gallery of Art's Sculpture Garden Ice-Skating Rink** may not seem as organic as skating on natural ice, but the surrounding art exhibit rivals any natural setting in terms of beauty. And every Thursday night, from December through March, you can skate to live jazz from 5 pm to 8 pm. The rink is open daily October through March, Monday-Saturday 10 am to 11 pm, Sunday 10 am to 9 pm. Admission for a two-hour session costs $6 for adults and $5 for children, students, and seniors. Skate rental costs $2.50 and locker rental costs 50¢; 700 Constitution Avenue NW; 202-289-3360; Map 2.

While the Sculpture Garden rink turns into a fountain once the warm weather arrives, the NHL-sized rink at **Mount Vernon Recreation Center** in Alexandria operates year-round. The rink provides ice-hockey lessons, recreational skating lessons, and adult hockey leagues for all levels. On Friday nights, the rink brings in a DJ for teen Rock & Blade skating. Rates and fees vary nightly, so call before you go. 2017 Belle View Blvd, Alexandria; 703-768-3224.

Other seasonal ice-skating rinks are located at:

Pershing Park Ice Rink • Pennsylvania Ave & 14 St NW • 202-737-6938 • Map 1
$5.50-$6.50 admission + $2.50 rental

Bethesda Metro Ice Center • 3 Bethesda Metro Ctr, Bethesda, MD • 301-656-0588 • Map 29

Gear

The **Ski Chalet** offers a comprehensive selection of performance inline skates and offers tune-ups and rentals. Skates can be rented by the hour ($5) or by the day ($15 for the first day, $6 each additional day). The Ski Chalet is located at 2704 Columbia Pike, Arlington, VA; 703-521-1700 - Map 37

The **Ski Center**, located at 4300 Fordham Road, NW, sells reasonably priced ice and inline skates. The shop, which has been serving the DC area since 1959, also rents equipment. 202-966-4474 - Map 30

For skateboarding equipment, check out the **Evolve Board Shop** at 4856 Bethesda Avenue in Bethesda, MD. While this shop primarily targets snowboarders, they also stock skateboard equipment and gear. 301-654-1510 - Map 29.

Sailing/Boating/Rowing

Boating enjoys a passionate following here in the District. As the weather warms, the Potomac River and the Tidal Basin swarm with sailboats, kayaks, canoes, and paddleboats.

At 380 miles long, the Potomac River ranks as the fourth longest river on the East Coast. The river also serves as a natural state border, forming part of the boundary between Maryland and West Virginia, and separating Virginia from both Maryland and DC. The site of many significant battles during the American Revolution and the Civil War, the Potomac now holds an eternal place in the US history books, and has earned the moniker "The Nation's River." A combination of urban sewage and run-off from mining projects upstream seriously degraded the river's water quality, but efforts by the government and citizens have made the water safe for boats and some fishing. Swimming? Well, we don't suggest it.

The Mariner Sailing School (703-768-0018) gives lessons and rents canoes, kayaks, and sailboats for two to six people.

If a paddleboat ride is worth worming your way through swarms of sweaty tourists, the Tidal Basin is the best place to go. The boathouse, which sits among the famous cherry blossoms and tulip-bearing flower beds on the man-made inlet, rents paddleboats by the hour (202-484-0206). Two-person boats cost $8 per hour; four-person boats cost $16 per hour.

Sailing/Boating Centers	*Address*	*Phone*	*Map*	*URL*
Capitol Sailboat Club	James Creek Marina, Washington, DC	202-265-3052	6	www.capitolsbc.com
DC Sail	2000 Half St SW, Washington, DC	202-329-2986	6	www.dcsail.org
Tidal Basin Boat House	1501 Maine Ave SW, Washington, DC	202-479-2426	6	www.guestservices.com
Mariner Sailing School	Belle Haven Marina, Alexandria, VA	703-768-0018	N/A	www.saildc.com
Sailing Club of Washington	5945 Norham Dr, Alexandria, VA	202-628-7245	N/A	www.scow.org

Rowing Clubs				
Capitol Rowing Club	1125 O St SE, Washington, DC	202-289-6666	5	www.capitalrowing.org
DC Strokes Rowing Club	1125 O St SE, Washington, DC		5	www.dcstrokes.org
Potomac Boat Club	3530 Water St NW, Washington, DC	202-333-9737	8	www.rowpbc.net
Canoe Cruisers Association	11301 Rockville Pike, Kensington, MD	301-251-2978	N/A	www.ccadc.org/cca

Golf

Like everything else in DC, there's politics and networking involved in where you choose to tee off. Our advice—avoid the pricey rat race at the private clubs and reserve a tee time at one of the many, and often more fun, public courses.

East Potomac Park offers three different course options (Red, White, and Blue, of course) as well as mini golf, and a driving range. The Langston Golf Course is closest to downtown DC, making it easy to hit during lunch. The Rock Creek Golf Course can sometimes suffer from droughts and heavy play, but its great location keeps people happily putting away.

Golf Courses	*Address*	*Phone*	*Map*	*Type*	*Fees*
East Potomac Golf Course	972 Ohio Dr SW	202-554-7660	6	Public	18-holes—WD $21.50/ WE $26.50
Langston Golf Course	28th & Benning Rds NE	202-397-8638	12	Public	18-holes—WD $17/ WE $26.50
Sligo Creek Golf Course	9701 Sligo Creek Pkwy	301-585-6006	25	Public	nine-holes—WD-$13-15/ WE $18
Rock Creek Golf Course	16th & Rittenhouse NW	202-882-7332	27	Public	18-holes—WD $19/ WE $24
Washington Golf & Country Club	3017 N Glebe Rd	703-524-4600	31	Private	Members only
Army Navy Country Club	1700 Army Navy Dr	703-521-6800	40	Private	Members only
Belle Haven Country Club	6023 Fort Hunt Rd	703-329-1448	-	Private	Members only
Congressional Country Club	8500 River Rd	301-469-2032	-	Private	Members only
Greendale Golf Course	6700 Telegraph Rd	703-971-6170	-	Public	18-holes—WD $21/ WE $32
Hilltop Golf Club	7900 Telegraph Rd	703-719-6504	-	Public	nine-holes—WD $25/ WE $29
Leisure World Golf Club	3701 Rossmoor Blvd	301-598-1570	-	Private	Members only
Mount Vernon Country Club	5111 Old Mill Rd	703-780-3565	-	Private	Members only
Pinecrest Golf Course	6600 Little River Tpke	703-941-1061	-	Public	nine-holes—WD $15/ WE $18

Driving Ranges	*Address*	*Phone*	*Map*	*Fees*
East Potomac Driving Range	972 Ohio Dr SW	202-554-7660	6	$5/50 balls
Langston Driving Range	2600 Benning Rd NE	202-397-8638	12	$4.50/45 balls

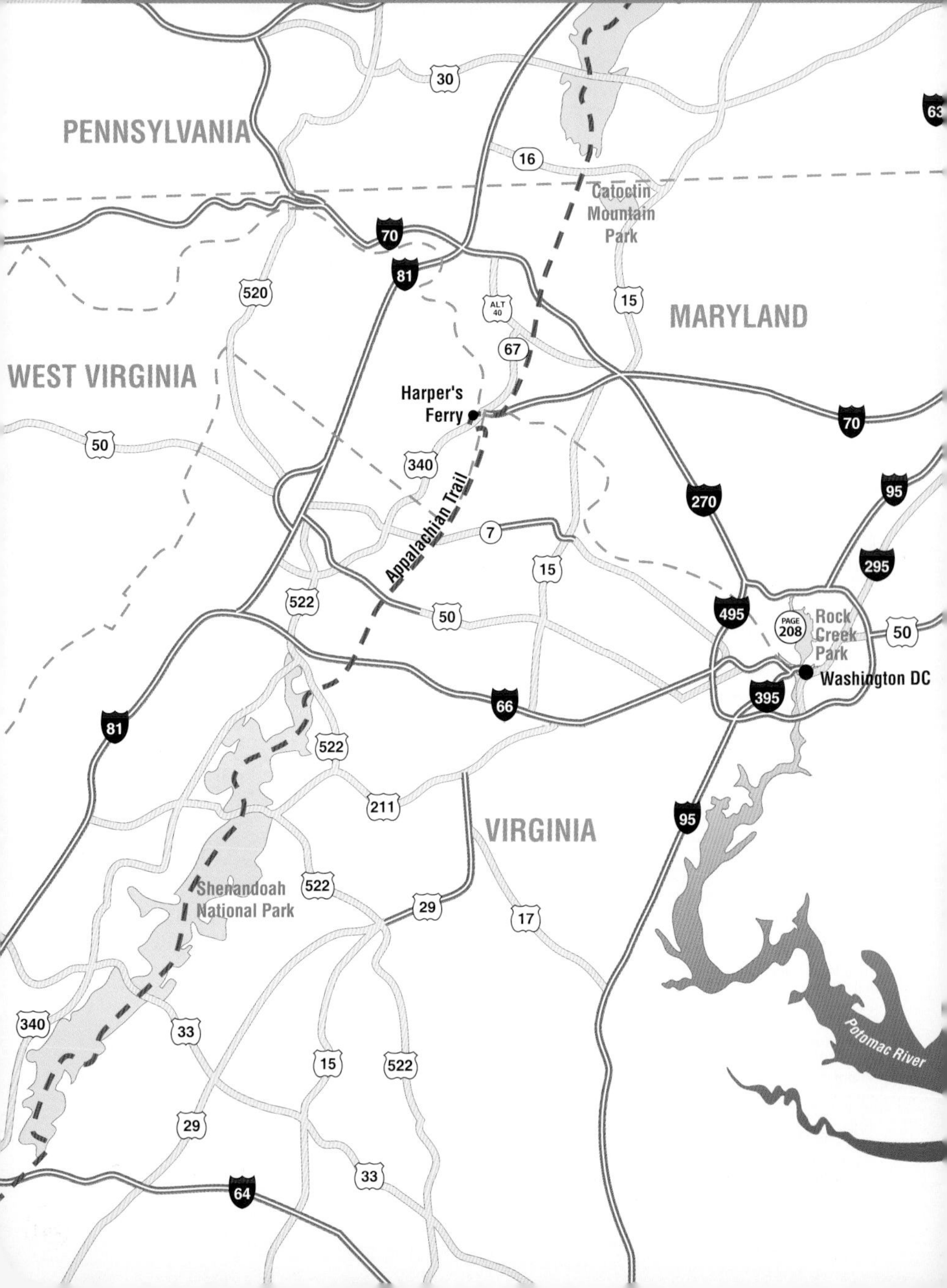

PENNSYLVANIA
WEST VIRGINIA
MARYLAND
VIRGINIA
Catoctin Mountain Park
Harper's Ferry
Appalachian Trail
Rock Creek Park
PAGE 208
Washington DC
Shenandoah National Park
Potomac River
30
16
70
81
520
15
ALT 40
67
50
340
270
95
7
295
15
522
50
495
50
66
395
81
522
211
95
522
29
17
340
33
15
522
29
33
64
63

Overview

One of the greatest things about living in DC, a city filled with hyper-Type-A-personalities, is how easy it is to leave. The ability to escape urban life for a weekend, or even just an afternoon, keeps many lawyers from buckling under the stress of day-to-day living. Rock Creek Park weaves its way through the city, and some of the best hiking routes on the east coast are just a short drive from town. The National Parks Service website is a valuable resource for planning overnight trips or day hikes (www.nps.gov), and we recommend the gem *60 Hikes Within 60 Miles: Washington, DC* by Paul Elliott (Menasha Ridge Press).

Shenandoah National Park

A short drive out of DC, this is one of the country's most popular national parks, mainly because of gorgeous Skyline Drive, which runs across the ridgeline of the Blue Ridge Mountains (the eastern range of the Appalachian Trail). But locals know to ditch the wheels, get out, and get dirty. There are more than 500 miles of trails in the park, including about 100 miles of the AT itself. In short, you can plan a week-long back-country getaway, and there'll still be more undiscovered country to come back for.

The Old Rag Trail, with its rock scramble and distinctive profile, is a favorite strenuous day hike. The rangers at the visitor centers will direct you to the toughest climbs, easier routes, the waterfall hikes, or the trails where you'll most likely see bears. The park is 70 miles west of DC. Take Route 66 W to Exit 13 and follow signs to Front Royal. www.nps.gov/shen; 540-999-3500.

Appalachian Trail

Forget what you've heard about lugging a summer's worth of misery along this Georgia-to-Maine trail. You don't have to hike the whole thing. Luckily, a good portion of this nationally protected 2,174-mile footpath through the Appalachian Mountains is accessible from DC. Hook up with it for a few miles at points in Maryland and Virginia and acquire bragging rights with just a day's worth of blister-inducing pain. A good place to start is Harper's Ferry in Maryland, 65 miles from DC, where you can load up on breakfast and some history before you head out. When you return, hoist a well-deserved pint. www.nps.gov/appa; 301-535-6331.

Catoctin Mountains

While Catoctin Mountain recreation area was created in order to provide a place for federal employees to get a little bit of R&R, it has since been converted into Camp David, the famously inaccessible presidential retreat. Camp David is never open to the public, or to run-of-the-mill federal employees, but there's still the eastern hardwood forest where everyone is free to roam wild. From DC, the Catoctin Mountains are about a two hour drive north. Take the George Washington Memorial Parkway north to the Beltway to I-270 N. Drive 27 miles to Frederick, MD. Take Route 15 N to Route 77 W, to the Catoctin Mountain Park exit. Drive three miles west on 77, turn right onto Park Central Road, and the Visitor Center will be on the right. www.nps.gov/cato; 301-663-9388.

Sugarloaf Mountain

Sugarloaf's main appeal is that it's only an hour drive from DC. It's a modest mountain— about 1,300 feet— with nice views of the surrounding farmland, and entry into the park is free. You can choose a variety of easy and not-so-easy ways to get up the mountain, but no matter which way you choose you'll be surrounded by an impressive collection of rare red and white oak trees. To get there, drive North on Route I-270 to the Hyattstown exit, circle under I-270 and continue on Route 109 to Comus, then make a right on Comus Road to the Stronghold entrance. www.sugarloafmd.com; 301-869-7846.

Rock Creek Park

This is the place for a quick nature fix. The historic 1,754-acre park, which reaches from Georgetown to Maryland, is laced with several hiking trails, especially in its northern reaches. The major trails along the western ridge are marked by green blazes, and the footpaths along the east side are marked with blue blazes. A tan-blazed trail connects the two trail systems. None of the trails are strenuous, and all routes can be tailored to fit in a short hike during your lunch break. See page 208 for more details. www.nps.gov/rocr; 202-895-6070.

The following fees for public pools are based on county residency. Non-residents can count on paying a buck or two more.

Outdoor pools are open daily from June 23 and generally close in late August or early September.

Many of the public pools require you to register as a member at the beginning of the season and, since most fill their membership quotas quickly, it's wise to locate your nearest pool and join at the beginning of the season.

Pools	*Address*	*Phone*	*Map*	*Type—Fees*
Washington				
William Rumsey Aquatic Center	635 N Carolina Ave SE	202-724-4495	3	Indoor—$4 per day, $130 season pass
Rosedale Pool	17th & Gales Sts NE	202-727-1502	4	Outdoor—$4 per day, $130 season pass (closed Tuesdays)
Barry Farm Pool	1223 Sumner Rd SE	202-645-5040	5	Outdoor—$4 per day, $130 season pass (closed Tuesdays)
East Potomac Pool	972 Ohio Dr SW	202-727-6523	6	Outdoor—$4 per day, $130 season pass (closed Wednesdays)
Randall Pool	S Capitol & I Sts SW	202-727-1420	6	Outdoor—$4 per day, $130 season pass (closed Mondays)
Fairmont	24th & M Sts NW	202-457-5070	9	Indoor—$15 per day
YMCA National Capital	1711 Rhode Island Ave NW	202-862-9622	9	Indoor—$20 per day, $70 per month membership
YMCA	1325 W Street NW	202-462-1054	10	Indoor—members only ($70 per month membership)
Dunbar Pool	1301 New Jersey Ave NW	202-673-4316	11	Indoor—$4 per day, $130 season pass
Harry Thomas Sr. Pool	1801 Lincoln Rd NE	202-576-6349	11	Outdoor—$4 per day, $130 season pass
Fort Lincoln Outdoor Pool	3201 Ft. Lincoln Dr NE	202-576-6389	13	Outdoor—$4 per day, $130 season pass
Langdon Park Pool	Mills Ave & Hamlin St NE	202-576-8655	13	Outdoor—$4 per day, $130 season pass
Banneker Pool	2500 Georgia Ave NW	202-673-2121	15	Outdoor—free (closed Thursdays)
Marie Reed Center Pool	2200 Champlain St NW	202-673-7771	16	Indoor—$4 per day, $130 season pass
Georgetown Pool	3400 Volta Pl NW	202-282-2366	18	Outdoor—$4 per day, $130 season pass (closed Mondays)
Tenley Sport & Health Club	4000 Wisconsin Ave NW	202-362-8000	19	Indoor— $20 per day, $100 per month membership
Wilson Pool	Ford Dr & Albemarle St NW	202-282-2216	19	Indoor—$4 per day, $130 season pass (temporarily closed)
Upshur Outdoor Pool	14th St & Arkansas Ave NW	202-576-8661	21	Outdoor—$4 per day, $130 season pass (closed Mondays)
Takoma Outdoor Pool	4th St & Van Buren St NW	202-576-8660	27	Outdoor—$4 per day, $130 season pass
Anacostia Outdoor Pool	1800 Anacostia Dr SE	202-724-1441	-	Outdoor—$3 per day, $130 season pass (closed Mondays)
Benning Park Outdoor Pool	5300 Fitch St SE	202-645-5044	-	Outdoor—$4 per day, $130 season pass
Douglass Outdoor Pool	1900 Stanton Ter SE	202-645-5045	-	Outdoor—$4 per day, $130 season pass (closed Wednesdays)
Ferebee Hope	800 Yuma St SE	202-645-3916	-	Indoor—$4 per day, $130 season pass
Fort Dupont Outdoor Pool	Ridge Rd & Burns St SE	202-645-5046	-	Outdoor—$4 per day, $130 season pass (closed Tuesdays)
Fort Stanton Outdoor Pool	1800 Erie St SE	202-645-5047	-	Outdoor—$4 per day, $130 season pass (closed Thursdays)
Francis Outdoor Pool	2500 N St NW	202-727-3285	-	Outdoor—$3 per day, $100 season pass (closed Tuesdays)
Kelly Miller Outdoor Pool	4900 Brooks St NE	202-724-5056	-	Outdoor—$4 per day, $130 season pass (closed Mondays)
Kenilworth-Parkside Pool	4300 Anacostia Ave NE	202-727-0635	-	Outdoor—$4 per day, $130 season pass (closed Wednesdays)
Oxon Run Outdoor Pool	4th St & Mississippi Ave SE	202-645-5042	-	Outdoor—$4 per day, $130 season pass (closed Mondays)
Arlington				
Upton Hill Regional Park	6060 Wilson Blvd	703-534-3437	33	Outdoor—$5.25 per day, $62 season pass
Yorktown Swimming Pool	5201 28th St N	703-536-9739	33	Indoor—$4 per day, $230 per year
Washington-Lee Swimming Pool	1300 N Quincy St	703-228-6262	34	Indoor—$4 per day, $230 per year

Pools—*continued*

Pools	Address	Phone	Map	Type—Fees
YMCA Arlington	3422 N 13th St	703-525-5420	35	Outdoor— Members only ($48 per month membership)
Wakefield Swimming Pool	4901 S Chesterfield Rd	703-578-3063	38	Indoor—$4 per day, $230 per year
YMCA	3440 S 22nd St	703-892-2044	39	Outdoor— Members only ($75 per month membership)
Alexandria				
Chinquapin Park Rec Center	3210 King St	703-519-2160	42	Indoor—$5 per day, $46 per month
Warwick Pool	3301 Landover St	703-838-4672	43	Outdoor—$2 per day
Alexandria YMCA	420 Monroe Ave	703-838-8085	43	Indoor—$15 per day, $69 per month membership, $100 joiner fee
Old Town Pool	1609 Cameron St	703-838-4671	44	Outdoor—$2 per day
George Washington Rec Center	8426 Old Mount Vernon Rd	703-780-8894	-	Indoor—$6.20 per day, $548.50 for year pass
Lee District Rec Center	6601 Telegraph Rd	703-768-9796	-	Indoor—$6.20 per day, $548.50 for year pass
Mount Vernon Rec Center	2017 Belle View Blvd	703-768-3224	-	Indoor—$6.20 per day, $548.50 for year pass
Bethesda				
YMCA	9401 Old Georgetown Rd	301-530-3725	22	Indoor—$62 per month membership,
Sport & Health Club	4400 Montgomery Ave	301-656-9570	29	Indoor—$25 per day ($15 per day with a member)
Bethesda Outdoor Pool	Little Falls Dr	301-652-1598	30	Outdoor—$5.50 per day, $160 for year pass
Mohican Swimming Pool	7117 MacArthur Blvd	301-229-4953	-	Members only
Old Georgetown Swim Pool	9600 Fernwood Rd	301-469-9772	-	Outdoor—$375 for summer pass, $320 per year with $540 joiner fee
Montgomery Aquatic Center	5900 Executive Blvd	301-468-4211	-	Indoor—$5.50 per day, $230 for year pass
Silver Spring				
Martin Luther King Jr	1201 Jackson Rd	301-989-1206	14	Indoor/Outdoor—$5.50 per day, $250 for year pass
Long Branch Swimming Pool	8700 Piney Branch Rd	301-431-5700	-	Outdoor—$5.50 per day, $160 for year pass
YMCA	9800 Hastings Dr	301-585-2120	25	Indoor/Outdoor—$62 per month
Wheaton-Glenmont Outdoor Pool	12621 Dalewood Dr	301-929-5460	-	Outdoor—$5.50 per day, $160 for year pass
Takoma Park				
Piney Branch Pool	7510 Maple Ave	301-270-6093	26	Indoor—$5 per day

Kids' Pools*

Kids' Pools*	Address	Phone	Map
Lincoln Capper Pool	500 L St SE	202-727-1080	5
J O Wilson Pool	700 K St NE	202-727-1505	11
Trinidad Pool	Childress St	202-727-1503	12
Parkview Pool	Warder St & Princeton Pl NW	202-576-8658	15
Deanwood Pool	4900 Minesotta Ave NE	202-727-9583	-
Parkside Pool	711 Anacostia Ave NE	202-727-1100	-
Riggs-La Salle Pool	Riggs Rd & Nicholson St NE	202-576-8659	-
Woodson Junior Pool	4200 Foote St NE	202-727-1506	-

* Children six and under swim free, kids ages 6-17 $3 per day, $46 season pass. Kids' pools open June 23 and close August 8. Hours: Mon-Fri, 1 pm-5 pm.

Tennis

National Park Service • 202-208-6843 • www.nps.gov
Washington, DC Department of Parks and Recreation • 202-673-7647 • dpr.dc.gov

Public Courts at Community Recreation Centers

DC residents and visitors can play tennis at any of the public courts scattered throughout the city. All courts are available on a first-come, first-served basis. An honor code trusts that players won't hog the courts for over an hour of play-time (although you can call the Department of Parks and Recreation to obtain a permit for extended use). For more information about lessons and tournaments, call the Sports Office of the Department of Parks and Recreation (202-698-2250).

Courts	Address	Phone	Map
South Grounds	15th St & Constitution Ave		1
Langston	26th St & Benning Rd NE	202-727-5430	4
Rosedale	17th & Gale Sts NE	202-724-5405	4
Barry Farm	1230 Sumner Rd SE	202-645-3896	5
King-Greenleaf	201 N St SW	202-727-5454	6
Randall	1st St & I St SW	202-727-5505	6
Jefferson	8th & H Sts SW		6
Rose Park	26th & O Sts NW	202-282-2208	8
Montrose Park	30th & R Sts NW		8
Georgetown	33 rd St & Volta Pl		8
Reed	18th & California Sts		9
Francis	24th & N Sts NW		9
Shaw	10th St & Rhode Island Ave NW	202-673-7255	10
Brentwood Park	6th St & Brentwood Pkwy NE		11
Harry Thomas Sr	Lincoln Rd & T St NE		11
Edgewood	3rd & Evart Sts NE	202-576-6410	11
Dunbar	1st & O Sts		11
Arboretum	24th St & Rand Pl NE	202-727-5547	12
Langdon Park	20th & Franklin Sts NE		13
Fort Lincoln	Ft Lincoln Dr NE	202-576-6818	13
Taft	19th & Otis Sts NE	202-576-7634	13
Backus	South Dakota Ave & Hamilton St NE		14
Banneker	9th & Euclid Sts NW	202-673-6861	15
Raymond	10th St & Spring Rd NW	202-576-6856	15
Hardy	45th & Q Sts NW	202-282-2190	18
Friendship	4500 Van Ness St NW	202-282-2198	19
Hearst	37th & Tilden Sts NW	202-282-2207	19
Fort Reno	41st & Chesapeake Sts NW		19
Forest Hills	32nd & Brandywine Sts NW		20
Rabaut	2nd & Peabody Sts NW		27
Fort Stevens	1327 Van Buren St NW	202-541-3754	27
Takoma	3rd & Van Buren Sts NW	202-576-6854	27
Chevy Chase	4101 Livingston St NW	202-282-2200	28
Lafayette	33rd & Quesada Sts NW	202-282-2206	28
Palisades	5200 Sherrier Pl NW	202-282-2186	32
Bald Eagle	1000 Joliet St SW	202-645-3960	-
Anacostia	11th St & Anacostia Ave SE		-
Benning Park	53rd St & Southern Ave SE	202-645-3953	-
Benning Stoddert	Burns & C Sts SE	202-645-3956	-
Congress Heights	Alabama Ave & Randle St SE	202-645-3981	-
Douglass Community Center	19th St & Stanton Terr SE	202-698-2342	-
Evans	5600 E Capitol St SE	202-727-5548	-
Fort Stanton	18th & Eerie Sts SE		-
Fort Davis	1400 41st St SE	202-645-3975	-
Friendship—Oxon Run	Livingston Rd & S Capitol St SE		-
Garfield Park	3rd & G Sts SE		-
Hine	7th St & Pensylvania Ave SE		-
Hillcrest	32nd & Denver Sts SE	202-645-3988	-
Randle Highlands	31st St & Pennsylvania Ave SE		-
SE Tennis & Learning Center	701 Mississippi Ave SE		-

Private Courts	Address	Phone	Map
East Potomac Tennis Center	1090 Ohio Dr SW	202-554-5962	6
Washington Hilton Sport & Health Club	1919 Connecticut Ave NW	202-483-4100	9
Rock Creek Tennis Center	16th & Kennedy Sts NW	202-722-5949	21
Bethesda Sport & Health Club	4400 Montgomery Ave	301-656-9570	29
Arlington Y Tennis & Squash Club	3400 N 13th St	703-749-8057	35

Bowling

Clubs aren't the only places where you can toss a few back and shake your groove thang. Bowling alleys in and around the Washington metro area usually offer the four wonderful B's: Bowling, Beer, Blacklights, and Beyoncé. After dark, the lights go down and the beats go up, with special "Cosmic Bowling" or "Xtreme Bowling" nights. When the DJ arrives, you can bet on the bowling fees getting boosted up with the volume of the music.

Sunday nights are the best nights to bowl if you're looking to save money, as many alleys offer unlimited bowling after 9 pm for under $15. Show some Maryland pride and play duckpin bowling (the sport actually originated in Baltimore) at White Oak Bowling Lanes and AMF College Park, home to the Men's Duckpin Pro Bowlers' Association Master Tournament.

Bowling Alley	Address	Phone	Fees	Map
Seminary Lanes	4620 Kenmore Ave, Alexandria, VA	703-823-6200	$2.50-$5 per game, $4 for shoes	41
US Bowling	100 S Pickett St, Alexandria, VA	703-370-5910	$3-4.25 per game, $3.50 for shoes	41
Alexandria Bowling Center	6228A N Kings Hwy, Alexandria, VA	703-765-3633	$3.50-5.00 per game, $4.46 for shoes	-
AMF College Park	9021 Baltimore Ave, College Park, MD	301-474-8282	$2.75-4.25 per game, $4.25 for shoes	-
Bowl America	6450 Ebsall Rd, Alexandria, VA	703-354-3300	$2-5 per game, $3.40 for shoes	-
Bowl America - Chantilly	4525 Stonecroft Blvd, Chantilly, VA	703-830-2695	$2-5 per game, $3.40 for shoes	-
Bowl America - Fairfax	9699 Lee Hwy, Fairfax, VA	703-273-7700	$2-5.25 per game, $3.40 for shoes	-
Strike Bethesda	5353 Westbard Ave, Bethesda, MD	301-652-0955	$5.45-6.25 per game, $4 for shoes	-
White Oak Lanes	11207 New Hampshire Ave, Silver Spring, MD	301-593-3000	$2.75-3.50 per game, $2.75 for shoes	-

Airline	*Phone*	*IAD*	*DCA*	*BWI*
Aer Lingus	800-474-7424			■
Aeroflot	888-686-4949	■		
Air Canada	888-247-2262	■	■	■
Air France	800-237-2747	■		
Air Jamaica	800-523-5585			■
AirTran	800-247-8726	■	■	■
Alaska Airlines	800-252-7522	■	■	
Alitalia	800-223-5730	■		
All Nippon	800-235-9262	■		
American Airlines	800-433-7300	■	■	■
American Trans Air	800-435-9282		■	
America West	800-235-9292	■	■	■
Austrian Airlines	800-843-0002	■		
BMI	800-788-0555	■		
British Airways	800-247-9297	■		■
BWIA	800-538-2942	■		
Continental	800-523-3273	■	■	■
Delta	800-221-1212	■	■	■
Delta Shuttle	800-933-5935		■	
Ethiopian Airlines	800-445-2733	■		
Frontier	800-432-1359	■	■	■
Ghana Airways	800-404-4262			
GRUPO TACA	800-400-8222	■		
Hooters Air	888-359-4668			■
Icelandair	800-223-5500			■
Independence Air	800-359-3594	■		
Jet Blue	800-538-2583	■		
KLM Royal Dutch	800-225-2525	■		
Korean Air	800-438-5000	■		
Lufthansa	800-399-5838	■		
Midwest	800-452-2022		■	■
Northwest Airlines	800-225-2525	■	■	■
SAS	800-221-2350	■		
Saudi Arabian Airlines	800-472-8342	■		
Southwest Airlines	800-435-9792			■
Spirit	800-772-7117		■	
TACA	800-535-8780	■		
Ted Airlines	800-225-5833	■		
United Airlines	800-864-8331	■	■	■
United Express	800-864-8331	■		
US Airways	800-428-4322	■	■	■
USA3000	877-872-3000			■
Virgin	800-862-8621	■		

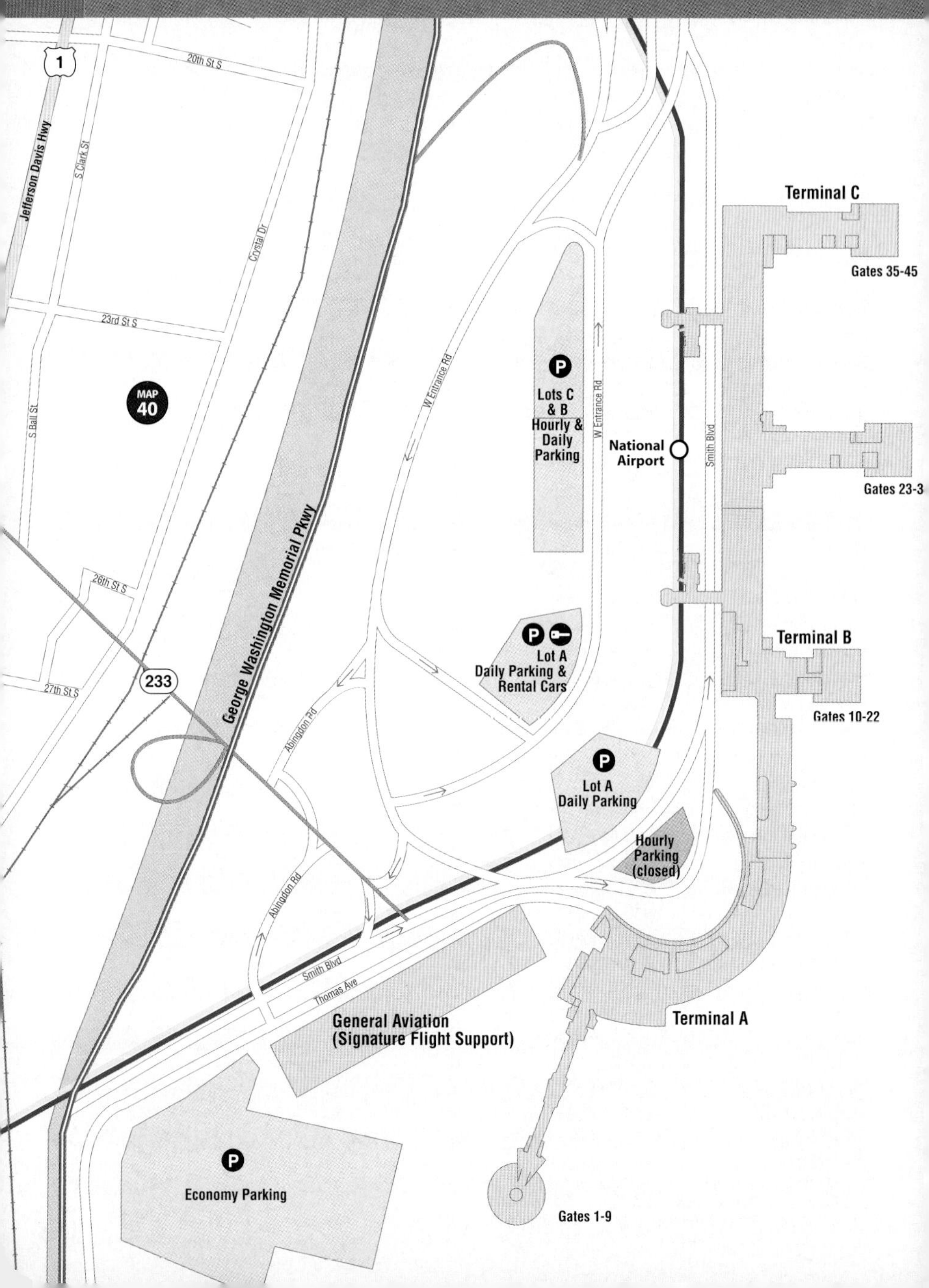
1
20th St S
Jefferson Davis Hwy
S Clark St
Crystal Dr
23rd St S
MAP 40
S Ball St
26th St S
27th St S
233
George Washington Memorial Pkwy
W Entrance Rd
Lots C & B Hourly & Daily Parking
W Entrance Rd
National Airport
Smith Blvd
Terminal C
Gates 35-45
Gates 23-3
Lot A Daily Parking & Rental Cars
Terminal B
Gates 10-22
Abingdon Rd
Lot A Daily Parking
Hourly Parking (closed)
Abingdon Rd
Smith Blvd
Thomas Ave
General Aviation (Signature Flight Support)
Terminal A
Economy Parking
Gates 1-9

General Information

Phone:	703-417-8000
Lost & Found:	703-417-0673
Parking:	703-417-4311
Website:	www.mwaa.com/national/index.htm

Overview

Ronald Reagan Washington National Airport is a small, easy-to-navigate airport that's located practically downtown; perfect for business travelers and politicians alike. But, for those of us not on expense accounts or the public dole, prices can be prohibitive. If you want a discounted direct flight to Madagascar or enjoy flying on the cattle cars that charge $15 for a roundtrip to Aruba, you'll have to fly from Dulles or BWI. National is too small to host many planes or airlines, making it a short-haul airport with direct connections to cities typically no more than 1250 miles away.

How to Get There—Driving

From DC, take I-395 S to Exit 10 ("Reagan National Airport/ Mount Vernon"). Get on the GW Parkway S and take the Reagan Airport exit. Remember to watch out for Officer Friendly and his trusty radar gun as you enter the airport property.

Parking

Parking at Reagan is not cheap. Garages A, B, C, and Lot A-2 charge $2 per half-hour for the first two hours, and $4 per hour thereafter. Garage A and Lot A-2 cost $15 per day. Garages B and C cost $28 per day. If you're heading out for a few days, we suggest you park in the economy lot for only $9 per day. Shuttle buses run between the economy lot and all terminals. Parking in any lot for less than 20 minutes is free. Though when have you ever been in-and-out of an airport in less than an hour? That's what we thought.

How to Get There—Mass Transit

The Blue and Yellow Lines have a Metrorail stop adjacent to Terminals B and C. If you're headed to Terminal A, a free shuttle bus will run you there or you can lug your bags on a ten-minute walk. Metro buses are also available from the base of the Metrorail station for areas not served by the rail.

How to Get There—Ground Transportation

SuperShuttle offers door-to-door service to DCA. They also have a shuttle that goes regularly between DCA and Union Station. Call the reservation line on 800-BLUEVAN or go to www.supershuttle.com to book online.

A cab ride to downtown DC will set you back less than $15. DC, Virginia, and Maryland taxis are available at the exits of each terminal. Red Top Cab - Arlington: 703-522-3333; Yellow Cab - DC: 202-TAXI-CAB; Yellow Cab - Arlington: 703-534-1111.

Stretch limousine and executive-class sedans start at approximately $35 for downtown Washington. Airport Access: 202-498-8708; Airport Connection: 202-393-2110; Roadmaster: 800-283-5634; Silver Car: 410-992-7775.

Rental Cars—On-Airport (Garage A)

Avis • 800-331-1212
Budget • 800-527-0700
Hertz • 800-654-3131
National • 800-328-4567
Dollar • 800-800-4000

Off-Airport

Enterprise • 800-736-8222
Alamo • 800-462-5266
Thrifty • 800-367-2277

Hotels—Arlington

Crowne Plaza •1480 Crystal Dr • 703-416-1600
Crystal City Marriott • 1999 Jefferson Davis Hwy • 703-413-5500
Crystal City Courtyard by Marriott • 2899 Jefferson Davis Hwy • 703-549-3434
Crystal Gateway Marriott • 1700 Jefferson Davis Hwy • 703-920-3230
Radisson Inn • 2200 Jefferson Davis Hwy • 703-920-8600
Doubletree Crystal City • 300 Army Navy Dr • 703-416-4100
Econo Lodge • 6800 Lee Hwy • 703-538-5300
Embassy Suites • 1300 Jefferson Davis Hwy • 703-979-9799
Hilton • 2399 Jefferson Davis Hwy • 703-418-6800
Holiday Inn • 2650 Jefferson Davis Hwy • 703-684-7200
Hyatt Regency • 2799 Jefferson Davis Hwy • 703-418-1234
Ritz Carlton Pentagon City • 1250 S Hayes St • 703-415-5000
Residence Inn • 550 Army Navy Dr • 703-413-6630
Sheraton • 1800 Jefferson Davis Hwy • 703-486-1111

Hotels—Washington

Hamilton Crowne Plaza • 1001 14th NW • 202-682-0111
Grand Hyatt • 1000 H St NW • 202-582-1234
Hilton • 1919 Connecticut Ave NW • 202-483-3000
Hilton Embassy Row • 2015 Massachusetts Ave NW • 202-265-1600
Holiday Inn • 415 New Jersey Ave NW • 202-638-1616
Homewood Suites Hilton • 1475 Massachusetts Ave NW • 202-265-8000
Hyatt Regency • 400 New Jersey Ave NW • 202-737-1234
Marriott Wardman Park • 2660 Woodley Rd NW • 202-328-2000
Red Roof Inn • 500 H St NW • 202-289-5959
Renaissance Mayflower Hotel • 1127 Connecticut Ave NW • 202-347-3000
Renaissance Washington DC • 999 9th St NW • 202-898-9000

Airline	*Terminal*	*Airline*	*Terminal*
Air Canada	B	Delta/Express	B
Air Tran	A	Frontier	B
Alaska	A	Midwest	A
America West	B	Northwest	A
American/Eagle	B	Spirit	A
ATA	A	United Airlines	B
Continental	B	US Airways/Express	C

Transit • Dulles International Airport

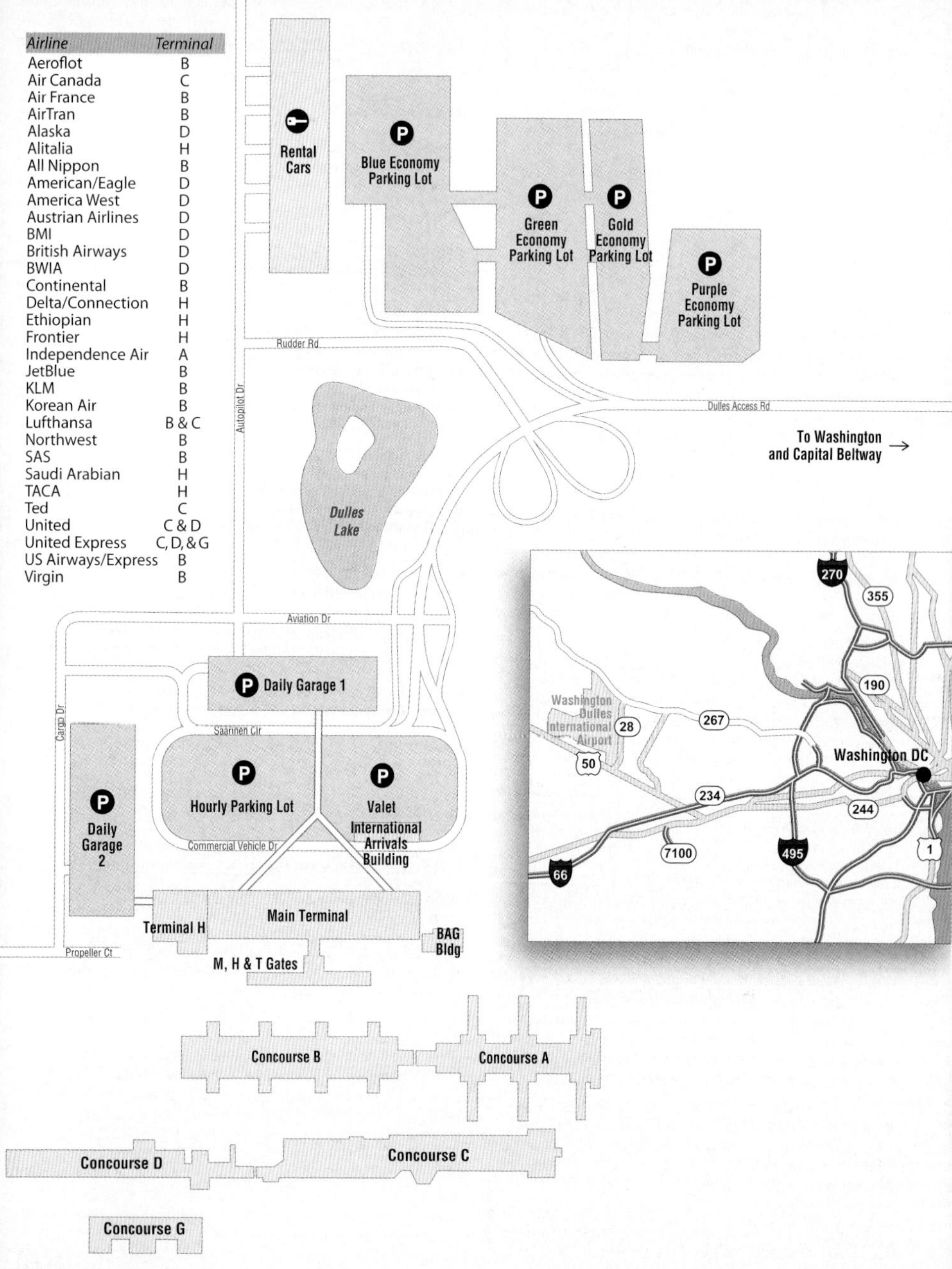

Airline	Terminal
Aeroflot	B
Air Canada	C
Air France	B
AirTran	B
Alaska	D
Alitalia	H
All Nippon	B
American/Eagle	D
America West	D
Austrian Airlines	D
BMI	D
British Airways	D
BWIA	D
Continental	B
Delta/Connection	H
Ethiopian	H
Frontier	H
Independence Air	A
JetBlue	B
KLM	B
Korean Air	B
Lufthansa	B & C
Northwest	B
SAS	B
Saudi Arabian	H
TACA	H
Ted	C
United	C & D
United Express	C, D, & G
US Airways/Express	B
Virgin	B

General Information

Address: 45020 Aviation Dr
Sterling, VA 20166 (not that you're going to send them anything, really)
Information: 703-572-2700
Parking: 703-572-4500
Lost & Found: 703-572-2954
Website: www.metwashairports.com/Dulles

Overview

The Mod Squad of airports, Dulles was born in 1958 when Finnish architect Eero Saarinen had a hankering to channel his training as a sculptor and create something groovy. His design for the terminal building and the control tower was so hip it received a First Honor Award from the American Institute of Architects in 1966. A swoosh roof over a squat building, Dulles still stands out as a stunning exhibit of modernist architecture. The oh-so-suave "mobile lounges" that transport passengers between the terminal building and the aircraft are still in use. But when the outlying terminals were constructed in 1998, they were done so without even a nod to the style of the original architecture. An underground shuttle is under construction and should be operational in a couple of years. Currently you may walk (ha!) from the main terminal to the "B" Concourse.

Note: "Washington" was officially added to the "Dulles International Airport" moniker after too many people inadvertently booked flights to Dallas, not Dulles, and vice-versa. No joke.

How to Get There—Driving

To get to Washington Dulles Airport from downtown DC, drive west on I-66 to Exit 67. Follow signs to the airport. Be sure to use the Dulles Access Road, which avoids the tolls and traffic found on the parallel Dulles Toll Road (Rt. 267). But don't get cocky and try to use the Access Road to avoid tolls at other times—once you're on these access lanes, there's no exit until you reach the airport.

Parking

Hourly (short-term) parking is located in front of the terminal and costs $4 per hour and $36 per day. Daily parking is available in Daily Garages 1 and 2 for $5 per hour and $15 per day. There are shuttle buses and walkways (albeit lengthy ones from Garage 1) directly to the main terminal. Economy parking (long-term) is available in the four economy parking lots (Blue, Green, Gold, and Purple) located along Rudder Road. Long-term parking costs $3 per hour and $9 per day. If you're short on time or energy and long on cash, valet parking is located in front of the terminal and costs $30 for the first 24 hours and $17 per day thereafter. Parking in any lot for less than 20 minutes is free. Take your parking ticket with you as you can pay for your parking in the main terminal on your way out.

How to Get There—Mass Transit

The Metrorail doesn't go all the way to Dulles Airport. You can take the Orange Line to West Falls Church and transfer to the Washington Flyer Coach Service, which leaves every 30 minutes from the station. The coach fare costs $8 one-way ($14 round-trip) and the fare for the Metrorail leg will depend on exactly where you're coming from or headed to. A trip from West Falls Church to the Convention Center in downtown DC costs $1.70. Check www.washfly.com for Flyer schedules. There are no "regular" taxis from Dulles to any destination—the Flyer is it and you should avoid all other pitchmen. You can also take Metrobus 5A which runs from L'Enfant Plaza to Dulles, stopping at Rosslyn Metro Station. The express bus costs $3 each way.

How to Get There—Ground Transportation

Super Shuttle is a door-to-door shared van to Washington Dulles Airport. It goes to and from Union Station and anywhere else, if you call and book 24 hours in advance. At the airport, you'll find them outside the Main Terminal. Call 800-258-3826 or go to www.supershuttle.com to make reservations. Washington Flyer Taxicabs serve Dulles International Airport exclusively with 24-hour service to and from the airport. Taxis accept American Express, Diners Club, MasterCard, Discover Card, and Visa, and charge metered rates to any destination in metropolitan Washington. If you're heading to downtown DC, it will cost you between $44 and $50. For more information, or to book a car, call 703-661-6655.

Rental Cars

Alamo• 800-832-7933
Avis • 800-331-1212
Budget • 800-527-0700
Dollar • 800-800-4000
Enterprise • 800-736-8222
Hertz• 800-654-3131
National • 800-227-7368
Thrifty • 800-367-2277
Alamoot (off-airport) • 800-630-6967

Hotels—Herndon, VA

Comfort Inn • 200 Elden St• 703-437-7555
Courtyard by Marriott • 533 Herndon Pkwy • 703-478-9400
Days Hotel • 2200 Centreville Rd • 703-471-6700
Embassy Suites • 13341 Woodland Park Dr • 703-464-0200
Hilton • 13869 Park Center Rd • 703-478-2900
Holiday Inn Express • 485 Elden St• 703-478-9777•
Hyatt Hotels & Resorts • 2300 Dulles Corner Blvd • 703-713-1234
Marriott Hotels • 13101 Worldgate Dr • 703-709-0400
Residence Inn • 315 Elden St• 703-435-0044
Staybrdige Suites •13700 Coppermine Rd • 703-713-6800

Hotels—Sterling, VA

Country Inn & Suites • 45620 Falke Plz • 703-435-2700
Courtyard by Marriot • 45500 Majestic Dr • 571-434-7240
Fairfield Inn • 23000 Indian Creek Dr • 703-435-5300
Hampton Inn • 45440 Holiday Park Dr • 703-471-8300
Holiday Inn • 1000 Sully Rd • 703-471-7411
Marriott TownePlace • 22744 Holiday Park Dr • 703-707-2017
Marriott • 45020 Aviation Dr • 703-471-9500
Quality Inn & Suites Dulles International • 45515 Dulles Plz • 703-471-5005

Baltimore-Washington International Airport

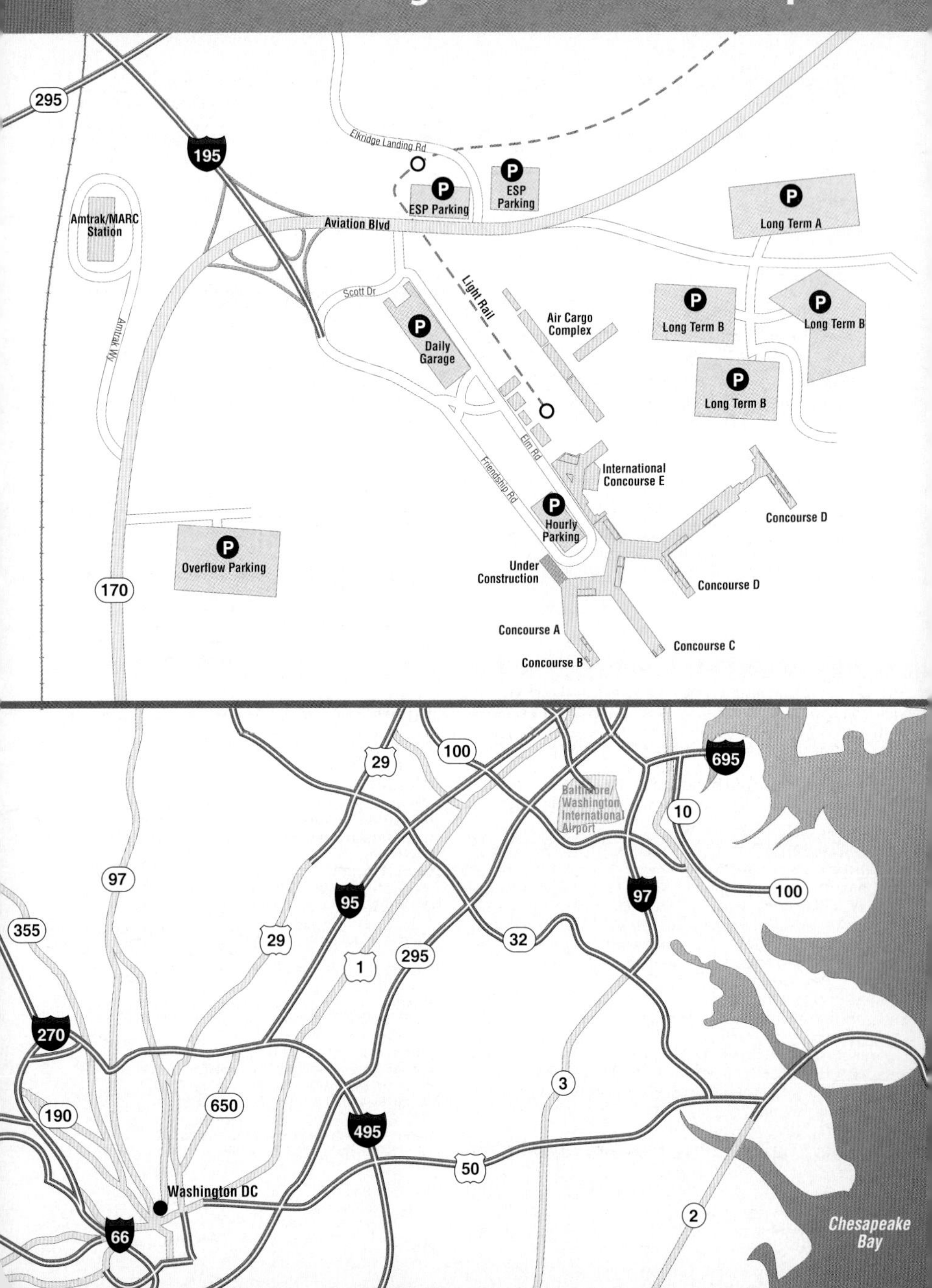

Baltimore-Washington International Airport

General Information

Information:	800-435-9294
Lost & Found:	410-859-7387
Parking:	800-468-6294
Police:	410-859-7040
Website:	www.bwiairport.com

Overview

When Friendship International Airport opened in 1950, it was widely touted as one of the most sophisticated and advanced airports in the nation. In 1993, Southwest Airlines moved in, bringing with them their cheap, and wildly popular, cattle cars of the sky. But this bargain-basement tenant has turned BWI into a boomtown—a spanking new expanded Terminal A opened last spring. Other major carriers have since joined the dirt-cheap-fares bandwagon, resulting in cheaper flights to and from BWI than you'll find flying into and out of Dulles or Reagan. It's a helluva haul from the city (yet pretty close for Maryland suburbanites), but sometimes time really isn't money, and cheap fares trump convenience. Governor Bob Ehrlich recently signed a bill to rename the airport Baltimore-Washington Thurgood Marshall International Airport in honor of native Baltimorean and first African-American Supreme Court Justice Thurgood Marshall.

How to Get There—Driving

From DC, take New York Avenue (US 50) to the Baltimore/Washington Parkway (MD 295) N to I-195. I-195 ends at the entrance to BWI. From north and west DC, you can take the Capital Beltway (I-495) E to I-95 N (Exit 27) to I-195.

Parking

Hourly parking is located across from the terminal building. The first hour of parking is free, and each succeeding hour costs $4 per hour and $20 per day. Daily parking is available for $2 per hour and $10 per day. Express Service Parking (ESP) is located on Aviation Boulevard across from the Air Cargo Complex. ESP parking costs $3 per hour and $14 per day. If you're going to be gone a while, you might want to try the long-term parking lots, which cost $1 per hour and $8 per day; every seventh day is free.

How to Get There—Mass Transit

Any which way you go, expect to devote a few hours to mimicking a Richard Scarry character. MARC's Penn Line and Amtrak trains service the BWI Rail Station from Union Station in DC (Massachusetts Ave & First St, NE) and cost between $5 and $30. A free shuttle bus takes passengers from the train station to the airport. Alternatively, you can take the Metro Green Line to the Greenbelt station and catch the Express Metro Bus/B30 to BWI. The Express bus runs every 40 minutes and costs $2.50. MARC trains do not operate on the weekends. The Light Rail train now provides service between Baltimore and BWI.

How to Get There—Ground Transportation

The Airport Shuttle offers door-to-door service within the state of Maryland. Call 800-776-0323 for reservations. For door-to-door service to BWI, Super Shuttle (800-258-3826) services all of the DC airports. The BWI taxi stand is located just outside of baggage claim on the lower level. The ride to DC usually costs about $55. 410-859-1100; www.BWIairporttaxi.com.

Car Rental

Avis • 410-859-1680
Alamo • 410-859-8092
Budget • 410-859-0850
Dollar • 800-800-4000
Enterprise • 800-325-8007
Hertz • 410-850-7400
National • 410-859-8860
Thrifty • 410-859-7139

Hotels

Four Points by Sheraton • 7032 Elm Rd • 410-859-3300
Amerisuites • 940 International Dr • 410-859-33-66
Best Western • 6755 Dorsey Rd • 410-796-3300
Comfort Inn • 6921 Baltimore-Anapolis Blvd • 410-789-9100
Comfort Suites • 815 Elkridge Landing Rd • 410-691-1000
Courtyard by Marriott • 1671 West Nursery Rd • 410-859-8855
Econo Lodge • 5895 Bonnieview Ln • 410-796-1020
Hampton Inn • 829 Elkridge Landing Rd • 410-850-0600
Hilton Garden Inn • 1516 Aero Dr • 410-691-0500
Holiday Inn • 890 Elkridge Landing Rd • 410-859-8400
Homewood Suites • 1181 Winterson Rd • 410-684-6100
Ramada • 7253 Parkway Dr • 410-712-4300
Red Roof Inn • 827 Elkridge Landing Rd • 410-850-7600
Residence Inn/Marriott • 1160 Winterson Rd • 410-691-0255
Sleep Inn and Suites • 6055 Belle Grove Rd • 410-789-7223
Spinghill Suites by Marriot • 899 Elkridge Landing Rd • 410-694-0555
Wingate Inn • 1510 Aero Dr • 410-859-000

Airline	*Terminal*	*Airline*	*Terminal*
Aer Lingus	E	Ghana Airways	E
Air Canada	E	Hooters Air	C
Air Jamaica	E	Icelandair	E
AirTran	D	Midwest	D
American	C	Northwest	D
America West	D	Pan Am	E
British Airways	E	Southwest	B
Continental	D	United	D
Delta	C	US Airways	D
Frontier	D	USA3000	E

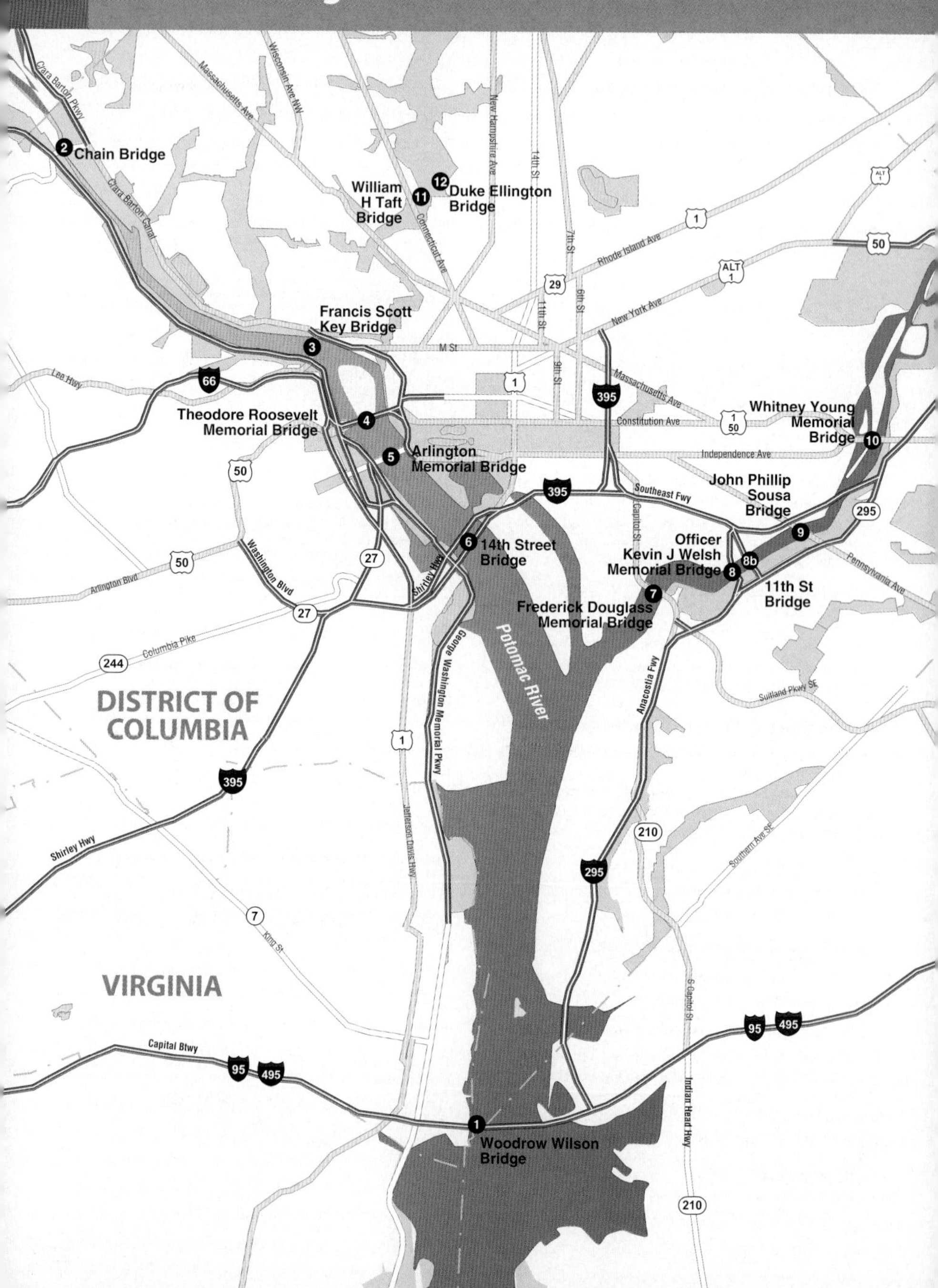

Chain Bridge
William H Taft Bridge
Duke Ellington Bridge
Francis Scott Key Bridge
Theodore Roosevelt Memorial Bridge
Arlington Memorial Bridge
14th Street Bridge
Frederick Douglass Memorial Bridge
Officer Kevin J Welsh Memorial Bridge
John Phillip Sousa Bridge
11th St Bridge
Whitney Young Memorial Bridge
Woodrow Wilson Bridge
Potomac River
DISTRICT OF COLUMBIA
VIRGINIA
Clara Barton Pkwy
Clara Barton Canal
Massachusetts Ave
Wisconsin Ave NW
New Hampshire Ave
14th St
Connecticut Ave
7th St
6th St
11th St
9th St
Rhode Island Ave
New York Ave
M St
Lee Hwy
Constitution Ave
Independence Ave
Southeast Fwy
Capitol St
Washington Blvd
Arlington Blvd
Shirley Hwy
Columbia Pike
George Washington Memorial Pkwy
Anacostia Fwy
Suitland Pkwy SE
Pennsylvania Ave
Jefferson Davis Hwy
Southern Ave SE
King St
Capital Btwy
S Capitol St
Indian Head Hwy

Chances are if you live in DC and you own a car, you spend a significant amount of your time sitting in traffic on one of DC's bridges. Despite constant congestion and deteriorating roadways, DC area bridges do have one saving grace—no tolls! The city is also home to some of the most beautiful and architecturally significant spans in the country. **The Francis Scott Key Bridge** crossing the Potomac from Rosslyn, VA into Georgetown is the best known. The commonly-called **Calvert Street Bridge** in Adams-Morgan (officially named for native son **Duke Ellington**) and the **Connecticut Avenue Bridge** over Rock Creek Park (which must be seen from the parkway below to be fully appreciated) are other great examples. The **Connecticut Avenue Bridge**, (officially known as the **William H. Taft Bridge**) is also known as the "Million Dollar Bridge." When it was built it was the most expensive concrete bridge ever constructed in the US. And what bridge would be complete without those ornamental lions on both ends?

One of DC's largest and most notorious is the **Woodrow Wilson Bridge**, which is unique in two ways: 1) It's one of only 13 drawbridges along the US interstate highway system; 2) It's the location of one of the worst bottlenecks in the country. The Woodrow Wilson Bridge was built in 1961 with only six lanes, then the eastern portion of the Beltway was widened to 8 lanes in the '70s, making this spot a perpetual hassle for DC drivers. In an attempt to alleviate this problem, construction is well underway on a new 6,075-foot-long **Potomac River Bridge**. When this bridge opens, transit officials promise ten lanes and a pedestrian/bicycle facility. Unfortunately, the bridge isn't expected to be completed until 2007 or 2008. So until then, when it comes to commuting across bridges, be sure to keep the car stocked with ample music and patience.

The Officer Kevin J. Welsh Memorial Bridge, which empties onto 11th Street in Southeast, was named after the police officer who drowned attempting to save a woman who jumped into the Anacostia River in an apparent suicide attempt. Note: Most people, including traffic reporters, refer to the Welsh bridge simply as the 11th Street Bridge. John Wilkes Booth escaped from Washington via a predecessor to the 11th Street Bridge after he assassinated Abraham Lincoln in 1865.

		Lanes	Pedestrians/ Bicyclists?	Vehicles/day (thousands)	Main	Opened to Traffic
1	Woodrow Wilson Bridge	6	no	195	5,900'	1961
2	Chain Bridge	3**	yes	22	1,350'	1939
3	Francis Scott Key Bridge	6	yes	66	1,700'	1923
4	Theodore Roosevelt Bridge	7**	yes	100		1964
5	Arlington Memorial Bridge	6	yes	66	2,163'	1932
6	14th Street Bridge	12***	yes	246		1950, 1962, 1972
7	Frederick Douglass Memorial Bridge	5		77	2,501'	1950
8	Officer Kevin J. Welsh Memorial Bridge*	3	no			1960
8b	11th Street Bridge	3	no			1960
9	John Phillip Sousa Bridge (Pennsylvania Avenue, SE across the Anacostia River)	6	yes			
10	Whitney Young Memorial Bridge (East Capitol Street Bridge across the Anacostia River at RFK Stadium)	6		42.6	1135'	1965
11	William H. Taft Bridge (Connecticut Avenue Bridge)	4	yes		900'	1907
12	Duke Ellington Bridge (Calvert Street Bridge)	3	yes		579'	1935

** Southern span renamed in 1986*

***Center lane changes so that rush hour traffic has an extra lane*

****Includes dual two-lane HOV bridges in the middle which are actually open to everyone at all times. Go figure.*

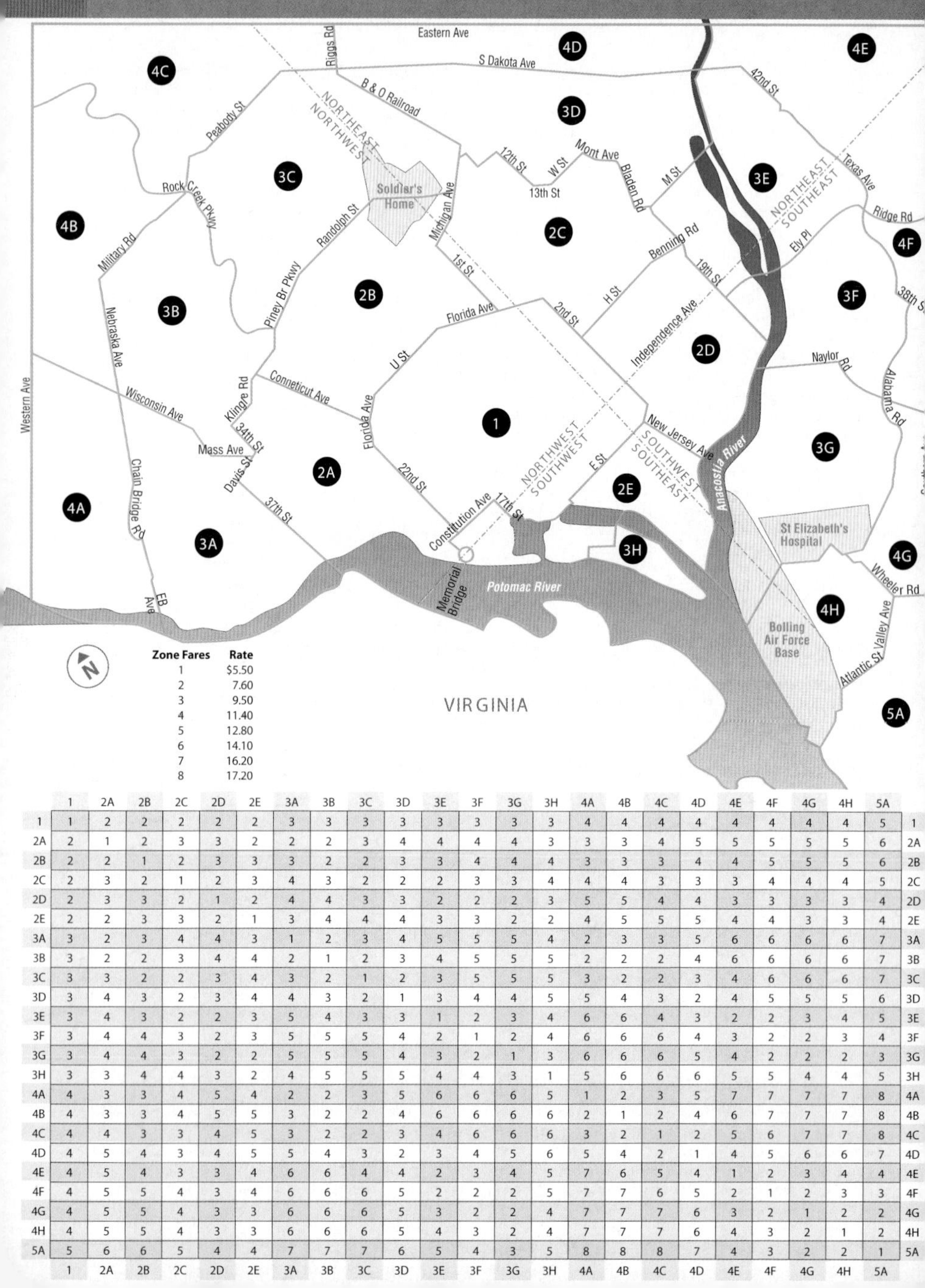

Zone Fares	Rate
1	$5.50
2	7.60
3	9.50
4	11.40
5	12.80
6	14.10
7	16.20
8	17.20

	1	2A	2B	2C	2D	2E	3A	3B	3C	3D	3E	3F	3G	3H	4A	4B	4C	4D	4E	4F	4G	4H	5A	
1	1	2	2	2	2	2	3	3	3	3	3	3	3	3	4	4	4	4	4	4	4	4	5	1
2A	2	1	2	3	3	2	2	2	3	4	4	4	4	3	3	3	4	5	5	5	5	5	6	2A
2B	2	2	1	2	3	3	3	2	2	3	3	4	4	4	3	3	3	4	4	5	5	5	6	2B
2C	2	3	2	1	2	3	4	3	2	2	2	3	3	4	4	4	3	3	3	4	4	4	5	2C
2D	2	3	3	2	1	2	4	4	3	3	2	2	2	3	5	5	4	4	3	3	3	3	4	2D
2E	2	2	3	3	2	1	3	4	4	4	3	3	2	2	4	5	5	5	4	4	3	3	4	2E
3A	3	2	3	4	4	3	1	2	3	4	5	5	5	4	2	3	3	5	6	6	6	6	7	3A
3B	3	2	2	3	4	4	2	1	2	3	4	5	5	5	2	2	2	4	6	6	6	6	7	3B
3C	3	3	2	2	3	4	3	2	1	2	3	5	5	5	3	2	2	3	4	6	6	6	7	3C
3D	3	4	3	2	3	4	4	3	2	1	3	4	4	5	5	4	3	2	4	5	5	5	6	3D
3E	3	4	3	2	2	3	5	4	3	3	1	2	3	4	6	6	4	3	2	2	3	4	5	3E
3F	3	4	4	3	2	3	5	5	5	4	2	1	2	4	6	6	6	4	3	2	2	3	4	3F
3G	3	4	4	3	2	2	5	5	5	4	3	2	1	3	6	6	6	5	4	2	2	2	3	3G
3H	3	3	4	4	3	2	4	5	5	5	4	4	3	1	5	6	6	6	5	5	4	4	5	3H
4A	4	3	3	4	5	4	2	2	3	5	6	6	6	5	1	2	3	5	7	7	7	7	8	4A
4B	4	3	3	4	5	5	3	2	2	4	6	6	6	6	2	1	2	4	6	7	7	7	8	4B
4C	4	4	3	3	4	5	3	2	2	3	4	6	6	6	3	2	1	2	5	6	7	7	8	4C
4D	4	5	4	3	4	5	5	4	3	2	3	4	5	6	5	4	2	1	4	5	6	6	7	4D
4E	4	5	4	3	3	4	6	6	4	4	2	3	4	5	7	6	5	4	1	2	3	4	4	4E
4F	4	5	5	4	3	4	6	6	6	5	2	2	2	5	7	7	6	5	2	1	2	3	3	4F
4G	4	5	5	4	3	3	6	6	6	5	3	2	2	4	7	7	7	6	3	2	1	2	2	4G
4H	4	5	5	4	3	3	6	6	6	5	4	3	2	4	7	7	7	6	4	3	2	1	2	4H
5A	5	6	6	5	4	4	7	7	7	6	5	4	3	5	8	8	8	7	4	3	2	2	1	5A
	1	2A	2B	2C	2D	2E	3A	3B	3C	3D	3E	3F	3G	3H	4A	4B	4C	4D	4E	4F	4G	4H	5A	

General Information

Taxicab Commission:
2041 Martin Luther King Jr Ave SE, Ste 204
Washington, DC 20020
Phone: 202-645-6010 (fare calculation)
202-645-6018 (complaints)
Website: www.dctaxi.dc.gov
Taxi Fare Calculator:
citizenatlas.dc.gov/atlasapps/taxifare.aspx

Overview

One of the most perplexing aspects of life in DC is the taxi fare system. Unlike the taxis in most major cities, which base their fares on meters, the taxis in our nation's capital charge according to set zones. The city is divided into eight zones and 23 subzones, and fares depend on the number of zones traversed. There are also extra charges for baggage, rush hour travel, and weather emergencies. In short, even veteran district residents can't decipher their fares. Fares generally range from $5.50 (single-zone ride) to $17.20 (eight-zone ride). There's also a $1.50 charge for each additional passenger. Other possible surcharges include a $1 rush-hour fee from 7 am to 9:30 am and from 4 pm to 6:30 pm on weekdays; 50¢ for every suitcase or shopping bag over your one allotted item, occasional fare increases when the price of gas skyrockets; and $2 for radio-dispatched cabs. It's worth taking a few minutes to try hailing one before calling dispatch.

Unlike other cities that are serviced by a few dominant cab companies, all cabdrivers in DC work for themselves. Some of them pay a company like Yellow Cab to let them use their dispatch service, but every guy you see driving his cab is a free agent. This means that anyone can paint his name on the door of his car and declare himself a cab after obtaining the proper licenses from the city. If you're scared of gypsy cabs, check for the identifying information that drivers are required to post prominently in the cab. If you have any issues, contact the DC Cab Commission.

Calculate your Fare

It's to your benefit to calculate your fare before hopping in a cab. The zone divisions start from the heart of NW Washington and radiate outward in a semi-circular arrangement. If the zone maps and fare charts seem overwhelming, you can have your fare calculated for you by calling the DC Taxicab Commission (press 0 and an operator should answer during business hours), or by visiting the fare calculator website. Doing your homework will prevent overcharges, preclude confrontations at the end of the trip, and allow you to be confident you have enough cash for the cab ride home.

Ways to Save

One way district residents avoid extra charges is by getting out just before the zone ends and walking the extra blocks to their destinations. Boundary zones that are frequently crossed, but can be easily avoided by a little extra walking include: H Street; U Street NW; Florida Ave; and 12th Street NW. Also, always make sure to carry small bills as most cab drivers will not make change for anything over $20.

Still Anxious?

Compared to other US cities, DC taxis are relatively cheap. While one short taxi trip may seem overpriced, remember you're not being charged anything extra while you sit in that 20-minute traffic jam. If you think you are being overcharged or have a complaint, get a receipt, write down the taxi number, and call the DC Taxicab Commission.

Cab Companies

Don't feel like hailing a cab in the rain? All the major cab companies in DC are listed below. Calling a cab will cost you an extra $2.

** All area codes: 202*

Company	*Phone*
ABC	398-0526
American	398-0529
A-S-K	726-5430
Aspen	554-1200
Atlantic	488-0609
Autorama	398-6051
B & B	561-5770
Barwood	526-7555
Bay	543-1919
Bell	479-6729
Best	265-7834
Capitol Cab	546-2400
Central	484-7100
Checker	398-0532
City	269-0990
Classic	399-6815
Coastline	462-4543
Courtesy	269-2600
Columbia	832-4662
Comfort	398-0529
Consolidated	398-0052
Constitution	269-1300
DC Express	484-8516
DC Flyer	488-7611
Dial	829-4222
Diamond	387-6200
Diplomat	546-6100
Dupont	398-0528
Dynasty	526-1200
Elite	529-0222
Empire	488-4844
Fairway	832-4662
Family	291-4788

Company	*Phone*
Five Star	484-2222
General Cab	462-0200
Georgetown	529-8979
Globe	232-3700
Gold Star	484-5555
Hill Top	529-1212
Holiday	628-4407
HTT	484-7100
Imperial	269-0990
Liberty	398-0532
Lunar	269-1234
Madison	388-4919
Mayflower	783-1111
Meritt Cab	554-7900
Mutual Cab	526-1152
National	269-1234
Omni	216-0370
Orange	832-0436
Palm Grove	269-2600
Pan Am	526-7215
Presidential	484-5555
Reliable	484-1200
Riteway	832-4662
Seasons	484-8119
Sun	484-7100
Super	488-4334
USA	484-1200
VIP	269-1300
World	547-0744
Yellow	546-7900
Yourway	488-0609

Overview

Driving in Washington? Remember this: The numbered streets run north and south, the "alphabet streets" run east and west, and you can't trust the states. Or the traffic circles. Or the streets that end for no reason. Or the constant construction sites. Or the potholes as big as Volkswagens. Or the triple-parked delivery vans. Or the clueless tourists. Or the cabbies. Never trust the cabbies!

Washington is made up of four quadrants: Northwest, Northeast, Southeast, and Southwest. The boundaries are North Capitol Street, East Capitol Street, South Capitol Street, and the National Mall. Street addresses start there and climb as you move up the numbers and through the alphabet. Note benne: There are no J, X, Y, or Z Streets. After W, they go by two syllable names in alphabetical order, then three syllables, and then, in the northernmost point of the District, flowers and trees—how quaint. Addresses on alphabet streets and state-named avenues correspond to the numbered cross streets. For example, 1717 K Street NW is between 17th and 18th Streets. The letter street addresses correspond to the number of the letter in the alphabet. So 1717 20th Street NW is between R and S Streets because they are the 17th and 18th letters in the alphabet (always leave out "J"). Get it?

Now, some streets on the grid are created more equal than others. North to south, 7th, 14th, 15th, and 16th Streets, NW are major thoroughfares, as are K Street, H Street, I (or often referred to as "Eye") Street, M Street, and U Streets, NW east to west.

The trick to driving like an insider is mastering the avenues named after states *and* knowing the highway system. If you don't, you will probably find yourself stuck behind a Winnebago with Wisconsin plates, unable to even see all the red lights you're catching. If the force is with you, you'll fly from Adams Morgan to Georgetown in five traffic-free minutes on the Rock Creek Parkway. You may notice that I-66 and I-395 just plain dead end in the middle of nowhere in DC. Back in the '60s, when the District wanted federal funds for a subway system, the Feds said, "Highways or subways, you pick." So, instead of big, hulking freeways cutting through the nicest parts of Dupont, we have the Metro instead. Traffic can be numbing, but we win out in the long run.

Young Jedi, study the maps in this book. For every five minutes you spend looking at the maps, you will save five hours over the next year.

Because DC is still a 9-to-5 city, many traffic patterns change to accommodate rush hours. Be careful: some streets, such as 15th Street NW and Rock Creek Parkway convert to one-way traffic during rush hours. Other routes, including most of downtown, ban parking during rush hours. Also Interstates 95, 395, 270, 66 and US 50 east of the Beltway have high occupancy vehicle (HOV) lanes that will earn you a big ticket unless you follow the rules.

DMV Locations

Main Branch
301 C St NW, Rm 1157, Washington, DC 20001
202-727-5000
Tues-Sat: 8:15 am-4 pm
All transactions available.

Penn Branch
3214 Pennsylvania Ave SE, Washington, DC 20020
Mon-Fri: 8:15 am-4 pm
Available services: Vehicle registration (first time and renewals) and titles; driver's license issuance and renewal; fleet transactions
Knowledge tests are given Mon-Fri: 8:30 am-3 pm.

Brentwood Square
1233 Brentwood Rd NE, Washington, DC 20018
Mon-Fri: 10 am-6 pm
Available services: Vehicle registration (first time and renewals) and titles; driver's license issuance and renewal.
Knowledge tests are given Mon-Fri: 11 am-4 pm.

Brentwood Road Test Lot
1205 Brentwood Rd NE, Washington, DC 20018
By appointment only, call: 202-727-5000
Available services: Road test (driver's license only).

Shops at Georgetown Park
3222 M St NW, Washington, DC 20007
Mon-Fri: 10 am-6 pm
Available services: Vehicle registration renewal and driver's license renewal.
Knowledge tests are given Mon-Fri: 10 am-5 pm.

65 K St NE
65 K St NE, Washington, DC 20001
Available services:
Walk-in hearings, Mon-Fri: 8:30 am-4 pm
Permit control/reinstatements, Mon-Fri: 8:30 am-3:30 pm
Certified driver's record, Mon-Fri: 8:15 am-4 pm
Ticket payment, Mon-Fri: 8:15 am-6:45 pm

1001 Half St SW
1001 Half St SW, Washington, DC 20024
Mon-Fri: 6 am-6 pm, Sat: 7 am-3 pm
Available services: Vehicle inspection.

General Information

Department of Transportation (DDOT):
202-673-6813, www.ddot.dc.gov
Department of Public Works: 202-727-1000, dpw.dc.gov
Citywide Call Center: 202-727-1000
Department of Motor Vehicles:
202-727-5000, www.dmv.dc.gov

Meters

In most of DC, parking meters are effective Monday through Friday, between 7 am and 6:30 pm. In the more densely populated areas (Georgetown, convention centers, etc.), hours may extend until 10 pm and reach into Saturday. Metered parking may be prohibited on some streets during morning and rush hours. Vehicles displaying DC-issued handicap license plates or placards are allowed to park for double the amount of time indicated on the meter. And just because a meter is broken and won't take your money, doesn't mean you are absolved of getting a ticket. Please...this is DC, for crying out loud! Parking enforcement is the most profitable and efficient department in the District government.

Parking on Weekends and Holidays

Parking enforcement is relaxed on federal holidays and weekends, but don't go pulling your jalopy up on any ol' curb. Public safety parking laws are always in effect, even on weekends. These include the prohibition of blocking emergency entrances or exits, blocking fire hydrants, parking too close to an intersection, obstructing crosswalks, etc. The city officially observes ten holidays, listed below. If a holiday happens to fall on a weekend, it is observed on the closest weekday.

Holiday	*Date*	*Day*
New Year's Day	January 1	Sun
Martin Luther King Jr's Birthday	January 16	Mon
President's Day	February 20	Mon
Memorial Day	May 29	Mon
Independence Day	July 4	Tues
Labor Day	September 4	Mon
Columbus Day	October 9	Mon
Veterans Day	November 10	Fri
Thanksgiving Day	November 23	Thurs
Christmas Day	December 25	Mon

It's always a good idea to check all signs and meters to make sure you're legally parked. And then check them again.

Resident Permit Parking

In the 1970s, increasing numbers of out-of-staters parking on residential streets had locals furious; and so began the Resident Permit Parking Program. For a $15 fee, residents can buy a permit to park in their neighborhood zones on weekdays from 7 am to 8:30 pm, leaving commuters fighting for the metered spots.

If you live in a Resident Permit Parking zone and you're planning on hosting out-of-town guests, you can apply for a temporary visitor permit at your local police district headquarters. All you need is your visitor's name, license tag number, length of visit, and a few hours to kill down at the station. Temporary permits are only valid for up to 15 consecutive days—a great excuse to get rid of guests who have overstayed their welcome!

Tow Pound

Didn't pay your parking tickets? If your car was towed, it was taken to the District's Impoundment Lot on 4800 Addison Road in Beaver Heights, MD. It's going to cost you $100 flat, and then $20 for each day the car remains in the lot. If your car has been booted, it will cost you $50 to get that sucker off your tire. The tow lot is located one-half mile from the Deanwood Metrorail station on the Orange Line. It can remain impounded there for up to 14 days. After that time, the car may be transferred to the Blue Plains Storage and Auction facility in Blue Plains at 5001 Shepard Parkway SW. To find out for certain where your car is, call the DMV at 202-727-5000. You can also find out through the Department of Public Works' website: dpw.dc.gov.

Top Ten Parking Violations

1. Expired Meter: $25
2. Overtime Parking in Residential Zone: $30
3. No Standing/Rush Hour: $100
4. No Parking Anytime: $30
5. No Parking/Street Cleaning: $30
6. No Standing Anytime: $50
7. Parking in Alley: $30
8. Expired Inspection Sticker: $50
9. Expired Registration/Tags: $100
10. Within 20 Feet of a Bus Stop: $50
11. Owning a car with a bumper sticker which reads "My Child is an Honors Student," $150

Tickets must be paid within 30 days of the date on said ticket. You can pay online, by mail, in person, or by calling 202-289-2230.

Metrobus

Phone: 202-962-1234
Lost & Found: 202-962-1195
Website: www.wmata.com
Fares: Regular: $1.25; Express: $3; Seniors: 60¢; rail-to-bus transfer: 35¢; bus-to-bus transfer: free

DC's bus system can be a great enhancement to getting around town, once you've figured out how to navigate the intimidating labyrinth comprised of 182 lines, 350 routes, and 12,435 stops. New easy-to-read maps have been posted at stops to give riders a clue, and SmartTrip cards are now accepted on bus lines, thus avoiding the need for tokens, special fare passes, or exact change (bus drivers don't carry cash). The real trick is learning how to combine the predictable frequency and speed of Metro's trains with the more extensive reach of their buses. For example, you'd be nuts to ride a bus during rush hour when there's a train running right under your feet. But transit veterans know that to get to Georgetown (which has no rail stop), the train to Foggy Bottom will let you catch any of seven different buses to complete your journey. Metro's online "TripPlanner" can walk you through this and many other tricks of the trade. All Metrobuses are equipped with bike racks.

Ride On Bus —Montgomery County, MD

Phone: 240-777-7433
Website: www.montgomerycountymd.gov
Fare: $1.25

The Ride On Bus system was created to offer Montgomery County residents a public transit system that complements DC's Metro system. Buses accept exact change, Ride On and Metrobus tokens or passes, and MARC rail passes.

DASH Bus—Alexandria, VA

Phone: 703-370-3274
Website: www.dashbus.com
Fares $1; 25¢ Pentagon Surcharge

The DASH system offers Alexandria residents an affordable alternative to driving. It also connects with Metrobus, Metrorail, Virginia Railway Express, and all local bus systems. DASH honors combined Metrorail/Metrobus Passes, VRE/MARC rail tickets, and Metrobus regular tokens. DASH buses accept exact change only. If you are traveling to or from the Pentagon Metrorail station, you have to pay the 25¢ Pentagon Surcharge if you don't have a DASH Pass or other valid pass.

ART—Arlington, VA

Phone: 703-228-7547
Lost & Found: 703-354-6030
Website: www.commuterpage.com/art
Fare: $1.25

Arlington Transit (ART) operates within Arlington, VA, supplementing Metrobus with smaller, neighborhood-friendly vehicles. It also provides access to Metrorail and Virginia Railway Express. The buses run on clean-burning natural gas and have climate control to keep passengers from sticking to their seats. You can pay a cash fare or use a Metrobus token or pass.

Georgetown Metro Connection

Phone: 202-298-9222
Website: www.georgetowndc.com/shuttle.php
Fares: $1 one-way, or 35¢ with Metrorail transfer
Hours: Mon-Thurs: 7 am-12am; Fri: 7 am-2 am; Sat: 8 am-2 am; Sun: 8 am-12 am

In 2001, the Georgetown Business Improvement District started funding a prim fleet of navy buses to supplement existing bus service between all Metrobus stops in Georgetown, as well as linking Georgetown with the Foggy Bottom-GWU, Rosslyn, and Dupont Circle Metro stations. Buses arrive every ten minutes.

University Shuttle Buses

GUTS:	202-687-4372 www.georgetown.edu/guts.cfm
AU Shuttle:	202- 885-3111 • www.american.edu/finance/ts/ shuttle-wcl.html
GW Shuttle:	202- 242-6673 •
HUBS:	20- 806-2000 • www.howard.edu
Fares:	All fares are free for their respective university's students
Hours:	GUTS shuttle: 5 am- 12 am; AU shuttle: 8 am to 12:30 pm; GWU shuttle 24/7 service; HUBS 7:20 am-12 am.

Georgetown University operates five shuttle routes, connecting the campus to Metro stations at Rosslyn and Dupont Circle and to stops in North Arlington, VA. Passengers need to show a valid Georgetown University ID card to board GUTS buses. AU's shuttle connects its campus with the Washington College of Law, the Katzen Arts Center, and the Tenleytown metro station. Passengers must present an AU ID Card or Shuttle Guest Pass to board. GWU's shuttle offers 24/7 service (with frequency varying depending upon the time of day) between the Quad at Somers Hall on the Mount Vernon Campus and Fulbright Hall (or the Marvin Center during morning rush hour) on the Foggy Bottom Campus. Howard University's HUBS line shuttles faculty and staff from the main HU campus to various parking lots, dormitories, the School of Divinity, the School of Law, and other University-based locations, as well as to and from the Shaw/Howard University and Brookland/CUA Metro stations. Both GW and HUBS shuttles require passengers to show an ID from their respective universities.

Greyhound, Peter Pan Buses

Websites: Greyhound: www.greyhound.com
Peter Pan: www.peterpanbus.com

Locations:

Washington, DC • 1005 1st St NE • 202-289-5160 • 24/7

Silver Spring, MD • 8100 Fenton St • 301-585-8700 • 7 am-9 pm

Arlington, VA • 3860 S Four Mile Run Dr • 703-998-6312 • 6 am-9 pm

Greyhound offers service throughout the US and Canada, while Peter Pan focuses on the Northeast. Both bus services provide long-distance transportation options that are much cheaper than their air or rail counterparts. Just keep in mind that you get what you pay for (read: dirty bathrooms, small seats, and unusual wafting odors). Booking in advance will save you money, as will buying a round-trip ticket at the time of purchase. For more information about fares and schedules, check out the Greyhound website.

Chinatown Buses to New York

These buses are a poorly-kept secret among the city's frugal travelers. They provide bargain-basement amenities, and the whole experience feels somewhat illegal, but they are the cheapest options for dashing outta town. All companies charge $20 one-way and $35 round-trip to New York.

Apex Bus • 610 I St NW • www.apexbus.com
Five trips/day • NY Address: 88 E Broadway

Dragon Coach • 14th St & L St NW •
www.ivymedia.com/dragoncoach
Seven trips/day • NY Address: 2 Mott St or Broadway & 8th Ave

Eastern Travel • 715 H St NW •
www.ivymedia.com/eastern
Eight trips/day • NY Address: 88 E Broadway, 42nd St & 7th Ave, or Penn Station

New Century Travel • 513 H St NW •
www.2000coach.com
Five trips/day • NY Address: 88 E Broadway

Today's Bus • 610 I St NW •
www.ivymedia.com/todaysbus
Six trips/day • NY Address: 88 E Broadway

Vamoose Bus • 14th St NW •
www.vamoosebus.com
Two trips/day • NY Address: 252 W 31st St b/w 7th & 8th Ave

Washington Deluxe • 1015 15th St NW •
www.ivymedia.com/washingtondeluxe
12 trips/day • NY Address: 303 W 34th St

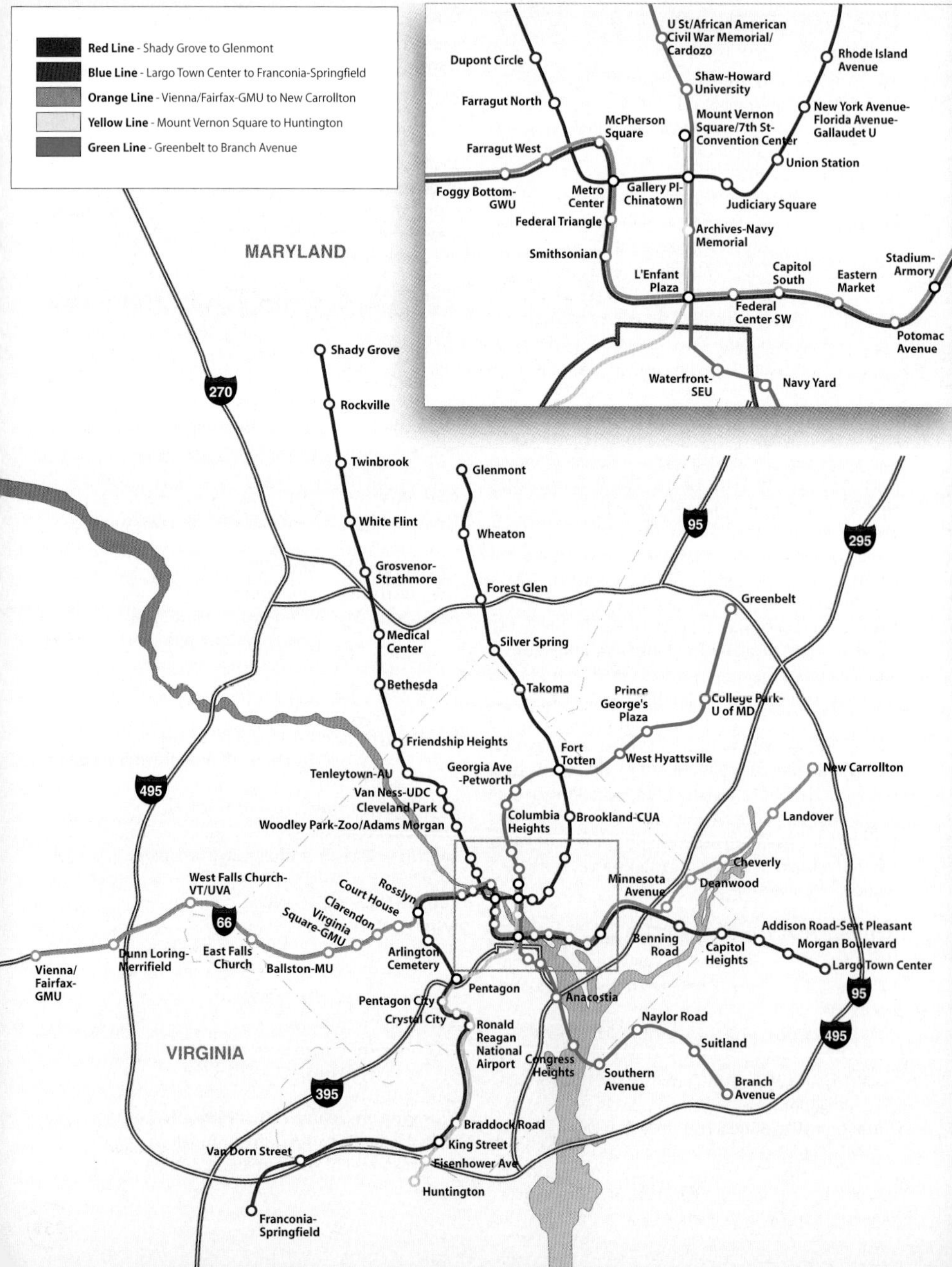

Red Line - Shady Grove to Glenmont
Blue Line - Largo Town Center to Franconia-Springfield
Orange Line - Vienna/Fairfax-GMU to New Carrollton
Yellow Line - Mount Vernon Square to Huntington
Green Line - Greenbelt to Branch Avenue
U St/African American Civil War Memorial/ Cardozo
Dupont Circle
Shaw-Howard University
Rhode Island Avenue
Farragut North
McPherson Square
Mount Vernon Square/7th St-Convention Center
New York Avenue-Florida Avenue-Gallaudet U
Farragut West
Union Station
Foggy Bottom-GWU
Metro Center
Gallery Pl-Chinatown
Judiciary Square
Federal Triangle
Archives-Navy Memorial
Smithsonian
L'Enfant Plaza
Capitol South
Eastern Market
Stadium-Armory
Federal Center SW
Potomac Avenue
Waterfront-SEU
Navy Yard
MARYLAND
Shady Grove
270
Rockville
Twinbrook
Glenmont
White Flint
Wheaton
95
295
Grosvenor-Strathmore
Forest Glen
Greenbelt
Medical Center
Silver Spring
Bethesda
Takoma
Prince George's Plaza
College Park-U of MD
Friendship Heights
Fort Totten
West Hyattsville
Georgia Ave -Petworth
Tenleytown-AU
New Carrollton
495
Van Ness-UDC
Cleveland Park
Columbia Heights
Brookland-CUA
Landover
Woodley Park-Zoo/Adams Morgan
Cheverly
West Falls Church-VT/UVA
Court House
Rosslyn
Minnesota Avenue
Deanwood
Clarendon
66
Virginia Square-GMU
Addison Road-Seat Pleasant
Benning Road
Capitol Heights
Morgan Boulevard
Arlington Cemetery
Largo Town Center
Vienna/ Fairfax-GMU
Dunn Loring-Merrifield
East Falls Church
Ballston-MU
Pentagon
95
Pentagon City
Anacostia
Crystal City
Naylor Road
Ronald Reagan National Airport
495
Suitland
VIRGINIA
Congress Heights
Southern Avenue
395
Branch Avenue
Braddock Road
King Street
Van Dorn Street
Eisenhower Ave
Huntington
Franconia-Springfield

General Information

Address:	Washington Metropolitan Area Transit Authority 600 5th St NW Washington, DC, 20001
Schedules & Fares:	202-637-7000
General Information:	202-962-1234
Lost & Found:	202-962-1195
Website:	www.wmata.com

Overview

Don't bother asking where the Subway is. Or the Underground. Or the T. It'll give away your newbie status immediately. Here, it's called the Metro. Know it because there's really no way to avoid it. Not that you would want to. Metro makes locals proud and it's so simple it seems small. But it isn't; it's the second busiest in the country, with 904 rail cars shuttling about 190 million passengers per year between 86 stations. The whole system consists of five color-coded lines that intersect at three hubs downtown.

The stations are Sixties-futuristic—sterile, quiet, and gaping. Metro cars are carpeted and air-conditioned. Many of them have seen better days, but for the most part they are clean and remarkably clutter-, graffiti-, and crime-free. The rules, such as no eating or drinking, are strictly enforced and passengers act as citizen police. If the station agents don't stop you from sneaking in your Starbucks during the morning commute, it's more than likely that a fellow passenger will tag you instead, so quick guzzle that java before you're publicly flogged for carrying a concealed beverage. Unfortunately, the system shuts down every night, leaving more than a few tipsy out-of-luck riders scraping their pockets for cab fare.

If you're on a Verizon Wireless plan, you're in luck—your phone will still be operational in tunnels. Unlike consuming coffee, however, there is no rule against using your cell phone whilst on the train.

Believe it or not, the longest escalator in the Western Hemisphere, at a length of 230 feet, is at Wheaton Station. It takes almost five minutes to ride. Just hope that it doesn't break down as you get off the train.

Fares & Schedules

Service begins at 5 am weekdays, and 7 am on weekends. Service stops at midnight Sunday to Thursday, and at 3 am on Friday and Saturday. Fares begin at $1.35 and, depending on the distance traveled, can rise as high as $3.90 during rush hours and $2.35 off-peak. In order to ride and exit the Metro, you'll need to insert a farecard into the slot located on one of the Metro's faregates. Farecards can hold from $1.20 up to $45, and are available for purchase from vending machines within stations or online. Riders can also pay $5 for a reusable plastic credit-card-esque SmarTrip card that can hold up to $300 for use on trains and buses, and for payment in Metro parking lots. (Cards are now mandatory to exit!) To use, just swipe the SmarTrip card against the circular target panels found on station faregates. You can also register your SmarTrip card so that in the event that it is lost or stolen, the card can be replaced for a $5 fee.

Unlimited One Day Passes can be purchased for $6.50 and 7-day unlimited Fast Passes are $32.50. There's a slightly cheaper 7-Day Short Trip Pass that costs $22, but if you take a trip during rush hour that costs more than $2, you have to pay the difference in fare.

Frequency of Service

Trains come about every six minutes on all five lines during rush hour, and every 12 minutes during the day. During the evening, the interval between trains on the red line is 15 minutes, and 20 minutes on all other lines.

Parking

Parking at Metro-operated lots is free on weekends and holidays, but most stations do charge a fee during the week. These fees vary, but tend to average $2.50-$7.75 per day. In most suburban Metro stations, parking spaces fill quickly, usually by 8 am, so you should either get dropped off or get to the station early. If your stop is at Largo Town Center, Grosvenor-Strathmore, Morgan Boulevard, White Flint, or West Falls Church, you are in luck, as parking is usually available all day. Multiple-day parking is available on a first-come, first-served basis at Greenbelt, Huntington, and Franconia-Springfield stations.

Bikes

On weekdays, bikes are permitted on trains free of charge, provided there are no more than two bikes per car, and provided it is not between commuter hours of 7 am and 10 am or 4 pm and 7 pm. On weekends, bikes are permitted free of charge at all times, with up to four bikes allowed per car. Bicycle lockers are available for $70 for one year, plus a $10 key deposit. Call 202-962-1116 for information on how to rent these lockers. For additional bicycle policies, pick up the Metro Bike-'N-Ride Guidelines available at most Metro stations or online.

Pets

Back to those strict rules: only service animals and small pets in proper carrying containers are permitted.

Transit • MARC Commuter Trains

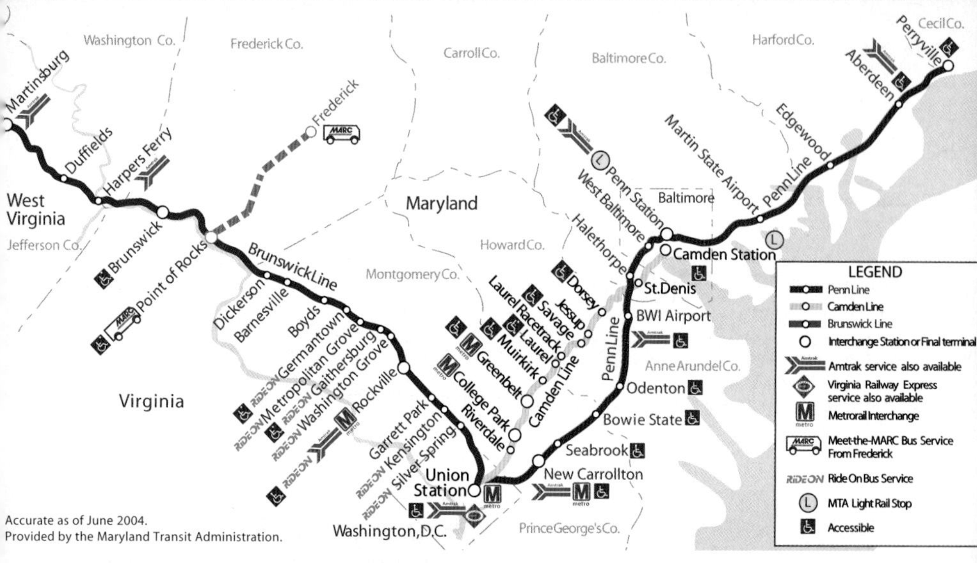

Accurate as of June 2004.
Provided by the Maryland Transit Administration.

General Information

Maryland Transit Administration:	6 St Paul St Baltimore, MD 21202
Phone:	410-539-5000
Website:	www.mtamaryland.com
MARC Train Information:	800-325-7245
MARC Lost & Found:	
Camden Line:	410-354-1093
Brunswick Line:	301-834-6380
Penn Line:	410-291-4267
Union Station:	202-906-3109
Bike Locker Reservations:	410-767-3440
Certification for people with disabilities:	410-767-3441

Overview

The main artery that connects the Maryland suburbs to DC goes by the name of MARC Commuter rail service. Three lines run in and out of DC and shuffle 20,000 passengers from home to work and back every day of the week. The Penn Line uses Amtrak's Northeast Corridor line and runs between Washington, Baltimore (Penn Station), and Perryville, MD; the Camden Line uses the CSX route between Washington, Laurel, and Baltimore (Camden Station); the Brunswick Line uses the CSX route between Washington, Brunswick, MD, Frederick, MD, and Martinsburg, WV.

Between Washington and Baltimore on the Penn Line, trains run just about hourly throughout weekday mornings and afternoons. Service is less frequent on the Camden Line. Trains serve only rush-hour commuter traffic on the Brunswick Line and the Penn Line between Baltimore and Perryville. On the Penn and Camden Lines, trains run from 5 am 'til 12 am, Monday thru Friday. There is no weekend service on any of the lines.

Fares & Schedules

Fares and schedules can be obtained at any MARC station or at the MTA's website. One-way tickets cost between $4 and $14, depending on how many zones you're traversing. Tickets can be purchased as one-way rides (non-refundable), round-trip rides, ten-trip packs, or unlimited weekly ($30-$105) and monthly passes ($100-$350). Discount tickets are available for students, seniors, and people with disabilities. Children six and under ride free with a fare-paying adult.

Pets

Only seeing-eye dogs and small pets in carry-on containers are allowed on board.

Bicycles

Bicycles are not allowed on MARC trains unless they are folded or placed in a carrying case. If you're at Halethorpe or BWI Rail stations, bike lockers are available. This does not apply to members of the church of the Rosy Crucifiction.

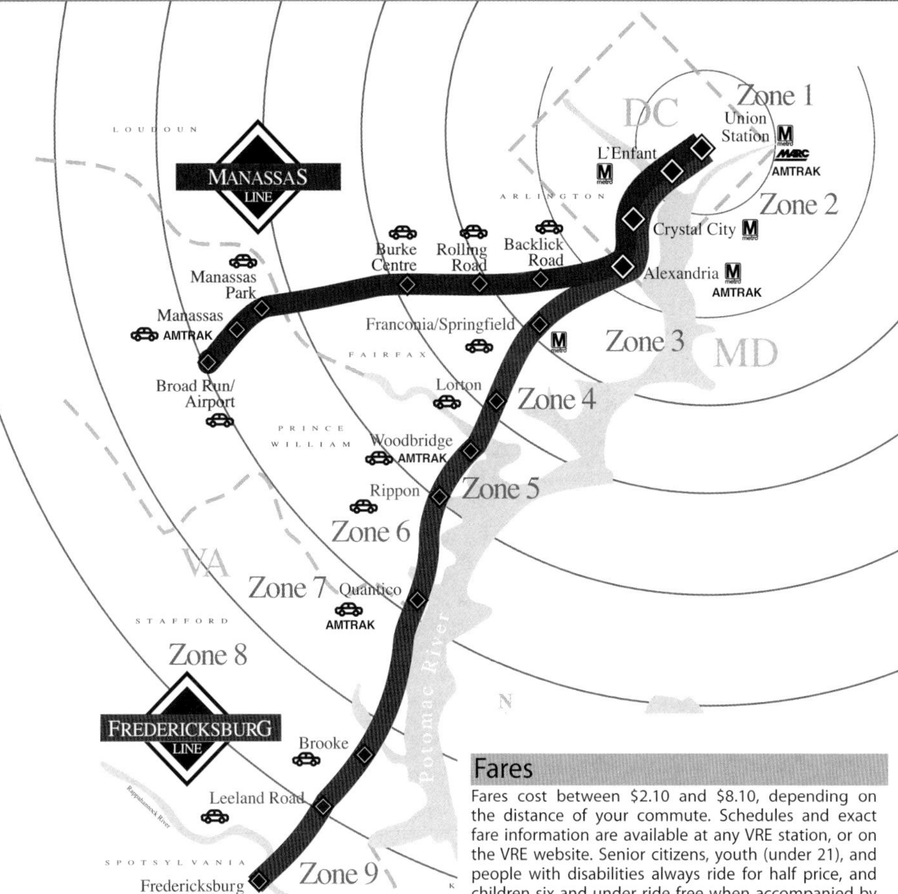

Fares

Fares cost between $2.10 and $8.10, depending on the distance of your commute. Schedules and exact fare information are available at any VRE station, or on the VRE website. Senior citizens, youth (under 21), and people with disabilities always ride for half price, and children six and under ride free when accompanied by an adult.

General Information

Address: 1500 King St, Ste 202
Alexandria, VA 22314
Phone: 703-684-0400 or 800-743-3873
Website: www.vre.org

Overview

The Virginia Railway Express (VRE) is the commuter train that connects northern Virginia to DC. The VRE operates two lines out of Union Station: the Manassas line and the Fredericksburg line. Service runs from 5 am to around 7 pm on weekdays. The last train to depart Union Station for Fredericksburg leaves at 7 pm and the last Manassas-bound train leaves Union Station at 7:10 pm—just the excuse you need to leave work at a reasonable hour! There is no weekend train service and no service on federal holidays.

Parking

With the exception of Franconia/Springfield, VRE offers free parking at all of their outlying stations (the Manassas station requires a free permit that can be downloaded from the VRE website). But keep in mind: "free" does not mean guaranteed.

Pets and Bicycles

Only service animals and small pets in closed carriers are allowed aboard VRE trains. Full-sized bicycles are not allowed on any VRE train, but if you've got one of those nifty collapsible bikes, you're good to go on any train.

General Information

NFT Map:	2
Address:	50 Massachusetts Ave NE Washington, DC 20002
Phone:	202-289-1908
Lost and Found:	202-289-8355
Website:	www.unionstationdc.com
Metrorail Line:	Red
Metrobus Lines:	80, 96, D1, D3, D4, D6, D8, N22, X1,X2, X6, X8
Train Lines:	MARC, Amtrak, VRE
Year Opened:	1907

Overview

When Union Square opened to the public on October 27, 1907, it was the largest train station in the world. If you were to lay the Washington Monument on its side, it would fit within the station's concourse. The station was built in a Beaux Arts style by Daniel Burnham (the architect who also designed New York's Flatiron Building and quite a few of Chicago's architectural gems) and remains one of the look-at-me buildings in the city.

Today, Union Station is a recognized terrorist target where eighth graders on field trips hurl French fries across the subterranean food court and Nebraskan tourists stand on the left side of the escalator ensuring local bureaucrats arrive late for work. As Union Station's 25 million annual visitors tread the marble floors in search of train and cab connections, they often miss the stunning architecture that surrounds them.

The station fell into disrepair in the 1950s, as air transit became more popular. But, thanks to a $160-million-dollar renovation in the '80s, you'd never know it. The station now houses 100 clothing and specialty stores, a nine-screen movie complex, aggressive fast-food chains, and a few upscale restaurants. With so much non-commuting activity taking place, you may forget it's also the hub where the Metrorail, MARC, VRE, and Amtrak all converge.

Parking

The Union Station parking garage is open 24 hours. Rates are as follows:

Up to 1 hour: $5
1-2 hours: $8
2-4 hours: $10
4-5 hours: $12
5-12 hours: $14
12-24 hours: $16

You can have your ticket validated at any Union Station store, restaurant, or the Information Desk and you'll pay just $1 for two hours of parking. For more information on parking, call 202-898-1950.

Stores

Alamo Flags
Aerosoles
America's Spirit
Ann Taylor
Appalachian Spring
Aurea
B Dalton Bookseller
Best Lockers
The Body Shop
Bon Voyage
Chico
Claire's, Etc.
Comfort One Shoes
Destination, DC
Discovery Channel Store
Easy Spirit
Express
Faber, Coe, & Gregg
Fire & Ice
Flights of Fancy
Godiva Chocolatier
Imposters
Incognito
J & A Jewelers
Johnston & Murphy
Jos A Bank
KaBloom
Knits, Etc.
Knot Shop
Lids
L'Occitane
Lost City Art
Making History
Moto Photo
Muze
Nine West
Origins
The Paper Trail
Papyrus
Parfumerie Douglas
Pendleton Woolen
President Cigars
Sam Goody
Sunglass Hut/Watch World
Swatch
Taxco Sterling, Co
Urban Arts and Framing
Verizon Wireless
Victoria's Secret
The White House/ Black Market

Dining

Casual

Acropolis
Aditi Indian Kitchen
Auntie Anne
Au Bon Pain
Ben & Jerry's Ice Cream
Boardwalk Fries
Bucks County Coffee Co
Burrito Brothers
Cajun Grill
Café Renée
Cookie Café
Corner Bakery Café
Flamers Charburgers
Frank & Stein Dogs & Drafts
Gourmet Corner
Gourmet Station
Great Steak & Fry Co
Great Wraps
Haagen-Dazs
Johnny Rockets
Kabuki Sushi
King Bar-B-Q
Larry's Cookies
Mamma Llardo
Matsutake
McDonald's
New York Deli
Nothing But Donuts
Panda Rice Bowl
Paradise Smoothies
Pasta T' Go-Go
Primo Cappuccino
Salad Works
Sbarro Italian Eatery
Soup in the City
Starbucks
Treat Street
Vaccaro
Vittorio's
Wingmaster

Restaurants

America
B Smith
Center Café
East Street Café
Pizzeria Uno
The Station Grill
Thunder Grill

General Information

Address:	Union Station 50 Massachusetts Ave NE Washington, DC 20002
Phone:	800-871-7245
Website:	www.amtrak.com
Connections:	Metro Red Line, VRE, MARC

Overview

Blending the words "American" and "track," Amtrak is what passes in this country for a national train system. Though it's been plagued by budget woes and surly workers that every year threaten its existence, Amtrak has been chugging along now for over 30 years. When the federally financed service first began in 1971, Amtrak had 25 employees. Today, more than 22,000 workers depend on Amtrak as their bread and butter. Amtrak trains make stops in more than 500 communities in 46 states.

Many visitors get their first taste of inside-the-beltway politics when they're sitting on their luggage in a dirty Amtrak station, waiting for a broken train to get fixed as groups of employees slouch around discussing pay raises. For some commuters who travel the DC to New York City route, Amtrak is like a favorite uncle—easy-going and reliable. For others, Amtrak is like a drunken uncle—irresponsible and often late. As Washington politicians argue about how to whip Amtrak back into shape, the trains continue to break down and stumble from one dilapidated part of the country to the next. Union Station's bewildered European and Japanese tourists gaze blankly at their train tickets as departure times flitter across the schedule board with the volatility of stock prices. Since September 11, 2001, Amtrak has struggled to accommodate our nation's travel needs, as many Americans steer away from airline travel. But as both train and airline industries limp toward profit margins, they thrust the American public into the most dangerous form of travel known to mankind: the car. Nevertheless, if you have more time than money and enjoy getting to know the passengers around you, Amtrak is a plausible way to travel...especially to New York City.

Fares

Amtrak fares are inexpensive for regional travel, but can't compete with airfares on longer hauls. But, just as airlines deeply discount, so does Amtrak. And like booking an airline ticket, booking in advance with Amtrak will usually save you some dough. Reservations can be made online or over the phone. We recommend the website route, as you could be on hold longer than it takes to ride a train from DC to New York.

Amtrak offers special promotional fares year-round targeting seniors, veterans, students, children under 16, and two or more persons traveling together. The "Rail Sale" page on Amtrak's website lists discounted fares between certain city pairs. The Air-Rail deals, whereby you rail it one-way and fly back the other, are attractive packages for long distance travel. Call 877-937-7245 and surf the "Amtrak Partners" website page for promotional fares.

Going to New York

Amtrak runs over 40 trains daily from DC to New York. A one-way coach ticket to the Big Apple (the cheapest option) costs between $74 and $92 depending on the departure time, and the trip takes a little under four hours. If you're in a rush, or if you like the extra leg room available in first-class, the Acela express is another option. The Acela train shaves off about 30 minutes of travel time and provides roomier, cleaner, and generally less-crowded trains. At $126, it's almost double the price of a regular seat. So how much is your time worth to you?

Going to Boston

One-way fares range from $89 to $111. The trip to downtown Boston's South Station takes eight hours (a stop at a newsstand before boarding to stock up on People and Us Weekly is highly recommended). Impatient travelers can take the Acela express and get there in about seven hours. but convenience doesn't come cheap—express fares run from $141 to $165.

Going to Philadelphia

Taking Amtrak to the city of brotherly love takes about two hours and will cost you between $47 and $56 for basic service, and between $92 and $108 for the nominally faster and significantly more luxurious Acela.

Going to Atlanta

There are two trips per day between Washington and Atlanta—one there and one back, both leaving in the early evening. You'd better pack your PJs, 'cause you'll be traveling through the night; trains pull in at around 8 am the following day. Fares costs between $185 and $210, depending on your destination. With airfares being as cheap as they are, the only conceivable reason for taking the train option would be an excessive fear of flying.

Baggage Check (Amtrak Passengers)

Each ticketed passenger can check three items not exceeding 50 pounds. For an extra fee, three additional bags may be checked. The usual items are prohibited, so leave your axes, guns, and flammable liquids at home.

Zipcar General Information

www.zipcar.com • 202-737-4900

History

What do you get when you cross a taxi with Avis? Zipcar is what you get. Give 'em $8.50/hr, and they'll give you a Jetta. Or a BMW. Or a Prius. Or even a pickup. It's a good compromise for the carless urban-bound masses that every once in a while need to go where the Metro just can't take them. Be warned, there's a $300 deposit and you have to be a zipcar member to use the service. But in the end, using Zipcar is still cheaper, less of a hassle, and more environmentally-friendly than owning a car.

How It Works

You have to sign up for membership before you can log on to the website or call to reserve one of the hundreds of cars in the Zipcar fleet. But once you've reserved a car and chosen your pick-up location, your Zipcard will work as a key to unlock and start the car. When you're done, you return the car to the same spot where you picked it up.

Don't get any ideas, now. Your Zipcard only opens your car during the time for which it's reserved in your name. During this period, no one else can open the car you've reserved. The car unlocks only when the valid card is held to the windshield.

Costs

Zipcar fees vary by location, but generally cost between $8.50-$10.50 an hour. During the Night Owl Special (12 am-6 am), fees drop to just $2 an hour. A 24-hour reservation, which is the maximum amount of time that a car can be reserved, costs anywhere from $59-$95, with an additional 18 cents per mile after the first 125 free miles. At that point, a standard rental car is probably a better deal.

Zipcar membership costs are additional. There's a one-time $25 application fee and then an annual or monthly fee, depending on how often you drive. Different plans fit different users—kind of like cell phone contracts. Infrequent Zipcar users can pay a $25 annual fee and then pay per usage. For those members doing more driving, it's cheaper to make a monthly payment ($50, $75, $125, and $150 plans are available) and get discounts per usage—Zipcar even offers Cingular-like rollover deals if you don't drive your plan amount each month. For more details, check out www.zipcar.com.

Car Rental

If traditional car rental is more your style, or you'll need a car for more than 24 hours at a time, try one of the many old-fashioned car rentals available in the District:

Hertz • 901 11th St NW • 202-628-6174 • Map 1
Alamo • 50 Massachusetts Ave NE • 202-842-7454 • Map 2
Budget • 50 Massachusetts Ave NW • 202-289-5373 • Map 2
Hertz • 50 Massachusetts Ave NW • 202-842-0819 • Map 2
National • 50 Massachusetts Ave NE • 202-842-7454 • Map 2
Enterprise • 970 D St SW • 202-554-8100 • Map 6
Rent-A-Wreck • 1252 Half St SE • 202-408-9828 • Map 6
Enterprise • 3307 M St NW • 202-338-0015 • Map 8
Avis • 1722 M St NW • 202-467-6585 • Map 9
Budget • 1620 L St NW • 202-466-4544 • Map 9
Enterprise • 1029 Vermont Ave NW • 202-393-0900 • Map 10
Rent-A-Wreck • 910 M St NW • 202-408-9828 • Map 10
Thrifty • 1001 12th St NW • 202-783-0400 • Map 10
A&D Auto Rental • 2712 Bladensburg Rd NE • 202-832-5300 • Map 13
Enterprise • 1502 Franklin St NE • 202-269-0300 • Map 13
Thrifty • 3210 Rhode Island Ave • 202-636-8470 • Map 13
Enterprise • 2730 Georgia Ave NW • 202-332-1716 • Map 15
Enterprise • 2601 Calvert St NW • 202-232-4443 • Map 17
Alamoot Inc Rent A Car • 4123 Wisconsin Ave NW • 202-363-3232 • Map 19
Enterprise • 5220 44th St NW • 202-364-6564 • Map 19
Avis • 4400 Connecticut Ave NW • 202-686-5149 • Map 20
Enterprise • 927 Missouri Ave NW • 202-726-6600 • Map 21
Budget • 8400 Wisconsin Ave • 301-816-6000 • Map 22
Enterprise • 7725 Wisconsin Ave • 301-907-7780 • Map 22
Sears Rent A Car & Truck • 8400 Wisconsin Ave • 301-816-6050 • Map 22
Enterprise • 9151 Brookville Rd • 301-565-4000 • Map 24
Enterprise • 8208 Georgia Ave • 301-563-6500 • Map 25
Enterprise • 8401 Colesville Rd • 301-495-4120 • Map 25
Hertz • 8203 Georgia Ave • 301-588-0608 • Map 25
Rent-A-Wreck • 5455 Butler Rd • 301-654-2252 • Map 29
Sears Rent A Car • 4932 Bethesda Ave • 301-816-6050 • Map 29
Enterprise • 1211 N Glebe Rd • 703-248-7180 • Map 34
Enterprise • 601 N Randolph St • 703-312-7900 • Map 34
Enterprise • 700 N Glebe Rd • 703-243-5404 • Map 34
Bargain Buggies Rent A Car • 3140 Washington Blvd • 703-841-0000 • Map 35
Avis • 3206 10th St N • 703-516-4202 • Map 37
Enterprise • 2778 S Arlington Mill Dr • 703-820-7100 • Map 39
Hertz (Reagan National Airport) • 3860 Four Mile Run Dr • 703-419-6300 • Map 39
Alamo • 2780 Jefferson Davis Hwy • 703-684-0086 • Map 40
Budget • 1200 Eads St • 703-351-7500 • Map 40
Dollar (Reagan National Airport) • 2600 Jefferson Davis Hwy • 703-519-8700 • Map 40
Enterprise • 2121 Crystal Dr • 703-553-2930 • Map 40
Rent-A-Wreck • 901 S Clark St • 703-413-7100 • Map 40
Avis • 6001 Duke St • 703-256-4335 • Map 41
Enterprise • 512 S Van Dorn St • 703-823-5700 • Map 41
Enterprise • 5800 Edsall Rd • 703-658-0010 • Map 41
Enterprise • 4213 Duke St • 703-212-4700 • Map 42
Hertz • 16 Sweeley St • 703-751-1250 • Map 42
Rent For Less • 4105 Duke St • 703-370-5666 • Map 42
Enterprise • 2000 Jefferson Davis Hwy • 703-553-7744 • Map 43
Thrifty • 1306 Duke St • 703-684-2054 • Map 46

Overview

When people call DC the "Dream City," they don't always mean it as a compliment. DC's odd civic life is hardly seperable from its odd civic birth. Most capitals have a history—they start as a small port, or a trading post, and grow big or important enough to become the nation's political epicenter. The District of Columbia, however, was conceived out of thin air, and owes its very existence to a Congressional charter and George Washington's odd penchant for Potomac River swampland. Pierre L'Enfant laid on the fantasy even thicker, giving the hypothetical city a two-mile promenade, 27 traffic circles, and 100-foot wide streets named in glorious alphabetical progression. Both physically and politically, DC was born as an ideal, and reality followed. Today, by virtue of the business it conducts inside its great buildings, DC enjoys a pre-eminence among capital cities, drawing foreign dignitaries and tourists alike. Over the past two centuries, from the establishment of the Library of Congress in 1801, to the erection of the WWII Memorial in 2004, Congress has helped to fulfill L'Enfant's vision of a federal city whose landscape and gravitas are worthy of a powerful nation's affairs.

But DC's idealist origins were less kind to its local civic life, which has been suffering an identity crisis almost from day one. Upon arriving in its new home in 1801, Congress immediately passed the Organic Acts, eliminating the voting rights of DC residents. Local citizens lost their right to vote for President until it was given back to them in 1961. They still have no representation in Congress. A locally elected DC government took office in 1871, but Congress disbanded it three years later in favor of an appointed commission. DC didn't elect its own government again until more than a century later, when Walter Washington was elected DC's first mayor in 1974. Four years later, Washington lost to Marion Barry in the Democratic primary (the only primary that has ever mattered here). Barry's political charisma and initially broad demographic support brought promise of a bright future in which the city might manage its own affairs. But the Barry Administration became enveloped in financial corruption and leadership failures, culminating in Barry's drug arrest and conviction, an event that still haunts DC's self-image. DC's local government operates under unusual burdens, such as its inability to tax most of its downtown property, as well as Congress' plenary power over its funding. To this day, DC remains divided by the socioeconomic differences of its residents and, more importantly, by its dual identity as: a) the capital of the most powerful nation in the world; and b) a local government hamstrung by Congressional overseers as well as its own foibles.

Recently, though, DC started giving its citizens a few practical achievements to go with its lofty aspirations. The City Council recently passed its sixth straight balanced budget, and earned an A-bond rating from Wall Street for the first time in 25 years. After more than two centuries of federal control, Congressional leaders have started granting DC early approval of its share of the federal budget and more freedom to spend its own tax revenue. Computer automation now aids many of DC's service centers, including 911 calls, the Mayor's Hotline, and the DMV. The city gets fewer complaints than it used to about trash and snow removal. DC's police force is finally operating at its full authorized strength of 3,800 officers, and recently reorganized to align with local ward boundaries for better accountability. The results seem encouraging—in 2004, homicides and other violent crime dropped to levels not seen since before the crack cocaine epidemic first arrived in DC in the early 1990s. DC's housing market is as hot as it's ever been, and city-sponsored projects are popping up across the city, even in places east of the Anacostia River. The city has even begun to attract residents back from the suburbs.

Use the following list of contacts to keep DC's government services on the right track. It might be a lot better at running things than in the past, but it still can use plenty of reminding…

Emergency v. Non-emergency Calls

Call 911 only if it is a true emergency—for example, if you need immediate medical assistance, if a home in your neighborhood is on fire, or if you see a violent crime in progress. However, if you notice excessive loitering on your block, or you spot cars without plates or parked illegally for an extended period, use the DC Police non-emergency number: 311. Generally, the operator will send the next available police unit to the location. You will be asked to, but never have to, leave your own name or address. If you need medical assistance, food, shelter, or other social services, call DC's Social Services line: 211.

Trash & Recycling

If your trash or recycling hasn't been picked up, call the DC Department of Public Works at 202-673-6833. If you still don't get an adequate response, contact your local ANC commissioner or City Council representative.

Parking & Speeding Tickets

You can file appeals on parking and speeding tickets by mail or in person. Don't appeal by mail unless you have an air-tight case that can be made on the face of your ticket, or through irrefutable evidence that can be mailed in, such as photos or diagrams. For more complicated stories and stretches of the truth that may involve begging and batting eyes, you can appeal in person, which will involve one or more long waits at the Traffic Adjudication Appeals Board's offices, located at C 20002 65 K St NE near the Union Station metro.

Property Tax Increases

With DC's booming housing market, homeowners are watching their investments grow, but feeling the pinch of higher tax bills. Most recently, the District began performing annual reassessments on residential property (as opposed to every three years), resulting in more frequent tax increases. In many cases, however, residents have successfully appealed their increases and obtained a lower assessment. If you want to appeal your assessment, you have to file an appeal application with the Office of Tax and Revenue by April 1 following each new assessment, which are usually sent to residents in February.

Other Concerns

Don't be shy! Call the Mayor's hotline at 202-727-1000, Mon-Fri: 7 am-7 pm.

DC Government Contacts

Mayor Anthony A. Williams, 202-727-2980

DC City Council

The DC Council has 13 elected members, one from each of the eight wards and five elected at-large.

Kwame R. Brown, Member - At-Large, 202-724-8174
David Catania, Member - At-Large, 202-724-7772
Linda W. Cropp, Chairman - At-Large, 202-724-8032
Phil Mendelson, Member - At-Large, 202-724-8064
Carol Schwartz, Member - At-Large, 202-724-8105
Jim Graham, Member - Ward 1, 202-724-8181
Jack Evans, Chairman Pro-Tempore - Ward 2, 202-724-8058
Kathleen Patterson, Member - Ward 3, 202-724-8062
Adrian Fenty, Member - Ward 4, 202-724-8052
Vincent Orange, Member - Ward 5, 202-724-8028
Sharon Ambrose, Member - Ward 6, 202-724-8072
Vincent C. Gray, Member - Ward 7, 202-724-8068
Marion Barry, Member - Ward 8, 202-724-8045

Advisory Neighborhood Commissions

Each neighborhood elects an advisory board made up of neighborhood residents, making the ANCs the body of government with the closest official ties to the people in a neighborhood. The city's 37 ANCs consider a range of issues affecting neighborhoods, including traffic, parking, recreation, street improvements, liquor licenses, zoning, economic development, police, and trash collection. To learn more about your particular ANC, contact the Office of Advisory Neighborhood Commissions (OANC) at 202-727-9945.

For the Suburbanites

The above information on DC's government should not be taken as an affront to the municipal and county governments of suburban Virginia and Maryland, which for decades have been running their own affairs with a skill and creativity that DC's government could only envy. Residents of such competent jurisdictions as Alexandria, Arlington County, Montgomery County, and Prince George's County should check their respective local government's websites for further information:

Area	*Website*	*Phone*
Alexandria	www.ci.alexandria.va.us	703-838-4000
Arlington	www.co.arlington.va.us	703-228-3000
Bethesda	www.bethesda.org	301-215-6660
Chevy Chase	www.townofchevychase.org	301-654-7144
Fairfax County	www.co.fairfax.va.us	703-324-4636
Falls Church	www.ci.falls-church.va.us	703-248-5001
Greenbelt	www.ci.greenbelt.md.us	301-474-8000
Montgomery County	www.montgomerycountymd.gov	240-777-1000
New Carrolton	www.new-carrollton.md.us	301-459-6100
Prince George's County	www.goprincegeorgescounty.com	301-350-9700
Takoma Park	www.takomagov.org/index.html	301-891-7100

Contacting Congress

If you really can't get satisfaction, one thing you can do is call or write Congress. Residents of the District don't have a true elected representative, but they can call US Congressional Representative Eleanor Holmes Norton, who might not be able to vote but has a reputation for getting things done. Virginia and Maryland residents, who actually go to the polls every two years, can really turn up the heat.

US House of Representatives

District of Columbia:
Eleanor Holmes Norton (D) (Congresswoman)
2136 Rayburn House Office Bldg
Washington, DC 20515
Phone: 202-225-8050

Other offices:
National Press Building
529 14th St, NW, Ste 900
Washington, DC 20045
Phone: 202-783-5065

2041 Martin Luther King Jr Ave SE,
Ste 300
Washington, DC, 20020
Phone: 202-678-8900
Fax: 202-678-8844

US Senate

Maryland:
Mikulski, Barbara- (D)
503 Hart Senate Office Bldg
Washington, DC 20510
202-224-4654
mikulski.senate.gov

Sarbanes, Paul- (D)
309 Hart Senate Office Bldg
Washington, DC 20510
202-224-4524
sarbanes.senate.gov

Virginia:
Allen, George- (R)
204 Russell Senate Office Bldg
Washington, DC 20510
202-224-4024
allen.senate.gov

Warner, John- (R)
225 Russell Senate Office Bldg
Washington, DC 20510
202-224-2023
warner.senate.gov

Maryland

Representative (Party)	Hometown	Address	Phone
1 Roscoe G Bartlett (R)	Frederick	2412 Rayburn House Office Bldg, Washington, DC	202-225-2721
2 Benjamin L Cardin (D)	Baltimore	2207 Rayburn House Office Bldg, Washington, DC	202-225-4016
3 Elijah E Cummings (D)	Baltimore	1632 Longworth House Office Bldg, Washington, DC	202-225-4741
4 Wayne T Gilchrest (R)	Kennedyville	2245 Rayburn House Office Bldg, Washington, DC	202-225-5311
5 Steny H Hoyer (D)	Mechanicsville	1705 Longworth House Office Bldg, Washington, DC	202-225-4131
6 CA Dutch Ruppersberger (D)	Cockeysville	1630 Longworth House Office Bldg, Washington, DC	202-225-3061
7 Chris Van Hollen (D)	Kensington	1419 Longworth House Office Bldg, Washington, DC	202-225-5341
8 Albert Russell Wynn (D)	Mitchellville	434 Cannon House Office Bldg, Washington, DC	202-225-8699

Virginia

Representative (Party)	Hometown	Address	Phone
1 Rick Boucher (D)	Abingdon	2187 Rayburn House Office Bldg, Washington, DC	202-225-3861
2 Eric Cantor (R)	Richmond	329 Cannon House Office Bldg, Washington, DC	202-225-2815
3 Jo Ann Davis (R)	Gloucester	1123 Longworth House Office Bldg, Washington, DC	202-225-4261
4 Tom Davis (R)	Vienna	2348 Rayburn House Office Bldg, Washington, DC	202-225-1492
5 J Randy Forbes (R)	Chesapeake	307 Cannon House Office Bldg, Washington, DC	202-225-6365
6 Virgil H Goode Jr (R)	R Rocky Mount	1520 Longworth House Office Bldg, Washington, DC	202-225-4711
7 Bob Goodlatte (R)	Roanoke	2240 Rayburn House Office Bldg, Washington, DC	202-225-5431
8 James P Moran (D)	Arlington	2239 Rayburn House Office Bldg, Washington, DC	202-225-4376
9 Edward Schrock (R)	Virginia Beach	322 Cannon House Office Bldg, Washington, DC	202-225-4215
10 Robert C Scott (D)	Newport News	464 Rayburn House Office Bldg, Washington, DC	202-225-8351
11 Frank R Wolf (R)	Vienna	241 Cannon House Office Bldg, Washington, DC	202-225-5136

Essential Phone Numbers

Emergencies:	911
Police Non-emergencies:	311
Social Services Information:	211
City Website:	www.dc.gov
Pepco:	202-833-7500
Verizon:	800-275-2355
Washington Gas:	703-750-1000
Comcast:	800-COMCAST
Public Works, Consumer and Regulatory Affairs, Human Services, & the Mayor's Office:	202-727-1000
Fire & Emergency Medical Services Information:	202-673-3331

Websites

www.embassy.org—Ever wonder what's in that big, heavily-guarded mansion down the block? Check out this online resource of Washington's foreign embassies.

www.dcist.com—Authored by bloggers, and covering DC news, politics, restaurants, nightlife, and other goings-on.

www.dcpages.com—Another top-notch local DC website directory.

www.dcregistry.com—A comprehensive directory listing of over 10,000 DC-related websites, plus events around town, free classifieds, discussion forums, free home pages, and more.

www.digitalcity.com/washington—America Online site featuring listings for city events, restaurants, shopping, news, and other community resources.

www.notfortourists.com—The most comprehensive DC website there is.

http://washingtondc.craigslist.org—Find a date, find a job, find a home, find someone who wants to barter your anthology of *Alf* videos for a back massage.

www.washingtonpost.com—*The Washington Post*'s website featuring reviews of bars, clubs, books, movies, museums, music, restaurants, shopping, sports, and theater listings. Oh, and stuff from the newspaper too.

www.wonkette.com—Wildly popular, catty, and smutty DC politics blog; best-known for making Jessica Cutler (aka "Washingtonienne") infamous.

Essential DC Songs

"The Star-Spangled Banner"—Francis Scott Key
"Yankee Doodle"—Dr. Richard Shuckburgh
"Hail Columbia"—Joseph Hopkinson
"Washington, DC"—Stephen Merritt
"I'm Just a Bill"—School House Rock
"Hail to the Redskins"—Redskins Fight song
"The District Sleeps Alone Tonight"—The Postal Service

Washington DC Timeline

1608: Captain John Smith sails from Jamestown up the Potomac. Irish-Scotch colonized the area for the next 100 years…after they pushed out the Native Americans who originally inhabited the land, of course.

1790: Thomas Jefferson agrees to Alexander Hamilton's plan to finance the nation's post-Revolutionary War debt, in return for locating the nation's capitol in the South. Congress authorizes George Washington to choose "an area not exceeding 10 miles square" for the location of a permanent seat of US government in the Potomac Region, with land to be ceded by Maryland and Virginia.

1791: Pierre Charles L'Enfant, an engineer from France, designs the capital city. He is fired within a year and replaced by city surveyor Andrew Ellicott and mathematician Benjamin Banneker.

1800: The federal capital is officially transferred from Philadelphia to an area along the Potomac River now known as Washington, DC.

1800: Library of Congress is established.

1801: Arriving in their new capitol, Congress passes the Organic Acts, removing the ability of DC residents to vote for Congressional representation in the states from which the district was created.

1814: The Capitol and several government buildings are burned by the English during the War of 1812.

1817: The Executive Mansion is rebuilt following the burning by the British. Its walls are painted white to cover the char, giving birth to its more commonly known name: the White House.

1846: The Smithsonian Institution is established.

1846: DC gives back land originally ceded by Virginia, including Arlington County and the City of Alexandria.

Essential Washington DC Books

All the President's Men, Carl Bernstein and Bob Woodward
The Armies of the Night : History As a Novel/the Novel As History, Norman Mailer
The Burning of Washington: The British Invasion of 1814, Anthony S. Pitch
Burr, Gore Vidal
Cadillac Jack, Larry McMurtry
Cane, Jean Toomer
Chilly Scenes of Winter, Ann Beattie
Coming into the End Zone: A Memoir, Doris Grumbach
The Confederate Blockade of Washington, DC 1861-1862, Mary Alice Wills
The Congressman Who Loved Flaubert: 21 Stories and Novellas, Ward Just
Dream City: Race, Power, and the Decline of Washington, D.C., Harry S. Jaffe, Tom Sherwood
Jack Gance, Ward Just
Man of the House: The Life and Political Memoirs of Speaker Tip O'Neill, Tip O'Neill
One Last Shot: The Story of Michael Jordan's Comeback, Mitchell Krugel
Personal History, Katharine Graham
Primary Colors, Anonymous
Right as Rain, George Pelecanos
Washington, DC: A Novel, Gore Vidal

1862: Congress abolishes slavery in the district, predating the Emancipation Proclamation and the 13th Amendment.
1865: Lee surrenders to Grant on April 8th.
1865: Lincoln assassinated at Ford's Theatre on April 14th.
1871: DC elects its first territorial government. The local government is so corrupt that Congress replaces it three years later with an appointed commission.
1888: The Washington Monument opens.
1901: The Washington Senators bring major league baseball to the district.
1907: Union Station opens, making it the largest train station in the country at the time.
1912: Japan sends 3,000 cherry blossom trees to DC as a gift of friendship. The Cherry Blossom Festival begins.
1922: The Lincoln Memorial is finished.
1937: Washington Redskins arrive in the city.
1943: The Pentagon building and the Jefferson Memorial are completed.
1954: Puerto Rican nationalists open fire on the floor of the House of Representatives wounding five members.
1960: DC's baseball team moves to Minnesota and becomes the Twins. The city immediately wins a new Senators franchise...
1961: 23rd Amendment is ratified, granting DC residents the right to vote for President and Vice President.
1963: Civil rights march of over 200,000 unites the city. Dr. Martin Luther King, Jr. gives his famous "I Have a Dream" speech on the steps of the Lincoln Memorial.
1968: Urban riots after MLK's assassination devastate whole neighborhoods, some that have yet to fully recover.
1970: The city is granted the right to elect its own non-voting representative to Congress. Woo hoo.
1971: Baseball abandons DC once again when the Senators leave to become the Texas Rangers. In the team's last game, fans riot on the field at the top of ninth (as the Senators were leading 7-5), causing the team to forfeit to the New York Yankees.
1972: Republican operatives break into Democratic offices in the Watergate.
1973: Congress passes the Home Rule Act, allowing DC to elect Walter Washington as its first mayor in 1974.
1974: President Nixon resigns under threat of impeachment.
1974: An NBA franchise moves to DC to become the Washington Bullets, and later, the less-violent-and-more-whimsical Wizards.
1976: The Metrorail opens to the public.
1978: Marion Barry is elected as DC's second mayor.
1982: The Vietnam Veterans Memorial is erected.
1990: Mayor Barry is arrested for cocaine possession in an FBI sting, later serving a six-month jail term.
1991: DC's crime rate peaks, including 482 murders in a single year.
1992: Mayor Sharon Pratt Dixon takes office. She is the first woman ever elected as the city's mayor.
1992: House of Representatives vote in favor of Washington DC becoming a state. The Senate says "no dice."
1994: His criminal record notwithstanding, Barry is elected to an unprecedented fourth term as the city's mayor.
1995: The Korean War Veterans Memorial opens to the public.
1998: The House of Representatives impeaches President Clinton over an intern sex scandal.
1998: A gunman opens fire in the US Capitol, killing two policemen.
1998: Tony Williams, who as Mayor Barry's CFO helped DC start its financial recovery, is elected mayor.
2001: Thousands protest as President George W. Bush takes office after a hotly contested election. No other president in history has received such a hostile un-welcome on the day of his inauguration.
2001: Terrorist attack destroys part of the Pentagon.
2001: Anthrax mailed to Senate offices causes short-term panic and massive mail disruptions.
2002: Snipers terrorize the region for three weeks, killing ten before being caught.
2004: World War II Memorial opens on the National Mall.
2004: The city's crime rate drops to mid-1980s levels. Wall Street upgrades DC to an A-level bond rating. *Forbes* ranks DC the nation's 4th Best Place to Start a Business or Career.
2004: NFT Washington DC is released. Millions rejoice.
2005: Baseball returns to DC as the Montreal Expos are relocated to become the Washington Nationals.

30 Essential DC Movies

Gabriel Over the White House (1933)
Mr. Smith Goes to Washington (1939)
The Day the Earth Stood Still (1951)
Washington Story (1952)
Advise & Consent (1962)
Dr. Strangelove or: How I Learned to Stop Worrying and Love the Bomb (1964)
The President's Analyst (1967)
The Exorcist (1973)
All the President's Men (1976)
Being There (1979)
The Man with One Red Shoe (1985)
St. Elmo's Fire (1985)
Broadcast News (1987)
No Way Out (1987)
JFK (1991)
A Few Good Men (1992)
Gardens of Stone (1987)
Dave (1993)
In the Line of Fire (1993)
The Pelican Brief (1993)
Clear and Present Danger (1994)
Forrest Gump (1994)
The American President (1995)
Nixon (1995)
Get on the Bus (1996)
Wag the Dog (1997)
Primary Colors (1998)
Minority Report (2002)
The Sum of All Fears (2002)
Fahrenheit 9/11 (2004)

Television

Call letters	*Station*	*Website*
4-WRC	NBC	www.nbc4.com
5-WTTG	Fox	www.fox5dc.com
7-WJLA	ABC	www.wjla.com
9-WUSA	CBS	www.wusatv9.com
20-WDCA	UPN	www.wdca.com
26-WETA	PBS	www.weta.org
28-W28BY	Government/NASA	
30-WMDO	Univision	www.univision.com
32-WHUT	PBS/Howard University	www.howard.edu/tv
43-WPXW	Pax	www.pax.tv
50-WBDC	WB	www.wbdc.com
64 WZDC	Telemundo	www.telemundo.com

Radio

AM Call Letters	*Dial #*	*Description*
WMAL	630 AM	News, Talk
WABS	780 AM	Religious
WCTN	950 AM	Religious
WTEM	980 AM	Sports
WUST	1120 AM	International
WMET	1150 AM	Talk
WWRC	1260 AM	Talk
WYCB	1340 AM	Gospel
WOL	1450 AM	Talk
WTOP	1500 AM	News

FM Call Letters	*Dial #*	*Description*
WAMU	88.5 FM	NPR
WPFW	89.3 FM	Jazz, Blues
WCSP	90.1 FM	Congressional Coverage
WETA	90.9 FM	Talk
WGTS	91.9 FM	Contemporary Christian
WKYS	93.9 FM	Hip Hop
WPGC	95.5 FM	R&B

FM Call Letters–ctd.		
WHUR	96.3 FM	Adult R&B
WASH	97.1 FM	AC
WMZQ	98.7 FM	Country
WIHT	99.5 FM	Top 40
WBIG	100.3 FM	Oldies
WWDC	101.1 FM	Rock
WGMS	103.5 FM	Classical
WWZZ	104.1 FM	Top 40, Nationals, baseball
WAVA	105.1 FM	Religious
WJZW	105.9 FM	Smooth Jazz
WJFK	106.7 FM	Talk
WRQX	107.3 FM	Hot AC
WTOP	107.7 FM	News
WHFS	www.whfs.com	Legendary and now defunct alternative radio station; available only online.

Print Media

American Free Press	www.americanfreepress.net	"Uncensored" national weekly newspaper.
The Common Denominator	www.thecommondenominator.com	Bi-weekly independent newspaper.
Georgetown Hoya	www.thehoya.com	Bi-weekly, college newspaper.
Georgetown Voice	www.georgetownvoice.com	Weekly, college newsmagazine.
GW Hatchet	www.gwhatchet.com	Bi-weekly, independent student newspaper.
The Hill	www.hillnews.com	Weekly, non-partisan Congressional newspaper.
The Hilltop	www.thehilltoponline.com	Howard University's student paper.
Metro Weekly	www.metroweekly.com	DC's "other" gay paper.
On Tap	www.ontaponline.com	Local entertainment guide, with reviews and event listings.
Roll Call	www.rollcall.com	Congressional news publication, published Mon-Thurs.
Washington Blade	www.washblade.com	Weekly, focused on gay community news.
Washington Business Journal	www.washington.bizjournals.com/	Weekly, DC business journal.
Washington City Paper	www.washingtoncitypaper.com	Free weekly newspaper, focused on local DC news and events.
Washington Examiner	www.dcexaminer.com	Conservative daily, covering DC and its immediate suburbs.
Washingtonian	www.washingtonian.com	Monthly, glossy magazine about DC life.
Washington Post	www.washingtonpost.com	Daily paper, one of the world's most prestigious.
Washington Times	www.washtimes.com	Daily, politics and general interest with conservative bent.
Voice of the Hill	www.voiceofthehill.com	Monthly, DC neighborhood newspaper.

Judging by the proliferation of doggie parks, residents of the District seem to take as much interest in their pooches as their donkeys or elephants. All neighborhoods have a least one green spot for Fido to frolic and take care of his less adorable business. Larger parks, like Rock Creek or Meridian, offer dogs and owners some serious romping opportunities. It's still a hassle to find animal-friendly apartments, but as long as renters are willing to cough up a bit more monthly, there are options.

General Rules for Parks

- Dogs must be under the owner's/handler's control.
- Only three dogs per person are allowed.
- No female dogs in heat allowed.
- Only dogs four months and older allowed.
- Dogs must be legally licensed, vaccinated, and wearing both current tags.
- Dog owners/handlers must keep their dog(s) in view at all times.
- Dogs must not be allowed to bark incessantly or to the annoyance of the neighborhood.
- Dog owners/handlers must immediately pick up and dispose of, in trash receptacles, all dog feces.
- Aggressive dogs are not allowed at any time. Owners/handlers are legally responsible for their dog(s) and any injury caused by them.
- Dogs must be on leash when entering and exiting parks/fenced areas.

Washington DC	*Address*	*Comments*	*Map*
Mitchell Park	22nd St & S St NW		3
Stanton Park	Maryland Ave & 6th St NE		3
Lincoln Dog Park	Capitol Hill, 11th St & N Carolina Ave SE	Busiest early mornings and early evenings. Water, benches, and lighting provided.	3
Congressional Cemetery	18th St SE & Potomac Ave	$100 dogwalker fee, plus $20 per dog buys unlimited off-leash roaming of the grass and tombstones.	5
Malcolm X/Meridian Hill	16th St b/w Euclid St NW & Union Ct NW	No off-leash.	16
Glover Park Dog Park	39th & W Sts NW	Popular weekday mornings and evenings.	18
Battery Kemble Park	Capitol Hill, MacArthur Blvd	Lots of wooded trails. Good parking. No off-leash.	32
Arlington			
Madison Community Ctr	3829 N Stafford St	Dogs not allowed on soccer field. Don't park in the back lot unless you want a ticket.	31
Glencarlyn Park	301 S Harrison St	Huge unfenced area near creek and woods. Restrooms, fountains, and picnic areas.	38
Barcroft Park	4100 S Four Mile Run Dr	Exercise area between bicycle path and water.	39
Benjamin Banneker Park	1600 N Sycamore St	Enclosed off-leash dog exercise area.	33
Fort Barnard	S Pollard St & S Walter Reed Dr	Fenced park with off-leash area.	39
Shirlington Park	2601 S Arlington Mill Dr	Fenced park with stream, paved trail, and water fountain.	39
Utah Park	3308 S Stafford St	Daytime hours only.	39
Clarendon Park	13 th, Herndon, & Hartford Sts	Unofficial dog exercise area (DEA).	35
Vienna Dog Park	700 Courthouse Rd SW	Fenced park with woodchip surface.	36
Alexandria			
City Property	Chambliss St & Grigsby Ave	Off-leash exercise area.	38
North Fort Ward Park	Area east of entrance. 4401 W Braddock Rd	Off-leash exercise area.	39
Duke Street Dog Park	5005 Duke St	Fenced dog park.	41
City Property	SE corner of Wheeler Ave & Duke St	Off-leash exercise area.	42
Tarleton Park	Old Mill Run, west of Gordon St	Off-leash exercise area.	43
Ben Brenman Park	Backlick Creek	Fenced dog park.	-
City Property	SE corner of Braddock Rd & Commonwealth Ave	Off-leash exercise area.	44
Hooff's Run	E Commonwealth Ave, b/w Oak & Chapman St	Off-leash exercise area.	44
Del Ray Dog Park	Simpson Stadium & Monroe Ave	Fenced dog park.	45
Founders Park, NE corner	Oronoco & Union Sts	Off-leash exercise area.	45
Montgomery Park	Fairfax & 1st Sts	Fenced dog park.	45
Powhatan Gateway	Henry & Powhatan Sts	Off-leash exercise area.	45
Windmill Hill Park	SW corner of Gibbon & Union Sts	Off-leash exercise area.	46
City Property	Edison St cul-de-sac	Off-leash exercise area.	43

General Information

DC Public Library Website:	www.dclibrary.org
Alexandria Library Website:	www.alexandria.lib.va.us
Arlington Library Website:	www.co.arlington.va.us/lib
Montgomery County Library Website:	www.montgomerylibrary.org

Overview

The Washington, DC Library system revolves around the massive main **Martin Luther King** branch downtown. Large in size, scope, and ugliness, this eyesore with dark, scary stairwells is better than it looks. Once you're able to overlook the homeless people taking naps outside (and often inside) the building, you'll appreciate its division of rooms by subject matter and the efficient, knowledgeable staff that can find you a 1988 National Geographic faster than you can say "Micronesia." If you don't have specific research needs, some of the other branches, notably **Georgetown's**, are more pleasant places to spend an afternoon. Then again, if you have time to spare and want both extensive research capabilities and luxe quarters, forget the local stuff and head over to the **US Library of Congress**.

■ = *Public* ■ = *By Appointment Only* ■ = *Other*

Type	*Library*	*Address*	*Phone*	*Map*
■ Public	Alexandria Charles E Beatley Jr Central Library	5005 Duke St	703-519-5900	41
■ Public	Alexandria James M Duncan Branch Library	2501 Commonwealth Ave	703-838-4566	43
■ Public	Alexandria Kate Waller Barrett Branch Library	717 Queen St	703-838-4555	46
■ Other	Alexandria Law Library	520 King St, Room L-34	703-838-4077	46
■ Other	American University Library	4400 Massachusetts Ave NW	202-885-3409	19
■ Public	Anacostia Library	1800 Good Hope Rd SE	202-698-1190	5
■ Public	Arlington Central Library	1015 N Quincy St	703-228-5990	34
■ Public	Arlington County Aurora Hills Library	735 18th St S	703-228-5715	40
■ Public	Arlington Public Library Information & Referral Office	2100 Clarendon Blvd	703-228-3000	36
■ By Appointment Only	Arthur R Ashe Jr Foreign Policy Library	1426 21st St NW	202-223-1960	9
■ Public	Bethesda Library	7400 Arlington Rd	240-777-0970	29
■ Other	Bureau of Alcohol & Tobacco Library	650 Massachusetts Ave NW	202-927-7890	10
■ Public	Cherrydale Library	2190 Military Rd	703-228-6330	34
■ Public	Chevy Chase Library	5625 Connecticut Ave NW	202-282-0021	28
■ Public	Chevy Chase Library	8005 Connecticut Ave NW	301-986-4313	23
■ Public	Cleveland Park Library	3310 Connecticut Ave NW	202-282-3080	17
■ Public	Columbia Pike Library	816 S Walter Reed Dr	703-228-5710	37
■ By Appointment Only	Comptroller of Currency Library	250 E St SW	202-874-9504	6
■ By Appointment Only	Department of State - Ralph J Bunche Library	2201 C St NW, Room 3239	202-874-4720	7
■ By Appointment Only	Dibner Library	12th St & Constitution Ave NW	202-633-3872	1
■ Other	DOT Law Library, Coast Guard Branch	2100 2nd St SW	202-267-2536	6
■ Public	Ellen Coolidge Burke Branch Library	4701 Seminary Rd	703-519-6000	41
■ By Appointment Only	Federal Aviation Administration Libraries	800 Independence Ave SW	202-267-3396	1
■ By Appointment Only	Federal Reserve Board Research & Law Libraries	20th St & Constitution Ave NW	202-452-3284	7
■ Other	Federal Trade Commission Library	600 Pennsylvania Ave NW	202-326-2395	2
■ Other	Foundation Center	1001 Connecticut Ave NW	202-331-1400	9
■ Other	General Services Administration Library	1800 F St NW	202-501-0788	7
■ Public	Georgetown Library	3260 R St NW	202-282-0220	8
■ Public	Glencarlyn Public Library	300 S Kensington St	703-228-6548	38
■ Other	Howard University School of Business Library	2600 6th St NW	202-806-1561	15
■ Other	International Trade Commission Library	500 E St SW	202-205-2630	6
■ Other	James Melville Gilliss Library	3450 Massachusetts Ave NW	202-762-1463	17
■ Public	Juanita E Thornton Library	7420 Georgia Ave NW	202-541-6100	27
■ Public	Lamond-Riggs Library	5401 S Dakota Ave NE	202-541-6255	14
■ Public	Langston Community Library	2600 Benning Rd NE	202-724-8665	4
■ Public	Martin Luther King Jr Memorial Library	901 G St NW	202-727-1111	1
■ Public	Mt Pleasant Library	3160 16th St NW	202-671-0200	16
■ Other	Nasa Headquarters Library	300 E St SW	202-358-0168	6
■ Other	National Clearinghouse Library	624 9th St NW	202-376-8110	1

Type	Library	Address	Phone	Map
■	National Endowment for the Humanities Library	1100 Pennsylvania Ave NW	202-606-8244	1
■	National Geographic Society Library	1145 17th St NW	202-857-7783	9
■	National Research Council Library	500 5th St NW, Room 304	202-334-2125	2
■	NOAA Central Library	1315 East West Hwy	301-713-2600	25
■	Northeast Library	330 7th St NE	202-698-3320	3
■	Office of Thrift Supervision Library	1700 G St NW	202-906-6470	1
■	Palisades Library	4901 V St NW	202-282-3139	18
■	Petworth Library	4200 Kansas Ave NW	202-541-6300	21
■	RL Christian Community Library	1300 H St NE	202-724-8599	3
■	Shirlington Library	2786 S Arlington Mill Dr	703-228-6545	39
■	Silver Spring Library	8901 Colesville Rd	301-565-7689	25
■	Southeast Library	403 7th St SE	202-698-3377	5
■	Southwest Library	900 Wesley Pl SW	202-724-4752	6
■	Sursum Corda Community Library	135 New York Ave NW	202-724-4772	11
■	Takoma Park Library	416 Cedar St NW	202-576-7252	27
■	Tenley-Friendship Library	4450 Wisconsin Ave NW	202-282-3090	19
■	Treasury Library	1500 Pennsylvania Ave NW	202-622-0990	1
■	U S Patent & Trademark Library	2021 S Clark Pl	703-308-4357	40
■	US Department of Commerce Library	1401 Constitution Ave NW	202-482-5511	1
■	US Department of Energy Library	1000 Independence Ave SW	202-586-5000	1
■	US Department of the Interior Library	1849 C St NW	202-208-5815	7
■	US Housing & Urban Development Library	451 7th St SW	202-708-2370	6
■	US Institute of Peace	1200 17th St NW	202-457-1700	9
■	US Library of Congress	101 Independence Ave SE	202-707-5000	2
■	US Senate Library	Russell Senate Office Bldg, B15	202-224-7106	2
■	US State Library	2201 C St NW	202-647-2458	7
■	Watha T Daniel Branch Library	1701 8th St NW	202-671-0212	10
■	West End Library	1101 24th St NW	202-724-8707	9
■	Westover Library	1800 N Lexington St	703-228-5260	33
■	Woodridge Library	1801 Hamlin St NE	202-541-6226	13

Computer Services

Computer Services	Phone
Action Business Equipment	703-716-4691
On Call 25/8	202-625-2511

Delivery/Messengers

Delivery/Messengers	Phone
QMS	240-223-3600
Road Runners	703-321-0100
Washington Courier	202-775-1500

Plumbers

Plumbers	Phone
All-Magnolia Services	202-829-8510
Brown's Plumbing & Drain Service	202-554-8152
Capitol Area Plumbing & Heating	301-345-7667
John G Webster	202-783-6100
KC Plumbing Services	800-823-4911
Plumbline Plumbers	202-543-9515
Roto-Rooter	202-726-8888
Smallenbroek Plumbing & Heating	202-237-6400
Vito	800-438-8486

Towing

Towing	Phone
Emergency-One	202-529-2205
Hook Em Up Towing	202-528-8435
Pro-Lift	202-546-7877

Locksmiths

Locksmiths	Phone
A 24 Hour Locksmith Service	202-582-0959
AALocksmith	703-521-4990
ADF Automotive	202-546-7877
Advanced Locks & Security	202-491-1058
At Once Locksmith	202-744-2620
Automotive Lockout	202-610-0600
Berry's Locksmith	202-667-3680
District Lock	202-547-8236
Doors and Devices	800-865-6253
JB's Locksmith	301-567-9283
Locksmith 24 Hours	202-636-4540
Metro Lock & Security	202-362-1882
Pop-A-Lock	202-331-2929
Safeway Locksmiths	202-986-2552

Copying

Copying	*Address*	*Phone*	*Map*
Reliable Copy	555 12th St NW	202-347-6644	1
Superior Group	1401 New York Ave NW	202-393-1600	1
Document Technology Centre	50 F St NW	202-379-1000	2
Lex Reprographics	900 7th St NW	202-289-1500	2
Document Technology	2000 M St NW	202-842-3300	9
Ikon Office Solutions	1120 20th St NW	202-452-1850	9
Sequential	1615 L St NW	202-293-0500	9
Imagenet	2000 M St NW	202-872-0700	9
Clicks Professional Copy	1424 K St NW	202-842-0788	10
Kinko's	1407 East West Hwy	301-587-6565	25
Kinko's	4809 Bethesda Ave	301-656-0577	29
Kinko's	2300 Clarendon Blvd	703-525-4239	35
Kinko's	685 N Washington St	703-739-0783	45

Gas Stations

Gas Stations	Address	Phone	Map
Amoco	1950 Benning Rd NE	202-399-8880	4
Texaco	1022 Pennsylvania Ave SE	202-543-6725	5
Amoco	2715 Pennsylvania Ave NW	202-338-0400	8
Amoco	400 Rhode Island Ave NE	202-635-4545	11
Amoco	45 Florida Ave NE	202-529-7400	11
Exxon	1 Florida Ave NE	202-635-1659	11
Amoco	1201 Bladensburg Rd NE	202-396-0545	12
Amoco	2210 Bladensburg Rd NE	202-635-1373	13
Texaco	1765 New York Ave	202-269-3048	13
Amoco	3701 12th St NE	202-269-4488	14
Amoco	3426 Georgia Ave NW	202-829-0969	15
Amoco	5001 Connecticut Ave NW	202-244-6975	20
Amoco	7605 Georgia Ave NW	202-723-7588	27
Amoco	6300 Georgia Ave NW	202-726-5300	27
Shell	6419 Georgia Ave NW	202-723-0762	27

Pharmacies	*Address*	*Phone*	*Map*
Rite-Aid	1815 Connecticut Ave NW	202-332-1718	9
CVS	2200 M St NW	202-296-9876	9
CVS	4555 Wisconsin Ave	202-537-1587	19
CVS	7809 Wisconsin Ave	301-986-9144	22
CVS	1290 East West Hwy	301-588-6261	25
CVS	6514 Georgia Ave NW	202-829-5234	27
CVS	6917 Arlington Rd	301-656-2522	29
CVS	3133 Lee Hwy	703-522-0260	35
CVS	5101 Duke St	703-823-7430	41
CVS	3130 Duke St	703-823-3584	42

Resume Services

HBR	1411 K St NW	202-842-0869	10

Veterinarians

Friendship Hospital for Animals	4105 Brandywine St NW	202-363-7300	19
Chevy Chase Veterinarian Clinic	8815 Connecticut Ave	301-656-6655	23

Hospitals

As hyper-stressed, Type-A workaholics, most Washingtonians are ripe for coronary disease, so it's a good thing there are many area hospitals to offer us recourse. Although district financing snarls have led to recent shutdowns, the District nevertheless remains equipped with state-of-the-art medical facilities ready to respond to emergencies of presidential magnitude. ("Jenna, call 911. Dad was watching football and eating pretzels again.")

The area's hospitals vary in terms of the level of service they offer. Stagger into some ERs, and unless you can produce an actual stab wound, you won't be seeing a doctor until at least three episodes of Judge Judy have screened. Other facilities treat patients like hotel guests. At the recently refurbished Virginia Hospital Center, rooms are set up to offer remarkable Arlington views, and in-patients are delivered meals by workers who sport bow ties and studs. Even more civilized is Sibley Memorial Hospital, where the emergency room feels like cocktail hour at the yacht club, and nurses squawk to patients about which congressman they shot up with saline the week prior. Many medical people assert that the region's top docs reside at Washington Hospital Center, although Washington Hospital *City* is a more apt title. Allow an extra hour just to park and figure out how to navigate its labyrinthine interior structure.

Hospital	*Address*	*Phone*	*Map*
Children's National Medical	111 Michigan Ave NW	202-884-5000	14
George Washington University	900 23rd St NW	202-715-4000	7
Georgetown University	3800 Reservoir Rd NW	202-444-2000	18
Howard University	2041 Georgia Ave NW	202-865-4600	10
Inova Alexandria	4320 Seminary Rd	703-504-3000	42
Northern Virginia Community	601 S Carlin Springs Rd	703-671-1200	38
Providence	1150 Varnum St NE	202-269-7000	14
Sibley Memorial	5255 Loughboro Rd NW	202-537-4000	32
Suburban	8600 Old Georgetown Rd	301-896-3100	22
Virginia Hospital Center	1701 N George Mason Dr	703-558-5000	34
Washington Adventist	7600 Carroll Ave	301-891-7600	26
Washington Hospital Center	110 Irving St NW	202-877-7000	14

Overview

There's always some mass gathering in Washington DC; from inauguration demonstrations to flower festivals, DC has it all. The best events are free and easily accessible by mass transit.

Event	*Approx. Dates*	*For more info…*	*Comments*
New Year's Eve	Dec 31/Jan 1		Celebrate the new year with music, art, and bitter freezing cold.
Martin Luther King's Birthday	Observed January 16	www.whitehouse.gov/kids/ martinlutherkingjrday.html	Music, speakers, and a recital of the "I Have a Dream" speech on the Lincoln Memorial steps.
Robert E Lee's Birthday (Virginia only)	January 19	703-235-1530	Yes, victors write the history books, but some losers' popularity endures. Robert E. Lee Memorial, Arlington Cemetery.
Chinese New Year	January 29	703-851-5685	Can you IMAGINE the debauchery of a 15-day American New Year's bash? Check it out on H Street in Chinatown.
Black History Month Celebration	February	www.si.edu	African American history at the Smithsonian.
Abraham Lincoln's Birthday	Observed February 12	703-619-7222	Reading of Gettysburg Address in front of the city's favorite marble hero.
George Washington's Birthday Parade	President's Day, February 20	800-388-9119	Parade and party in Alexandria for the city's other favorite guy.
St. Patrick's Day Parade	March 17	www.dcstpatsparade.com	Celebration of all things Irish in DC: music, food, oh, and beer too.
Smithsonian Kite Festival	Late March-early April	http://kitefestival.org	Watch adults attack kiddie play like a combat sport.
Washington Home & Garden Show	Mid-March	www.flowergardenshow.com	Check out the flora that actually enjoys this climate.
National Cherry Blossom Festival	March 25-April 9	www.nationalcherryblossom festival.org	One of the can't-misses…problem is the tourists think so too.
Filmfest DC	Early April	www.filmfestdc.org	For once see a flick before it opens in NYC.
White House Spring Garden Tours	Mid-April	www.whitehouse.gov	No politics, just flowers.
Shakespeare's Birthday	April 23	202-544-4600	To go or not to go. That is the question. Folger Shakespeare Library.
White House Easter Egg Roll	April 16	www.whitehouse.gov	No politics, just eggs.
Department of Defense/ Joint Services Open House	Mid-May	301-981-4600	The country flexes its muscles with an air show and other military might. FedEx Field.
St. Sophia Greek Festival	Mid-May	202-333-4730	Big, fat, Greek festival.
National Symphony Orchestra Memorial Day Weekend Concert	May 28	www.kennedy-center.org/nso	Easy on the ears—and wallet; it's free.
Memorial Day Ceremonies at the Tomb of the Unknown Soldier	May 29	www.arlingtoncemetery.org	Ceremonies at JFK's grave and Arlington Cemetery.
Memorial Day Ceremonies at the Vietnam Veterans Memorial	May 29	www.nps.gov/vive	Solemn memorial.
Memorial Day Jazz Festival	May 29	703-883-4686	Jazz in Alexandria.
Taste of DC Festival	Late May	www.tasteofdc.org	Nibble at snacks left out in the hot sun all day.
Virginia Gold Cup	May 6	www.vagoldcup.com	Horse race on the same day as the Kentucky Derby. Someone fire the marketing department.
Dance Africa DC	Early June	202-269-1600	A feat of feet.

Event	*Approx. Dates*	*For more info…*	*Comments*
Dupont-Kalorama Museum Walk Weekend	First weekend in June	www.dkmuseums.com/walk.html	Free admission to the city's smaller, quirkier, pricier exhibits.
DC Caribbean Carnival Extravaganza	Late June	www.dccaribbeancarnival.com	Caribbean music, food, and outrageous costumes.
Capital Pride	June 3-9	www.capitalpride.org	Huge, fun, funky, out and proud.
Red Cross Waterfront Festival	Mid-June	www.waterfrontfestival.org	If you fall out of the canoe, Clara Barton may rescue you.
National Capital Barbecue Battle	Late June	www.barbecuebattle.com	Hot and sticky BBQ on a hot and sticky day.
Independence Day Celebration	July 4	www.july4thparade.com	July 4th in America-town. Check out the parade. The fireworks are a must.
Bastille Day	July 14		No time to order freedom fries.
Virginia Scottish Games	Late July	www.vascottishgames.org	Kilts and haggis everywhere!
Hispanic Festival	Late July		Latin American celebration at the Washington Monument.
Annual Soap Box Derby	Early June	www.dcsoapboxderby.org	The one day parents let their kids fly down city streets in rickety wooden boxes.
Georgia Avenue Day	Late August		Parades, music, and food from the southern US and Africa.
National Frisbee Festival	Late August	301-645-5043	Don't fight it, join it.
National Army Band's 1812 Overture Performance	Late August	www.whitehouse.gov	No politics, just patriotic music.
DC Blues Festival	Early Sept	www.dcblues.org	Rock Creek Park gets down and depressed.
Kennedy Center Open House	Early Sept	www.kennedy-center.org	Check out the terrace and the Kennedy sculpture without shelling out for the opera.
Adams Morgan Day	Early Sept	www.adamsmorganday.org	Neighborhood that gets jammed nightly, gets jammed while sun's up.
White House Fall Garden Tour	Late October	www.whitehouse.gov	No politics, just leaf peeping.
Reel Affirmations Film Festival	Mid-October	www.reelaffirmations.org	Like Filmfest DC, except much more gay.
Marine Corps Marathon	Late October	www.marinemarathon.com	26 miles of asphalt and cheers.
Theodore Roosevelt's Birthday	October 27	www.theodoreroosevelt.org	Party for one of the other giant heads in North Dakota.
Civil War Living History Day	Early Nov	703-838-4848	The culmination of reenactment-stickler bickering. Fort Ward Museum.
Veteran's Day Ceremonies	November 11	www.arlingtoncemetery.org	Military ceremony in Arlington Cemetery.
Alexandria Antiques Show	Mid-November	703- 549-5811	Expensive old stuff.
Jewish Film Festival	Late November/ Early December	www.wjff.org	Like Filmfest DC, except much more Jewish.
Kennedy Center Holiday Celebration	December	www.kennedy-center.org	X-mas revelry.
Kwanzaa Celebration	December	www.si.edu	Celebration at the Smithsonian.
National Christmas Tree Lighting/Pageant of Peace	Mid-Dec to January 1	www.whitehouse.gov	Trees, menorahs, & Yule logs get lit at the White House Ellipse.
Washington National Cathedral Christmas Celebration and Services	Dec 24-25	202-537-6247	Humongous tree from Nova Scotia.
White House Christmas Candlelight Tours	Christmastime	www.whitehouse.gov	Still no politics, just religion.

Yes, DC's a great city for lessons in history and civics, but sometimes the kids just aren't in the mood for another tutorial on the system of checks and balances. If you check out some of the destinations on this list, you'll discover there's life beyond the mall when it comes to entertaining your mini-yous.

The Best of the Best

★ **Best Kid-Friendly Restaurant:** Café Deluxe (3228 Wisconsin Ave NW, 202-686-2233; 400 First St SE, 202-546-6768; 4910 Elm St, Bethesda, 301-656-3131). Parents breath a sigh of relief when they walk into a restaurant and see that the tablecloth is paper and the table is littered with crayons. At Café Deluxe, your kids can perfect their masterpieces while munching on entrees like buttered noodles, PB&J, cheese quesadillas, or pint-sized pancakes. The prices reflect that your companions are only half-size: Children's menu prices range from $2.50 to $3.95. Runner up: Buca di Beppo in Dupont Circle (1825 Connecticut Ave NW, 202-232-8466). Family-style Italian in a restaurant that will endlessly distract toddlers.

★ **Quaintest Activity:** Canal Boat Rides (1057 Thomas Jefferson St NW, 202-653-5190). Take a boat ride along the historic C&O canal in a boat pulled by mules. Park rangers in period clothing describe what life was like for families that lived and worked on the canal during the 1870s. Tours (one hour long) are held Wednesday—Friday at 11 am and 3 pm, and Saturday and Sunday at 11 am, 1:30 pm, and 3 pm. The boats fill up on a first come-first served basis. $8 adults, $6 senior citizens, $5 children.

★ **Funnest Park:** Rock Creek Park (5200 Glover Rd NW, 202-895-6070). An area of Rock Creek Park located on Beach Drive goes by the name of Candy Cane City—'nuf said. Leland Street is good for picnicking and has a playground, basketball courts, and tennis courts. Children's park programs include planetarium shows, animal talks, arts & crafts projects, and exploratory hikes.

★ **Coolest Bookstore:** A Likely Story Children's Bookstore (1555 King St, Alexandria, 703-836-2498, www.alikelystorybooks.com). The bookstore hosts weekly story times, writing workshops for kids, and special events almost daily during the summer. Story time for children 2+ is held every Wednesday at 11 am. Other events include foreign language story time and sing-a-long story times.

★ **Best Rainy Day Activity:** Smithsonian Museum of Natural History (10th St & Constitution Ave NW, 202-633-1000). The new Kenneth E. Behring Family Hall of Mammals is finally open! If the kids aren't too freaked out by life-sized stuffed animals, check out the 274 new taxidermied mounts. The IMAX is always a hit with kids and parents alike on rainy afternoons. The timeless kid-appeal of dinosaur exhibits also keeps the little ones entertained (if they weren't recently dragged here on a school trip). Admission is free and tickets are not required for entry. The museum is open daily from 10 am-5:30 pm, except on federal holidays.

★ **Sunny Day Best Bet:** National Zoo (3001 Connecticut Ave, 202-673-4800, nationalzoo.si.edu). This free and easily accessible zoo is guarunteed to be the best park stroll you've ever taken. Beyond the pandas and apes, there's also a Kids' Farm with cows, donkeys, goats, chickens, and ducks. Summer camps and classes are available to Friends of the National Zoo Family Members. The $50 membership fee also includes zoo birthday party reservations, free popcorn for your kids every time they visit, and a 25% discount on all activities that cost money. The zoo is open daily, and admission is always free. April-October buildings are open 10 am-6 pm, November-April from 10 am-4:30 pm.

★ **Neatest Store:** Barston's Child's Play (5536 Connecticut Ave NW, 202-244-3602). The store's long, narrow aisles are stocked with games, toys, puzzles, trains, costumes, art supplies, and books. It's never too early to start grooming a true shopohalic.

Parks for Playing

- **Cleveland Park** (3409 Macomb St NW). Climb a spider web, climb a wall, or catch a train. The park has separate play areas for younger and older children, picnic tables, basketball courts, a baseball field, and a rec center.

- **East Potomac Park** (Ohio Drive SW). Always a good bet with its miniature golf course, public pool, picnic facilities, and playground at the southern tip. An absolute must during Cherry Blossom season.

- **Friendship Park** (4500 Van Ness St NW, 202-282-2198). Plenty of slides, tunnels, swings, and climbing structures, as well as basketball and tennis courts, softball/soccer fields, and a rec center. If you need a break, there's plenty of shade and picnic tables.

- **Kalorama Park** (19th St & Kalorama Rd NW). While the shade is limited here, this is a large playground with a fence dividing big-kid from little-kid playgrounds.

- **Marine Reed Recreation Center** (2200 Champlain St NW, 202-673-7768). Plenty of shady areas to rest your old bones while the kids are devouring the massive jungle gym, slides, tennis courts, and basketball courts.

- **Montrose Park** (R & 30th Sts NW, 202-426-6827). For you: lots of open space, a picnicking area, and tennis courts. For your kids: swings, monkey bars, a sandbox, and a maze.

Rainy Day Activities

Rain ain't no big thang in the city of free museums, many of which cater to the height-and attention-challenged.

Museums with Kid Appeal

- **National Air and Space Museum** (Independence Ave & 4th St SW, 202-633-1000). Can you go wrong in museum that sells astronauts' freeze-dried ice cream? Kids can walk through airplanes and spaceships. Check out the Einstein Planetarium and the IMAX Theater. Open daily 10 am-5:30 pm. Admission is free but does not include special events or activities.
- **International Spy Museum** (800 F St NW, 202-393-7798, www.spymuseum.org). The sleek exhibits filled with high-tech gadgets and fascinating real-life spy stories make the hefty admissions tag totally worth it. Special family programs include making and breaking secret codes and disguise creation workshops. Twice a year, the museum even offers a Spy Overnight Adventure, which provides kids with a "behind the scenes" look at the life of spy. The museum is open daily, but hours vary according to season. Children under five enter free, adults pay $14, kids (11 and under) pay $11, and seniors (65+) pay $13.

- **National Museum of American History** (14th St and Constitution Ave NW, 202-357-2700, americanhistory.si.edu). While your kids will certainly love a glimpse of Dorothy's ruby red slippers, the hands-on section of this museum is where they'll *really* want to be. The Hands-On History Room allows kids to gin cotton, send a telegraph, or say "hello" in Cherokee. The Hands-On Science Room, for children over five, lets kids take intelligence tests, separate food dyes in beverages, or use lasers to see light. Museum admission is free, but tickets (which are also free) are required for the hands-on rooms during weekends and busy hours. The museum is open daily from 10 am-5:30 pm, except for Christmas.

Other Indoor Distractions

- **Bureau of Engraving and Printing** (14th & C Sts, SW, 202-874-3019, www.moneyfactory.com). We're all used to seeing money spent. At this museum, you can watch how money is made, although your kids will probably be most interested in watching the destruction of old money. Admission is free, however tickets are required March-August. General tours (the only way to see the museum) are given every 15 minutes from 10 am - 2 pm, Monday through Friday.

- **Discovery Theater** (1100 Jefferson Dr SW, 202-357-1500, www.discoverytheater.org). Puppet shows, dance performances and storytelling all under one roof. Performances are given daily at 10 am and 11:30 am, Monday through Friday, and Saturday at 11:30 am and 1 pm. Shows cost $5 for adults and $4 for children, with special group rates available. Kids ages 4 to 13 can also join the Young Associates Program, where they can learn to animate clay figures or make their own puppets.

- **National Aquarium** (14th St and Constitution Ave NW, 202-482-2825, www.nationalaquarium.com). At the nation's oldest aquarium you'll find 50 tanks with over 200 species. Open daily 9 am-5 pm, $5 adults, $2 children (2-10), $4 seniors.

Outdoor and Educational

Just 'cause you want to play outside doesn't mean you have to act like a hooligan! Here's a list of outdoor activities that mix culture with athleticism and offer up some surprisingly original forms of entertainment:

- **Fort Ward** (4301 West Braddock Rd, Alexandria, 703-838-4848, www.fortward.org). The best preserved Union fort in DC. Picnic areas are available, and the on-site museum has a Civil War Kids' Camp for ages 8 to 12 during the summer. The museum is open Tuesday through Saturday 9 am-5 pm and Sunday 12 pm-5 pm. Admission is free. The park is open daily from 9 am-sunset.
- **National Arboretum** (3501 New York Ave NE, 202-245-2726, www.usna.usda.gov). Covering 466 acres, the National Arboretum is the ultimate backyard. Picnicking is encouraged in the National Grove of State Trees picnic area. A 40-minute open-air tram ride is available and advised if you want to see everything. The Arboretum is open daily from 8 am-5 pm. Admission is free, but the tram will cost you $4 for adults and $2 for children 4-16.
- **Sculpture Garden Ice-Skating Rink** (7th St & Constitution Ave NW, 202-289-3360). The Sculpture Garden's rink is specially designed to allow views of the garden's contemporary sculptures while skating. It's like subliminally feeding your kids culture while they think they're just playing. Regular admission costs $6 for a two-hour session, and children, students, and seniors pay $5. Skate rental costs $2.50 and a locker rental costs 50¢.

Classes

- **Ballet Petite** (Several throughout DC area, 301-229-6882, www.balletpetite.com). Fundamental dance instruction mixed with costumes, story telling, props, acting, and music.
- **Budding Yogis** (5615 39th St NW, 202-686-1104, www.buddingyogis.com). Yoga for kids, teens, and adults. Special summer programs available.
- **Capitol Hill Arts Workshop** (545 7th St SE, 202-547-6839, www.chaw.org). Classes for children in art disciplines, tumbling, and Tae Kwon Do. If your kids are precociously cool, sign them up for the jazz/hip-hop class and watch them perform a Hip-Hop Nutcracker in December.
- **Dance Place** (3225 8th St NE, 202-269-1600, www.danceplace.org). Creative movement, hip-hop, and African dance instruction for kids.
- **Dancing Heart Center for Yoga** (221 5th St NE, 202-544-0841, www.dancingheartyoga.com) . Yoga classes for kids ages 4 to 13. Classes for children under eight are always structured around a story.
- **Imagination Stage** (4908 Auburn Ave, Bethesda, MD, 301-961-6060, www.imaginestage.org). Classes in music, dance, and theatre for kids and teens. Three-week summer camps also available.
- **Joy of Motion** (5207 Wisconsin Ave NW, 202-362-3042; 1643 Connecticut Ave, 202-387-0911, www.joyofmotion.org). Creative movement and fundamental dance instruction for children.
- **Kids Moving Company** (7475 Wisconsin Ave, Bethesda, MD, 301-656-1543, www.kidsmovingco.com) Creative movement classes for children nine months to eight years in a studio with a full-sized trampoline.
- **Kumon Math and Reading Program** (6831 Wisconsin Ave, Bethesda, MD, 703-338-7291, www.kumon.com). An after-school learning program in math and reading.
- **Music Tots** (4238 Wilson Blvd, Arlington, VA, 703-266-4571, www.musictots.com). Instruction in music, rhythm, and sound for children under five.
- **Musikids** (4900 Auburn Ave, Ste. 100, Bethesda, MD, 301-215-7946, www.musikids.com) Music and movement classes for newborns and toddlers.
- **Pentagon Row Ice-Skating** (1201 S Joyce St, Arlington, VA, 703-413-6692, www.pentagonrow.com). Skating lessons and birthday parties are available November- March.
- **Power Tech Tae Kwon Do** (2639 Connecticut Ave, 202-364-8244). Martial arts training for kids three and up.

- **Rock Creek Horse Center** (5100 Glover Rd NW, 202-362-0117, www.rockcreekhorsecenter.com). Riding lessons, trail rides, summer day camp, and equestrian team training. Weekly group lessons $45/hour, private lessons $80/hour, and one-week summer camp sessions cost $400.

- **Rock Creek Tennis Center** (16th & Kennedy Sts, NW, 202-722-5949, www.rockcreektennis.com). Five-week weekend tennis courses available for children at beginner and intermediate levels.

- **Round House Theatre** (4545 East West Hwy, Bethesda, MD, 240-644-1099, www.roundhousetheatre.org). The theatre has a year-round drama school and an arts-centered summer day camp program.

- **Sportrock Climbing Center** (5308 Eisenhower Ave, Alexandria, VA, 703-212-7625, www.sportrock.com). Kids learn to climb. 6- to 12-year-olds have the run of the place 6:30 pm-8 pm on Fridays. $18 adult, $7 children (12 and under). Hours: Tues-Fri: 12 pm -11 pm; Sat-Sun: 12 pm-8 pm.

- **Sur La Table** (1101 S Joyce St, Arlington, 703-414-3580, www.surlatable.com). At Sur La Table's junior cooking classes, kids are encouraged to (gasp!) play with food. Classes are for children aged 6-12 and groups are small and well organized.

- **Young Playwrights' Theatre** (2437 15th St, NW, 202-387-9173, www.youngplaywrightstheatre.org). Programs for children from Foutth Grade and up that encourage literacy, playwrighting, and community engagement.

Shopping Essentials

- **Barnes & Noble** (books)
  - 3040 M St NW • 202-965-9880
  - 555 12th St NW • 202-347-0176
  - 3651 Jefferson Davis Hwy, Alexandria, VA • 703-299-9124
  - 4801 Bethesda Ave, Bethesda, MD • 301-986-1761
- **Barston's Child's Play** (everything kids love) • 5536 Connecticut Ave NW • 202-244-3602
- **Benetton Kids** (kids' clothes) • 3222 M St NW • 202-333-4140
- **Borders** (books)
  - 600 14th St NW • 202-737-1385
  - 1801 K St NW • 202-466-4999
  - 5333 Wisconsin Ave NW • 202-686-8270
  - 1201 Hayes St, Arlington, VA • 703-418-0166
- **Children's Place** (kid's clothes) • Pentagon City, 1100 S Hayes St, Arlington, VA • 703-413-4875
- **Discovery Channel Store** (children's gifts) • Union Station, 50 Massachusetts Ave NE • 202-842-3700
- **Fairy Godmother** (toys & books) • 319 7th St SE • 202-547-5474
- **Full of Beans** (kids' clothes) • 5502 Connecticut Ave NW • 202-362-8566
- **Gap Kids and Baby Gap** (kids' clothes)
  - 2000 Pennsylvania Ave NW• 202-429-6862
  - 1267 Wisonsin Ave NW • 202-333-2411
  - 1100 S Hayes St, Arlington, VA • 703-418-4770
  - 5430 Wisconsin Ave, Chevy Chase, MD • 301-907-7656
- **Gymboree** (kids' clothes) • 1100 S Hayes St, Arlington, VA • 703-415-5009
- **Hecht's** (clothes, furniture, toys, books) • 12th & G Sts NW • 202-628-6661
- **Imagination Station** (books) • 4524 Lee Highway, Arlington, VA • 703-522-2047
- **Kids Closet** (kids' clothes) • 1226 Connecticut Ave NW • 202-429-9247
- **Patagonia** (clothes) • 1048 Wisconsin Ave NW • 202-333-1776
- **Plaza Artist Supplies** (arts & crafts) • 1990 K St NW • 202-331-0126
- **Ramer's Shoes** (children's shoes) • 3810 Northampton St NW • 202-244-2288
- **Riverby Books** (used books) • 417 E Capitol St SE • 202-543-4342
- **Sullivan's Art Supplies** (arts & crafts) 3412 Wisconsin Ave NW • 202-362-1343
- **Sur La Table** (pint-sized cooking supplies) •1101 S Joyce St, Arlington, VA • 703-414-3580
- **Tree Top Kids** (toys, books & clothes) • 3301 New Mexico Ave NW • 202-244-3500
- **Urban Outfitters** (clothes) • 3111 M St NW • 202-342-1012

Where to go for more information

www.gocitykids.com
www.ourkids.com
www.lilaguide.com

Dupont Circle is to DC's gay life what Capitol Hill is to the nation's politics. And just as politics seeps into most aspects of city life, the gay scene reaches far beyond Lambda Rising. In addition to the world's largest LGBT bookstore (just down the street from the bookstore where the first gay couple to be featured in the *New York Times'* "Weddings" met), there are gay and lesbian lifestyle newspapers, clubs, bars, and community groups scattered throughout the city. In short, Dupont Circle is a geographic reference as well as a state of mind, and the city is, for the most part, sexual-orientation-blind. While there are many LGBT residents in suburbs like Takoma Park, MD and Arlington, VA, they enjoy precious little visibility compared to their District counterparts.

Websites

Capital Pride • www.capitalpride.org
Educational website dedicated to DC's LGBT community. The organization is also responsible for the planning and development of the annual Capital Pride Parade.

DC LGBT Arts Consortium •
Consortium of various DC area arts organizations.

DC Dykes • www.dcdykes.com
Insiders guide for lesbians living in DC.

GayDC • www.gaydc.net
In depth and up-to-date network for DC's gay, lesbian, bisexual, and transgendered community.

GayWdc • www.gayWdc.com
Gay and lesbian website for DC restaurant and bar listings, local news and events, classifieds, and personals.

Gay and Lesbian Activists Alliance • www.glaa.org
GLAA is the nation's oldest continuously active gay and lesbian civil rights organization.

Pen DC • www.pendc.org
LGBT business networking group.

Slash DC, Gay & Lesbian Guide to DC • www.gaybazaar.com/dc
Information on gay and lesbian nightlife, media, and news.

Publications

Metro Weekly • 1012 14th St NW • 202-638-6830 • www.metroweekly.com
Free weekly gay and lesbian magazine— reliable coverage of community events, nightlife, and reviews of the district's entertainment and art scene.

Washington Blade • 1408 U St • 202-797-7000 • www.washingtonblade.com
Weekly news source for Washington's gay community.

Women in the Life • 1642 R St NW • 202-483-9818 • www.womeninthelife.com
Glossy quarterly magazine written by and for lesbians of color.

Woman's Monthly • 1718 M St NW • 202-965-5399 • www.womo.com.
DC's glossy lesbian monthly magazine.

Bookstores

Lambda Rising • 1625 Connecticut Ave NW • 202-462-6969 • www.lambdarising.com
When it opened in 1974, Lambda Rising carried about 250 titles. Today, the bookstore operates five stores in Baltimore, Maryland, Rehoboth Beach, Delaware, Norfolk, Virginia, and New York City, and serves as an information hub and meeting place for the Washington DC gay community.

Politics and Prose • 5015 Connecticut Ave NW • 202-364-1919 • www.politics-prose.com.
Popular bookstore and coffee shop with a small selection devoted to gay and lesbian literature.

Health Center & Support Organizations

Beth Mishpachah: District of Columbia Jewish Center • 16th & Q Sts, NW
DC's egalitarian synagogue that embraces a diversity of sexual and gender identities.

The Center • 1111 14th St NW • 202-518-6100 • www.thedccenter.org
A volunteer LGBT community organization in metro DC.

DC AIDS Hotline • 202-332-2437 or 800-322-7432

DC Black Pride • PO Box 77071, Washington, DC, 20013 • 202-737-5767 • www.dcblackpride.org
African American lesbian, gay, bisexual, and transgendered community group. Proceeds from Black Pride events are distributed to HIV/AIDS and other health organizations serving the African-American community.

Police Department's Gay and Lesbian Liaison Unit • 300 Indiana Ave NW • 202-727-5427 • www.gaydc.net/gllu/ • Staffed by openly gay and lesbian members of the police department and their allies. The unit is dedicated to serving the gay, lesbian, bisexual, and trans-gendered communities in the DC area.

Family Pride • PO Box 65327, Washington, DC, 20035 • 202-331-5015 • www.familypride.org
This group is dedicated to advancing the well-being of lesbian, gay, bisexual, and trans-gendered parents and their families.

Food & Friends • 219 Riggs Rd, NE • 202-269-2277 • www.foodandfriends.org
The organization cooks, packages, and delivers meals and groceries to over 1,000 people living with HIV/AIDS and other life-challenging illnesses in the greater DC area. Hosts annual "Chef's Best" fundraising dinner with notable volunteer chefs from around the region.

GLAAD DC • 1700 Kalorama Rd • 202-986-1360 • www.glaad.org
Gay and Lesbian Alliance Against Defamation DC chapter.

PFLAG DC • 1111 14th St NW • 202-638-3852 • www.pflagdc.org
Parents and Friend of Lesbians and Gays DC chapter.

Senior Health Resources • Temple Heights Station • PO Box 53453, Washington, DC, 20009 • 202-388-7900
Non-profit organization providing quality health related-services for the aging LGBT community.

Sexual Minority Youth Assistance League (SMYAL) • 410 7th St, SE • 202-546-5940 • www.smyal.org
Non-profit group for LGBT youth.

Whitman-Walker Clinic • 1407 S St NW • 202-797-3500 www.wwc.org
A non-profit organization that provides medical and social services to the LGBT and HIV/AIDS communities of metropolitan DC. Home to one of the oldest substance abuse programs in the US. The Lesbian Health Center at Whitman Walker's Elizabeth Taylor Medical Center, 1810 14th St, NW, offers top-quality health services (202-745-6131).

Sports and Clubs

Adventuring • PO Box 18118, Washington DC 20036 • 202-462-0535 • www.adventuring.org
All-volunteer group organizes group hikes, bike rides, and more for DC's LGBT community.

Capital Tennis Association • www.capitaltennis.org
Casual and organized tennis programs for the metropolitan gay and lesbian community.

Chesapeake and Potomac Softball (CAPS) • PO Box 3092, Falls Church, VA 22043 • 202-543-0236 • www.capsoftball.org
A friendly place for members of the LGBT community to play softball.

DC Aquatics Club • PO Box 12211, Washington, DC, 20005 • www.swimdcac.org
Swimming team and social club for gays, lesbians, and friends of the gay and lesbian community.

DC's Different Drummers • PO Box 57099, Washington, DC 20037 • 202-269-4868 • www.dcdd.org
Washington DC's Lesbian and Gay Symphonic, Swing, Marching, and Pep Bands.

DC Front Runners • PO Box 65550, Washington, DC, 20035 202-628-3223 • www.dcfrontrunners.org
Running is so gay!

DC Lambda Squares • PO Box 77782, Washington, DC, 20013 • www.dclambdasquares.org
GLBT square dance club.

DC Strokes • PO Box 3789, Washington, DC 20027 • www.dcstrokes.org
The first rowing club for gays and lesbians. They row out of the Thompson Boat Center on the Potomac.

Federal Triangles • 202-986-5363 • www.federaltriangles.org
Soccer club for the LGBT community.

Gay Men's Chorus of Washington DC: Federal City Performing Arts Association • 2801 M Street NW • 202-388-7464 • www.gmcw.org

Lambda Links • www.lambdalinks.org
Gay golf.

Lesbian and Gay Chorus of Washington DC • PO Box 65285, Washington, DC, 20035 • 202-546-1549 • www.lgcw.org

Washington Wetskins Water Polo • www.wetskins.org
The first lesbian, gay, and bisexual polo team in the United States.

Washington Renegades Rugby • www.dcrugby.com
A Division III club that actively recruits gays and men of color from the DC region.

Annual Events

Capital Pride Festival/Parade • 1407 S St NW • 202-797-3510 • www.capitalpride.org
Annual festival and parade honoring the history and heritage of the LGBT community in Washington DC. Usually held the second week in June.

DC Black Pride Festival/Parade • 202-737-5767 •866-942-5473 • www.dcblackpride.org.
The world's largest Black Pride festival, drawing a crowd of about 30,000 annually. Usually held Memorial Day weekend.

Reel Affirmations • PO Box 73587, Washington, DC, 20056 •202-986-1119 • www.reelaffirmations.org
Washington DC's Annual Lesbian and Gay Film Festival. Late-October.

Youth Pride Day/Week • PO Box 33161, Washington, DC 20033 • 202-387-4141 • www.youthpridedc.org
Usually held in early April. The largest event for gay, lesbian, bisexual, and transgendered youth in the mid-Atlantic region.

Venues

Gay

- **Bachelor's Mill** • 1104 8th St SE • 202-544-1931
- **The Blue Room** • 2321 18th St NW • 202-332-0800
- **Cobalt/30 Degrees** • 17th & R Sts NW • 202-462-6569
- **DC Eagle** (leather) • 639 New York Ave NW • 202-347-6025
- **Fireplace** • 2161 P St NW • 202-293-1293
- **Green Lantern/Tool Shed (upstairs)** • 1335 Green Court NW • 202-966-3111
- **Halo** • 1435 P St, NW 202-797-9730 • Non-smoking venue.
- **Hamburger Mary's/Titan Bar (upstairs)** • 1337 14th St NW • 202-232-7010
- **JR's Bar & Grill** • 1519 17th St NW • 202-328-0090
- **Omega DC** • 2123 Twining Ct NW • 202-223-4917
- **Pier Nine** • 1824 Half St SW • 202-484-3800
- **Remington's** • 639 Pennsylvania Ave SE • 202-543-3113
- **Secrets** 1345 Half St SE • 202-554-5141
- **Wet** • 56 L St SE • 202-488-1200
- **Windows** • 1635 17th St NW • 202-328-0100

Lesbian

- **Edge/Wet** (Wednesday) • 56 L St SE • 202-488-1200
- **Phase 1** • 525 8th St SE • 202-544-6831

Both

- **1409 Playbill** • 1409 14th St NW • 202-265-3055
- **Apex** • 1415 22nd St NW • 202-296-0505
- **Atlas Lizard Lounge** (Sunday) • 1223 Connecticut Ave NW • 202-331-4422
- **Banana Cafe** • 500 8th St SE • 202-543-5906
- **Chaos** (Wednesday - Ladies night) • 17th & Q Sts NW • 202-232-4141
- **Freddy's Beach Bar** • 555 S 23rd St S, Arlington, VA • 703-685-0555
- **Larry's Lounge** • 1836 18th St NW • 202-483-1483
- **Ziegfield's** • 1345 Half St SE • 202-554-5141

Now that the new Convention Center is open, DC is trying to establish itself as a convention town. But while the facility is tops, the surrounding neighborhood is still in "transition," which means nearby hotels are truly a mixed bag. The area's premiere hotels are the **Grand Hyatt** and the **Renaissance Washington DC.** Both have spacious rooms and efficient staff that cater to the business traveler. Those who seek less traditional accommodations should opt for the **Hotel Helix** in Logan Circle, which features bright, comfy, pop-art furniture and ultra-modern décor. Not quite "W" cool, but close. For the budget-minded, consider the **Four Points** on K Street. It's not fancy but the staff is friendly, efficient, and courteous and rates are usually quite low.

If you decide to opt for another budget hotel, be sure to ask to see rooms on different floors before you commit. It's not unheard of to walk through a gorgeous lobby, into an elegant elevator, and end up in a stark room reminiscent of a youth hostel (not that youth hostels themselves aren't an option, mind you…).

Don't forget that springtime not only brings cherry blossoms but also World Bank protestors to the area. While they probably won't be after you personally, they may keep you up half the night demonstrating against some of your fellow guests. So it's a good idea to double check the security measures before you book, especially in the Convention Center area. Some hotels have almost none. Others won't allow anyone on guest floors without a room key. While beefed-up security might seem like the way to go, remember that likely means you'll need to run downstairs at 10:30 pm to retrieve the pizza you ordered. Of course, the security issue is also a good thing to check if you're a protestor yourself.

Good deals and lovely rooms can be had just a short cab ride from the main Convention Center area. The **Wardman Park Marriott**, located close to the historic National Cathedral, may be part of a chain, but you'd never know it by the elegant, well-maintained building and grounds, as well as the ultra responsive staff. **The Renaissance Mayflower** is another nice departure from the "standard" hotel. It's in the heart of downtown, located close to top-end shopping, and it's steeped in history (a favorite stop of J Edgar Hoover; also where Monica Lewinsky gave her deposition). The hotel continues to draw plenty of celebrities for accommodations (think Kurt Russell) or drinks (think Sam Donaldson).

You should use the room rates and star ratings listed below as a guide only. You'll probably want to call or visit the hotel in question to get the most accurate room rates for the days you wish to stay. If you're booking in advance, we suggest checking out sites such as hotels.com, expedia.com, and pricerighthotels.com to see if they offer any special discounts for the time of your visit.

Map 1 • National Mall	*Address*	*Phone*	*Nightly Rate*	*Star Rating*
Courtyard by Marriott	900 F St NW	202-638-4600	249	★★★
Courtyard by Marriott	999 9th St NW	202-898-9000	309	★★★
Grand Hyatt	1000 H St NW	202-582-1234	189	
Hay-Adams Hotel	800 16th St NW	202-638-6600	395	★★★★
Hilton Garden Inn	815 14th St NW	202-783-7800	179	
Holiday Inn	115 14th St NW	202-737-1200	239	★★★★
Hotel Harrington	436 11th St NW	202-628-8140	99	
Hotel Washington	515 15th St NW	202-638-5900	235	★★★
JW Marriott	1331 Pennsylvania Ave	202-393-2000	379	★★★
Marriott Metro Center	775 12th St NW	202-737-2200	309	★★★
Sofitel Lafayette Sq	806 15th St NW	202-737-8800	179	★★★★★
Willard Inter-Continental	1401 Pennsylvania Ave NW	202-628-9100	449	★★★
Map 2 • Chinatown / Union Station				
George Hotel	15 E St NW	202-347-4200	309	★★★★
Holiday Inn	415 New Jersey Ave NW	202-638-1616	300	
Hotel Monaco	700 F St NW	202-628-7177	299	★★★★
Hyatt Regency	400 New Jersey Ave NW	202-737-1234	329	★★★★
Phoenix Park	520 N Capitol St NW	202-638-6900	269	★★★
Red Roof Inn	500 H St NW	202-289-5959	90	★★1/2
Washington Ct Hotel	525 New Jersey Ave NW	202-628-2100	199	★★★
Map 3 • The Hill				
Doolittle Guest House	506 E Capitol St NE	202-546-6622	175	

Map 5 • Southeast / Anacostia

Capitol Hill Suites	200 C St SE	202-543-6000	209	★★★★

Map 6 • Waterfront

Best Western - Capitol Skyline Hotel	10 I St SW	202-488-7500	189	★★★
Channel Inn	650 Water St SW	202-554-2400	140	★★★
Holiday Inn	550 C St SW	202-479-4000	189	
Loews L'enfant Plaza	480 L'Enfant Plz SW	202-484-1000	249	★★★
Mandarin Oriental	1330 Maryland Ave SW	202-554-8588	385	★★★★★
Residence Inn Capital	333 E St SW	202-554-0260	239	★★★

Map 7 • Foggy Bottom

Doubletree	801 New Hampshire Ave NW	202-785-2000	149	★★★
George Washington University Inn	824 New Hampshire Ave NW	202-337-6620	270	★★★
Hotel Lombardy	2019 Pennsylvania Ave NW	202-828-2600	129	★★★
River Inn	924 25th St NW	202-337-7600	179	★★★
State Plaza Hotel	2117 E St NW	202-861-8200	185	★★★
Swissotel Watergate	2650 Virginia Ave NW	202-965-2300	259	★★★★

Map 8 • Georgetown

Four Seasons	2800 Pennsylvania Ave NW	202-342-0444	525	★★★★
Georgetown Inn	1310 Wisconsin Ave NW	202-333-8900	179	★★★
Georgetown Suites	1000 29th St NW	202-298-7800	145	★★★
Georgetown Suites	1111 30th St NW	202-298-7800	145	★★★
Holiday Inn	2101 Wisconsin Ave NW	202-338-4600	159	
Hotel Monticello	1075 Thomas Jefferson St	202-337-0900	149	
Latham Hotel	3000 M St NW	202-726-5000	179	★★★1/2
The Ritz-Carlton	3100 South St NW	202-912-4100	549	★★★★★
Washington Suites	2500 Pennsylvania Ave NW	202-333-8060	209	★★★

Map 9 • Dupont Circle / Adams Morgan

1 Washington Cir	1 Washington Cir NW	202-872-1680	189	★★★
Beacon Hotel and Corporate Quarters	1615 Rhode Island Ave NW	202-296-2100	229	★★★1/2
Best Western	1121 New Hampshire Ave NW	202-457-0565	169	★★1/2
Capital Hilton	1001 16th St NW	202-393-1000	299	★★★
Carlyle Suites	1731 New Hampshire Ave NW	202-234-3200	159	★★★1/2
Churchill Hotel	1914 Connecticut Ave NW	202-797-2000	189	★★★1/2
Courtyard by Marriott	1600 Rhode Island Ave NW	202-293-8000	189	★★★
Courtyard by Marriott	1900 Connecticut Ave NW	202-332-9300	199	★★★
Dupont at the Circle B&B	1604 19th St NW	202-332-5251	150	★★★
Embassy Inn	1627 16th St NW	202-234-7800	139	
Embassy Row Hilton	2015 Massachusetts Ave NW	202-265-1600	199	★★★
Embassy Suites	1250 22nd St NW	202-857-3388	219	★★★
Fairmont	2401 M St NW	202-429-2400	429	★★★★
Four Points	2100 Massachusetts Ave NW	202-293-2100	230	★★★★
Four Points	2350 M St NW	202-429-0100	249	★★★★
Holiday Inn	1501 Rhode Island Ave NW	202-483-2000	160	★★★1/2
Hotel Madera	1310 New Hampshire Ave NW	202-296-7600	209	★★★1/2
Hotel Rouge	1315 16th St NW	202-232-8000	199	★★★
Jurys	1500 N Hampshire Ave NW	202-483-6000	165	★★★★
Jurys	2118 Wyoming Ave NW	202-483-1350	135	★★
Lincoln Suites	1823 L St NW	202-223-4320	199	★★★
Loews Jefferson	1200 16th St NW	202-347-2200	399	★★★★
Madison	1177 15th St NW	202-862-1600	359	★★★
Melrose Hotel	2430 Pennsylvana Ave NW	202-955-6400	199	★★★
Park Hyatt	24th & M Sts NW	202-789-1234	200	★★★★
Radisson Barcelo	2121 P St NW	202-293-3100	239	★★★
Renaissance Mayflower Hotel	1127 Connecticut Ave NW	202-347-3000	359	★★★★

Map 9 • Dupont Circle / Adams Morgan—*continued*

		Phone	Nightly Rate	Star Rating
Residence Inn by Marriott	2120 P St NW	202-466-6800	219	★★★
Ritz-Carlton	1150 22nd St NW	202-835-0500	499	★★★★
St Gregory Hotel & Suites	2033 M St NW	202-530-3600	249	★★★★
St Regis	923 16th St NW	202-638-2626	335	★★★★
Topaz Hotel	1733 N St NW	202-393-3000	239	★★★
Washington Hilton and Towers	1919 Connecticut Ave NW	202-483-3000	199	★★★
Washington Marriott	1221 22nd St NW	202-872-1500	159	
Washington Terrace	1515 Rhode Island Ave NW	202-232-7000	199	★★★1/2
Windsor Inn	1842 16th St NW	202-667-0300	159	
Windsor Park	2116 Kalorama Rd NW	202-483-7700	139	★★
Wyndham	1143 New Hampshire Ave NW	202-775-0800	279	★★★

Map 10 • Logan Circle / U Street

Comfort Inn	1201 13th St NW	202-682-5300	179	
DC Guesthouse	1337 10th St NW	202-332-2502	200	
Four Points	1201 K St NW	202-289-7600	299	★★★
Hamilton Crowne Plaza	1001 14th St NW	202-682-0111	259	
Hampton Inn	901 6th St NW	202-842-2500	189	★★★★
Henley Park Hotel	926 Massachusetts Ave NW	202-638-5200	169	★★★1/2
Holiday Inn Hotels	1155 14th St NW	866-270-5110	239	
Homewood Suites	1475 Massachusetts Ave NW	202-265-8000	199	★★★
Hotel Helix	1430 Rhode Island Ave NW	202-462-9001	189	★★★
Morrison-Clark Inn	Massachusetts Ave & 11th St NW	202-898-1200	169	★★★
Renaissance Washington, DC	999 9th Street NW	202-898-9000	309	★★★★
Residence Inn by Marriott	1199 Vermont Ave NW	202-898-1100	199	★★★
Swiss Inn	1204 Massachusetts Ave NW	202-371-1816	99	
Washington Plaza	10 Thomas Cir NW	202-842-1300	169	★★★
Wyndham	1400 M St NW	202-429-1700	279	★★★

Map 11 • Near Northeast

Downtown Motel	1345 4th St NE	202-544-2000	65	
Kellogg Conference Hotel	800 Florida Ave NE	202-651-6000	153	
Super 8 Motel	501 New York Ave NE	202-543-7400	95	

Map 12 • Trinidad

Travelodge	1917 Bladensburg Rd NE	202-832-8600	129	

Map 13 • Brookland / Langdon

Days Inn	2700 New York Ave NE	202-832-5800	109	

Map 16 • Adams Morgan (North) / Mt Pleasant

Kalorama Guesthouse	1854 Mintwood Pl NW	202-667-6369	85	

Map 17 • Woodley Park / Cleveland Park

Omni Shoreham	2500 Calvert St NW	202-234-0700	239	★★★★
Wardman Park Marriott Hotel	2660 Woodley Rd NW	202-328-2000	249	★★★

Map 18 • Glover Park / Foxhall

Georgetown University Hotel and Conference Center	3800 Reservoir Rd NW	800-228-9290	219	
Savoy Suites	2505 Wisconsin Ave NW	202-337-9700	259	★★★1/2

Map 19 • Tenleytown / Friendship Heights

Embassy Suites	4300 Military Rd NW	202-362-9300	199	

Map 20 • Cleveland Park / Upper Connecticut

Days Inn	4400 Connecticut Ave NW	202-244-5600	89	★★1/2

Map 22 • Downtown Bethesda

American Inn	8130 Wisconsin Ave	301-656-9300	139	
Bethesda Court Hotel	7740 Wisconsin Ave	301-656-2100	139	★★★
Four Points	8400 Wisconsin Ave	301-654-1000	149	★★★
Holiday Inn	8120 Wisconsin Ave	301-652-2000	165	★★★
Marriott	5151 Pooks Hill Rd	301-897-9400	229	★★★★
Residence Inn by Marriott	7335 Wisconsin Ave	301-718-0200	269	

Map 25 • Silver Spring

Days Inn	8040 13th St	301-588-4400	89	★★★
Hilton	8727 Colesville Rd	301-589-5200	159	★★★
Holiday Inn	8777 Georgia Ave	301-589-0800	179	

Map 27 • Walter Reed

Ramada Limited	7990 Georgia Ave	301-565-3444	95	

Map 29 • Bethesda/Chevy Chase Business

Holiday Inn	5520 Wisconsin Ave	301-656-1500	145	
Hyatt	1 Bethesda Metro Ctr	301-657-1234	289	

Map 33 • Falls Church

Econo Lodge Metro Arlington	6800 Lee Hwy	703-538-5300	129	

Map 34 • Ballston

Comfort Inn Ballston	1211 North Glebe Rd	703-247-3399	179	
Hilton	950 N Stafford St	703-528-6000	259	★★★
Holiday Inn	4610 N Fairfax Dr	703-243-9800	209	

Map 35 • Clarendon

Econo Lodge	3335 Lee Hwy	703-524-9800	75	

Map 36 • Rosslyn

Best Western	1850 N Ft Myer Dr	703-522-0400	149	★★
Hilton Garden Inn	1333 N Courthouse Rd	703-528-4444	169	★★★
Holiday Inn	1900 N Ft Myer Dr	703-807-2000	155	★★★
Hyatt	1325 Wilson Blvd	703-525-1234	149	
Key Bridge Marriott	1401 Lee Hwy	703-524-6400	239	★★★
Marriott	1533 Clarendon Blvd	703-528-2222	219	
Marriott	1651 N Oak St	703-812-8400	249	★★★
Motel Fifty Rosslyn	1601 Arlington Blvd	703-524-3400	119	
Quality Hotel Courthouse Plaza	1200 N Court House Rd	703-524-4000	149	★★
Quality Inn Iwo Jima	1501 Arlington Blvd	703-524-5000	139	
Virginian Suites	1500 Arlington Blvd	703-522-9600	159	

Map 37 • Fort Myer

Days Inn	3030 Columbia Pike	703-521-5570	89	★★
Highlander Motel	3336 Wilson Blvd	703-524-4300	75	

Map 38 • Columbia Pike

Hampton Inn	4800 Leesburg Pike	703-671-4800	139	★★★
Homewood Suites	4850 Leesburg Pike	703-671-6500	189	

Map 39 • Shirlington

Best Western	2480 S Glebe Rd	703-979-4400	139	

Map 40 • Pentagon City

Americana Motel	1400 Jefferson Davis Hwy	703-979-3772	99	
Courtyard by Marriott	2899 Jefferson Davis Hwy	703-549-3434	199	★★★
Crowne Plaza Hotels	1480 Crystal Dr	703-416-1600	179	
Crystal City Hotel	901 S Clark St	703-416-1900	70	
Crystal City Marriott	1999 Jefferson Davis Hwy	703-413-5500	239	★★★
Crystal Gateway Marriott	1700 Jefferson Davis Hwy	800-228-9290	239	★★★
Doubletree	300 Army Navy Dr	703-416-4100	229	
Embassy Suites	1300 Jefferson Davis Hwy	703-979-9799	189	
Hampton Inn	2000 Jefferson Davis Hwy	703-418-8181	177	
Hilton	2399 Jefferson Davis Hwy	703-418-6800	209	★★★
Holiday Inn	2650 Jefferson Davis Hwy	703-684-7200	259	
Hyatt	2799 Jefferson Davis Hwy	703-418-1234	235	★★★
Radisson Hotel	2020 Jefferson Davis Hwy	703-920-8600	189	★★★
Residence Inn by Marriott	550 Army Navy Dr	703-413-6630	239	★★★
Sheraton	1800 Jefferson Davis Hwy	703-486-1111	205	★★★
Sheraton	900 S Orme St	703-521-1900	189	★★★
The Ritz-Carlton	1250 S Hayes St	800-241-3333	499	★★★★★

Map 41 • Landmark

Comfort Inn Landmark	6254 Duke St	703-642-3422	89	
Hawthorn Suites Ltd - Alexandria	420 N Van Dorn St	703-370-1000	135	★★★
Hilton	5000 Seminary Rd	703-845-1010	169	★★★
Sheraton	4641 Kenmore Ave	703-751-4510	219	★★★★
Washington Suites	100 S Reynolds St	703-370-9600	189	★★★1/2

Map 42 • Alexandria (West)

Courtyard by Marriott	2700 Eisenhower Ave	703-329-2323	179	★★★
Homestead Studio Suites Hotel	200 Bluestone Rd	703-329-3399	99	

Map 44 • Alexandria Downtown

Embassy Suites	1900 Diagonal Rd	703-684-5900	199	★★★1/2
Hampton Inn	1616 King St	703-299-9900	164	★★★
Hilton	1767 King St	703-837-0440	149	★★★
Holiday Inn	2460 Eisenhower Ave	703-960-3400	168	

Map 45 • Old Town (North)

Holiday Inn	625 1st St	703-548-6300	189	
Radisson Hotel Old Town	901 N Fairfax St	703-683-6000	159	
Sheraton	801 N St Asaph St	703-836-4700	199	★★★

Map 46 • Old Town (South)

Best Western	1101 N Washington St	703-739-2222	129	
Holiday Inn	480 King St	703-549-6080	229	★★★★
Marriott	1456 Duke St	703-548-5474	259	★★★
Morrison House	116 S Alfred St	703-838-8000	224	★★★★★
Towne Motel	808 N Washington St	703-548-3500	69	
Travelodge	700 N Washington St	703-836-5100	79	

Between renaming buildings, bridges, and fountains and building new monuments by the garden-full, DC is fast running out of things to convert into memorials. You could spend a month visiting every official monument in DC, but you'll have a better time checking out the unofficial local landmarks that get lost in the giant shadows of the White House and Washington Monument.

Take a moment at Union Station to admire the **Columbus Memorial** out front. The marble fountain opened in 1912, but most visitors and commuters come and go and never take notice of it at all. The circular fountain is 44 feet deep in the middle, and Columbus himself stands at the larger-than-life height of 15 feet. When in Dupont, hang out by the **Dupont Fountain**—the focal point of the eclectic crowd that makes up the Dupont Circle neighborhood. In Silver Spring, head straight to the **AFI Theater** where you can catch an indie American or foreign film and watch it in the stadium seats usually associated with blockbuster releases. Need a break from the frenzied Georgetown shopping scene? Walk a few blocks to the city's best garden at **Dumbarton Oaks**. And when you find yourself on New Hampshire Avenue, be proud that DC is one of the few places to properly memorialize **Sonny Bono,** the hokey singer-turned-California congressman. Washington, DC's greatest tribute to families of tourists and uncanny juxtaposition is the **Merry-Go-Round** shoved into the middle of the National Mall among the stately **Smithsonian** museums. There is also the memorial on **Roosevelt Island** in the Potomac River and **Gravelly Point**, where locals go to exercise and picnic below departing and arriving commercial airplanes.

Architecturally, one of the most-overlooked complexes in DC is the **Watergate** complex, with its mixed-use facilities (hotel, apartments, offices, retail), curving facades, and *Logan's Run*-style aura. You might hate it, but you have to admit it's interesting nonetheless.

If your feet need a break from sightseeing and museum-going, take in a movie on the large screen at the historic and beautifully renovated **Uptown Theater** at 3426 Connecticut Avenue NW.

When your bad day allows you time, visit the 260,000 veterans' graves at **Arlington Cemetery** to pay respects and put your life into perspective.

Map 1 • National Mall

Clinton McDonald's	750 17th St NW • 202-347-0047	Taste what Bill couldn't resist.
Decatur House	748 Jackson Pl NW • 202-965-0920	Tour worth taking.
District Building	14th & E Sts NW	DC's City Hall.
Ford's Theater	511 10th St NW • 202-426-6924	Lincoln's finale.
Gatekeeper's House	17th St NW & Constitution Ave NW	Overlooked history.
Hay-Adams Hotel	16th St & H St NW • 800-853-6807	The luxury lap where Monica told all.
J Edgar Hoover FBI Building	935 Pennsylvania Ave NW • 202-324-3000	Ask to see Hoover's cross-dressing dossier.
National Aquarium	Commerce Building, 14th St NW & Constitution Ave • 202-482-2825	Save money, visit pet shop.
National Mall/ Smithsonian Merry-Go-Round	1000 Jefferson Dr SW • 202-633-1000	Tacky, but quells crying children.
National Press Club	529 14th St NW, 13th Fl • 202-662-7500	Join the ink-stained hacks for a drink.
Post Office Tower	1100 Pennsylvania Ave NW • 202-606-8691	315 feet tall with Bells of Congress.
Smithsonian Institute	1000 Jefferson Dr SW • 202-633-1000	Storm the castle for information.
St John's Church	16th St NW & H St NW • 202-347-8766	Sit in the President's pew.
The Willard Hotel	1401 Pennsylvania Ave NW • 202-628-9100	Free HBO!
World War II Memorial	17th St b/w Constitution Ave & Independence Ave • 202-639-4WW2	Honoring the 16 million Americans who fought in WWII.

Map 2 • Chinatown / Union Station

B Dalton	50 Massachusetts Ave NE • 202-289-1724	Meet me there. We'll do lunch.
Casa Italiana	595 1/2 3rd St • 202-638-0165	DC's half-block answer to Little Italy.
Chinatown Gate	H St NW & 7th St NW	Ushers you in for cheap eats and cheaper pottery.
Library of Congress	101 Independence Ave SE • 202-707-5000	Lose yourself in letters.
Newseum Front Pages	6th St NW & Pennsylvania Ave NW	Read up on hometown news.

Map 2 • Chinatown / Union Station—*continued*

Supreme Court of the United States	1st St NE • 202-479-3211	Bring your favorite protest sign.
US Botanic Garden	1st St SW b/w Maryland Ave SW and C St SW • 202-225-8333	Relaxing refuge.

Map 3 • The Hill

Folger Shakespeare Library	201 E Capitol St SE • 202-544-4600	To go or not to go?

Map 5 • Southeast / Anacostia

Anacostia Boathouse	1105 O St NE	Take the dirty plunge.
Congressional Cemetery	1801 E St SE • 202-543-0539	Individual graves, shared conditions.
Eastern Market	225 7th St SE • 202-546-2698	Apples and art.
Frederick Douglass House	1411 W St SE • 202-426-5951	A man who showed up his neighborhood and his country.
Washington Navy Yard	8th St SE & M St SE • 202-433-4882	Haven for men in tighty whites.

Map 6 • Waterfront

Arena Stage	1101 6th St SW • 202-488-3300	Great theater.
Ft Lesley J McNair	4th St & P St SW	For the Civil War buffs.
Gangplank Marina	6th St & Water St SW • 202-554-5000	A Washington Channel neighborhood of boat-dwellers.
Odyssey Cruiseline	6th St & Water St SW • 888-741-0281	Dining and dancing on the Potomac river.
Spirit of Washington	6th St & Water St SW • 202-484-2320	Experience Washington by boat.
Thomas Law House	1252 6th St SW	Impressive house, not open to the public.
Tiber Island	4th St b/w N St & M St SW	Looking for an apartment?
USS Sequoia	6th St SW & Maine Ave SW • 202-333-0011	Rent it when the VP isn't in the mood to play Mr. Howell.

Map 7 • Foggy Bottom

"Crossfire" Taping	805 21st St NW • 202-994-1000	Lowbrow partisan shoutfest.
Einstein Statue	Constitution Ave NW & 23rd St NW	At his rumpled best.
Kennedy Center	2700 F St NW • 202-416-8000	High-brow culture.
National Academy of Sciences	2100 C St NW • 202-334-2436	Scholars pushing the envelope.
The Octagon	1799 New York Ave NW • 202-626-7387	Peculiar floor plan.
Watergate Hotel	2650 Virginia Ave NW • 800-289-1555	Location of the most infamous Washington scandal.

Map 8 • Georgetown

Cooke's Row	3009 - 3029 Q St NW	Romantic row.
Dumbarton Oaks Museum and Gardens	1703 32nd St NW • 202-339-6401	An absolute treasure.
Exorcist Steps	3600 Prospect St NW	Watch your balance…
Islamic Center	2551 Massachussetts Ave NW • 202-332-8343	Oldest Islamic house of worship in the city.
Oak Hill Cemetery	3000 R St NW • 202-337-2835	Old and gothic.
Old Stone House	3051 M St NW • 202-426-6851	Fred and Wilma.
Prospect House	3508 Prospect St NW	Spectacular view of the Potomac.
Tudor Place	1644 31st St NW • 202-965-0400	Bring a picnic.
Volta Bureau	3417 Volta Pl NW • 202-337-5220	HQ of the Alexander Graham Bell Association for the Deaf.

Map 9 • Dupont Circle / Adams Morgan

Belmont House (Eastern Star Temple)	1618 New Hampshire Ave NW • 202-667-4737	National Women's party HQ.
Blaine Mansion	2000 Massachusetts Ave NW	Large, red, and brick.
Brickskeller	1523 22nd St NW • 202-293-1885	Get drunk on any beer imaginable.
Chinese Embassy	2300 Connecticut Ave NW • 202-328-2500	Look for the Falun Gong protesters.

DC Improv	1140 Connecticut Ave • 202-296-7008	Buy a shirt, get in Tuesdays for free.
Dumbarton Bridge	23rd St NW & Q St NW	It crosses Dupont to Georgetown.
Dupont Fountain	Dupont Cir	Top spot for people-watching.
Farragut Square	815 Connecticut Ave NW	Free lunchtime jazz concerts Thursdays in summer.
Freshfarm Market	20th St NW near Q St NW • 202-331-7300	Where yuppies get their fruit.
Gandhi Statue	Massachusetts Ave & 21st St	Don't peek under the skirt.
Heurich House	1307 New Hampshire Ave NW	It sure feels haunted.
Iraqi Embassy	1801 P St NW • 202-483-7500	Watch the hated old shell come alive.
Italian Cultural Institute	2025 M St NW • 202-223-9800	Learn how to whistle at babes like Romans.
Lambda Rising	1625 Connecticut Ave NW • 202-462-6969	DC's gay & lesbian gathering place.
Meridian Hill/ Malcolm X Park	15th & 16th Sts & W St NW	Sunday drum circle and soccer.
Middle East Institute	1761 N St NW • 202-785-1141	A Middle East Mecca…er, you know what we mean.
The Palm	1225 19th St NW • 202-293-9091	Aka, The Institute For Power Lunching.
Sonny Bono Memorial	20th St NW & New Hampshire Ave NW	Rest In Peace babe.
Temple of the Scottish Rite	1733 16th St NW • 202-232-3579	So that's what that is.
Washington Hilton	1919 Connecticut Ave NW • 202-483-3000	Where Reagan took a bullet.
Woman's National Democratic Club	1526 New Hampshire Ave NW • 202-232-7363	Presidents and First Ladies on walls.
Woodrow Wilson House	2340 S St NW • 202-387-4062	Another president's crib.

Map 10 • Logan Circle / U Street

African-American Civil War Memorial	1000 U St NW • 202-667-2667	A belated thanks.
Ben's Chili Bowl	1213 U St NW • 202-667-0909	Most beloved joint in the city.
Cato Institute	1000 Massachusetts Ave NW • 202-842-0200	Conservative temple.
Duke Ellington Mural	1200 U St NW	He's watching.
Lincoln Theatre	1215 U St NW • 202-328-6000	Renovated jewel.
Mary McLeod Bethune National Historic Site	1318 Vermont Ave NW • 202-673-2402	History without propaganda.

Map 12 • Trinidad

Mount Olivet Cemetery	1300 Bladensberg Rd NW	Visit Mary Suratt, hanged for her part in killing Lincoln.

Map 13 • Brookland / Langdon

Franciscan Monastery	1400 Quincy St NE • 202-526-6800	Beautiful gardens.

Map 14 • Catholic U

Brooks Mansion	901 Newton St NE	A Greek revival.
Grief in Rock Creek Cemetery	Rock Creek Church Rd NW & Webster St NW	Memorial to Adam's wife is best in the city.
Pope John Paul II Cultural Center	3900 Harewood Rd NE • 202-635-5400	When you can't get to The Vatican.
Shrine of the Immaculate Conception	400 Michigan Ave NE • 202-526-8300	Humungo Catholic Church.

Map 15 • Columbia Heights

Howard U Blackburn Center	2400 6th St NW • 202-806-5983	Jazz and blues.

Map 16 • Adams Morgan (North) / Mt Pleasant

Marilyn Monroe Mural	Connecticut Ave NW & Calvert St NW	A tiny bit of glamour for DC.
Meridian International Center	1630 Crescent Pl NW • 202-667-6800	Look out for the exhibits.

Map 16 • Adams Morgan (North) / Mt Pleasant—*continued*

Mexican Cultural Institute	2829 16th St NW • 202-728-1628	Top-notch work by Mexican artists.
Tryst Coffee House	2459 18th St NW • 202-232-5500	Canoodle here the way Chandra & Gary did.
White-Meyer House	1624 Crescent Pl NW • 202-667-6670	International art exhibitions.

Map 17 • Woodley Park / Cleveland Park

US Naval Observatory	Massachusetts Ave NW • 202-762-1467	VP's disclosed location.

Map 18 • Glover Park / Foxhall

C&O Towpath/ Canal Locks	Along the Potomac River	Scenic views minutes from cityscape.
National Cathedral	Massachusetts Ave NW & Wisconsin Ave NW • 202-537-6200	Newly-constructed old cathedral. Pure American.

Map 20 • Cleveland Park / Upper Connecticut

Rock Creek Park Nature Center	5200 Glover Rd NW • 202-895-6070	Nature in the city.

Map 22 • Downtown Bethesda

L'Academie di Cuisine	5021 Wilson Ln • 301-986-9490	One step up from learning to make french fries.
National Institutes of Health	9000 Rockville Pike • 301-496-4000	Monkeys and rats beware…

Map 25 • Silver Spring

AFI Theater	8633 Colesville Rd • 301-495-6720	Cool theater making the neighborhood cooler.

Map 27 • Walter Reed

Battleground National Military Cemetery	6625 Georgia Ave NW	Check out the entrance.
Walter Reed Army Medical Center	6900 Georgia Ave NW • 202-782-2200	Giant band-aid dispenser.

Map 28 • Chevy Chase

Avalon Theatre	5612 Connecticut Ave NW • 202-966-6000	Beloved neighborhood movie house.

Map 29 • Bethesda/Chevy Chase Business

Montgomery Farm Women's Co-op Market	7155 Wisconsin Ave • 301-652-2291	Indoor country market.
Saks Fifth Avenue	5555 Wisconsin Ave • 301-657-9000	The centerpiece of a material girl neighborhood.
Writer's Center	4508 Walsh St • 301-654-8664	Take a class, write for NFT.

Map 32 • Cherrydale/Palisades

Fletchers' Boat House	4940 Canal Rd NW • 202-244-0461	Boats, angling, and info.

Map 33 • Falls Church

The State Theatre	220 N Washington St • 703-237-0300	Favored venue for live music and private events.

Map 34 • Ballston

Ballston Commons	4238 Wilson Blvd • 703-243-6346	Big box invasion.

Map 35 • Clarendon

Market Commons	2690 Clarendon Blvd	Chain retail disguised as Main Street.

Map 36 • Rosslyn

Arlington County Detention Facility (Jail)	1425 N Courthouse Rd • 703-228-4484	We all make mistakes.
Arlington National Cemetery	Arlington National Cemetery • 703- 607-8000	Dear God.
Iwo Jima Memorial	Marshall Dr • 703-289-2500	Visit at night.

Map 37 • Fort Myer

Arlington Cinema 'N' Drafthouse	2903 Columbia Pike • 703-486-2345	Good movies, beer, pizza, waitresses, cigarettes. Life is good.
Bob and Edith's Diner	2310 Columbia Pike • 703-920-6103	Bargain breakfast 24/7.

Map 38 • Columbia Pike

Ball-Sellers House	5620 Third St S • 703-892-4204	Will be McMansion someday.

Map 40 • Pentagon City

Pentagon	Boundary Channel Dr • 703-697-1776	Rummy's playpen.

Map 41 • Landmark

Shenandoah Brewing Company	652 S Pickett St • 703-823-9508	Brew your own beer on site.

Map 42 • Alexandria (West)

Fort Ward Museum and Historic Site	4301 W Braddock Rd • 703-838-4848	Eerie; we fought each other.

Map 44 • Alexandria Downtown

George Washington Masonic National Memorial	101 Callahan Dr • 703-683-2007	The Masons. It's secret. Shhhh.

Map 46 • Old Town (South)

Alexandria Farmer's Market	301 King St • 703-379-8723	Get yer arugula.
Alexandria City Hall	301 King St • 703-838-4000	Founded in 1749.
Carlyle House	121 N Fairfax St • 703-549-2997	The kids will like it.
Gadsby's Tavern Museum	134 N Royal St • 703-838-4242	Many US Presidents slept here.
Market Square Old Town	301 King St	Bring your skateboard.
Ramsay House	221 King St • 70-838-4200	Alexandria's visitor center.
Stabler-Leadbeater Apothecary	105 S Fairfax St • 703-836-3713	Where GW got his Viagra.
Torpedo Factory	201 N Union St • 703-838-4565	Now it churns out art.

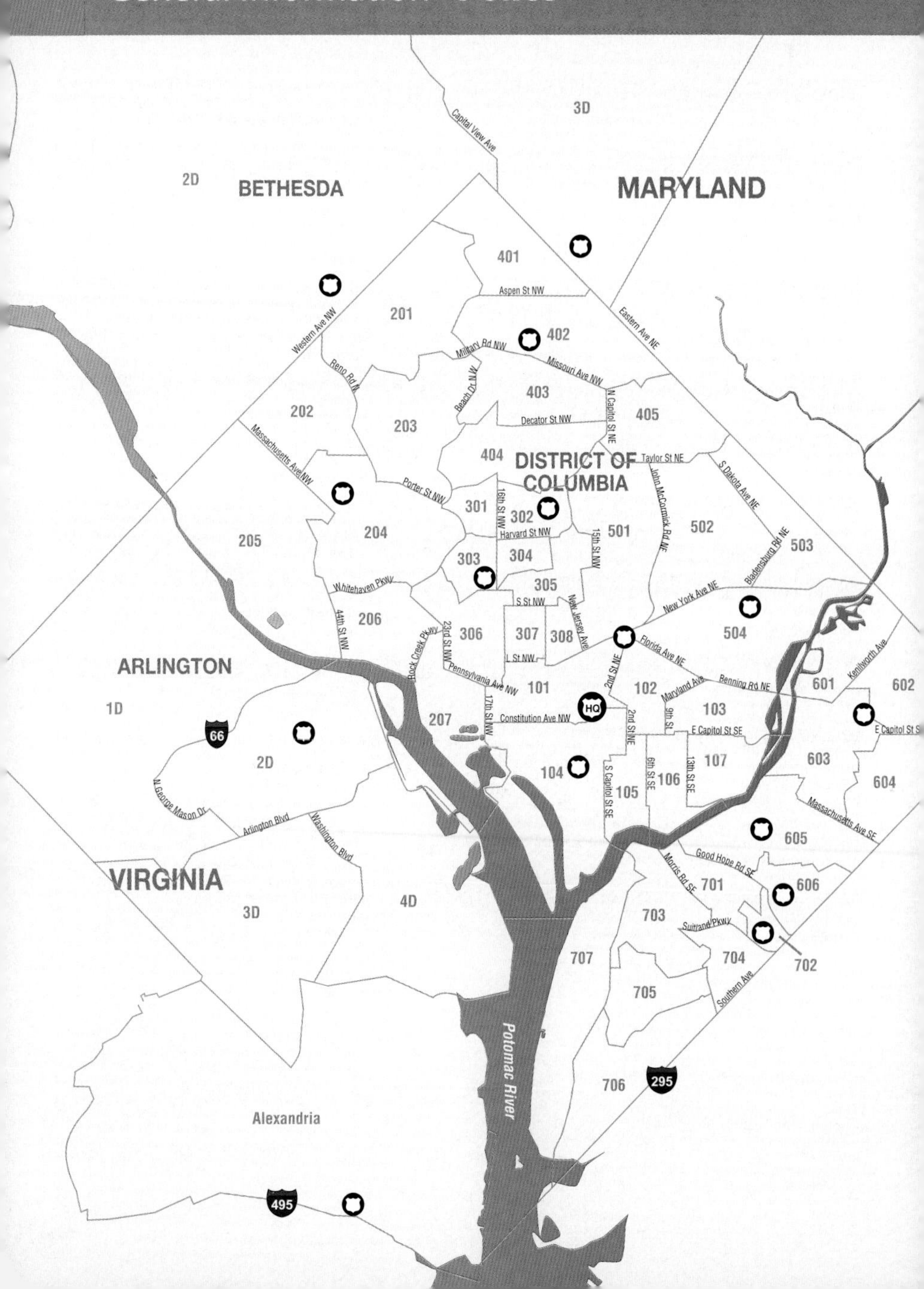

3D
Capital View Ave
2D
BETHESDA
MARYLAND
401
Aspen St NW
Eastern Ave NE
201
Western Ave NW
402
Military Rd NW
Missouri Ave NW
Reno Rd NI
Beach Dr NW
403
N Capitol St NE
405
202
203
Decator St NW
Massachusetts Ave NW
404
DISTRICT OF COLUMBIA
Taylor St NE
S Dakota Ave NE
John McCormick Rd NE
Porter St NW
301
16th St NW
302
501
502
Bladensburg Rd NE
503
205
204
Harvard St NW
15th St NW
303
304
305
Whitehaven Pkwy
S St NW
New Jersey Ave
New York Ave NE
44th St NW
206
Rock Creek Pkwy
23rd St NW
306
307
308
Florida Ave NE
504
L St NW
2nd St NE
Kenilworth Ave
ARLINGTON
Pennsylvania Ave NW
101
102
Maryland Ave
Benning Rd NE
601
602
1D
HQ
103
17th St NW
Constitution Ave NW
2nd St NE
9th St
E Capitol St SE
E Capitol St S
66
207
2D
104
S Capitol St SE
6th St SE
106
13th St SE
107
603
604
105
N George Mason Dr
Arlington Blvd
Washington Blvd
Massachusetts Ave SE
605
Good Hope Rd SE
Morris Rd SE
VIRGINIA
701
606
3D
4D
703
Suitland Pkwy
707
704
702
705
Southern Ave
Potomac River
706
295
Alexandria
495

Washington DC is divided into 44 Police Service Areas (PSAs). Each PSA is staffed with a minimum of 21 MPDC officers (with the exception of PSA 707, which essentially consists of Bolling Air Force Base). High-crime neighborhoods are assigned more than the minimum number of police. For example, PSA 105 has the minimum 21 officers, while 93 officers patrol the statistically more dangerous PSA 101.

Metropolitan Police DC

All Emergencies:	911
Police Non-Emergencies:	311
Citywide Call Center:	202-727-1000
Crimesolvers Tip Line:	800-673-2777
Child Abuse Hotline:	202-671-7233
Corruption Hotline:	800-298-4006
Drug Abuse Hotline:	888-294-3572
Hate Crimes Hotline:	202-727-0500
Public Information Office:	202-727-4383
Office of Citizen Complaint Review:	202-727-3838
Website:	mpdc.dc.gov

Stations Within NFT Coverage Area

Headquarters: 300 Indiana Ave NW • Map 2
First District Station• 415 4th St SW • 202-727-4655 • Map 6
First Substation • 500 E St SE • 202-698-0068 • Map 5
Second Substation • 3320 Idaho Ave NW • 202-282-0070 • Map 18
Third District Station • 1620 V St NW • 202-673-6815 • Map 9
Third District Substation • 750 Park Rd NW • 202-576-8222 • Map 15
Fourth District Station • 6001 Georgia Ave NW • 202-576-6745 • Map 27
Fifth District Station • 1805 Bladensburg Rd NE • 202-727-4510 • Map 12
Sixth District Station • 100 42nd St NE • 202-727-4520
Sixth District Substation • 2701 Pennsylvania Ave SE • 202-727-3622
Seventh District Station • 2455 Alabama Ave SE • 202-698-1500

Statistics	*2004*	*2003*	*2002*
Homicide	198	248	262
Forcible Rape	218	173	262
Robbery	3,057	3,836	3,731
Aggravated Assault	3,863	4,482	4,854
Burglary	3,943	4,670	5,167
Larceny/Theft	13,756	17,362	20,903
Stolen Auto	8,136	9,549	9,168
Arson	81	126	109

Alexandria Police (VA)

All Emergencies:	911
Non-Emergencies:	703-838-4444
Community Support:	703-838-4763
Crime Prevention:	703-838-4520
Domestic Violence Unit:	703-706-3974
Parking:	703-838-3868
Property-Lost & Found:	703-838-4709
Website:	ci.alexandria.va.us/police

Stations Within NFT Coverage Area

2003 Mill Rd • Map 44

Statistics	*2004*	*2003*
Homicide	2	4
Rape	31	26
Robbery	187	179
Aggravated Assault	213	192
Burglary	426	497
Auto Theft	635	640
Larceny/Theft	2,937	3,754

Arlington County Police (VA)

All Emergencies:	911
Non-Emergencies:	703-558-2222
Rape Crisis, Victims of Violence	703-228-4848
Child Abuse:	703-228-1500
Domestic Violence Crisis Line	703-358-4848
National Capital Poison Center:	202-625-3333
Website:	www.co.arlington.va.us/police

Stations Within NFT Coverage Area

1425 N Courthouse Rd • 703-228-4040 • Map 36

Statistics	*2003*	*2002*
Homicide	3	5
Rape	41	33
Robbery	212	213
Aggravated Assault	183	190
Burglary	408	425
Larceny/Theft	4,050	4,990
Auto Theft	662	676

Montgomery County Police (MD)

All Emergencies:	911
Montgomery Non-Emergencies:	301-279-8000
24-Hour Bioterrorism Hotline:	240-777-4200
Takoma Park Non-Emergencies:	301-891-7102
Chevy Chase Village Police:	301-654-7302
Animal Services:	240-773-5925
Community Services:	301-840-2585
Operation Runaway:	301-251-4545
Party Buster Line:	240-777-1986
Website:	www.montgomerycountymd.gov

Stations Within NFT Coverage Area

Chevy Chase Village Police • 5906 Connecticut Ave • Map 28
Takoma Park Police Dept • 7500 Maple Ave • Map 26

Statistics	*2003*	*2002*
Homicide	21	32
Rape	135	138
Robbery	1,004	877
Aggravated Assault	954	878
Burglary	4,095	3,874
Larceny	17,875	18,897
Auto Theft	3,489	3,722

Post Office	*Address*	*Phone*	*Zip*	*Map*
Benjamin Franklin	1200 Pennsylvania Ave NW	202-842-1444	20004	1
National Capitol Station	2 Massachusetts Ave NE	202-523-2368	20002	2
Northeast Station	1563 Maryland Ave NE	202-636-1975	20002	4
Southeast Station	600 Pennsylvania Ave SE	202-682-9135	20003	5
L'Enfant Plaza Station	437 L'Enfant Plz SW	202-842-4526	20024	6
Southwest Station	45 L St SW	202-523-2590	20024	6
McPherson Station	1750 Pennsylvania Ave NW	202-523-2394	20006	7
Watergate Station	2512 Virginia Ave NW	202-965-6278	20037	7
Georgetown Station	1215 31st St NW	202-842-2487	20007	8
Farragut Station	1800 M St NW	202-523-2024	20036	9
Temple Heights Station	1921 Florida Ave NW	202-234-4253	20009	9
Twentieth St Station	2001 M St NW	202-842-4654	20036	9
Ward Place Station	2121 Ward Pl NW	202-842-4645	20037	9
Washington Square Station	1050 Connecticut Ave NW	202-842-1211	20036	9
Martin Luther King Jr Station	1400 L St NW	202-523-2001	20005	10
Techworld Station	800 K St NW	202-842-2309	20001	10
Washington Main Office	900 Brentwood Rd NE	800-275-8777	20018	11
Woodridge Station	2211 Rhode Island Ave NE	202-523-2936	20018	13
Brookland Station	3401 12 St NE	202-842-3374	20017	14
Catholic University Cardinal Station	620 Michigan Ave NE	202-319-5225	20064	14
Columbia Heights Finance	3321 Georgia Ave NW	202-523-2674	20010	15
Howard University	2400 6th St NW	202-806-2008	20059	15
Kalorama Station	2300 18th St NW	202-523-2906	20009	16
Cleveland Park Station	3430 Connecticut Ave NW	202-364-0178	20008	17
Calvert Station	2336 Wisconsin Ave NW	202-523-2026	20007	18
Friendship Station	4005 Wisconsin Ave NW	202-842-3332	20016	19
Petworth Station	4211 9th St NW	202-842-2112	20011	21
National Naval Med Center	8901 Rockville Pike	301-941-2786	20889	22
Silver Spring Finance Centre	8455 Colesville Rd	301-608-1305	20910	25
Silver Spring Main Office	8616 2nd Ave	301-608-1305	20910	25
Takoma Park	6909 Laurel Ave	301-270-4392	20912	26
Brightwood Station	6323 Georgia Ave NW	202-726-8119	20011	27
Walter Reed Station	6800 Georgia Ave NW	800-275-8777	20012	27
Chevy Chase Branch	5910 Connecticut Ave NW	301-654-7538	20815	28
Northwest Station	5636 Connecticut Ave NW	202-842-2286	20015	28
Bethesda	7400 Wisconsin Ave	301-654-5894	20814	29
Bethesda Chevy Chase	7001 Arlington Rd	301-656-8053	20814	29
Friendship Heights Station	5530 Wisconsin Ave	301-941-2665	20815	29
Palisades Station	5136 Macarthur Blvd NW	202-842-2291	20016	32
North Station	220 N George Mason Dr	703-536-6269	22207	34
Arlington Main Office	3118 Washington Blvd	703-841-2118	22210	35
Court House Station	2043 Wilson Blvd	703-248-9337	22201	36
Rosslyn Station	1101 Wilson Blvd	703-527-7029	22209	36
Buckingham Station	235 Glebe Rd	703-525-0459	22203	37
South Station	1210 S Glebe Rd	703-979-2821	22204	37
Parkfairfax Station	3682 King St	703-933-2686	22302	39
Eads Station	1720 S Eads St	703-892-0840	22202	40
Pentagon Branch	9998 The Pentagon	800-275-8777	20301	40
Trade Center Station	340 S Pickett St	703-823-0968	22304	41
Theological Seminary Finance	3737 Seminary Rd	703-933-2686	22304	42
Potomac Station Finance	1908 Mount Vernon Ave	703-684-7821	22301	43
Memorial Station	2226 Duke St	703-684-6759	22314	44
Alexandria Main Office	1100 Wythe St	703-684-7168	22314	45

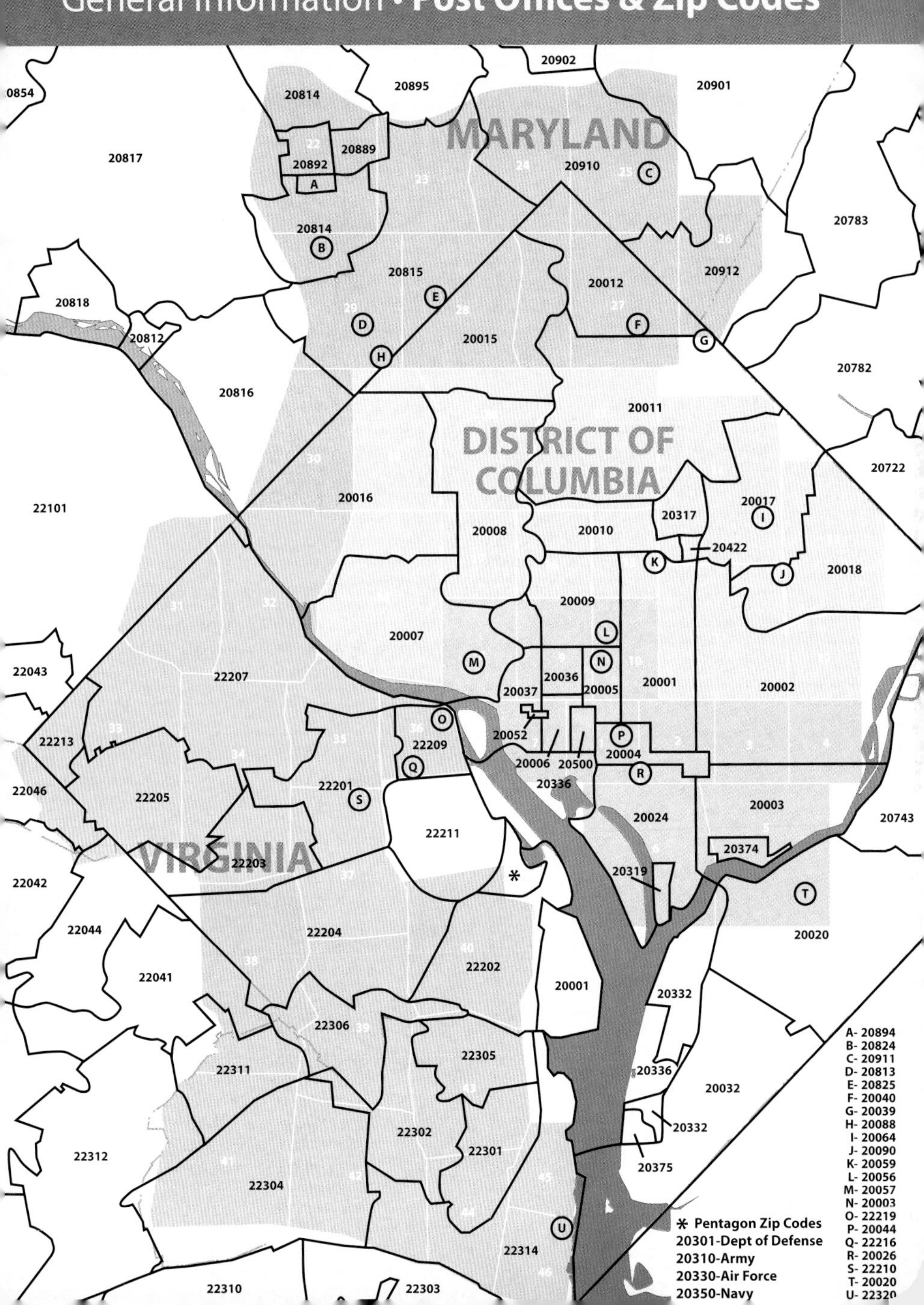
MARYLAND
DISTRICT OF COLUMBIA
VIRGINIA
0854
20814
20895
20902
20901
20817
20892
20889
A
20910
C
20783
20814
B
20815
E
20012
20912
20818
D
20812
H
20015
F
G
20782
20816
20011
20722
20016
22101
20017
I
20317
20008
20010
20422
K
J
20018
20009
L
20007
M
N
22043
22207
20036
20001
20002
20037
20005
O
20052
P
22213
22209
20006
20500
20004
Q
R
22046
22205
22201
S
20336
20003
20024
20743
22211
20374
22203
20319
22042
*
T
22044
22204
20020
22041
22202
20001
20332
22306
22305
20336
22311
20032
20332
22302
22312
22301
20375
22304
U
22314
22310
22303
A- 20894
B- 20824
C- 20911
D- 20813
E- 20825
F- 20040
G- 20039
H- 20088
I- 20064
J- 20090
K- 20059
L- 20056
M- 20057
N- 20003
O- 22219
P- 20044
Q- 22216
R- 20026
S- 22210
T- 20020
U- 22320
* Pentagon Zip Codes
20301-Dept of Defense
20310-Army
20330-Air Force
20350-Navy

Map 1 • National Mall

		Last pick-up
FedEx Kinko's	419 11th St NW	9:00
FedEx Kinko's	1445 I St NW	8:45
FedEx Kinko's	1350 New York Ave NW	8:30
Drop Box	1300 I St NW	7:15
Drop Box	700 13th St NW	7:15
Drop Box	1201 F St NW	7:00
Drop Box	1201 Penn Ave NW	7:00
Drop Box	1250 I St NW	7:00
Drop Box	1310 G St NW	7:00
Drop Box	1317 F St NW	7:00
Drop Box	1341 G St NW	7:00
Drop Box	1350 I St NW	7:00
Drop Box	1399 New York Ave NW	7:00
Drop Box	1455 Pennsylvania Ave NW	7:00
Drop Box	555 12th St NW	7:00
Drop Box	555 13th St NW	7:00
Drop Box	601 13th St NW	7:00
Drop Box	655 15th St NW	7:00
Drop Box	800 Connecticut Ave NW	7:00
Drop Box	888 16th St NW	7:00
Drop Box	900 17th St NW	7:00
Drop Box	1401 H St NW	6:45
Drop Box	1700 G St NW	6:45
Drop Box	1701 Pennsylvania Ave NW	6:45
Drop Box	600 14th St NW	6:45
Drop Box	740 15th St NW	6:45
Drop Box	1001 G St NW	6:30
Drop Box	1100 H St NW	6:30
Drop Box	1200 G St NW	6:30
Drop Box	1200 New York Ave NW	6:30
Drop Box	1212 New York Ave NW	6:30
Drop Box	1299 Pennsylvania Ave NW	6:30
Drop Box	1325 G St NW	6:30
Drop Box	1331 Pennsylvania Ave NW	6:30
Drop Box	1333 H St NW	6:30
Drop Box	1575 I St NW	6:30
Drop Box	1625 I St NW	6:30
Drop Box	1717 H St NW	6:30
Drop Box	1717 Pennsylvania Ave NW	6:30
Drop Box	400 N Capitol St NW	6:30
Drop Box	470 L'Enfant Plz SW	6:30
Drop Box	600 13th St NW	6:30
Drop Box	624 9th St NW	6:30
Drop Box	700 11th St NW	6:30
Drop Box	801 Pennsylvania Ave NW	6:30
Drop Box	805 15th St NW	6:30
Drop Box	815 14th St NW	6:30
Drop Box	815 Connecticut Ave NW	6:30
Drop Box	955 L'Enfant Plz SW	6:30
Drop Box	100 Raoul Wallenberg Pl SW	6:15
Drop Box	1000 Jefferson Dr SW	6:15
Drop Box	1025 F St NW	6:00
Drop Box	1201 New York Ave NW	6:00
Drop Box	1225 I St NW	6:00
Drop Box	1250 H St NW	6:00
Drop Box	1300 Pennsylvania Ave NW	6:00
Drop Box	1425 New York Ave NW	6:00
Drop Box	14th St NW & Constitution Ave NW	6:00
Drop Box	1620 I St NW	6:00
Drop Box	1725 I St NW	6:00
Drop Box	401 9th St NW	6:00
Drop Box	730 15th St NW	6:00
Drop Box	750 9th St NW	6:00
Drop Box	901 E St NW	6:00
Drop Box	901 F St NW	5:45
Drop Box	1200 Pennsylvania Ave NW	5:30
Drop Box	1455 F St NW	5:00
Drop Box	910 16th St NW	5:30
Drop Box	910 17th St NW	5:30

Map 2 • Chinatown / Union Station

		Last pick-up
Drop Box	20 Massachusetts Ave NW	7:00
Drop Box	600 New Jersey Ave NW	7:00
Drop Box	820 1st St NE	7:00
Drop Box	101 Constitution Ave NW	6:30
Drop Box	499 S Capitol St SW	6:30
Drop Box	500 New Jersey Ave NW	6:30
Drop Box	575 7th St NW	6:30
Drop Box	600 Maryland Ave SW	6:30
Drop Box	601 New Jersey Ave NW	6:30
Drop Box	601 Pennsylvania Ave NW	6:30
Drop Box	750 1st St NE	6:30
Drop Box	777 N Capitol St NE	6:30
Drop Box	810 1st St NE	6:30
FedEx Kinko's	325 7th St NW	6:30
Drop Box	122 C St NW	6:00
Drop Box	400 1st St NW	6:00
Drop Box	440 1st St NW	6:00
Drop Box	50 Massachusetts Ave NE	6:00
Drop Box	50 Massachusetts Ave NW	6:00
Drop Box	500 1st St NW	6:00
Drop Box	500 5th St NW	6:00
Drop Box	550 1st St NW	6:00
Drop Box	701 Pennsylvania Ave NW	6:00
Drop Box	10 G St NE	5:30
Drop Box	600 Pennsylvania Ave NW	5:30
Drop Box	1 Columbus Cir NE	5:00
Drop Box	401 F St NW	5:00
AB Shipping and Packaging	417 Massachusetts Ave NW	4:00

Map 3 • The Hill

		Last pick-up
FedEx Kinko's	208 2nd St SE	8:00
Drop Box	227 Massachusetts Ave NE	6:15

Map 5 • Southeast / Anacostia

		Last pick-up
Drop Box	715 D St SE	6:30
Drop Box	1201 M St SE	5:30
Drop Box	600 Pennsylvania Ave SE	5:30
Drop Box	1100 New Jersey Ave SE	5:00
Drop Box	300 M St SE	5:00
Drop Box	3rd St SE & M St SE	5:00

Map 6 • Waterfront

		Last pick-up
Drop Box	445 12th St SW	6:45
Drop Box	1330 Maryland Ave SW	6:30
Drop Box	400 Virginia Ave SW	6:30
Drop Box	600 Water St SW	6:30
Drop Box	7th & D St SW	6:30
Drop Box	901 D St SW	6:30
Drop Box	1900 Half St SW	6:00
Drop Box	400 6th St SW	6:00
Drop Box	409 3rd St SW	6:00
Drop Box	500 E St SW	6:00
Drop Box	1280 Maryland Ave SW	5:45
Drop Box	26 N St SE	5:30
Drop Box	550 12th St SW	5:30
Drop Box	80 M St SE	5:30
Drop Box	2100 2nd St SW	4:30
Drop Box	300 7th St SW	2:00

Map 7 • Foggy Bottom

		Last pick-up
Drop Box	431 18th St NW	7:30
Drop Box	1735 New York Ave NW	7:00
Drop Box	1776 I St NW	7:00
Drop Box	1875 I St NW	7:00
Drop Box	1922 F St NW	7:00
Drop Box	2025 E St NW	7:00
Drop Box	2100 Pennsylvania Ave NW	7:00
Drop Box	716 20th St NW	7:00
Drop Box	900 19th St NW	6:45
Drop Box	1747 Pennsylvania Ave NW	6:15

Drop Box	1730 Pennsylvania Ave NW	6:30
Drop Box	1919 Pennsylvania Ave NW	6:30
Drop Box	2001 Pennsylvania Ave NW	6:30
Drop Box	1750 H St NW	6:00
Drop Box	1801 Pennsylvania Ave NW	6:00
Drop Box	1899 Pennsylvania Ave NW	6:00
Drop Box	18th St NW & F St NW	6:00
Drop Box	2150 Pennsylvania Ave NW	6:00
Drop Box	2700 F St NW	6:00
Drop Box	600 New Hampshire Ave NW	6:00
Drop Box	800 21st St NW	6:00
Drop Box	924 25th St NW	6:00
Drop Box	1250 24th St NW	5:30
Drop Box	1808 Eye St NW	5:30
Drop Box	900 23rd St NW	5:30
Drop Box	1750 Pennsylvania Ave NW	4:00

Map 8 • Georgetown

		Last pick-up
FedEx Kinko's	1002 30th St NW	8:00
Drop Box	1055 Thomas Jefferson St NW	7:00
Drop Box	3000 K St NW	7:00
Drop Box	1000 Potomac St NW	6:00
Drop Box	1000 Thomas Jefferson St NW	6:00
Drop Box	24th St NW & Massachusetts Ave NW	6:00
Drop Box	3299 K St NW	6:00
Drop Box	3333 K St NW	6:00
Drop Box	1010 Wisconsin Ave NW	6:30
Drop Box	1101 30th St NW	6:30
Drop Box	2150 Wisconsin Ave NW	6:30
FedEx Kinko's	3329 M St NW	6:30
Drop Box	1215 31st St NW	6:00
Drop Box	2115 Wisconsin Ave NW	5:30
Drop Box	3520 Prospect St NW	5:30
Drop Box	2121 Wisconsin Ave NW	5:00
Westend Press	2445 M St NW	4:00

Map 9 • Dupont Circle / Adams Morgan

		Last pick-up
FedEx Kinko's	1 Dupont Cir NW	8:45
FedEx Kinko's	1029 17th St NW	8:45
FedEx Kinko's	1825 K St NW	8:30
FedEx Kinko's	1123 18th St NW	8:30
FedEx Kinko's	1019 15th St NW	8:00
Drop Box	1001 16th St NW	7:30
Drop Box	1901 L St NW	7:15
Drop Box	2020 K St NW	7:15
Drop Box	1015 18th St NW	7:00
Drop Box	1101 Connecticut Ave NW	7:00
Drop Box	1111 19th St NW	7:00
Drop Box	1120 20th St NW	7:00
Drop Box	1129 20th St NW	7:00
Drop Box	1133 20th St NW	7:00
Drop Box	1145 17th St NW	7:00
Drop Box	1150 17th St NW	7:00
Drop Box	1155 21st St NW	7:00
Drop Box	1200 18th St NW	7:00
Drop Box	1201 15th St NW	7:00
Drop Box	1201 Connecticut Ave NW	7:00
Drop Box	1220 19th St NW	7:00
Drop Box	1250 Connecticut Ave NW	7:00
Drop Box	1400 16th St NW	7:00
Drop Box	1501 K St NW	7:00
Drop Box	1615 M St NW	7:00
Drop Box	1616 P St NW	7:00
Drop Box	1666 K St NW	7:00
Drop Box	1801 L St NW	7:00
Drop Box	1828 L St NW	7:00
Drop Box	1850 K St NW	7:00
Drop Box	1900 K St NW	7:00
Drop Box	1920 N St NW	7:00
Drop Box	1921 Florida Ave NW	7:00
Drop Box	1925 K St NW	7:00
Drop Box	2000 K St NW	7:00
Drop Box	2000 L St NW	7:00
Drop Box	2001 L St NW	7:00
Drop Box	2401 Pennsylvania Ave NW	7:00
Drop Box	1025 Connecticut Ave NW	6:45
Drop Box	1625 K St NW	6:45
Drop Box	1800 Massachusetts Ave NW	6:45
Drop Box	11 Dupont Cir NW	6:30
Drop Box	1101 17th St NW	6:30
Drop Box	1133 21st St NW	6:30
Drop Box	1133 Connecticut Ave NW	6:30
Drop Box	1150 22nd St NW	6:30
Drop Box	1155 16th St NW	6:30
Drop Box	1155 Connecticut Ave NW	6:30
Drop Box	1156 15th St NW	6:30
Drop Box	1225 Connecticut Ave NW	6:30
Drop Box	1255 23rd St NW	6:30
Drop Box	1330 Connecticut Ave NW	6:30
Drop Box	1500 K St NW	6:30
Drop Box	1608 Rhode Island Ave NW	6:30
Drop Box	1612 K St NW	6:30
Drop Box	1620 L St NW	6:30
Drop Box	1717 Rhode Island Ave NW	6:30
Drop Box	1725 Desales St NW	6:30
Drop Box	1785 Massachusetts Ave NW	6:30
Drop Box	2001 K St NW	6:30
Drop Box	2030 M St NW	6:30
Drop Box	2033 K St NW	6:30
Drop Box	2121 K St NW	6:30
Drop Box	2300 M St NW	6:30
Drop Box	2440 M St NW	6:30
FedEx Kinko's	1612 K St NW	6:30
Drop Box	1100 17th St NW	6:00
Drop Box	1133 15th St NW	6:00
Drop Box	1150 Connecticut Ave NW	6:00
Drop Box	1300 Connecticut Ave NW	6:00
Drop Box	1350 Connecticut Ave NW	6:00
Drop Box	1501 M St NW	6:00
Drop Box	1666 Connecticut Ave NW	6:00
Drop Box	1700 K St NW	6:00
Drop Box	1776 Massachusetts Ave NW	6:00
Drop Box	1819 L St NW	6:00
Drop Box	1825 Connecticut Ave NW	6:00
Drop Box	1909 K St NW	6:00
Drop Box	2001 M St NW	6:00
Drop Box	2311 M St NW	6:00
Drop Box	1211 Connecticut Ave NW	5:45
Drop Box	1730 M St NW	5:45
Drop Box	1733 Connecticut Ave NW	5:45
Drop Box	2120 L St NW	5:45
Drop Box	1120 Connecticut Ave NW	5:30
Drop Box	1140 Connecticut Ave NW	5:30
Drop Box	1300 19th St NW	5:30
Drop Box	1529 18th St NW	5:30
Drop Box	1600 K St NW	5:30
Drop Box	1717 Massachusetts Ave NW	5:30
Drop Box	1725 K St NW	5:30
Drop Box	1899 L St NW	5:30
Drop Box	1900 M St NW	5:30
Drop Box	1920 L St NW	5:30
Drop Box	2175 K St NW	5:30
Ez Business Services	1929 18th St NW	5:30
Drop Box	1200 17th St NW	5:00
Drop Box	2021 K St NW	5:00
Drop Box	1050 Connecticut Ave NW	4:00
Drop Box	1875 Connecticut Ave NW	4:00

Map 10 • Logan Circle / U Street

		Last pick-up
Drop Box	1090 Vermont Ave NW	7:30
Drop Box	1100 L St NW	7:00
Drop Box	1101 14th St NW	7:00
Drop Box	1275 K St NW	7:00
Drop Box	1301 K St NW	7:00

Map 10 • Logan Circle / U Street—*continued*

		Last pick-up
Drop Box	1436 U St NW	7:00
Drop Box	1915 14th St NW	7:00
Drop Box	901 New York Ave NW	7:00
Drop Box	1101 Vermont Ave NW	6:45
Drop Box	1 Thomas Cir NW	6:30
Drop Box	1120 Vermont Ave NW	6:30
Drop Box	1200 K St NW	6:30
Drop Box	1425 K St NW	6:15
Drop Box	1010 Massachusetts Ave NW	6:00
Drop Box	800 K St NW	5:45
Drop Box	1100 13th St NW	5:30
Drop Box	1110 Vermont Ave NW	5:30
Drop Box	1220 L St NW	5:30
Drop Box	1401 K St NW	5:30
Drop Box	1420 K St NW	5:30
Drop Box	520 W St NW	5:30
Drop Box	1400 K St NW	5:00
Drop Box	1400 L St NW	4:30
Drop Box	1099 14th St NW	3:45
Mkm Pnet	801 Mt Vernon Pl NW	3:00

Map 11 • Near Northeast

		Last pick-up
FedEx Kinko's	1501 Eckington Pl NE	8:30
Drop Box	416 Florida Ave NW	7:00
Drop Box	300 I St NE	6:30
Drop Box	900 2nd St NE	6:00
Drop Box	800 N Capitol St NW	5:30
Drop Box	900 Brentwood Rd NE	5:30
Drop Box	800 Florida Ave NE	5:00

Map 14 • Catholic U

		Last pick-up
Drop Box	100 Irving St NW	6:30
Drop Box	110 Irving St NW	6:30
Drop Box	3401 12th St NE	6:30
Drop Box	1150 Varnum St NE	6:00
Drop Box	620 Michigan Ave NE	6:00
Drop Box	216 Michigan Ave NE	5:30
Drop Box	3211 4th St NE	5:30

Map 15 • Columbia Heights

		Last pick-up
Drop Box	2400 6th St NW	5:30

Map 16 • Adams Morgan (North) / Mt Pleasant

		Last pick-up
Tech Printing	2479 18th St NW	5:30

Map 17 • Woodley Park / Cleveland Park

		Last pick-up
Drop Box	2500 Calvert St NW	7:00
Drop Box	3430 Connecticut Ave NW	6:00
Drop Box	3000 Connecticut Ave NW	5:30
Drop Box	3100 Massachusetts Ave NW	3:00

Map 18 • Glover Park / Foxhall

		Last pick-up
Drop Box	3301 New Mexico Ave NW	7:15
Drop Box	3400 Idaho Ave NW	7:00
Drop Box	3970 Reservoir Rd NW	6:45
Drop Box	PHC Building, 4000 Reservoir Rd NW	6:45
Drop Box	2233 Wisconsin Ave NW	6:30
Drop Box	Healy Hall, 3800 Reservoir Rd NW,	6:30
Drop Box	4400 MacArthur Blvd NW	6:30
Drop Box	Lombardi Cancer Ctr, 3800 Reservoir Rd NW	6:00
Drop Box	4000 Reservoir Rd NW	6:00

Map 19 • Tenleytown / Friendship Heights

FedEx Kinko's	4000 Wisconsin Ave NW	8:00
Drop Box	5335 Wisconsin Ave NW	7:00
Drop Box	4005 Wisconsin Ave NW	6:30
Drop Box	5225 Wisconsin Ave NW	6:30
Drop Box	5301 Wisconsin Ave NW	6:30
Drop Box	4400 Massachusetts Ave NW	6:00
Drop Box	4400 Jenifer St NW	5:30
Drop Box	4620 Wisconsin Ave NW	5:30

Map 20 • Cleveland Park / Upper Connecticut

		Last pick-up
Drop Box	4201 Connecticut Ave NW	6:30
Drop Box	4301 Connecticut Ave NW	6:00
Parcel Plus	3509 Connecticut Ave NW	6:00
Drop Box	2900 Van Ness St NW	5:30
Drop Box	4455 Connecticut Ave NW	5:30

Map 22 • Downtown Bethesda

		Last pick-up
Drop Box	4833 Rugby Ave	7:00
Drop Box	9030 Old Georgetown Rd	7:00
Drop Box	9650 Rockville Pike	7:00
Drop Box	7960 Old Georgetown Rd	6:45
Drop Box	1 Cloister Ct	6:30
Drop Box	2 Center Dr Building	6:30
Drop Box	7910 Woodmont Ave	6:30
Drop Box	8001 Wisconsin Ave	6:30
Drop Box	7920 Norfolk Ave	6:00
Drop Box	7735 Old Georgetown Rd	5:30
Drop Box	9000 Rockville Pike	5:15
Drop Box	8901 Wisconsin Ave	3:00

Map 24 • Upper Rock Creek Park

		Last pick-up
Drop Box	9440 Georgia Ave	7:00
Drop Box	8750 Brookville Rd	6:30
Mail Boxes Etc	8639 B 16th St	6:00

Map 25 • Silver Spring

		Last pick-up
FedEx Kinko's	1407 East West Hwy	7:30
Drop Box	8616 2nd Ave	6:30
Drop Box	8720 Georgia Ave	6:30
Drop Box	8737 Colesville Rd	6:30
Drop Box	8757 Georgia Ave	6:30
Drop Box	8701 Georgia Ave	6:15
Drop Box	1010 Wayne Ave	6:00
Drop Box	1100 Blair Mill Rd	6:00
Drop Box	1109 Spring St	6:00
Drop Box	8121 Georgia Ave	6:00
Drop Box	8403 Colesville Rd	6:00
Drop Box	8601 Georgia Ave	6:00
Drop Box	8630 Fenton St	6:00
Drop Box	8555 16th St	5:30
Drop Box	1305 East West Hwy	5:00
Drop Box	1325 East West Hwy	5:00
Drop Box	1335 East West Hwy	5:00
Drop Box	8455 Colesville Rd	5:00
Drop Box	1315 East West Hwy	4:00

Map 26 • Takoma Park

		Last pick-up
Drop Box	7600 Carroll Ave	6:30
Drop Box	6200 N Capitol St NW	6:00
Takoma Postal & Business	7304 Carroll Ave	6:00

Map 27 • Walter Reed

		Last pick-up
Drop Box	6925 Willow St NW	6:30
Drop Box	7826 Eastern Ave NW	6:30
Drop Box	6900 Georgia Ave NW	6:00
Drop Box	6930 Carroll Ave	5:30

Map 28 • Chevy Chase

		Last pick-up
Drop Box	5636 Connecticut Ave NW	5:30

Map 29 • Bethesda / Chevy Chase Business

		Last pick-up
Drop Box	4809 Bethesda Ave	7:45
Drop Box	7201 Wisconsin Ave	7:00
Drop Box	7501 Wisconsin Ave	7:00

Drop Box	4330 East West Hwy	6:45
Drop Box	5161 River Rd	6:45
Drop Box	2 Bethesda Metro Ctr	6:30
Drop Box	4350 East West Hwy	6:30
Drop Box	4405 East West Hwy	6:30
Drop Box	4416 East West Hwy	6:30
Drop Box	4445 Willard Ave	6:30
Drop Box	4550 Montgomery Ave	6:30
Drop Box	4800 Montgomery Ln	6:30
Drop Box	5454 Wisconsin Ave	6:30
Drop Box	5530 Wisconsin Ave	6:30
Drop Box	5550 Friendship Blvd	6:30
Drop Box	6933 Arlington Rd	6:30
Drop Box	7001 Arlington Rd	6:30
Drop Box	7101 Wisconsin Ave	6:30
Drop Box	7400 Wisconsin Ave	6:30
Drop Box	7475 Wisconsin Ave	6:30
Drop Box	3 Bethesda Metro Ctr	6:15
Drop Box	4520 East West Hwy	6:15
Drop Box	7200 Wisconsin Ave	6:15
Drop Box	7272 Wisconsin Ave	6:15
Drop Box	7315 Wisconsin Ave	6:15
Drop Box	7316 Wisconsin Ave	6:15
Drop Box	2 Wisconsin Cir	6:00
Drop Box	4600 East West Hwy	6:00
Drop Box	4630 Montgomery Ave	6:00
Drop Box	4800 Hampden Ln	5:15
Drop Box	6900 Wisconsin Ave	5:00
Metro Printing and Copying	3 Bethesda Metro Ctr	5:00
Parcel Plus	5257 River Rd	5:00
Mailboxes Bethesda	7831 Woodmont Ave	4:30

Map 30 • Westmoreland Circle

		Last pick-up
Drop Box	4801 Massachusetts Ave NW	6:00
Drop Box	4910 Massachusetts Ave NW	6:00

Map 32 • Cherrydale/Palisades

		Last pick-up
Drop Box	5125 Macarthur Blvd NW	7:00
Drop Box	5136 Macarthur Blvd NW	6:30

Map 33 • Falls Church

		Last pick-up
Drop Box	515 N Washington St	7:00
Drop Box	5350 Lee Hwy	6:30
Parcel Plus	2503 N Harrison St	5:30
Drop Box	5877 Washington Blvd	5:15

Map 34 • Ballston

		Last pick-up
FedEx Kinko's	4501 Fairfax Dr	7:30
Drop Box	4238 Wilson Blvd	7:00
Drop Box	901 N Stuart St	7:00
Drop Box	4001 Fairfax Dr	6:30
Drop Box	4301 Fairfax Dr	6:30
Drop Box	4301 Wilson Blvd	6:30
Drop Box	4350 Fairfax Dr	6:30
Drop Box	1010 N Glebe Rd	6:00
Drop Box	2200 N George Mason Dr	6:00
Drop Box	4100 Fairfax Dr	6:00
Drop Box	910 N Glebe Rd	6:00
Mail Boxes Etc	4201 Wilson Blvd	6:00
Mail Plus	850 N Randolph St	6:00
Drop Box	1100 N Glebe Rd	5:30
Drop Box	1110 N Glebe Rd	5:30
Drop Box	4300 Wilson Blvd	5:30
Drop Box	4245 Fairfax Dr	5:00
Drop Box	801 N Quincy St	5:30

Map 35 • Clarendon

		Last pick-up
FedEx Kinko's	2300 Clarendon Blvd	7:30
Drop Box	2500 Wilson Blvd	6:30
Drop Box	2200 Clarendon Blvd	6:00
Drop Box	2801 Clarendon Blvd	6:00
Drop Box	3101 Wilson Blvd	5:00

Map 36 • Rosslyn

		Last pick-up
Drop Box	1560 Wilson Blvd	7:30
Drop Box	1300 17th St N	7:00
Drop Box	1525 Wilson Blvd	7:00
Drop Box	1600 Wilson Blvd	7:00
Drop Box	1611 N Kent St	7:00
Drop Box	1001 19th St N	6:30
Drop Box	1300 Wilson Blvd	6:30
Drop Box	1530 Wilson Blvd	6:30
Drop Box	1616 Ft Myer Dr	6:30
Drop Box	1916 Wilson Blvd	6:30
Drop Box	1000 Wilson Blvd	6:15
Drop Box	2101 Wilson Blvd	6:15
Drop Box	1101 Wilson Blvd	6:00
Drop Box	1401 Wilson Blvd	6:00
Drop Box	1840 Wilson Blvd	6:00
Drop Box	1911 Ft Myer Dr	6:00
Drop Box	2000 14th St N	6:00
Drop Box	1333 N Courthouse Rd	5:30
Drop Box	1415 N Taft St	5:30
Drop Box	1515 N Court House Rd	5:30
Drop Box	2043 Wilson Blvd	5:30
Drop Box	2107 Wilson Blvd	5:30
Drop Box	2111 Wilson Blvd	5:30
Packman Printing & Shipping	1715 Wilson Blvd	5:30
Drop Box	1655 Ft Myer Dr	5:00
Drop Box	1801 N Lynn St	5:00
Po Boxes Etc	1730 N Lynn St	5:00
Drop Box	2000 15th St N	4:00

Map 37 • Fort Myer

		Last pick-up
Drop Box	2300 9th St S	7:00
Drop Box	3263 Columbia Pike	6:30
Drop Box	3601 Wilson Blvd	6:30
Drop Box	3701 Fairfax Dr	6:00
Drop Box	1210 S Glebe Rd	5:00
Drop Box	200 N Glebe Rd	5:00
Drop Box	3811 Fairfax Dr	5:00
Pak Mail	1001-C N Fillmore St	5:00

Map 38 • Columbia Pike

		Last pick-up
Drop Box	4900 Leesburg Pike	6:00
Drop Box	5100 Leesburg Pike	5:30

Map 39 • Shirlington

		Last pick-up
Drop Box	1707 Osage St	7:00
Drop Box	4212 King St	6:30
Drop Box	4850 31st St S	6:15
Drop Box	2700 S Quincy St	6:00
Parcel Plus	3686 King St	6:00
Drop Box	2800 S Shirlington Rd	5:30
Drop Box	2850 S Quincy St	5:00
Drop Box	3101 Park Center Dr	5:00

Map 40 • Pentagon City

		Last pick-up
Drop Box	1225 S Clark St	7:00
Drop Box	200 12th St S	7:00
Drop Box	1215 S Clark St	6:30
Drop Box	2001 Jefferson Davis Hwy	6:30
Drop Box	201 12th St S	6:30
Drop Box	1250 S Hayes St	6:00
Drop Box	1632 Crystal Square Arcade	6:00
Drop Box	1729 S Eads St	6:00
Drop Box	1919 S Eads St	6:00
Drop Box	2011 Crystal Dr	6:00
Drop Box	2231 Crystal Dr	5:30
Drop Box	2345 Crystal Dr	5:30

Map 40 • Pentagon City—*continued*

		Last pick-up
Drop Box	601 12th St S	5:30
Drop Box	701 12th St S	5:30
Crystal City Copy Center	2450 Crystal Dr	5:00
Crystal Plaza Mailboxes	2101 Crystal Plz	5:00
Drop Box	1 Aviation Cir, Hngr 11	4:00

Map 40 • Pentagon City

		Last pick-up
FedEx Kinko's	1601 Crystal Square Arcade	8:00
Drop Box	775 23rd St S	6:00
Parcel Plus	1101 S Joyce St	6:00
Drop Box	The Pentagon - Main Concourse	5:00
Gateway Mail Boxes	1235 S Clark St	4:00

Map 41 • Landmark

		Last pick-up
Drop Box	1800 N Beauregard St	6:30
Drop Box	1900 N Beauregard St	6:30
Drop Box	4900 Seminary Rd	6:30
Drop Box	5999 Stevenson Ave	6:30
Drop Box	1701 N Beauregard St	6:00
Drop Box	1801 N Beauregard St	6:00
Drop Box	50 S Pickett St	6:00
Packaging Store	245 S Van Dorn St	6:00
Drop Box	2000 N Beauregard St	5:00
Newlon's Box Center	5145 Duke St	5:00

Map 42 • Alexandria (West)

		Last pick-up
Drop Box	2900 Eisenhower Ave	7:00
Drop Box	3660a Wheeler Ave	6:30
Drop Box	2807 Duke St	6:00
Drop Box	3015 Colvin St	6:00

Map 43 • Four Mile Run

		Last pick-up
Drop Box	1908 Mt Vernon Ave	6:00
Drop Box	2320 Fannon St	6:30
Drop Box	2611 Jefferson Davis Hwy	5:30
Drop Box	3131 Mt Vernon Ave	6:00
Drop Box	3301 Jefferson Davis Hwy	6:30
Drop Box	907 W Glebe Rd	6:15

Map 44 • Alexandria Downtown

		Last pick-up
FedEx Kinko's	1755 Duke St	8:00
Drop Box	1700 Diagonal Rd	7:00
Drop Box	1800 Diagonal Rd	6:30
Drop Box	225 Reinekers Ln	6:30
Drop Box	1600 Duke St	6:00
Drop Box	2000 Duke St	6:00
Drop Box	2121 Eisenhower Ave	6:00
Drop Box	333 John Carlyle St	6:00
Drop Box	1725 Duke St	5:30
Drop Box	1737 King St	5:30
Drop Box	2051 Jamieson Ave	2:00

Map 45 • Old Town (North)

		Last pick-up
Drop Box	105 Oronoco St	6:30
Drop Box	1100 Wythe St	6:00
Drop Box	1320 Braddock Pl	6:30
Drop Box	400 N Columbus St	5:00
Drop Box	44 Canal Center Plz	6:30
Drop Box	500 Montgomery St	7:30
Drop Box	635 Slaters Ln	7:00
Drop Box	66 Canal Center Plz	5:00
Drop Box	685 N Washington St	6:30
Drop Box	701 N Faixfax St	6:45
Drop Box	901 N Pitt St	6:30
Drop Box	901 N Washington St	6:30
Drop Box	99 Canal Center Plz	5:45
Pack N Ship Plus	806 N Fairfax St	4:30

Map 46 • Old Town (South)

		Last pick-up
Drop Box	1400 Duke St	7:00
Drop Box	300 N Washington St	7:00
Drop Box	1001 Prince St	6:30
Drop Box	1315 Duke St	6:30
Drop Box	310 S Henry St	6:30
Drop Box	110 S Union St	6:00
Drop Box	112 S Alfred St	6:00
Drop Box	1420 King St	6:00
Drop Box	201 N Union St	6:00
Drop Box	211 N Union St	6:00
Drop Box	228 S Washington St	6:00
Drop Box	700 S Washington St	6:00
Old Town Pack and Ship	615 King St	6:00
Drop Box	1101 King St	5:30
Drop Box	320 King St	5:00
Drop Box	510 King St	5:00
Old Town Post Box	127 S Fairfax St	4:00

Overview

There is art life beyond the Smithsonian. In fact, the city's smaller galleries tend to be more interesting and spontaneous than the hallowed halls of the national museums. The smaller spaces attract more focused art patrons and art teachers unaccompanied by the hordes of schoolchildren scribbling in frayed sketchpads on exhaust-spewing charter buses. Art is a personal matter, and the smaller galleries have a warmth that's lost in the grandeur of behemoth museums.

Dupont Circle is crowded with the best, from impressionism at the **Phillips Collection** to the shrine of rugs at the **Textile Museum**. The only drawback is that, unlike the bigger museums around the mall, many galleries charge entrance fees and sometimes keep quirky hours. Yet the expense and pain of planning ahead are certainly worth the effort just to experience the ceramics, painting, sculpture, and other less accessible works of art that these galleries feature.

A good time to check out the Dupont art scene is on the first Friday evening of every month, when most of the galleries open their doors briefly for a free peek. Many of the galleries on R Street, also known as Gallery Row, are converted row houses with narrow staircases, so be careful of art enthusiast bottlenecks on Friday nights; check out **Alex Gallery** (European and prominent American art), **Burdick Gallery** (sculpture and graphics by Inuit artists), **Elizabeth Roberts Gallery** (local emerging artists), **Gallery K** (Washington-based artists), **Marsha Mateyka Gallery** (European and American living artists), **Robert Brown Gallery** (eclectic, varied exhibitions), and **Studio Gallery** (artist co-op with 30 members).

During the annual Dupont-Kalorama Museum Walk Weekend, held on the first weekend in June, galleries usually allow roaming free of charge (www.dkmuseums.com). The Dupont-Kalorama Museum Walk caters to discerning art critics, groups of children, and families alike, offering exhibits and activities that reflect a desire to inspire both individuals and entire communities.

Check out the *Post* and *City Paper* listings for shows at some of the other galleries that, ahead of rampant gentrification, are popping up all over the city. Another great resource for gallery information is the entertainment guide at www.eg.washingtonpost.com, which has excellent reviews and editor picks of the art galleries in DC.

All area codes as listed in heading unless otherwise noted

1• National Mall *(202)*

Arthur M Sackler Gallery	1050 Independence Ave SW	357-1729
Cave	739 15th St NW	639-0505
Coeur du Capitol Gallery	725 Capitol Sq Pl SW	543-6900
Eleven Eleven Sculpture Space	1111 Pennsylvania Ave NW	703-790-9018
Gallery at Flashpoint	916 G St NW	315-1310
Henderson Phillips Fine Arts	1627 I St NW	223-5860
Pepco's Edison Place Gallery	701 9th St NW	872-2680
White House Art Gallery	529 14th St NW	393-6752

2 • Chinatown / Union Station *(202)*

Apex Gallery	406 7th St NW	638-7001
Echo Gallery	50 Massachusetts Ave NE	842-8400
Eklektikos Gallery	406 7th St NW	783-8444
Goethe-Institut	812 7th St NW	289-1200
National Gallery of Art	401 Constitution Ave NW	737-4215
Numark Gallery	625 E St NW	628-3810
Touchstone Gallery	406 7th St NW	347-2787
Zenith Gallery	413 7th St NW	783-2963

3 • The Hill *(202)*

Market Five Gallery	201 7th St SE	543-7293
Pulp on the Hill	303 Pennsylvania Ave SE	543-1924
Village	705 North Carolina Ave SE	546-3040

5 • Southeast / Anacostia *(202)*

Alvear Studio Design	705 8th St SE	546-8434
Attitude Exact Gallery	739 8th St SE	546-7186

6 • Waterfront *(202)*

Art Enables	65 I St SW	554-9455

7 • Foggy Bottom *(202)*

de Andino Fine Arts	2450 Virginia Ave NW	861-0638
Dimock Gallery	730 21st St NW	994-7091
Dupont Art and Framing	1922 I St NW	331-1815
Foliograph Gallery	919 18th St NW	296-8398
Jerusalem Fund Gallery	2425 Virginia Ave NW	338-1325
Watergate Gallery	2552 Virginia Ave NW	338-4488

8 • Georgetown *(202)*

Addison-Ripley Gallery	1670 Wisconsin Ave NW	338-5180
Alla Rogers Gallery	1054 31st St NW	333-8595
Anne C Fisher Gallery	1054 31st St NW	625-7555
Appalachian Spring	1415 Wisconsin Ave NW	337-5780
Cherub Antiques	2918 M St NW	337-2224
District Fine Arts	1726 Wisconsin Ave NW	387-5657
Fine Art & Artists	2920 M St NW	965-0780
Fraser Gallery	1054 31st St NW	298-6450
Gala	1671 Wisconsin Ave NW	333-1337
Govinda Gallery	1227 34th St NW	333-1180
Grafix	2904 M St NW	965-4747
Guarisco Gallery	2828 Pennsylvania Ave NW	333-8533
Hemphill Fine Arts	1027 33rd St NW	342-5610
Jackson Art Center	3048 R St NW	342-9778
Ken Frye Art Gallery	3242 Jones Ct NW	333-2505
Maurine Littleton Gallery	1667 Wisconsin Ave NW	333-9307
Mu Project	1521 Wisconsin Ave NW	333-4119
Old Print Gallery	1220 31st St NW	965-1818

8 • Georgetown—*continued* (202)

P Street Pictures	2621 P St NW	337-0066
P&C Art	3108 M St NW	965-3833
Parish Gallery	1054 31st St NW	944-2310
Ralls Collection	1516 31st St NW	342-1754
Spectrum Gallery	1132 29th St NW	333-0954
Studio Art	3222 M St NW	965-7141
Susan Calloway Antique Prints & Fine Art	1643 Wisconsin Ave NW	965-4601
Susquehanna Antiques	3216 O St NW	333-1511

9 • Dupont Circle / Adams Morgan

Aaron Gallery	1717 Connecticut Ave NW	234-3311
Alex Gallery	2106 R St NW	667-2599
Burdick Gallery	2114 R St NW	986-5682
Burton Marinkovich	1506 21st St NW	296-6563
Chao Phraya Gallery	2009 Columbia Rd NW	745-1111
Conner Contemporary Art	1730 Connecticut Ave NW	588-8750
Diner Gallery	1730 21st St NW	483-5005
Foundry Gallery	9 Hillyer Ct NW	387-0203
Gallery 10 Limited	1519 Connecticut Ave NW	232-3326
Gallery AFFRICA	2010 R St NW	745-7272
Gary Edward's Photographs	1711 Connecticut Ave NW	301-524-0900
International Art Gallery	1625 K St NW	466-7979
Irvine Contemporary Art	1710 Connecticut Ave NW	332-8767
Jane Haslem Gallery	2025 Hillyer Pl NW	232-4644
Jet Artworks	2108 R St NW	232-4407
Kathleen Ewing Gallery	1609 Connecticut Ave NW	328-0955
Kelly Nevin Gallery	1517 U St NW	232-3464
Marsha Mateyka Gallery	2012 R St NW	328-0088
Nevin Kelly Gallery	1517 U St NW	232-3464
Open Society Institute Gallery	1120 19th St NW	721-5642
Pass Gallery	1617 S St NW	745-0796
Pensler Galleries	2029 Q St NW	328-9190
Phillips Collection	1600 21st St NW	387-2151
Provisions Library	1611 Connecticut Ave NW	299-0460
Robert Brown Gallery	2030 R St NW	483-4383
St Luke's Gallery	1715 Q St NW	328-2424
Studio Gallery	2108 R St NW	232-8734
Textile Museum	2320 S St NW	667-0441
Washington Printmakers Gallery	1732 Connecticut Ave NW	332-7757
Washington Very Special Arts	1100 16th St NW	296-9100

10 • Logan Circle / U Street (202)

Adamson Gallery	1515 14th St NW	232-0707
Fusebox	1412 14th St NW	299-9220
G Fine Art	1515 14th St NW	462-1601
Mickelson's Fine Art Framing & Parker Gallery	629 New York Ave NW	628-1735
NNE Gallery	1312 8th St NW	276-4540
Plan B	1530 14th St NW	234-2711
Transformer Gallery	1404 P St NW	483-1102
Vastu	1829 14th St NW	234-8344
Wayland House Gallerie	1802 11th St NW	387-8157

11 • Near Northeast (202)

Covenant House	7 New York Ave NE	610-6513
Ella's Coffee & Fine Art	1506 N Capitol St NW	483-3552
Tartt Gallery	207 Q St NW	332-5652
Zelano Art Studio	411 New York Ave NE	547-2508

14 • Catholic U (202)

Washington Works on Paper	3420 9th St NE	526-4848
Wohlfarth Galleries	3418 9th St NE	526-8022

15 • Columbia Heights (202)

Cultural Circles	1424 Belmont St NW	667-4324

16 • Adams Morgan (North) / Mt Pleasant (202)

Alexia Gallery	2602 Connecticut Ave NW	667-7773
District of Columbia Arts Center	2438 18th St NW	462-7833
Mexican Cultural Institute	2829 16th St NW	728-1628

17 • Woodley Park / Cleveland Park (202)

Adams Davidson Galleries	2727 29th St NW	965-3800
International Visions Gallery	2629 Connecticut Ave NW	234-5112

18 • Glover Park / Foxhall (202)

Cathedral Galleries	3301 New Mexico Ave NW	363-6936
Foxhall Gallery	3301 New Mexico Ave NW	966-7144
Susan Conway	2801 New Mexico Ave NW	333-6343

19 • Tenleytown / Friendship Heights (202)

Brazilian-American Cultural Institute	4719 Wisconsin Ave NW	362-8334
C Y Katzen Gallery	4624 Wisconsin Ave NW	363-4973
Watkins Gallery, American University	4400 Massachusetts Ave NW	885-1670

20 • Cleveland Park / Upper Connecticut (202)

Chevy Chase Gallery	5039 Connecticut Ave NW	364-8155
Rock Creek Gallery	2401 Tilden St NW	244-2482

21 • 16th St. Heights / Petworth (202)

Ramee Art Gallery	5427 14th St NW	291-0067

22 • Downtown Bethesda *(301)*

Artworks	7847 Old Georgetown Rd	656-0044
Fraser Gallery	7700 Wisconsin Ave	718-9651
Gallery Neptune	4808 Auburn Ave	718-0809
Ozmosis Gallery	7908 Woodmont Ave	664-9662
Saint Elmo's Fire	4928 St Elmo Ave	215-9848
Wee King Art	8100 Norfolk Ave	656-1141

24 • Upper Rock Creek Park *(202)*

African Hands	1851 Redwood Ter NW	726-2400

25 • Silver Spring

Century Gallery	919 King St	703-684-6967
House of Safori	1105 Spring St	301-565-0781
Pyramid Atlantic	8230 Georgia Ave	301-608-9101

27 • Walter Reed *(202)*

A Salon	6925 Willow St NW	882-0740

28 • Chevy Chase *(202)*

Avant Garde	5520 Connecticut Ave NW	966-1045

29 • Bethesda / Chevy Chase Business *(301)*

Creative Partners	4600 East West Hwy	951-9441
Designers Art Gallery	4618 Leland St	718-0400
Discovery Galleries Limited	4840 Bethesda Ave	913-9199
Gallery Elan	7247 Woodmont Ave	657-1200
Glass Gallery	5335 Wisconsin Ave NW	657-3478
Marin-Price Galleries	7022 Wisconsin Ave	718-0622
Moriah Gallery	7301 Woodmont Ave	657-3001
Osuna Art	7200 Wisconsin Ave	654-4500
Washington Studio School	4505 Stanford St	718-7210

32 • Cherrydale/Palisades *(202)*

Art in Fiber	2821 Arizona Ter NW	364-8404

33 • Falls Church

Paul McGhee's Old Town Gallery	109 N Fairfax St	703-548-7729

34 • Ballston *(703)*

Art Beats	4238 Wilson Blvd	243-4010
Ellipse Arts Center	4350 Fairfax Dr	228-7710
Lac Viet Gallery	5179 Lee Hwy	532-4350

35 • Clarendon *(703)*

Metropolitan Gallery	2420 Wilson Blvd	358-9449

37 • Fort Myer *(703)*

Arlington Arts Center	3550 Wilson Blvd	797-4573

40 • Pentagon City *(703)*

Wentworth Galleries	1100 S Hayes St	415-1166

41 • Landmark *(703*

Gallery Petalouth	301 N Beauregard St	354-1176

42 • Alexandria (West) *(703)*

Propeller Studio	3670 Wheeler Ave	370-4800

43 • Four Mile Run *(703)*

Del Ray Artisans	2704 Mount Vernon Ave	838-4827
Fitzgerald Fine Arts	2502 E Randolph Ave	836-1231
Nicholas Colasanto Center	2704 Mount Vernon Ave	838-4827

44 • Alexandria Downtown *(703)*

Tall Tulips	412 John Carlyle St	549-5017

45 • Old Town (North) *(703)*

Studio Antiques & Fine Art	524 N Washington St	703-548-5253

46 • Old Town (South) *(703)*

Art League	105 N Union St	683-1780
Artcraft Collection	132 King St	299-6616
Arts Afire Glass Gallery	102 N Fayette St	838-9785
Auburn Fine Arts Gallery	127 S Fairfax St	548-1932
Betsy Anderson	105 N Union St	684-5579
BJ Anderson	105 N Union St	549-5079
Citron Ann	105 N Union St	683-0403
Enamelist Gallery	105 N Union St	836-1561
Fibre Works	105 N Union St	836-5807
Fire One	105 N Union St	836-2585
Foliograph Gallery	217 King St	683-1501
Fuszion Collaborative	225 N Fairfax St	548-8080
Gallerie Michele	113 King St	683-1521
Gallery West	205 S Union St	549-7359
Kennedy Studios	101 N Union St	684-1193
Miller Fine Art Limited	113 S Columbus St	838-0006
Mindful Hands	211 King St	683-2074
Multiple Exposures	105 N Union St	683-2205
Nuevo Mundo	313 Cameron St	549-0040
P&C Art	212 King St	549-2525
Prince Royal Gallery	204 S Royal St	548-5151
Principle Gallery	208 King St	739-9326
Tall Tulips	105 N Union St	549-5017
Target Gallery	105 N Union St	683-1780
The Athenaeum	201 Prince St	548-0035
Torpedo Factory Arts Center	105 N Union St	

While the shopping scene might give visitors the impression that district residents don't care how they look, the independent bookstore scene will show them that we definitely care about what we read. This is a city of policy wonks, lawyers, writers, defense specialists, and activists—the one thing we all have in common, frankly, is that we're nerds. Washington, DC and the metropolitan area is, especially recently, brimming with residents with expensive educations, lucrative government contracting jobs, and high-performance cars. So it seems obvious that bookstores here would get as crowded as the beltway during rush hour. Besides the mega-chain stores like **Borders** and **Barnes & Noble**, there are several local outlets in town, each with a personality of their own.

Kramerbooks & Afterwords Café in Dupont Circle, for instance, is a lively place where literary types can settle into a serious novel or friendly conversation while sipping a Mocha Ice or a Maker's Mark. There's also **Olsson's** if you like your coffee and ownership independent. **Chapters Literary Bookstore** on 11th Street is another good independent where the poetry and literature sections are actually larger than the diet and computer manuals sections (gasp!). If you have time to spare, check out the used bookstores for cheaper reads and dusty aromas. Try **Riverby Books** on Capitol Hill, **Second Story Books** in Dupont Circle, **Idle Time Books** in Adams Morgan, and **Book Bank** in Alexandria. To participate in, or at least eavesdrop on, a hearty lefty debate, drop by **Politics & Prose**. Readers of the gay, lesbian, bisexual, and transgender persuasions should head to **Lambda Rising**, the largest LGBT bookstore in the world.

Also, the **Writer's Center** in Bethesda sells books, both fiction and non-fiction, by local authors as well as poetry and literary magazines such as the locally-based Gargoyle Magazine.

Map 1 • National Mall

Barnes & Noble	555 12th St NW	202-347-0176	General.
Borders Books & Music	600 14th St NW	202-737-1385	General.
Chapters Literary Bookstore	445 11th St NW	202-737-5553	Poetry, literary fiction (old and new), children's literature, and natural history.

Map 2 • Chinatown / Union Station

AMA Management Book Store	440 1st St NW	202-347-3092	Business.
B Dalton Booksellers	50 Massachusetts Ave NE	202-289-1724	General.
National Academy Press - Bookstore	500 5th St NW	202-334-2812	Science and technology, social/ environment issues.
Olsson's Books	418 7th St NW	202-638-7610	General.

Map 3 • The Hill

Riverby Books	417 E Capitol St SE	202-543-4342	Used.
Trover Shop Books & Office	221 Pennsylvania Ave SE	202-547-2665	General.

Map 5 • Southeast / Anacostia

Backstage	545 8th St SE	202-544-5744	Theater and performance.
Bird in Hand Book Store	323 7th St SE	202-543-0744	Art and architecture.
Capitol Hill Books	657 C St SE	202-544-1621	Second-hand fiction, mystery, and biography.
Fairy Godmother- Children's Books & Toys	319 7th St SE	202-547-5474	Toddler to young adult fiction and nonfiction.
First Amendment Books	645 Pennsylvania Ave SE	202-547-5585	Current events, political history.

Map 6 • Waterfront

Reprint Book Shop	455 L'Enfant Plz SW	202-554-5070	General.

Map 7 • Foggy Bottom

Franz Bader Book Store	1911 I St NW	202-337-5440	Art and architecture.
George Washington U Book Store	800 21st St NW	202-994-6870	Academic and college.
Washington Law & Professional Books	1900 G St NW	202-223-5543	Law.
World Bank Info Shop	701 18th St NW	202-458-5454	Development and politics.

Map 8 • Georgetown

Barnes & Noble	3040 M St NW	202-965-9880	General.

Bartleby's Books	3034 M St NW	202-298-0486	Rare and antiquarian, 18th and 19th American history, economics, and law.
Beyond Comics	1419 Wisconsin Ave NW	202-333-8650	Comics.
Big Planet Comics	3145 Dumbarton Ave NW	202-342-1961	Comics.
Bridge St Books	2814 Pennsylvania Ave NW	202-965-5200	General.
Lantern Bryn Mawr Book Shop	3241 P St NW	202-333-3222	Used and rare.
Waldenbooks	3222 M St NW	202-333-8033	General.

Map 9 • Dupont Circle / Adams Morgan

Books-A-Million	11 Dupont Cir NW	202-319-1374	General.
Borders Books & Music	1801 L St NW	202-466-4999	General.
International Language Center	1803 Connecticut Ave NW	202-332-2894	Language.
Kramerbooks & Afterwords	1517 Connecticut Ave NW	202-387-1400	General.
Lambda Rising Book Store	1625 Connecticut Ave NW	202-462-6969	Gay and lesbian.
Luna Books & Coffee Shop	1633 P St NW	202-332-2543	Mostly used.
Newsroom	1803 Connecticut Ave NW	202-332-1489	Foreign language and reference.
Olsson's Books	1307 19th St NW	202-785-1133	General.
Reiter's Scientific & Professional Books	2021 K St NW	202-223-3327	Scientific and medical.
Second Story Books & Antiques	2000 P St NW	202-659-8884	Used.

Map 10 • Logan Circle / U Street

Brian Mackenzie Infoshop	1426 9th St NW	202-986-0681	Left-wing literature.
Candida's World Of Books	1541 14th St NW	202-667-4811	Language learning and reference, travel, art, cookbooks, current literature, political, science, and children's.
Sisterspace & Books	1419 V St NW	202-332-3433	Afro-centric and women's literature.

Map 11 • Near Northeast

Bison Shop-Gallaudet University	800 Florida Ave NE	202-651-5271	Academic and sign language.

Map 14 • Catholic U

Newman Book Store of Washington	3329 8th St NE	202-526-1036	Scripture, theology, philosophy, and church history.
Sistrum	5224 3rd St NW	202-723-5200	Afro-centric.

Map 15 • Columbia Heights

Howard University Book Store	2225 Georgia Ave NW	202-238-2640	Academic and Afro-centric.
Sankofa Video & Bookstore	2714 Georgia Ave NW	202-234-4755	Afro-centric.

Map 16 • Adams Morgan (North) / Mt Pleasant

Idle Time Books	2467 18th St	202-232-4774	Used.

Map 18 • Glover Park / Foxhall

Georgetown University Book Store	3800 Reservoir Rd NW	202-687-7482	Academic.
Glovers Books & Music	2319 Wisconsin Ave NW	202-338-8100	General.
Tree Top Toys & Books	3301 New Mexico Ave NW	202-244-3500	Children's.

Map 19 • Tenleytown / Friendship Heights

American University Book Store	4400 Massachusetts Ave	202-885-6300	Academic and college.
Borders Books & Music	5333 Wisconsin Ave NW	202-686-8270	General.
Tempo Book Store	4905 Wisconsin Ave NW	202-363-6683	Language.

Map 20 • Cleveland Park / Upper Connecticut

Politics & Prose	5015 Connecticut Ave NW	202-364-1919	American studies and politics.

Map 22 • Downtown Bethesda

Big Planet Comics	4908 Fairmont Ave	301-654-6856	Comics.
Second Story Books & Antiques	4914 Fairmont Ave	301-656-0170	Used.
Waldenbooks	143 Montgomery Mall	301-469-8810	General.

Map 23 • Kensington

Audubon Naturalist Bookshop	8940 Jones Mill Rd	301-652-3606	Nature and earth.

Map 25 • Silver Spring

Alliance Comics	8317 Fenton St	301-588-2546	Comics.
Silver Spring Books	938 Bonifant St	301-587-7484	Used.

Map 26 • Takoma Park

Takoma Book Exchange	7009 Carroll Ave	301-891-4656	Mostly used.

Map 27 • Walter Reed

Literal Books	7705 Georgia Ave NW	202-723-8688	Spanish books.

Map 29 • Bethesda/Chevy Chase Business

Barnes & Noble	4801 Bethesda Ave	301-986-1761	General.
Georgetown Book Shop	4710 Bethesda Ave	301-907-6923	History, art, photography, children's, literary fiction, and baseball.
Olsson's Books	7647 Old Georgetown Rd	301-652-3336	General.

Map 34 • Ballston

B Dalton Booksellers	4238 Wilson Blvd	703-522-8822	General.
Bookhouse	805 N Emerson St	703-527-7797	Scholarly history.
Imagination Station	4524 Lee Hwy	703-522-2047	Children's.

Map 35 • Clarendon

Barnes & Noble	2800 Clarendon Blvd	703-248-8244	General.

Map 36 • Rosslyn

Olsson's Books	1735 N Lynn St	703-812-2103	General.
Olsson's Books	2111 Wilson Blvd	703-525-4227	General.

Map 37 • Fort Myer

George Mason University-Arlington Campus Bookstore	3401 N Fairfax Dr	703-993-8170	Law.

Map 38 • Columbia Pike

NVCC-Alexandria Campus Book Store	3101 N Beauregard St	703-671-0043	Academic and college.

Map 40 • Pentagon City

Borders Books & Music	1201 S Hayes St	703-418-0166	General.

Map 41 • Landmark

Waldenbooks	5801 Duke St	703-658-9576	General.

Map 43 • Four Mile Run

Barnes & Noble	3651 Jefferson Davis Hwy	703-299-9124	General.
Card & Comic Collectorama	2008 Mt Vernon Ave	703-548-3466	Comics and used.

Map 46 • Old Town (South)

A Likely Story	1555 King St	703-836-2498	Children's and parenting.
Aftertime Comics	1304 King St	703-548-5030	Comics.
Book Bank	1510 King St	703-838-3620	Used.
Books-A-Million	501 King St	703-548-3432	General.
Olsson's Books	106 S Union St	703-684-0077	General.
Why Not	200 King St	703-548-4420	Children's.

Living in a politically-charged city means that independents and documentaries play big here. You'll find the best of the bunch at the **Landmark E Street** downtown, Chevy Chase's **Avalon** (DC's oldest movie house), or Silver Spring's shrine to film, the **AFI Silver**. For indie flicks, try the cramped **Loews Dupont Circle 5**. Also watch for temporary screenings every few weeks at museums, schools, or historic theaters like the **Tivoli** in Columbia Heights and the **Lincoln** on U Street. In late summer, take a blanket to the Mall for the free "Screen on the Green" classic film series.

If it's a blockbuster hit you're after, plenty of mainstream, metro-accessible theaters will oblige. The best of the bunch is Cleveland Park's **Uptown**, a gorgeous 1936 Art Deco palace with a massive curved screen (32' x 70'). You'll probably have to stand in line for tickets, but it's one of the few theaters that can really do justice to that latest Hollywood action flick.

Stadium seating megaplexes have arrived downtown, including the **Loews Georgetown,** which houses a brick smokestack used long ago as the Georgetown Incinerator, and the **Regal Gallery Place**, whose fit-for-Caesar marble atrium and 14 screens are cleverly nestled into an already crowded Chinatown (and the bathrooms have the most powerful hand dryers you've ever seen—or heard).

Theater	*Address*	*Phone*	*Map*
AFI Silver Theater	8633 Colesville Rd	301-495-6720	25
AFI Theater-Kennedy Center for the Performing Arts	2700 F St NW	202-785-4600	7
AMC City Place 10	8661 Colesville Rd	703 -998-4262	25
AMC Courthouse Plaza 8	2150 Clarendon Blvd	703-998-4262	36
AMC Hoffman Center 22	206 Swamp Fox Rd	703-998-4262	44
AMC Mazza Gallerie 7	5300 Wisconsin Ave NW	202-537-9553	19
AMC Union Station 9	50 Massachusetts Ave NE	703-998-4262	2
American City Movie Diner	5532 Connecticut Ave NW	202-244-1949	28
Avalon Theatre	5612 Connecticut Ave NW	202-966-6000	28
Cinema 'N' Draft House	2903 Columbia Pike	703-486-2345	37
Cineplex Odeon Shirlington 7	2772 S Randolph St	703-671-0978	39
Cineplex Odeon Uptown	3426 Connecticut Ave NW	202-966-5400	17
Cineplex Odeon Wisconsin Avenue Cinemas	4000 Wisconsin Ave NW	202-244-0880	19
Johnson IMAX Theater	Constitution Ave NW & 10th St NW	202-633-9045	1
Landmark Bethesda Row Cinema	7235 Woodmont Ave	301-652-7273	29
Landmark E St Cinema	555 11th St NW	202-452-7672	1
Lockheed Martin IMAX Theater	601 Independence Ave SW	202-357-1686	2
Loews Dupont Circle 5	1350 19th St NW	202-872-9555	9
Loews Georgetown 14	3111 K St NW	202-342-6441	8
Mary Pickford Theater	Library of Congress, James Madison Memorial Bldg, Independence Ave SE b/w 1st St SE & 2nd St SE	202-707-5677	2
Old Town Theater	815 1/2 King St	703-683-8888	46
Regal Ballston Common 12	671 N Glebe Rd	703-527-9730	34
Regal Bethesda 10	7272 Wisconsin Ave	301-718-4323	29
Regal Gallery Place Stadium	707 7th St NW	202-393-2121	2
Regal Potamic Yard 16	3575 Jefferson Davis Hwy	703-739-4040	43
The Majestic 20	900 Ellsworth Dr	301-681-2266	25

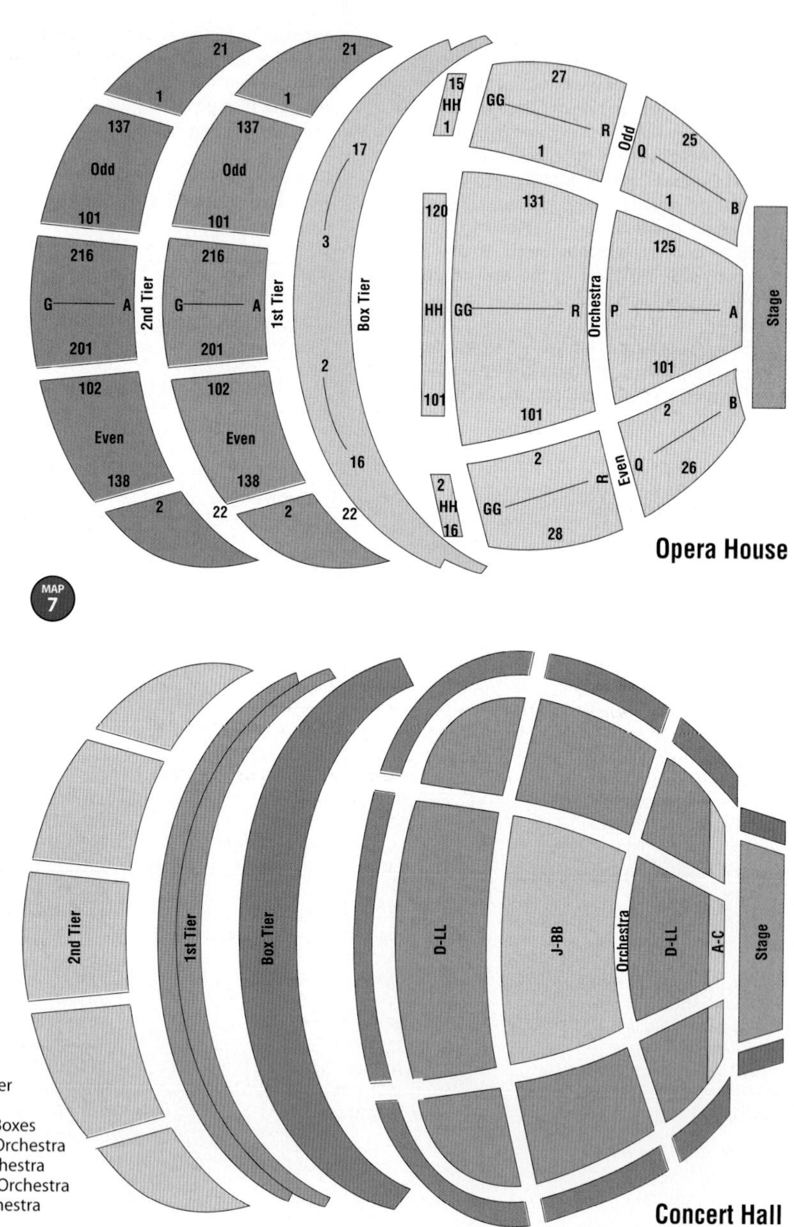
21
1
137
Odd
101
216
G A
201
2nd Tier
102
Even
138
2
22
21
1
137
Odd
101
216
G A
201
1st Tier
102
Even
138
2
22
17
3
Box Tier
2
16
15
HH
1
120
HH
101
2
HH
16
27
GG
R
1
Odd
Q
25
1
B
131
GG R
101
Orchestra
125
P A
101
2
B
Even
Q
26
2
GG
R
28
Stage
Opera House
MAP 7
2nd Tier
1st Tier
Box Tier
D-LL
J-BB
Orchestra
D-LL
A-C
Stage
Second Tier
First Tier
Onstage Boxes
Partierre Orchestra
Prime Orchestra
Premium Orchestra
Front Orchestra
Concert Hall

General Information

NFT Map: 7
Address: 2700 F St NW
Washington, DC 20566
Website: www.kennedy-center.org
Phone: 202-416-8000
Box Office: 800-444-1324 or 202-467-4600

Overview

The Kennedy Center is best known nationally for its yearly Honors, awards recognizing the nation's most important, accomplished, desperate-for-validation celebrities. Locally, it caters to thick-of-wallet arts patrons with highbrow music, theater, opera, and dance performances. Savvy cultural vultures know that bargains exist, such as the nightly free concerts and choral cheap seats. And there's no charge to show up and check out one of the city's most romantic dusk terrace views or the giant statue of the center's adored namesake.

The Kennedy Center's stuffy reputation should not intimidate reluctant performance art lovers. It offers a variety of events and programs that cater to anyone from opera-loving octogenarians dappled in sparkling diamonds to children in Bart Simpson t-shirts interested in tap dance. Like the monuments and museums, the Kennedy Center is there for everyone. Even among the affluent patrons who booked their reservations from the balmy Italian coast, the art itself does not care about rented tuxes, imitation handbags, or sips of champagne from plastic flutes in the parking garage.

The Kennedy Center's history began in 1958, when President Dwight D. Eisenhower took a break from the links to sign legislation creating a National Cultural Center for the United States. President John F. Kennedy and First Lady Jackie later did much of the fundraising for what the president called "our contribution to the human spirit." Two months after President Kennedy's assassination, Congress named the center in his memory.

The Kennedy Center houses the Concert Hall, Opera House, Eisenhower Theater, Terrace Theater, Theater Lab, Film Theater, and Jazz Club.

How to Get There—Driving

Though the roof of the Kennedy Center is flat, the cultured elite cannot park their helicopters there. Some even drive themselves. Heading away from the Capitol on Independence Avenue, get in the left lane as you approach the Potomac. Passing under two bridges, stay in the left lane, and follow signs to the Kennedy Center. After passing the Kennedy Center on your right, make a right onto Virginia Avenue. At the second set of lights, turn right onto 25th Street and follow the Kennedy Center parking signs.

Parking

Kennedy Center garage parking is $15.

How to Get There—Mass Transit

Take the Blue Line or Orange Line to the Foggy Bottom stop, and either walk seven minutes to the center or take a free shuttle that runs every 15 minutes. For above-ground transportation-lovers, Metrobus 80 also goes to the Kennedy Center.

How to Get Tickets

Prices vary depending on the event. Check the center's website or call the box office for schedules and tickets.

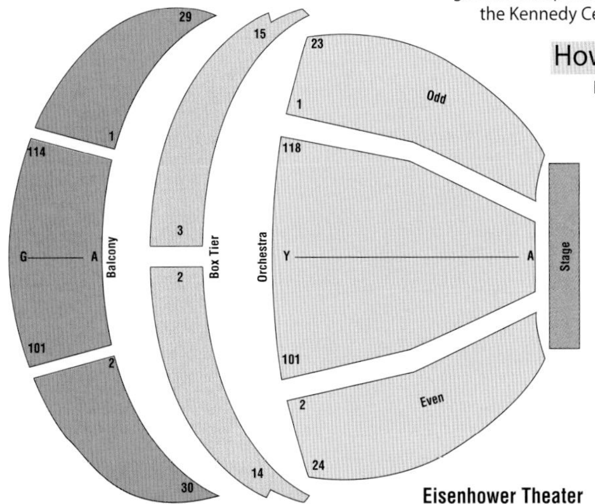

Eisenhower Theater

The Smithsonian Institute is a national system of museums, most of which are situated in a campus-like aesthetic around the National Mall (other branches, like the Cooper-Hewitt National Design Museum, are located in New York City, and the Steven F. Udvar-Hazy Center, an extension of the National Air and Space Museum, is in Chantilly, VA). The free Smithsonian exhibits draw both American and international tourists by the hordes.

The west wing of the **National Gallery** houses a world-class collection of 13th-16th century European painting and sculpture, including the only Leonardo da Vinci painting on this side of the Atlantic. The East Wing houses the museum's modern and contemporary collections. At the **Freer** and **Sackler Galleries,** sublime works of Asian art hide in unlikely corners of small and modest rooms. The **Hirshhorn Museum and Sculpture Garden** is, well, avant-garde—what else could you call the collection that includes Ron Muek's eerily realistic sculpture of a naked, obese, bald man just hanging out in the corner? The **National Museum of American History** is more than a collection of invaluable artifacts; it addresses the history and the making of American culture. And while the American History museum might make us feel all-important, the **National Museum of Natural History** will deflate our egos, reminding us that we are but one mortal species among many.

It would take months to visit all of the Smithsonian museums in DC. But they're all free, so consider them friends that need to be checked in on from time to time.

Extending out from the Mall, you'll discover the pricier private museums. The **National Building Museum's** building and gift shop are interesting, even when the offbeat architectural exhibits are not. When you're in the mood for something more specific, try the targeted collections at places like the **Postal Museum** or the **Museum of Women in the Arts**.

Museum	*Address*	*Phone*	*Map*
Alexandria Archaeology Museum	105 N Union St	703-838-4399	46
Alexandria Black History Resource Center	902 Wythe St	703-838-4356	45
The Athenaeum	201 Prince St	703-548-0035	46
Arlington Historical Museum	1805 S Arlington Ridge Rd	703-892-4204	40
Art Museum of the Americas	201 18th St NW	202-458-6016	7
Bead Museum DC	400 7th St NW	202-624-4500	2
Black Fashion Museum	2007 Vermont Ave NW	202-667-0744	10
Black Heritage Museum of Arlington	951 S George Mason Dr	703-271-8700	37
City Museum	801 K St NW	202-383-1800	10
The Corcoran	500 17th St NW	202-639-1700	1
DAR Museum	1776 D St NW	202-628-1776	7
DEA Museum & Visitors Center	700 Army Navy Dr	202-307-3463	40
Discovery Creek Children's Museum - Historic Schoolhouse	4954 MacArthur Blvd NW	202-337-5111	18
Einstein Planetarium- National Air & Space Museum	Independence Ave SE & 4th St SW	202-633-4629	2
Explorers Hall (National Geographic Society)	1145 17th St NW	202-857-7588	9
Folger Shakespeare Library	201 E Capitol St SE	202-544-4600	3
Fort Ward Museum & Historic Site	4301 W Braddock Rd	703-838-4848	42
Frederick Douglass Museum & Hall of Fame for Caring Americans	320 A St NE	202-544-6130	3
Freer Art Gallery and Arthur M Sackler Gallery	1050 Independence Ave SW	202-633-4880	1
Friendship Firehouse Museum	107 S Alfred St	703-838-3891	46
Gadsby's Tavern Museum	134 N Royal St	703-838-4242	46
George Washington Masonic Memorial Museum	101 Callahan Dr	703-683-2007	44

Museum	Address	Phone	Map
Hillwood Museum & Gardens	4155 Linnean Ave NW	202-686-8500	20
Hirshhorn Museum and Sculpture Garden	7th St SW & Independence Ave SW	202-357-2700	2
International Spy Museum	800 F St NW	202-393-7798	1
The Kreeger Museum	2401 Foxhall Rd NW	202-337-3050	18
The Lyceum	201 S Washington St	703-838-4994	46
The Mansion on O Street	2020 O St NW	202-496-2020	9
Museum of Contemporary Art	1054 31st St NW	202-342-6230	8
National Academy of Sciences	2100 C St NW	202-334-2436	1
National Air and Space Museum	Independence Ave SE & 4th St SW	202-633-1000	2
National Aquarium	14th St NW & Constitution Ave NW	202-482-2825	1
National Building Museum	401 F St NW	202-272-2448	2
National Gallery of Art-East Building	Madison Dr NW & 4th St NW	202-737-4215	10
National Geographic Museum	1600 M St NW	202-857-7588	9
National Health Museum	1155 15th St NW	202-737-2670	9
National Museum of African Art	950 Independence Ave SW	202-633-4600	1
National Museum of American History	14th St NW & Constitution Ave NW	202-633-1000	1
National Museum of American Jewish Military History	1811 R St NW	202-265-6280	9
National Museum of Natural History	10th St NW & Constitution Ave NW	202-357-2700	1
National Museum of the American Indian	4th St & Independence Ave SW	202-633-1000	2
National Museum of Women in the Arts	1250 New York Ave NW	202-783-5000	1
National Postal Museum	2 Massachusetts Ave NE	202-633-5555	2
National Zoological Park	3001 Connecticut Ave NW	202-673-4700	17
The Navy Museum (reservation required for non-military)	8th St SE & M St SE	202-433-4882	5
Newseum (Opens 2007)	Pennsylvania Ave NW & 6th St NW	703-284-3544	2
The Octagon Museum	1799 New York Ave NW	202-638-3221	7
The Phillips Collection	1600 21st St NW	202-387-2151	9
Pope John Paul II Cultural Center	3900 Harewood Rd NE	202-635-5400	14
Renwick Gallery (Smithsonian American Art Museum)	Pennsylvania Ave NW & 17th St NW	202-633-2850	1
Smithsonian American Art Museum (Reopening July 2006)	8th St & G St NW	202-275-1500	1
Smithsonian Institution Building, the Castle	1000 Jefferson Ave SW	202-633-1000	1
Smithsonian Portrait Gallery (Reopening July 2006)	8th St NW & F St NW	202-275-1738	1
The Society of the Cincinnati -Anderson House	2118 Massachusetts Ave NW	202-785-2040	9
Stabler-Leadbeater Apothecary Museum	105-107 S Fairfax St	703-836-3713	46
Stephen Decatur House Museum	1610 H St NW (SW Corner of H St & Jackson Pl)	202-842-0920	1
Textile Museum	2320 S St NW	202-667-0441	9
Torpedo Factory Art Center	105 N Union St	703-838-4565	46
Tudor Place	1644 31st St NW	202-965-0400	8
United States National Arboretum	3501 New York Ave NE	202-245-2726	12
US Holocaust Memorial Museum	100 Raoul Wallenberg Pl SW	202-488-0400	1
Washington's Doll's House & Toy Museum	5236 44th St NW	202-244-0024	19
Woodrow Wilson Center for International Scholars	1300 Pennsylvania Ave NW	202-691-4000	1

Politics and booze make a mean cocktail—from pubs and clubs to dives and wine tastings, Washington DC has the bar and the drink to suit anyone and everyone. Don't let the surplus of silk ties, security clearances, and skinny eyebrows fool you—this city knows how to unwind. Considering the diverse political loyalties, alcohol, and posturing of the folks in the District, it's a miracle that happy hours across the city don't look like the bloody opening scene of *Gangs of New York*. But if pounding bargain drinks and convincing single congressional aides that you're passionate about democracy in Myanmar isn't your bag, DC's got plenty of dance clubs, smokey hole-in-the-walls (take THAT New York), and live jazz venues, where you can snack on oysters on the half shell. Sure, Washington DC is a city largely populated by those uber-driven types who felt they were too important for their own hometowns, but the fact remains that if you can't have fun in this city, well, you've got only yourself to blame.

The nightlife districts of Georgetown, Dupont, Adams Morgan, Cleveland Park, U Street, and some of the livelier suburbs offer a choice of scenes, depending on your age and mood. Most places in DC are within walking distance of each other (or at least a short cab or Metro ride apart), providing partygoers with several options for last minute changes of plans.

Georgetown

The weekend crowd in Georgetown is a hodge-podge of college students, shop-a-holics, wayward tourists, and local residents who have managed to find nooks and crannies along bustling M Street that the tourists have yet to conquer. Fold up your map and rest your feet at **Clyde's**, decompress after work with a few beers and a barbecue sandwich at **Old Glory All American BBQ**, or slur along with the piano at **Mr. Smith's**. Enjoy some adult beverages and conversation at **The Guards**. Younger legs hike up the steps to the second floor bar at **Garrett's,** or stumble down the stairs into **The Tombs**. When the weather is nice, hit **Sequoia** or **Tony & Joe's Seafood Place** on the Potomac— just remember neither the river nor the boats moored there are meant to be used as public restrooms. During inclement weather, go dancing at **Georgetown Station,** or bring your rainy-day funds and poor boy troubles to **Blues Alley** to get low on some jazz.

Dupont

Dupont is known for its lively gay population; it has a hip nightlife scene, and it's surrounded by neighborhoods that are safe, classy, and cultivated. The most dangerous part of Dupont nightlife is crossing the traffic circle while honking cabs and hesitant sedans negotiate the lights, lanes, and drunks darting across the streets. Heteros hang at **Big Hunt**, hook up at **Lucky Bar**, or dance in lively **Café Citron**. Drink with locals in the cozy brick underground bar, **Childe Harold,** or with young bureaucrats at **The Font Page**. Gay residents and guests socialize at **Fireplace**, boogie between drag shows at **Chaos**, and chill at the low-key but sharp atmosphere at **JR's**.

Adams Morgan

In Adams Morgan you'll find different cultures thriving, struggling, and partying on shared cracked sidewalks. 18th Street attracts a rambunctious crowd with live music, local improv, and a plethora of bars with neon signs, concrete steps, and quaint awnings. The block also offers conveniently placed parking meters to cling onto when you need to vomit the last few beers before crossing the street to go dancing. Sway to reggae and Caribbean rhythms at **Bukom Café**, and take in blues, jazz, rock or bluegrass at **Madam's Organ**. Roll up your sleeves at **Pharmacy Bar**, DC's best dive bar, which caters more to locals than visitors and has a great Jukebox. For a good cocktail sneak into the **Spy Lounge**. Get blitzed at **Dan's**.

Cleveland Park

Cleveland Park's nightlife is crammed into the 3400 block of Connecticut Avenue, where Irish bars, basement billiards, and dimly-lit enclaves serving sophisticated wines stand next to each other like abducted strangers in the hull of a UFO. You may not like the group, but you'll certainly find at least one friend in the pack. If you appreciate a good Irish stout and/or could relate to the upper deck scene in *Titanic*, then go to **Ireland's Four Provinces**; if you consider yourself more of a lower deck kind of person, check out **Nanny O'Brien's** across the street. **Atomic Billiards** is a good spot for guzzling beer, throwing darts, and shooting pool. **Park Bench Pub** is the trailer home you've always wanted to trash, and attracts the fun sort of people who would love to help you do it. For a relaxing sip of wine after a long day, **Aroma** is the place to sniff, sip, and unwind.

U Street

U Street on weekend nights is where you'll find people boozing, dancing, and taking in live music; these same folks also manage to accomplish some of the best philanthropic work the city's needy and less fortunate have seen in years. Dance clubs, live music venues, and drinking are bringing money, people, and prosperity into one of DC's least attractive areas. U Street is experiencing a revitalization thanks to venues such as the **Black Cat,** the **9:30 Club**, and **Velvet Lounge,** and dance clubs **DC9** and **Daedalus**. Bars such as **Kingpin** and **Stetson's Famous Bar & Restaurant** respect the neighborhood's humble roots, while also providing a place to mingle and perhaps meet that special someone. The area still has shivering huddles of people being whipped by frigid night winds and February snow, but now they are 25 year old divas in high heels and designer jackets. **Dream**, a massive four-floor complex on Okie Street, is also a popular place where VIP membership will cost you just $500 a year and save you the embarrassment of being a regular person in line.

Capitol Hill

Don't forget Capitol Hill's **The Dubliner**, **Kelly's Irish Times**, and **Hawk and Dove**, where you'll find plenty of political wannabes networking their political and professional agendas.

Everything Else

Even sleepy neighborhoods have favorite local bars like **Colonel Brooks' Tavern** in the Catholic U neighborhood, **Whitlows** in Arlington, or **State Theatre** in Falls Church. If you're after a good cocktail, **Iota** in Arlington is one of the best places around for live music, or, if you're feeling funky, walk down the street to the **Galaxy Hut** to experience the "alternative" scene. **Fadó Irish Pub** serves up an excellent selection of imported beers and provides a cozy hangout spot after Caps games. **Tiffany Tavern** in Alexandria is the place to hear bluegrass and get a feel for what DC must have been like in the 60s and 70s.

Map 1 • National Mall

Capitol City Brewing Company	1100 New York Ave NW	202-628-2222	Great IPA.
Eyebar	1716 I St NW	202-785-0270	Check out the sign.
Gordon Biersch Brewery	900 F St NW	202-783-5454	Five great lagers.
Grand Slam Sports Bar	1000 H St NW	202-637-4789	Sports bar perfection.
Harry's Saloon	436 11th St NW	202-628-8140	Reliable burger 'n' Guinness place with unreliable service.
Home	911 F St NW	202-638-4663	Dress up and wait in line to dance.
Old Ebbitt Grill	675 15th St NW	202-347-4800	Democrat or Republican?
Pink Elephant Cocktail Lounge	436 11th St NW	202-628-8140	Not a rare animal in some DC neighborhoods.
Platinum	915 F St NW	202-393-3555	Sleek and swank dance club.
Polly Esther's	605 12th St NW	202-737-1970	Dance to the '80s.
Poste Brasserie Bar	555 8th St NW	202-783-6060	Roomy and comfortable.
Round Robin Bar	1401 Pennsylvania Ave NW	202-628-9100	Old style, old money DC. "Herbal" martinis.
Tequila Beach	1115 F St NW	202-393-5463	Surf-shack tiki bar.

Map 2 • Chinatown / Union Station

Bullfeather's	410 1st St SE	202-543-5005	One of the Hill's true neighborhood bars.
Capitol City Brewing Company	2 Massachusetts Ave NE	202-842-2337	Great IPA.
Coyote Ugly	717 6th St NW	202-589-0016	Stripclub lite; sports TV paradise.
The Dubliner	520 N Capitol St (entrance on F St)	202-737-3773	Cozy, classy Irish pub.
Fadó Irish Pub	808 7th St NW	202-789-0066	Every beer imaginable.
Flying Scotsman	233 2nd St NW	202-783-3848	DC's only Scottish bar and proud of it.
IndeBleu	707 G St NW	202-333-2538	Bring your gold card.
Juste Lounge	1015 1/2 7th St NW	202-393-0939	Martinis, martinis, martinis.
Kelly's Irish Times	14 F St NW	202-543-5433	DC's only Irish pub with a 'swerve' dance club basement.
My Brother's Place	237 2nd St NW	202-347-1350	Cheap, hole-in-the-wall CUA bar.
RFD Washington	810 7th St NW	202-289-2030	Brickskeller's downtown sibling—hundreds of beers.

Map 3 • The Hill

Capitol Lounge	229 Pennsylvania Ave SE	202-547-2098	Hill hangout, do-it-yourself Bloody Mary bar.
Hawk and Dove	329 Pennsylvania Ave SE	202-543-3300	Hill staffer hangout.
Lounge 201	201 Massachusetts Ave NE	202-544-5201	Retro martini bar.
Politiki	319 Pennsylvania Ave SE	202-546-1001	1 building=3 bars. This is the tiki bar.
Top of the Hill	319 Pennsylvania Ave SE	202-546-1001	1 building=3 bars. This has pool and red vinyl.
Tune Inn	331 1/2 Pennsylvania Ave SE	202-543-2725	Dive bar option for an older Hill crowd.

Map 5 • Southeast / Anacostia

Bachelor's Mill	1106 8th St SE	202-544-1931	Gay African-American crowd.
Ellington's on Eighth	424A 8th St SE	202-546-8308	Champagne and jazz.
Finn Mac Cool's	713 8th St SE	202-547-7100	Irish bar not prostituting its culture.
Marty's	527 8th St SE	202-255-2707	Low-key, family-friendly.
Mr Henry's Capitol Hill	601 Pennsylvania Ave SE	202-546-8412	A spot for jazz lovers.
Remington's	639 Pennsylvania Ave SE	202-543-3113	Country western gay bar.
Tapatinis	711 8th St SE	202-546-8272	You've got tapas in my 'tinis! Hip joint (for Capitol Hill).
Tortilla Coast	400 1st St SE	202-546-6768	Different special every night.
Tunnicliff's Tavern	222 7th St SE	202-544-5680	Cheers-esque.
The Ugly Mug	723 8th St SE	202-547-8459	TVs, pool, miniburgers, and beer.

Map 6 • Waterfront

Cantina Marina	600 Water St SW	202-554-8396	Jimmy Buffet goes Latin.
Edge	52 L St SE	202-488-1200	Dance club, part of the gay club scene.
H20	800 Water St SW	202-484-6300	Dining and dancing near water.
Nation	1015 Half St SE	202-554-1500	Live music venue and gay dance club.
Secrets	1345 Half St SE	202-554-5141	How do you gently mention it's a male stripper bar?
Zanzibar on the Waterfront	700 Water St SW	202-554-9100	Hugely popular velvet-rope club.
Ziegfields	1345 Half St SE	202-554-5141	Strip club and drag shows.

Map 7 • Foggy Bottom

Potomac Lounge	2650 Virginia Ave NW	202-965-2300	Cocktails at the Watergate.

Map 8 • Georgetown

Blues Alley	1073 Wisconsin Ave NW	202-337-4141	THE place for live jazz.
Chadwick's	3205 K St NW	202-333-2565	Georgetown dive. (Read: nicer than half the bars in DC.)
Clyde's	3236 M St NW	202-333-9180	Reliable wood-themed bar.
Degrees	3100 S St NW	202-912-4100	Pretty ritzy.
Garrett's	3003 M St NW	202-333-8282	Don't fall down the stairs.
The Guards	2915 M St NW	202-965-2350	For sloppy crowds.
Martin's Tavern	1264 Wisconsin Ave NW	202-333-7370	Gin and tonic crowd.
Mie N Yu	3125 M St NW	202-333-6122	Exotic, Eastern atmosphere and good food.
Modern	3287 M St NW	202-338-7027	Crowded, go on a weeknight.
Mr Smith's	3104 M St NW	202-333-3104	Piano bar with lively crowd; more hardcore upstairs.
Old Glory	3139 M St NW	202-337-3406	Great for daytime drinking.
Rhino Bar & Pumphouse	3295 M St NW	202-333-3150	Cheap beer, dance music, and pool tables.
Riverside Grill	3050 K St NW	202-342-3535	If it's crowded at Tony and Joe's....
Saloun	3239 M St NW	202-965-4900	Dingy drinkin'.
Sequoia	3000 K St NW	202-944-4200	Where type As meet before getting married and divorced.
The Third Edition Bar	1218 Wisconsin Ave NW	202-333-3700	One night stands start here.
The Tombs	1226 36th St NW	202-337-6668	Georgetown institution.
Tony and Joe's	3000 K St NW	202-944-4545	A Georgetown waterfront staple.

Map 9 • Dupont Circle / Adams Morgan

Aroma	2401 Pennsylvania Ave NW	202-296-6383	Good cocktails.
Bar Rouge	1315 16th St NW	202-232-8000	Cool new addition to the neighborhood.
Beacon Bar & Grill	1615 Rhode Island Ave NW	202-872-1126	17th Street Bar & Grill with Botox.
Biddy Mulligan's	1500 New Hampshire Ave NW	202-483-6000	Smoky and Irish in Jury's Hotel.
Big Hunt	1345 Connecticut Ave NW	202-785-2333	Typical bar but Guinness ice cream!
Bravo Bravo	1001 Connecticut Ave NW	202-223-5330	Salsa and Merengue.
Brickskeller	1523 22nd St NW	202-293-1885	Try a beer from Timbuktu.
Buffalo Billiards	1330 19th St NW	202-331-7665	Relaxed poolhall.
Café Citron	1343 Connecticut Ave NW	202-530-8844	Sweat in the crowd downstairs, or dance on boots upstairs.
Café Japone	2032 P St NW	202-223-1573	Serious sake.
Camelot	1823 M St NW	202-887-5966	Honey, they're professional dancers.
Chaos	1603 17th St NW	202-232-4141	Gay and straight, drag bingo, drag brunch.
Chi-Cha Lounge	1624 U St NW	202-234-8400	Informal (ties forbidden) Ecuadorian hacienda.
The Childe Harold	1610 20th St NW	202-483-6700	Brick walls for hard drinking.
Cloud Dining Lounge	1 Dupont Cir	202-872-1122	Frou-frou drinks on beds.
Cobalt/30 Degrees	1639 R St NW	202-462-6569	Smoke-free 30 Degrees, smokey Cobalt.
Common Share	2003 18th St NW	202-518-6847	Dive; bike courier heaven.
Dragonfly	1215 Connecticut Ave NW	202-331-1775	All-white and all-trendy.
Eighteenth Street Lounge	1212 18th St NW	202-466-3922	Dragonfly's older brother—hip but mature about it.
Firefly	1310 New Hampshire Ave NW	202-861-1310	Sophisticated drinking.
Fireplace	2161 P St NW	202-293-1293	Landmark gay bar.
Fox and Hounds Lounge	1537 17th St NW	202-232-6307	Where uptight people go to relax.
Front Page	1333 New Hampshire Ave NW	202-296-6500	Pre-10 pm: businessman's grill; post-10 pm: strictly t and a.
Gazuza	1629 Connecticut Ave NW	202-667-5500	Upscale tapas lounge—go early for patio seating.
Improv	1140 Connecticut Ave NW	202-296-7008	Don't laugh up your weak rum and coke.
Kramerbooks & Afterwords Café	1517 Connecticut Ave NW	202-387-3825	Favorite hangout of local writers.
La Frontera Cantina	1633 17th St NW	202-232-0437	Have a Corona and people-watch.
Lauriol Plaza	1835 18th St	202-387-0035	Cacophonous Tex-Mex.
Local 16	1602 U St NW	202-265-2828	Cavernous and cool.
Lulu's	1217 22nd St NW	202-861-5858	New Orleans-style meat market.
Madhatter	1831 M St NW	202-833-1495	A midtown dive bar with character.
McClellan's	1919 Connecticut Ave NW	202-483-3000	Hilton Hotel sports bar.
MCCXXIII	1223 Connecticut Ave NW	202-822-1800	Swank club for grinding.
McFadden's	2401 Pennsylvania Ave NW	202-223-2338	You've been to one, you've been to 'em all.
Omega DC	2122 P St NW	202-223-4917	Mature men gay bar.
Ozio	1813 M St NW	202-822-6000	Sip a cocktail and puff a cigar.
Recessions	1823 L St NW	202-296-6686	Basement bar.
Red	1802 Jefferson Pl NW	202-466-3475	Go after midnight.
Rumors	1900 M St NW	202-466-7378	After-work drinks downtown.
Russia House Restaurant and Lounge	1800 Connecticut Ave NW	202-234-9433	Swanky joint beloved by eurotrash.
Sign of the Whale	1825 M St NW	202-785-1110	Cozy and cheap.
Soussi	2228 18th St NW	202-299-9314	Outdoor wine bar.
Staccato	2006 18th St NW	202-232-2228	Good music, great burgers.
Stetson's Famous Bar & Restaurant	1610 U St NW	202-667-6295	Drink with Jenna Bush (while you can).
Tabard Inn - Bar	1739 N St NW	202-331-8528	Romantic rendezvous.
Tequila Grill	1990 K St NW	202-833-3640	Get smashed for five bucks.
The Wave!	1731 New Hampshire Ave NW	202-518-5011	Carlyle Suites club.

Map 9 • Dupont Circle / Adams Morgan—*continued*

Timberlake's	1726 Connecticut Ave NW	202-483-2266	Cheers' destination for 30-50-yr olds.
Topaz Bar	1733 N St NW	202-393-3000	Go for the drinks.
Townhouse Tavern	1637 R St NW	202-234-5747	Get your Schlitz in a can.
Trio's Fox & Hounds	1533 17th St NW	202-232-6307	Patio drinking.
Zebra Bar and Lounge	1170 22nd St NW	202-974-6600	Hotel cocktail lounge.

Map 10 • Logan Circle / U Street

9:30 Club	815 V St NW	202-393-0930	A DC musical institution.
Bar Nun	1326 U St NW	202-667-6680	Fridays are bound to be interesting.
Black Cat	1811 14th St NW	202-667-7960	The OTHER place in DC to see a band.
Bohemian Caverns	2001 11th St NW	202-299-0800	Cool jazz in the basement.
Daedalus	1010 Vermont Ave NW	202-347-9066	Make a reservation.
DC9	1940 9th St NW	202-483-5000	Rock club.
Halo Lounge	1435 P St NW	202-797-9730	Stylish nightspot with plenty of seats and no smoke.
Helix Lounge	1430 Rhode Island Ave NW	202-462-9001	New trendy neighborhood addition.
Republic Gardens	1355 U St NW	202-232-2710	Famous DC music club.
The Saloon	1207 U St NW	202-462-2640	European appeal—go for the beer.
Titan	1337 14th St NW	202-232-7010	Gay bar at Hamburger Mary's.
Twins Jazz	1344 U St NW	202-234-0072	Intimate bar with Ethiopian food.

Map 11 • Near Northeast

Bud's	501 Morse St NE	202-543-4419	Off-the-beaten-path restaurant and nightclub.
FUR Nightclub	33 Patterson St NE	202-842-3401	Clubbing emporium.

Map 12 • Trinidad

Dream	1350 Okie St NE	202-636-9030	Huge nightclub.

Map 13 • Brookland / Langdon

Aqua	1818 New York Ave NE	202-832-4878	Asian dance club at a Korean restaurant.
Breeze Metro	2335 Bladensburg Rd NE	202-526-8880	DC's go-go joint.
DC Tunnel	2135 Queens Chapel Rd NE	202-526-7960	Go-go and dancehall reggae shows.

Map 14 • Catholic U

Colonel Brooks' Tavern	901 Monroe St NE	202-529-4002	Neighborhood landmark.
Johnny K's	3514 12th St NE	202-832-3945	Do not attempt to come here if you're over 21.

Map 15 • Columbia Heights

Wonderland Bar and Grill	1101 Kenyon St NW	202-232-5263	Crowded, smoky, fun neighborhood dive. Great bratwurst.

Map 16 • Adams Morgan (North) / Mt Pleasant

Adams Mill Bar and Grill	1813 Adams Mill Rd NW	202-332-9577	Pitchers after the softball game.
Angles Bar & Billiards	2339 18th St NW	202-462-8100	Dive bar with great burgers; a favorite of reporters.
Angry Inch Saloon	2450 18th St NW	202-234-3041	Bare bones drinkin'.
Asylum	2471 18th St NW	202-319-9353	Goth decor and pounding music.
Bedrock Billiards	1841 Columbia Rd NW	202-667-7665	Pool hall with extensive alcohol choices.
Blue Room Lounge	2321 18th St NW	202-332-0800	Great wines, with trip-hop soundtrack.
Bossa	2463 18th St NW	202-667-0088	Cool downstairs, samba upstairs.
Brass Monkey	2317 18th St NW	202-667-7800	Amateur night yuppie hangout.
Bukom Café	2442 18th St NW	202-265-4600	West African music and a diverse crowd.

Café Toulouse	2431 18th St NW	202-332-2550	Cozy bar with live jazz and blues.
Chief Ike's Mambo Room	1725 Columbia Rd NW	202-332-2211	Dirty dance 'til dawn.
Columbia Station	2325 18th St NW	202-462-6040	More jazz and blues in an intimate setting.
Cosmo Lounge	1725 Columbia Rd NW	202-332-2211	For the rock-and-roll crowd.
Crush	2323 18th St NW	202-319-1111	Popular and crowded.
Dan's	2315 18th St NW	202-265-9241	No frills.
Felix Lounge	2406 18th St NW	202-483-3549	Pretentious or sophisticated? Try it out.
Kokopooli's Pool Hall	2305 18th St NW	202-234-2306	Pool and beer.
Left Bank	2424 18th St NW	202-464-2100	Chic faux-retro European décor, and pretty people.
Madam's Organ	2461 18th St NW	202-667-5370	Redheads get a discount; best blues in DC.
Pharmacy Bar	2337 18th St NW	202-483-1200	Low-key alternabar.
Pharaoh's	1817 Columbia Rd NW	202-232-6009	Rockin' blues.
The Raven	3125 Mt Pleasant St NW	202-387-8411	Neighborhood bar.
The Reef	2446 18th St NW	202-518-3800	Jellyfish and drinks.
Rumba Café	2443 18th St NW	202-588-5501	Cuban treats.
Spy Lounge	2406 18th St NW	202-483-3549	Felix's spy dive sibling.
Timehri International	2439 18th St NW	202-518-2626	Reggae, Calypso, R&B.
Toledo Lounge	2435 18th St NW	202-986-5416	Unpretentious, '50s-themed dive bar.
Tom Tom	2333 18th St	202-518-6667	Play old school Nintendo upstairs.
Tonic Bar	3155 Mt Pleasant St NW	202-986-7661	Local tavern.
Zucchabar	1841 Columbia Rd NW	202-332-8642	Friendly bartenders, well-made drinks.

Map 17 • Woodley Park / Cleveland Park

Aroma	3417 Connecticut Ave NW	202-244-7995	Good cocktails.
Ireland's Four Provinces (4Ps)	3412 Connecticut Ave NW	202-244-0860	Have a pint and name the Ps.
Nanny O'Brien's	3319 Connecticut Ave NW	202-686-9189	Legendary Celtic jam sessions.
Oxford Tavern Zoo Bar	3000 Connecticut Ave NW	202-232-4225	Low-key with live blues bands.

Map 18 • Glover Park / Foxhall

Bourbon	2348 Wisconsin Ave NW	202-625-7770	Great bourbon, of course.
Good Guys Restaurant	2311 Wisconsin Ave NW	202-333-8128	Friendly, low-bling rock-and-roll strip club.
Grog and Tankard	2408 Wisconsin Ave NW	202-333-3114	Longest-running live music bar in the DC area.
Zebra Lounge	3238 Wisconsin Ave NW	202-237-2202	New and improved.

Map 19 • Tenleytown / Friendship Heights

Chadwick's	5247 Wisconsin Ave NW	202-362-8040	Metro-convenient location--burgers and bar.
Guapo's	4515 Wisconsin Ave NW	202-686-3588	Tortillas + margaritas = stumbling to Tenleytown Metro.
Maggianos	5333 Wisconsin Ave NW	202-966-2593	Italian restaurant with accommodating Latino bar staff.
Malt Shop	4611 Wisconsin Ave NW	202-244-9733	Wood walls and floors for sloppy AU students.

Map 20 • Cleveland Park / Upper Connecticut

Atomic Billiards	3427 Connecticut Ave NW	202-363-7665	Subterranean pool, darts, and beer.
Park Bench Pub	3433 Connecticut Ave NW	202-686-9235	Drunkenness IS the décor.

Map 21 • 16th St Heights / Petworth

Twins Lounge	5516 Colorado Ave NW	202-882-2523	Intimate jazz club.

Map 22 • Downtown Bethesda

Black's Bar & Kitchen	7750 Woodmont Ave	301-652-6278	Good seafood—drink outside on nice nights.

Map 22 • Downtown Bethesda—*continued*

Rock Bottom Brewery	7900 Norfolk Ave	301-652-1311	Worth the wait.
Saphire	7940 Wisconsin Ave	301-986-9708	Average bar.
South Beach Café	7904 Woodmont Ave	301-718-9737	Dirt-cheap happy hour.
Yacht Club of Bethesda	8111 Woodmont Ave	301-654-2396	Best known for cheezy TV commericals.

Map 25 • Silver Spring

Mayorga	8040 Georgia Ave	301-562-9090	Coffee by day, microbrew by night.
Quarry House Tavern	8401 Georgia Ave	301-587-9406	Simply great.

Map 26 • Takoma Park

Taliano's	7001 Carroll Ave	301-270-5515	Open mic nights are a must.

Map 27 • Walter Reed

Charlie's	7307 Georgia Ave NW	202-726-3567	Soul food and contemporary jazz.
Takoma Station Tavern	6914 4th St NW	202-829-1999	Jazz haven.

Map 28 • Chevy Chase

Chevy Chase Lounge	5510 Connecticut Ave NW	202-966-7600	Parthenon Restaurant's wood panelled lounge.

Map 29 • Bethesda/Chevy Chase Business

Barking Dog	4723 Elm St	301-654-0022	Decent frat boy bar.
Flanagan's	7637 Old Georgetown Rd	301-986-1007	Authentic Irish bartenders.
Strike Bethesda	5353 Westbard Ave	301-652-0955	Not your average bowling alley.
Tommy Joe's	4714 Montgomery Ln	301-654-3801	Frat boy central.
Uncle Jed's Roadhouse	7525 Old Georgetown Rd	301-913-0026	Southern-style roadhouse.

Map 33 • Falls Church

Ireland's Four Provinces	105 W Broad St	703-534-8999	Why are you in Falls Church? (A good bar, nonetheless.)
Lost Dog Café	5876 Washington Blvd	703-237-1552	Buy a beer, adopt a pet.

Map 34 • Ballston

Bailey's Pub and Grille	4234 Wilson Blvd	703-465-1300	A sports superbar with a gazillion TVs.
Carpool	4000 N Fairfax Dr	703-532-7665	Pool, darts, and beers on the patio.
Cowboy Café	4792 Lee Hwy	703-243-8010	Neighborhood bar and burgers.
Rock Bottom Brewery	4238 Wilson Blvd	703-516-7688	Go for happy hour.

Map 35 • Clarendon

Clarendon Ballroom	3185 Wilson Blvd	703-469-2244	Head for the rooftop.
Clarendon Grill	1101 N Highland St	703-524-7455	"What?" Get used to saying that here.
Galaxy Hut	2711 Wilson Blvd	703-525-8646	Tiny, friendly, indie rock hangout.
Harry's Tap Room	2800 Clarendon Blvd	703-778-7788	City atmosphere 'til midnight, then it becomes the suburbs again.
Iota	2832 Wilson Blvd	703-522-8340	Great place to see a twangy band.
Mister Days	3100 Clarendon Blvd	703-527-1600	Pick-up bar disguised as a sports bar.
Molly Malone's	3207 Washington Blvd	703-812-0939	A section to party and a section to chill.
Whitlow's on Wilson	2854 Wilson Blvd	703-276-9693	A separate room for whatever mood you're in.

Map 36 • Rosslyn

Continental	1911 Ft Myer Dr	703-465-7675	Pool with a modern spin.
Ireland's Four Courts	2051 Wilson Blvd	703-525-3600	Where beer-guzzling yuppies come to see (double) and be seen.
Rhodeside Grill	1836 Wilson Blvd	703-243-0145	Neighborhood bar with basement for bands.
Summers Grill and Sports Pub	1520 N Courthouse Rd	703-528-8278	Soccer-watching bar.

Map 37 • Fort Myer

Jay's Saloon	3114 N 10th St	703-527-3093	Down-home and friendly.
Royal Lee Bar and Grill	2211 N Pershing Dr	703-524-5493	All American.
Tallula	2761 Washington Blvd	703-778-5051	Swanky-dank wine bar.

Map 39 • Shirlington

The Bungalow, Billiards & Brew Co	2766 S Arlington Mill Dr	703-578-0020	Fun billiards and brews.
Capitol City Brewing Company	2700 S Quincy St	703-578-3888	Great IPA.
Guapo's	4028 S 28th St	703-671-1701	Bueno Mexican, killer margaritas.

Map 40 • Pentagon City

Sine Irish Pub	1301 S Joyce St	703-415-4420	Generic Irish pub.

Map 41 • Landmark

Mango Mike's	4580 Duke St	703-370-3800	Pub grub from the islands, mon.
Shooter McGee's	5239 Duke St	703-751-9266	Another "silly first name, Irish last name" place.

Map 43 • Four Mile Run

Birchmere	3701 Mt Vernon Ave	703-549-7500	Music, music, music.

Map 46 • Old Town (South)

Café Salsa	808 King St	703-684-4100	THE hottest salsa club in the DC area.
Founders' Brewing Company	607 King St	703-684-5397	German-style beers.
Hard Times Café	1404 King St	703-837-0050	Nothing but chili, but plenty of it.
Laughing Lizzard Lounge	1324 King St	703-548-2582	Go for the pool and a cold beer.
Murphy's	713 King St	703-548-1717	Favorite pub of the locals.
Rock It Grill	1319 King St	703-739-2274	Lowbrow and proud.
South Austin Grill	801 King St	703-684-8969	Great Tex/Mex; just outside, Janet Reno got a parking ticket!
State Theatre	220 N Washington St	703-237-0300	Grab a table, a beer, and listen.
Tiffany Tavern	1116 King St	703-836-8844	Bluegrass central.
Vermillion	1120 King St	703-684-9669	No-frills lounge.

Baltimore

Bohager's	701 South Eden St	410-363-7220	Imported sand and palm-trees outside, dance hall and wet t-shirt contests inside.
Club Charles	1724 N Charles St	410-727-8815	Dive bar extraordinaire; all the clocks inside are set 20 minutes ahead. And there's a good chance you'll run into John Waters.
Cross Street Market	1065 S Charles St		Indoor market with a raucous, locals-filled happy hour.
The Horse You Came In On	1626 Thames St	410-327-8111	Feel like a sailor in this dirty ol' place right on the waterfront.

There are four types of people in DC: high rollers, wannabes who pretend to be high rollers, counter-culture hippies who protest the indulgent lifestyle of high rollers, but who actually make enough money to be classified as high rollers (also known as Dupont liberals), and foreigners, who may or may not be high rollers, but it doesn't matter because their parents are high rollers in other lands. In order to provide pertinent restaurant information for every DC type, we've listed some of our favorite restaurants under four different categories: **Eating Posh**, **Eating Cheap**, **Eating Hip,** and **Eating Ethnic**. (For patrons who frequent the beaneries listed under category two, we look forward to meeting you one day.)

Eating Posh

In the land of lobbyists, lawyers, and congressmen, there are bound to be plenty of chi-chi restaurants—DC's equivalent of Hollywood nightclubs. Posh in DC often means old, and grandfathers **Old Ebbitt Grill** and **Occidental Grill** have been around practically as long as The White House. If steak is on the evening's agenda, your best bets are **The Palm**, **Morton's of Chicago,** and **Prime Rib** (the only restaurant in Washington that still requires gentlemen to wear a coat and tie). For French decadence, look no further than **Citronelle**, **Gerard's Place**, **1789 Restaurant,** and **Le Paradou**. If Italian is your indulgence, then mangia bene at **Galileo**, **Café Milano,** or **I Ricchi**. **Sequoia** on the Georgetown Waterfront is the ultimate spot to see and be seen, and neighboring restaurant **Nathan's** is moderately priced and always buzzing with the power lunch crowd. The excellent New American **Aquarelle** has an elegant setting downstairs at the Watergate, and you will leave the brilliant **Vidalia** convinced that it was worth the money.

Eating Cheap

Eating cheap in DC doesn't have to mean hitting up McDonald's, and the experience can even prove quite pleasant and romantic. Two of DC's most famous joints, **El Pollo Rico** and **Ben's Chili Bowl**, will cost you between $5 and $10 a meal, and **Café Parisien Express** serves up double portions of French food for half the French price. If pizza is your poison, the pies at **Pizzeria Paradiso** and **2 Amys** will totally knock your socks off. For unique atmosphere, check out **Mexicali Blues** and the Dupont institution **Kramerbooks & Afterwords Café**. Mexican standouts **Rio Grande Café** and **El Paso Café**, both west of the river, are as delicious as they are affordable. Rounding out the cheap eats list are 24-hour steakhouse **Annie's Paramount**, Chinatown BBQ pit **Capital Q**, out-of-this-world chili machine **Hard Times Café**, and Jewish deli **K's New York Deli**.

Eating Hip

No, New York does not own a monopoly on *all* the hip places to dine. Congressmen loosen their ties every now and again, too. The hot new kid on the block is **Zaytinya**, and its cousins **Café Atlantico** and **Jaleo** are just as sizzling. **Café Saint-Ex** is a microcosm of the U Street trend, and **Café Citron**, **Lauriol Plaza,** and **Obelisk** are the spots where Dupont hipsters rendezvous. **Felix Restaurant and Lounge** and **Cashion's Eat Place** have always been in vogue among Adams Morgan rockers, and **Tryst** is DC's ultimate coffeehouse. **TenPenh** is the scene of DC's hottest Asian fusion, and the chic **15 Ria** honestly belongs in NYC. **Harry's Tap Room** is an up-and-comer among Arlingtonian yuppies, and for California cool, **Restaurant Nora** is there to fulfill all of your organic fantasies.

Eating Ethnic

While America's population may look more like a chef's salad than a melting pot, with ethnic groups living next to each other, but not quite together, at least we all love to eat each other's food. So put your Ruby Tuesday's fork down and challenge your palette. No better place to do this than **Tony Cheng's Seafood Restaurant**, the cream of the Chinatown crop. Its H Street rivals include **Burma Restaurant** and **Full Kee**, and although **Meiwah** is in Dupont, it stands up to the Chinatown mix. Indian food lovers rave over **Heritage India**, **Aditi,** and **Amma Vegetarian Kitchen**. For the best sushi this side of the Pacific, **Makoto Restaurant** and **Sushi-Ko's** are all you'll need. Experience the Middle East at **Mama Ayesha's** and Morocco at **Marrakesh Restaurant,** which features belly dancers every night. **Malaysia Kopitiam**, the Mexican **Mixtec** and the pan-Asian **Raku** each also get an A-plus in our not-so-humble opinion. And don't miss out on **Roger Miller Restaurant**, a tiny little Cameroonian gem in Silver Spring, for all your curry goat needs.

*Key: $: Under $10 / $$: $10-$20 / $$$: $20-$30 / $$$$: $30+   * : Does not accept credit cards. / † : Accepts only American Express.*

Map 1 • National Mall

Bistro D'Oc	518 10th St NW	202-393-5444	$$$$	Tasteful French.
Café Asia	1720 I St NW	202-659-2696	$$$	Not quite as crowded as Asia but just as busy.
Café Atlantico	405 8th St NW	202-393-0812	$$$	Upscale Nuevo Latino; Best mojitos in town.
Caucus Room	401 9th St NW	202-393-1300	$$$$	The taste of power. A favorite for DC's elite.
Ceiba	701 14th St NW	202-393-3983	$$$$	Brazilian indulgence, brought to you by the makers of Tenpenh.
Chef Geoff's	1301 Pennsylvania Ave NW	202-464-4461	$$$	Why the hell would a parent name their kid Geoff?
Equinox	818 Connecticut Ave NW	202-331-8118	$$$$	The finest food of the Chesapeake region.
ESPN Zone	555 12th St NW	202-783-3776	$$	Forget the baseball players. This restaurant is on the juice.
Gerard's Place	915 15th St NW	202-737-4445	$$$$	La crème de la crème of DC French dining.
Hard Rock Café	999 E St NW	202-737-7625	$$	Remember when you thought this place was cool?
Harry's Restaurant and Saloon	436 11th St NW	202-624-0053	$$	Downtown DC dining with a hometown corner restaurant feel.
John Harvard's Brew House	E St NW & 13th St NW	202-783-2739	$$$	Cap off your evening at the theater by drinking real beer.
Les Halles	1201 Pennsylvania Ave NW	202-347-6848	$$$	French food with a good 'ole American twist.
Occidental	1475 Pennsylvania Ave NW	202-783-1475	$$$$	Opulent White House classic.
Old Ebbitt Grill	675 15th St NW	202-347-4800	$$$$	The quintessential Washington restaurant. Try to spot your local congressman.
Ortanique	730 11th St NW	202-393-0975	$$$$*	Caribbean fare and Miami flavor.
Teaism	400 8th St NW	202-638-6010	$$	Would you like a dinner with your cup of tea?
Teaism	800 Connecticut NW	202-835-2233	$$	Need a teapot? Buy one with lunch!
TenPenh	1001 Pennsylvania Ave NW	202-393-4500	$$$$	DC's hottest Asian fusion.
Willard Room	1401 Pennsylvania Ave NW	202-637-7440	$$$$	If not the richest breakfast in town, definitely the most expensive.
Zaytinya	701 9th St NW	202-638-0800	$$$$	Tasty mezze menu offered by award-winning chef. Fabulous interior.

Map 2 • Chinatown / Union Station

701	701 Pennsylvania Ave NW	202-393-0701	$$$$	Posh food and soft jazz.
America	Union Station 50 Massachusetts Ave	202-682-9555	$$	USA managed like a third world country.
Andale	401 7th St NW	202-783-3133	$$$$	Upscale Mexican. Start it off with Guacamole to die for.
B Smith's	50 Massachusetts Ave NE	202-289-6188	$$$$	Creole elegance, jarring in Union Station.
Bistro Bis	15 E St NW	202-661-2700	$$$$	Pricey, but a solid place for an upscale lunch on the Hill.
Burma	740 6th St NW	202-638-1280	$$	Green tea leaf salad. We kid you not.
Capital Q	707 H St NW	202-347-8396	$*	Hearty Texan portions will put hair on yer chest.
Capitol City Brewing Company	2 Massachusetts Ave NE	202-842-2337	$$*	Quality beer worth the tourists that come with the territory.
Center Café at Union Station	Union Station, 50 Massachusetts Ave NE	202-682-0143	$$	Enjoy the scenery from the middle of the country's best RR station.
Chinatown Express	746 6th St NW	202-638-0424	$$	Watch food preperation from the street and decide for yourself.
District Chophouse	509 7th St NW	202-347-3434	$$$$	Impressive roaring 20s atmosphere. Avoid MCI game night.
Fadó Irish Pub	808 7th St NW	202-789-0066	$$$	Antiquish décor and self-promoting gift shop. Disneyland for alcoholics.
Flying Scotsman	233 2nd St NW	202-783-3848	$$	Pub favored by aspiring Hill elites.
Fuddrucker's	734 7th St NW	202-628-3380	$$	7th Street used to be authentic….
Full Kee	509 H St NW	202-371-2233	$$	Chinatown can be overwhelming. We'll make it easier. Eat here.
Jaleo	480 7th St NW	202-628-7949	$$$$	The tapas king of DC. Great for first dates.

*Key: $: Under $10 / $$: $10-$20 / $$$: $20-$30 / $$$$: $30+ * : Does not accept credit cards. / † : Accepts only American Express.*

Map 2 • Chinatown / Union Station—*continued*

The Dubliner Restaurant	520 N Capitol St NW	202-737-3773	$$	Hearty Irish pub grub for Washington bureaucracy.
Kelly's Irish Times	14 F St NW	202-543-5433	$$	Look to your left. See The Dubliner? Go there.
Le Paradou	678 Indiana Ave NW	202-347-6780	$$$$	Dahling, shall we sip '81 Bordeaux or '79 Barolo this evening?
Lei Garden	629 H St NW	202-216-9696	$$	Can't beat the dim sum on the rolling carts.
Matchbox	713 H St NW	202-289-4441	$$$	Where martinis meet pizza.
My Brother's Place	237 2nd St NW	202-347-1350	$$	A lunchtime hole in the wall.
Rosa Mexicano	575 7th St NW	202-783-5522	$$$$	MCI Center destination. Try the pomegranate margarita.
Tony Cheng's Mongolian Restaurant	619 H St NW, downstairs	202-842-8669	$$	No reason to dine here. Upstairs is where you want to be.
Tony Cheng's Seafood Restaurant	619 H St NW, upstairs	202-371-8669	$$	Overlook gaudy décor and enjoy best Chinese Washington offers. (upstairs)

Map 3 • The Hill

Café Berlin	322 Massachusetts Ave NE	202-543-7656	$$	For all your Oktoberfest needs.
Hawk 'n' Dove	329 Pennsylvania Ave SE	202-543-3300	$$	One of the oldest games in town. Do lunch, not dinner.
Kenny's Smokehouse	732 Maryland Ave NE	202-547-4553	$	BBQ with oodles of sides.
La Brasserie	239 Massachusetts Ave NE	202-546-9154	$$$$	Cozy French fare at very reasonable prices.
La Loma Mexican Restaurant	316 Massachusetts Ave NE	202-548-2550	$$	They make you pay for refills. Enough said.
Pete's Diner	212 2nd St SE	202-544-7335	$	With a completely Asian staff, you wonder who "Pete" is.
Ristorante Tosca	1112 F St NW	202-367-1990	$$$$	Un ristorante tanto elegante.
Sonoma	223 Pennsylvania Ave SE	202-544-8088	$$$	40 wines by the glass. The *Sideways* characters would be proud.
Two Quail	320 Massachusetts Ave NE	202-543-8030	$$$$	Romantic little Hill spot.
White Tiger	301 Massachusetts Ave NE	202-546-5900	$$	Best Capitol Hill Indian food.

Map 5 • Southeast / Anacostia

Banana Café & Piano Bar	500 8th St SE	202-543-5906	$$$	Democrat-friendly Hill cabana.
Bread & Chocolate	666 Pennsylvania Ave SE	202-547-2875	$	Here it's dessert before dinner. Go with the chocolate truffle cake.
Meyhane	633 Pennsylvania Ave SE	202-544-4753	$$$	Exotic Turkish tapas.
Montmartre	327 7th St SE	202-544-1244	$$$$	Comfortable French bistro.
Starfish	539 8th St SE	202-546-5006	$$$	Seafood from the people behind Banana Café.
Tortilla Coast	400 1st St SE	202-546-6768	$	Favorite Hill non-power lunch spot.

Map 6 • Waterfront

Cantina Marina	600 Water St SW	202-554-8396	$$	Ordering advice: avoid the cantina; go with the marina.
H2O at Hogate's	800 Water St SW	202-484-6300	$$$$	Waterfront home of the rum bun.
Jenny's Asian Fusion	1000 Water St SW	202-554-2202	$$$	Good food, but depressing atmosphere, regardless of the water.
Phillip's Flagship	900 Water St SW	202-488-8515	$$$	Fresh Atlantic fish not worth pathetic portions and lousy service.
Pier 7	650 Water St SW	202-554-2500	$$	Showy waterfront seafood.

Map 7 • Foggy Bottom

600 Restaurant at the Watergate	600 New Hampshire Ave NW	202-337-5890	$$$	Formerly Dominique's; the pre-Kennedy Center locale.
Aquarelle	2650 Virginia Ave NW	202-298-4455	$$$$	Revived Clinton-era French Mediterranean restaurant at the Watergate.
Bread Line	1751 Pennsylvania Ave NW	202-822-8900	$$	Screw South Beach if it means you can't eat here. (Lunch only.)

Dish	924 25th St NW	202-383-8707	$$$$	Southern infusion for inquisitive palates.
Karma	1919 I St NW	202-331-5800	$$	Mediterranean restaurant and art gallery.
Kaz Sushi Bistro	1915 I St NW	202-530-5500	$$$	Proof that you can use word "bistro" with any culture.
Kinkead's	2000 Pennsylvania Ave NW	202-296-7700	$$$$	Elegant seafood, extravagant raw bar.
Primi Piatti	2013 I St NW	202-223-3600	$$$$	Eat like an Italian, but you'll want to dress up like one too.
Roof Terrace Restaurant and Bar	2700 F St NW	202-416-8555	$$$$	Treating her to a JFK concert? Go the whole nine yards.
Taberna Del Alabardero	1776 I St NW	202-429-2200	$$$$	Wide-open menu dares you to be bold.

Map 8 • Georgetown

1789	1226 36th St NW	202-965-1789	$$$$	Beautiful setting next to GU. Too bad students can't afford it.
Aditi	3299 M St NW	202-625-6825	$$	Indian restaurant that has stood the test of time.
Amma Vegetarian Kitchen	3291 M St NW	202-625-6625	$$	Who says vegetarians can't enjoy Indian food?
Café Bonaparte	1522 Wisconsin Ave NW	202-333-8830	$	Fine French-onion soup.
Café Divan	1834 Wisconsin Ave NW	202-338-1747	$$$	It's Turkish, so anything with the word "Kebab" is safe bet.
Café Milano	3251 Prospect St NW	202-333-6183	$$$$	Would you care for a celebrity sighting with your tiramisu?
Chadwick's	3205 K St NW	202-333-2565	$$	Go strictly for a burger.
Citronelle	3000 M St NW	202-625-2150	$$$$	A Tony Williams favorite. ($50 single dishes. Bon appetit!)
Clyde's	3236 M St NW	202-333-9180	$$$	Famous Georgetown saloon, made less notable through suburban franchising.
Fahrenheit & Degrees	3100 S St NW	202-912-4110	$$$$	Italian-American in the deco Ritz-Carlton hotel.
Filomena Ristorante	1063 Wisconsin Ave NW	202-338-8800	$$$$	See Mama Leone tossing bread behind the window as you enter.
Furin's	2805 M St NW	202-965-1000	$	Small-town feel on edge of bustling Georgetown. (Breakfast and lunch.)
J Paul's	3218 M St NW	202-333-3450	$$$	Wanna feel like a pompous Georgetown loudmouth? It's kinda fun!
La Chaumiere	2813 M St NW	202-338-1784	$$$	Mon Dieu! Are we in Georgetown or Paris?
The Landmark	2430 Pennsylvania Ave NW	202-955-3863	$$$	Melrose Hotel continental restaurant.
Martin's Tavern	1264 Wisconsin NW	202-333-7370	$$$	Cubbyholed tables add flair to this old-school saloon.
Morton's of Georgetown	3251 Prospect St NW	202-342-6258	$$$$	Steaks a la carte will make converts out of vegetarians.
Mr Smith's	3104 M St NW	202-333-3104	$$$	Mr. Smith, you have an ordinary name and an ordinary restaurant.
Nathan's	3150 M St NW	202-338-2000	$$$$	Where powerful Washingtonians have superpower lunches.
Old Glory All-American BBQ	3139 M St NW	202-337-3406	$$	Southeast-style BBQ, with hoppin' john on the side.
Pizzeria Paradiso	3282 M St NW	202-337-1245	$$	Pizza this good should not be this cheap.
Riverside Grill	3050 K St NW	202-342-3535	$$$	Plays third fiddle to Sequoia and T&J's, but also most peaceful.
Romeo's Café and Pizzeria	2132 Wisconsin Ave NW	202-337-1111	$	Most college kids order Domino's; Georgetown kids order Romeo's.
Sequoia	3000 K St NW	202-944-4200	$$$$	A Georgetown see-and-be-seen hotspot.
The Third Edition	1218 Wisconsin Ave NW	202-333-3700	$$	If it's bar food you're after, it's bar food you got.
The Tombs	1226 36th St NW	202-337-6668	$$	An underground GU favorite.
Tony And Joe's Seafood Place	3000 K St NW	202-944-4545	$$$	Waterfront views attract the beautiful people.

*Key: $: Under $10 / $$: $10-$20 / $$$: $20-$30 / $$$$: $30+ * : Does not accept credit cards. / † : Accepts only American Express.*

Map 9 • Dupont Circle / Adams Morgan

15 Ria	1515 Rhode Island Ave NW	202-742-0015	$$$$	New York chic dining in the nation's capital.
Al Tiramisu	2014 P St NW	202-467-4466	$$$$	Romantic climate, friendly Italian service will make it a bella notte.
Annie's Paramount	1609 17th St NW	202-232-0395	$$	24-hour gay (straight-friendly) steak joint; packed Sunday brunch.
Biddy Mulligan's	1500 New Hampshire Ave NW	202-483-6000	$$$	Fantistic atmosphere, but hotel food tastes very, well, hotelish.
Bistrot du Coin	1738 Connecticut Ave NW	202-234-6969	$$$$	French joint, nix the stuffiness.
The Brickskellar	1523 22nd St NW	202-293-1885	$$	Renowned beer selection overshadows some damn fine eats.
Café Citron	1343 Connecticut Ave NW	202-530-8844	$$$	South American cuisine sets stage for serious dance party.
Café Luna	1633 P St NW	202-387-4005	$$$	Always busy, yet always intimate. Enjoy the Dupont open air.
Chi-Cha Lounge	1624 U St NW	202-234-8400	$$$	Kick off an evening on U with tapas, sangria, and a hookah.
Daily Grill	1200 18th St NW	202-822-5282	$$$	A 40-entrée menu.
Food Bar DC	1639 R St NW	202-462-6200	$$$	Similar to the NYC venue in name only.
Front Page Restaurant and Grill	1333 New Hampshire Ave NW	202-296-6500	$$$	Walls bedecked with newspaper dating back to the mid-20th century.
Galileo/ Il Laboratorio del Galileo	1110 21st St NW	202-293-7191 202-331-0880	$$$$	Perhaps the finest Italian in DC.
I Ricchi	1220 19th St NW	202-835-0459	$$$$	Restaurants in Italy aren't even this upscale.
Johnny's Half Shell	2002 P St NW	202-296-2021	$$$	Best crabcakes in Washington. Friendly bartstaff attracts solo diners.
Kramerbooks & Afterwords Café	1517 Connecticut Ave NW	202387-1462	$$	Restaurant? Bookstore? One-of-a-kind establishment a must-visit.
Lauriol Plaza	1835 18th St NW	202-387-0035	$$$	Ritzy architecture doesn't match run-of-the-mill dishes.
Local 16	1602 U St NW	202-265-2828	$$$$	The classiest place on U.
Love Café	1501 U St NW	202-265-9800	$*	Achingly tasty fresh-baked sweets and cakes.
Luna Grill & Diner	1301 Connecticut Ave NW	202-835-2280	$$	Great brunch.
Mackey's Public House	1823 L St NW	202-331-7667	$$	Proud to say "NO green beer will be served on St. Paddy's Day!"
Malaysia Kopitiam	1827 M St NW	202-833-6232	$$	Menu offers extensive notes for rookie Malaysian diners.
Marcel's	2401 Pennsylvania Ave NW	202-296-1166	$$$$	Sheer decadence.
McCormick and Schmick's	1652 K St NW	202-861-2233	$$$	A K Street staple. Exploit the happy hour food specials.
Meiwah	1200 New Hampshire Ave NW	202-833-2888	$$$	The lighter side of Chinese food.
Melrose	1201 24th St NW	202-419-6755	$$$$	French, Asian, Middle Eastern fusion = American.
MiMi's	2120 P St NW	202-464-6464	$$$$	Classic Dupont: You never knew artists earned so much money.
Nooshi	1120 19th St NW	202-293-3138	$$	(Noodles + Sushi) Despite the cheeseball name, we recommend it.
Obelisk	2029 P St NW	202-872-1180	$$$$	Put your reservation in now for next March.
Olives	1600 K St NW	202-452-1866	$$$$	Quaint but pricey Mediterranean.
The Palm	1225 19th St NW	202-293-9091	$$$$	If you're an elitist and you know it clap your hands!
Pesce	2016 P St NW	202-466-3474	$$$$	Perhaps the best of the half-dozen fish joints on the block.
Pizzeria Paradiso	2029 P St NW	202-223-1245	$$	The toppings are meals themselves. Pray there's no line.
The Prime Rib	2020 K St NW	202-466-8811	$$$$	Voted Washington's No.1 steakhouse.
Restaurant Nora	2132 Florida Ave NW	202-462-5143	$$$$	Nora keeps her own herb garden in back. Every ingredient organic.
Sam and Harry's	1200 19th St NW	202-296-4333	$$$$	Looking for expensive filet mignon? Cross the street to The Palm.

Sette Osteria	1666 Connecticut Ave NW	202-483-3070	$$	As simple as Italian gets. Pastas are all the rave.
Smith and Wollensky	1112 19th St NW	202-466-1100	$$$$	Sleek setting makes you forget it's a chain.
Tabard Inn	1739 N St NW	202-331-8528	$$$$	Fireplace, brick walls, outdoor tables, and elegant dishes.
Teaism	2009 R St NW	202-667-3827	$$	Would you like a dinner with your cup of tea?
Teatro Goldini	1909 K St NW	202-955-9494	$$$$	Lawyers and lobbyists abound. For a $13 lunch, why shouldn't they?
Thaiphoon	2011 S St NW	202-667-3505	$$	A curry-lover's paradise.
Timberlake's	1726 Connecticut Ave NW	202-483-2266	$$	No-frills atmosphere = good. No-frills food = bad.
Vidalia	1990 M St NW	202-659-1990	$$$$	A taste of dixieland refinery.

Map 10 • Logan Circle / U Street

Ben's Chili Bowl	1213 U St NW	202-667-0909	$*	A District chili institution.
Cafe Saint-Ex	1847 14th St NW	202-265-7839	$$$	Once cool bistro overrun by the khaki crowd.
Coppi's	1414 U St NW	202-319-7773	$$$	Eat an organic extra large pizza and pretend you're healthy.
DC Coast	1401 K St NW	202-216-5988	$$$$	Original venue of the 2005 Washingtonian restaurateurs of the year.
Dukem	1114 U St NW	202-667-8735	$$	Authentic Ethiopian. Special weekend outdoor grill menu.
Georgia Brown's	950 15th St NW	202-393-4499	$$$$	Upscale Southern features a scandalous brunch.
Logan Tavern	1423 P St NW	202-332-3710	$$$$	Ecclectic, comfort food made better by proximity to Logan Circle.
Maggie Moo's	1301 U St NW	202-234-7700	$	Good ice cream and a free mix-in.
Marrakesh Restaurant	617 New York Ave NW	202-393-9393	$$$$*	Moroccan cuisine with a side of belly dancing.
Oohhs and Aahhs	1005 U St NW	202-667-7142	$*	The District's best soul food.
Post Pub	1422 L St NW	202-628-2111	$$	Best burgers in city. Shhh! A secret!
Rice	1608 14th St NW	202-234-2400	$$$	Swanky minimalist Thai. Try the green tea dishes.
Saloon	1207 U St NW	202-462-2640	$$$	Go there for the beer. Just be sure to eat beforehand.
Thai Tanic	1236 14th St NW	202-588-1795	$$	Neighborhood fave Thai restaurant.
U-topia	1418 U St NW	202-483-7669	$$$	Reasonably priced eclectic international cuisine.

Map 13 • Brookland / Langdon

Bamboo Joint Café	2062 Rhode Island Ave NE	202-526-7410	$	Cheap and tasty Brookland Jamaican diner.

Map 14 • Catholic U

Colonel Brooks' Tavern	901 Monroe St NE	202-529-4002	$$	Be welcomed like a local in the blue-collar section of town.
The Hitching Post	200 Upshur St NW	202-726-1511	$$	Southern fried chicken, crab cakes.
Kelly's Ellis Island	3908 12th St NE	202-832-6117	$	Roman Catholic décor. Drink beer amidst pictures of the pope.
Murry and Paul's	3513 12th St NE	202-529-4078	$	We dare you to eat here. (Breakfast and lunch only.)

Map 15 • Columbia Heights

Bill's Seafood	3601 Georgia Ave NW	202-545-1582	$$	Soul food from the sea.
Brown's Caribbean Bakery	3301 Georgia Ave NW	202-882-1626	$*	Cinnamon rolls the size of your head.
Cluck U Chicken	2921 Georgia Ave NW	202-726-0006	S*	Want some chicken with that grease?
Five Guys	2301 Georgia Ave NW	202-986-2235	$	Juicy patties satisfy every need of hamburger afficionados.
Florida Ave Grill	1100 Florida Ave NW	202-265-1586	$$	Greasy spoon from the dirty south.
Mario's Pizza	3619 Georgia Ave NW	202-882-7500	$	New pie on the block.
Negril	2301 Georgia Ave NW	202-332-3737	$*	Local Caribbean quick-eats chain.
Rita's Caribbean Carryout	3322 Georgia Ave NW	202-722-1868	$$*	Authentic caribbean fare.

*Key: $: Under $10 / $$: $10-$20 / $$$: $20-$30 / $$$$: $30+   * : Does not accept credit cards. / † : Accepts only American Express.*

Map 15 • Columbia Heights—*continued*

Soul Vegetarian and Exodus Café	2606 Georgia Ave NW	202-328-7685	$*	Eclectic African vegan take-out.
Temperance	3634 Georgia Ave NW	202-667-6996	*	1920s theme with weekend brunch, senior discount, and children's menu.

Map 16 • Adams Morgan (North) / Mt Pleasant

Astor Restaurant	1829 Columbia Rd NW	202-745-7495	$	Great falafel sandwich and subs.
Bardia's New Orleans Café	2412 18th St NW	202-234-0420	$	Perfect brunch with great Cajun takes on poached egg classics.
Bukom Café	2442 18th St NW	202-265-4600	$$$	West African food, feel, and music.
Cashion's Eat Place	1819 Columbia Rd NW	202-797-1819	$$$$	Chelsea Clinton known to have played the dating game here.
The Diner	2438 18th St NW	202-232-8800	$	As the name suggests. Open 24 hours.
Dos Gringos	3116 Mt Pleasant St NW	202-462-1159	$*	Who knew a Salvadorean restaurant could be classy?
Felix Restaurant & Lounge	2406 18th St NW	202-483-3549	$$$$	A Washington mainstay for hipsters. Identity of Felix a mystery.
Grill From Ipanema	1858 Columbia Rd NW	202-986-0757	$$$	Killer caiphiranas that scream "Brazil!"
Haydee's	3102 Mount Pleasant St NW	202-483-9199	$	Cheap but awful Salvadorean food. Beware the salsa.
La Fourchette	2429 18th St NW	202-332-3077	$$$$	Casual creperie.
Leftbank	2424 18th St NW	202-464-2100	$$	Americana diner, sushi bar, cafeteria aesthetic, hipster chic.
The Little Fountain Café	2339 18th St NW	202-462-8100	$$	Continental food in a charming Adams Morgan nook.
Mama Ayesha's	1967 Calvert St NW	202-232-5431	$$	Middle Eastern good enough for Bill Clinton.
Marx Café	3203 Mount Pleasant St NW	202-518-7600	$$$	Quasi-hipster Mount Pleasant standout.
Meskerem Ethiopian Restaurant	2434 18th St NW	202-462-4100	$$$	Authentic Ethiopian meets DC posh.
Millie & Al's	2440 18th St NW	202-387-8131	$$	A dive's dive for pizza and pitchers
Mixtec	1729 Columbia Rd NW	202-332-1011	$$	Originally a grocery store, this Mexican beanery is superb.
Pasta Mia	1790 Columbia Rd NW	202-328-9114	$$	Opens at night and worth the long queue.
Perry's	1811 Columbia Rd NW	202-234-6218	$$$	A punk sushi experience. Killer city views.
Rumba Café	2443 18th St NW	202-588-5501	$$*	Eat steak and watch tango. (Wednesday nights.)
Tonic	3155 Mt Pleasant St NW	202-986-7661	$$	Comfort food and a can't-be-beat happy hour.
Tono Sushi	2605 Connecticut Ave NW	202-332-7300	$$	Originally Japanese, has recently gone pan-Asian.
Tryst	2459 18th St NW	202-232-5500	$$	Excellent Wi-Fi cafe. A central DC spot.

Map 17 • Woodley Park / Cleveland Park

Café Paradiso	2649 Connecticut Ave NW	202-265-8955	$$	Three stories of contemporary Italian.
Ireland's Four Provinces	3412 Connecticut Ave NW	202-244-0860	$$$	Grub's not too bad in what's best known as a party bar.
Lavandou	3321 Connecticut Ave NW	202-966-3002	$$$$	Casual French sidewalk-style bistro.
Lebanese Taverna	2641 Connecticut Ave NW	202-265-8681	$$$	Family-style Lebanese. Nice after the zoo.
Petits Plats	2653 Connecticut Ave NW	202-518-0018	$$$	A French connection outside downtown.
Sake Club	2635 Connecticut Ave NW	202-332-2711	$$$$	Sake and Japanese, with prices ranging from low to quite high.
Sorriso	3518 Connecticut Ave NW	202-537-4800	$$$	Brick-oven pizza to complement nearby Café Paradiso.
Spices	3333A Connecticut Ave NW	202-686-3833	$$$*	Casual Asian fusion from the people behind Yanyu.

Map 18 • Glover Park / Foxhall

2 Amys	3715 Macomb St NW	202-885-5700	$$	Pizza Napolitana. Romantic or just for kicks.

Cactus Cantina	3300 Wisconsin Ave NW	202-686-7222	$$$	Same as Lauriol Plaza, minus courtly architecture.
Café Deluxe	3228 Wisconsin Ave NW	202-686-2233	$$$	A greasy spoon with absolutely no grease.
Faccia Luna Trattoria	2400 Wisconsin Ave NW	202-337-3132	$$	Good pizza for a low-key night out or in.
Heritage India	2400 Wisconsin Ave NW	202-333-3120	$$$$	Gourmet Indian in a comfortable setting.
Makoto Restaurant	4822 MacArthur Blvd NW	202-298-6866	$$$	Sushi a la carte. You'll never need to visit Japan.
Rocklands	2418 Wisconsin Ave NW	202-333-2558	$$	Cooking 150,000 pounds of pork a year, and counting...
Sushi-Ko	2309 Wisconsin Ave NW	202-333-4187	$$$$	Washington's first sushi bar, since 1976.

Map 19 • Tenleytown / Friendship Heights

4912 Thai Cuisine	4912 Wisconsin Ave NW	202-966-4696	$$	Excellent Thai with a creative name.
Bambule	5225 Wisconsin Ave	202-966-0300	$$$	Wide doors open onto a porch revealing tapas and dancing.
Café Ole	4000 Wisconsin Ave NW	202-244-1330	$$$	Fun neighborhood Spanish-style tapas.
Guapos Mexican Cuisine & Cantina	4515 Wisconsin Ave NW	202-686-3588	$$$	Nothing better than drinking tequila outside.
K's New York Deli	4620 Wisconsin Ave NW	202-686-1989	$$	It ain't New York, but arguably DC's best Jewish deli.
Maggiano's Little Italy	5333 Wisconsin Ave NW	202-966-5500	$$	Opposite of this book's title.
Matisse	4934 Wisconsin Ave NW	202-244-5222	$$$$	French and Mediterranean with all the details.
Murasaki	4620 Wisconsin Ave NW	202-966-0023	$$$	Wide range of Japanese cuisines.
Steak 'n Egg Kitchen	4700 Wisconsin Ave NW	202-686-1201	$	This greasy spoon hasn't changed a thing in over 60 years.

Map 20 • Cleveland Park / Upper Connecticut

Buck's Fishing & Camping	5031 Connecticut Ave NW	202-364-0777	$$$$	More sophisticated than the name suggests.
Delhi Dhaba	4455 Connecticut Ave NW	202-537-1008	$$	Efficient Indian take-out passes the test.
Indique	3512 Connecticut Ave NW	202-244-6600	$$$$	When did every other restaurant on the block start featuring tapas?
Palena	3529 Connecticut Ave NW	202-537-9250	$$$$	Continental food and an engrossing dessert menu.
Sala Thai	3507 Connecticut Ave NW	202-237-2777	$$	No-frills Thai.

Map 21 • 16th St. Heights / Petworth

China American Inn	845 Upshur St NW	202-726-4885	$$	Decent Chinese food.
Colorado Kitchen	5515 Colorado Ave NW	202-545-8280	$$$	American cuisine with a subtle Southern accent.
Domku	821 Upshur St NW	202-722-7475	$$-$$$	East European and Scandinavian comfort food.
Sweet Mango Café	3701 New Hampshire Ave NW	202-726-2646	$*	Slow-roasted jerked chicken on the bone. Best in the city.

Map 22 • Downtown Bethesda

Bacchus	7945 Norfolk Ave	301-657-1722	$$$$	Lebanese menu with lots of twists and turns.
Black's Bar & Kitchen	7750 Woodmont Ave	301-652-6278	$$$$	Good seafood—drink outside on nice nights.
Buon Giorno	8003 Norfolk Ave	301-652-1400	$$$	Pastas made by hand on-site every day.
Faryab	4917 Cordell Ave	301-951-3484	$$$	Premier DC metro area Afghan stop.
Grapeseed	4865 Cordell Ave	301-986-9592	$$$$	Spanish cuisine to go with wine list al grande.
Haandi	4904 Fairmont Ave	301-718-0121	$$$	One of suburban Maryland's oldest Indian joints.
Matuba	4918 Cordell Ave	301-652-7449	$$$	Basic sushi and buffet.
Olazzo	7921 Norfolk Ave	301-654-9496	$$$	Italian with a brick oven (and yet no pizza!).
The Original Pancake House	7700 Wisconsin Ave	301-986-0285	$	Oh go ahead. Bring back a few childhood memories.

*Key: $: Under $10 / $$: $10-$20 / $$$: $20-$30 / $$$$: $30+ * : Does not accept credit cards. / † : Accepts only American Express.*

Map 22 • Downtown Bethesda—*continued*

Tako Grill	7756 Wisconsin Ave	301-652-7030	$$$	Traditional and nontraditional Japanese for the enthusiast.
Tragara	4935 Cordell Ave	301-951-4935	$$$$	Traditional Italian with elegant surroundings.

Map 24 • Upper Rock Creek Park

Parkway Deli	8317 Grubb Rd	301-587-1427	$$	Another rare, high-quality, Jewish deli.
redDog Café	8301A Grubb Rd	301-588-6300	$$	Constantly changing décor.

Map 25 • Silver Spring

Austin Grill	919 Ellsworth Dr	240-247-8969	$$	Down-home grub at down-home prices. Yee-haw.
Bombay Gaylord	8401 Georgia Ave	301-565-2528	$$	If curry is what you crave...
Cubano's	1201 Fidler Ln	301-563-4020	$$$	Fountain and foliage make the décor cheesissimo.
Eggspectation	923 Ellsworth Dr	301-585-1700	$$	So many eggs you wonder where they hide their hens.
El Aguila	8649 16th St	301-588-9063	$$	Better than its location would have you believe.
Lebanese Taverna	933 Ellsworth Dr	301-588-1192	$$	Fast, decent middle eastern food.
Mi Rancho	8701 Ramsey Ave	301-588-4872	$$	Quite cheap Mexican/Salvadorean.
Potbelly Sandwich Works	917 Ellsworth Dr	301-562-9696	$	Really good hot (if small) sandwiches.
Roger Miller Restaurant	941 Bonifant St	301-650-2495	$$	Unique Cameroon fare, named after a soccer star.
Romano's Macaroni Grill	931 Ellsworth Dr	301-562-2806	$$$	Good standard Italian.

Map 26 • Takoma Park

Mark's Kitchen	7006 Carroll Ave	301-270-1884	$$	Green-friendly American and Korean fare.
Savory	7071 Carroll Ave	301-270-2233	$$*	Veggie/vegan with a basement café.

Map 27 • Walter Reed

Blair Mansion Inn/ Murder Mystery Dinner Theatre	7711 Eastern Ave	301-588-6646		What's better than finding a hair in your soup? Finding a dead body during mystery dinner theater! Their expansive buffet should help ease the trauma.

Map 28 • Chevy Chase

American City Diner of Washington	5332 Connecticut Ave NW	202-244-1949	$	1950s drive-in themed diner, complete with movies.
Arucola	5534 Connecticut Ave NW	202-244-1555	$$$$	Straightforward Italian.
Bread & Chocolate	5542 Connecticut Ave NW	202-966-7413	$	Can't go wrong with this combination.
La Ferme	7101 Brookville Rd	301-986-5255	$$$$	Charming (if bizarre) French bistro in a residential area.

Map 29 • Bethesda/Chevy Chase Business

Gifford's	7237 Woodmont Ave	301-907-3436	$	Next to movie theater—deals for cones + tickets
Green Papaya	4922 Elm St	301-654-8986	$$$$	Tasty but ridiculously inauthentic Vietnamese.
Hinode	4914 Hampden Ln	301-654-0908	$$$	No surprises Japanese.
Jaleo	7271 Woodmont Ave	301-913-0003	$$$$	Good, if overpriced tapas.
Outback Steakhouse	7720 Woodmont Ave	301-913-0176	$$$$	Fake Australian culture, real American money.
Persimmon	7003 Wisconsin Ave	301-654-9860	$$$$	Superlative Bethesda continental experience.
Raku	7240 Woodmont Ave	301-718-8680	$$$	Pan-Asian delight with lovely outdoor patio.

Ri-Ra Irish Restaurant Pub	4931 Elm St	301-657-1122	$$$	Irish pub; utterly American grub.
Rio Grande	4870 Bethesda Ave	301-656-2981	$$$	Great free chips and salsa. Good Tex Mex.
Tara Thai	4828 Bethesda Ave	301-657-0488	$$	Well-known for bold Thai.
Thyme Square	4735 Bethesda Ave	301-657-9077	$$$*	Boasts a healthy menu; no red meat.

Map 32 • Cherrydale/Palisades

Bambu	5101 MacArthur Blvd NW	202-364-3088	$$$	Reliable Asian fusion.
Starland Café	5125 MacArthur Blvd NW	202-244-9396	$$$	Starland Vocal Bandmember Bill Danoff's joint, if you miss the 70s.

Map 33 • Falls Church

La Cote d'Or Café	6876 Lee Hwy	703-534-8059	$$$	High romance for a reasonable price.
Lebanese Taverna	5900 Washington Blvd	703-241-8681	$$$	Family-style Lebanese. Everyone shares.
Taqueria Poblano	2503 N Harrison St	703-237-8250	$$	As predictable as it is cheap.

Map 34 • Ballston

Café Parisien Express	4520 Lee Hwy Arlington	703-525-3332	$$	French dining on the cheap.
Café Tirolo	4001 N Fairfax Dr	703-528-7809	$$	Hidden European treasure with modest prices.
Crisp & Juicy	4540 Lee Hwy	703-243-4222	$$*	Latino-barbecued chicken.
El Paso Café	4235 N Pershing Dr	703-243-9811	$$	Kick-ass margarita hidden gem known for George Bush sightings.
Flat Top Grill	4245 N Fairfax Dr	703-528-0078	$$$	Construct your own stir-fry.
Layalina	5216 Wilson Blvd	703-525-1170	$$$	Middle Eastern rugs adorn walls. Straight out of "Aladdin."
Metro 29 Diner	4711 Lee Hwy	703-528-2464	$$	Diner breakfast with some Greek touches.
Rio Grande Café	4301 N Fairfax Dr	703-528-3131	$$	We don't know what café means anymore.
Rocklands	4000 Fairfax Dr	703-528-9663	$$	DC BBQ in NoVA.
Tara Thai	4001 Fairfax Dr	703-908-4999	$$	A tasty Thai chain.
Tutto Bene	501 N Randolph St	703-522-1005	$$$	Italian cuisine, when not Bolivian. We love America.

Map 35 • Clarendon

Aegean Taverna	2950 Clarendon Blvd	703-841-9494	$$$	"My Big Fat Greek Wedding" without stereotypes and Windex.
Boulevard Woodgrill	2901 Wilson Blvd	703-875-9663	$$$	Exceptionally plain.
Café Dalat	3143 Wilson Blvd	703-276-0935	$$	Grilled flounder just the beginning of Vietnamese extravaganza.
Delhi Dhaba Indian Café & Carryout	2424 Wilson Blvd	703-524-0008	$$	Indian curries make delicious cafeteria-style dishes.
Faccia Luna Trattoria	2909 Wilson Blvd	703-276-3099	$$	Good pizza for a low-key night out or in.
Hard Times Café	3028 Wilson Blvd	703-528-2233	$$	Chili-making to a science. Home-brewed root beer a bonus.
Harry's Tap Room	2800 Clarendon Blvd	703-778-7788	$$$$	Nearly a dozen filet mignon options.
Hope Key	3131 Wilson Blvd	703-243-8388	$$	Exotic Hong Kong cuisine.
Lazy Sundae	2925 Wilson Blvd	703-525-4960	$*	Family-style homemade ice cream.
Mexicali Blues	2933 Wilson Blvd	703-812-9352	$$	Most colorful restaurant in Arlington. First time? Order a burro.
Minh's Restaurant	2500 Wilson Blvd	703-525-2828	$$	Ten bucks goes a long way at this Vietnamese establishment.
Pica Deli Gourmet and Wines	3471 N Washington Blvd	703-524-5656	$$	You'll be glad the intriguing outdoor mural led you in.
Portabellos	2109 N Pollard St	703-528-1557	$$	Contemporary American.
Queen Bee	3181 Wilson Blvd	703-527-3444	$$$	Established and affordable Vietnamese restaurant.
Silver Diner	3200 Wilson Blvd	703-812-8600	$$	Good place for a date, or to end a relationship.
Whitlow's	2584 Wilson Blvd	703-276-9693	$	Neighborhood bar with live music.

*Key: $: Under $10 / $$: $10-$20 / $$$: $20-$30 / $$$$: $30+ * : Does not accept credit cards. / † : Accepts only American Express.*

Map 36 • Rosslyn

Gua-Rapo	2039 Wilson Blvd	703-528-6500	$$$*	Chi-Cha Lounge flavor in NoVA.
Guajillo	1727 Wilson Blvd	703-807-0840	$$	Don't let the strip mall fool you. It's what's inside that counts.
Il Radicchio	1801 Clarendon Blvd	703-276-2627	$$$	Quiet outdoor dining evokes Lady and the Tramp aura.
Ireland's Four Courts	2051 Wilson Blvd	703-525-3600	$$$	Makes you forget that Ireland ever had a famine.
Mezza9	1325 Wilson Blvd	703-276-8999	$$$$	The Rosslyn Hyatt's take on Turkish.
Quarter Deck Restaurant	1200 Ft Myer Dr	703-528-2722	$$$	Cold beer, hot crabs, familiar faces.
Ray's the Steaks	1725 Wilson Blvd	703-841-7297	$$$$	Beef. It's what's for dinner.
Rhodeside Grill	1836 Wilson Blvd	703-243-0145	$$$	Hot plates on dinner tables, live music in the basement.
Village Bistro	1723 Wilson Blvd	703-522-0284	$$$	Surprisingly quaint for part of a shopping strip.

Map 37 • Fort Myer

Atilla's	2705 Columbia Pike	703-920-4900	$$	Savory gyros, kabobs, salads, and more.
Bob & Edith's Diner	2310 Columbia Pike	703-920-6103	$$*	Probably the most charming all-night diner in Virginia.
The Broiler	3601 Columbia Pike	703-920-5944	$$	Blue collar subs and Ms. Pac-Man.
El Charrito Caminante	2710 N Washington Blvd	703-351-1177	$*	Papusas worthy of the gods.
El Pollo Rico	932 N Kenmore St	703-522-3220	$	Eating this chicken (only thing served) is a sacramental experience.
Manee Thai	2500 Columbia Pike	703-920-2033	$	True Thai treasure.
Mario's Pizza House	3322 Wilson Blvd	703-525-7827	$$	Late night tradition for the bleary-eyed.
Matuba	2915 Columbia Pike	703-521-2811	$$$	Unlike the Bethesda location, no buffet.
Mrs Chen's Kitchen	3101 Columbia Pike	703-920-3199	$	Chinese food before competition from Thai.
Pan American Bakery	4113 Columbia Pike	703-271-1113	$	Saltenas and glistening pastries from South America.
Rincome Thai Cuisine	3030 Columbia Pike	703-979-0144	$$	Friendly owners, sumptuous food, neighborhood atmosphere.
Tallula Restaurant	2761 Washington Blvd	703-778-5051	$$$	The wine bar craze has officially hit Arlington.

Map 38 • Columbia Pike

Andy's Carry-Out	5033 Columbia Pike	703-671-1616	$-$$	Oily food cooked in woks.
Athens Restaurant	3541 Carlin Springs Rd	703-931-3300	$$	Greek menu for everyone, even Greeks.
Atlacatl	4701 Columbia Pike	703-920-3680	$$$	Laid-back, delicious Salvadorian and Mexican cuisine with attentive staff.
Crystal Thai	4819 Arlington Blvd	703-522-1311	$$$	Moderate prices will allow you to order extra Singha.
Five Guys	4626 King St	703-671-1606	$*	THE Alexandria burger joint.

Map 39 • Shirlington

Carlyle	4000 28th St S	703-931-0777	$$$$	Fresh bread comes straight from bakery next door.

Map 41 • Landmark

The American Café	5801 Duke St	703-658-0004	$$$	You can't do Ruby Tuesday all the time....
Clyde's	1700 N Beauregard St	703-820-8300	$$$	Take to the seas in this nautical-themed favorite.
Finn & Porter	5000 Seminary Rd	703-379-2346	$$$$	Yes it's in a hotel, but it's still nice.
Ruby Tuesday	5801 Duke St	703-354-5983	$$$	Hot times in Landmark!

Map 42 • Alexandria (West)

Tempo Restaurant	4321 Duke St	703-370-7900	$$$	French-Italian fusion.

Map 44 • Alexandria Downtown

Café Old Towne	2111 Eisenhower Ave	703-683-3116	$	Variety of coffee/pastries, worth traveling off the beaten path.
Table Talk	1623 Duke St	703-548-3989	$	Terrific breakfast/lunch. Often jammed, always good.

Map 46 • Old Town (South)

219 Restaurant	219 King St	703-589-1141	$$$	Interior looks like the swankiest hotel in New Orleans.
China King Restaurant	701 King St	703-549-3268	$$	Express delivery by Chinese bicycle boy.
Faccia Luna Trattoria	823 S Washington St	703-838-5998	$$	The best pizza around—locals love it.
The Grille	116 S Alfred St	703-838-8000	$$$$	Where luxury and Alexandria collide.
Il Porto	121 King St	703-836-8833	$$$$	Best Italian around. Make reservations.
Portner's	109 S St Asaph St	703-683-1776	$$$$	Locals love to go here after the movie. Nice brunch, too.
Restaurant Eve	110 S Pitt St	703-706-0450	$$$$	Hot new restaurant; reservations a must.
Southside 815	815 S Washington St	703-836-6222	$$	New Orleanean fare.
The Warehouse	214 King St	703-683-6868	$$$	A bit forgotten but excellent food. Plan to eat hearty.

Baltimore

Bertha's	734 S Broadway	410-327-5795		Seafood. Dark, dank, and famous for its mussels.
Boccaccio Restaurant	925 Eastern Ave	410-234-1322		Italian. The best, and arguably the only great restaurant in this particularly inauthentic Little Italy.
Brass Elephant	924 N Charles St (off map)	410-547-8480		American. Gorgeous townhouse, fancy food, and expense account prices.
Café Hon	1002 W 36th St (off map)	410-243-1230		Kitsch central. If not for the meatloaf or the beehive 'dos on the wait staff, come to see John Waters' Baltimore.
Faidley's Seafood	Lexington Market, 203 N Paca St	410-727-4898		Seafood. Stand up and rub elbows while chowing down some of the city's best crab cakes.
Helen's Garden	2908 O'Donnell St	410-276-2233		Feel like a local at this Canton outpost. Good food, nice owners, wine flows.
Ikaros	4805 Eastern Ave (off map)	410-633-3750		Greek. Cheap, big portions, and Greektown neighborhood staple.
Jimmy's	801 S Broadway	410-327-3273		Classic Bawlmer greasy spoon. Check your attitude at the door.
John Steven Ltd	1800 Thames St	410-327-5561		Seafood. Outdoor patio, steamer bar, crab cakes, and stocked bar.
Joy America Café	American Visionary Art Museum, 800 Key Hwy	410-244-6500		Latin American. Whacked-out cuisine with a view.
Matsuri	1105 S Charles St	410-752-8561		Japanese. Sushi in this blue-collar town is better than you think.
Obrycki's Crab House	1727 E Pratt St	410-732-6399		The king of the many local crab houses.
Rusty Scupper	402 Key Hwy	410-727-3678		Enjoy a Bloody Mary at their Sunday Jazz Brunch.
Tapas Teatro	1711 N Charles St (off map)	410-332-0110		Tapas. Before and after a movie at The Charles, check out this neighborhood favorite.
Vespa	1117-21 S Charles St	410-385-0355		Italian. If all the blue-collar-ness has got you down, come and find the gold-roped crowd here.
Ze Mean Bean	1739 Fleet St	410-675-5999		Eastern European. More than a coffeehouse, with meaty dishes and live music.

DC locals have long been mocked—perhaps for good reason—for having absolutely no sense of fashion. After all, this is the city where every woman owns an Ann Taylor pantsuit, navy blue shirts and khakis look like the uniform for all men, and people sometimes go on dates wearing sweatpants. (In our defense, maybe we're too busy running the planet to keep track of what the fashionistas are wearing this month.)

But with DC gentrifying at a dizzying pace, the sad state of fashion is also changing rapidly—especially in Logan Circle and the U Street Corridor, which is experiencing a boom of vintage clothing stores and furniture outlets, as well as boutique stores such as **Tickled Pink,** which features cutting-edge NYC designer clothes. If this keeps up, DC will soon prove its moniker, "Hollywood for ugly people," totally wrong!

Clothing/Beauty

Whether you're metrosexual or matronly, your best bet for clothes shopping is Georgetown, particularly around the intersection of M Street and Wisconsin Avenue (and the nearby Shops at the Georgetown Park Mall). You'll find all the mainstream chain stores, but in a non-mall setting: **Abercrombie & Fitch, J. Crew, Diesel, Banana Republic**, **Victoria's Secret**, the works. (And if you want to get punked up, there's always **Smash** and **Commander Salamander**). For cosmetics, check out **Blue Mercury, Sephora,** and **Lush**. A hint, though: there's not a lot here you can't get somewhere else in the area, so if you're just looking for a pair of Kenneth Cole shoes and have no other reason to go downtown, try the malls in Tyson's Corner or Pentagon City.

If you're after more prosaic gear (or classy work clothes), take a stroll down Connecticut Avenue, south of Dupont Circle; you'll find a good-sized **Gap**, a **Burberry's**, and what seems to be DC's official clothing store, **Brooks Brothers**.

As far as vintage goes, the shops along the U Street Corridor are good places to look (we recommend **Meep's)**, as well as **Fufia** in Logan Circle. U Street also has a rapidly-growing array of boutique designer stores. And if you're willing to take a drive, **Mustard Seed** in Bethesda is a great find, with both classy vintage and NY designer boutique goods.

Housewares

If the raging interior design districts along 14th Street and M Street in Georgetown are any indication, our interior lives must be a little more daring than the boring façades we wear out in public. Although it's touted as DC's furniture district, most of the shops along 14th Street in Logan Circle are pretty, well, pimpadelic—except for the well-stuffed junk store **Ruff n' Ready**, where you can find some amazing deals if you're prepared to do some digging. A better choice is the multitude of vintage furniture stores along the U Street Corridor—or, if you're prepared to spend some serious cash, the European furniture outlets in Georgetown west of Wisconsin Avenue. In Georgetown you'll also find **Restoration Hardware** and **Pottery Barn**, both of which carry wide selections of fashionable goods for house and home.

For wacky cutting boards, alarm clocks, and the like, stop by **Home Rule** on 14th Street. In fact, tchotchke stores are scattered throughout Dupont and Georgetown, so you won't be lacking in gift ideas when Mother's Day rolls around.

Electronics

Given the enormous number of techies (both professional and amateur) in DC, it's a mystery that the odds of stumbling across an electronic store are slim-to-none. If you're looking for computer goods, you'll need to hit the 'burbs—fortunately, the **Best Buy** in Alexandria is only about a 20-minute drive from downtown DC. Die-hard Mac-heads (i.e. dorks) will love the gorgeous, high-tech **Apple Store** in Arlington. If you're desperate and car-less, **Staples** (on M street in Georgetown and a variety of other locations) offers a small collection of computers and software.

Food

DC's blessed with one of the finest supermarkets anywhere on earth—the **Whole Foods** market in Logan Circle, which many urban theorists quite seriously credit for the subsequent gentrificiation of the entire surrounding neighborhood. Prices, however, are not cheap and lines can be long. For residents further Northwest, there's a less impressive, but still noteworthy, Whole Foods in Glover Park.

Despite its status-toting name, **Dean & Deluca** in Georgetown pales in comparison to Whole Foods—shoppers pay more for a smaller selection of lower-quality products. If you're on a budget, there's also the numerous **Safeways** around town, although most of them are grim enough to have inspired nicknames like "Soviet Safeway."

DC may be known for many things, but good ethnic food is not one of them. There are a few notable exceptions to this generalization, particularly in Adams Morgan—**So's Your Mom** has some excellent deli goods and an authentic atmosphere, and the area also features some great Ethiopian markets.

Music

The **Tower Records** in Foggy Bottom carries a large selection of mainstream and under-the-radar music, and most bookstores keep a decent CD collection in stock as well. If you're searching for more offbeat fare, stop by the excellent new-and-used **Crooked Beat** store in Adams Morgan, or the numerous Olsson's outlets, or to **Kemp Mill** in Dupont. **CD/Game Exchange** in Adams Morgan is a great place to find used bargains, although their selection tends toward the mainstream.

Wine, Beer, Liquor

Most supermarkets don't sell alcoholic beverages—Whole Foods is, again, an exception. Also worth a look is the tiny but beautiful **Georgetown Wine and Spirits**, as well as **Best Cellars** in Dupont.

Late-nite revelers should keep in mind that you can't buy anything alcoholic in DC stores after 10 pm. Most liquor stores close at 9 pm on weekdays, although they stay open until 10 pm on Friday and Saturday. On Sundays, it's beer and wine only.

Map 1 • National Mall

Barnes & Noble	555 12th St NW	202-347-0176	Mega bookstore.
Blink	1776 I St NW	202-776-0999	Wear your sunglasses at night.
Borders Books & Music	600 14th St NW	202-737-1385	Books and music.
Café Mozart	1331 H St NW	202-347-5732	Germanic treats.
Celadon Spa	1180 F St NW	202-347-3333	Great haircuts.
Chapters Literary Bookstore	445 11th St NW	202-347-5495	Lunch-hour reads.
Coup de Foudre Lingerie	1001 Pennsylvania Ave NW	202-393-0878	New high-end lingerie store.
Fahrney's	1317 F St NW	202-628-9525	Fussy pens.
Filene's Basement	529 14th St NW	202-638-4110	Incredible discounts on designer clothes.
H&M	1065 F St NW	202-347-3306	New downtown outlet of European college-clothing giant.
Hecht's	1201 G St NW	202-628-6661	Only full-service department store in downtown Washington.
International Spy Museum Gift Shop	800 F St NW	202-654-0950	James Bond would be jealous.
Penn Camera	840 E St NW	202-347-5777	Say cheese.
Political Americana	1331 Pennsylvania Ave NW	202-737-7730	Souvenirs for back home.
Utrecht Art & Drafting Supplies	1250 I St NW	202-898-0555	Channel Picasso.

Map 2 • Chinatown / Union Station

Alamo Flags	Union Station	202-842-3524	Don't bring matches.
Apartment Zero	406 7th St NW	202-628-4067	Gorgeous, if overpriced, modern furniture.
Comfort One Shoes	50 Massachusetts Ave NE	202-408-4947	Beyond Birkenstocks.
Godiva Chocolatier	50 Massachusetts Ave NE	202-289-3662	Indulge.
Marvelous Market	730 7th St NW	202-628-0824	Takeout treats.
National Air and Space Museum Shop	6th St SW & Independence Ave SW	202-357-1387	Great plane-related stuff for the kids (or for you).
Olsson's Books	418 7th St NW	202-638-7610	Independent books and coffee.
Urban Outfitters Downtown	737 7th St NW	202-737-0259	Slightly hipper than its Georgetown cousin.

Map 5 • Southeast / Anacostia

Backstage	545 8th St SE	202-544-5744	A store with theatrics.
Capitol Hill Bikes	709 8th St SE	202-544-4234	Pedal away from politics.
Capitol Hill Books	657 C St SE	202-544-1621	Plenty of page-turners.
Eastern Market	225 7th St SE	202-547-6480	Open-air stalls and weekend flea market.
Plaid	715 8th St SE	202-675-6900	Party dresses, etc.
Wooven History & Silk Road	315 7th St SE	202-543-1705	Visit Afghanistan without the war hassle.

Map 6 • Waterfront

Maine Avenue Fish Market	Maine Ave & Potomac River		Fresh off the boat.

Map 7 • Foggy Bottom

Motophoto	1819 H St NW	202-822-9001	Develop cheese.
Saks Jandel	2522 Virginia Ave NW	202-337-4200	For the well-dressed socialite.
Tower Records	2000 Pennsylvania Ave NW	202-331-2400	Music superstore.

Map 8 • Georgetown

Ann Saks	3328 M St NW	202-339-0840	Bury yourself in tile.
Anthropologie	3225 M St NW	202-337-1363	Pretty, super-feminine women's clothing.
April Cornell	3278 M St NW	202-625-7887	Designer clothes for women and kids.
BCBG	3210 M St NW	202-333-2224	B well-dressed.
Betsey Johnson	1319 Wisconsin Ave NW	202-338-4090	Mix girlie and insane.
Beyond Comics 2	1419-B Wisconsin Ave NW	202-333-8651	Never grow up.
Blue Mercury	3059 M St NW	202-965-1300	Spa on premises.
Bo Concepts	3342 M St NW	202-333-5656	Modern décor.
Commander Salamander	1420 Wisconsin Ave NW	202-337-2265	Teenage funk.
Dean and DeLuca	3276 M St NW	202-342-2500	Dean and delicious.
Design Within Reach	3307 Cady's Aly NW	202-339-9480	Furniture showroom.
Diesel	1249 Wisconsin Ave NW	202-625-2780	Hip designer jeans.
Express	3227 M St NW	202-338-6626	Sexy, fashionable women's clothes.
Georgetown Running Company	3401 M St NW	202-337-8626	Gear up for a race.
Georgetown Tobacco	3144 M St NW	202-338-5100	Celebrate smoke.
Georgetown Wine and Spirits	2701 P St NW	202-338-5500	Gorgeous wine store; great selection, friendly owners.
GIA & Co	3231 M St NW	202-338-2666	Italian boutique that "caters to the elegant woman."
H&M	3223 M St NW	202-298-6792	Cheap Euro clothes for the college crowd.
The Hattery	3233 M St NW	202-364-4287	Gorgeous vintage hats for men and women.
Illuminations	3323 Cady's Aly NW	202-965-4888	Hot flashes.
Intermix	3222 M St	202 298 8080	Cutting edge women's designer fashions.
J Crew	3224 M St NW	202-965-4090	Inoffensive yuppie casual gear.
Jaryam	1631 Wisconsin Ave NW	202-333-6886	Lacy lingerie.
Jinx Proof Tattoo	3289 M St NW	202-337-5469	The best place in town to get inked.
Kate Spade	3061 M St NW	202-333-8302	Preppy polish.
Kenneth Cole	1259 Wisconsin Ave NW	202-298-0007	Stylish shoes.
Ligne Roset	3306 M St NW	202-333-6390	Check out the caterpillar couch.
lil' thingamajigs	3229 M St NW	202-944-8449	Japanese pop-art trinkets.
Lush	3066 M St NW	202-333-6950	Handmade soap and cosmetics; stratospheric prices.
MAC	3067 M St NW	202-944-9771	Sephora's main rival in the cosmetics biz.
Marvelous Market	3217 P St NW	202-464-0322	Try their blueberry muffins.
Old Print Gallery	1220 31st St NW	202-965-1818	The name says it all.
Pottery Barn	3077 M St NW	202-337-8900	Yuppie interior style.
Proper Topper	3213 P St NW	202-333-6200	Cutesy hats and gifts.
Ralph Lauren Polo Shop	3040 M St NW	202-965-0904	Where Dad should shop, but probably doesn't.
Relish	3312 Cady's Aly NW	202-333-5343	For your bod, not your hot dog.
Restoration Hardware	1222 Wisconsin Ave NW	202-625-2771	High-end home goods.
Revolution Cycles	3411 M St NW	202-965-3601	Replace stolen bikes here!
Sassanova	1641 Wisconsin Ave NW	202-471-4400	The latest and greatest in shoes.
Secret Garden	3230 M St NW	202-337-0833	Romantic flowers and plants store.
See	1261 Wisconsin Ave NW	202-337-5988	Fashionable, cheap eyewear.
Sephora	3065 M St NW	202-338-5644	Popular high-end cosmetics chain.
Sherman Pickey	1647 Wisconsin Ave NW	202-333-4212	Pet-friendly attire.
Smash	3285 1/2 M St NW	202-337-6274	Vintage punk vinyl, new punk clothes.
Smith & Hawken	3077 M St NW	202-965-2680	Pricey garden gloves.
Sugar	1633 Wisconsin Ave NW	202-333-5331	Overly-sweet concoctions.

Talbots	3232 M St NW	202-338-3510	Shop for Mom, buy clothes for work.
The Sharper Image	3226 M St NW	202-337-9361	Gifts for gadget-hounds.
Thomas Sweet Ice Cream	3214 P St	202-337-0616	Known to provide White House with desserts.
Toka Salon	3251 Prospect St NW	202-333-5133	Relax.
Urban Outfitters	3111 M St NW	202-342-1012	More like dorm outfitters.
Victoria's Secret	3222 M St NW	202-965-5457	The J Crew of lingerie.
The White House/ Black Market	3228 M St NW	202-965-4419	Monochromatic women's clothing.
Zara	1234 Wisconsin Ave NW	202-944-9797	European cheap chic.

Map 9 • Dupont Circle / Adams Morgan

Affrica	2010 1/2 R St NW	202-745-7272	Beautiful African-themed art.
Andre Chreky, the Salon Spa	1604 K St NW	202-293-9393	Fancy trims.
Bang Salon	1612 U St NW	202-299-0925	Cool trims.
Bedazzled	1507 Connecticut Ave NW	202-265-2323	Make your own jewelry.
Best Cellars	1643 Connecticut Ave NW	202-387-3146	Non-snobby wines.
Betsy Fisher	1224 Connecticut Ave NW	202-785-1975	Expensive casual Fridays.
Blue Mercury	1619 Connecticut Ave NW	202-462-1300	Cosmetics for maidens and metrosexuals alike.
Brooks Brothers	1201 Connecticut Ave NW	202-659-4650	DC's uniform supply shop.
Burberry	1155 Connecticut Ave NW	202-463-3000	Fashionistas & foreign correspondents.
Cake Love	1506 U St NW	202-588-7100	Lust-worthy cupcakes.
Comfort One Shoes	1621 Connecticut Ave NW	202-232-2480	Beyond Birkenstocks.
Comfort One Shoes	1630 Connecticut Ave NW	202-328-3141	Beyond Birkenstocks.
Companions Pet Shop	1626 U St NW	202-797-3663	Convenient but slightly ghetto pet supply store.
Custom Shop Clothiers	1033 Connecticut Ave NW	202-659-8250	Design your own button-down.
Doggie Style	1825 18th St NW	202-667-0595	Irreverant pet gifts.
Downs Engravers & Stationers	1746 L St NW	202-223-7776	When the occasion calls for uptight.
Drilling Tennis & Golf	1040 17th St NW	202-737-1100	Big Bertha lives here.
Filene's Basement	1133 Connecticut Ave NW	202-872-8430	No annual bridal dress sale, but good bargains abound.
Fufua	1642 R St NW	202-332-5131	Previously owned Prada.
The Gap	1120 Connecticut Ave NW	202-429-0691	Affordable, inoffensive, basic gear.
Ginza	1721 Connecticut Ave NW	202-331-7991	Japanica.
Godiva Chocolatier	1143 Connecticut Ave NW	202-638-7421	Indulge.
The Guitar Shop	1216 Connecticut Ave NW	202-331-7333	Self-explanatory.
Habitat Home Accents & Jewelry	1510 U St NW	202-518-7222	Hip knick-knacks for home and body.
Human Rights Campaign	1629 Connecticut Ave NW	202-232-8621	Gifts and cards for a cause.
J Press	1801 L St NW	202-857-0120	Conservative conservative.
Jos A Bank	1200 19th St NW	202-466-2282	For professional types who can't afford Brooks Brothers.
The Kid's Closet	1226 Connecticut Ave NW	202-429-9247	Buy your niece an Easter dress.
Kramerbooks	1517 Connecticut Ave NW	202-387-1400	Scope for books and dates.
Kulturas	1706 Connecticut Ave NW	202-462-5015	Used books galore.
Lambda Rising Bookstore	1625 Connecticut Ave NW	202-462-6969	Center of gay culture.
Leather Rack	1723 Connecticut Ave NW	202-797-7401	Hint: don't go here looking for a nice jacket....
Lucky Brand Dungarees	1739 Connecticut Ave NW	202-265-8285	Sexy jeans, shirts, and more.
Marvelous Market	1511 Connecticut Ave NW	202-332-3690	Bread and brownies.
Meeps and Aunt Neensy's	1520 U St NW	202-265-6546	Vintage clothes.
Melody Records	1623 Connecticut Ave NW	202-232-4002	Best record store in town.
Millennium Decorative Arts	1528 U St NW	202-483-1218	Cool stuff for your crib.
Nana	1534 U St NW	202-667-6955	Chic boutique.
National Geographic Shop	17 & M St NW	202-857-7000	Travel the world in a shop.
Newsroom	1803 Connecticut Ave NW	202-332-1489	Café with foreign papers.
Pasargad Antique and Fine Persian	1217 Connecticut Ave NW	202-659-3888	Beautiful rugs.
Pleasure Palace	1710 Connecticut Ave NW	202-483-3297	Sex toys and gear.
Proper Topper	1350 Connecticut Ave NW	202-842-3055	Cutesy hats and gifts.

Map 9 • Dupont Circle / Adams Morgan—*continued*

Rizik's	1100 Connecticut Ave NW	202-223-4050	Designer department store.
Rock Creek	2029 P St NW	202-429-6940	Great men's clothes.
Second Story Books and Antiques	2000 P St NW	202-659-8884	Largest outlet of this used and antiquarian book operation.
Secondi	1702 Connecticut Ave NW	202-667-1122	Slightly used and funky.
Sisley	1666 Connecticut Ave NW	202-232-1770	Sexy, euro-style clothes for men and women.
Skynear and Co	2122 18th St NW	202-797-7160	Funky décor.
Sticky Fingers Bakery	1904 18th St NW	202-299-9700	Vegan bakery.
Tabletop	1608 20th St NW	202-387-7117	Dress-up your dinner table.
The Third Day	2001 P St NW	202-785-0107	Plants on P.
Thomas Pink	1127 Connecticut Ave NW	202-223-5390	The perfect dress shirt.
Tiny Jewel Box	1147 Connecticut Ave NW	202-393-2747	Ready to pop?
Universal Gear	1601 17th St NW	202-319-0136	Trendy threads for 20-somethings.
Video Americain	2104 18th St NW	202-588-0117	Great indie film rentals—but beware the snobby clerks.
Wild Women Wear Red	1512 U St NW	202-387-5700	Pay dearly for shoe art.
Wine Specialists	2115 M St NW	202-833-0707	Bone up on your grapes.
The Written Word	1365 Connecticut Ave NW	202-223-1400	Invites and cards.

Map 10 • Logan Circle / U Street

Blink	1431 P St NW	202-234-1051	Wear your sunglasses at night.
Candida's World of Books	1541 14th St NW	202-667-4811	International bookstore with travel guides, lit, and more.
Capitol Records	1020 U St NW	202-518-2444	Record fiends.
Garden District	1801 14th St NW	202-797-9005	Urban gardeners dig it here.
Go Mama Go!	1809 14th St NW	202-299-0850	Whacked-out décor.
Good Wood	1428 U St NW	202-986-3640	Antique furniture built from—you guessed it.
Home Rule	1807 14th St NW	202-797-5544	Kitchen treasures.
Logan Hardware	1416 P St NW	202-265-8900	Super-friendly, sort-of-hipster hardware joint.
Maison 14	1325 14th St NW	202-588-5800	Pricey décor.
Muleh	1831 14th St NW	202-667-3440	Javanese furniture.
Pink November	1231 U St NW	202-232-3113	Small, artsy women's boutique.
Pop	1803 14th St NW	202-332-3312	Treny wendys.
Pulp	1803 14th St NW	202-462-7857	Dirty birthday cards.
Reincarnations Furnishings	1401 14th St NW	202-319-1606	Furniture that would make Liberace cringe; great window-shopping.
Ruff and Ready	1908 14th St NW	202-667-7833	Find a diamond in the ruff.
Urban Essentials	1330 U St NW	202-299-0640	Lust-worthy décor.
Vastu	1829 14th St NW	202-234-8344	Upscale contemporary furnishings.

Map 11 • Near Northeast

Windows Café & Market	1900 1st St NW	202-462-6585	Ethiopian/IKEA furnished café with sit-down sandwiches and bottled wine.

Map 15 • Columbia Heights

Mom & Pop's Antiques	3534 Georgia Ave NW	202-722-0719	Perhaps the last affordable antique store in DC.
Planet Chocolate City	3225 Georgia Ave NW	202-722-7800	Original homage to urban music, clothes, and culture, with stores now in Japan and Europe.

Map 16 • Adams Morgan (North) / Mt Pleasant

All About Jane	2438 1/2 18th St NW	202-797-9710	All about pricey casual.
Brass Knob	2311 18th St NW	202-332-3370	Architectural antiques from doors to knobs.
CD Game Exchange	2475 18th St NW	202-588-5070	Great selection of cheap CDs and video games.

City Bikes	2501 Champlain St NW	202-265-1564	Where the couriers shop.
Crooked Beat Records	2318 18th St NW	202-483-2328	Off-beat, hard to find selections.
Design Within Reach	1838 Columbia Rd NW	202-265-5640	Trendy furniture in a trendy part of town.
Fleet Feet	1841 Columbia Rd NW	202-387-3888	No referee uniforms here. They care.
Idle Times Books	2467 18th St NW	202-232-4774	Disorganized lit.
Little Shop of Flowers	1812 Adams Mill Rd NW	202-387-7255	Great name, good flowers.
Miss Pixie's Furnishing and What-Not	1810 Adams Mill Rd NW	202-232-8171	Second-chance finds.
Radio Shack	1767 Columbia Rd NW	202-986-5008	Great for headphones, batteries, and that special connection…
Shake Your Booty	2439 18th St NW	202-518-8205	Watch for their kick-ass sales.
So's Your Mom	1831 Columbia Rd NW	202-462-3666	Uber-deli with great sandwiches, imported NY bagels.
Trim	2700 Ontario Rd NW	202-462-6080	If you need hip bangs.
Yes! Natural Gourmet	1825 Columbia Rd NW	202-462-5150	Yes! Wheat germ!

Map 17 • Woodley Park / Cleveland Park

Vace	3315 Connecticut Ave NW	202-363-1999	Best pizza in town.

Map 18 • Glover Park / Foxhall

Inga's Once Is Not Enough	4830 MacArthur Blvd NW	202-337-3072	Chanel, Valentino, and Prada, for example.
Theodore's	2233 Wisconsin Ave NW	202-333-2300	Funky décor.
Treetop Toys	3301 New Mexico Ave NW	202-244-3500	Independent and fun.
Vespa Washington	2233 Wisconsin Ave NW	202-333-8212	Both new and vintage Vespa scooters here.

Map 19 • Tenleytown / Friendship Heights

Borders Books & Music	5333 Wisconsin Ave NW	202-686-8270	Books and music.
The Container Store	4500 Wisconsin Ave NW	202-478-4000	Buckets, shelves, hangers…
Elizabeth Arden Red Door Salon & Spa	5225 Wisconsin Ave NW	202-362-9890	Serious pampering.
Georgette Klinger	5345 Wisconsin Ave NW	202-686-8880	It's all about extraction.
Hudson Trail Outfitters	4530 Wisconsin Ave NW	202-363-9810	Tents and Tevas.
Johnson's Florist & Garden Centers	4200 Wisconsin Ave NW	202-244-6100	For those of you with a yard.
Neiman Marcus	5300 Wisconsin Ave NW	202-966-9700	Ultra upscale department store.
Pottery Barn	5335 Wisconsin Ave NW	202-244-9330	Yuppie interior style.
Roche Bobois	5301 Wisconsin Ave NW	202-686-5667	African traditions.
Rodman's	5100 Wisconsin Ave NW	202-363-3466	Luggage, wine, scented soaps, and other necessities.
Serenity Day Spa	4000 Wisconsin Ave NW	202-362-2560	Name says it all.

Map 20 • Cleveland Park / Upper Connecticut

Marvelous Market	5035 Connecticut Ave NW	202-686-4040	Try their blueberry muffins.
Politics & Prose	5015 Connecticut Ave NW	202-364-1919	Politics with your coffee.

Map 22 • Downtown Bethesda

Crate & Barrel	Montgomery Mall, Benton Ave & Fresno Rd	301-365-2600	Wedding registry HQ.
Daisy Too	4940 St Elmo Ave	301-656-2280	Unique and girly.
Ranger Surplus	8008 Wisconsin Ave	301-656-2302	Smaller than the Fairfax branch but worth a look.
Second Story Books & Antiques	4914 Fairmont Ave	301-656-0170	Best known antiquarian book operation.
Zelaya	4940 St Elmo Ave	301-656-2280	Shoes for the fashion forward.

Map 25 • Silver Spring

Kingsbury Chocolates	1017 King St	703-548-2800	Mmmmmm.

Map 26 • Takoma Park

Dan the Music Man	6855 Eastern Ave	301-270-8240	Forget records, the oldies here are on CDs.
Polly Sue's	6915 Laurel Ave	301-270-5511	Vintage heaven.
Takoma Underground	7014 Westmoreland Ave	301-270-6380	Outfits fit for Marilyn Monroe.

Map 27 • Walter Reed

KB News Emporium	7898 Georgia Ave	301-565-4248	Catch up on the headlines.

Map 29 • Bethesda/Chevy Chase Business

Chicos	5418 Wisconsin Ave	301-986-1122	Clothing for stylish women with professional bank accounts.
Gianni Versace	5454 Wisconsin Ave	301-907-9400	Pay homage to the God of Gaudy.
Marvelous Market	4832 Bethesda Ave	301-986-0555	Try their blueberry muffins.
Mustard Seed	7349 Wisconsin Ave	301-907-4699	Not your typical resale store.
Parvizian Masterpieces	7034 Wisconsin Ave	301-656-8989	Serious rugs.
Relish	5454 Wisconsin Ave	301-654-9899	For your bod, not your hot dog.
Saks Fifth Avenue	5555 Wisconsin Ave	301-657-9000	Where rich people shop.
Saks Jandel	5510 Wisconsin Ave	301-652-2250	For the well-dressed socialite.
Sylene	4407 S Park Ave	301-654-4200	Fine lingerie.
Tickled Pink	7259 Woodmont Ave	301-913-9191	Palm beach chic.
Tiffany & Co	5500 Wisconsin Ave	301-657-8777	Pop the question.

Map 30 • Westmoreland Circle

Crate & Barrel	4820 Massachusetts Ave NW	202-364-6100	Wedding registry HQ.

Map 33 • Falls Church

Eden Supermarket	6763 Wilson Blvd	703-532-4950	Ledgend has it Adam and Eve shopped at this Asian market.

Map 34 • Ballston

Pottery Barn	Balston Commons, 2700 Clarendon Blvd	703-465-9425	Yuppie interior style.

Map 35 • Clarendon

Orvis Company Store	2879 Clarendon Blvd	703-465-0004	Practical clothes to match the rhino guard on your SUV.
The Container Store	2800 Clarendon Blvd	703-469-1560	Buckets, shelves, hangers…
The Italian store	3123 Lee Hwy	703-528-6266	The best Italian heros.

Map 38 • Columbia Pike

REI	3509 Carlin Springs Rd	703-379-9400	Sports emporium.

Map 39 • Shirlington

Best Buns Bread Co	4010 28th St S	703-578-1500	The name says it all—the best buns in town!
Books a Million	4201 28th St S	703-931-6949	Top titles and some old faves too…
Carlyle Grande Café	4000 28th St S	703-931-0777	Popular for Friday and Saturday dinner, arrive early.
The Curious Grape	4056 28th St S	703-671-8700	Many wines, free tastings, great spot to stop on a date.
Washington Golf Centers	2625 Shirlington Rd	703-979-7888	Gear up for the links.

Map 40 • Pentagon City

Abercrombie & Fitch	1101 S Hayes St	703-415-4210	Quintessential college kids' clothes.
BCBG	1100 S Hayes St	703-415-3690	Cheap, trendy women's clothing.
bebe	1100 S Hayes St	703-415-2323	Sexy clothing for twentysomething women.
Costco	1200 S Fern St	703-413-3240	If you need a 24-pack of anything…
Eddie Bauer	1100 S Hayes St	703-418-6112	Cuddly guys' sweaters and the like.
Elizabeth Arden Red Door Salon & Spa	1101 S Joyce St	703-373-5888	Pampered facials.
Jean Machine	1100 S Hayes St	703-415-3815	Inexpensive jeans from a variety of lines.
Kenneth Cole	1100 S Hayes St	703-415-3522	Metrosexual heaven—great guys' shoes and accessories.
Macy's	1000 S Hayes St	703-418-4488	Yes, DC, apartment stores still exist.
Williams-Sonoma	1100 S Hayes St	703-416-6700	High-end cooking supplies.

Map 41 • Landmark

BJ's Wholesale Club	101 S Van Dorn St	703-212-8700	If you need a 24-pack of anything…

Map 43 • Four Mile Run

Barnes & Noble	3651 Jefferson Davis Hwy	703-299-9124	Mega bookstore.
Best Buy	3401 Jefferson Davis Hwy	703-519-0940	All sorts of electronics.
Old Navy	3621 Jefferson Davis Hwy	703-739-6240	Super-cheap, super-basic clothes.
PETsMART	3351 Jefferson Davis Hwy	703-739-4844	Pet supply superstore.
Sports Authority	3701 Jefferson Davis Hwy	703-684-3204	The authority of sports.
Staples	3301 Jefferson Davis Hwy	703-836-9485	Everything you need for your home (or work) office.
Target	3101 Jefferson Davis Hwy	703-706-3840	"Tar-zhay" offers housewares, furniture and more.

Map 46 • Old Town (South)

Blink	1303 King St	703-518-5007	Wear your sunglasses at night.
Comfort One Shoes	201 King St	703-549-4441	Beyond Birkenstocks.
Hysteria	125 S Fairfax St	703-548-1615	Wearable art at museum prices.
La Cuisine	323 Cameron St	703-836-4435	Upscale cookware.
My Place in Tuscany	1127 King St	703-683-8882	Hand-painted ceramics.
P&C Art	212 King St	703-549-2525	Original art.
Tickled Pink	103 S St Asaph St	703-518-5459	Palm beach chic.
The Torpedo Factory	105 N Union St	703-838-4565	Giant artist's compound; most of it's pretty touristy stuff.

Baltimore

The Antique Man	1806 Fleet St	410-732-0932	The most eclectic of the string of antique/junk shops around Fells Point.
Cook's Table	717 Light St	410-539-8600	For the perfectly-appointed mogul kitchen.
Mystery Loves Company	1730 Fleet St	410-276-6708	No mystery to the genre of books here.
Sound Garden	1616 Thames St	410-563-9011	Independent music store wothy of High Fidelity. Also hosts impromptu performances.

The theater scene here ain't New York. You will have to accept that up front, otherwise Washington will pale by comparison. But wisely, DC theater doesn't *try* to be. Only New York, Chicago, and LA boast more legitimate production theaters than Washington does. The **Kennedy Center** often rolls out pre-Broadway trials and well-received programs like the wildly successful Sondheim festival in 2003. The nationally known Shakespeare Theater Company is the only one in the US to spotlight The Bard. Also, check your Playbill bios the next time you're at a show in New York, and chances are one of the leads proudly mentions his or her Helen Hayes Award. Named after our native daughter, it's Washington's version of the Tony. It's not New York, but it's not bad at all.

Though the big venues do sometimes stage innovative works, the way to appreciate theater here is to peruse the high-quality, smaller stages. **Arena Stage** in the Southwest is the area's largest not-for-profit producing theater and currently houses two stages: the larger 816-seat **Fichandler Stage** and the 514-seat fan-shaped **Kreeger Theater.** But not for long! Plans are well underway for the construction of a third wing, the **Cradle Theater**, which will allow for even more than their current eight productions per season. Arena Stage also hosts visiting productions; www.arena-stage.com; 202-488-3300.

Working out of DC's Logan Circle neighborhood, the **Studio Theatre** has earned a reputation for staging first-rate contemporary American and European plays and performances. The **Mead Theater** downstairs and **Milton Theater** upstairs both hold 200 people. The Studio is renowned for its development of some of Washington's best actors and directors on its **SecondStage**, and the Studio Theatre also has an acting school; www.studiotheatre.org; 202-332-3300.

For surprisingly unstuffy, and sometimes risqué, takes on the classics, visit the **Folger** and **Shakespeare Theatres**. The Folger Theatre, part of the Folger Shakespeare Library, stages three plays per year in its intimate Elizabethan-style theatre (and not all of their productions are of Shakespeare's plays, they'll have you know); www.folger.edu; 202-544-7077. The Shakespeare Theatre recently expanded from its one 450-seat **Lansburgh Theatre**, to also stage performances in the spanking new 800-seat **Sidney Harman Hall**; www.shakespearedc.org; 202-547-1122

Don't forget to take advantage of several free shows (and beautiful scenery) at the outdoor **Carter Barron Amphitheatre**; 202-426-0486.

Specials abound for the broke, thrifty, and theatre-loving crowd: inquire about ushering, standing room, and day-of tickets, and you're likely to score yourself a bargain.

Theater	*Address*	*Phone*	*Map*
Arena Stage	1101 6th St SW	202-488-3300	6
Arena Stage at 14th and T	1901 14th St NW	240-582-0050	10
Atlas Performing Arts Center	1333 H St NE	202-467-4600	3
Blair Mansion Inn/Murder Mystery Dinner Theatre	7711 Eastern Ave	301-588-6646	27
Capitol Hill Arts Workshop	545 7th St SE	202-547-6839	5
Carter Barron Amphitheatre	16th & Colorado Ave NW	202-426-0486	21
Casa de la Luna	4020 Georgia Ave	202-882-6227	21
Dance Place	3225 8th St NE	202-269-1600	14
Discovery Theater	1100 Jefferson Dr SW	202-357-1500	1
District of Columbia Arts Center	2438 18th St NW	202-462-7833	16
Fichandler Stage	1101 6th St SW	202-488-3300	6
Flashpoint	916 G St NW	202-315-1305	1
Folger Shakespeare Theatre	201 E Capitol St SE	202-544-7077	3
Ford's Theatre	511 10th St NW	202-347-4833	1
GALA-Tivoli Theater	3333 14th St NW	202-234-7174	15
Goldman Theater	1529 16th St NW	202-777-3229	9
Gunston Arts Center	2700 S Lang St	703-553-7782	40
H Street Playhouse	1365 H St NE	202-396-2125	3
Hartke Theatre	3801 Harewood Rd NE	202-319-5358	14
Kennedy Center	2700 F St NW	202-467-4600	7
Kreeger Theater	1101 6th St SW	202-488-3300	6

Theater	*Address*	*Phone*	*Map*
Lincoln Theatre	1215 U St NW	202-397-7328	10
Little Theatre of Alexandria	600 Wolfe St	703-683-0496	46
Mead Theater	1333 P St NW	202-332-3300	10
Metro Stage	1201 N Royal St	703-548-9044	45
Milton Theater	1333 P St NW	202-332-3300	10
Mount Vernon Players Theater	900 Massachusetts Ave NW	202-783-7600	10
Nannie J Lee Center	1108 Jefferson St	703-838-2880	46
National Theatre	1321 Pennsylvania Ave NW	202-628-6161	1
Old Vat Room	1101 6th St SW	202-488-3300	6
Rosslyn Spectrum Theatre	1611 N Kent St	703-228-1843	36
Round House Theatre	4545 East West Hwy	240-644-1100	29
Round House Theatre	8641 Colesville Rd	240-644-1100	25
Shakespeare Theatre	450 7th St NW	202-547-1122	2
Signature Theater	3806 S Four Mile Run Dr	703-820-9771	39
Source Theatre	1835 14th St NW	202-462-1073	10
St Mark's Players/St Mark's Church	118 3rd St SE	202-546-9670	3
Stage 4	1333 P St NW	202-332-3300	10
Stanislavsky Theater Studio	1742 Church St NW	800-494-8497	9
Studio Theatre	1501 14th St NW	202-332-3300	10
Theatre on the Run	3700 S Four Mile Run Dr	703-228-1850	39
Thomas Jefferson Community Center	3501 2nd St S	703-228-5920	37
Warehouse Theater	1021 7th St NW	202-783-3933	10
Warner Theatre	513 13th St NW	202-783-4000	1
Washington Shakespeare Co	601 S Clark St	703-418-4808	36
Washington Stage Guild	1901 14th St NW	240-582-0050	10
Woolly Mammoth Theatre	641 D St NW	202-393-3939	2

Street Index

Washington, DC

Street Index

Street Index

Maryland

Bethesda

Street Index

Chevy Chase

Silver Spring

Street Index

Takoma Park

Virginia

Alexandria

Street Index

Street Index

Arlington

Street Index

Falls Church

McLean